CATHOLIC DICTIONARY

CATHOLIC DICTIONARY

JOHN A. HARDON, SJ

AN ABRIDGED AND UPDATED EDITION OF
MODERN CATHOLIC DICTIONARY

IMAGE

NEW YORK

An Image Book

Copyright © 1980 by John A. Hardon
New material copyright © 2013 by Inter Mirifica

Excerpts from *The Jerusalem Bible,* copyright © 1966 by Darton, Longman & Todd, Ltd.,
and Doubleday & Company, Inc. Used by permission of the publisher.

1980 Edition:

Imprimi Potest:	Michael J. Lavelle, S.J.
	Provincial, Detroit Province
	December 3, 1979
Nihil Obstat:	William B. Smith, S.T.D.
	Censor Librorum
Imprimatur:	Joseph T. O'Keefe
	Vicar General, Archdiocese of New York
	December 13, 1979

Updated 2013 Edition:

Nihil Obstat:	Monsignor Francis J. McAree, S.T.D.
Imprimatur:	Bishop Gerald T. Walsh, Archdiocese of
	New York
	March 19, 2013

The Nihil Obstat and Imprimatur are official declarations that this book
is free of doctrinal or moral error. No implication is contained therein that those who
have granted the Nihil Obstat and Imprimatur agree with the content,
opinions, or statements expressed.

Published in the United States by Image Books, an imprint of the Crown Publishing
Group, a division of Random House, Inc., New York.

Image and the Image colophon are registered trademarks of Random House, Inc.

Originally published in hardcover in slightly different form as *Modern Catholic
Dictionary* in 1980 and subsequently published as an abridged paperback edition as
Pocket Catholic Dictionary in 1985 in the United States by Image Books, a division of
Random House, Inc., New York.

Library of Congress Catalog Card Number: 77–82945
Library of Congress Cataloging-in-Publication Data
Hardon, John A.
Modern Catholic dictionary.
1. Catholic Church—Dictionaries. 2. Theology—Dictionaries. I. Title.
BX841.H36 282'.03

ISBN 978-0-307-88634-7
eISBN 978-0-307-88635-4

Cover design: Nupoor Gordon
Cover photograph: © Ben Pipe/Robert Harding World Imagery/Getty Images

Printed in the United States of America

1   3   5   7   9   10   8   6   4   2

Updated 2013 Image Edition

CONTENTS

A NOTE ON THE 2013 EDITION

It is with great pleasure that Image books presents this updated version of the long-out-of-print *Modern Catholic Dictionary*, originally published to great acclaim in 1980. Though Father Hardon passed away in 2000, his prose and insight have been appreciated by the faithful and the curious for decades now. It is our hope that this updated edition will introduce this excellent book to a whole new generation of readers.

We are grateful and thankful to John O'Connell, who oversaw the editing of this book. His patience, guidance, and love for the material were a blessing to us.

Gary Jansen
Senior Editor, Image Books
New York, 2013

INTRODUCTION

1980

The need for a modern Catholic dictionary seems obvious. Much has happened in the Catholic Church since the opening of the Second Vatican Council in 1962. The council itself was a historic event whose sixteen documents, confirmed by Pope Paul VI, have deeply influenced the thinking of all the faithful. As a result, new words and expressions have entered the Catholic vocabulary, and old terms have taken on a fresh and more profound meaning.

Moreover, the world in which the faithful live has undergone major changes, some would say among the most profound in Christianity since the apostolic age. Secularism is no longer a mere theory; it is the chosen way of life of large segments of Western society. Marriage and the family are on trial for their existence; abortion and now euthanasia are being legalized in one country after another. This has placed a grave strain on Catholicism, and the effects are showing across a wide spectrum of thought and practice, again with corresponding impact on the language of people who "instead of the spirit of the world," as St. Paul says, "have received the Spirit that comes from God."

No dictionary is ever complete, and the present one makes no claim to comprehensiveness. There are too many terms in what may be called the Catholic vocabulary to even cover them all, let alone give an extensive treatment of each one. This is plainly to be a dictionary and not an encyclopedia. Yet, unlike other lexicons, a Catholic dictionary should be more than a mere listing of definitions. It cannot, in the name of objectivity, remain neutral on things on which the Catholic Church has an established position. Otherwise it would not merit being called Catholic.

Many terms have been included from psychology and the social sciences—but always defined (or described) from a Catholic point of view. They were included because they underlie distinctively Catholic principles, or in order to indicate how the Church understands the world in which her faithful live and are working out their salvation.

All the while, however, the main focus of the dictionary and the bulk of its contents are definably, even exclusively, Roman Catholic. An effort was made to include every significant concept of the Church's doctrine in faith and morals, ritual and devotion, canon law and liturgy, mysticism and spirituality, ecclesiastical history and organization.

Special attention has been given to the Second Vatican Council and the most important documents that explain the conciliar teaching.

Events in the life of the Church over the centuries have been screened to include such as are necessary or at least useful for a balanced grasp of Catholic Christianity. There has endured a stable tradition that proves the Church's divine origin and guidance. But there has also been development, and therefore change. The dictionary seeks to reflect both dimensions: the Catholic, and therefore the Church's continuity, and the modern, and therefore her progress, in a marvelous paradox that is borne out in no other institution in the annals of the human race.

Wherever feasible, exact Scripture references or even citations have been given to enable the reader to go back to the Bible to see the defined term in its full biblical context. So, too, precise references, often with quotations, are given for the Church's doctrines, which may then be traced to their original sources, mainly in papal documents or the canons and decrees of ecumenical councils.

Equivalent terms have not been multiplied beyond measure, but enough of them are available to help the reader find what is sought, perhaps defined under a heading different from the one that first comes to mind.

Special attention was given to Catholic shrines and prayers. With so many hallowed places of pilgrimage and forms of popular piety in the Catholic world, the author felt that these should be duly considered. They reflect one side of the Church's existence that may be overlooked—namely, the people's sentiment and affections, with particular emphasis on their devotion to the Blessed Virgin Mary. Likewise the praying side of Catholicism has been highlighted with many of the better-known prayers and hymns. These appear with a brief history and, in most cases, the full text of the prayer or song in question.

There are really two parts to the dictionary, of unequal length. The first and major part is the lexicon of terms, over five thousand, directly or indirectly dealing with Catholic faith, worship, morals, history, canon law, and spirituality.

The second part is the Appendix, which contains the Credo of the People of God and a listing of popes from Peter to Benedict XVI.

Priests and teachers, whether in the pulpit, in the classroom, or in the home, will find in the dictionary an invaluable aid to communicating the riches and beauty of the Catholic religion. It is the author's hope that this book will bring everyone who reads it closer to the One who is beyond all definition, and for whose honor and glory it was written.

—John A. Hardon, S.J.

GUIDE TO THE USE OF THE DICTIONARY

In order to help the reader derive full benefit from this dictionary, it is worth noting certain features that the author had in mind when doing the research and assembling the data. The years of planning that went into the composition of the present volume were mainly directed to accuracy of content, conciseness of treatment, and facility of use. The following information is offered especially to facilitate the use of the *Catholic Dictionary*.

Key to Sources

Most of the sources of quotations in the dictionary are self-explanatory. Some, however, call for further comment.

Denzinger

The full title of this source is *Enchiridion Symbolorum* (Handbook of Creeds), originally edited by Henry Denzinger and first published in 1854. The book has gone through upwards of forty editions and is the standard collection, in one volume, of the most important documents of the Catholic Church on faith and morals from the first century to the present time. The numbers following Denzinger are also standard and correspond to sections that are regularly cited in all the official statements of the popes or the organs of the Holy See. The *Enchiridion* is in Latin.

Second Vatican Council

Conciliar documents are quoted extensively and generally in their Latin titles. Numbers following a document correspond to the official subsection of the Latin original.

Postconciliar Documents

These were issued by Venerable Pope Paul VI to implement formally the sixteen basic documents of the Second Vatican Council. They cover the whole spectrum of Catholic faith, worship, and morality and range in dignity from apostolic constitutions of the pope through the numerous directives and decrees of the Vatican congregations.

Code of Canon Law

The new Code of Canon Law, issued by Blessed Pope John Paul II on January 25, 1983, is a summary synthesis of the legislation of the Roman Catholic Church.

The Catechism of the Catholic Church

The new *Catechism of the Catholic Church* was promulgated by Blessed Pope John Paul II, who declared it to be "a sure norm for teaching the faith." This edition incorporates references to the *Catechism of the Catholic Church*.

Etymology

Many of the entries are given short etymologies. Their purpose is to bring out more clearly the meaning of a term by placing it in historical context. Biblical names often symbolize the person named; Greek derivatives relate the word to its scriptural or first-century origin; and the many Latin sources indicate the role of the Church in standardizing the language of Catholicism.

Cross-References

Although this work is not an encyclopedia, every effort was made to make it as complete as limitations of space would allow. One method to achieve this was to correlate the entries. Where another entry is more or less synonymous, this is indicated by "See" after a single term. When further information is elsewhere available in the dictionary, this appears as "See also" after the entry.

Biographies

Every entry about a person includes his or her biographical dates of birth and death and, in the case of popes, of the years of their reign. Where the exact dates are disputed among scholars, this is shown by "c." (Latin *circa,* "about") or a choice by the author of the most probable date. Some persons are given these biographical dates several times in different entries, whenever this was considered helpful to understand the subject treated.

The only biographies, as such, are those of biblical personages. This was not for lack of appreciation of the many important characters of Catholic Church history but because of the intended purpose of the volume: to concentrate on the objective faith and data of the Church's faith and practice and not enter the vast arena of her life and biographical activity.

On the other hand, biblical persons are treated at some length. Both Old and New Testament characters are given entries. In the light of the Catholic Church's new emphasis on the Scriptures, this was considered an essential part of the *Catholic Dictionary*. Supporting these biblical figures are also a number of important places that belong to historic and contemporary Palestine.

Organizations and Societies

It was clearly impossible to include more than a fraction of the thousands of archaic and present-day societies within Catholic Christianity. There are, for example, some four thousand religious institutes of men and women in the Church today. Within the dictionary itself are separate entries for about fifty institutes of Christian perfection that are of historic importance and that fairly set the pattern for similar religious communities throughout the world.

Even more limited is the number of other Catholic organizations that are given special entries. The relatively few given are those of an international character or that have particular significance for the Catholic Church in modern times.

Abbreviations

Built into the sequence of entries are several hundred standard abbreviations for Catholic use, especially for use in the liturgy, canon law, and formal writing. While most of the terms are in current use, others were included from the Church's practice before the Second Vatican Council to give the reader a handy reference source for identifying many terms that appear in print from preconciliar days.

Scholastic Philosophy and Theology

Special attention was paid to including as many basic terms from scholastic philosophy and theology as feasible. These terms are the backbone, as it were, of the Church's official teaching of faith and morals. They derive mainly from the Middle Ages, notably from St. Thomas Aquinas, and are necessary to appreciate the genius of Catholicism in its fundamental grasp of revealed and naturally knowable truth. It is impossible to understand the Catholic Church in her own deepest understanding of herself without some familiarity with this language of scholastic thought.

DICTIONARY OF TERMS

AARON. The founder and first head of the Hebrew priesthood for almost forty years. Son of Amram and Jochebed, he was the brother of Moses and Miriam (Exodus 6:20). He married Elisheba, and one of his sons, Eleazar, succeeded him in heading the priesthood. Aaron was associated with Moses in every enterprise (Exodus 6:23) and acted as his brother's spokesman because of his eloquence (Exodus 4:16). In the early Pentateuch narratives, his role was mentioned in connection with the Exodus, the making of the golden calf, and taunting Moses for marrying his Ethiopian wife. Apparently he was punished for doubting God's ability to cause water to spring from the rock at Meribah. After a long life he died and was buried at Mount Hor (Numbers 20:27–29).

ABBA. "Father," transliterated from the Aramaic. St. Paul says, "It is the spirit of sons, and it makes us cry out 'Abba, Father'" (Romans 8:15).

ABBESS. Feminine counterpart of abbot. The spiritual and temporal superior of a community of nuns, symbolizing her role as mother of the religious women under her care. Over the centuries an abbess has enjoyed some extraordinary privileges, such as wearing a special ring and bearing the crosier as a sign of her rank. But an abbess does not have ecclesiastical jurisdiction corresponding to that of an abbot. See also ABBOT.

ABBEY. Canonically erected and independent monastery with a required minimum of religious. Occupied by monks, it is ruled by an abbot; if by nuns, ruled by an abbess. With the exception of Carthusian abbeys, which provide cottages for individual monks, most abbey buildings are constructed around a quadrangle and consist of a novitiate, guest house, choir, conference room, infirmary, kitchen, refectory, cells, dormitory, oratory for prayer, almonry for alms distribution, cellars for storage, calefactory (or warming room), locutory (or parlor), and a chapter house for business and private meetings with the superior. Most abbeys are either Benedictine or Cistercian.

ABBOT. Superior of a monastery of monks having a settled location; a title definitely fixed by St. Benedict. The abbot is elected, usually for life, by the professed members of the community in a secret ballot. The authority of an abbot is, first, paternal, administering the property of the abbey and maintaining discipline in the observance of rule, and, second, is quasi-episcopal in conferring a certain territorial jurisdiction. The rule of the order determines the qualifications of its abbot. His insignia are the pectoral cross and a ring. (Etym. Aramaic *abba*, father.) See also ABBESS.

ABEL. The second son of Adam and Eve, slain by his brother, Cain, who was jealous because Abel's offering to God was more acceptable than Cain's. Abel was a shepherd and his brother a farmer (Genesis 4:2, 4:8). During his ministry Jesus made references to Cain's offense when he warned the Scribes and Pharisees, ". . . you will draw down on yourselves the blood of every holy man that has been shed on earth, from the blood of Abel the Holy to the blood of Zechariah . . ." (Matthew 23:35).

ABJURATION. In Church law, the formal renunciation of apostasy, heresy, or schism. While still in effect in exceptional cases, persons now entering the Catholic Church are not required to abjure their former doctrinal errors. Their positive profession of the Catholic faith implies their abjuration of whatever they may have once held contrary to this faith. (Etym. Latin *abiuratio*, a foreswearing, abjuration; from *ab*, from + *iurare*, to swear: *abiurare*, to swear away from, to deny on oath.)

ABLUTION. Liturgical washing with water. In the Latin Rite baptism is generally conferred by ablution—i.e., the pouring of water over the person's head. Also the ritual washing of the thumbs and index fingers of the celebrant at Mass; the cleansing of the chalice used during Mass; and the washing of feet in the Holy Thursday ceremony. In the Greek Church ablution refers to the public washing of newly baptized persons. (Etym. Latin *ablutio*, a washing away or cleansing; a spiritual cleaning.)

ABORTION. In Catholic morality, abortion is either direct (induced) or indirect. Direct abortion is any destruction of the product of human conception, whether before or after implantation in the womb. A direct abortion is one that is intended either as an end in itself or as a means to an end. As a willful attack on unborn human life, no matter what the motive, direct abortion is always a grave objective evil.

Indirect abortion is the foreseen but merely permitted evacuation of a fetus that cannot survive outside the womb. The evacuation is not the intended or directly willed result, but the side effect, of some legitimate procedure. As such it is morally allowable.

The essential sinfulness of direct abortion consists in the homicidal intent to kill innocent life. This factor places the controverted question as to precisely when human life begins outside the ambit of the moral issue; as it also makes the now commonly held Catholic position that human life begins at conception equally outside the heart of the Church's teaching about the grave sinfulness of direct abortion.

Abortion was condemned by the Church since apostolic times. *The Teaching of the Twelve Apostles,* composed before A.D. 100, told the faithful, "You shall not procure abortion. You shall not destroy a newborn child" (II, 2). Direct abortion and infanticide were from the beginning placed on the same level of malice.

Hundreds of ecclesiastical documents from the first century through the present testify to the same moral doctrine, with such nuances as time, place, and circumstances indicated. The Second Vatican Council declared: "Life must be protected with the utmost care from the moment of conception" so that "abortion and infanticide are abominable crimes" (*Pastoral Constitution on the Church in the Modern World,* IV, 51). Venerable Pope Paul VI confirmed this teaching in 1974. "Respect for human life," he wrote, "is called for from the time that the process of generation begins. From the time that the ovum is fertilized, a life is begun which is neither that of the father nor of the mother. It is rather the life of a new human being with its own growth. It would never be made human if it were not human already." Consequently, "divine law and natural reason exclude all right to the direct killing of an innocent human being" (*Declaration on Procured Abortion,* III, 12).

Blessed Pope John Paul II confirmed, especially in his encyclical *Evangelium Vitae,* the constant teaching of the Church condemning the practice of direct abortion (*EV,* 62). The *Catechism of the Catholic Church* also affirms the Church's traditional prohibition against direct abortion (2270–2275). (Etym. Latin *abortivus,* born prematurely, abortive; from *aboriri,* to miscarry.)

ABRAHAM. Born in the twentieth or nineteenth century B.C., in Ur of the Chaldeans on the Euphrates River. His father, Terah, named him Abram. The family migrated to Haran, where Terah died (Genesis 11:26–31). At God's behest, Abram, his wife, Sarah, his nephew, Lot, and all their followers moved on to Canaan (Genesis 12:4). When Abram was ninety-nine years old, God made a covenant with him, changing his name to Abraham and promising to make him the "father of a multitude of nations . . . [Genesis 17:1–5] I will make you into nations and your issue shall be kings. . . . I will give to you and your descendants the land you are living in, the whole land of Canaan, to own in perpetuity, and I will be your God" (Genesis 17:5–8). Hence he has been called the founder of the Hebrew people. Abraham's dedication to the will of God was tested when he was told to take his son, Isaac, to the land of Moriah (which later became the site of the Jerusalem Temple) and sacrifice his son as a burnt offering. He obeyed without hesitation, but Isaac was spared at the last moment (Genesis 22). In his final days Abraham arranged to have his son marry Rebekah, one of his kinfolk (Genesis 24), and left Isaac all his possessions before he died at the age of 175 (Genesis 25).

ABROGATION. In ecclesiastical law the total abolition of a law, right, duty, or privilege. (Etym. Latin *abrogare*, to repeal a law, abrogate.)

ABSOLUTE. That which is independent or not related to anything else; or that which is total and complete in itself.

Applied to God, who is the Absolute, it is equivalent to the divine transcendence in two ways. He is absolutely independent of all creation for his own existence and perfections. They totally depend upon him, but he is completely self-sufficient in himself, since his essence is his existence. He is the Being who cannot not be, whereas all others are contingent beings whose existence depends wholly on him who alone is necessary Being.

But God is also absolutely perfect. He is the infinite Being whose attributes are without limitation and whose perfections are without restriction. He is almighty and all good, omniscient and all holy. In a word he is the One in whom there is no potency that can be actualized and no possibility that can still be realized.

Applied to beings other than God, a thing is said to be absolute when it is considered or conceived in itself and apart from its relation to something else. Thus, absolutely speaking, sin is an unmitigated evil. But considered from the viewpoint of Divine Providence, sin can be the occasion of much good in the world.

ABSOLUTION. In the sacrament of penance, the act by which a qualified priest, having the necessary jurisdiction, remits the guilt and penalty due to sin. The new formula of absolution, since the Second Vatican Council, is: "God, the Father of mercies, through the death and resurrection of His Son, has reconciled the world to Himself and sent the Holy Spirit among us for the forgiveness of sins; through the ministry of the Church may God give you pardon and peace, and I absolve you from your sins in the name of the Father, and of the Son, and of the Holy Spirit." To which the penitent answers, "Amen." In this formula the essential words are: "I absolve you." For centuries, the Church used the deprecatory form of absolution, e.g.: "May God absolve you from your sins." This was really declarative in meaning, as is clear from the fact that in the whole of tradition the priest who absolved was looked upon as a judge who actually absolved, even though he used the subjunctive mood to express his affirmative judgment. (Etym. Latin *absolvere,* to free from; to absolve, acquit.)

ABSOLUTION OF THE DYING. Special faculties conferred by the Church's common law, for any priest, even though laicized or not approved for confessions, can validly and licitly absolve any penitent in danger of death. The absolution covers any sin and censure, even in the presence of a priest who is approved for confessions.

ABSTINENCE. The moral virtue that inclines a person to the moderate use of food or drink as dictated by right reason or by faith for his own moral and spiritual welfare.

As commonly understood, abstinence refers to refraining from certain kinds of food or drink and may be undertaken by a person spontaneously or it may be prescribed by ecclesiastical law, whether for the universal Church or for certain territories. Institutes of Christian perfection may also have special provisions for abstinence according to their rule of life.

The Jewish Law contained elaborate food prohibitions that, however, were abrogated by the New Dispensation, the only apparent exceptions being blood and things strangled (Acts 15:20). From early Christian times, other kinds of abstinence were practiced, especially among the hermits. Thus St. Antony of Egypt and his followers abstained from all food except bread, water, and salt, and many contemplative orders still observe a severe abstinence for all or most of the year. (Etym. Latin *abstinere,* to refrain from, to keep away.) See also FASTING.

ACCIDENTS. Things whose essence naturally requires that they exist in another being. Accidents are also called the appearances, species, or properties of a thing. These may be either physical, such as quantity, or modal, such as size or shape. Supernaturally, accidents can exist, in the absence of their natural substance, as happens with the physical properties of bread and wine after Eucharistic consecration.

ACCLAMATION. 1. One of the ways of electing a pope in which the cardinals unanimously, without consultation or balloting, proclaim one of the candidates Supreme Pontiff. 2. Liturgical acclamations at the coronation of a pope or the election of a bishop.

Acclamations were sent as compliments to the emperors from the early Church councils and were found in the coronation rites of secular princes and kings. Sepulchral monuments carried them as inscriptions. Brief liturgical formulas such as *"Deo gratias"* (thanks to God) may be classified as acclamations. (Etym. Latin *ac-,* to + *clamare,* to cry out: *acclamare:* proclaim, declare, invoke.)

ACOLYTE. A ministry to which a person is specially appointed by the Church to assist the deacon and to minister to the priest. His duty is to attend to the service of the altar and to assist as needed in the celebration of the Mass. He may also distribute Holy Communion as an auxiliary minister at the Eucharistic liturgy and to the sick. An acolyte may be entrusted with publicly exposing the Blessed Sacrament for adoration but not with giving benediction. He may also, to the extent needed, take care of instructing other faithful who by appointment assist the priest or deacon by carrying the missal, cross, candles, and similar functions. The ministry of acolyte is reserved to men and conferred by the bishop of the diocese or, in clerical institutes of religious, by the major superior, according to the liturgical rites composed for the purpose by the Church. Women may be delegated to perform some of the functions of an acolyte. (Etym. Greek *akolouthos,* attendant follower.) See also ALTAR SERVER.

ACTA APOSTOLICAE SEDIS. Acts of the Apostolic See. An official journal, published periodically. Established September 29, 1908, it contains all the principal decrees, encyclical letters, decisions of Roman congregations, and notices of ecclesiastical appointments. The contents are to be considered promulgated when published and effective three months from date of issue.

ACTIVISM. Preoccupation with activity instead of mental reflection. As a philosophical theory, it emphasizes the active character of the mind. The principal value of thinking is to serve man and society outside the mind. Activism is part of the philosophy of Marxist-Leninism, which holds that the main purpose of thought is not to discover and contemplate the truth but to change reality, especially social reality, in the world.

ACTS OF THE APOSTLES. The book of the New Testament, written by St. Luke, which narrates some of the important events in the lives of Sts. Peter and Paul and, to a lesser degree, of the Apostles John, the two Jameses, and Barnabas. The Acts are a historical narrative that describes the founding of the Church on Pentecost, the influence of the Holy Spirit on the early Christians, the persecution of the faithful, the miracles worked in confirmation of their faith, and the rapid expansion of Christianity throughout the eastern Mediterranean world. The Acts were written about A.D. 63, in Greek, and most probably while Luke was in Rome.

ACTUAL GRACE. Temporary supernatural intervention by God to enlighten the mind or strengthen the will to perform supernatural actions that lead to heaven. Actual grace is therefore a transient divine assistance to enable man to obtain, retain, or grow in supernatural grace and the life of God. See also EFFICACIOUS GRACE, GRACE, HABITUAL GRACE, JUSTIFYING GRACE, SACRAMENTAL GRACE, SANCTIFYING GRACE, SUFFICIENT GRACE.

ACTUAL SIN. Any thought, word, deed, or omission contrary to God's eternal law. All actual sins are classified on the basis of this division, where sinful thoughts are essentially desires, the words may either be spoken or otherwise articulated, the deeds involve some external manifestation, and omissions are failures to do what should have been done by a person in a given set of circumstances.

Sin is a human act that presumes three elements: objective malice in the action performed, or at least the person considers it wrong; actual advertence of mind by which the sinner is at least confusedly aware of the malice of his conduct; and consent of the will, which formally constitutes actual sin and without which the sin is said to be only material.

Every sin is a genuine offense against God. There is consequently no such thing as merely philosophical sin, which offends against right reason but is not at the same time a deliberate transgression of the divine law. Sin is theological by its very nature. See also OMISSION, ORIGINAL SIN, SIN.

ADAM. The first man. Created in the image of God. His wife was Eve and his sons Cain, Abel, and Seth. They lived in the Garden of Eden but were expelled because Adam and Eve disobeyed God's command not to eat the fruit of a certain tree (Genesis 1, 2). In early accounts of Adam's life he is referred to not by a specific name but as "the man" (Genesis 3). Not until his descendants were given (Genesis 4:25) was the proper noun "Adam" applied to him. Many doctrines in the New Testament are traced back to the life of the first man, notably original sin and the concept of Jesus as the second Adam bringing redemption to the human race.

ADAPTATION. Legitimate adjustment of basic principles to time, place, and circumstances. Used by the Second Vatican Council to distinguish external accommodation from internal renewal. Adaptation is secondary to renewal and corresponds to updating in accidentals for the sake of greater effectiveness. (Etym. Latin *adaptatio;* from *adaptare,* to fit to.)

ADDICTION. The state of being physically dependent on something, generally alcohol or drugs, but it can be any material object or experience. Addiction means increased tolerance but also greater difficulty in withdrawal. In fact, the fear of withdrawal symptoms is the main obstacle even in persons who are convinced on moral grounds that they should overcome an addiction. The study of addiction has contributed to a major development in Catholic moral theology, through a better understanding of subjective guilt and a more effective pastoral care of persons with bad moral habits. (Etym. Latin *addicere,* to give one's consent to a thing.)

AD GENTES DIVINITUS. Decree of the Second Vatican Council on the Church's missionary activity. The Church's mission is defined as "the evangelization and the implanting of the Church among peoples or groups in which it has not yet taken root." Among the surprising recommendations is that the young churches of the newly evangelized take part "in the universal mission of the Church as soon as possible" and send "missionaries to preach the Gospel throughout the whole world, even though they are themselves short of clergy." Special stress is placed on adequate training of missionaries, their sanctity of life, and cooperation among themselves in the apostolate (December 7, 1965).

AD MAJOREM DEI GLORIAM. "For the greater glory of God," abbreviated A.M.D.G. The motto of the Society of Jesus, but commonly used by Christians everywhere.

ADOLESCENCE. Physiologically the period of development from puberty to full adulthood. But theologically the operations of divine grace are quite independent of this physical process. Not only can adolescents live a deep life of faith, but they are capable of reaching a high degree of sanctity, as testified by the Church's canonization of such young persons as St. Stanislaus Kostka (1550–68), St. Dominic Savio (1842–57), and St. Maria Goretti (1890–1902). (Etym. Latin *adolescentia,* time of youth; from the fifteenth year to the thirtieth, between the *puer* and the *iuvenis.*)

ADORATION. The act of religion by which God is recognized as alone worthy of supreme honor because he is infinitely perfect, has supreme dominion over humans, and the right for all humans to be totally dependent on him as their Creator. It is at once an act of mind and will, expressing itself in appropriate prayers, postures of praise, and acts of reverence and sacrifice. (Etym. Latin *ad-,* to + *orare,* to pray; or *os, oris,* mouth, from the pagan custom of expressing preference for a god by wafting a kiss to the statue: *adoratio,* worship, veneration.)

ADORATION OF THE EUCHARIST. Acknowledgment that, because the whole Christ is really present in the Blessed Sacrament, he is to be adored in the Eucharist as the incarnate God. The manner of showing this homage differs among countries and has varied through the ages. The postconciliar legislation for the Latin Rite requires that the Blessed Sacrament, whether in the tabernacle or exposed on the altar, is to be venerated by genuflecting on one knee.

ADULT. A person who has reached the age of maturity. In ecclesiastical terms the age varies; e.g., sixteen years is adult for men and fourteen for women to marry. But adult baptism means that one has reached the age of reason. A person is a canonical minor (Canon 97) until the completion of the eighteenth year.

ADULTERY. Sexual intercourse of a married person and another who is not the wife or husband. Forbidden by the sixth commandment of the Decalogue, it was extended in meaning by Christ, who forbade divorce with the right to remarry during the lifetime of one's legitimate spouse. (Etym. Latin *adulterium,* adultery, carnal or spiritual.)

ADVENT WREATH. A band or circle of green foliage surrounding four candles that may be enclosed in glass and are lighted successively in the four weeks of the Advent season. They symbolize the coming celebration of Christmas, when Christ the Light of the World was born in Bethlehem. The wreath originated in Germany, and in some countries there is a special ceremony, with prayers and hymns, associated with the lighting of the candles on the Sundays of Advent.

AFFECTIONS. A broad variety of human sentiments that are distinguished from strictly mental or cognitive experiences. Affections pertain to the will, desires, and feelings—i.e., the outgoing activities. In the spiritual life they are identified with those movements of the soul that reach out to God and with the invisible world of angels and saints. Affections are acts of the infused virtues of hope and charity. (Etym. Latin *affectus,* condition, situation; affectionate state or inclination; faculty of desire.)

AFFINITY. An invalidating impediment to marriage with certain blood relatives of a deceased husband or wife, unless a dispensation is granted. No dispensation is given for marriage in the direct line—i.e., with any of his or her ancestors or descendants. In the collateral line, the impediment extends to the second degree—first cousin, uncle or aunt, nephew or niece—and dispensations are granted for both the first and second degrees of affinity. (Etym. Latin *affinitas,* relationship, nearness; from *affinis,* bordering on, nearby family relationship.)

AGAPE. The most distinctively Christian form of love. Used by Christ to describe the love among the persons of the Trinity, it is also the love he commanded his followers to have for one another (John 13:34–35).

It is totally selfless love, which seeks not one's own advantage but only to benefit or share with another.

As a proper noun, Agape is the so-called love feast celebrated in the early Church (I Corinthians 11:20–22, 33–34). At first these were often joined with the Eucharistic liturgy, but in time they were separated from the Mass because of the disorder and scandal they provoked. Legislation against the Agape was passed by the Council of Carthage (397), and by the eighth century the practice disappeared. Since the Second Vatican Council a limited use of the Agape has been encouraged (*Decree on the Apostolate of Lay People*, 8). (Etym. Greek *agapē*, love.)

AGE OF DISCRETION. Sometimes refers to the age at which a person reaches adulthood and can make lifetime decisions, especially regarding one's state of life. But more commonly it is the age when a child is capable of making free acts of the will and therefore becomes morally responsible for his actions. This was St. Pius X's understanding as regards the age for receiving the sacraments of penance and Holy Communion. In general, it is about seven years of age.

AGE OF REASON. The time of life at which a person is assumed to be morally responsible and able to distinguish between right and wrong. It is generally held to be by the end of the seventh year, although it may be earlier. With the mentally disabled it will vary.

AGILITY. Quality of the glorified human body, which St. Paul says is sown in weakness and is raised in strength (I Corinthians 15:42). This is commonly understood to mean that the body is totally submissive to spirit, in movement through space, with the speed of thought. (Etym. Latin *agilis*, nimble; lit., easily driven about.)

AGNOSTICISM. The theory that either knowledge or certitude about ultimates is impossible. In practice, it stresses uncertainty about the nature or substance of things, the existence of an immortal soul, the origin of the universe, life after death, and the existence and perfections of a personal God. (Etym. Greek *agnōstos*, unknown, unknowable.)

AGNUS DEI. A sacramental consisting of a small piece of wax, blessed by the pope, stamped with the figure of a lamb on one side and with the coat of arms of the pope on the reverse side. It is a symbol of the

Lamb of God as the Savior. It is used as a protection against Satan, sickness, temptations, fire, tempests, and sudden death, and, for pregnant women, for safe delivery. Its use is not indulgenced. Except as minute particles of the one blessed by the pope on the Wednesday of Holy Week in the first year and every succeeding seventh year of his pontificate, no other Agnus Deis are to be distributed among the faithful.

AGNUS DEI (LITURGY). The invocation "Lamb of God" is sung or recited at Mass during the breaking of the bread and the commingling. It may be repeated as often as necessary, but the conclusion is always "Dona nobis pacem"—"Grant us peace."

AGONY IN THE GARDEN. The bloody sweat of Christ in the Garden of Gethsemane, described by the third evangelist (Luke 22:43). Although Matthew and Mark also narrate the event, only Luke mentions the sweat of blood and the visitation of the angel. Catholic tradition has understood the bloody perspiration literally. Medical testimony indicates that, although rare, the phenomenon is neither impossible nor, by itself, miraculous. Commemoration of the event forms the first of the sorrowful mysteries of the Rosary. (Etym. Latin *agonia;* from Greek, contest, anguish, from *agōn,* contest, from *agein,* to drive.)

ALB. A full-length white linen vestment secured with a cincture used at Mass. An adaptation of the undertunic of the Greeks and Romans of the fourth century. It is blessed before being worn. It symbolizes the garment in which Christ was clothed by Herod and the purity of the soul with which the Sacrifice of the Mass should be offered. "Make me white O Lord and cleanse my heart that, made white by the Blood of the Lamb, I may be able to serve Thee" is said by the priest as he puts on the alb. It is also the white garment worn by the newly baptized person from Holy Saturday to the Sunday after Easter, Divine Mercy Sunday, sometimes called the "Sunday in white." (Etym. Latin *albus,* white.)

ALBIGENSIANISM. A modified form of the Manichaean heresy that flourished in Southern France in the twelfth and thirteenth centuries. It claimed that a good deity created the world of the spirit and an evil god the material world, including the human body, which is under its control. The good deity sent Jesus Christ, as a creature, to deliver human souls from their imprisonment. Albigensians favored suicide and advocated abstaining from marriage. A crusade was organized against them as a menace to society, and was opposed by Raymond of Toulouse. In Belgium, France, and Germany the war against them continued even after their defeat, contrary to the wishes of Pope Innocent III. By the fifteenth century they had disappeared as a political force, but their Manichaean ideas reappeared in the Reformation.

ALCOHOLISM, MORALITY OF. Habitual excessive consumption of alcoholic beverages. It is characterized by an abnormal and persistent desire to drink ethyl alcohol to excess, and also describes the condition that results from such drinking. Chronic alcoholism may have begun as a moral weakness or disorder, but in time it produces psychic instability. It causes psychological and structural changes. One of its most serious effects is to lessen the willpower that is needed to stop. In time all higher faculties are impaired and, not infrequently, undoubted insanity results. Overcoming alcoholism is a major social problem in many societies. Treatment is effective only if a person is sufficiently motivated to practice total abstinence.

ALLELUIA. Hebrew *hallelujah* "praise YHWH." Ancient liturgical form of jubilation especially in the Psalms, now in the Divine Office and Eucharistic liturgy. Best known in the Easter chant and in the Alleluia verse at Mass. (Etym. Hebrew *halelu jah,* praise ye YHWH; praise to him who is.)

ALL SAINTS. A feast now celebrated on November 1 as a holy day of obligation. It originated in the West in 609, when Pope Boniface IV dedicated the Pantheon to the Blessed Virgin Mary. At first celebrated in Rome on May 13, Pope Gregory III (731–41) changed the date to November 1, when he dedicated a chapel in honor of All Saints in the Vatican Basilica. Gregory IV later extended the feast to the whole Church.

ALL SOULS. A feast commemorating on November 2 the faithful departed. Begun by Abbot Odo of Cluny in his monasteries in 998, it was gradually adopted by the whole Church. Pope Benedict XV granted all priests the privilege of offering three masses on this day: one for all the poor souls, another for the pope's intentions, and a third for the intentions of the priest. When the feast falls on Sunday, it is observed on November 3.

ALMS. Material or financial assistance given to a needy person or cause, prompted by Christian charity. Almsgiving is recognized by the Church as one of the principal forms of penance, especially since the mitigation of the laws on fast and abstinence.

ALPHA AND OMEGA. A symbol witnessing to the divinity of Christ. Words spoken by Jesus of himself: "I am the Alpha and the Omega, the beginning and the end, who is, who was, and who is to come, the Almighty" (Revelation 1:8). This combined symbol is often used in conjunction with the cross and together are favorite symbols in ecclesiastical decorations on altars, walls, and vestments.

ALTAR. A table or stand on which sacrifice is offered. In Catholic churches the table on which the Sacrifice of the Mass is offered. One or more relics of martyrs are commonly set into the altar. In the primitive church and in the catacombs, the altar was usually a niche covered with a slab over the tomb of a martyr. "Altar" in the Greek Rite is synonymous with "sanctuary" in the Latin Rite. It may also refer to a secondary side space or section dedicated to a saint in the transept of the church. (Etym. Anglo-Saxon *altare*, altar; Latin *altar* or *altare*, an altar, high place.)

ALTAR BELL. A small bell, originally kept at the epistle side of the altar, rung at the Sanctus and Elevation during Mass as an invitation to those present to alert them to the solemnity of the Eucharistic consecration. In some countries, the bell was also rung first before the consecration, and before the Communion of the priest and the faithful. Although no longer prescribed by the rubrics for the Ordinary Form of the Roman Rite, it is a laudable and approved practice to ring the altar bell at least at the Elevation of the Host and the chalice.

ALTAR BREAD. Round wafers of wheaten bread, unleavened in the Latin, Maronite, and Armenian Rites, used at Mass for consecration.

ALTAR RAIL. Horizontal bar of wood, marble, or metal, supported by vertical posts and generally ornamented. Its immediate purpose is to separate the sanctuary from the body of the church. It also serves as a communion rail when the Eucharist is given to kneeling communicants (*Eucharisticum Mysterium*, 1967, No. 34).

ALTAR SERVER. Server at the altar at the Mass, Vespers, and other liturgical functions.

ALTAR STEPS. Wood, stone, or brick steps extending around an altar on three sides. High altars commonly had three, five, or seven steps; side altars were required to have at least one.

ALTAR STONE. A small flat stone, consecrated by a bishop, that contains in a hollowed-out cavity relics of two canonized martyrs. The stone is usually inserted in the center of an altar that is not entirely consecrated. It constitutes the altar proper and can be moved from one altar table to another. The host and chalice during the Sacrifice of the Mass are placed on it.

AMEN. Solemn prayerful affirmation, taken over by the Christians from the synagogue for scriptural and liturgical use in apostolic times. It was often spoken by Christ, and is given as one of his names (Revelation 3:14). Now used as an acclamation of assent or religious confirmation of the speaker's own thoughts. (Etym. Latin *amen;* Greek *amen,* verily; Hebrew *amen,* verily, sobeit; from *aman,* to confirm.)

AMERICANISM. The movement propagated in the United States in the late nineteenth century that claimed that the Catholic Church should adjust its doctrines, especially in morality, to the culture of the people. Emphasizing the "active" virtues of social welfare and democratic equality, it underrated the "passive" virtues of humility and obedience to ecclesiastical authority. Americanism was condemned by Pope Leo XIII in an apostolic letter, *Testem Benevolentiae* (January 22, 1899), addressed to Cardinal Gibbons.

AMICE. A short, oblong vestment of white linen, worn beneath the alb to cover the shoulders of the priest while celebrating Mass. Now optional in the Latin Rite. When putting on the amice, the priest says, "Put on my head, O Lord, the helmet of salvation in order to repel the assaults of the devil." (Etym. Latin *amictus,* garment, mantle, cloak; from *amicire,* to throw around.)

AMNIOCENTESIS. A medical technique sometimes used during pregnancy (after the fourteenth to sixteenth weeks) whereby a hollow needle is inserted through the abdomen and into the mother's womb to pierce the amniotic sac (the so-called "bag of waters" that surrounds the fetus) in order to withdraw some of the liquid to examine it for chromosomal evidence of the sex of the unborn child as well as evidence of certain diseases or defects of the developing infant. The risk to the unborn child is statistically low, but the damage that may be induced is grave. Moreover, it is often used as a prenatal screening to determine whether to abort an unborn child who is diseased or defective. When performed for such reasons, amniocentesis is forbidden on Catholic moral principles. But even for a good purpose it is morally questionable because of the risk to the life of the unborn child.

AMOS. Third among the minor prophets. He describes Israel as steeped in national prosperity and reveling in sin. The central theme of his book is a threefold prophecy that extends through nine chapters. The first part (1–2) foretells God's judgment on the nations surrounding Israel and then on Israel itself. The second part (3–6) develops the divine judgment against Israel in three separate discourses. The third part (7–9) records five visions, of which the fifth describes the glorious anticipation of messianic blessings. Amos is the prophet of God's sovereign lordship over all creation.

ANANIAS. A member of the early Christian community with his wife, Sapphira. In obedience to the ideal that the community owned everything in common, Ananias sold his property but connived with his wife to turn over to the Apostles only part of the proceeds. Peter rebuked him for his deception: "It is not to men you have lied but to God." Ananias dropped dead. His wife arrived later and, not knowing her husband's fate, repeated the lie. She, too, died on the spot. This incident originated the familiar use of the name Ananias to represent a liar (Acts 5:1–10).

ANARCHISM. The theory that laws are an invasion of the rights of free, intelligent beings; that individuals have the right to unlimited self-expression; and that the self-interest of the individual, if intelligently pursued, will best serve the common good. Its origins are traceable to the French Revolution and to Pierre Joseph Proudhon (1809–65). Some anarchists are evolutionary, believing that propaganda and the ballot will gradually eliminate (or make obsolete) most laws. Others are revolutionary, urging the establishment of anarchism by violence. Nihilists are extreme revolutionary anarchists. The basis of anarchism is an unreasoning optimism about the goodness of unrestrained human nature. Anarchism has been more than once condemned by the Catholic Church, e.g., in the *Syllabus of Errors* of Pope Pius IX in 1864. (Etym. Latin *anarchia;* from Greek *anarchos,* having no ruler.)

ANATHEMA. Solemn condemnation, of biblical origin, used by the Church to declare that some position or teaching contradicts Catholic faith and doctrine.

"If anyone," Paul wrote to the Galatians, "preach to you a gospel besides what you have received, let him be anathema" (Galatians 1:9). Reflecting the Church's concern to preserve the integrity of faith, the Fathers anathematized heretics in a variety of terms. Polycarp called Marcion the firstborn of the devil. Ignatius saw in heretics poisonous plants, or animals in human form. Justin (c. 100–65) and Tertullian (160–220) called their teachings an inspiration of the Evil One. Theophilus compared them to barren and rocky islands on which ships were wrecked, and Origen said they were pirates placing lights on cliffs to lure and destroy vessels in search of refuge. These primitive views were later tempered in language, but the implicit attitudes remained and were crystallized in solemn conciliar decrees. The familiar *anathema sit* (let him be anathema, or excommunicated) appears to have been first applied to heretics at the Council of Elvira (Spain) in 300–306, and became the standard formula in all the general councils of the Church, as against Arius (256–336) at I Nicaea (325), Nestorius at Ephesus (431), Eutyches at Chalcedon (451), and the Iconoclasts at II Nicaea in 787. (Etym. Greek *anathema,* thing devoted to evil, curse; an accursed thing or person; from *anatithenai,* to set up, dedicate.)

ANDREW. A fisherman and follower of John the Baptist. He was in John's company when he saw Jesus for the first time and stayed with him for the rest of the day. Convinced that Jesus was the Messiah, he took his brother, Simon Peter, to meet him the next day. This was the occasion on which Jesus told Andrew's brother that from being called Simon his name would be changed to Cephas, meaning the Rock (John 1:35–42). The two brothers were the first apostles chosen by Jesus; they accepted his summons to become fishers of men and abandoned their fishing nets (Mark 1:16–18). The miracle of the loaves that Jesus performed at Tiberias followed Andrew's report of a boy with five loaves and two fishes (John 6:5–10). According to tradition, Andrew was crucified in Achaea on a *crux decussata* (x), which thereafter was called St. Andrew's cross. His feast day is November 30. (Etym. Greek *andreas,* manly.)

ANGEL. A pure, created spirit, called angel because some angels are sent by God as messengers to humans. An angel is a pure spirit because he has no body and does not depend for his existence or activity on matter. The Bible tells us that the angels constitute a vast multitude, beyond human reckoning. They differ in perfection of nature and grace. Each is an individual person. According to Christian tradition, they form three major categories in descending order. The word "angel" is commonly applied only to those who remained faithful to God, although the devils are also angels by nature. Moreover, "angel" is the special name for the choir of angelic spirits, from whom guardian angels are sent to minister to human needs. The existence of angels has been twice defined by the Church: at the Fourth Lateran Council (Denzinger 800) and the First Vatican Council (Denzinger 3002). (Etym. Latin *angelus,* an angel; Greek *angelos,* messenger.)

ANGELIC SALUTATION. First part of the Hail Mary, repeating the words of the archangel Gabriel to the Blessed Virgin, up to and including the name "Jesus."

Hail Mary, full of grace,
the Lord is with thee!
Blessed art thou among women,
and blessed is the fruit of thy womb, Jesus.

ANGELS (SYMBOLS). Depicted in various forms to express the will of God, of which they are the mediators. Shown as messengers, in worship, and in executing justice, they appeared in Western art before A.D. 600. Before Constantine their appearance without wings was mainly with a staff indicative of their office as messengers. The nine choirs are distinctively represented. Angels in art are represented with a variety of articles, musical instruments, thuribles, shields, scrolls, and in a few instances emblems of the Passion, though they are usually represented in worship before the Blessed Sacrament on earth and before the throne of God in heaven. Archangels are variously depicted: Michael driving Satan into hell; Gabriel announcing the Incarnation to Mary; Raphael healing the blind Tobit. The thrones are shown kneeling in adoration. Seraphim symbolize fire and love with their six red wings and eyes; cherubim, with four-eyed wings of blue and holding a book, indicate their great knowledge; dominations, in royal robes, are crowned for authority; virtues, two-eyed, are charged with dispensing celestial miracles; the powers, holding swords, indicate their conquest of the evil spirits shown under their feet; the principalities carry scepters to assist in their direction of God's commands. The emblem of St. Frances of Rome is her guardian angel, whom she saw daily in visible form.

ANGELUS. Devotion in honor of the Incarnation, commemorating the archangel Gabriel's annunciation to the Blessed Virgin. Recited approximately at 6 A.M., noon, and 6 P.M., "Angelus" is the opening word of the prayer "*Angelus Domini nuntiavit Mariae*" (the angel of the Lord declared unto Mary). The evening Angelus probably owes its origin to the curfew bell, a signal for evening prayer. The morning recital began as a prayer for peace. The noon Angelus was first said only on Friday. It is replaced by the prayer *Regina Coeli Laetare* (Queen of Heaven, Rejoice) during the Easter season. The text of the Angelus follows:

The Angel of the Lord declared unto Mary,
And she conceived by the power of the Holy Spirit. (Hail Mary)
Behold the handmaid of the Lord.
Be it done unto me according to Thy word. (Hail Mary)
And the Word was made flesh,
And dwelt among us. (Hail Mary)
Pray for us, O Holy Mother of God,
That we may be made worthy of the promises of Christ.
Let us pray.
Pour forth, we beseech Thee, O Lord, Thy grace into our hearts; that we,
to whom the Incarnation of Christ Thy Son was made known by the
message of an angel, may by His Passion and Cross be brought to the
glory of His Resurrection. Through the same Christ, our Lord. Amen.
See also *REGINA COELI.*

ANGELUS BELL. Consists of three strokes of a bell each followed by a pause, then nine strokes while the Angelus prayer is being finished.

ANGER. An emotional sense of displeasure and usually antagonism, aroused by real or apparent injury. The anger can be either passionate or nonpassionate, depending on the degree to which the emotions are excited, strongly in one case and mildly in the other.

ANGLICAN COMMUNION. The churches in communion with the See of Canterbury. It originated with Henry VIII's Act of Supremacy, 1534, declaring "the king's majesty justly and rightfully is and ought to be the supreme head of the Church of England." But the complete rupture with Catholicism did not come until 1563, when the Elizabethan Parliament made the Thirty-nine Articles of Religion obligatory on all citizens under heavy penalties.

Since then the Thirty-nine Articles have played a major role in shaping the doctrine of Anglicanism. Among typical features, the Bible is declared to contain all that is necessary for salvation, general councils are said not to be infallible, transubstantiation is denied, and the civil ruler is given authority over the Church. To this day the Church of England retains its State Establishment.

Even more influential has been the Book of Common Prayer. This is the official service book of the Church of England and contains, among other things, the forms for the administration of the sacraments and the Ordinal. Mainly the creation of Thomas Cranmer, Archbishop of Canterbury, the Book of Common Prayer has been the single most cohesive force in shaping world Anglicanism.

ANGLICANORUM COETIBUS. An apostolic constitution, along with complementary norms, promulgated by Pope Benedict XVI in response to petitions from groups of Anglicans to be received into the Catholic Church. It provides for personal ordinariates for Anglicans entering into full communion with the Catholic Church (November 4, 2009). "The Ordinate has the faculty to celebrate the Holy Eucharist and the other Sacraments, Liturgy of the Hours and other liturgical celebrations according to the liturgical books proper to the Anglican tradition, which have been approved by the Holy See, so as to maintain the liturgical, spiritual, and pastoral traditions of the Anglican Communion within the Catholic Church."

ANIMA CHRISTI (SOUL OF CHRIST). A hymn written in the fourteenth century by an unknown author. There are numerous translations in all the modern languages. It was a favorite prayer of St. Ignatius Loyola. The translation of Cardinal Newman reads:

Soul of Christ, be my sanctification;
Body of Christ, be my salvation;

Blood of Christ, fill all my veins;
Water of Christ's side, wash out my stains;
Passion of Christ, my comfort be;
O good Jesu, listen to me;
In Thy wounds I fain would hide,
Ne'er to be parted from Thy side;
Guard me, should the foe assail me;
Call me when my life shall fail me;
Bid me come to Thee above,
With Thy saints to sing Thy love,
World without end. Amen.

ANNO DOMINI. "In the year of our Lord." Abbreviated A.D., it is based on the supposed year of Christ's birth devised by Dionysius Exiguus (d. 550). Modern scholarship agrees that the actual birth was several years earlier, either between 7 and 4 B.C., based on the death of Herod the Great (Matthew 2:19) in 4 B.C., or at A.D. 6, based on the great taxation under Quirinius (Luke 2:1–2).

ANNUAL CONFESSION. The duty to receive the sacrament of penance at least once a year. First decreed by the Fourth Lateran Council in 1215, it has been reconfirmed many times since, especially by Pope St. Pius X in 1910 and Pope Paul VI since the Second Vatican Council. It is binding by ecclesiastical law on "everyone of the faithful of both sexes, after he has reached the age of discretion," and therefore also children or those with only venial sins. It is also binding by divine law on those with mortal sins committed since their last worthy confession and sacramental absolution.

ANNULMENT. Official declaration by competent authority that, for lawful reasons, a previous act or contract was invalid and consequently null and void. In ecclesiastical law, annulments mainly apply to marriage contracts over which the Church has the right to determine their validity. (Etym. Latin an-, to + nullus, none; anullare, to annihilate, to annul.) See also DECLARATION OF NULLITY.

ANNUNCIATION. The feast, observed on March 25, commemorating the announcement of the Incarnation by the archangel Gabriel to the Virgin Mary. There are references to the feast as early as the fifth century. Its date was finally determined by the date of Christmas on December 25. It is considered a feast of the Blessed Virgin and, in the revised liturgy, is a solemnity. (Etym. Latin *annuntiatio*, an announcing, announcement.)

ANOINTED. The meaning of "Christ," derived from the Greek *Christos,* corresponding to the Hebrew *Mashijah* (Messiah). (Etym. Latin *inunctio,* besmearing, an anointing.)

ANOINTING. Literally the pouring of oil on someone or something in a religious ceremony. Its biblical purpose was to make sacred the object anointed. Thus kings were anointed (I Samuel 10:1), priests (Exodus 28:41), and prophets (I Kings 19:16). The reference to anointing in the New Testament as a sacred rite pertains to the sacrament of anointing the sick, but the verb here used (James 5:14), *aleipho,* is unique. It therefore has a different meaning from "to make sacred," as elsewhere in the Bible. In the Catholic Church, holy oils are used in the administration of the three sacraments, which impart a permanent character (baptism, confirmation, and holy orders) and with a different purpose, in the anointing of the sick. Oil is used in the blessing of altars, bells, and sacred vessels. There are also a number of blessed oils, e.g., in honor of St. Serapion (fourth century), that are used as sacramentals. (Etym. Latin *inunguere; in-,* upon + *unguere,* to smear, anoint.)

ANOINTING OF THE SICK. Sacrament of the New Law, instituted by Christ to give the sick spiritual aid and strength and to perfect spiritual health, including, if need be, the remission of sins. Conditionally it also restores bodily health to Christians who are seriously ill. It consists essentially of the anointing by a priest of the forehead and the hands, while pronouncing the words "Through this holy anointing and His most loving mercy, may the Lord assist you by the grace of the Holy Spirit, so that freed from your sins, He may save you and in His goodness raise you up." In case of necessity, a single anointing of the forehead or of another suitable part of the body suffices. Olive oil, blessed by a bishop, is normally used for the anointing, but any vegetable oil may be substituted in case of emergency.

The institution of anointing by Christ is an article of the Catholic faith, defined by the Council of Trent (Denzinger 1716). The Church further teaches that this sacrament is implied in Gospel reference to Christ sending out the disciples, who "anointed many sick people with oil and cured them" (Mark 6:13); moreover that the sacrament was promulgated by the Apostle James when he wrote, "Is anyone among you sick? Let him bring in the presbyters of the Church and let them pray over him, anointing him with oil in the name of the Lord. And the prayer of faith will save the sick man and the Lord will raise him up and if he be in sins, they shall be forgiven him" (James 5:14–15).

See also EXTREME UNCTION.

ANTHEM. A hymn of acclamation and loyalty, it may be a musical composition set to a sacred text, or a patriotic song expressing celebration and praise. (Etym. Latin *antiphona,* an anthem; Greek *antiphona,* sounding in response to; from the alternate singing of the half-choirs.)

ANTI-CATHOLICISM. Concerted and coordinated opposition, on principle, to the Roman Catholic Church. Its origins are lost in obscurity, but its modern development was one of the fruits of the Reformation. The rise of the modern secular state has intensified the conflict. The Catholic Church's insistence on operating her own schools and welfare institutions, and her uncompromising position on such issues as abortion and marital morality, are logically opposed by those who disagree with the Church and have the power to enforce their views.

ANTICHRIST. The chief of Christ's enemies. The New Testament specifically names him only in I John 2:18, 2:22, 4:3, and II John 7, where he is identified with unbelievers who deny the Incarnation. Over the centuries the Antichrist has been variously associated with historical persons, e.g., Caligula, Simon Magus, and Nero, or again with organized movements such as Arianism. The more common Catholic interpretation says that he is not merely symbolic or an embodiment of the anti-Christian. The Antichrist is a real person. (Etym. Greek *antichristos,* against Christ.)

ANTIPOPE. A false claimant to the Holy See in opposition to the pope canonically elected. There have been more than thirty in the Catholic Church's history. (Etym. Latin *antipapa;* Greek *anti,* against + *papas,* father.)

ANTI-SEMITISM. Feelings of prejudice and hostility toward the Jews. The term was used in 1879 in a pamphlet attacking the Jews as descendants of the biblical Shem. On this subject the Second Vatican Council stated that the Catholic Church "deplores all hatreds, persecutions, displays of antisemitism leveled at any time or from any source against the Jews" (*Decree on the Relation of the Church to Non-Christian Religions,* 4). (Etym. Greek *anti-,* against + Hebrew *Shēm,* son of Noe.)

ANTITYPE. A person or thing typified or prefigured by a biblical person or object. Christ is the antitype of the Old Testament figures of Noah, Moses, David; the Blessed Virgin is the antitype of Eve. (Etym. Greek *anti-,* corresponding to + *typos,* a mold, type.)

See also TYPES, SCRIPTURAL.

APOCALYPSE. The book of Revelation, commonly attributed to St. John the Apostle. It was written to encourage the persecuted Christians by foretelling the fall of Rome and the final victory of Christ and his church. It is also a prophetical work, describing in anticipation the many trials of the followers of Christ and their eventual triumph over Satan and the forces of the Antichrist. It is also eschatological, in predicting the glories of the Heavenly Jerusalem in the City on High. The Apocalypse is the most image-laden book of the New Testament, rich in allegory and subject to numerous, legitimate interpretations. (Etym. Latin *apocalypsis,* a disclosing, revelation; Greek *apokalypsis,* a revelation.)

APOCRYPHA. Originally writings that claimed a sacred origin and were supposed to have been hidden for generations; later, a well-defined class of literature with scriptural or quasi-scriptural pretensions, but lacking genuineness and canonicity, composed during the two centuries before Christ and the early centuries of our era. Protestants apply the term improperly to denote also Old Testament books not contained in the Jewish canon but received by Catholics under the name of deuterocanonical. The following is a list of the Apocrypha:

Apocrypha of Jewish Origin
Jewish Apocalypses: Book of Henoch; Assumption of Moses: Fourth Book of Esdras; Apocalypse of Baruch; Apocalypse of Abraham. *Legendary Apocrypha of Jewish Origin:* Book of Jubilees, or Little Genesis; Third Book of Esdras; Third Book of Maccabees; History of Maxims of Ahikar the Assyrian. *Apocryphal Psalms and Prayers:* Psalms of Solomon; Prayer of Manasses. *Jewish Philosophy:* Fourth Book of Maccabees.

Apocrypha of Jewish Origin with Christian Accretions
Sibylline Oracles; Testaments of the Twelve Patriarchs; Ascension of Isaias.

Apocrypha of Christian Origin
Apocryphal Gospels of Catholic Origin: Protoevangelium Jacobi, or Infancy Gospel of James, describing the birth, education, and marriage of the Blessed Virgin; Gospel of the Pseudo-Matthew; Arabic Gospel of the Infancy; History of Joseph the Carpenter; Transitus Mariae, or Evangelium Joannis, describing the death and assumption of the Blessed Virgin. *Judaistic and Heretical Gospels:* Gospel according to the Hebrews; Gospel according to the Egyptians; Gospel of Peter; Gospel of Philip; Gospel of Thomas; Gospel of Marcion; Gospel of Bartholomew; Gospel of Matthias; Gospel of Nicodemus; Gospel of the Twelve Apostles; Gospel of Andrew; Gospel of Barnabas; Gospel of Thaddeus; Gospel of Philip; Gospel of Eve; Gospel of Judas Iscariot. *Pilate Literature and Other Apocrypha Concerning Christ:* Report of Pilate to the Emperor; Narrative of Joseph of Arimathea; Pseudo-Correspondence of Jesus and Abgar, King of Edessa. *Gnostic Acts of the Apostles:* Acts of Peter; Acts of John; Acts of Andrew; Acts and Martyrdom of Matthew; Acts of Thomas; Acts of Bartholomew. *Catholic Apocryphal Acts of the Apostles:* Acts of Peter and Paul; Acts of Paul; Acts of Paul and Thecla; Acts of Philip; Acts of Matthew; Acts of Simon and Jude; Acts of Barnabas; Acts of James the Greater. *Apocryphal Doctrinal Works:* Testamentum Domini Nostri Jesu; Preaching of Peter, or Kerygma Petri. *Apocryphal Epistles:* Pseudo-Epistles of Paul; Pseudo-Epistles to the Laodiceans; Pseudo-Correspondence of Paul and Seneca. *Christian Apocryphal Apocalypses:* Apocalypse of Peter; Apocalypse of Paul. (Etym. Latin *apocryphus,* uncanonical, apocryphal; from Greek *apokryphos,* hidden.)

See also GOSPELS, APOCRYPHAL.

APOLOGETICS. The science that aims to explain and justify religious doctrine. It shows the reasonableness of such doctrine in the face of the objections offered by those who refuse to accept any religion, especially Christianity and more particularly Roman Catholicism. Also called fundamental theology, as the science that establishes the credibility of Christian revelation on the evidence of miraculous phenomena and the testimony of unbiased history. (Etym. Greek *apologetikos,* a defense.)

APOSTASY. The total rejection by a baptized person of the Christian faith he once professed. The term is also applied in a technical sense to "apostates from religious life," who without authorization leave a religious institute after perpetual vows with no intention of returning. (Etym. Latin *apostasia,* falling away or separation from God; from Greek *apostasis,* revolt, literally, a standing off.)

APOSTLE. A messenger and authorized representative of the sender. Broadly used in Scripture, it refers to many followers of Jesus who spread his message. More precisely, however, it applies to the original twelve men chosen by Jesus to be his immediate aides. They are referred to as disciples during the period in which he was instructing them, but following his Ascension they are always called Apostles. After Pentecost they spoke and acted with confidence and assurance in teaching others what he had taught them and in assuming leadership roles in the early church. They were ordained priests by Christ at the Last Supper and were commissioned by him to preach the Gospel to all mankind (Matthew 28:19–20). (Etym. Latin *apostolus,* an apostle; Greek *apostolos,* one who is sent off.)

APOSTLES' CREED. A formula of belief, in twelve articles, containing the fundamental doctrines of Christianity, whose authorship (in substance if not in words) tradition ascribes to the Apostles. Its full text reads:

> I believe in God the Father Almighty,
> Creator of heaven and earth.
> And in Jesus Christ,
> His only Son our Lord,
> who was conceived by the Holy Spirit,
> born of the Virgin Mary,
> suffered under Pontius Pilate,
> was crucified, died, and was buried.
> He descended into hell.
> The third day He arose again from the dead.
> He ascended into heaven,
> and sits at the right hand of God the Father Almighty.
> From thence He shall come to judge the living and the dead.
> I believe in the Holy Spirit,
> the holy, catholic Church,
> the communion of saints,
> the forgiveness of sins,

the resurrection of the body,
and life everlasting. Amen.

Eastern Christians do not use the Apostles' Creed in their liturgy. At a very early date the Western Church required catechumens to learn and recite the Apostles' Creed before admission to baptism.

APOSTLESHIP OF PRAYER. Worldwide organization, founded at Vals, France, in 1844, to promote devotion to the Sacred Heart of Jesus. Basic requirements for membership are the recitation of the Daily Offering and inscription of one's name in the Apostleship. The members are asked to pray for the particular intentions of the Holy Father, which are specified each month in two forms. There is a general and a mission intention, and both are made publicly known a year ahead of time. The Apostleship publishes *The Messenger of the Sacred Heart* in many countries.

APOSTOLATE. The work of an apostle, not only of the first followers of Christ but of all the faithful who carry on the original mission entrusted by the Savior to the Twelve to "make disciples of all the nations" (Matthew 28:19). The apostolate belongs essentially to the order of grace. Its purpose is not temporal welfare, however noble, but to bring people to the knowledge and love of Christ and, through obedience to his teaching, help them attain life everlasting.

APOSTOLICAE CURAE. Encyclical of Pope Leo XIII, issued on September 13, 1896, in which Anglican orders were declared invalid because of defect in both the form (rite) and intention.

APOSTOLICAM ACTUOSITATEM. Second Vatican Council's Decree on the Apostolate of Lay People (November 18, 1965). The document is a practical expression of the Church's mission, to which the laity are specially called in virtue of their baptism and incorporation into Christ. One of its important provisions is the recognition that, while preserving the necessary link with ecclesiastical authority, the laity have the right to establish and direct associations and to join existing ones. In effect the decree provides for three kinds of corporate lay apostolates: 1. those which "owe their origin to the free choice of the laity and are run at their own discretion," but always having "the approval of legitimate ecclesiastical authority"; 2. those specially chosen by the bishops and "without depriving the laity of their rightful freedom" nevertheless have received a "mandate" from the hierarchy;

3. those so closely associated with the hierarchy that they are "fully subject to the superior ecclesiastical control in regard to the exercise of these charges."

APOSTOLIC DELEGATE. A papal representative who has the right and duty of supervising the status of the Church in the area assigned to him and keeping the pope informed of the same. He has certain faculties delegated to him by the Holy See. Where established relations exist with a civil government, he is a papal representative with diplomatic status; otherwise his role is purely ecclesiastical. His duties do not interfere with the jurisdiction of local ordinaries but rather strengthen the general condition of the Church throughout the territory by unifying and facilitating the work of the bishops. He does not constitute a tribunal of justice, but he may decide certain conflicts according to Church law. The delegate takes precedence in honor over the bishops not cardinals in his territory. He also enjoys other concessions of an honorary nature.

APOSTOLICITY. That quality of the Catholic Church by which she is derived from the Apostles. There is an apostolicity of origin, since the Church was first organized by the apostles chosen by Christ; of teaching, because what the Church teaches now is essentially what was taught by the Apostles; and of succession in office, since there has been an unbroken historical transmission of episcopal powers, through ordination, from the Apostles to all the bishops in communion with the Bishop of Rome today.

APOSTOLIC SEE. Title given to Rome since the first Christian centuries. It applies to the pope and the persons and offices directly under his authority. It implies that, as successor of St. Peter, the Prince of the Apostles, he has the primary duty of extending the Christian faith to all the world. See also HOLY SEE.

APOSTOLIC SUCCESSION. The method by which the episcopacy has been derived from the Apostles to the present day. Succession means successive consecration by the laying on of hands, performing the functions of the Apostles, receiving their commission in a lineal sequence from the Apostles, succession in episcopal sees traced back to the Apostles, and successive communion with the Apostolic See, i.e., the Bishop of Rome. The Eastern Orthodox and others share in the apostolic succession in having valid episcopal orders, although they are not in collegial union with the Roman Catholic hierarchy.

APPARITION. Supernatural vision. It is a psychical experience in which a person or object not accessible to normal human powers is seen and ordinarily also heard. When apparitions are claimed, the Church's policy is to require proof of the fact, since illusions and hallucinations are so common, and the influence of the evil spirit is also to be taken into account. Yet from the Scriptures on, there have been numerous, well-attested apparitions that were certainly of divine origin.

APPROPRIATION. A manner of speaking in which the properties and activities of God, though common to the three divine persons, are attributed to an individual person. The purpose of appropriation is to manifest the differences in the divine properties and persons. Four kinds of appropriations are known from Scripture and sacred tradition: 1. substantive names of God (*Theos*), applied to the Father, and of Lord (*Kurios*), applied to the Son; 2. absolute attributes of God, namely power, unity, and eternity applied to the Father; wisdom, equality, and beauty applied to the Son; goodness, harmony, and happiness applied to the Holy Spirit; 3. works of God, namely efficient cause (Father), exemplary cause (Son), and final cause (Holy Spirit); 4. worship of God, with the Father as recipient of adoration and sacrifice, and the Son and Holy Spirit as mediators between God and man. (Etym. Latin *appropriatio*, ascribing, the attributing of a special characteristic.)

ARAMAIC. Named from Aram, a country in southwestern Asia. A Semitic language spoken by the Jews during and after the Babylonian exile (606–536 B.C.). It was spoken by Christ and the Apostles, since in New Testament times Hebrew was cultivated only by the learned. To meet the needs of the Jewish faithful, the Hebrew Bible was made available in Aramaic paraphrases called Targums.

ARCHANGEL. A chief or ruling angel. The term occurs twice in the New Testament (Jude 5:9; I Thessalonians 4:16) and has two meanings in the Catholic vocabulary. In its wider sense, an archangel is any angel of higher rank, so that St. Michael is an archangel although he is the prince of the Seraphim. But more strictly, archangels are those angelic spirits who belong to the eighth or second to last of nine choirs of angels. As distinct from guardian angels, archangels are messengers of God to men in matters of greater significance. Thus Raphael delivered Tobias' wife from demonic obsession (Tobit 12:6, 15) and traditionally is identified with the angel who moved the waters of the pool, where Christ worked his miracle (John 5:1–4). Gabriel was the angel of the Annunciation. St. Michael is the leader of the heavenly host, who fought and won against the rebellious spirits (Revelation 12:7–9).

ARCHBISHOP. A bishop who presides over one or more dioceses. He may call the bishops to a provincial council, having the right and duty to do so, and he may act as first judge of appeal over a decision of one of his bishops. His immediate jurisdiction, however, pertains solely to his own diocese. He is often styled "metropolitan" because of the importance of his see city or ecclesiastical province.

ARCHIVES, VATICAN. Collections of documents pertaining to the affairs of the Holy See. Since apostolic times, the popes preserved writings of importance, but most of the material before Pope Innocent III (1161–1216) has been destroyed or has disappeared. Pope Paul V (1552–1621) established a central repository of documents of the Holy See. In 1881, Pope Leo XIII opened these archives to scholars for consultation. The Vatican Archives are connected with the Archivist School, which before 1968 was the annual Archivist Institute, first established by Pope Pius XI in 1923. The archives of the Holy See contain tens of thousands of documents and are the most important center of historical research in the world.

ARIANISM. A fourth-century heresy that denied the divinity of Jesus Christ. Its author was Arius (256–336), a priest of Alexandria, who in 318 began to teach the doctrine that now bears his name. According to Arius there are not three distinct persons in God, co-eternal and equal in all things, but only one person, the Father. The Son is only a creature, made out of nothing, like all other created beings. He may be called God but only by an extension of language, as the first and greatest person chosen to be divine intermediary in the creation and redemption of the world.

In the Arian system, the Logos or Word of God is not eternal. There was a time when he did not exist. He is not a son by nature but merely by grace and adoption. God adopted him in prevision of his merits, since he might have sinned but did not. In a word, instead of being God he is a kind of demiurge who advanced in virtue and merit and thus came to be closely associated with the Father. But his nature is not of the same substance as the Father's.

Boldly anti-Trinitarian, Arianism struck at the foundations of Christianity by reducing the Incarnation to a figure of speech. If the Logos was created and not divine, God did not become man or redeem the world, and all the consequent mysteries of the faith are dissolved.

The First Council of Nicaea was convoked in 325 to meet the Arian crisis. Since the signature lists are defective, the exact number of prelates who attended the council is not known. However, at least two hundred twenty bishops, mostly from the East but also from Africa, Spain, Gaul, and Italy, signed the creed that affirmed the divinity of Christ and condemned Arius as a heretic. "We believe," the formula read, "in one God, the Father Almighty, Creator of all things visible and invisible. And in one Lord Jesus Christ, the Son of God, the only-begotten of the Father, that is, of the *substance of the Father;* God from God, light from light, true God from true God; begotten, not created, consubstantial [Greek *Homo ousion*] with the Father." The soul of the council was St. Athanasius (296–373), Bishop of Alexandria, whose resolute character and theological insight were the main obstacle to the triumph of Arianism in the East.

Since the fifth century, Arian churches have remained in existence in many countries, although some of them were absorbed by Islam. A principal tenet of these churches is the recognition of Christ as Messiah but denial that he is the natural Son of God.

ARK. The chest containing the tablets of the Law. God ordered Moses to construct it of acacia wood, telling him the exact dimensions. "Inside the ark you must place the Testimony I shall give you" (Exodus 25:10–22). This Ark of the Covenant became a dramatic symbol in Israelite history, accompanying the people on their wilderness journeys and throughout Joshua's rule. Later it was seized by the Philistines but surrendered in fear to Israel. David brought the ark to Jerusalem, where it remained until the first Temple was destroyed. At that point it disappeared from history.

ARTICLE OF FAITH. A term used by the catechism of the Council of Trent, speaking of the Apostles' Creed: "The chief truths which Christians must hold are those which the holy Apostles, the leaders and teachers of the faith, inspired by the Holy Spirit have divided into the twelve Articles of the Creed." But the term "article" has a long history and designates whatever a Catholic must believe, whether defined by the Church as revealed or commonly held by the Church's ordinary and universal magisterium as revealed in Scripture or sacred tradition. (Etym. Latin *articulus,* a joint, member, part; literally, a small joint.)

ARTIFICIAL INSEMINATION. Any process by which the male spermatozoa and the female ovum are brought together apart from and wholly distinct from an act of natural intercourse. Long used in animal husbandry, the practice presents no moral problem in the lower forms of life. The Catholic Church teaches that among humans artificial insemination constitutes such a violation of the dignity of the person and the sanctity of marriage as to be contrary to the natural and divine law. Catholic teaching on artificial insemination (among humans) was summed up by Venerable Pope Pius XII in an address to Catholic physicians (September 29, 1949). The various dimensions of the immorality involved include: in-donor insemination (insemination with the active element of a donor); the third-party invasion of the exclusive marriage covenant in a kind of mechanical adultery; the irresponsibility of the donor fathering a child for which he can fulfill no paternal responsibility; and the deordination of his masturbation in order to thus donate his paternal seed. Even if insemination could be artificially achieved with the husband's semen properly collected (without masturbation) the papal teaching still points out that any process that isolates the sacred act of human generation from the beautiful and intimate conjugal union of the marriage act itself is inconsistent with the holiness and intimate personalism of that two-in-one-flesh union which alone is appropriate for the generation of a child. As long, however, as the integrity of the marriage act is preserved, various clinical techniques designed to facilitate the process are not to be condemned. The *Catechism of the Catholic Church* reiterates the Church's moral prohibition of artificial insemination (2376, 2377).

ASCENSION. Christ's going up to heaven forty days after his Resurrection from the dead. All the creeds affirm the fact, and the Church teaches that he ascended into heaven in body and soul (Denzinger 801). He ascended into heaven by his own power, as God in divine power and as man in the power of his transfigured soul, which moves his transfigured body, as it will. In regard to the human nature of Christ, one can also say, with the Scriptures, that it was taken up or elevated into heaven by God (Mark 16:19; Luke 24:51; Acts 1:9, 11).

Rationalism has denied the doctrine since the earliest times—e.g., Celsus in the second century. It tries to explain the Ascension as a borrowing from the Old Testament or from pagan mythology, but in doing so omits the basic differences.

Doctrinally the Ascension means the final elevation of Christ's human nature into the condition of divine glory. It is the concluding work of redemption. According to the Church's common teaching, the souls of the just from the pre-Christian era went with the Savior into the glory of heaven. Christ's Ascension is the archetype and pledge of our own ascension into heaven. (Etym. Latin *ascensio,* an ascending, ascent.)

ASCETICAL THEOLOGY. The science of the saints based on a study of their lives. It is aimed to make people holy by explaining what sanctity is and how to attain it. It is the science of leading souls in the ways of Christian perfection through growth in charity and the practice of prayer leading to contemplation. It is that part of spiritual theology which concentrates on man's cooperation with grace and the need for human effort to grow in sanctity.

ASCETICISM. Spiritual effort or exercise in the pursuit of virtue. The purpose is to grow in Christian perfection. Its principles and norms are expanded in ascetical theology. (Etym. Greek *askētikos,* literally, given to exercise; industrious; applied to hermits who strictly exercised themselves in religious devotion.)

ASH WEDNESDAY. The first day of Lent. Named from the custom of signing the foreheads of the faithful with blessed ashes. Its date depends on the date of Easter. In the early Church, public penitents were liturgically admitted to begin their penance on this day. And when this fell into disuse, from the eighth to the tenth centuries, the general penance of the whole community took place. This was symbolized by the imposition of ashes on the heads of the clergy and laity alike.

ASPERGES. The first word in the Latin of the Psalm "Thou shall sprinkle me, O Lord, with hyssop" gave its name to the ceremony of sprinkling the people with holy water before the principal Mass on Sunday. During the paschal season the *Asperges* is replaced by the *Vidi Aquam*. (Etym. Latin *asperges,* thou wilt sprinkle; from *aspergere,* to sprinkle.)

ASPIRATION. Short formalized prayer of about a dozen words. It is expressed in choice language, sometimes poetic, its purpose being to help one maintain a spirit of recollection in God's presence during the day. Such prayers are generally indulgenced by the Church. (Etym. Latin *aspirare,* literally, to breathe upon.)

ASSUMPTION. The doctrine of Mary's entrance into heaven, body and soul. As defined by Venerable Pope Pius XII in 1950, the dogma declares that "Mary, the immaculate perpetually Virgin Mother of God, after the completion of her earthly life, was assumed body and soul into the glory of heaven."

While there is no direct evidence of the Assumption in the Bible, implicitly the Church argues from Mary's fullness of grace (Luke 1:28). Since she was full of grace, she remained preserved from the consequence of sin, namely corruption of the body after death and postponement of bodily happiness in heaven until the last day.

The Church does not rely on the Scriptures for belief in Mary's Assumption. The doctrine is rather part of the oral tradition, handed down over the centuries. It was therefore certainly revealed because, in reply to the questions, the Catholic bishops of the world all but unanimously expressed the belief that this was part of the divine revelations. In explaining the grounds for the Church's belief, Venerable Pius XII singled out the fact that Mary was the Mother of God; as the body of Christ originated from the body of Mary (*caro Jesu est caro Mariae*); that her body was preserved unimpaired in virginal integrity, and therefore it was fitting that it should not be subject to destruction after death; and that since Mary so closely shared in Christ's redemptive mission on earth, she deserved to join him also in bodily glorification.

ASTROLOGY. A form of divination based on the theory that the planets and stars influence human affairs. Until Copernicus (1473–1543), much of the lore of astrology was a partial basis for astronomy. Since Copernicus, astrology and astronomy separated. In astrology a horoscope is a map of the heavens at the time of birth, using the chart of the zodiac. The "house," or sign in the ascendancy at the time of one's birth, is said to determine one's temperament, tendencies to disease, and liability to certain fortunes or calamities.

It is normally wrong to believe in astrology or to direct one's life and conduct according to its supposed predictions. The reasons are that astrology involves contradictions, since it claims uniform influence on persons born on the same day and in the same place, and who later on prove to be unmistakably different; it claims to predict accurately the free future—i.e., happenings that depend on the exercise of man's free will—whereas such knowledge is unknown to anyone except God; it is against the doctrine of free will, for it leads to fatalistic views of man's destiny; and it is against belief in Divine Providence, which includes the influence of divine grace and the value of intercessory prayer.

Astrology has been more than once formally condemned by the Church, as at the Council of Trent, which expressly forbade the faithful to read books on astrology dealing with "future contingent achievements, with fortuitous events and such actions as depend on human freedom, but daring to claim certitude about their occurrence" (*Regulae Tridentinae,* 9). Those who believe in astrology expose themselves to a weakening of their Christian faith. (Etym. Greek *astron,* star + *logia,* science, knowledge.)

ATHANASIAN CREED. Profession of faith dating from the late fourth century and attributed to St. Athanasius (296–373). It differs from the other standard creeds in its extraordinary length and in embodying anathemas against those who would deny the doctrines it professes. Its opening word *Quicumque* is also the Latin title of the creed, whose first sentence declares, "If anyone wishes to be saved, before everything else he must hold the Catholic faith."

ATHEISM. Denial of a personal God who is totally distinct from the world he created. Modern atheism has become so varied and widespread that the Second Vatican Council identified no less than eight forms of disbelief under the single term *atheismus:* "Some people expressly deny the existence of God. Others maintain that man cannot make any assertion whatsoever about Him. Still others admit only such methods of investigation as would make it seem quite meaningless to ask questions about God. Many, trespassing beyond the boundaries of the positive sciences, either contend that everything can be explained by the reasoning process used in such sciences or, on the contrary, hold that there is no such thing as absolute truth. With others it is their exaggerated idea of man that causes their faith to languish; they are more prone, it would seem, to affirm man than to deny God. Yet others have such a faulty notion of God that when they disown this product of the imagination their denial has no reference to the God of the Gospels. There are also those who never inquire about God; religion never seems to trouble or interest them at all, nor do they try to see why they should bother about it" (*Church in the Modern World*, I, 19). In the light of this array of infidelity, it was only logical for the Council to declare that atheism is one of the greatest problems facing mankind in the world today. (Etym. Greek *atheos,* denying the gods, without a god.)

ATONEMENT. The satisfaction of a legitimate demand. In a more restricted sense it is the reparation of an offense. This occurs through a voluntary performance that outweighs the injustice done. If the performance fully counterbalances the gravity of the guilt, the atonement is adequate. And if the atonement is done by someone other than the actual offender, but in his stead, it is vicarious.

Applied to Christ the Redeemer, through his suffering and death he rendered vicarious atonement to God for the sins of the whole human race. His atonement is fully adequate because it was performed by a divine person. In fact, it is superabundant because the positive value of Christ's expiation is actually greater than the negative value of human sin. (Etym. Middle English *at one,* to set at one, to reconcile; of one mind, in accord.)

ATTACHMENT. An emotional dependence, either of one person on another, or of a person on some real or illusory object. Attachments play an important role in spiritual development, since the first condition for progress in sanctity is some mastery over one's inordinate attachments.

ATTRITION. Imperfect contrition, because this form of sorrow for sins is based on motives that are self-interested and not based on the perfect love of God. (Etym. Latin *ad,* to + *terere,* to rub: *attritio,* rubbing, imperfect grinding; incomplete compunction of heart.) See also IMPERFECT CONTRITION.

AUDIENCES, PAPAL. Receptions given to interested persons, clerical or lay, who have business with the Holy See. Audience requests are presented to the Maestro di Camera, even for bishops, ambassadors, or heads of religious institutions. Religious orders are received on stated days. Cardinal prefects of the sacred congregations are received regularly by the pope, at which time counsel is given and decrees are signed. Rulers of nations are received in formal audience. Special or private audiences for groups of individuals follow a definite order. Generally a letter of recommendation from the bishop of a home diocese is received by some responsible personage in Rome, who transmits the request to the Master of the Chamber. If the audience is granted, the required ticket for admission, with specified date and time, is communicated to the one(s) working on the request. Public and general audiences are a recent development. They are held in the Audience Hall, built in 1971, in the Basilica or Piazza of St. Peter's, or at the papal summer residence, Castel Gondolfo.

AUGUSTINIANS. A general name for a number of religious institutes of men and women who base their way of life on the Rule of St. Augustine. Among the men are Augustinian canons, since the eleventh century; Augustinian hermits or friars, to whom Martin Luther had belonged; Augustinian recollects, or discalced hermits; and Augustinians of the Assumption, better known as Assumptionists.

AURICULAR CONFESSION. The obligation by divine law of confessing one's grave sins, committed after baptism, to a qualified priest. It is called auricular confession because normally the manifestation of sins is done by word of mouth and heard by the priest before he gives absolution. (Etym. Latin *auricula*, the external ear.)

AURIESVILLE. Shrine of the North American Martyrs, near Albany, New York, on the Mohawk River. In 1642 Father Isaac Jogues (1607–47) and a Jesuit lay brother, René Goupil (1606–42), newly arrived from France and trying to run supplies to the famished Huron Indians, were captured by the Iroquois tribe and cruelly tortured at Ossernenon, present Auriesville. René Goupil died as a result. Jogues recovered and was persuaded to return to France, but 1646 saw him back again in the same place with John La Lande, a nineteen-year-old French boy. Both received the crown of martyrdom in 1647. Auriesville, as the original Ossernenon, has been verified by documentary evidence and excavations on the six hundred acres of rolling land. The first pilgrimage was made in 1885. The small oratory soon became too small to care for the crowds. The second church seated five hundred, to be replaced in 1931 by a vast amphitheater built to accommodate sixteen thousand. Four altars facing the points of the compass are in the center of this buff-colored brick building, and during the summer and fall the rising tiers of seats are often filled to capacity for Mass and benediction. Auriesville is a year-round retreat center. A museum adjacent to the church houses some important relics of the missionaries and their Indian converts. Jogues, Goupil, and La Lande were canonized in 1930 together with Brébeuf (1593–1649), Lallemant (1610–49), Garnier (1643–1730), Chabanel (1613–49), and Daniel (1601–48), their companions who died as martyrs trying to convert the Canadian Indians. Their composite feast day is commemorated on October 19, except in Canada and for those celebrating the Extraordinary Form of the Mass, when the feast is celebrated on September 26.

AUTHENTIC TEACHING. Official teaching of the hierarchical Church. Its authenticity depends on its authorization, which means the assurance of divine guidance, as vested in the duly ordained successors of the Apostles united with the Bishop of Rome. Authentic teaching is also infallible when the hierarchy (pope or bishops with the pope) intends it universally to bind the consciences of the faithful.

AUTHORITY. The right of a society to direct and compel the members to cooperate toward the attainment of the end of that society. Ultimately all authority in a society comes from God but in different ways, depending on the kind of society.

In a conventional society, founded by the free agreement of men and women who set its purpose and choose its means, God is the final source of authority, but indirectly, in the sense that he is the source of everything. He created the persons who form the society and gave them the faculties by which to direct the society.

In natural societies, such as the family and state, God is the source of authority directly and immediately. He established the natural law that requires that people organize themselves. The authority passes from God directly to the society and not through the personalities of the founders.

In theocratic societies, such as the Catholic Church, God founded a particular society by supernatural revelation. He specified its structure and determined its leaders. Here God is most directly and immediately the source of authority, not only in governing but also in teaching the faithful who belong to the society. (Etym. Latin *auctoritas,* source, authorship; authority, weight, might, power.)

AUTONOMOUS MORALITY. The theory that each person imposes the moral law on himself. It is opposed to heteronomous morality, which holds that the moral law is imposed from outside of man by another, and ultimately by the divine Other, who is God, which makes the moral law theonomous.

Developed into a system by Immanuel Kant (1724–1804), autonomous morality in effect deifies each person's free will. In the Kantian understanding of freedom, liberty means not only freedom of choice but freedom of independence, on the assumption that one cannot retain free will and still be under the command of another's law. To save freedom, Kant demanded autonomy, but by demanding autonomy he destroyed all real obligation and therefore all real law. (Etym. Greek *autonomos,* free, living by one's own laws; Latin *moralis,* relating to conduct.)

AUXILIARY BISHOP. One deputed by the Holy See to assist a diocesan bishop in the performance of pontifical functions. As such, he does not have ordinary jurisdiction in a diocese, nor does he have the right of succession to a diocesan see.

AVARICE. An excessive or insatiable desire for money or material things. In its strict sense, avarice is the inordinate holding on to possessions or riches instead of using these material things for some worthwhile purpose. Reluctance to let go of what a person owns is also avarice.

Of itself, avarice is venially sinful. But it may become mortal when a person is ready to use gravely unlawful means to acquire or hold on to his possessions, or when because of his cupidity he seriously violates his duty of justice or charity. (Etym. Latin *avaritia,* greediness, covetousness, avarice.)

AVE MARIA. The title for the Hail Mary in Latin, which reads:
Ave Maria, gratia plena, Dominus tecum.
Benedicta tu in mulieribus, et benedictus fructus ventris tui Jesus.
Sancta Maria, Mater Dei, ora pro nobis peccatoribus,
nunc et in hora mortis nostrae. Amen.

AVOIDING SIN. The moral responsibility of not exposing oneself unnecessarily to occasions of sin. Three principles are standard in Catholic moral teaching: 1. no one is obliged to avoid the remote occasions of sin. This is true because the danger of sin is slight and otherwise it would be impossible to live in the world; 2. everyone is obliged to avoid voluntary proximate occasions of sin, where "voluntary" means that it can easily be removed or avoided; 3. anyone in a necessary proximate occasion of sin is obliged to make the occasion remote. An occasion is necessary when the person's state of life or profession or circumstances make it morally impossible to avoid exposure to certain enticements. What is a proximate danger to sinning can be rendered remote by such means as prayer, the sacraments, and custody of the senses, especially of the eyes.

BAD EXAMPLE. The external performance of some morally evil action that scandalizes other people and encourages them to do the same. Bad example refers especially to leaders in the Church or human society who are expected to practice above-ordinary virtue and whose conduct is under constant public scrutiny. Their misconduct, therefore, inevitably gives a bad example to people who look to them for guidance and inspiration.

BAD FAITH. The condition of a person who either acts against the dictates of his or her conscience or who has not sought to enlighten conscience before making a moral decision. The term is also applied to one who has acquired another person's property and does not take reasonable means either to find the owner or to restore the owner's possessions. People are likewise said to be in bad faith when they do not embrace Catholicism although convinced of its truth, or when they do not take appropriate measures to learn what is the true faith.

BALTIMORE CATECHISM. Originally the "Catechism of Christian Doctrine, Prepared and Enjoined by Order of the Third Council of Baltimore." It was the Plenary Council of 1884 that authorized this manual, first published in 1885, after a committee of six bishops was entrusted with the composition. The question of a uniform textbook of Catholic doctrine had been considered by the American hierarchy since First Provincial Council in 1829, but it took fifty years to see the project to completion. After the catechism was issued, various editions were published, with word meanings, explanatory notes, and even different arrangements, so that in a few decades there was great diversity in the books that were called the Baltimore Catechism.

BANNEUX. The shrine of Our Lady of the Poor, near the city of Liège in the Flemish village of Banneux. Devotion to Mary began as a result of an apparition to a poor twelve-year-old Belgian child in the garden of her home on January 16, 1933. Our Lady told her that she had come to relieve the ills and sufferings of the poor of all nations. A painting on the wall of the village's chapel made according to the child's description shows Mary robed in white with a blue sash and with a rosary over her right arm. On January 18, 1933, the child's father, an avowed atheist, accompanied his daughter to the garden, and although he did not see the Virgin he was instantly converted, overwhelmed in the presence of an unseen power. After years of investigation, the Holy See authorized public devotion to Our Lady of Banneux, patroness of the poor, in 1942. Formal approval was given by the Bishop of Liège in 1949, and a statue of that title was solemnly crowned in 1956. Pilgrims from many countries came to worship at the shrine. Over one hundred shrines throughout the world are dedicated to Our Lady of Banneux.

BANNS. Public announcements of an intended marriage. Their purpose is to discover matrimonial impediments if any exist. Unless a dispensation has been secured, three publications are required on three Sundays or holy days in the churches of the marrying parties. Anyone knowing of such impediments is bound in conscience to make the same known to the clergy concerned. Similar announcements are required for those about to receive holy orders. (Etym. Anglo-Saxon *gebann*, a proclamation.)

BAPTISM. The sacrament in which, by water and the word of God, a person is cleansed of all sin and reborn and sanctified in Christ to everlasting life. (Etym. Latin *baptisma*; from Greek *baptisma*, a dipping.)

BAPTISMAL GRACES. The supernatural effects of the sacrament of baptism. They are 1. removal of all guilt of sin, original and personal; 2. removal of all punishment due to sin, temporal and eternal; 3. infusion of sanctifying grace along with the theological virtues of faith, hope, and charity, and the gifts of the Holy Spirit; 4. incorporation into Christ; 5. entrance into the Mystical Body, which is the Catholic Church; and 6. imprinting of the baptismal character, which enables a person to receive the other sacraments, to participate in the priesthood of Christ through the sacred liturgy, and to grow in the likeness of Christ through personal sanctification. Baptism does not remove two effects of original sin, namely concupiscence and bodily mortality. However, it does enable a Christian to be sanctified by his struggle with concupiscence and gives him the title to rising in a glorified body on the last day.

BAPTISMAL NAME. The name that a person receives at baptism. It is prescribed by the Church's ritual, as when the celebrant asks the parents or sponsors at infant baptism, "What name do you wish to give the infant?" According to the Church's tradition, the baptismal name "should be taken from some person whose eminent sanctity has given him a place in the catalogue of the saints. The similarity of name will stimulate each one to imitate the virtues and holiness of the Saint and, moreover, to hope and pray that the one who is the model for one's imitation will also be his advocate and watch over the safety of his body and soul" (*Catechism of the Council of Trent*, Baptism).

BAPTISMAL VOWS. Profession of the Christian faith by an adult candidate for baptism or by the godparent in the name of the infant to be baptized. The solemn renewal of these promises is a widespread act of piety usually at the close of a mission or retreat or when receiving First Communion or the sacrament of confirmation. It is a part of the Eucharistic liturgy at the Easter Vigil and on the Feast of the Baptism of the Lord.

BAPTISMAL WATER. The water used for the administration of the sacrament of baptism. For the valid conferral of baptism any ordinary natural water may be used. But for licit administration of solemn baptism, the water should be ritually blessed. Normally, the water is blessed for this purpose during the Easter Vigil on Holy Saturday. But it may be blessed at each baptism by the one who confers the sacrament. Three ritual blessings of the water are provided by the Roman ritual, two of which include a symbolic touching of the water by the priest and alternate responses by the people.

BAPTISM OF BLOOD. Martyrdom in the case of a person who died for the Christian faith before he or she could receive the sacrament. The effects of martyrdom of blood are the complete remission of all sin and the title to immediate entrance into heaven. The expression entered the Christian vocabulary during the first three centuries when many catechumens awaiting baptism and pagans who had suddenly converted to the Christian faith were martyred before they could receive formal baptism of water.

BAPTISM OF DESIRE. The equivalent of sacramental baptism of water, which in God's Providence is sufficient to enable a person to obtain the state of grace and to save his or her soul. According to the Church's teaching, "Those who through no fault of their own, do not know the Gospel of Christ or His Church, but who nevertheless seek

God with a sincere heart, and, moved by grace, try in their actions to do His will as they know it through the dictates of their conscience—those too may achieve eternal salvation" (Second Vatican Council, Dogmatic Constitution on the Church, I, 16).

BARABBAS. "A notorious prisoner," Matthew described him (Matthew 27:16–17). John called him "a brigand" (John 18:40–41). Mark and Luke both said that he was in prison as a rioter and a murderer (Mark 15:7–15; Luke 23:19–25). When Pilate questioned Jesus at his trial and could find him guilty of nothing, he offered the people the choice of freeing Christ or Barabbas, hoping that the latter's notorious reputation would induce them to release Christ. But, whipped into fury by their chief priests, they insisted that the guilty man be freed and the innocent die. (Etym. Aramaic *bar' abba,* son of the father.)

BAR-JONAH. Simon Peter's surname. Peter was the son of Jonah. Jesus hailed him by his family name at the time he bestowed on him his new name. "You are Peter and on this rock I will build my Church" (Matthew 16:18). (Etym. Greek *bar ionas,* from Aramaic *bar yonah,* son of Jonah; Hebrew *yonah,* dove.)

BARNABAS. Otherwise known as Joseph, a Levite of Cyprus (Acts 4:36–37). He became a member of the primitive Church. Paul's acceptance by the Christians in Jerusalem was largely due to Barnabas's eloquence in persuading them of Paul's sincerity and the miraculous conversion at Damascus. The two traveled together in the work of the Church in obedience to the Holy Spirit: "I want Barnabas and Saul set apart for the work to which I have called them" (Acts 13:2). They were especially successful in the year they spent together in Antioch, converting many (Acts 11:25–26). The team of Paul and Barnabas was finally disrupted by a "violent quarrel." On Paul's next projected journey Barnabas wanted his nephew, Mark, to accompany them, but Paul disagreed. The consequence was that Paul chose Silas to accompany him, while Barnabas and Mark traveled to Cyprus (Acts 15:36–40). This new partnership paved the way for Mark's development as Peter's disciple and the second evangelist. (Etym. Greek *barnabas,* from Aramaic word, popular meaning "son of consolation.")

BARTHOLOMEW. One of the Twelve Apostles mentioned each of the four times they are listed in the New Testament (Matthew 10:3;

Mark 3:18; Luke 6:14; Acts 1:13). Otherwise his name does not appear. Writers speculate that he may be the Nathanael discussed in John's Gospel (John 1:45–48), but there is no definite proof. (Etym. Greek *bartholomaios;* from Aramaic *bar talmai,* son of Tolmai.)

BARUCH. Trusted friend and amanuensis of the prophet Jeremiah, living in the seventh century B.C. God delivered lengthy warnings to Jeremiah about the Israelites. Chapter 36 in the book of Jeremiah describes in detail how he dictated these messages to Baruch and ordered him to read them to the people in the Temple. King Jehoiakim listened to the warnings with displeasure and ordered them destroyed. Jeremiah repeated the dictation of the messages, so determined was he that the people be enlightened. Both Jeremiah and Baruch fled the kingdom. The book of Baruch is in the Catholic Bible. Its first five chapters are the prophecy with which Baruch consoled the Jewish exiles. Chapter 6 is the Epistle of Jeremiah, which seems to have been authored by Jeremiah rather than Baruch.

BASILIANS. A general name for various religious institutes. Orthodox monks are sometimes called Basilians because they have inherited the spirit of St. Basil (329–79), although they have no uniform rule. There are five Catholic Basilian orders of men and four congregations of women, all of pontifical status. A congregation of the Priests of St. Basil was founded in 1822 at Annonay in France for educational and parochial work.

BASILICA. A lengthy oblong religious edifice, rectangular in shape with an apse at one end. This name was originally given to certain ancient churches in Rome, the Holy Land, and elsewhere that were converted from pagan edifices to Christian use. The width of a basilica building is never greater than one half of its length. It is divided by rows of columns into a central nave and a surrounding aisle, or ambulatory. The upper part of the nave is lighted by clerestory windows overlooking the roof over the aisles. Similar lower windows light the aisle sections. The altar is placed within or before the apse arching from the nave and opening into the transept, or cross hall. At the main entrance to the basilica is the narthex, beyond which the early neophytes were not admitted. St. John Lateran, the Mother Church, is the archbasilica for the patriarch of the West, the pope; St. Peter's for the patriarch of Constantinople; St. Paul's Outside the Walls for the patriarch of Alexandria; St. Mary Major for the patriarch of Antioch;

St. Lawrence Outside the Walls, for the patriarch of Jerusalem. Each of these major basilicas has an altar exclusively for the pope's use, and by others only with his permission. Adjoining their basilicas were the former residences of the various patriarchs when they were in Rome. St. Francis of Assisi's church is also a major basilica with a papal altar and a throne. Eleven churches in Rome and many others throughout the world have been designated by the pope as minor basilicas, e.g., at Loreto and Padua in Italy, Lourdes in France, Lough Derg in Ireland. The clergy who serve in them enjoy a title of honor that gives them certain ceremonial rites. (Etym. Latin *basilicus*, royal.)

BASILICA OF ST. PETER. The patriarchal church adjoining the Vatican Palace of the pope. In A.D. 67, St. Peter was executed in the circus of Nero near the foot of the obelisk that was brought from Egypt and that stands in the center of the piazza in front of St. Peter's Basilica. In A.D. 90, Pope St. Anacletus marked the grave by building a small oratory over the spot that Constantine, destroying the old circus, hoped to place within the foundations of the new cathedral. This first basilica had lasted for eleven hundred years when Pope Nicholas V determined to build a more pretentious edifice. Work progressed very slowly. Successive popes engaged Rosselino (1439–1507), Alberti (1474–1515), Bramante (1444–1514), Michelangelo (1475–1564), Maderna (1556–1629), and Bernini (1598–1680). The basilica was finally finished after being in the process of construction for 176 years. It was dedicated with great ceremony by Pope Urban VIII in 1626. The famed colonnade surrounding the piazza, four columns deep, was designed by Bernini. The top is surmounted by 126 statues of saints each twelve feet in height. Over the front entrance is the Loggia della Benedizione, from which the pope imparts benediction. From the portico five entrances lead into the basilica—the first is the Porta Santa, opened only during the Holy Year. The central entrance has the noted bronze doors from the first cathedral depicting the life of Christ and the Virgin. The nave is the longest in the world, flanked by fluted pillars with the niches that contain the huge sculptured statues of the founders of the religious orders. This leads to the high altar, with its bronzed and gilt-ornamented canopy done by Bernini in 1633. In front of it is the circular marble balustrade, with its ninety-five lamps burning day and night, leading below to the bronze sarcophagus above which is the gold cross of St. Peter. At the left as one ascends from the Confessio is the fifth-century bronze statue of the first pope from the first basilica of A.D. 445. The right foot of bronze has been worn and polished by the millions who, passing by, have kissed Peter's foot. Beyond the transept is the tribune that contains the bronze reliquary enclosing the ancient episcopal wooden chair of the first Vicar of Christ. Numerous papal tombs are in the tribune and aisles, notably Pope Paul III's, considered the finest of the monuments in St. Peter's. The world-famous Michelangelo *Pietà* is in the first chapel of the right aisle with the youthful Mother and her dead Son. In the crypt, in the thirteen feet between the pavement of the new and old cathedrals, are the tombs of many popes, including Pope Adrian IV, the only Englishman to be a successor of Peter, and St. Pius X, best known as the Pope of the Blessed Sacrament. St. Peter's body lies in a vault beneath the high altar. Scientific excavations have established authenticity of his remains.

BEATIFICATION. A declaration by the pope as head of the Church that one of the deceased faithful lived a holy life and/or died a martyr's death and is now dwelling in heaven. As a process, the beatification consists of a years-long examination of the life, virtues, writings, and reputation for holiness of the servant of God under consideration. This is ordinarily conducted by the bishop of the place where he or she resided or died. For a martyr miracles worked through the person's intercession need not be considered in this primary process. The second, or Apostolic, process is instituted by the Holy See when the first process reveals that the servant of God practiced virtue in a heroic degree or died a martyr for the faith. Beatified persons are called "Blessed" and may be venerated by the faithful but not throughout the universal Church. (Etym. Latin *beatificatio,* the state of being blessed; from *beatus,* happy.)

BEATIFIC VISION. The intuitive knowledge of God that produces heavenly beatitude. As defined by the Church, the souls of the just "see the divine essence by an intuitive vision and face to face, so that the divine essence is known immediately, showing itself plainly, clearly and openly, and not mediately through any creature" (Denzinger 1000–1002). Moreover, the souls of the saints "clearly behold God, one and triune, as He is" (Denzinger 1304–6). It is called vision in the mind by analogy with bodily sight, which is the most comprehensive of human sense faculties; it is called beatific because it produces happiness in the will and the whole being. As a result of this immediate vision of God, the blessed share in the divine happiness, where the beatitude of the Trinity is (humanly speaking) the consequence of God's perfect knowledge of his infinite goodness. The beatific vision is also enjoyed by the angels, and was possessed by Christ in his human nature even while he was in his mortal life on earth. (Etym. Latin *beatificus,* beatific, blissful, imparting great happiness or blessedness; from *beatus,* happy.)

BEATITUDES. The promises of happiness made by Christ to those who faithfully accept his teaching and follow his divine example. Preached in the Sermon on the Mount, they are recorded in St. Matthew (5:3–11) and in St. Luke (6:20–22). In Matthew there are eight (or nine) blessings of a spiritual nature, applicable to all Christians; in Luke there are four blessings of a more external character, addressed to the disciples. Luke's version also includes four maledictions threatened on those who do the opposite. In both versions, the beatitudes are expressions of the New Covenant, where happiness is assured already in this life, provided a person totally gives himself to the imitation of Christ.

In the Gospel of Matthew
"How happy are the poor in spirit: theirs is the kingdom of heaven.
Happy the gentle: they shall have the earth for their heritage.
Happy those who mourn: they shall be comforted.
Happy those who hunger and thirst for what is right: they shall be satisfied.
Happy the merciful: they shall have mercy shown them.
Happy the pure in heart: they shall see God.
Happy the peacemakers: they shall be called sons of God.
Happy those who are persecuted in the cause of right: theirs is the kingdom of heaven.
Happy are you when people abuse you and persecute you and speak all kinds of calumny against you on my account. Rejoice and be glad, for your reward will be great in heaven; this is how they persecuted the prophets before you." (Matthew 5:3–12)

In the Gospel of Luke
"How happy are you who are poor: yours is the kingdom of God.
Happy you who are hungry now: you shall be satisfied.
Happy you who weep now: you shall laugh.
Happy you when people hate you, drive you out, abuse you, denounce your name as criminal, on account of the Son of Man. Rejoice when

that day comes and dance for joy, for then your reward will be great in heaven. This was the way their ancestors treated the prophets.
But alas for you who are rich: you are having your consolation now.
Alas for you who have your fill now: you shall go hungry.
Alas for you who laugh now: you shall mourn and weep.
Alas for you when the world speaks well of you! This was the way their ancestors treated the false prophets." (Luke 6:20–26)

BEAUPRÉ, ST. ANNE DE. World famous shrine to the mother of the Blessed Virgin in Quebec, Canada. Its origins are dated from the reported miraculous cure of the cripple Louis Grimont, March 16, 1658. The small chapel was gradually enlarged, and the present structure was declared a minor basilica in 1888. In the north transept of the church is a golden reliquary containing an authenticated wristbone of St. Anne. Many miracles are reported annually, with thousands of pilgrims praying there the year round, but especially on July 26, the feast day of the saint.

BEFORE CHRIST (B.C.). The era of human history from the origin of man to the coming of Christ. Sometimes called "Before the Christian Era" (B.C.E.).

BENEDICTINES. The men and women religious who follow the Rule of St. Benedict (480–547). Founded about 529 at Monte Cassino, some eighty miles south of Rome, the Benedictine Order early included both monks and nuns. The latter were separately established by St. Benedict with the help of his sister, St. Scholastica (480–543). Originally each monastery was an independent and self-sustaining unit, and this principle remains substantially in effect to the present day.

It is customary to distinguish four stages in the history of the Benedictines: 1. from St. Benedict to St. Gregory the Great who died in A.D. 604. The latter as monk who became pope extended the Benedictine ideal into other countries and through his *Dialogues* developed the ascetical principles of the founder; 2. from the sixth century to the foundation of the Cistercians at Cîteaux by St. Bernard of Clairvaux (1090–1153), who began a form of Benedictinism that was more austere; 3. from Cîteaux to the Council of Trent. During this period a grouping of monasteries and a development of the monastic way of life took place, affecting the whole of Western Europe. There was also decadence due to the inroads of the pagan renaissance; 4. from Trent to the Second Vatican Council. The Council of Trent passed decrees regulating monastic life, e.g., election of superiors, administration of property, prescriptions on poverty and common life. These had the salutary effect of joining autonomous monasteries into confederations and thus giving the Benedictine way of life a coordinated unity that St. Benedict assumed was necessary to grow in sanctity and the love of God.

BENEDICTION OF THE BLESSED SACRAMENT. A Eucharistic devotion in the Catholic Church of the Latin Rite. In its traditional form, a priest, vested in surplice, stole, and cope, places on the altar or in the niche above it the consecrated Host in the ostensorium, or monstrance, and then incenses it. "O Salutaris Hostia" or similar hymn is usually sung at the beginning of exposition, followed by a period of meditation, praise, and adoration by priest and people. At the conclusion of the ceremony the "Tantum Ergo" hymn is chanted, with another incensation, and followed by blessing the people with the raised monstrance in the form of a cross. During the blessing the priest wears the humeral veil covering his hands. A small bell is rung during the blessing. The Divine Praises are then sung or recited by priest and people, and the Blessed Sacrament is reposed in the tabernacle. Benediction is commonly held on major feasts and Sundays, Divine Mercy Sunday, also during Lent, during a mission, or retreat or during forty hours' devotions. Other days may be designated by individual bishops. Since the Second Vatican Council the Holy See has simplified the traditional ritual, allowing for a variety of options in the prayers, songs, and readings "to direct the attention of the faithful to the worship of Christ the Lord" (*Eucharistiae Sacramentum*, 1973, No. 95).

BETHLEHEM. Called Ephrathah to designate it as the birthplace of King David, it is one of the oldest towns in Palestine, twelve miles southeast of Jerusalem. In the center of the village is the Church of the Nativity, whose sanctuary is directly above the traditional cave where Christ was born. Two stairways lead to it from the basilica. The large cathedral doors have been blocked to prevent Moslem desecration. Built by Constantine in A.D. 330, the Church of the Nativity is one of the oldest Byzantine structures and one of the earliest Christian churches. In the underground cave in a large niche is the altar of the Nativity. Underneath the altar table is the silver star in the marble floor whose center opening reveals the original stone floor of the cave below. Around the opening are the words "Here Jesus Christ was born of the Virgin Mary." Fifty-three lamps burn there day and night. In this grotto the Christmas Mass is celebrated every day, the faithful kneeling on the marble floor. (Etym. Hebrew *beth lechem,* house of bread or house of [the god] Lahm.)

BIBLE. The collection of books accepted by Christian churches as the authentic, inspired record of the revelations made to mankind by God about himself and his will for men. It is divided into the Old Testament and the New Testament to distinguish between the Jewish tradition and the Christian. In the New Testament, the Old is generally spoken of as "the Scriptures" or "the sacred writings" (Matthew 21:42). Gradually the word has been used in the singular and "Scripture" has become a synonym for the Bible (Acts 8:32). "Testament" has the meaning of "covenant" with reference to the two covenants God established with his people in each period of human history.

Books of the Bible
Texts, Translation, and Authenticity
The Catholic Church has more than once taught what books are to be regarded as inspired and therefore belong to the Bible. At the Council of Trent, in 1546, the biblical canon was solemnly defined and the Vulgate declared to be authentic:

> The council follows the example of the orthodox Fathers and with the same sense of devotion and reverence with which it accepts and venerates all the books both of the Old and the New Testament, since one God is the author of both, it also accepts and venerates traditions concerned with faith and morals as having been received orally from Christ or inspired by the Holy Spirit and continuously preserved in the Catholic Church. It judged, however, that a list of the Sacred Books should be written into this decree so that no one may doubt which books the council accepts. The list is here given.
>
> The Old Testament: five books of Moses, that is, Genesis, Exodus, Leviticus, Numbers, Deuteronomy; Joshua, Judges, Ruth, four books of Kings, two of Paralipomenon; the first book of Esdras and the second, which is called Nehemias; Tobias, Judith, Esther, Job, David's Psalter of one hundred and fifty Psalms, Proverbs, Ecclesiastes, the Canticle of Canticles, Wisdom, Ecclesiasticus, Isaias, Jeremias with Baruch, Ezechiel, Daniel; the twelve minor prophets, that is Osee,

Joel, Amos, Abdias, Jonas, Micheas, Nahum, Habacuc, Sophonias, Aggeus, Zacharias, Malachias; two books of Machabees, the first and the second.

The New Testament: the four Gospels, according to Matthew, Mark, Luke, and John; the Acts of the Apostles, written by the evangelist Luke; fourteen epistles of the Apostle Paul: to the Romans, two to the Corinthians, to the Galatians, to the Ephesians, to the Philippians, to the Colossians, two to the Thessalonians, two to Timothy, to Titus, to Philemon, to the Hebrews; two epistles of the Apostle Peter, three of the Apostle John, one of the Apostle James, one of the Apostle Jude; and the Apocalypse of the Apostle John. Moreover, if anyone does not accept these books as sacred and canonical in their entirety, with all their parts, according to the text usually read in the Catholic Church and as they are in the ancient Latin Vulgate, but knowingly and willfully contemns the traditions previously mentioned: let him be anathema.

Moreover, since the same sacred council has thought that it would be very useful for the Church of God if it were known which one of all the Latin editions that are in circulation is the authentic edition, it determines and decrees that the ancient Vulgate, which has been approved in the Church by the use of many centuries, should be considered the authentic edition in public readings, disputations, preaching, and explanations; and that no one should presume or dare to reject it under any pretext whatever (Denzinger 1501–6).

Almost four centuries later (1943), Pope Pius XII in the encyclical *Divino Afflante Spiritu,* reconfirmed the biblical canon and the authenticity of the Vulgate. But he made some important declarations that gave the primary impetus to the publication of totally new editions of the Bible. They are new because they are based on Hebrew and Greek manuscripts beyond the Vulgate, and because new translations into the vernacular were made from the original languages and not merely from the Latin Vulgate.

According to Pius XII:

"[T]he Vulgate, as the Church has understood and does now understand, is free from all error in matters of faith and morals. Consequently, as the Church herself testifies, it can be safely quoted, without the least fear of erring, in disputations, public readings, and sermons. Its *authenticity* should not be called *critical,* but *juridical.* The authority the Vulgate enjoys in doctrinal matters does not by any means proscribe—and in modern times it fairly demands—that this same doctrine be corroborated by the original texts. Nor does it mean that the original texts cannot be continually used to help clarify and explain more and more the proper meaning of Sacred Scripture. Nor does the decree of the Council of Trent forbid that translations be made into the vernacular so that the faithful may use them and profit by them and understand more readily the meaning of the divine message. These translations may be made from the original texts (Denzinger 3825).

A standard listing of the books of the Bible, according to the directives of Pope Pius XII, shows a number of variants in the titles of the books, their division and sequence, as follows:

Books of the Bible in Biblical Order
Old Testament
Genesis Gn
Exodus Ex
Leviticus Lv
Numbers Nb
Deuteronomy Dt
Joshua Jos
Judges Jg
Ruth Rt
I Samuel I S
II Samuel II S
I Kings I K
II Kings II K
I Chronicles I Ch
II Chronicles II Ch
Ezra Ezr
Nehemiah Ne
Tobit Tb
Judith Jdt
Esther Est
I Maccabees I M
II Maccabees II M
Job Jb
Psalms Ps
Proverbs Pr
Ecclesiastes Qo
Song of Songs Sg
Wisdom Ws
Ecclesiasticus Si

Old Testament, cont.
> Isaiah Is
> Jeremiah Jr
> Lamentations Lm
> Baruch Ba
> Ezekiel Ezk
> Daniel Dn
> Hosea Ho
> Joel Jl
> Amos Am
> Obadiah Ob
> Jonah Jon
> Micah Mi
> Nahum Na
> Habakkuk Hab
> Zephaniah Zp
> Haggai Hg
> Zechariah Zc
> Malachi Ml

New Testament
> Matthew Mt
> Mark Mk
> Luke Lk
> John Jn
> Acts Ac
> Romans Rm
> I Corinthians I Co
> II Corinthians II Co
> Galatians Ga
> Ephesians Ep
> Philippians Ph
> Colossians Col
> I Thessalonians I Th
> II Thessalonians II Th
> I Timothy I Tm
> II Timothy II Tm
> Titus Tt
> Philemon Phm
> Hebrews Heb
> James Jm
> I Peter I P

II Peter II P
I John I Jn
II John II Jn
III John III Jn
Jude Jude
Revelation Rv

Books of the Bible in Alphabetical Order
Old Testament

Amos Am
Baruch Ba
I Chronicles I Ch
II Chronicles II Ch
Daniel Dn
Deuteronomy Dt
Ecclesiastes Qo
Ecclesiasticus Si
Esther Est
Exodus Ex
Ezekiel Ezk
Ezra Ezr
Genesis Gn
Habakkuk Hab
Haggai Hg
Hosea Ho
Isaiah Is
Jeremiah Jr
Job Jb
Joel Jl
Jonah Jon
Joshua Jos
Judges Jg
Judith Jdt
I Kings I K
II Kings II K
Lamentations Lm
Leviticus Lv
I Maccabees I M
II Maccabees II M
Malachi Ml
Micah Mi

Old Testament, cont.
    Nahum Na
    Nehemiah Ne
    Numbers Nb
    Obadiah Ob
    Proverbs Pr
    Psalms Ps
    Ruth Rt
    I Samuel I S
    II Samuel II S
    Song of Songs Sg
    Tobit Tb
    Wisdom Ws
    Zechariah Zc
    Zephaniah Zp

New Testament
    Acts Ac
    Colossians Col
    I Corinthians I Co
    II Corinthians II Co
    Ephesians Ep
    Galatians Ga
    Hebrews Heb
    James Jm
    John Jn
    I John I Jn
    II John II Jn
    III John III Jn
    Jude Jude
    Luke Lk
    Mark Mk
    Matthew Mt
    I Peter I P
    II Peter II P
    Philemon Phm
    Philippians Ph
    Revelation Rv
    Romans Rm
    I Thessalonians I Th
    II Thessalonians II Th
    I Timothy I Tm

II Timothy II Tm
Titus Tt

Books of the Bible in Alphabetical Order of Abbreviations

Ac Acts
Am Amos
Ba Baruch
I Ch I Chronicles
II Ch II Chronicles
I Co I Corinthians
II Co II Corinthians
Col Colossians
Dn Daniel
Dt Deuteronomy
Ep Ephesians
Est Esther
Ex Exodus
Ezk Ezekiel
Ezr Ezra
Ga Galatians
Gn Genesis
Hab Habakkuk
Heb Hebrews
Hg Haggai
Ho Hosea
Is Isaiah
Jb Job
Jdt Judith
Jg Judges
Jl Joel
Jm James
Jn John
I Jn I John
II Jn II John
III Jn III John
Jon Jonah
Jos Joshua
Jr Jeremiah
Jude Jude
I K I Kings
II K II Kings

Books of the Bible in Alphabetical Order of Abbreviations, cont.
Lk Luke
Lm Lamentations
Lv Leviticus
I M I Maccabees
II M II Maccabees
Mi Micah
Mk Mark
Ml Malachi
Mt Matthew
Na Nahum
Nb Numbers
Ne Nehemiah
Ob Obadiah
I P I Peter
II P II Peter
Ph Philippians
Phm Philemon
Pr Proverbs
Ps Psalms
Qo Ecclesiastes
Rm Romans
Rt Ruth
Rv Revelation
I S I Samuel
II S II Samuel
Sg Song of Songs
Si Ecclesiasticus
Tb Tobit
I Th I Thessalonians
II Th II Thessalonians
I Tm I Timothy
II Tm II Timothy
Tt Titus
Ws Wisdom
Zc Zechariah
Zp Zephaniah

BIBLICAL THEOLOGY. Systematic exposition of the teachings of the Bible. There are two principal forms of biblical theology. One stresses subordination to Christian dogmatics. It works through the material furnished by exegesis, correlates ideas with facts, synthesizes them on the basis of an organic principle consistent with their nature and respective value, and places them into the stream of the history of revelation.

The other form of biblical theology sees the development of exegesis into theology as the work of reason enlightened by faith. Its purpose is to enter, through grace, into more intimate contact with transcendent reality as revealed in the sacred text. In this sense biblical theology is an ideal that always tends toward a goal without stopping at the results already achieved.

The two forms of biblical theology, as auxiliary to dogma and as instruments to religious insight, are not incompatible. They are mutually conducive to heighten the value of both Scripture and dogma, by integrating two areas of religious knowledge that derive from a common, divine source.

BIGAMY. Contracting a marriage while a former one remains undissolved. An older use of the term calls bigamy any valid marriage after the death of a first spouse. (Etym. Latin *bi*, double + Greek *gamos*, marriage: Latin *bigamia*.)

BIOETHICS. The study of ethical questions arising from the development of the biological sciences. This study may be of two kinds, either resolving problems created by the rapid growth of the life sciences, or analyzing the prospects of new developments in ethical practice consistent with the Christian principles of morality. Examples of the first are genetic engineering and artificial insemination; examples of the second are organ transplantation and natural family planning. (Etym. Greek *bios*, life + *ēthos*, custom, moral nature.)

BIORHYTHM. The scientifically determined cycle of changes in a person, depending on his or her temperament and physical condition. The cycle basically occurs in the functions of the organs and organism, but the changes also affect a person's emotions, following various rhythms in both men and women each month. Biorhythm has considerable implications in the moral order, as a mechanism that influences one's feelings and indirectly the degree of imputability in human actions.

BIRTH CONTROL. A synonym for contraception, introduced into the vocabulary by professed contraceptionists in order to equate control of population with preventing conception through artificial means.

BISHOP. A successor of the Apostles who has received the fullness of Christ's priesthood. His most distinctive power, that of ordaining priests and other bishops, belongs uniquely to a bishop. Moreover, in spite of some disputed cases in history, it is highly probable that a priest would not be authorized by the Holy See to ordain another priest. A priest certainly cannot consecrate a bishop.

In the ordination of a bishop the "matter" is the imposition of hands on the head of the bishop-elect by the consecrating bishops, or at least by the principal consecrator, which is done in silence before the consecratory prayer; the "form" consists of the words of the consecratory prayer, of which the following pertains to the essence of the order, and therefore is required for the validity of the act: "Now pour out upon this chosen one that power which flows from you, the perfect Spirit whom He gave to the apostles, who established the Church in every place as the sanctuary where your name would always be praised and glorified." (Etym. Greek *episkopos,* a bishop, literally, overseer.)

BLASPHEMY. Speaking against God in a contemptuous, scornful, or abusive manner. Included under blasphemy are offenses committed by thought, word, or action. Serious contemptuous ridicule of the saints, sacred objects, or of persons consecrated to God is also blasphemous because God is indirectly attacked. Blasphemy is a grave violation of charity toward God. Its gravity may be judged by the capital punishment in the Old Testament, and by severe penalties of the Church and in many cases also of the State for blasphemous speech or conduct. In order for a person to sin gravely in this manner, he must use blasphemous expressions and realize the contemptuous meaning of what he says or does. (Etym. Latin *blasphemia,* blasphemy; from Greek *blasphēmein,* to speak ill of.)

BLESSED. In general, a person, place, or object associated with God and implying a divine favor: 1. a sacramental as a blessed article; 2. a deceased person who has been beatified by an official declaration of the Church; 3. believers in Christ who respond to his beatitudes; 4. all Christians insofar as they receive the grace of God; 5. all who are in heaven. (Etym. Anglo-Saxon *blētsian,* to consecrate by blood.)

BLESSED SACRAMENT. The Eucharist as one of the seven sacraments instituted by Christ to be received by the faithful. Unlike the other sacraments, however, the Eucharist is not only a sacrament to be received but also a sacrament to be adored before, during, and after reception. It is therefore a permanent sacrament, since Christ remains in the Eucharist as long as the physical properties of the species of bread and wine remain essentially unchanged.

BLESSED VIRGIN MARY. Mother of Jesus Christ and greatest of the Christian saints. The name "Mary" occurs only once in the Old Testament as the name of Moses's sister (Exodus 15:20). Its etymology has been variously traced to mean beautiful, bitter, rebellion, illuminatrix, lady, and beloved of God. Scholars prefer the last meaning, derived from the Egyptian, which may be explained by the four hundred years' sojourn of the Israelites in Egypt.

The Gospel account of Mary's life begins with the appearance of the archangel Gabriel in Nazareth to announce the choice of her as mother of the Messiah. Though espoused to Joseph, she intended to remain a virgin and asked for an explanation. The angel assured her that this would be done by the power of the Most High, at which Mary gave her consent: "Be it done to me according to your word."

On her visit to Elizabeth, Mary sang the Magnificat, "My soul magnifies the Lord," which recalls the canticle of Anna, mother of Samuel the prophet (I Kings 2:1–10). When Mary returned to Nazareth, Joseph realized that she was pregnant and thought of putting her away privately until an angel appeared to him and revealed the mystery.

In obedience to a census decree of Augustus, Mary and Joseph, who were both of Davidic descent, went to David's city of Bethlehem, where Jesus was born in a stable. Forty days later Mary, in the company of Joseph, came to the Temple in Jerusalem to be purified according to the Law of Moses, and to offer her son to the Lord together with a sacrifice of a pair of turtledoves or two young pigeons. At this presentation, the old man Simeon took Jesus in his arms and foretold Mary's share in the future sufferings of her son.

During the hidden life of Christ, the Gospels are silent about Mary except for one dramatic incident when Jesus was twelve years old. Finding him in the Temple in the midst of the doctors, his mother asked him why he had done this. In their first recorded dialogue, Jesus replied that he must be about his Father's business.

Mary was with Christ at the beginning of his public life, when through her intercession he changed water into wine at the marriage feast in Cana of Galilee. She was in his company at Capharnaum for a short time, and on occasion followed him in his ministry.

She stood beneath the Cross on Calvary and was placed in the care of the Apostle John, being told, "Behold your son." After the Ascension of Christ into heaven, Mary waited in Jerusalem with the Apostles and disciples for the coming of the Holy Spirit. From then on there are no further biographical data about Mary in the New Testament, except for the mystical references to the "woman" in St. John's Apocalypse, and St. Paul's description to the Galatians of Christ as "made of a woman."

According to tradition, Mary lived for a time in or near Ephesus, but her permanent home after Pentecost seems to have been Jerusalem. There is no certain place or date for Mary's death, although most likely it occurred at Ephesus, twelve years after Christ's Ascension.

BLESSING. As found in Scripture, it means praise, the desire that good fortune go with a person or thing, dedication of a person or thing to God's service and a gift. In liturgical language a blessing is a ritual ceremony by which an authorized cleric in major orders sanctifies persons or things to divine service, or invokes divine favor on what he blesses. The Church's ritual provides for over two hundred such blessings, some of which are reserved to bishops or members of certain religious institutes.

BLOOD OF ST. JANUARIUS. A famous relic in the Cathedral of Naples. The blood of this martyr (died about 305), preserved in a glass phial, liquifies several times each year when the reliquary is exposed and placed near the saint's head. No natural explanation has been found for the phenomenon.

BLUE ARMY. An organization founded in 1946 to pray and sacrifice for the conversion of Russia and for world peace. The society is a response to one of the requests made by Our Lady at Fátima, Portugal, in 1917, recommending the recitation of the Rosary and urging mortification for the conversion of sinners. The Blue Army was established after Pope Pius XII in 1942 consecrated the world to the Immaculate Heart of Mary.

BODILY IMMORTALITY. The immunity from disease and bodily death that was enjoyed by Adam and Eve before the Fall. It was a special privilege that was to have been passed on to their descendants. Since man is naturally mortal in body, this privilege was preternatural. It conferred the capacity not to die. Its purpose was to enable mankind to better use the gift of sanctifying grace in serving God.

BODILY RESURRECTION. The reunion of the soul of each human being with his own body on the last day. Christ taught the resurrection from the dead (Matthew 22:29–32; Luke 14:14; John 5:29, 6:39–40, 11:25), and the Apostles preached the doctrine as a cardinal mystery of the Christian faith (I Corinthians 15:20; Revelation 20:12). Belief in resurrection is professed in all the ancient creeds. "The human beings that rise again are the identical persons who lived before, though their vital processes are performed in a different way. Now their life is mortal, then it will be immortal. . . . [But] they still are of the same kind and are still the same individuals as before. . . . They do not assume a heavenly or ghostly kind of body. Their bodies remain truly human, though they are invested with an immortality coming from a divine strength which enables them so to dominate the body that corruption cannot enter" (St. Thomas, *Compendium Theologiae*, 155).

BODY OF THE CHURCH. The visible, organized commonwealth of the faithful. As the Holy Spirit is the soul of the Church, so her human members on earth are the body. One of the corollaries of this fact is that anyone who culpably remains outside the body of the Church cannot participate in the life of grace that comes to the Church from the Holy Spirit.

BOLSHEVISM. A term derived from the Russian *bolshinstvo* (majority) and originally used to designate the radical left among the Communists. The professed aim of Bolshevism is the overthrow of existing governments and the substitution of Communism under the dictatorship of the proletariat. It has been several times condemned by name in papal documents. Pope Pius XI declared, "We have exposed the errors and the violent deceptive tactics of Bolshevistic and atheistic Communism" (encyclical *Divini Redemptoris*, III, 25).

BORN AGAIN. Spiritual rebirth at baptism, as commanded by Christ: "Unless a man be born again of water and the Spirit, he cannot enter the Kingdom of God" (John 3:5). The term is used in Catholic theology to describe the spiritual change worked by divine grace, by which a person, from having been conceived and born in sin, is regenerated into a new creature, a child of God and heir of heaven. It is synonymous with supernatural regeneration. In some Protestant circles the expression refers to a new experiential knowledge in Christ, wrought by baptism or by a sudden and lasting conversion from sin to a fervent service of God.

BRAIN DEATH. A form of medical evidence of bodily death, when the death of the cerebral cortex is shown by flat tracings on an electroencephalograph. Sometimes called cerebral death or irreversible coma, it is useful as a scientific confirmation of death. The further question of how long a flat electroencephalogram must last to be sure of death is still debated, although five hours has been recommended in the case of organ transplants. On moral grounds, other proven criteria must also be used to establish clinical death.

BREAD (LITURGICAL USE). 1. An element in the Eucharistic Sacrifice of the Christian liturgy. It is made of wheaten flour, either unleavened, as in the Latin Rite, or leavened, in the other rites of the Catholic Church; 2. a symbol of union, when two loaves are presented to the celebrant at the Offertory of the Mass, while celebrating the canonization of a saint or the consecration of a bishop, or when bread blessed at the Offertory is distributed to the people for consumption at home; 3. a symbol of sacrifice when bread brought by the faithful is blessed at the Sunday parochial Mass.

BREAKING OF THE HOST. The liturgical breaking of the consecrated Host at Mass. Its purpose is first practical, to facilitate consuming by the priest. It is also a symbol that through the body of Christ the faithful become one with him and with one another.

BREVIARY. The liturgical book containing the Divine Office of the Roman Catholic Church. Formerly the various "hours" of the office were in different books, e.g., the Psaltery, the Hymnary, and the Lectionary. But from the eleventh century they began to be combined in one book. The complete text of the Liturgy of the Hours is published in four consecutive volumes. These volumes are divided according to the following calendar year: Advent and Christmas season, Lent and Easter season, the first through the seventeenth, and the eighteenth through the thirty-fourth weeks of the year. (Etym. Latin *breviarium*, a summary, abridgment.) See also DIVINE OFFICE.

BROTHERS. A generic name that originally referred to all members of a religious community but is now generally used to identify those men religious who do not or will not receive holy orders. The term is also applied in some institutes to students for the priesthood who are not yet ordained.

BULL, PAPAL. The most solemn and weighty form of papal letter. The name is derived from the Latin *bulla,* the disklike leaden seal attached to such a document. It is used by the pope in appointing a bishop. Formerly all papal letters of major importance, including canonization decrees, were called bulls, but the current *Acta Apostolicae Sedis* gives some of these papal letters various names.

BURIAL, CHRISTIAN. Interment of a deceased person with the Church's funeral rites in consecrated ground. Since it is an honor granted by the Church, it follows that the Church may determine who is worthy of it. The general practice of the Church is to interpret certain prohibitions of Christian burial as mildly as possible. Doubtful cases are referred to a bishop. If the burial is to take place in a cemetery that has not been consecrated, the grave must be individually blessed before a Catholic person is interred.

BURSE. A stiff pocket about twelve inches square in which the folded corporal is carried to and from the altar. Part of a set of vestments, it is made of matching material. It is placed upon the chalice at the beginning and end of Mass and on the altar at Benediction. The leather case containing the pyx, in which the Holy Eucharist is brought to the sick, is called a burse. It is also the name for an endowment or foundation fund especially for scholarships for candidates for the priesthood. (Etym. Latin *bursa,* purse or pouch.)

BYZANTINE RITE. Ritual and ecclesiastical policy followed by the Church of Constantinople. The second most widely used rite after the Roman, it has three forms: 1. the liturgy of St. James the Elder, modified by St. Basil and named after him; 2. St. John Chrysostom's later modification, which became the common Eucharistic service of Constantinople. Though it did not displace the original St. Basil's, it did limit its use; 3. the liturgy of the Presanctified, essentially the distribution of the Blessed Sacrament consecrated on the preceding Sunday.

C

CAIAPHAS. Son-in-law of Annas and his successor as High Priest of Jerusalem (A.D. 18–37) (Luke 3:2). It was his ominous observation to the chief priests and Pharisees that presaged the death of Jesus. "You don't seem to have grasped the situation at all; you fail to see that it is better for one man to die for the people than for the whole nation to be destroyed" (John 11:49–50). Jesus, after Annas had questioned him, was brought to the palace of Caiaphas (John 18:24), who sent him to Pilate for official condemnation. (Etym. Greek *kaiaphas*, rock or depression.)

CAIN. The elder son of Adam and Eve. He tilled the soil, while his brother, Abel, was a shepherd. When each offered the product of his work to YHWH, Abel's offering was more favorably accepted. In his resentment, Cain slew his brother (Genesis 4). Condemned by YHWH, he became "a fugitive and a wanderer over the earth" (Genesis 4:14). His wife bore him a son, Enoch, and when Cain later built a town, he named it after his son (Genesis 4:17).

CALUMNY. Injuring another person's good name by lying. It is doubly sinful, in unjustly depriving another of his good name and in telling an untruth. Since calumny violates justice, it involves the duty of making reparation for the foreseen injury inflicted. Hence the calumniator must try not only to repair the harm done to another's good name but also to make up for any foreseen temporal loss that resulted from the calumny—for example, loss of employment or customers. (Etym. Latin *calumnia*, a false accusation, malicious charge; from *calvi*, to deceive.)

CALVARY. Golgotha, or the place where Jesus was crucified (Luke 23). It was so called because it resembled a head or skull. Mount Calvary was near Jerusalem and was the place where criminals were normally executed.

CALVINISM. The religious system introduced by John Calvin (1509–64), French reformer, in opposition to the doctrine of the Catholic Church on the meaning of humanity's predestination. In the Calvinist system, as a result of Adam's fall, man no longer has any internal freedom of the will; he is a slave of God. Everyone is eternally predestined, either for heaven or for hell, absolutely independent of his personal efforts. Consequently the elect cannot be lost. The basic principles of Calvinism are set forth in the *Institutes of the Christian Religion,* in which Calvin argues that since God is absolutely infinite he is the only real agent in the universe, and creatures are merely his instruments.

CANA. A village in Galilee where Jesus performed the miracle of turning water into wine at the marriage feast (John 2:1–11). Later, when he returned to Cana, he performed another miracle in curing the dying son of a court official (John 4:46–53). (Etym. Hebrew *qanah,* reed; Greek *kana.*)

CANDLE. A sacramental used in the Church's liturgy. Candles were first used to dispel darkness in predawn services and in the catacombs. They have since become part of the liturgy and their symbolism part of the Church's tradition. Candles are an emblem of God, the giver of life and enlightenment. Being pure, they represent Christ's spotless body, the flame a figure of the Divine Nature. Candles are blessed solemnly on the feast of the Purification of the Blessed Virgin or Candlemas Day (February 2). Candles are required at the public administration of the sacraments, at Mass and Benediction, at funerals and at other church ceremonies.

CANDLEMAS. Synonymous with the feast of the Purification of Mary, February 2, commemorating the purification of the Blessed Virgin, according to Mosaic Law, forty days after Christ's birth and the presentation of the Child Jesus in the Temple. Candles are blessed on that day, and a lighted candle procession is held to commemorate Christ as the light of revelation to the Gentiles, and to represent his entry into the Temple. In Scotland it is the legal term day on which interests and rents are payable. See also PURIFICATION.

CANON. An established rule for guidance, a standard, or a list of such rules: 1. in biblical usage the catalogue of inspired writings known as the Old and New Testaments, identified as such by the Church; 2. in ecclesiastical usage, a short definition of some dogmatic truth, with attached anathema, made as a rule by general councils; 3. the Eucharistic Prayer, which is the essential part of the Sacrifice of the Mass; 4. in religious life, certain orders of men with specific duties often attached to a particular church, shrine, or ecclesiastical function; 5. in music a composition that repeats the same melody by one or more voices in turn, producing harmony; 6. in printing a size type, namely 4 line pica 48 point, used in printing church books or the Canon of the Mass; 7. catalogue of canonized saints; 8. rules of certain religious orders and the books that contain them; 9. in art and architecture the established rule, which is periodically specified in ecclesiastical matters by Church directives or legislation; 10. a member of the clergy attached to a cathedral or other large church, with specific duties such as the choral recitation of the Divine Office. (Etym. Latin *canon*, rule, standard of conduct; summary, record; from Greek *kanōn*, rod, rule.)

CANONICAL FORM. The requisite conditions for a valid marriage in which one or both parties are Catholic. For the marriage of a Catholic to be valid, there must be present 1. a bishop or a parish priest in his parish or another priest duly delegated, and 2. two witnesses. A dispensation from the canonical form can be obtained for mixed marriages.

CANONIZATION. Declaration by the pope that a deceased person is raised to the full honors of the altar, i.e., a saint after previously having been beatified. Two miracles credited to the beatus (feminine: beata) are usually required before canonization to attest the heroic virtue of the saint. Beatification allows veneration of the blessed, canonization requires it. The canonization is celebrated at St. Peter's and is usually followed by a solemn triduum in another church in the city or elsewhere within a limited time. (Etym. Latin *canonizare*, to canonize; from *canon*, catalogue of saints.)

CANON LAW. The authentic compilation of the laws of the Catholic Church. Two major compilations have been made in the Church's history, Gratian's Decree, assembled about A.D. 1140 by the Italian Camaldolese monk Gratian, and the Code of Canon Law, promulgated by Pope Benedict XV in 1917 and effective on Pentecost, May 19, 1918. A new Code of Canon Law was promulgated on January 25, 1983, by Blessed Pope John Paul II.

CANTICLE. In the Divine Office a sacred chant from Scripture apart from the Psalms. In the Roman Breviary there are many canticles from the Old Testament. The three evangelical canticles of the New Testament recited daily in the Divine Office are the Benedictus of

Zechariah, the Magnificat of the Blessed Virgin, and the Nunc Dimittis of Simeon. (Etym. Latin *canticulum*, a little song.)

CANTICLE OF CANTICLES. An allegorical love poem in the Bible that has several layers of meaning. Basically it expresses the special love of God for the Chosen People; prophetically the espousal of Christ with his church; universally the love of God for a devoted soul; by accommodation the delight of God with the soul of the Blessed Virgin. It was read in the Jewish liturgy on the octave of the Passover. Traditionally ascribed to Solomon, the imagery of the two lovers, united and then separated, sought and then found, reflects the changing relationships of God and his people, depending on their varying loyalty to him.

CANTICLE OF THE SUN. The best-known poem of praise of St. Francis of Assisi (1181–1226). It was begun in 1225, but the final verses about Sister Death were added shortly before he died. His biographer, Thomas of Celano (1200–55), says that the saint's last words were: "Welcome, my Sister Death." The praise in the canticle is not addressed to the creatures but to God, their Creator. The full text of this great hymn reads:

Most high, all-powerful, all good, Lord!
    All praise is yours, all glory, all honor
    And all blessing.
To you, alone, Most High, do they belong.
    No mortal lips are worthy
    To pronounce your name.
All praise be yours, my Lord, through all that you have made,
    And first my lord Brother Sun,
    Who brings the day; and light you give to us through him.
How beautiful is he, how radiant in all his splendor!
    Of you, Most High, he bears the likeness.
All praise be yours, my Lord, through Sister Moon and Stars;
    In the heavens you have made them, bright
    And precious and fair.
All praise be yours, my Lord, through Brothers Wind and Air,
    And fair and stormy, all the weather's moods,
    By which you cherish all that you have made.
All praise be yours, my Lord, through Sister Water,
    So useful, lowly, precious and pure.
All praise be yours, my Lord, through Brother Fire,

Through whom you brighten up the night.
How beautiful is he, how gay! Full of power and strength.
All praise be yours, my Lord, through Sister Earth, our mother,
Who feeds us in her sovereignty and produces
Various fruits with colored flowers and herbs.
All praise be yours, my Lord, through those who grant pardon
For love of you; through those who endure
Sickness and trial.
Happy those who endure in peace,
By you, Most High, they will be crowned.
All praise be yours, my Lord, through Sister Death,
From whose embrace no mortal can escape.
Woe to those who die in mortal sin!
Happy those She finds doing your will!
The second death can do no harm to them.
Praise and bless my Lord, and give him thanks,
And serve him with great humility.

CANTOR. The chief singer of an ecclesiastical choir, who leads the singing and often selects the music. In the Divine Office the cantor intones the antiphons and starts the Psalms. He is also called the precentor. (Etym. Latin *cantor,* singer.)

CAPITAL PUNISHMENT. The death penalty imposed by the state for the punishment of grave crimes. It is certain from Scripture that civil authorities may lawfully put malefactors to death. Capital punishment was enacted for certain grievous crimes in the Old Law, e.g., blasphemy, sorcery, adultery, and murder. Christian dispensation made no essential change in this respect, as St. Paul expressly says: "The state is there to serve God for your benefit. If you break the law, however, you may well have fear: the bearing of the sword has its significance" (Romans 13:4). Among the errors of the Waldenses condemned by the Church in the early thirteenth century was the proposition that denied the lawfulness of capital punishment (Argentré, *Collectio de Novis Erroribus,* I, 86). St. Thomas Aquinas (1225–74) defends capital punishment on the grounds of the common good. The state, he reasons, is like a body composed of many members, and as a surgeon may cut off one corrupt limb to save the others, so the civil authority may lawfully put a criminal to death and thus provide for the common good.

Theologians further reason that, in receiving its authority from

God through the natural law, the state also receives from him the right to use the necessary means for attaining its end. The death penalty is such a means. If even with capital punishment crime abounds, no lesser penalty will suffice.

The practical question remains of how effective a deterrent capital punishment is in some modern states, when rarely used or only after long delays.

The *Catechism of the Catholic Church*, while reaffirming the Church's traditional teaching permitting capital punishment, goes on to say that if "non-lethal means are sufficient to defend and protect people's safety from the aggressor, authority will limit itself to such means" (2267).

CAPITAL SINS. Those sins to which man's fallen nature is mainly inclined and that are, as a result, the source of all other human failings. The name "capital" does not mean that they are necessarily grave sins. They are leading tendencies toward sin and are seven in number: pride, avarice, lust, envy, gluttony, anger, and sloth. Theology justifies the number by pointing to the goods that human nature seeks to attain or the evils it wants to avoid. The goods desired and the evils disliked can be material or spiritual, and either real or imaginary. Thus, pride and vainglory come from wanting to be held in high honor and glory, and from preening oneself in the imagination. Gluttony comes from individual high living, lust from sexuality inborn to preserve the race, and avarice from the gathering of wealth. The repulsions are about good things wrongfully regarded as threatening our own proper good and that therefore are grieved over or actively combatted. Spiritual values menace our physical pleasure and ease, hence sloth or boredom about spiritual values. Envy is much the same; it resents another's good qualities because they may lower our own self-esteem. To flare out at others is anger. (Etym. Latin *capitalis,* principal, acting in the manner of a head.) See also DEADLY SINS.

CAPITAL VIRTUES. The seven principal virtues that are contrary to the seven capital sins, namely: 1. humility (pride), 2. liberality (avarice), 3. chastity (lust), 4. meekness (anger), 5. temperance (gluttony), 6. brotherly love (envy), 7. diligence (sloth).

CAPUCHINS. One of three autonomous branches of the Franciscans, founded in 1525 by Matteo di Bassi of Urbano (d. 1552), an Observant friar who wished to return to the primitive poverty and simplicity of the order. Its members wear a pointed cowl (capuche), with optional sandals and beard. They were one of the most powerful instruments of the Counter-Reformation where they gained wide respect as popular preachers, confessors, and missionaries.

CARD. Cardinal.

CARDINAL. A high official of the Roman Catholic Church ranking next to the pope. He is a member of the Sacred College and is appointed by the Sovereign Pontiff to assist and advise him in the government of the Church. The names of newly created cardinals are usually announced at a papal consistory. They may wear a specially designed red hat and cassock. They are the ones who elect a pope, who, for centuries now, has always been a cardinal before his election. The Code of Canon Law, promulgated in 1918, decreed that all cardinals must be priests. In 1962, Blessed Pope John XXIII provided that they should all be bishops; however, the Pope may dispense a person from this requirement. (Etym. Latin *cardo,* hinge.)

CARDINAL VIRTUE. One of the four principal virtues of human morality, to which the others are necessarily related. These four central virtues are prudence, justice, temperance, and fortitude. Each of the cardinal virtues has subjective, potential, and integral parts. The subjective parts are such acts and dispositions of soul as are necessary for the full possession of that virtue, as foresight is needed for prudence and patience for fortitude. The potential parts are virtues related to the cardinal virtue but yet distinct from it, as truthfulness is a potential part of justice. The integral parts are species of a cardinal virtue, as chastity is a species of temperance.

CARITAS IN VERITATE. Encyclical of Pope Benedict XVI on integral human development in charity and truth (June 29, 2009). Pope Benedict XVI examines the message of Venerable Pope Paul VI's encyclical *Populorum Progressio* in light of our times. The encyclical affirms that authentic human development cannot occur apart from God. Charity and truth are at the heart of the Church's social doctrine, which "illuminates with an unchanging light the new problems in society that are constantly emerging." Pope Benedict XVI also teaches that work for human development depends upon the underlying system of morality to which the Church's social teaching has much to contribute because it recognizes the "inviolable dignity of the human person and the transcendent value of natural moral norms."

CARMELITE ORDER. The Order of Our Lady of Mount Carmel, founded at about 1154 in Palestine by St. Berthold (d. 1195). It claims continuity with hermits on Mount Carmel from ancient times, and even to the prophet Elijah. The original rule, set down in 1209 by the Latin Patriarch of Jerusalem, Albert of Vercelli (1149–1214), was very severe, prescribing absolute poverty, total abstinence from meat, and solitude. After the Crusades, the Englishman St. Simon Stock (d. 1265) reorganized the Carmelites as mendicant friars. The laxity of the sixteenth century brought reforms among the women under St. Teresa of Avila (1515–82) and the men under St. John of the Cross (1542–91). This created the two independent branches of the order, the Calced, or Shod, Carmelites (of the Old Observance) and the Discalced, or Unshod, following the Teresian Reform. The main purpose of the order is contemplation, missionary work, and theology. Carmelite nuns devote themselves to prayer, especially of intercession for priests, and to a life of hidden sacrifice. The canonization of St. Thérèse de Lisieux (1873–97) in 1925 and her designation as patroness of the missions have done much to make the Carmelites' ideal known and imitated throughout the Catholic world.

CARTESIANISM. The principles embodied in the teaching of René Descartes (1596–1650). Its outstanding feature is the notion of universal methodical doubt. Cartesianism begins by calling into doubt whatever knowledge a person has acquired and then seeking to find a truth so evident that it cannot be doubted. This truth it claims to find in each person's intuition of his own thought and existence. Within the Cartesian system are several principles, all at variance with the Catholic faith, which Descartes professed to believe, namely: occasionalism, which disowns free will for man; ontologism, which denies that a person can perceive ideas within his mind or objects directly in themselves; and angelism, which regards man as if he were a pure spirit within a body, as if thought must be intuitive and not deductive, and independent of things but evolved from one's own consciousness.

CARTHUSIANS. The strictly contemplative order founded by St. Bruno (1032–1101) in 1084 at the Grande Chartreuse in Dauphiné. At first there was no special rule except that the monks were expected to practice perfect mortification and renunciation of the world. Essentially hermits, the Carthusians were vowed to silence, with conventual Mass. In 1133, a form of life called the Carthusian Customs was approved by Pope Innocent II, and this has remained to the present day substantially unchanged. The Carthusian way of life is a combination of Benedictine monasticism and eremitical asceticism.

The order also includes a number of monasteries of nuns who live under a similar rule, but they have separate cells instead of cottages and are under the direction of the Carthusian monks. (Etym. French *Chartreuse*.)

CASTI CONNUBII. An encyclical letter of Pope Pius XI on Christian marriage, published in 1930. Its clear, outspoken teaching on marital indissolubility and on the evil of contraception makes it a landmark in the Church's doctrine on the sanctity of matrimony. The Second Vatican Council built on this document in its treatment of Christian marriage in the *Pastoral Constitution on the Church in the Modern World*.

CATACOMBS. Subterranean galleries used as burial grounds by the Christians of the first centuries. Here, by Roman law, they were immune from disturbance. The tombs of the martyrs buried there became altars for the celebration of the divine mysteries. The disposition and maintenance of the catacombs are now reserved to the Holy See. The best known of these rediscovered cemeteries are in Rome. (Etym. Italian *catacomba*, a sepulchral vault.)

CATECHESIS. That form of ecclesiastical action that leads both communities and individual members of the faithful to maturity of faith. Because of varied circumstances and multiple needs, catechetical activity takes on various forms.

In regions that have been Catholic from past ages, catechesis most often takes the form of religious instruction given to children and adolescents in schools or outside a school atmosphere. Also found in those regions are various catechetical programs for adults, whether in preparation for baptism or reception into the Church, or to deepen one's understanding of the faith. Sometimes the actual condition of the faithful demands that some form of evangelization of the baptized precede catechesis.

In churches that have been established recently, special importance is placed on evangelizing in the strict sense. This becomes the well-known catechumenate for those who are being introduced to the faith in preparation for baptism.

For individuals whose minds are open to the message of the Gospel, catechesis is an apt means to understand God's plan in their own lives and in the lives of others. Having come to know this divine plan, they can more effectively cooperate with God's grace and become better instruments for the extension of Christ's kingdom. (Etym. Greek *katechizo*, to teach by word of mouth.)

CATECHISM. A popular manual of instruction in Christian doctrine. In the early Church, catechetical instruction was standardized in preparation for baptism as in the writings of St. Augustine (354–430) and St. Gregory of Nyssa (330–95). After the invention of printing, books of catechetical instruction multiplied. For centuries, the best known catechisms in the Catholic Church were St. Peter Canisius's *Summa of Christian Doctrine* (1555) and the *Catechism of the Council of Trent,* or *Roman Catechism* (1566). Numerous catechisms were published in various countries authorized by their respective hierarchies, e.g., the so-called *Penny Catechism* in Great Britain and the series of Baltimore Catechisms in the United States. Since the Second Vatican Council, all catechisms published by ecclesiastical authority must also be "submitted to the Apostolic See for review and approval" (*General Catechetical Directory,* 119). Blessed Pope John Paul II ordered the development and publishing of a new *Catechism of the Catholic Church.* On September 8, 1997, Blessed John Paul II formally promulgated the *editio typica* (the definitive Latin text) of the *Catechism of the Catholic Church.*

CATECHUMENATE. The period of instruction in the faith before baptism and admission of converts to the Catholic Church. The Second Vatican Council set down specific directives on the catechumenate by: 1. distinguishing between the more intense and normally prolonged catechumenate in mission lands; 2. stressing the importance of not only instruction but training in the practice of virtue; 3. pointing out the responsibility of the whole Christian community to cooperate in the preparation of catechumens; and 4. directing that the catechumenate be integrated with the liturgical year and the celebration of the Paschal Mystery (*Ad Gentes Divinitus,* 13–14). (Etym. Latin *catechumenus;* from Greek *katēkhoumenos,* from *katēkhein,* to catechize.)

CATHEDRAL. The official church of a bishop, where his permanent episcopal throne is erected. It is the mother church of a diocese, and its clergy have precedence. The cathedral must be consecrated, and the date of consecration and the date of its titular feast must be observed liturgically. (Etym. Latin *cathedra*, a chair, stool, throne; Greek *kathedra*, seat.)

CATHOLIC. Its original meaning of "general" or "universal" has taken on a variety of applications in the course of Christian history. First used by St. Ignatius of Antioch (A.D. 35–107) (Letter to the Smyrneans, 8, 2), it is now mainly used in five recognized senses: 1. the Catholic Church as distinct from Christian ecclesiastical bodies that do not recognize the papal primacy; 2. the Catholic faith as the belief of the universal body of the faithful, namely that which is believed "everywhere, always, and by all" (Vincentian Canon); 3. orthodoxy as distinguished from what is heretical or schismatical; 4. the undivided Church before the Eastern Schism of 1054; thereafter the Eastern Church has called itself orthodox, in contrast with those Christian bodies that did not accept the definitions of Ephesus and Chalcedon on the divinity of Christ.

In general, today the term "Catholic" refers to those Christians who profess a continued tradition of faith and worship and who hold to the apostolic succession of bishops and priests since the time of Christ (Etym. Latin *catholicus*, universal; Greek *katholikos*, universal.)

CATHOLIC ACTION. The apostolate of the laity under the guidance of the hierarchy. Since Catholic Action became an established feature of the Church in modern times, it has undergone several stages of development. The necessary role of the laity in the Church's mission of evangelization and education is one of the principal doctrines of the Second Vatican Council. They are seen as not mere supplements to make up for what is wanting among the clergy, nor even as mere assistants. Their function in the Church's mission to the world is co-ordinate with that of priests and religious, while they serve in the corporal and spiritual works of mercy in deference to the divinely established hierarchy. Consistent with the Church's development of the concept of subsidiarity, laypeople are to be given every opportunity to make their own distinctive contribution to the Catholic apostolate. Moreover, with the progress in social communications they are to work cooperatively among themselves in groups and organizations that are always respectful of the local hierarchy but also conscious of their larger, even international responsibility (under the Holy See) to Christianize all of human society.

CATHOLICISM. The faith, ritual, and morals of the Roman Catholic Church as a historical reality, revealed in Jesus Christ and destined to endure until the end of time. It comprehends all that the Church teaches must be believed and lived out in order to be saved and, beyond salvation, in order to be sanctified. This system of doctrine, cultus, and practice is called Catholic (universal) because it is intended for all mankind, for all time, contains all that is necessary, and is suitable in every circumstance of human life.

CATHOLICITY. Universality of the Church founded by Christ. In the Nicene Creed the Church is said to be "one, holy, *catholic,* and apostolic." The Church's catholicity is first of all spatial, on account of her actual extension over the whole earth. This kind of catholicity may be actual, when the Church is actually extended everywhere; it is virtual in that Christ's intention was to have the Church present among all peoples. Actual catholicity is said to be physical if it embodies all persons of the earth, even if not literally every individual. It is moral if it includes only the greater part of them. Although moral catholicity suffices for the Church's universality, it is Christ's will that the Church constantly endeavor to extend. The ideal toward which the Church strives is physical catholicity. A common position among apologists holds that moral catholicity demands that the Church extend over the whole earth simultaneously. Thus after a certain time of development, moral catholicity will be realized and from that time on is to be perpetuated.

CELIBACY. The state of being unmarried and, in Church usage, of one who has never been married. Catholicism distinguishes between lay and ecclesiastical celibacy, and in both cases a person freely chooses for religious reasons to remain celibate.

Lay celibacy was practiced already in the early Church. The men were called "the continent" (*continentes*) and women "virgins" (*virgines*). They were also known as ascetics who were encouraged to follow this form of life by St. Paul. According to the Apostle, "An unmarried man can devote himself to the Lord's affairs, all he need worry about is pleasing the Lord. . . . In the same way an unmarried woman, like a young girl, can devote herself to the Lord's affairs; all she need worry about is being holy in body and spirit" (I Corinthians 7:32, 34). Throughout history the Church has fostered a celibate life in the lay state. Towering among the means of sanctity available to the laity, declared the Second Vatican Council, "is that precious gift of divine grace given to some by the Father to devote themselves to God alone more easily with an undivided heart in virginity or celibacy. This perfect continence for love of the kingdom of heaven has always been held in high esteem by the Church as a sign and stimulus of love, and as a singular source of spiritual fertility in the world" (Dogmatic Constitution on the Church, 42).

Ecclesiastical celibacy was a logical development of Christ's teaching about continence (Matthew 19:10–12). The first beginnings of religious life were seen in the self-imposed practice of celibacy among men and women who wished to devote themselves to a lifetime following Christ in the practice of the evangelical counsels. Celibacy was one of the features of the earliest hermits and a requirement of the first monastic foundations under St. Pachomius (c. 290–346). Over the centuries religious celibacy has been the subject of the Church's frequent legislation. The Second Vatican Council named chastity first among the evangelical counsels to be practiced by religious and said that "it is a special symbol of heavenly benefits, and for religious it is a most effective means of dedicating themselves wholeheartedly to the divine service and the works of the apostolate" (*Decree on the Up-to-date Renewal of Religious Life*, 12). (Etym. Latin *caelibatus*, single life, celibacy.)

CENSURE, ECCLESIASTICAL. A penalty by which a baptized person, gravely delinquent and obstinate, is deprived of certain spiritual benefits until he gives up his obstinacy. The Church's right to inflict censure follows from her existence as a perfect society, and the main purpose of censures is corrective. Three main kinds of censures are imposed by Church law: excommunication, interdict, and suspension. Some censures take effect as soon as some grave external sin (such as professing heresy) is committed. Others take effect only on being personally imposed. Moreover, a person can be absolved from his sin through a good confession and yet have the censure remain until removed by legitimate authority. But in the case of a censure that prevents the reception of the sacraments, the censured person cannot be absolved from the sins until he or she has first been absolved from the censure.

CHAINED BIBLES. An institution of the medieval Church to protect copies of the Bible from thievery. Before the advent of printing, the rarity of books made them available only to the wealthy. They were often locked away in chests. The Church, wishing to make the Bible available to all the faithful and still to ensure it against loss, chained it to a desk or lectern near a window. There even poor students had its use, and it was in popular demand. Bias and ignorance have interpreted this chaining as proof that the Church withheld the Bible from the laity.

CHAIR OF PETER. A portable chair preserved at the Vatican, believed to have been used by St. Peter the Apostle. The feast of the Chair of St. Peter commemorates the date of his first service in Rome. A similar feast of the Chair of St. Peter commemorates the foundation of the See of Antioch.

CHALICE. The cup-shaped vessel or goblet used at Mass to contain the Precious Blood of Christ. For centuries it was made of precious material; if it was not of gold, the interior of the cup was gold-plated. Since the Second Vatican Council, chalices may be made of other materials, but the materials used must be noble and durable. A chalice is consecrated with holy chrism by a bishop. Regilding the inside does not destroy the consecration. Sometimes the word "chalice" designates its contents. (Etym. Latin *calix,* cup, goblet, drinking vessel, chalice.)

CHALICE VEIL. A covering for the chalice used at Mass. According to the Church's prescription, since the Second Vatican Council "the chalice should be covered with a veil, which can always be white in color" (*Eucharistiae Sacramentum,* IV, 80).

CHANCE. That which is thought to happen without apparent purpose. But from the standpoint of the Catholic faith nothing ever merely happens; everything has a divinely ordained purpose because it is somehow part of God's universal Providence. Chance, therefore, is the admission of ignorance as to why something unexplainable takes place, rather than a denial that every event has a reason for taking place. (Etym. Latin *cadere,* to fall.)

CHANCERY, DIOCESAN. The administrative branch of a diocese under the authority of the local ordinary; it handles the official documents pertaining to the ecclesiastical affairs of the diocese.

CHAPEL. A relatively small place for liturgical worship by the members of a private or religious family. Sometimes it is an oratory in another, larger building or a small, consecrated detached room or building having an altar. Side chapels in churches often have a special purpose, as for the reservation of the Blessed Sacrament or as a shrine. (Etym. Latin *cappella,* originally a shrine in which was preserved the *capa* or cloak of St. Martin of Tours.)

CHAPLAIN. A priest who serves a chapel or oratory or is appointed to exercise the sacred ministry in an institution, such as a convent or orphanage, hospital or prison. Also a priest or other sacred minister appointed to serve special classes of persons, such as the armed forces, or authorized to lead religious services in the assemblies of fraternal organizations, legislatures, and other bodies. (Etym. Latin *cappellanus;* from *cappella,* shrine.)

CHARACTER. Moral qualities of a person, founded on his or her temperament and developed by free choices, which distinguish one as an individual; a person's habitual virtues and failings that make one a distinct moral individual. In a praiseworthy sense, character is the integration of a person's nature and nurture in one's moral habits and the expression of these in daily living. (Etym. Latin *character;* from Greek *charaktēr,* an engraved or stamped mark.)

CHARISMATIC MOVEMENT. A modern revival of Pentecostalism in many Christian churches, including Roman Catholic. The term "charismatic" is preferred in Catholic circles to "Pentecostal," which is more commonly used by Protestant leaders of the movement.

CHARITY. The infused supernatural virtue by which a person loves God above all things for his own sake and loves others for God's sake. It is a virtue based on divine faith or a belief in God's revealed truth, and is not acquired by mere human effort. It can be conferred only by divine grace. Because it is infused along with sanctifying grace, it is frequently identified with the state of grace. Therefore, a person who has lost the supernatural virtue of charity has lost the state of grace, although he may still possess the virtues of hope and faith.

CHASTITY. The virtue that moderates the desire for sexual pleasure according to the principles of faith and right reason. In married people, chastity moderates the desire in conformity with their state of life; in unmarried people who wish to marry, the desire is moderated by abstention until (or unless) they get married; in those who resolve not to marry, the desire is sacrificed entirely.

Chastity and purity, modesty and decency are comparable in that they have the basic meaning of freedom from whatever is lewd or salacious. Yet they also differ. Chastity implies an opposition to the immoral in the sense of lustful or licentious. It suggests refraining from all acts or thoughts that are not in accordance with the Church's teaching about the use of one's reproductive powers. It particularly stresses restraint and an avoidance of anything that might defile or make unclean the soul because the body has not been controlled in the exercise of its most imperious passion. (Etym. Latin *castus,* morally pure, unstained.)

CHASUBLE. A sleeveless outer garment worn by a priest at Mass. It is worn over all other vestments and is made of silk, velvet, or other rich material usually decorated with symbols. The arms are to be free when it is worn. It symbolizes the yoke of Christ and signifies charity. (Etym. Latin *casula,* a little house; hence a mantle.)

CHEATING. Deception by trickery or fraud in order to gain materially, socially, or psychologically. Cheating is always sinful. Its gravity depends on the harm inflicted on the person defrauded or on some third party. True repentance for cheating requires at least the willingness to make restitution for the harm that may have been caused.

CHILDLIKENESS. The quality of guileless openness that Christ declared is one of the conditions for attaining salvation (Matthew 18:3). It is the virtue of humility, at once ready to do God's will and having no selfish interests of one's own.

CHOIR. 1. The part of a church reserved for choristers; 2. an organized body of singers who perform or lead the musical part of a church service; 3. in monasteries where the Divine Office is chanted, the stalls accommodating the monks or nuns and separated from the sanctuary by carved low partitions; 4. one of the nine orders of angels. (Etym. Latin *chorus,* a choir; Greek *choros,* a dance, a band of dancers or singers.)

CHRISM. A consecrated mixture of olive oil and balsam. Blessed by a bishop, it is used in the public administration of baptism, confirmation, and holy orders; in the blessing of tower bells and baptismal water, and in the consecration of churches, altars, chalices, and patens. (Etym. Middle English *chrisom,* short for chrism cloth.)

CHRIST, NEW TESTAMENT NAMES AND TITLES. The following is a list of names and titles of Christ, together with their biblical citations, that appear in the New Testament:

I John 2:1	Advocate
Revelation 1:8; 22:13	Alpha and Omega
Revelation 3:14	Amen
Hebrews 3:1	Apostle and High Priest of our religion
Luke 2:12	Baby
Matthew 12:18	Beloved
John 6:33	Bread of God
John 6:35	Bread of life
John 6:50	Bread that comes down from heaven
John 3:29	Bridegroom
Mark 6:3	Carpenter
Matthew 13:55	Carpenter's son
I Peter 5:4	Chief shepherd
Matthew 2:20	Child
Luke 23:35	Chosen One
Matthew 16:20	Christ
I Timothy 1:15; Colossians 1:1	Christ Jesus
Luke 9:20	Christ of God
Luke 2:12	Christ the Lord
Romans 9:5	Christ who is above all
Hebrews 2:9	Crowned with glory and splendor
Romans 8:29	Eldest of many brothers
Revelation 1:5; 3:14	Faithful witness
Matthew 12:18	Favorite
Revelation 1:17; 2:8	First and the Last
Revelation 1:5	Firstborn from the dead
Colossians 1:15	Firstborn of all creation
Luke 2:7	Firstborn (Son)
I Corinthians 15:20	First fruits
Matthew 11:19	Friend of tax collectors and sinners

John 10:7	Gate of the sheepfold
John 10:11, 14	Good Shepherd
John 12:41	Glory
Luke 2:32	Glory of your people Israel
Hebrews 7:22	Greater Covenant
Hebrews 13:20	Great Shepherd of the sheep
Ephesians 4:16	Head
Colossians 1:18	Head of the Church (Now the Church is his body, he is its head)
I Corinthians 11:3	Head of every man
Colossians 2:10	Head of every Sovereignty and Power
Revelation 2:17	Hidden manna
Hebrews 3:1; 4:14; 7:26	High priest
Acts 2:27	Holy One
Mark 1:25	Holy One of God
Acts 4:27	Holy servant Jesus
I Timothy 1:2	Hope
John 8:58	I am
II Corinthians 4:5	Image of God
Colossians 1:15	Image of the unseen God
Matthew 1:23	Immanuel
II Corinthians 9:15	Inexpressible gift
I Peter 3:18	Innocent
Luke 2:25	Israel's comforting
Matthew 1:21	Jesus
I John 2:1	Jesus Christ who is just
Hebrews 6:20	Jesus has entered before us
John 18:5	Jesus the Nazarene
Acts 7:52	Just One
Matthew 21:5	King
John 1:50	King of Israel
Revelation 17:14; I Timothy 6:15	King of kings
Revelation 15:3	King of nations
Hebrews 7:2	King of righteousness
Matthew 2:2	King of the Jews
John 1:29, 37	Lamb of God
Revelation 5:12	Lamb that was sacrificed
I Peter 1:20	Lamb without spot or stain
I Corinthians 15:45	Last Adam

Matthew 2:6	Leader
Acts 5:31	Leader and Savior
Hebrews 2:10	Leader who would take them to their salvation
Romans 11:26	Liberator
John 14:6; Colossians 3:4	Life
John 12:35	Light
John 1:4	Light of men
John 8:12	Light of the world
Luke 2:32	Light to enlighten the pagans
Revelation 5:5	Lion of the tribe of Judah
John 6:51	Living Bread
I Peter 2:4	Living stone
Luke 1:25	Lord
John 20:28	Lord and my God
Romans 14:9	Lord both of the dead and of the living
Acts 7:59; I Corinthians 12:3	Lord Jesus (Jesus is Lord)
Acts 10:36	Lord of all men
I Corinthians 2:9	Lord of Glory
I Timothy 6:15	Lord of lords
II Thessalonians 3:16	Lord of peace
Ephesians 2:21	Main cornerstone
John 19:6	Man, The
I Timothy 2:5	Mediator
John 1:41; 4:25	Messiah
Hebrews 8:2	Minister of the sanctuary and of the True Tent of Meeting
II Peter 1:20; Revelation 2:29	Morning Star
Matthew 2:23	Nazarene
Hebrews 1:12	Never change
Revelation 22:16	Of David's line
Ephesians 4:5	One Lord
John 10:16	One shepherd
John 1:14	Only Son of the Father
I Corinthians 5:8	Passover
Hebrews 1:3	Perfect copy of his (God's) nature
I Corinthians 1:25	Power and the wisdom of God
Luke 1:69	Power for salvation
I Peter 2:6	Precious cornerstone

Hebrews 5:6	Priest for ever (You are a priest of the order of Melchizedek, and for ever)
Acts 3:15	Prince of life
Luke 1:76	Prophet of the Most High
John 20:17	Rabbuni
Hebrews 1:3	Radiant light of God's glory
I Timothy 2:6	Ransom
Romans 3:25	Reconciliation
Hebrews 7:25	Remains for ever
John 11:25	Resurrection
II Timothy 4:8	Righteous judge
Luke 1:78	Rising Sun
Revelation 22:16	Root of David
I Timothy 6:15	Ruler of all
Revelation 1:5	Ruler of the kings of the earth
II Peter 2:20; 3:18	Savior
I John 4:14; John 4:42	Savior of the world
Romans 15:8	Servant of circumcised Jews
I Peter 2:24	Shepherd and guardian of your souls
Philippians 2:7	Slave
Galatians 4:5	Son
Matthew 1:1	Son of Abraham
Matthew 1:1	Son of David
Luke 1:36	Son of God
John 1:45	Son of Joseph
John 5:27	Son of Man
Mark 6:3	Son of Mary
Mark 14:61, 62	Son of the Blessed One
II John 3	Son of the Father
Matthew 16:17	Son of the living God
Luke 1:32	Son of the Most High
Mark 5:7	Son of the Most High God
Colossians 1:14	Son that he loves
Matthew 17:5	Son, the Beloved
I Corinthians 10:4	Spiritual rock
I Peter 2:8	Stone rejected
I Peter 2:8	Stone to stumble over
Matthew 23:11	Teacher

Hebrews 9:16	Testator
I John 5:20	True God
John 1:9	True light
John 15:1	True vine
John 14:6	Truth
Revelation 3:15	Ultimate source of God's creation
John 14:6	Way
John 12:24	Wheat grain
I Corinthians 1:25	Wisdom of God
John 1:1	Word
Revelation 19:14	Word of God
John 1:14	Word was made flesh
I John 1:1	Word who is life

CHRISTIAN. A person who is baptized. A professed Christian also believes in the essentials of the Christian faith, notably in the Apostles' Creed. A Catholic Christian further accepts the teachings of the Roman Catholic Church, participates in the Eucharistic liturgy and sacraments of Catholic Christianity, and gives allegiance to the Catholic hierarchy and especially to the Bishop of Rome.

CHRISTIAN CHURCH. The community of believers in Christ. Three approaches to the meaning of the Christian Church are distinguishable in Catholic teaching. Before the Eastern Schism in 1054 the accepted definition of the Church was the whole body of the faithful united under allegiance to the pope. With the rise of Eastern Orthodoxy, which redefined the Church without obedience to the pope, Catholicism began to stress the term Roman Catholic Church in order to emphasize the need for allegiance to the Bishop of Rome.

With the rise of Protestantism in the sixteenth century, the Catholic Church sensed the need to bring out the visible nature of the Church, challenged by the Reformers. Accordingly there entered the stream of Catholic theology the definition of the Church based on the words of St. Robert Bellarmine (1542–1621). "The one and true Church," he said, "is the assembly of men, bound together by the profession of the same Christian faith, and by the communion of the same sacraments, under the rule of legitimate pastors, and in particular of the one Vicar of Christ on earth, the Roman Pontiff." In modern times, Pope Pius XII defined the Church on earth as the Mystical Body of Christ, according to the teaching of St. Paul that the faithful followers of Christ are joined together in a mysterious union, of which Christ himself is the invisible head. The Second Vatican Council added the title "People of God" to describe the Christian world. Without abandoning the earlier definitions the Council offered this one to bring out the fact that all Christians belong by special title to God, who calls them to faith in Christ, and that they form a people—i.e., a chosen community—on whom God confers his special blessings for the benefit of mankind.

CHRISTIAN DECALOGUE. The Ten Commandments as part of the Christian religion. Christ on several occasions confirmed the binding character of the Decalogue (Matthew 5:21–27; Mark 7:10, 10:19; John 7:19) and even made them more stringent. He deepened and supplemented them in the Sermon on the Mount, and summed up their obligations in the double precept of loving God and one's neighbor (Matthew 12:29–31).

From the beginning the Church considered the Ten Commandments a standard way of teaching the faithful. At the Council of Trent the theory was condemned that "the Ten Commandments do not pertain at all to Christians" (Denzinger 1569).

There are two arrangements of the Decalogue in use among Christians. The Catholic Church, along with certain Protestants (e.g., Lutherans) follow the Massoretic (traditional) text in combining the two prohibitions about false worship into one. The number ten is made up by dividing the precept against covetousness into the last two commandments. See also DECALOGUE, JEWISH DECALOGUE, TEN COMMANDMENTS.

CHRISTIAN EDUCATION. Development of the whole person, body, mind, and spiritual powers according to the norms of reason and revelation and with the help of divine grace, in order to prepare him or her for a happy and useful life in this world and for eternal beatitude in the world to come.

CHRISTIANITY. The religion of Jesus Christ. It is a composite of the faith he inspired, the teachings and moral practices he communicated, the spirituality he urged on his followers, and the consequent form of civilization that for two millennia has been called Christian. It is above all the objective principles of belief, worship, and human conduct that give substance to this civilization, which is only as Christian as these principles are known and put into practice.

CHRISTIAN MARRIAGE. The sacrament that bestows on a baptized man and woman who have made the required contract the graces that will enable them to fulfill their marital obligations.

The marital contract is an agreement that is freely made but that once made imposes a serious obligation to share the rights and duties of the married state. The agreement or consent must be internal (sincere), simultaneous with the making of the contract, externally manifested and perfectly voluntary.

Moreover, the contract must be made lawfully. Both the man and woman must be baptized, and they must be free from invalidating impediments and also from illicit impediments.

Husband and wife receive actual graces to fulfill their matrimonial obligations. These duties arise from the very nature of matrimony and cannot be altered by any subjective ideas of the contracting parties. They are the procreation of children and the fostering of mutual love between husband and wife to meet their respective material and spiritual needs.

CHRISTIAN TEMPERANCE. The supernatural virtue that moderates the desire for pleasure. It is inspired by faith and motivated by charity. Its purpose is the imitation of Christ and the pursuit of sanctity. Supernatural temperance may call for practices that are more than moderation to the natural man, such as fasting and mortification, or total abstinence and celibacy.

CHRISTMAS. Feast of the Nativity of Jesus Christ. In the early Church the feast was celebrated along with the Epiphany. But already in A.D. 200 St. Clement of Alexandria (150–215) refers to a special feast on May 20, and the Latin Church began observing it on December 25. The privilege of priests offering three Masses on Christmas Day goes back to a custom originally practiced by a pope who, about the fourth century, celebrated a midnight Mass in the Liberian Basilica (where traditionally the manger of Bethlehem is preserved); a second in the Church of St. Anastasia, whose feast falls on December 25; and a third at the Vatican Basilica. Many of the present customs in various countries are traceable to the Church's Christianizing the pagan celebrations associated with the beginning of winter and the new year. (Etym. Anglo-Saxon *Cristes Maesse,* Christ's Mass.)

CHRIST THE KING. A feast originally established by Pope Pius XI in 1925, to be celebrated with special solemnity on the last Sunday of

October. It is now observed on the last Sunday of the liturgical year; except it continues to be celebrated on the last Sunday of October in the 1962 calendar, which is used when celebrating the Extraordinary Form of the Roman Rite. Its object is to worship Christ's Lordship of the Universe, both as God and Man, and it was instituted to meet the crisis of faith in the Savior's authority, exercised by the Church, of which he is the invisible head.

CHRISTUS DOMINUS. Decree on the Pastoral Office of Bishops in the Catholic Church, of the Second Vatican Council. A unique document because of its extensive decrees. Its focus is on two things: to urge bishops to cooperate with one another and with the Bishop of Rome for the welfare of the universal Church, and to legislate in detail the ways in which bishops are to work together in the modern communication-conscious world (October 28, 1965).

CHRONICLES, BOOKS OF. See PARALIPOMENON.

CHURCH. The faithful of the whole world. This broad definition can be understood in various senses all derived from the Scriptures, notably as the community of believers, the kingdom of God, and the Mystical Body of Christ.

As the community of believers, the Church is the assembly (*ekklesia*) of all who believe in Jesus Christ; or the fellowship (*koinonia*) of all who are bound together by their common love for the Savior. As the kingdom (*basileia*), it is the fulfillment of the ancient prophecies about the reign of the Messiah. And as the Mystical Body it is the communion of all those made holy by the grace of Christ. He is their invisible head, and they are his visible members. These include the faithful on earth, those in purgatory who are not yet fully purified, and the saints in heaven.

Since the Council of Trent, the Catholic Church has been defined as a union of human beings who are united by the profession of the same Christian faith, and by participation of and in the same sacraments under the direction of their lawful pastors, especially of the one representative of Christ on earth, the Bishop of Rome. Each element in this definition is meant to exclude all others from actual and vital membership in the Catholic Church, namely apostates and heretics who do not profess the same Christian faith, non-Christians who do not receive the same sacraments, and schismatics who are not submissive to the Church's lawful pastors under the Bishop of Rome.

At the Second Vatican Council this concept of the Church was recognized as the objective reality that identifies the fullness of the Roman Catholic Church. But it was qualified subjectively so as to somehow include all who are baptized and profess their faith in Jesus Christ. They are the People of God, whom he has chosen to be his own and on whom he bestows the special graces of his Providence. (Etym. Greek *kyriakon,* church; from *kyriakos,* belonging to the Lord.)

CHURCHING. A liturgical ceremony of thanksgiving by which mothers thank God for the blessing of motherhood. More appropriately the ritual is called "the blessing of a woman after childbirth," to remove any suspicion that, in giving birth, the mother incurred a legal defilement, as in ancient Judaism. The ceremony may begin at the door of a church, although it has become customary to perform the rite near the altar. Taking hold of the priest's stole, the mother is symbolically led into the church to express her gratitude. The prayer of the priest concludes with the petition that "she and her offspring may deserve to attain to the joys of eternal blessedness." In imitation of Mary at her Purification, the mother offers some gift to the church, according to her means.

CHURCH MILITANT. The Church on earth, still struggling with sin and temptation, and therefore engaged in warfare (Latin, *militia*) with the world, the flesh, and the devil.

CHURCH SUFFERING. The Church of all the faithful departed who are saved but are still being purified in purgatorial sufferings.

CHURCH TRIUMPHANT. The Church of all those in heavenly glory who have triumphed over their evil inclinations, the seductions of the world, and the temptations of the evil spirit.

CIBORIUM. A covered container used to hold the consecrated small Hosts. It is similar to a chalice but covered and larger, used for small Communion hosts of the faithful. It is made of various precious metals, and the interior is commonly gold or gold-plated. Also synonymous with baldachino as the dome-shaped permanent canopy over a high altar, supported by columns and shaped like an inverted cup. (Etym. Latin *ciborium;* from Greek *kibōrion,* cup.)

CISTERCIANS. A strict order of monks following the Rule of St. Benedict, founded in 1098 by St. Robert of Molesme (1024–1110) at Cîteaux. Its original purpose was to establish Benedictinism on austere lines along what was considered the primitive spirit. Its most famous member, often considered its second founder, was St. Bernard of Clairvaux (1090–1153). Before the end of the twelfth century, 530 Cistercian abbeys had been established and another 150 during the next century. The Cistercian way of life was to be one of silence, in a community devoted mainly to the liturgy and prayer. Monasteries were to be in secluded places, churches were to be plain, and sacred vessels not ornate. Strict rules of diet were to be followed, as also those rules relative to manual labor made by the Cistercian pioneers in agriculture, in which they gradually trained others. Their carefully structured constitutions deeply influenced other medieval orders. A period of decline after the thirteenth century was followed by a rise of new reformed groups of Cistercians, of which the most notable was the monastery group at La Trappe founded by Armand de Rancé (1626–1700).

CIVIL LAW. Legislation promulgated by the government in a political society. In general, it is morally binding in conscience, as the Church's tradition since biblical times testifies. "For the sake of the Lord," Peter told the first-century Christians, "accept the authority of every social institution: the emperor as the supreme authority, and the governors as commissioned by him to punish criminals and praise good citizenship" (I Peter 2:13).

What is less certain is the precise nature of the moral obligation of civil laws and under what conditions they are binding in conscience. They are certainly obligatory insofar as they sanction or determine a higher law, whether natural or revealed, as when they forbid murder and stealing or specify the rights of ownership. They are certainly not obligatory when the laws are unjust, notably when they are contrary to the laws of God and of the Church, when they do not proceed from legitimate authority, when they are not directed to the common welfare, and when they violate distributive justice.

Thus a person is not permitted to obey a law that commands acts against the moral law. Yet if an unjust law does not lead one to commit illicit actions, one may in practice obey it or even be obliged to do so for reasons of general welfare beyond the immediate scope of the law. Moreover, once a law has been passed by the civil government, it should be considered just unless the contrary is clear from the nature of the law or from the declaration of ecclesiastical authority.

CLAIRVOYANCE. Seeing or knowing events occurring at a distance without the use of sensibly perceptible means of communication. As with telepathy, the available evidence indicates that this is a rare but natural phenomenon. Its exercise and evaluation should therefore be based on the same principles as other human actions.

Clairvoyance is one of the familiar physical phenomena of mysticism. But the Church's custom is to be very circumspect about admitting anything more than natural psychic powers and cautious in warning the faithful about the possibility of demonic intervention. (Etym. French *clairvoyant,* clear seeing.)

CLARITY. A quality of the glorified human body in being totally free from every deformity and filled with resplendent radiance and beauty. The prototype is the transfigured body of Christ on Mount Tabor (Matthew 17:2) and after the Resurrection (Acts 9:3). The source of the transfiguration lies in the overflowing of the beauty of the beatified soul onto the body. Each person's clarity will vary according to the degree of glory in the soul, and this in turn will depend on a person's merit before God (I Corinthians 15:41–49).

CLERGY. Those specially ordained for Divine Service as deacons, priests, or bishops. In this sense the clergy form the Church's hierarchy. Entrance into the clerical state now takes place when a man is ordained deacon. Formerly it was at the time he received first tonsure. (Etym. Latin *clericus;* from Greek *kleros,* lot, portion; the clergy whose portion is the Lord.)

CLERICAL CELIBACY. The practice of not being married, among those in major orders in the Church. Voluntary celibacy among the clergy goes back to the first century of the Christian era. In time, two different traditions arose in the Catholic Church. In the East, the tendency was toward having a married clergy, and as early as the Council of Nicaea (A.D. 325) the proposal to make celibacy obligatory on all the clergy was not accepted. The canonical position, in general, is that priests and deacons may marry before ordination but not after. Bishops, however, must be celibate. In the West, the canonical position of the Church has remained constant from as early as the Spanish Council of Elvira (A.D. 306). In 386, Pope St. Siricius ordered celibacy for "priests and Levites." The same legislation was passed by Pope St. Innocent I (r. 402–17). In spite of numerous failures in observance, and even concerted opposition in some quarters, the Catholic Church has remained constant in her teaching on clerical celibacy. Enacted into canon law in 1918, the legislation was not changed by the Second Vatican Council. In its *Decree on the Ministry and Life of Priests,* it declared, "Celibacy was at first recommended to priests. Then, in the Latin Church, it was imposed by law on all who were to be promoted to sacred orders. This legislation, to the extent to which it concerns those who are destined for the priesthood, this most holy Synod once again approves and confirms" (*Presbyterorum Ordinis,* III, 16). When a man is ready for the diaconate, he is ordained either to the transient diaconate with a view to the priesthood or to the permanent diaconate. If he is going on to the priesthood, he binds himself to celibacy for life. If he is to become a permanent deacon and is unmarried, he also binds himself to celibacy and cannot marry in the future, although he can later become a priest. If he is a married man, he may be ordained to the permanent diaconate. Then, should his wife die, he must remain unmarried and may go on for the priesthood.

CLERICAL DRESS. The normal distinctive ecclesiastical garb of Catholic priests in the Western Church is a black cassock indoors and a clerical collar and suit for outdoors. In some countries this varies somewhat, but the Church's legislation about priests wearing a garb that distinguishes them from the laity is mandatory. The Catholic Eastern clergy in Western countries follow the pattern of the place where they reside. In other places they may wear a black gown, turban, and similar characteristic dress.

CODE OF CANON LAW. The new Code, issued by Blessed Pope John Paul II in 1983, contains seven "books" of unequal length. They deal, in sequence, with General Norms, People of God, Teaching Office of the Church, Office Sanctifying in the Church, Temporal Goods of the Church, Sanctions in the Church, and Processes. The books are divided into parts, titles, chapters, articles, and finally canons, of which there are 1,752, compared with 2,414 canons in the former Code of 1918. As explained by the pope when promulgating the present Code, it shows certain elements that characterize the true and genuine image of the Church, namely, as (1) the people of God, (2) with a hierarchical authority as service, (3) to form a communion between particular churches and the universal church, and between papal primacy and episcopal collegiality, (4) whose members share in the threefold priestly, prophetic, and kingly office of Christ, (5) all of whom, especially the laity, have certain rights and duties, (6) in a Church committed to ecumenism.

Although only the Latin text is official, the new Code is available in vernacular translations approved by the Holy See.

COLISEUM. A building in Rome also known as the Flavian Amphitheater. It was begun in A.D. 72 by Vespasian (9–79) and completed in A.D. 80 by Titus (39–81). It is now in ruins. Its form is elliptical, 620 feet long, 525 feet wide, built four stories 157 feet in height. A special terrace was reserved for privileged spectators, a private gallery for the emperor, seats in tiers for ordinary citizens, and standing room for all the rest. It could seat forty-five thousand. During the Middle Ages it was used as a stronghold by the Frangipani; later it came into possession of the municipality. Much of its walls were removed for their stone until Pope Clement X declared it a shrine, sanctuary of the martyrs who gave their lives within its limits during the persecutions. It is now a place of pilgrimage for visitors to Rome. (Etym. Latin *colisseus*, huge, gigantic, colossal.)

COLLEGE, APOSTOLIC. The Apostles as a group, forming one moral hierarchical body, not a body of equals, under St. Peter as their visible head (Matthew 10, 11, 16; Luke 22). After the death of Judas, in order to remain what Christ wanted them to be, a community of immediate witnesses of the Master, they immediately (even before Pentecost) elected Matthias "to take over this ministry and apostolate" (Acts 1:25).

COLLEGE OF CARDINALS. The cardinals of the Catholic Church considered as an organized community of prelates serving the Bishop of Rome. Also the cardinals when they meet in conclave to elect a new pope.

COLLEGIALITY. The bishops of the Roman Catholic Church, united under the pope as an episcopal community. According to the Second Vatican Council, "St. Peter and the other Apostles constitute a single apostolic college. In like manner, the Roman Pontiff, Peter's successor, and the bishops, successors of the Apostles, are linked together" (Dogmatic Constitution on the Church, III, 21). This community of pope and bishops, and the bishops among themselves, was created by Christ and therefore belongs by divine right to the nature of the Church he founded.

COLOSSIANS, LETTER TO THE. Written by St. Paul while he was in prison, probably in Rome or at Ephesus. The Church at Colossae, on the Lycus, was founded not by Paul but by Epaphras, yet Paul wrote to the converts there to teach them about the primacy of Christ, head of the Church and Redeemer of mankind. Faith in Christ delivers believers from the false wisdom of the world and vain observance. This letter anticipated the centuries-old conflict that the Church would have with Gnosticism.

COMMAND. In moral theology, a rational order or directive to do something. It may be given to oneself, whenever an act of the reason prompted by the will directs a person in some human activity or in carrying out one's decisions. Or it may be an act of the reason of a lawgiver or superior requiring those under legitimate authority to take some definite action for the common good. On rare occasion, it may be an order imposed by authority on a person for his or her own private good.

COMMITMENT. Pledging oneself by vow, promise, or simple resolution to the performance of some action or allegiance to a cause or cooperation with a person or group of persons. The obligation is morally binding, depending on the gravity of the commitment and the formality under which it is made. (Etym. Latin *committere*, to join, connect, entrust: *com-*, together + *mittere*, to send.)

COMMUNAL PENANCE. Group celebration of the sacrament of penance in one of several different ways, authorized by Pope Paul VI in 1973. One form has a communal penitential service, with individual confession of sins with absolution. Another form is entirely communal, including general absolution. When general absolution is given in exceptional circumstances, the penitents are obliged to make a private confession of their grave sins, unless it is morally impossible, at least within a year.

COMMUNICABLE ATTRIBUTE. Divine perfection that can be shared by someone other than God, as life, goodness, and wisdom.

COMMUNICANT. One who receives Holy Communion. The term also applies to all faithful and active members of a church, as distinct from merely nominal Catholics. (Etym. Latin *communicare,* to participate in, have in common; to inform, make generally known.)

COMMUNICATION OF PROPERTIES. Attributing to Christ two series of predicates, one divine and one human. Since we attribute properties and activities to one person, and since Christ is one person in two natures, we may attribute either divine or human qualities and actions to the same Christ. We may correctly say that Christ is God and that he is man, that God was born of Mary and that infinite truth died on the Cross. However, only concrete names may be used in this way because abstract names "abstract" from the existence of something in a particular individual or person. It would be wrong, therefore, to say that Mary is the mother of the divinity.

COMMUNION. In Christian parlance the most sacred expression for any one of different forms of togetherness. As communion between God and the human soul in the divine indwelling; between Christ and the recipient of the Eucharist in Holy Communion; among all who belong to the Mystical Body in heaven, purgatory, and on earth in the Communion of Saints; and among those who belong to the Catholic Church as a communion of the faithful. (Etym. Latin *communio,* sharing unity, association; participation.)

COMMUNION AND LIBERATION. An ecclesial movement founded by the Servant of God, Father Luigi Giussani (d. 2005) in Milan, Italy, in 1954, whose purpose is the education to Christian maturity and collaborating in the mission of the Church. Several groups have emerged out of the Communion and Liberation experience, including the Fraternity of Communion and Liberation, the *Memores Domini,* the Priestly Fraternity of the Missionaries of St. Charles Borromeo, the Congregation of the Sisters of Charity of the Assumption, and the Fraternity of St. Joseph.

COMMUNION, FREQUENT. The daily reception of Holy Communion, as Pope St. Pius X explained the meaning of "frequent." The conditions required for daily Communion are freedom from conscious, unconfessed mortal sin, and the right intention, namely to honor God, grow in Christian charity, and overcome one's sinful tendencies. In the early Church, daily Communion was common. Later on it fell into disuse, and only in modern times is the practice being gradually restored. The Church's grounds for urging the faithful to communicate daily are based on patristic tradition. "We are bidden in the Lord's Prayer," wrote St. Pius X, "to ask for our daily bread. The holy fathers of the Church all but unanimously teach that by these words must be understood not so much the material bread to support the body as the Eucharistic Bread which should be our daily food" (*Sacra Tridentina Synodus,* December 20, 1905).

COMMUNION, SPIRITUAL. The conscious desire to receive Holy Communion, which should precede the actual reception of the sacrament. Spiritual Communion, made in acts of faith and love during the day, is highly recommended by the Church. According to the *Catechism of the Council of Trent,* the faithful who "receive the Eucharist in spirit" are "those who, inflamed with a lively faith that works in charity, partake in wish and desire of the celestial Bread offered to them, receive from it, if not the entire, at least very great benefits" (*On the Eucharist*).

COMMUNION OF CHILDREN. In ancient times in Eastern churches children received Communion immediately after baptism; in the West little children received it only when dying. The Fourth Lateran Council (in 1215) and the Council of Trent (1551) laid the precept of Easter Communion and Viaticum on children after attaining the years of discretion. After years of neglect of this legislation, St. Pius X prescribed frequent Communion also for children (1905) and restored early Communion along with the sacrament of penance on reaching the age of reason (1910).

COMMUNION OF SAINTS. The unity and cooperation of the members of the Church on earth with those in heaven and in purgatory. They are united as being one Mystical Body of Christ. The faithful on earth are in communion with one another by professing the same faith, obeying the same authority, and assisting one another with their prayers and good works. They are in communion with the saints in heaven by honoring them as glorified members of the Church, invoking their prayers and aid, and striving to imitate their virtues. They are in communion with the souls in purgatory by helping them with their prayers and good works.

COMMUNION PATEN. A saucer-shaped plate usually of precious metal similar to the Mass paten but having a projecting handle. It is held under the chin of the communicant to catch any particle of the Sacred Host that may fall. It is not blessed.

COMMUNISM. The social doctrine that affirms the community of goods and denies the right to ownership of private property. As analyzed in numerous papal documents since Pope Pius IX in 1846, Communism is based on a philosophy, a theory of history, and a definable strategy or methodology. The philosophy is dialectical materialism, which claims that matter and not spirit, and least of all the infinite Spirit who is God, is the primary reality in the universe; and that material forces in conflict (dialectic) explain all the progress in the world. The Communist theory of history claims that economics is the sole basis of human civilization, making all ethical, religious, philosophical, artistic, social, and political ideas the result of economic conditions. The strategy of Communism is a shifting expediency that defies analysis but has two constants that never really change: massive indoctrination of the people and ruthless suppression of any ideas or institutions that threaten totalitarian control by the Communist Party.

COMMUNITY. A group of persons who share the same beliefs, live together under authority, and cooperate in pursuing common interests for the benefit of others besides their own members. The degree of common belief, living, and activity determines the intensity of the community and its distinctive identity as a human society. (Etym. Latin *communitas,* community, common possession; association; congregation, parish; generality.)

COMPARATIVE RELIGION. The science that compares one religion with another in order to find their common elements and to trace their development from primitive forms to their present beliefs and practices. The Catholic Church encourages such study, provided its purpose is not to disprove the unique character of Christianity or to try to prove that the Christian religion naturally evolved from previous religious systems.

COMPLINE. The concluding hour of the Divine Office. Its origins in the West are commonly ascribed to St. Benedict (480–547). At first it was recited after the evening meal or before retiring. It now follows

Vespers. As Night Prayer it consists of a hymn, one or two Psalms, a short reading from Scripture, a versicle and response, the Nunc Dimittis of Simeon, and a concluding prayer followed by the Salve Regina. (Etym. Latin *completorium,* complement.)

CONCELEBRANT. A priest who offers Mass jointly with one or more other priests. The liturgy provides for three distinct parts in a concelebrated Mass: those to be said by the principal celebrant, those to be said by all the celebrants together (e.g., the words of consecration), and those that may be said by one or another concelebrant.

CONCEPTION. The beginning of human life. From the time that an ovum is fertilized a new life begins that is that of neither the father nor the mother. It is rather the life of a new human being with his own growth. It would never become human if it were not human already (Sacred Congregation for the Doctrine of the Faith, *Declaration on Procured Abortion,* December 5, 1974).

CONCLAVE. The enclosure of the cardinals while electing a pope. To avoid interference from the outside, Pope Gregory X, in 1274, ordered the papal election to take place in conclave. Gregory's own election was preceded by a record vacancy of two years and nine months. On occasion (e.g., Pope Leo XIII) popes have permitted the cardinals, by majority vote, to dispense with conclave in case of emergency. Pope Paul VI, in the apostolic constitution *Romano Pontifici Eligendo* (October 1, 1975), introduced numerous changes in the laws governing the election of the Roman Pontiff. Thus: 1. only persons who have been named cardinals of the Church may be electors of the pope; 2. the number of electors is now limited to 120, allowing each cardinal to bring two or three assistants to the conclave; 3. while the conclave is not strictly required for validity, it is the normal way a pope is elected, during what may be called a sacred retreat made in silence, seclusion, and prayer; 4. three forms of election are allowed—i.e., by acclamation of all the electors, by compromise in which certain electors are given authority to act in the name of all, and by voting ballot; 5. if the newly elected person is a bishop, he becomes pope at once, but if he is not yet a bishop, he is to be ordained to the episcopacy immediately; 6. if no one is elected after three days, the conclave is to spend a day in prayer while allowing the electors freedom to converse among themselves; 7. secrecy is to be strictly observed under penalty of excommunication; 8. if an ecumenical council or synod of bishops is in progress, it is automatically suspended until authorized by the newly elected pontiff to proceed.

Blessed Pope John Paul II, in the apostolic constitution *Universi Dominici Gregis* (February 22, 1996), made significant changes to the papal elections, including the change that although normally two-thirds of the votes are necessary to elect a new pope, after a long succession of ballots are taken, the cardinals could chose to change that rule so the pope could be elected by a simple majority of the electors. In addition, the new pope may no longer be elected by acclamation or by compromise where certain electors could be given authority to act in the name of all. Pope Benedict XVI issued a *motu proprio* that once again requires that two-thirds of the vote is always necessary to elect a new pope.

(Etym. Latin *con-*, with + *clavis,* key: *conclave,* a room that can be locked up.)

See also POPE, ELECTION.

CONCOMITANCE. The doctrine that explains why the whole Christ is present under each Eucharistic species. Christ is indivisible, so that his body cannot be separated from his blood, his human soul, his divine nature, and his divine personality. Consequently he is wholly present in the Eucharist. But only the substance of his body is the specific effect of the first consecration at Mass; his blood, soul, divinity, and personality become present by concomitance, i.e., by the inseparable connection that they have with his body. The Church also uses the term "substance" of Christ's body because its accidents, though imperceptible, are also present by the same concomitance, not precisely because of the words of consecration.

In the second consecration, the conversion terminates specifically in the presence of the substance of Christ's blood. But again by concomitance his body and entire self become present as well. (Etym. Latin *concomitantia,* accompaniment.)

CONCORDAT. An official agreement between the pope, in his spiritual capacity as visible head of the Catholic Church, and the temporal authority of a state. Commonly accepted as a contract between Church and State, it is a treaty governed by international laws and has been used by the Holy See since the early Middle Ages. The earliest agreement called such was the Concordat of Worms (1122), by which Pope Calixtus II and Emperor Henry V (1081–1125) put an end to the struggle over lay investiture. The best known in modern times was the Lateran Treaty of 1929. After World War II a number of concordats were abrogated by Communist regimes. (Etym. Latin *concordatus,* a thing agreed on.)

CONCUPISCENCE. Insubordination of man's desires to the dictates of reason, and the propensity of human nature to sin as a result of original sin. More commonly, it refers to the spontaneous movement of the sensitive appetites toward whatever the imagination portrays as pleasant and away from whatever it portrays as painful. However, concupiscence also includes the unruly desires of the will, such as pride, ambition, and envy. (Etym. Latin *con-,* thoroughly + *cupere,* to desire: *concupiscentia,* desire, greed, cupidity.)

CONCUPISCENCE OF THE EYES. Unwholesome curiosity and an inordinate love of this world's goods. The first consists in an unreasonable desire to see, hear, and know what is harmful to one's virtue, inconsistent with one's state of life, or detrimental to higher duties. As an inordinate love of money, it is the desire to acquire material possessions irrespective of the means employed, or merely to satisfy one's ambitions, or to nurture one's pride.

CONCUPISCENCE OF THE FLESH. The inordinate love of sensual pleasure, to which fallen man is naturally prone. It is inordinate when pleasure is sought as an end in itself and apart from its divinely intended purpose: to facilitate the practice of virtue and satisfy one's legitimate desires.

CONFESSION. The voluntary self-accusation of one's sins to a qualified priest in order to obtain absolution from him. This accusation must be an external manifestation. It must be objectively complete in that the penitent confesses every mortal sin according to number and kinds that he has committed since his last worthy reception of the sacrament of penance. In extraordinary circumstances a subjectively complete confession is sufficient, that is, when circumstances prevent a person from accusing himself of all his grave sins. He is nevertheless obliged to confess all his mortal sins in a later reception of the sacrament.

When there are no mortal sins to confess, it is sufficient to confess any previous sins from one's past life or any present venial sins of which a person has been guilty, in order to obtain absolution and the grace of the sacrament of penance. (Etym. Latin *con-*, thoroughly + *fateri*, to acknowledge: *confessio*, confession.)

CONFESSOR. A priest qualified to hear the confessions of the faithful and grant sacramental absolution. A confessor is also empowered to grant certain dispensations and absolve from censures, according to the provisions of ecclesiastical law.

CONFESSOR (LITURGICAL). A Christian in the early Church who had suffered much for the sake of Christ but did not die as a result of torture or ill treatment. Such a person "confessed" his or her faith under trial and persecution. In present-day vocabulary, all the men saints who are not martyrs are called confessors.

CONFIRMATION. The sacrament in which, through the laying on of hands, anointing with chrism, and prayer, those already baptized are strengthened by the Holy Spirit in order that they may steadfastly profess the faith and faithfully live up to their profession. Confirmation is not strictly necessary for salvation, but it is eminently important in contributing to Christian perfection and there is a grave obligation to receive it in due time. (Etym. Latin *con-*, thoroughly + *firmare*, to make firm: *confirmatio*, fortification, strengthening.)

CONFITEOR. "I confess." The act of repentance that from the earliest Christian times was part of the Church's Eucharistic liturgy. In its usual form before the Second Vatican Council the confession was made to God, the Blessed Virgin Mary, St. Michael, St. John the Baptist, Sts. Peter and Paul, and all the other saints. The present form declares: "I confess to Almighty God, and to you my brothers, that I have sinned exceedingly in thought, word, act and omission: through my fault, through my fault, through my most grievous fault. Therefore I beseech the Blessed Mary ever Virgin, all the angels and saints, and you, brethren, to pray for me to the Lord our God." (Etym. Latin *confiteor*, I confess.)

CONGREGATIONALISTS. Those Protestants who believe that each local church (congregation) is to be independent and autonomous. They profess to represent the principle of democracy in church government, a policy, they hold, claiming that Christ alone is the head of the Church he founded.

Since the members of the Church are baptized Christians, they are all priests of God. No one, therefore, may claim to have priestly powers that others do not profess, or the right to teach or rule in Christ's name, except insofar as he or she is delegated by the congregation. Where two or three are gathered together in his name, he is in their midst, and the local church comes into existence as an expression and representation of the Church Universal. Congregationalists say that this system of church structure is the most primitive in Christianity and all other forms are later human additions and changes.

Although the Congregationalist principle began with Luther (1483–1546), it was not put into consistent practice until the English Reformation. With the rise of Anglicanism various separatists broke with the parent English Church to form what eventually became the Congregational Churches of Anglo-Saxon Protestantism. In the United States, most local Protestant groups of churches follow the Congregational pattern, even when they have other denominational names.

CONGREGATION, RELIGIOUS. Institutes of Christian perfection whose members take simple vows, as distinguished from religious orders in which solemn vows are made. Congregations are a modern development in the Catholic Church, among the first being the English Ladies, approved in 1703, and the Passionists, approved in 1741. They are either diocesan or pontifical, depending on whether they are subject immediately to a local bishop or to the Holy See. Since 1908, the special approbation as a pontifical community has been given by the Vatican's Congregation for Religious.

The term "congregation" is also applied to groups of monasteries that have arisen since the Middle Ages to facilitate discipline and intercommunication. Such groups may be united under an abbot general. Examples are the Cassinese Congregation, dependent on Monte Cassino, and various national congregations.

CONJUGAL CHASTITY. The virtue of chastity to be practiced by the married. This means marital fidelity between husband and wife, which forbids adultery; mutual respect of each other's dignity, which forbids any unnatural sexual activity, or sodomy; and the practice of natural intercourse that does not interfere with the life process, which forbids contraception.

CONJUGAL LOVE. The affection of husband and wife that should be both unitive and, unless virginal, procreative. It is unitive for the married spouses and procreative from them, as potential parents of the offspring God may wish to give them. (Etym. Latin *conjugalis;* from *conjux,* husband, wife; from *conjungere,* to join, unite in marriage.)

CONJUGAL RIGHTS. Principally the mutual rights to marital intercourse between husband and wife. In the words of St. Paul, "The husband must give his wife what she has a right to expect, and so too the wife to the husband. The wife has no rights over her own body; it is the husband who has them. In the same way, the husband has no rights over his body; the wife has them. Do not refuse each other except by mutual consent, and then only for an agreed time, to leave yourselves for prayer; then come together again in case Satan should take advantage of your weakness to tempt you" (I Corinthians 7:3–5). In a broader sense, conjugal rights include all that husband and wife may justly expect of each other in terms of attention, affection, cooperation, and patient forbearance.

CONSCIENCE. The judgment of the practical intellect deciding, from general principles of faith and reason, the goodness or badness of a way of acting that a person now faces.

It is an operation of the intellect and not of the feelings or even of the will. An action is right or wrong because of objective principles to which the mind must subscribe, not because a person subjectively feels that way or because his will wants it that way.

Conscience, therefore, is a specific act of the mind applying its knowledge to a concrete moral situation. What the mind decides in a given case depends on principles already in the mind.

These principles are presupposed as known to the mind, either from the light of natural reason reflecting on the data of creation or from divine faith responding to God's supernatural revelation. Conscience does not produce these principles; it accepts them. Nor does conscience pass judgment on the truths of reason and divine faith; it uses them as the premises from which to conclude whether something should be done (or should have been done) because it is good, or should be omitted (or should have been omitted) because it is bad. Its conclusions also apply to situations in which the mind decides that something is permissible or preferable but not obligatory.

Always the role of conscience is to decide subjectively on the ethical propriety of a specific action, here and now, for this person, in these circumstances. But always, too, the decision is a mental conclusion derived from objective norms that conscience does not determine on its own, receiving it as given by the Author of nature and divine grace.

CONSECRATED LIFE. A life consecrated by profession of the evangelical counsels of chastity, poverty, and obedience. There are two basic forms of consecrated life in the Catholic Church, namely religious institutes and secular institutes.

CONSECRATION. The words of institution of the Eucharist, pronounced at Mass, by which is accomplished the very sacrifice that Christ instituted at the Last Supper. The formula of consecration is uniform for all the approved canons of the Mass and reads, in literal translation: "Take this, all of you, and eat it: this is my body which will be given up for you. . . . Take this, all of you, and drink it: this is the cup of my blood, the blood of the new and everlasting covenant. It will be shed for you and for all so that sins may be forgiven. Do this in memory of me." (Etym. Latin *consecratio;* from *consecrare,* to render sacred.)

CONSECRATION TO MARY. An act of devotion, promoted by St. Louis de Montfort (1673–1716), that consists of the entire gift of self to Jesus through Mary. It is, moreover, a habitual attitude of complete dependence on Mary in one's whole life and activity. In making the act of consecration, a person gives himself or herself to Mary and through her to Jesus as her slave. This means that a person performs good works as one who labors without wages, trustfully hoping to receive food and shelter and have other needs satisfied by the master, to whom one gives all one is and does, and on whom one depends entirely in a spirit of love. The act of consecration reads, in part:

I, [Name], faithless sinner, renew and ratify today in your hands the vows of my baptism; I renounce forever Satan, his pomps and works; and I give myself entirely to Jesus Christ, the Incarnate Wisdom, to carry my cross after Him all the days of my life, and to be more faithful to Him than I have ever been before.

In the presence of all the heavenly court I choose you this day for my mother and queen. I deliver and consecrate to you, as your slave, my body and soul, my goods, both interior and exterior, and even the value of all my good actions, past, present, and future; leaving to you the entire and full right of disposing of me, and all that belongs to me, without exception, according to your good pleasure, for the greater glory of God, in time and in eternity. Amen.

CONSECRATION TO THE SACRED HEART. Formal dedication of oneself, of one's family, community, society, or even of the whole human race to the Sacred Heart of Jesus. Consecration implies a total surrender to the Savior in gratitude for his blessings in the past and as a pledge of fidelity in the future. One of the oldest known acts of consecration and reparation to the Sacred Heart dates from the fifteenth century and was popularized by the Benedictine monks at the Abbey of St. Matthias at Trier in the German Rhineland. After St. Margaret Mary, the practice of consecration to the Heart of Jesus became widespread in the Catholic world. Personal consecration of the individual can be made often and informally, and in fact, the Morning Offering of the Apostleship of Prayer is a daily act of consecration. Family consecration has been strongly recommended by the modern popes— e.g., Pope Pius XII, who declared, "It is our heartfelt desire that the love of Jesus Christ of which His Heart is the fountain, should again take possession of private and public life. May our divine Savior reign over society and home life through His law of love. That is why we make a special appeal to Christian families to consecrate themselves to the Sacred Heart." Group consecrations go back to at least 1720, when the city of Marseilles, through its bishop and civil officials, made the dedication. Pope Leo XIII consecrated the world to the Sacred Heart in 1899 in anticipation of the Holy Year at the turn of the century. In 1925, Pope Pius XI ordered a formal *Act of Consecration of the Human Race to the Sacred Heart of Jesus,* to be publicly recited annually on the feast of Jesus Christ the King.

CONSENT. A free act in which a person agrees to do, accept, or reject something. Commonly distinguished from assent, which properly belongs in the mind. Consent of the will may be partial or total, and only when total, or complete, is a person held fully responsible for his or her actions. Thus it requires full consent for a gravely wrong action to become a mortal sin. (Etym. Latin *consentire,* to agree to.)

CONSUMMATED MARRIAGE. A marriage in which after the matrimonial contract is made husband and wife have marital intercourse. Contraceptive intercourse does not consummate Christian marriage. (Etym. Latin *consummare,* to bring into one sum, to perfect.)

CONTEMPLATION. The enjoyable admiration of perceived truth (St. Augustine). Elevation of mind resting on God (St. Bernard). Simple intuition of divine truth that produces love (St. Thomas). (Etym. Latin *contemplatio,* simple gazing of the mind at manifest truth; from *con-,* with + *templum,* open space for observation [by augurs]: *contempari,* to observe, consider.)

CONTEMPLATIVE LIFE. Human life insofar as it is occupied with God and things of the spirit. Compared with the active life, it stresses prayer and self-denial as a means of growing in the knowledge and love of God. As a form of religious life, it identifies "institutes which are entirely ordered towards contemplation, in such wise that their members give themselves over to God alone in solitude and silence, in constant prayer and willing penance" (*Perfectae Caritatis,* 7).

CONTEMPLATIVE PRAYER. In general, that form of mental prayer in which the affective sentiments of the will predominate, as distinct from discursive reflections of the mind. Or again, it is that prayer which looks at God by contemplating and adoring his attributes more than by asking him for favors or thanking him for graces received.

CONTINENCE. The virtue by which a person controls the unruly movements of sexual desire or other bodily emotions. It is connected with the virtue of temperance. It generally means the chastity to be observed by the unmarried. But it may also refer to the abstinence, in marriage, voluntarily agreed upon by both parties or forced by circumstances to abstain from marital intercourse. (Etym. Latin *continentia,* holding together, coherence; containing in itself, inclusion, restraint.)

CONTINGENT. Whatever can be or not be other than it is; that which need not exist. Thus all creatures are contingent beings, since they come into existence out of nothing, and they are changeable realities that depend totally on the sustaining power of God.

CONTINUITY. Applied to the Church's teaching, it is the uninterrupted proclamation of the mysteries of faith from apostolic times to the present. The perdurance of revealed truth, maintained by the Church's teaching authority (magisterium).

CONTRACEPTION. Deliberate interference with marital intercourse in order to prevent conception. It is the performance of the marriage act with the positive frustration of conception. Also called conjugal onanism, from the sin of Onan, referred to in the Bible (Genesis 38:8–10); Neo-Malthusianism from the name of the English sociologist Malthus (1766–1834); it is popularly termed birth control, where those concerned with high birthrates have come to equate contraception with population control.

The Catholic Church has forbidden contraception from earliest times, and the number of papal statements dealing with the subject indicates the Church's constant tradition. In modern times the most significant document was *Humanae Vitae* in 1968 by Pope Paul VI. After referring to the long history of the Church's teaching, he declared that the "direct interruption of the generative process already begun," even though done for therapeutic reasons, is to be "absolutely excluded as a licit means of regulating birth." Equally to be excluded is direct sterilization for contraceptive reasons. "Similarly excluded is every action that, either in anticipation of the conjugal act, or in its accomplishment, or in the development of its natural consequences, purposes, whether as an end or as a means, to render procreation impossible" (*Humanae Vitae*, II, 14).

Few aspects of Christian morality in modern times have given rise to more difficulties of conscience than the Catholic doctrine on contraception. This was reflected in Paul's admission, shortly after *Humanae Vitae*: "How many times we have trembled before the alternatives of an easy condescension to current opinions."

One of the results of the Church's teaching on contraception has been to emphasize her right to teach the faithful, even to binding them gravely in conscience, in matters that pertain to the natural law. Yet the basic motivation offered to married people to live up to this difficult teaching is highly supernatural, namely the prospect of loving one another in such a way that they will share the fruits of their affection with another person whom their mutual love will bring into being.

CONTRACEPTIVE STERILIZATION. Depriving the body of its generative powers in order to prevent the conception or fetal development of undesired offspring, for the satisfaction of a person's wishes and/ or the relief of an economic or social need. Its morality falls under the same category as contraception. It is forbidden by the natural law.

CONTRACT. Mutual agreement upon sufficient consideration concerning the transfer of a right. A contract is an agreement because there must be consent of at least two wills to the same object. It is mutual because the consent on one side must be given in view of the consent on the other side; it cannot be a mere coincidence that two people happen to want the same thing. The contracting parties transfer a right and so bind themselves in commutative justice, as person to person. By natural law a tangible consideration or compensation is not necessary in all contracts, because there can be gratuitous contracts such as a gift or promise. Even here, however, some intangible consideration in the form of affection or gratitude is normally expected. Finally the obligation in justice may be on both sides or only on one side, so contracts can be bilateral (as in marriage) or unilateral (as in the promise of a donation). In either case the consent must always be on both sides.

CONTRITION. The act or virtue of sorrow for one's sins. The virtue of contrition is a permanent disposition of soul. However, only an act of contrition is required for the remission of sin, whether with or without sacramental absolution.

The act of contrition is a free decision involving a detestation of and grief for sins committed and also a determination not to sin again. This detestation is an act of the will that aims at past sinful thoughts, words, deeds, or omissions. In practice it means that a sinner must retract his past sins, equivalently saying he wished he had not committed them. The grief for sins is also an act of the will directed at the state of greater or less estrangement from God that results from sinful actions. Concretely, it means the desire to regain the divine friendship, either lost or injured by sin. There must also be a determination not to sin again, which is an act of the will resolving to avoid the sins committed and take the necessary means to overcome them.

Four qualities permeate a genuine act of contrition and affect all three constituents of the act, the detestation, the grief, and the determination not to sin again. A valid contrition is internal, supernatural, universal, and sovereign.

Contrition is internal when it is sincere and proceeds from the will, when it is not the result of a mere passing mood or emotional experience. It is supernatural when inspired by actual grace and based on a motive accepted on faith. It is universal when the sorrow extends to all mortal sins, and for valid sacramental absolution there must be sorrow for whatever sins are confessed. It is finally sovereign if the sinner freely recognizes sin as the greatest of all evils and is willing to make amends accordingly. (Etym. Latin *contritio*, grinding, crushing; compunction of heart; from *conterere*, to rub together, bruise.)

CONVERSION. Any turning or changing from a state of sin to repentance, from a lax to a fervent way of life, from unbelief to faith, and from a non-Christian religion to Christianity. Since the Second Vatican Council the term is not used to describe a non-Catholic Christian becoming a Catholic. The preferred term is "entering into full communion with the Church." (Etym. Latin *conversio*, a turning, overturning, turning around; turning point; change.)

COOPERATION IN EVIL. The concurrence with another in a sinful action. This concurrence may be done in several ways: by acting with another in the same sin, as when a person joins another in perpetrating a robbery; by supplying a person what is helpful in performing a sinful action, such as providing a gun or other deadly weapon; and by commanding or suggesting that one do something sinful, by encouraging him or her or suggesting means of carrying it into effect.

CO-REDEMPTRIX. A title of the Blessed Virgin, a cooperator with Christ in the work of human redemption. It may be considered an aspect of Mary's mediation in not only consenting to become the Mother of God but in freely consenting in his labors, sufferings, and death for the salvation of the human race. As Co-Redemptrix, she is in no sense equal to Christ in his redemptive activity, since she herself required redemption and in fact was redeemed by her Son. He alone merited man's salvation. Mary effectively interceded to obtain subjective application of Christ's merits to those whom the Savior had objectively redeemed.

CORINTHIANS, LETTERS TO THE. Two letters of St. Paul written from Ephesus to his converts at Corinth. The first was occasioned by certain problems that Paul sought to resolve. He therefore spoke of the need for unity (1:10–4:21), sins against chastity (5:1–6:20), marriage and sacrifices to idols (7:1–11:1), Christian worship and the gifts (11:2–14:40), the hymn on charity (13), and the resurrection of the dead (15:1–58). In the second letter, St. Paul confronts his enemies at Corinth. He defends his apostolate, recounts the achievements God worked through him in spite of his own weakness and incompetence, asks funds for the Christians in Jerusalem, and once again defends his call as an Apostle and the extraordinary gifts the Lord conferred on him. It is very probable that St. Paul wrote four letters to the Corinthians, of which only two are extant.

CORPORAL. A square white linen cloth on which the Host and Chalice are placed during Mass. When not in use it may be kept in a burse. It is also used under the monstrance at Benediction or under the Blessed Sacrament at any time. (Etym. Latin *corporalis,* bodily; from *corpus,* body.)

CORPORAL WORKS OF MERCY. The seven practices of charity, based on Christ's prediction of the Last Judgment (Matthew 5:3–10) that will determine each person's final destiny. They are 1. to feed the hungry; 2. to give drink to the thirsty; 3. to clothe the naked; 4. to shelter the homeless; 5. to visit the sick; 6. to visit those in prison; and 7. to bury the dead.

CORPUS CHRISTI. The Feast of the Blessed Sacrament, established in 1246 by Bishop Robert de Thorote of Liège, at the suggestion of St. Juliana of Mont Cornillon (1192–1258). Its observance was extended to the Universal Church by Pope Urban IV in 1264. The office for the day was composed by St. Thomas Aquinas, and the customary procession was approved by Popes Martin V and Eugene IV. Now celebrated as the solemnity of the Body and Blood of Christ on the first Thursday (or Sunday) after the feast of the Holy Trinity.

CORRECT CONSCIENCE. The judgment of the mind when it concludes correctly from true principles that some act is lawful or sinful. Also called true conscience.

COSMIC CHRIST. The Second Person of the Trinity, made man, seen as the origin or beginning and end or purpose of creation. This concept of a "world-Christ," that some have mistakenly understood in a pantheistic sense, is a favored theme of St. Paul. He describes Christ as "the image of the unseen God and the first-born of all creation, for in Him were created all things in heaven and on earth: everything visible and everything invisible, Thrones, Dominations, Sovereignties, Powers—all things were created through Him and for Him" (Colossians 1:12–14). The "Cosmic Christ" is sometimes distinguished from the "Redemptive Christ" and understood in the sense that God would have become man even though man had not sinned, out of sheer love of man and for the perfection of the universe.

The term was used by Pierre Teilhard de Chardin (1881–1955), according to whom the whole universe, with Christ as Ruler, is the true fullness of Christianity. As a result, all things are already permeated with a special presence of God, and correspondingly the whole world shares in the fruits of salvation. (Etym. Greek *kosmos,* order; the world, universe.)

COUNTER-REFORMATION. A period of Catholic revival from 1522 to about 1648, better known as the Catholic Reform. It was an effort to stem the tide of Protestantism by genuine reform within the Catholic Church. There were political movements pressured by civil rulers, and ecclesiastical movements carried out by churchmen in an attempt to restore genuine Catholic life by establishing new religious orders, such as the Society of Jesus, and restoring old orders to their original observances, such as the Carmelites under St. Teresa of Avila (1515–82). The main factors responsible for the Counter-Reformation, however, were the papacy and the Council of Trent (1545–63). Among church leaders, St. Charles Borromeo (1538–84), Archbishop of Milan, enforced the reforms decreed by the council, and St. Francis de Sales of Geneva (1567–1622) spent his best energies in restoring genuine Catholic doctrine and piety. Among civil rulers sponsoring the needed reform were Philip II of Spain (1527–98) and Mary Tudor (1516–58), his wife, in England. Unfortunately this aspect of the Reformation led to embitterment between England and Scotland, England and Spain, Poland and Sweden, and to almost two centuries of religious wars. As a result of the Counter-Reformation, the Catholic Church became stronger in her institutional structure, more dedicated to the work of evangelization, and more influential in world affairs.

COVENANT, BIBLICAL. In the Old Testament an agreement between God and Israel in which God promised protection to the Chosen People in return for exclusive loyalty. "If you obey my voice and hold fast to my covenant, you of all the nations will be my very own" (Exodus 19:5). Moses presented YHWH's offer to his people, who promptly "answered as one, 'All that YHWH has said we will do.'" The compact was sealed (Exodus 19:8). Many years later Jeremiah prophesied that a new covenant would be offered. "Deep within them," YHWH promised, "I will plant my law, writing it on their hearts" (Jeremiah 31:31–34). Ezekiel foresaw that God would "make a covenant of peace with them, an eternal covenant" (Ezekiel 37:26). Its universal character was foreshadowed by Isaiah, to whom it was revealed by YHWH "so that my salvation may reach to the ends of the earth" (Isaiah 49:6). In the New Testament, when Paul was explaining to the Corinthians the institution of the Eucharist at the Last Supper, he repeated Christ's words: "This cup is the new covenant in my blood. Whenever you drink it, do this as a memorial of me" (I Corinthians 11:25). This master idea of the New Testament is reinforced in the Letter to the Hebrews: "It follows that it is a greater covenant for which Jesus has become our guarantee" (Hebrews 7:22). Christ himself is the new covenant between God and his people. (Etym. Latin *convenire*, to agree, to come together.)

COVETOUSNESS. A strong desire for possessions, especially material possessions. It implies that the desire is inordinate, with allusion to the prohibition in the Ten Commandments not to covet what belongs to someone else. Often synonymous with avarice, although referring more to the wrongfulness of the desire for possession and less (as in avarice) to its eagerness or intensity.

CREATION. The production of material and spiritual things in their whole substance, done by God and of nothing. God creates out of nothing both because he starts with no pre-existing matter and because he parts with nothing of his own being in the act of creation. Thus creation in the proper sense (first creation) is to be distinguished from the so-called second creation described in Genesis, by which is understood the shaping of formless matter and giving it life and activity.

CREDIBILITY. The reasonable grounds for believing something to be true. Credibility is generally applied to the evidence from experience, history, and reason for the truthfulness of Christian revelation, either in general or of a particular mystery like Christ's divinity or his Resurrection. There are three logical stages for establishing the credibility of a mystery of faith: 1. the existence of God is proved by reason; 2. God's worthiness of being believed, if he makes a revelation, is likewise seen from reason, since a perfect God is all-knowing and trustworthy; 3. the fact that he actually made a revelation is then proved from the miracles he performs to confirm the testimony of those who claim to speak in his name. (Etym. Latin *credibilis,* from *credere,* to believe, entrust.)

CREDO. I believe. A creed or code of beliefs; also applied to any one article of faith. (Etym. Latin *credo,* I believe.)

CREMATION. The act of destroying the human body by fire after death. Christians followed the Jews in disposing of corpses by burial rather than by cremation, thinking of the latter as an unnatural and violent destruction of the human body, the repository of the Holy Spirit during life on earth. Since no principle of faith would be jeopardized by cremation, it has always been allowed with permission when public health required it. The Catholic Church has always opposed it, though, when it meant a defiance of belief in the resurrection of the body, and for centuries excommunicated those who ordered cremation for themselves or for others. At present, to meet changing world conditions, the Church is more lenient in her views on this method of disposal of the dead, while still preferring burial. (Etym. Latin *cremare,* to burn.)

CRITICISM, BIBLICAL. The scientific study and analysis of the human elements that have entered into the composition and preservation of the Scriptures. This study has been encouraged and fostered by the Church. The two outstanding papal documents urging Catholic scholars to engage in a scientific study of the Bible were Pope Leo XIII's *Providentissimus Deus* (1893) and Pope Pius XII's *Divino Afflante Spiritu* (1943). In all biblical criticism the Catholic Church insists on her scholars' recognizing that the Bible is the inspired word of God and consequently may not be treated as merely a human piece of writing. Moreover, the Church considers herself the divinely authorized custodian and interpreter of Sacred Scripture. Catholic scholars must therefore recognize that the Church's magisterium has the final word on the conclusions reached by biblical criticism. (Etym. Greek *kritikos,* able to discern or judge.)

CROSS. Primarily the instrument of suffering on which Christ died and redeemed the world. It also stands for whatever pain or endurance that a Christian undergoes, and voluntarily accepts, in order to be joined with Christ and cooperate in the salvation of souls. The Cross is, therefore, a revealed mystery, taught by Christ when he said,

"If anyone wants to be a follower of mine, let him renounce himself and take up his cross and follow me" (Matthew 16:24). The mystery of the Cross is one of the principal themes of St. Paul's writings (Romans 5:8; I Corinthians 1:17; Galatians 4:16; and Philippians 2:6–11).

CRUCIFIX. A cross bearing the image of Christ. It must be placed on or over an altar where Mass is offered. Due reverence is always given to it. It is sometimes carried as a procession cross leading a line of clergy. Depicting the dead or suffering Christ, the crucifix did not come into general use until after the Reformation. The earlier ones represented Our Lord as the High Priest crowned, robed, and alive. Some men and women religious wear the crucifix as part of their habit. A crucifix is attached to the rosary beads, and many liturgical blessings are to be given with it. A blessed crucifix is a sacramental and is commonly displayed in Catholic hospitals, homes, and institutions. (Etym. Latin *crucifixus,* the crucified.)

CRUCIFIXION. Execution of a criminal by nailing or binding to a cross. Originally used in the East, it was adopted by the Romans and was commonly inflicted on any condemned person who could not prove Roman citizenship. Normally preceded by scourging, it was later (from A.D. 69) imposed on certain lower-class citizens. Emperor Constantine abolished this method of capital punishment.

The crucifixion of Christ between two thieves is recorded by all four evangelists. According to tradition, the Cross of Christ was a *crux immissa,* with the upright extending above the transom. Also, most probably, Christ was fixed to the Cross with four nails and covered with a loincloth, as prescribed by the Talmud.

CULT. A definite form of worship or of religious observance, sometimes rendered "cultus," especially when referring to the worship of the saints. Also a particular religious group centered around some unusual belief, generally transient in duration and featuring some exotic or imported ritual and other practices. (Etym. Latin *cultus,* care, adoration; from *colere,* to cultivate.)

CURIA, ROMAN. The whole ensemble of administrative and judicial offices through which the pope directs the operations of the Catholic Church. Since the Second Vatican Council the Roman Curia has been extensively changed, with the merger of certain offices, the suppression of others, and the creation of entirely new ones. More than once in postconciliar statements the pope has defended the Curia against critics who would distinguish between the papacy and the curial officials. Pope John XXIII spoke of the Curia as his right hand, through which the Vicar of Christ mainly exercises his primacy over the universal Church.

CURSILLO MOVEMENT. A method of Christian renewal originated by a group of laymen, assisted by Bishop Hervas y Benet, on the island of Mallorca, Spain, on January 7, 1949. *Cursillo* literally means a "little course," and the program itself comes in three stages of three days each: preparation (Pre-Cursillo), the course proper (Cursillo), and the follow-up (Post-Cursillo). Its objective is to change the world by changing one's mind according to the mind of Christ, and then reshaping one's life accordingly. The Cursillo proper is an intensive weekend built around some fifteen talks, of which ten are given by laymen, and living together as a close Christian community. Those who participate are called Cursillistas, who meet regularly after the initial program in what is called the Ultreya, in small groups to pray, share their experiences, and plan apostolic action. An essential part of the Cursillo, as conceived by Bishop Hervas, is the Spiritual Exercises of St. Ignatius, to give doctrinal foundation and spiritual structure to the movement.

CZĘSTOCHOWA. Shrine of the Black Madonna, also called Our Lady of Jasna Gora, chief Marian sanctuary of Poland. There is a legend that the picture of Our Lady and her Son at the shrine was painted by St. Luke on a tabletop made by Jesus himself when he was an apprentice carpenter to St. Joseph. Hidden during the early persecutions, it was brought by St. Helena (255–330) to Constantinople. In the troubled eighth century it was stealthily taken from that city to a forest in eastern Poland. From there it was removed to Częstochowa. In 1430 a great Gothic cathedral was built around the precious relic, but in the war with the Hussites they stole the picture. When their horses refused to move their cargo beyond the village boundaries, they threw the picture by the roadside, where it lay broken. All attempts to repair the damage have failed. In the next three hundred years the Polish people believed that their welfare was identified with this miraculous picture. When the Turks were at the gates of Vienna, Sobieski (1624–96), the Polish king, dedicated his crusade to Mary, and the West was saved. Under Adolf Hitler (1889–1945) the people came secretly on their pilgrimages to Częstochowa, and in 1945, at the end of World War II, they came 500,000 strong to thank Mary for their liberation. In 1947 over 1,500,000 came there to beg Mary to save them from Communism. Blessed Pope John Paul II during his pontificate made five historic visits to the shrine, in 1979, 1983, 1987, 1991, and 1997.

D

DAMNATION. The conscious eternal loss of the vision of God. The state of being damned by reason of one's own deliberate estrangement from God. This is the lot of the demons and of those who die in mortal sin. It is damnation because it is the result of a just sentence pronounced by God on those who are guilty. It is eternal because it is irrevocable, being pronounced to be unending in its consequences (Matthew 25). The condemned are no longer in a state of probation, and no longer able to expiate or repent (Luke 16). (Etym. Latin *damnatio,* condemnation; from *damnum,* damage, loss, fine.)

DANCING, LITURGICAL. Moving rhythmically to music as part of a religious ceremony. Certain forms of dancing have at various times been introduced into Catholic worship, but the Church has set down two conditions. First, to the extent to which the body is a reflection of the soul, dancing has to express sentiments of faith and adoration in order to become a prayer. And second, dancing must be under the discipline of competent Church authority. "Concretely, there are cultures in which this is possible in so far as dancing is still reflective of religious values and becomes a clear manifestation of them. Such is the case among the Ethiopians. In their cultures, even today, there is the religious ritualized dance, clearly distinct from the martial dance and from the amorous dance." The same is found among Christians in the Syriac and Byzantine traditions. "However, the same criterion and judgment cannot be applied in the Western culture. Here dancing is tied in with love, with diversion, with profaneness, with unbridling of the senses; such dancing, in general, is not pure. For that reason it cannot be introduced into liturgical celebrations of any kind whatever."

What about dancing outside the liturgy? This is permissible, but only under certain conditions. Thus "if the proposal for a religious dance in the West is to be acceptable, care must be taken that this occurs *outside of the liturgy,* in assembly areas that are not strictly liturgical. Moreover, priests must always be excluded from the dance" (Sacred Congregation for the Sacraments and Divine Worship, *Notitiae,* 1975, 11, pp. 202–5).

DANIEL, BOOK OF. A prophetic book of the Old Testament, in fourteen chapters, among which three languages are represented. The preliminary section (1, 2, and 4) is in Hebrew and describes Daniel's capture and education. The first part of his prophecies (2, 5, and 7), in Aramaic, refers to world power in relation to God's people, notably the dream of the great statue and the vision of the four beasts. The second part of Daniel's prophecies (7 to 12), in Hebrew, describes the fortunes of the Jews with respect to world power. The book concludes with the so-called deuterocanonical parts (12 to 14) that are missing in the Jewish Bible but endorsed by the Septuagint Greek translation. In this section are found the narrative of the chaste Susanna, the idol Bel, the dragon destroyed by Daniel, and a second peril in the lions' den. In telling the future the prophet is very precise. Christ quotes from Daniel, foretelling the fall of Jerusalem and the last day (Matthew 24:15–25). The Church has embodied all fourteen chapters of the book in her biblical canon.

DARK NIGHT OF THE SOUL. General term in mystical theology to identify every form of purification through which God leads persons whom he is calling to a high degree of sanctity. It is called "night" to distinguish a person's normal spiritual condition of seeing, although dimly, by the light of faith; whereas in mystical purification a person is deprived of much of this light. There is a "groping in the night." It is called a "dark" night to emphasize the intensity of withdrawal of God's illuminating grace. The purpose of such purification is to cleanse the soul of every vestige of self-love and unite a person more and more closely with God. As the intellect is thus mortified, the will becomes more firmly attracted to God and more securely attached to his divine will. This purification, however, is only a means to an end, namely, 1. to give greater glory to God, who is thereby loved for himself and not for the benefits he confers; 2. to lead the one thus purified to infused contemplation and even ecstatic union with God; 3. to enable the mystic to be used more effectively by God for the spiritual welfare of others, since the more holy a person is the more meritorious are that person's prayers and sacrifices for the human race.

DAVID. Hebrew king who ruled 1000–961 B.C. A shepherd boy, he was the son of Jesse, a Bethlehemite (Ruth 4:22). He was introduced to the court of King Saul because of his skill as a harpist. Then he achieved unexpected fame in his duel with Goliath, when he killed the gigantic soldier with a slingshot (I Samuel 17). His feats as a warrior continued to win him such admiration that Saul felt overshadowed and tried to kill David (I Samuel 18:6–11). The latter had to flee and become a roving outlaw with a band of soldiers he organized (I Samuel 19). After Saul and his sons died (I Samuel 31:6), David became king of both Judah and Israel for a period of forty years (II Samuel 5:4–5). Perhaps his most historic achievement was the capture of Jerusalem from the Philistines and its establishment as the religious capital of all Israel. The most shameful episode in David's life was his conspiracy to kill Uriah the Hittite in order to marry his widow, Bathsheba. Nathan, the prophet, delivered YHWH's stern rebuke to David for this crime. As a punishment, Bathsheba's child died within a week of its birth. A later son of David and Bathsheba, however, was accepted by YHWH and lived to become King Solomon (II Samuel 11, 12). David's life was a mixture of good and evil, but the judgment of history has been that, on balance, he was a great king, loyal to YHWH, a great military figure, and a resourceful administrator (I Kings 2:12).

DAYS OF ABSTINENCE. The days prescribed for the universal Church on which the faithful are forbidden to take flesh meat or anything made from meat. All Fridays of the year, except holy days of obligation, are days of abstinence; but since 1966 there is an option to substitute another form of penance. Abstinence must be observed on Ash Wednesday and Good Friday, and all the Fridays in Lent. Abstinence becomes binding at the age of fourteen, and it is loosed after the age of fifty-nine.

DEACON. A man specially ordained to the service of the Church's ministry. In the ordination of deacons the "matter" is the imposition of a bishop's hands on individual candidates, which is done before the consecratory prayer; the "form" consists of the words of the consecratory prayer, of which the following pertain to the essence of the order and therefore are required for the validity of the act: "Lord, we pray, send forth upon them the Holy Spirit so that by the grace of your seven gifts they may be strengthened by Him to carry out faithfully the work of the ministry." The role of deacons is to assist priests in preaching, the conferral of baptism, performance of marriage, the administration of parishes, and similar duties. (Etym. Latin *diaconus;* from Greek *diakonos,* a servant, a deacon.)

DEADLY SINS. Another name for the seven capital sins. They may be called deadly because there are tendencies to those basic sins that, if deliberately and fully consented to, deprive a person of the supernatural life of God in the soul. See also CAPITAL SINS.

DEAD SEA SCROLLS. A collection of manuscripts and numerous fragments excavated in 1947 at the site of the ancient Qumran community, located close to the Dead Sea in Palestine. The principal texts include a set of rules for a monastic community, namely, *The Manual of Discipline, A Zadokite Document* (discovered earlier in Cairo), and a *Formulary of Blessings;* two collections of hymns; several commentaries on the books of Micah, Nahum, and Habakkuk; a long oration of Moses; an epic on *The War of the Sons of Light and the Sons of Darkness;* and a manual for the future congregation of Israel, the so-called Messianic Banquet. Conservative scholarship holds that the scrolls were composed at various dates between 170 B.C. and A.D. 68. There is in the Dead Sea Scrolls no trace of any of the principal doctrines of Christianity: the Incarnation or the universality of the Messianic Kingdom. But there are many affinities that have shed much light on the meaning of the Christian faith, notably in revealing the existence of an ascetical community, similar to the Essenes, in first-century Palestine.

DEATH. The cessation of the bodily functions of a human being through the departure of the soul. It is part of revelation that, in the present order of Divine Providence, death is a punishment for sin. According to the teaching of the Church, death is a consequence of Adam's sin, as declared by St. Paul: "Sin entered the world through one man, and through sin death" (Romans 5:12). In the case of those justified by grace, death loses its penal character and becomes a mere consequence of sin. All human beings, therefore, are subject to death, although in the case of Christ and his Mother, because of their freedom from sin, death was neither a punishment for sin nor a consequence of sin. Yet, as they were truly human, death was natural for them.

Death is also the end of human probation or testing of one's loyalty to God. It ends all possibility of merit or demerit.

Properly speaking, only the body dies when separated from its principle of life, which is the soul. However, the Bible speaks of a second death (Revelation 20:6), referring to the souls in hell, who are separated from their principle of supernatural life, which is God.

DECADE. The popular name given to each of the five divisions into which each chaplet of the Rosary is subdivided. It is called a decade because each contains ten Hail Marys, together with an Our Father and, normally, a Glory Be to the Father. Since each decade is a unit by itself, having its own mystery to commemorate, it may be said individually, even when the whole chaplet is not recited. In order to gain the Rosary indulgence, however, all five decades must be recited in sequence.

DECALOGUE. The Ten Commandments, given to Moses by God at Mount Sinai (Exodus 20). They were inscribed on two tablets of stone (Deuteronomy 4:13). In the New Testament Jesus accepted them as the basis of his teaching and promised to carry them to completion. "Not one dot, not one little stroke, shall disappear from the Law until its purpose is achieved" (Matthew 5:18). (Etym. Greek *deka,* ten + *logos,* a speech, saying: *dekalogos,* the Ten Commandments.)

See also CHRISTIAN DECALOGUE, JEWISH DECALOGUE, TEN COMMANDMENTS.

DECENCY. The social aspect of the virtue of modesty. It implies due concern for what society in general or people in particular consider proper in the external practice of chastity. As the morality of a culture falls below the objective norms of Christian chastity, the standards of decency tend to be formed by the prevalent customs of the people. (Etym. Latin *decere,* to be fitting.)

DECLARATION OF NULLITY. The Church's official declaration that an apparently valid marriage is actually null and void because of an invalidating impediment (such as a previous marriage), lack of due consent (absence of adequate knowledge or freedom), or a defect of required form (prescribed conditions for the actual celebration of marriage).

See also ANNULMENT.

DECREE, ECCLESIASTICAL. Generally legislative enactments of the pope, a council of the Church, or a congregation of the Holy See. Papal decrees are found in constitutions, apostolic letters, apostolic epistles, and *motu proprios.* Judicial decrees are all the rulings of an ecclesiastical court not included in incidental and final decisions. Nonjudicial decrees range from the regulations made in an episcopal visitation to such formal acts as removing or transferring a pastor. Roman congregations also issue decrees, but their decisions also take other forms.

DEFAMATION. Unjust injury of a person's good name. It consists in telling facts that harm another's reputation. In defamation, there is at least an implicit intention to harm the reputation of another, who is absent and therefore not a witness to being defamed.

Defamation may be committed in two ways: by spreading injurious facts that are true but not publicly known or by saying things that are false.

Since defamation violates commutative justice, it involves the duty of making reparation for the foreseen injury inflicted. Hence the defamer must try not only to repair the harm done to another's good name but also to make up any foreseen temporal injury that resulted from the defamation, such as the loss of employment or of customers.

A number of reasons would release a person from the obligation of repairing the damage done to someone's good name; for example, the injury no longer exists, or reparation is physically or morally impossible to make, or the one defamed has excused the defamer, or reparation would cause the defamer a far greater injury than the one inflicted, or if there is good likelihood that a calumnious defamation was not believed by those to whom it was said.

DEFENSOR VINCULI. Latin term for "Defender of the Bond." He is the member of an ecclesiastical matrimonial court whose duty is to uphold the validity of a disputed marriage until sufficient evidence is given to prove its nullity. If he is not satisfied with the court's ruling, he must appeal to a higher tribunal.

DE FIDE. A term meaning "of faith," used to identify those doctrines of the Church that are infallibly true. Their infallible certitude derives ultimately from divine revelation, but proximately from the fact that they have either been solemnly defined by the Church's magisterium or have been taught by her ordinary universal teaching authority as binding on the consciences of all the faithful.

DEFILEMENT. The condition of uncleanness. In biblical and ecclesiastical usage it means to render unclean by contact with unclean things, by eating forbidden foods, by polluting sexually through adultery. Its most important meaning is to be stained with sin.

DEISM. The theory that accepts the existence of God on purely rational grounds but denies (with Blount and Tindal) or doubts (with Hume) or rejects as incredible (with Voltaire and Rousseau) Christianity as a supernatural religion. Accordingly revelation, miracles, grace, and mysteries are excluded from acceptance by what is called "the rational man." Yet deism differs from rationalism in stressing its acceptance of a personal God and adherence to what is called natural religion, but with no recognition of a supernatural order. (Etym. Latin *Deus,* God.)

DEI VERBUM. Dogmatic Constitution on Divine Revelation of the Second Vatican Council. Its five sections treat divine revelation itself; the transmission of divine revelation through the faith of believers and the custody of the Church; Sacred Scripture as God's inspired word to be interpreted under the Church's guidance; the Old Testament as fulfilled in and also shedding light on the New Testament as the completion of God's self-disclosure; and the importance of Sacred Scripture in the life of the Church. Treated at length is the development of doctrine, which means the Church's ever deeper and clearer understanding of what God has once and for all revealed to the human race (November 18, 1965).

DELUGE. The biblical account of God's punishment of humankind by incessant rain that finally destroyed all except those persons who were with Noah in the ark (Genesis 6–9). The Deluge need not, however, have physically covered the whole earth. (Etym. Latin *diluvium,* flood, a washing away.)

DEMOCRACY. As defined in Catholic social philosophy, that form of civil government which is not only for the people and of the people but also by the people. Every political society, by the natural law, should be for the people, since its purpose is the common good. It should also be of the people, since it arises from their consent and with their authorization. But it need not be, unless the citizens so desire, also by the people. In a democracy, the governing heads are elected with equal right by all the people, and there exists the widest individual liberty consistent with the common good. Democracy is either limited or unlimited, depending on whether all the citizens or only a part of them have equal right to public offices. Democracy may also be direct or indirect. In a direct democracy the people as a whole possess full power and exercise directly all governing functions, which is possible only in a small social community. Indirect democracy, or representative government, is that in which the people are governed through the legitimate representatives whom they elected. (Etym. Greek *dēmos,* people + *kratia,* to rule: *dēmokratia,* popular government, rule by the people.)

DEMON. Originally a spirit between the gods and men. In the New Testament a demon is the same as an evil spirit, which may be translated as "devil." It consequently means a malevolent, invisible being, which the pre-Christian word "demon" did not imply. (Etym. Latin *daemon*, evil spirit; Greek *daimōn*, a god, genius, spirit.)

DEMYTHOLOGY. The theory that claims that the whole language and spirit of the New Testament are mythical in character. The evangelists assume that miracles occur and that the world is affected by supernatural powers. In order to discover the real facts of Christ's life and teaching, therefore, it is necessary to strip the New Testament, especially the Gospels, of this layer of mythology. (Etym. Latin *de*, reverse of + Greek *mythologein*, to relate legends, myths.)

DENIAL OF FAITH. Any word, sign, or action by which a person who is a professed Catholic denies what the Church teaches must be believed by her faithful. The denial is direct when what is said or done by its nature contains a rejection of the true faith. It is indirect when the rejection is implied under the circumstances. Every deliberate denial of one's faith is a grave sin.

DE PROFUNDIS. Psalm 129 (130), "Out of the depths," which is one of the fifteen Gradual Psalms and one of the seven Penitential Psalms. It is part of the Divine Office, generally recited or sung at Vespers, and always in the Office of the Dead. In the revised *Handbook of Indulgences* there is a partial indulgence granted for every recitation of *De Profundis*. Its theme is a plea for divine mercy and the expression of confident trust in God. In some countries this Psalm is recited to the ringing of the bell at about 9 P.M., and in Ireland it was regularly said at Mass after the Last Gospel for the victims of former religious persecutions.

DESACRALIZATION. The conscious removal or reduction of sacred symbols from religious life and worship. In Christianity it is a practical consequence of the demythology of the Bible and tradition. As the faith of a people is less concerned with revealed mysteries pertaining to God, their religious ceremonial becomes desacralized.

DESCENT INTO HELL. The coming of Christ before his Resurrection to deliver the souls of the just detained in the limbo of the Fathers. The purpose of this coming of Christ's soul was to deliver all the saved who had died before then by applying the fruits of the Redemption. They were immediately given the beatific vision. The doctrine is taught in all the early creeds and was defined by the Fourth Lateran Council (Denzinger 429).

DESECRATION. The profanation of a sacred person, place, or thing. Churches are desecrated by notorious crimes committed within them, such as willful murder or use of the sacred edifice for godless and sordid purposes. A desecrated church must first be reconciled before Divine Services can be held there. (Etym. Latin *dis,* the opposite of + *sacrare,* to declare or set apart as sacred.)

DESPAIR. The sin by which a person gives up all hope of salvation or of the means necessary to reach heaven. It is therefore not mere anxiety about the future or fear that one may be lost. It is rather a deliberate yielding to the idea that human nature cannot cooperate with God's grace, or that the despairing person is too wicked to be saved, or that God has cast one away. It is a grave crime against God's goodness. Experience also shows that a tendency to despair can seriously injure one's physical and mental health, and ironically can lead to all kinds of sinful indulgence. (Etym. Latin *de,* the opposite of + *sperare,* to hope: *desperatio,* hopelessness, despair.)

DETERMINANTS OF MORALITY. The factors in human conduct that determine whether it is good or bad. There are three such determinants of morality, namely the object, the end, and the circumstances.

By *object* is meant *what* the free will chooses to do—in thought, word, or deed—or chooses not to do. By *end* is meant the purpose for which the act is willed, which may be the act itself (as one of loving God) or some other purpose for which a person acts (as reading to learn). In either case, the end is the motive or the reason *why* an action is performed. By *circumstances* are meant all the elements that surround a human action and affect its morality without belonging to its essence. A convenient listing of these circumstances is to ask: *who? where? how? how much? by what means? how often?*

Some circumstances so affect the morality of an action as to change its species, as stealing a consecrated object becomes sacrilege and lying under oath is perjury. Other circumstances change the degree of goodness or badness of an act. In bad acts they are called aggravating circumstances, as the amount of money a person steals.

To be morally good, a human act must agree with the norm of

morality on all three counts: in its nature, its motive, and its circumstances. Departure from any of these makes the action morally wrong.

DETRACTION. Revealing something about another that is true but harmful to that person's reputation. It is forbidden to reveal another person's secret faults or defects, unless there is proportionate good involved. The fact that something is true does not, of itself, justify its disclosure. Detraction is a sin against justice. It robs one of what most people consider more important than riches, since a person has a strict right to his or her reputation whether it is deserved or not. (Etym. Latin *detractio,* a withdrawal.)

DEUS CARITAS EST. First encyclical of Pope Benedict XVI on the love of God (December 25, 2005). The encyclical is divided into two parts. The first part is entitled "The Unity of Love in Creation and Salvation History." In this part, Pope Benedict XVI discusses the nature of love and speaks about the love that God offers to man and, because God has first loved us, our ability to respond by loving God and neighbor. In the second part, entitled "The Practice of Love by the Church," Pope Benedict XVI teaches that the Church must practice corporate works of charity to be true to her mission. He further reflects on the relationship between justice and charity, proclaiming that justice does not eliminate the need for charity.

DEUTEROCANONICAL. Referring to those books and passages of the Old and New Testaments about which there was controversy at one time in early Christian history. In the Old Testament they are Tobit, Judith, Wisdom, Ecclesiasticus, Baruch, I and II Maccabees, parts of Esther (10:4–16) and Daniel (3:24–90, 13, 14). In the New Testament are Hebrews, James, II Peter, II and III John, Revelation, and Mark 16:9–20. All of these are recognized by the Catholic Church as part of the biblical canon. Among Protestants the deuterocanonical books of the Old Testament are rejected as apocryphal, along with the last twelve verses of Mark's Gospel.

DEUTERONOMY. The fifth book of the Bible. Its name (Greek *deuteros,* second; *nomos,* law) is a misnomer, since it contains no new legislation but is rather a partial repetition of previous laws with an urgent exhortation to keep them. The first discourse reviews the events that followed the promulgation of the Law (1–4). The second discourse is the longest (5–26) and recalls the covenant, covering the duties of the Jews toward God (5–11), the Lord's representatives, and their neighbors. The third discourse is a plea to observe the Law, a renewal of the alliance with YHWH, and Moses's prophetic canticle, while designating Joshua as his successor.

DEVELOPMENT OF DOCTRINE. Growth in the Church's understanding of the truths of divine revelation. Also called dogmatic progress or dogmatic development, it is the gradual unfolding of the meaning of what God has revealed. Always presumed is that the substantial truth of a revealed mystery remains unchanged. What changes is the subjective grasp of the revealed truth.

The source of this progressive understanding is the prayerful reflection of the faithful, notably of the Church's saints and mystics; the study and research by scholars and theologians; the practical experience of living the faith among the faithful; and the collective wisdom and teaching of the Church's hierarchy under the Bishop of Rome.

Implicit in the development of doctrine is the will of God that the faithful not only assent to what he revealed but also grow in the depth, clarity, and certitude of their appropriation of divine faith.

DEVIL. A fallen angel or evil spirit, especially the chief of the rebellious angels, Lucifer or Satan (Matthew 25). Adorned at his creation with sanctifying grace, he sinned by pride and along with many other angelic beings was denied the beatific vision. His abode is hell and he does not enjoy the benefits of Christ's redemption. Yet the devil remains a rational spirit, confirmed in evil, who is allowed by God to exercise some influence on living and inanimate creatures. (Etym. Greek *diabolos,* slanderer.)

DEVOTION. The disposition of will to do promptly what concerns the worship and service of God. Although devotion is primarily a disposition or attitude of the will, acts of the will that proceed from such disposition are also expressions of devotion. Essential to devotion is readiness to do whatever gives honor to God, whether in public or private prayer (worship) or in doing the will of God (service). A person who is thus disposed is said to be devoted. His devotedness is ultimately rooted in a great love for God, which in spiritual theology is often called devotion. (Etym. Latin *devotio,* state, act, or expression of being devoted; from *devovere,* to vow.)

DIALECTICAL MATERIALISM. The philosophy founded by Karl Marx (1818–83) and Friedrich Engels (1820–95), and condemned as such by the Catholic Church. It is materialism because it holds not only that matter is real but that matter is prior to mind both in time and in fact. Thus mind is said to appear only as an outgrowth of matter and must be explained accordingly. Space and time are viewed as forms of the existence of matter. It is dialectical in claiming that everything is in constant process of self-transformation. Everything is made up of opposing forces whose internal conflict keeps changing what the thing was into something else. Applied to society, the conflicts among people are essential to the progress of humanity, and to be fostered, as preconditions for the rise of the eventual classless society of perfect Communism.

DIDACHE **(TEACHING OF THE TWELVE APOSTLES).** A first-century treatise, written before A.D. 100. It was rediscovered in 1833 by Bryennios, Greek Orthodox Metropolitan of Nicomedia, in the codex from which in 1875 he had published the full text of the Epistles of St. Clement I. The *Didache* is divided into three parts: 1. the Two Ways, the Way of Life, and the Way of Death; 2. a liturgical manual treating of baptism, fasting, confession, and Holy Communion; 3. a treatise on the ministry. Doctrinal teaching is presupposed. The Way of Life is the love of God and of neighbor; the Way of Death is a list of vices to be avoided. There is a brief instruction on baptism, references to apostles, bishops, and deacons, and an exhortation to watch and be prepared for the coming of Christ.

DIGNITATIS HUMANAE. Decree on Religious Liberty, of the Second Vatican Council. The scope of this document is the religious liberty to believe in God, worship him, and serve him according to one's conscience. There are two aspects of this freedom, as explained in the document: the freedom from coercion in the light of reason, based on each one's dignity as a person, and the freedom of exercise and evangelization founded on Christian revelation. The main thrust of the decree is the affirmation of a divine right, that "the Church claims freedom for herself in human society and before every public authority" (December 7, 1965).

DIRECTION, SPIRITUAL. The guidance voluntarily sought by a person who is intent on progress in the spiritual life. The need for some spiritual direction for anyone seriously striving for sanctity is recognized in the Church's long history. In essence, spiritual direction is the positive assistance that a person receives from someone who is specially qualified by education, experience, or personal sanctity to discern the will of God in the practice of Christian virtue.

DISARMAMENT. The act of disarming, or the policy of reducing a nation's production of military weapons in the interests of regional or international peace. The policy was strongly advocated by the Second Vatican Council: "True peace must be born of mutual trust between peoples instead of being forced on nations through dread of arms; all must work to put an end to the arms race and make a real beginning of disarmament, not unilaterally indeed but at an equal rate on all sides, on the basis of agreements and backed up by genuine and effective guarantees" (Pastoral Constitution on the Church in the Modern World, 82).

DISCERNMENT OF SPIRITS. The ability to distinguish whether a given idea or impulse in the soul comes from the good spirit or from the evil spirit. It may be an act of the virtue of prudence, or a special gift of supernatural grace, or both. In persons who are seriously intent on doing God's will, the good spirit is recognized by the peace of mind and readiness for sacrifice that a given thought or desire produces in the soul. The evil spirit produces disturbance of mind and a tendency to self-indulgence. An opposite effect is produced by both spirits toward sinners. (Etym. Latin *discernere*, to distinguish between, determine, resolve, decide.)

DISMAS. The traditional name of the Good Thief, who was crucified with Christ and to whom Christ promised Paradise (Luke 23:39–43). A portion of the cross on which Dismas is said to have died is preserved at the Church of Santa Croce in Rome, and he is the patron of those condemned to death.

DISPENSATION. A relaxation of the Church's law in a particular case. It is neither an abrogation of the law nor an excuse from observing the law but a release from its observance, temporarily or permanently, by competent authority, for good reasons. The pope can dispense from all purely ecclesiastical laws. Other Church authorities can dispense from the laws that they or their predecessors have passed. Only those can dispense from the laws of a higher superior who are granted the power either by the Church's general legislation or by a special delegation. (Etym. Latin *dispensatio,* distribution, administration; freeing, release: from *dis-* + *pendere,* to weigh: *dispendere,* to weigh out.)

DISSENT, DOCTRINAL. The theory that a professed Catholic may legitimately disagree with an official teaching of the Catholic Church and, in fact, should disagree in order to advance the Church's interests. It is based on one of several erroneous premises—e.g., Modernism, which denies that divine faith is an assent of the mind to God's revealed truth, or process theology, which postulates an evolving deity and therefore also an everchanging truth. Most often the dissent applies to some doctrine of Christian morals that, though infallibly true, because taught by the Church's universal ordinary magisterium, has not been solemnly defined.

DISTRIBUTION OF COMMUNION. Liturgical reception of Holy Communion by the faithful. Communion is to be received either kneeling, and then "no other sign of reverence to the Blessed Sacrament is required," or standing, in which case a sign of reverence should be made before receiving.

DIVINATION. The art of knowing and declaring future events or hidden things by means of communication with occult forces. It is always an act of a religious nature. There is no divination if the religious element is missing, as in any scientific investigation. The occult forces in divination are always created rational powers that the Church identifies as diabolical. Implicit in this judgment is the belief that neither God nor the spiritual powers friendly to God would lend themselves to frivolous practices or subject themselves to any evoking human force. Hence, evoking these powers, whether explicitly or even implicitly, is considered an appeal to Satan's aid. It is therefore a grave offense against God to attribute to the devil a sure knowledge of the contingent future, which, as depending on free will, is known to God alone.

This explains the strong prohibition in the Bible of any divining practices. "Do not have recourse," the people were told, "to the spirits of the dead or to magicians; they will defile you. I am YHWH your God" (Leviticus 19:31). And again: "Any man or woman who is necromancer or magician must be put to death by stoning; their blood shall be on their own heads" (Leviticus 20:27).

In the history of Christianity every form of divination has been condemned by the Church. Among the more common are augury (Latin *augurare,* to predict) by the interpretation of omens such as watching the flight of birds or inspecting the entrails of sacrificed animals; axinomancy (Greek *axine,* axhead + *manteia,* divination) by means of the movements of an ax placed on a post; belomancy (Greek *belos,* dart) by drawing arrows at random from a container; bibliomancy (Greek *biblion,* book) by superstitiously consulting books, notably the Bible; capnomancy (Greek *kapnos,* smoke) by studying the ascent and descent of smoke and concluding that it was a good omen if the smoke rose vertically, especially from a sacrifice; chiromancy (Greek *cheir,* hand) by inspecting the lines of the hand, also called palmistry; necromancy (Greek *necros,* dead person) by consulting the dead or conjuring up the souls of the dead to inquire of them some secrets from the past or into the future, more commonly known as Spiritualism. (Etym. Latin *devinare,* to foresee, predict, prophesy.)

DIVINE ATTRIBUTES. The perfections of God, which, according to a human way of thinking, proceed from and belong to the essence of God. In reality the divine attributes are identical among themselves and with the divine essence. Theology distinguishes the attributes from the essence because they correspond, in human language, to different properties in creatures that reflect, so to speak, the perfections of God.

DIVINE LAW. The eternal law of Gõd, or the divine reason as governing the whole universe. God conceived as the Ruler of the Universe. The plan of government that he has in his mind bears the character of law, and because it is conceived in eternity and not in time, it is said to be the eternal law. This eternal law embraces both the physical and moral laws. Both have in common the idea of some norm to be fulfilled. In physical laws, this norm is fulfilled necessarily, as happens with gravity or the expansion of matter by heat. In moral laws, the norm may or may not be fulfilled depending on the free decision of human beings.

    The eternal moral law has been manifested to the human race in two ways, naturally and supernaturally. In the first case, human beings come to know the eternal law from created nature through the light of native reason; this is natural law in the full scope of its meaning. In the second case, human beings come to know the eternal law from divine revelation to which they can respond with the help of God's grace. This is the revealed law that spans the whole ambit of

God's special communication of his will "through the prophets" in times past and in our own time "through His Son" (Hebrews 1:1).

Since human beings are both individual and social beings, they are obliged by the eternal law on both levels of their existence. The duties that they have as individuals are of course never totally separable from their responsibilities as members of the human family. They are consequently always social by implication. But within the larger community of the human race are two societies that Catholicism has designated as "perfect" or "complete," in the sense that they are divinely provided with the necessary means to fulfill their respective reasons for existence. They are the civil society of the State and the ecclesiastical society of the Church.

Accordingly, each of these societies has the right to make its own laws and bind its members in conscience to obedience. Civil laws oblige all baptized persons who have reached the age of discretion and are therefore able to make rational decisions; yet the Church may also obligate children below that age in matters that pertain to the common good of the faithful.

DIVINE MERCY. The love of God beyond what humankind deserves. In one sense, every manifestation of God's love is an expression of mercy, since absolutely speaking, God is not obligated even to create. But more properly, mercy is the exercise of divine charity toward those who have sinned. Mercy, then, is God's continued love of humans although they have sinned, his forgiving love that invites them to be reconciled with the God against whom they have sinned, his condoning love that mitigates and is even willing to remove all the punishment due to sin, and his superabundant love that mysteriously blesses the repentant sinners beyond what they might have received from God had they not sinned.

DIVINE MERCY, DEVOTION. The modern form of devotion to Divine Mercy derives from the private revelations received from Sister (now Saint) Faustina Kowalska, a Polish religious. There are five practices or forms of the devotion as revealed to Saint Faustina: Divine Mercy Sunday, the Divine Mercy Image, the Chaplet of Divine Mercy, the Novena of Divine Mercy, and observance of the Hour of Great Mercy (3 o'clock P.M.).

DIVINE OFFICE. The group of Psalms, hymns, prayers, and biblical and spiritual readings formulated by the Church for chant or recitation at stated times every day. Its origins go back to apostolic times, when it consisted almost entirely of Psalms and readings from the Scriptures. Priests are obliged to say the full daily office, and religious who are not priests are obligated according to their rule of life. The latest edition of the Divine Office was promulgated by Pope Paul VI by the apostolic constitution *Laudis canticum* in 1970. It represents a complete revision of the text and arrangement of the Hours of the Liturgy according to the directives of the Second Vatican Council (Constitution on the Sacred Liturgy, IV, 83–101). As contained in the Breviary, the office is divided into the Proper of the Season, with biblical readings and homilies; Solemnities of the Lord as they occur during the year; the Ordinary or normal framework of the office; the Psalter, or Psalms assigned to each hour of the day on the basis of four weeks; the Proper of the Saints, as their feasts occur in sequence; Common Offices, corresponding to votive Masses in the Eucharistic liturgy; and the Office of the Dead. A supplement contains canticles and Gospel readings for vigils, brief intercessory prayers, and detailed indices. See also MORNING PRAYER, EVENING PRAYER, NIGHT PRAYER, PRAYER DURING THE DAY, OFFICE OF READINGS.

DIVINE PRAISES. A series of praises, recited for generations after the Benediction of the Blessed Sacrament. They are thought to have been originally compiled in 1797 in reparation for blasphemy and profane language. Praise of the Immaculate Conception, her bodily Assumption into heaven, the Sacred Heart, St. Joseph, and the Precious Blood have been added since the middle of the nineteenth century. The present text reads:

Blessed be God.
Blessed be his holy Name.
Blessed be Jesus Christ, true God and true man.
Blessed be the name of Jesus.
Blessed be his most Sacred Heart.
Blessed be his most Precious Blood.
Blessed be Jesus in the most holy Sacrament of the Altar.
Blessed be the Holy Spirit, the Paraclete.
Blessed be the great Mother of God, Mary most holy.
Blessed be her holy and Immaculate Conception.
Blessed be her glorious Assumption.
Blessed be the name of Mary, Virgin and Mother.
Blessed be St. Joseph, her most chaste spouse.
Blessed be God in his angels and in his saints.

DIVINI REDEMPTORIS. Encyclical letter of Pope Pius XI, published in 1937, condemning atheistic Communism and identifying its principal errors: dialectical materialism, utopian messianism, progress through class conflict, denial of personal liberty, and the negation of all human rights.

DIVORCE. Legal separation of husband and wife, or the release by civil authority from any one or more of the bonds of matrimony between them. Imperfect divorce is the separation of husband and wife so that the duty of living together, and sometimes the support, is relaxed, but giving them no right to remarry. Also called separation from bed and board, but not the severance of the primary bond of marriage, which is the exclusive lifelong fidelity in the use of marital rights. (Etym. Latin *divortium;* from *divertere,* to part, separate, turn aside.)

DOCTOR OF THE CHURCH. A title given since the Middle Ages to certain saints whose writing or preaching is outstanding for guiding the faithful in all periods of the Church's history. Originally the Western Fathers of the Church—Gregory the Great, Ambrose, Augustine, and Jerome—were considered the great doctors of the Church. But the Church has officially added many more names to the original four, including Sts. Thomas Aquinas (1224–74), Catherine of Siena (1347–80), Teresa of Avila (1515–82), and Thérèse of Lisieux (1873–97).

Doctors of the Church

ST. ALBERT THE GREAT (1200–80). Dominican. Patron of natural scientists; called Doctor Universalis, Doctor Expertus.

ST. ALPHONSUS LIGUORI (1696–1787). Patron of confessors and moralists. Founder of the Redemptorists.

ST. AMBROSE (340–97). One of the four traditional Doctors of the Latin Church. Opponent of Arianism in the West. Bishop of Milan.

ST. ANSELM (1033–1109). Archbishop of Canterbury. Father of Scholasticism.

ST. ANTHONY OF PADUA (1195–1231). Franciscan Friar. Evangelical Doctor.

ST. ATHANASIUS (297–373). Bishop of Alexandria. Dominant opponent of Arianism. Father of Orthodoxy.

ST. AUGUSTINE (354–430). Bishop of Hippo. One of the four traditional Doctors of the Latin Church. Doctor of Grace.

ST. BASIL THE GREAT (329–79). One of the Three Cappadocian Fathers. Father of monasticism in the East.

ST. BEDE THE VENERABLE (673–735). Benedictine priest. Father of English history.

ST. BERNARD OF CLAIRVAUX (1090–1153). Cistercian. Called Mellifluous Doctor because of his eloquence.

ST. BONAVENTURE (1217–74). Franciscan theologian. Seraphic Doctor.

ST. CATHERINE OF SIENA (1347–80). Mystic. Second woman Doctor.

ST. CYRIL OF ALEXANDRIA (376–444). Patriarch. Opponent of Nestorianism. Made key contributions to Christology.

ST. CYRIL OF JERUSALEM (315–87). Bishop and opponent of Arianism in the East.

ST. EPHRAEM SYRUS (306–73). Biblical exegete and ecclesiastical writer. Called Harp of the Holy Spirit.

ST. FRANCIS DE SALES (1567–1622). Bishop, leader in Counter-Reformation. Patron of Catholic writers and the Catholic press.

ST. GREGORY I THE GREAT (540–604). Pope. Fourth and last of the traditional Doctors of the Latin Church. Defended papal supremacy and worked for clerical and monastic reform.

ST. GREGORY OF NAZIANZEN (330–90). Called the Christian Demosthenes because of his eloquence and, in the Eastern Church, the Theologian. One of the Three Cappadocian Fathers.

ST. HILARY OF POITIERS (315–68). Bishop. Called the Athanasius of the West.

ST. HILDEGARD OF BINGEN (1098–1179). Abbess. German Benedictine mystic.

ST. ISIDORE OF SEVILLE (560–636). Archbishop, theologian, historian. Regarded as the most learned man of his time.

ST. JEROME (343–420). One of the four traditional Doctors of the Latin Church. Father of biblical science.

ST. JOHN CHRYSOSTOM (347–407). Bishop of Constantinople. Patron of preachers and called Golden-Mouthed because of his eloquence.

ST. JOHN DAMASCENE (675–749). Greek theologian. Called Golden Speaker because of his eloquence.

ST. JOHN OF AVILA (1500–1569). Priest. Spanish Evangelical preacher.

ST. JOHN OF THE CROSS (1542–91). Joint founder of the
  Discalced Carmelites. Doctor of Mystical Theology.
ST. LAWRENCE OF BRINDISI (1559–1619). Vigorous preacher
  of strong influence in the post-Reformation period.
ST. LEO I THE GREAT (400–61). Pope. Wrote against Nestorian
  and Monophysite heresies and errors of Manichaeism and
  Pelagianism.
ST. PETER CANISIUS (1521–97). Jesuit theologian. Leader in the
  Counter-Reformation.
ST. PETER CHRYSOLOGUS (400–50). Bishop of Ravenna.
  Called Golden-Worded.
ST. PETER DAMIAN (1007–72). Benedictine. Ecclesiastical and
  clerical reformer.
ST. ROBERT BELLARMINE (1542–1621). Jesuit. Defended
  doctrine under attack during and after the Reformation.
  Wrote two catechisms.
ST. TERESA OF AVILA (1515–82). Spanish Carmelite nun and
  mystic. First woman Doctor.
ST. THÉRÈSE OF LISIEUX (1873–97). French Carmelite nun.
  Doctor of the Little Way.
ST. THOMAS AQUINAS (1225–74). Dominican philosopher and
  theologian. Called Angelic Doctor. Patron of Catholic schools
  and education.

DOCTRINE. Any truth taught by the Church as necessary for acceptance by the faithful. The truth may be either formally revealed (as
the Real Presence), or a theological conclusion (as the canonization
of a saint), or part of the natural law (as the sinfulness of contraception). In any case, what makes it doctrine is that the Church authority
teaches that it is to be believed. This teaching may be done either solemnly in ex cathedra pronouncements or ordinarily in the perennial
exercise of the Church's magisterium or teaching authority. Dogmas
are those doctrines that the Church proposes for belief as formally
revealed by God. (Etym. Latin *doctrina*, teaching.)

DOGMATIC THEOLOGY. The science of Christian doctrine. It treats
the teachings of the Church systematically as a whole and considers
each article of faith in its own right and in relation to other dogmas
of Catholic Christianity. It proves the doctrines of the Church from
Scripture and tradition, illustrates them by suitable comparisons,

and shows that they are in harmony with reason. It answers objections from philosophy and other sciences and above all deduces theological consequences from the truths of faith.

DOLORS, SEVEN. The seven sorrows of the Blessed Virgin Mary. They are traditionally identified with the sorrows that Mary experienced in her association with Christ: the prophecy of Simeon (Luke 2:34–35), the flight into Egypt (Matthew 2:13–21), the three-day separation from Jesus in Jerusalem (Luke 2:41–50), and the four incidents related to Christ's Passion, as described or implied by the evangelists; namely, Mary's meeting Jesus on the way to Calvary, the Crucifixion, the removal of Christ's body from the Cross, and the burial in the tomb. There were two feasts in honor of the seven sorrows: the Friday after Passion Sunday, extended to the universal Church by Pope Benedict XIII in 1727; and September 15, first granted to the Servite Order in 1668 and extended in 1814 to the whole Church by Pope Pius VII. In the revised Roman calendar, only the feast on September 15 is observed, but its name has been changed to Our Lady of Sorrows. (Etym. Latin *dolor,* pain, sorrow.)

DOMINICANS. The Order of Preachers, founded by St. Dominic (1170–1221), whose form took definite shape at two general chapters held in Bologna in 1220 and 1221. Also known as Friars Preachers and in England as Black Friars. Specially devoted to preaching and teaching, they were the first major order to substitute intellectual work for manual labor. At Dominic's request, the order was to practice not only individual but corporate poverty. In 1475, Pope Sixtus IV revoked the law of corporate poverty and allowed the Dominicans to hold property and have permanent sources of income.

The chief apostolate is educational. There is a carefully organized system of teaching that culminates in the *Studia Generalia,* connected with a college or university. It was especially the Dominicans who adapted Aristotle (384–322 B.C.) to the service of Christianity, following the lead of St. Albertus Magnus (1200–80) and St. Thomas Aquinas (1225–74).

The popes have used the Dominicans on many missions, including preaching the Crusades and diplomatic service. The Inquisition was regularly staffed by Dominicans, who were therefore called "watchdogs of orthodoxy." In the Age of Discovery, they established many pioneer missions in the Eastern and Western Hemispheres.

There are two orders attached to the Friars Preachers. The Second Order consists of nuns who follow a rule similar to that of the friars but are cloistered and live a contemplative life. Most of the Third Order Sisters live an active life, with apostolic work outside the community. In 1852, Jean Baptiste Lacordaire (1802–61) founded a Third Order for priests with simple vows, which was destroyed by the French anticlerical laws of 1901.

DOORS, HOLY. The doors of the basilicas of St. Peter, St. John Lateran, St. Paul, and St. Mary Major, which are not opened except during the years of a jubilee. The pope opens the doors of St. Peter's to officially begin a Holy Year, and closes them at the end of a jubilee. Cardinals are commissioned to do the same at the three other basilicas. The custom dates back to the jubilee of 1450, under Pope Nicholas V. Between jubilees the holy doors are closed by two partitions of brick, between which are placed commemorative medals and a parchment recalling the jubilee just completed.

DOUAY BIBLE. The sixteenth- and seventeenth-century English translation of the Bible, begun at the English College, Douai, Flanders. The college was later moved to Reims, where the New Testament was completed and published. The Old Testament translation was issued some years later, when the college returned to Douai. The translation, which sought for accuracy rather than literary style, was made from the Latin Vulgate, carefully compared with the original Hebrew and Greek. It was mainly the work of Gregory Martin (d. 1582). In the eighteenth century it was considerably revised by Bishop Challoner (1691–1781) and until the mid-twentieth century was commonly used by Catholics in English-speaking countries.

DOUBLE CONSECRATION. The separate consecration of the bread and wine into the body and blood of Christ. This separate consecration constitutes the essence of the Mass as a renewal of Calvary. It symbolizes the death of Christ caused by the separation of his body and blood. All other parts of the Mass are not absolutely essential, even the priest's Communion, which, though gravely binding, belongs rather to the integrity than to the essence of the Eucharistic Sacrifice.

DOUBLE EFFECT. The principle that says it is morally allowable to perform an act that has at least two effects, one good and one bad.

It may be used under the following conditions: 1. the act to be done must be good in itself or at least morally indifferent; by the act to be done is meant the deed itself taken independently of its consequences; 2. the good effect must not be obtained by means of the evil effect; the evil must be only an incidental by-product and not an actual factor in the accomplishment of the good; 3. the evil effect must not be intended for itself but only permitted; all bad will must be excluded from the act; 4. there must be a proportionately grave reason for permitting the evil effect. At least the good and evil effects should be nearly equivalent. All four conditions must be fulfilled. If any one of them is not satisfied, the act is morally wrong.

A classic example of the principle of double effect is the moral acceptability of treatment for an ectopic pregnancy (where the fertilized egg implants in the wall of the fallopian tube) by removing part of the fallopian tube. The removal of part of the fallopian tube to prevent or stop internal bleeding of the mother is not evil per se. The preborn baby is not directly aborted; the embryo will die, for it is too young for viability outside the mother's womb. The purpose of the procedure is not to abort the ectopic pregnancy. The damaged tube is a potentially life-threatening condition for the woman. All four conditions called for by the principle of double effect are met in this example.

DOUBTING FAITH. The theory that, at least in modern times, it is quite possible to remain a good Catholic while positively doubting one or more articles of the faith. Implicit in the theory, condemned by the First Vatican Council, is the claim that "doubt is a spiritual exercise" that presupposes "permanent openness to truth." It ignores the fact that God always gives sufficient grace to believe, without either denial or doubt that what he revealed is certainly true.

DREAMS. The effect of psychic activity protracted in sleep. Their religious significance derives from many sources, not the least of which is the frequency with which the Scriptures speak of dreams, in the Old and New Testaments, and which indicate that sometimes God uses this means of communicating with human beings.

Dream representations are largely expressed in visual form, but auditory, olfactory, and taste dreams also occur. Although the structure of dreams is disorganized, nevertheless dreams do contain a latent meaning. They may be considered as a symbolic transference of situations, ideas, and sentiments previously experienced by the dreamer.

DRUG ABUSE, MORALITY OF. The use of any drug, although medicinal in original purpose, has grave moral implications, to the degree that it seriously affects a person's social adjustment and physical or mental health.

DRUNKENNESS. Overindulgence in alcoholic beverages. On Catholic moral principles, the degree of sinfulness in excessive drinking depends on how this excess is known to affect this particular drinker. It is a grave matter if it is foreseen that this drink will cause one to lose the use of one's senses or will put one in such a state that he or she is no longer able to distinguish right from wrong. It is a venial matter if one has reason for believing that this amount of drinking, though actually excessive, will neither deprive one of the use of one's senses or of the power to distinguish right from wrong.

E

EASTER COMMUNION. Reception of the Holy Eucharist, as prescribed by the Church, during the Easter season, which differs among countries, but generally between Ash Wednesday (or the first Sunday of Lent) and Trinity Sunday. Also called "Easter Duty," it includes the reception of the sacrament of penance. Children (*puberes*) are also to make their Easter Duty, and the obligation rests on parents, guardians, and the pastor to see that this duty is fulfilled.

EASTERN CHURCHES. Christian churches whose members follow the Eastern rites as a body. Historically they were the Patriarchates of Constantinople, Alexandria, Antioch, and Jerusalem before the schism in the thirteenth century. They follow the ceremonies originally used by the Patriarch of Constantinople. The groups not in communion with Rome are called the separated Eastern Churches; the others are Catholic Churches of their respective Eastern rites.

EASTERN SCHISM. Separation of the Christian Churches of the East from unity with Rome. The schism was centuries in the making and finally became fixed in 1054, when the Patriarch of Constantinople, Michael Cerularius (d. 1059), was excommunicated by the papal legates for opposing the use of leavened bread by the Latin Church and removing the pope's name from the diptychs or list of persons to be prayed for in the Eucharistic liturgy. A temporary reunion with Rome was effected by the Second Council of Lyons (1274) and the Council of Florence (1439) but never stabilized.

EASTER VIGIL. The ceremonies of Holy Saturday and the most solemn memorial of the liturgical year. They consist of four parts: Service of the Light, Liturgy of the Word, Liturgy of Baptism, and Liturgy of the Eucharist. The entire celebration takes place at night, and therefore it should not begin before nightfall and should end before dawn on Easter Sunday. In the early Church the night before Easter was celebrated by the illumination of the churches and even of whole cities. The revised Easter Vigil services include ceremonies that go back to the first centuries of the Christian era and stress the Church's joy in commemorating the night that Christ rose from the dead.

ECCLESIAL. Pertaining to the Church as the community of believers, with stress on their faith and union through love, and on the invisible operations of divine grace among the faithful.

ECCLESIASTES. A book of the Old Testament, called in Hebrew *Koheleth* or in English "the Preacher." Once held to have been written by Solomon, now agreed that the author is unknown. The theme of the book is the transient character of all earthly goods, compared with the true wisdom that is found in the fear of the Lord. Though sober in tone, it is not pessimistic, since hope for happiness is held out to those who direct their lives according to reason and the will of God. (Etym. Greek *ekklēsiastes*, preacher; Hebrew *Qōheleth*.)

ECCLESIASTICAL LAW. An ordinance issued by legitimate authority in the Catholic Church. The legislators for the entire Church are the Roman Pontiff alone, or the pope through the Roman Curia, or an ecumenical council together with the pope; the bishops for their individual dioceses, or conferences of bishops for the territories under their jurisdiction; and the major superiors of institutes of perfection for their members, according to the respective constitutions.

The Catholic Church has always professed her right to pass laws that are binding on the consciences of the faithful. This right is believed to be of divine origin, since "the Church, our most prudent Mother, by the constitution received from her Founder, Christ, was endowed with all the qualities suitable to a perfect society. So, too, from her very beginning, since she was to obey the Lord's command to teach and govern all nations, she has undertaken to regulate and protect by the laws the discipline of clergy and laity alike" (Benedict XV, *Providentissima Mater Ecclesia*, May 27, 1917).

Every baptized person, even if one is not a professed Catholic, is subject to ecclesiastical laws except in such cases as are indicated in the law. The obligation stems from the fact that by the sacrament of baptism "we are made members of Christ and of his body, the Church" (*Council of Florence*, Denzinger 1314). Baptism is, in fact, the *janua Ecclesiae*, the door of the Church. Since the baptismal character is indelible, a person once baptized always remains subject to the Church into which he or she was incorporated by this sacrament of water and the Holy Spirit.

ECCLESIASTICAL TRADITION. The revealed word of God as entrusted to the Church to be faithfully preserved, resolutely defended, authentically interpreted, validly developed, and effectively applied in the lives of the People of God.

ECCLESIASTICUS. A book of the Old Testament, also known as "The Wisdom of Jesus, Son of Sirach." Originally written in Hebrew, it was highly prized by the Jews, particularly of the Diaspora, and by the early Christians, next to the Psalms and the Gospels. It is the longest didactic book of the Old Testament. After an exhortation to seek wisdom, it offers a series of practical precepts. The transition 42:15 to 43:28 is a sublime hymn extolling God's work in nature. In the second part (44 to 50:23) God is praised in the lives of the heroes of Israel. Noteworthy is chapter 24, introducing uncreated wisdom, speaking as a divine person, although the idea of a distinct substance is not expressed. New Testament references to Ecclesiasticus are numerous.

ECSTASY. In general, the state of being beside oneself through some overpowering experience. As a mystical phenomenon, it includes two elements, one interior and the other exterior. The invisible element consists of the mind being riveted on a religious subject. The corporeal aspect means that the activity of the senses is suspended, so that not only are external sensations unable to influence the soul, but these sensations become very difficult to awaken. Many saints have received ecstasies as a supernatural gift from God, although ecstasy of itself is not a criterion of holiness. (Etym. Greek *ekstasis;* from *ex-*, out + *histanai,* to cause to stand: *existanai,* to derange.) See also RAPTURE.

ECUMENICAL. Literally "universal" and commonly used to identify the general councils of the Church. With the rise of the movement for Christian unity, it has become synonymous with "striving for re-unification" among the separated Churches of Christendom. (Etym. Latin *oecumenicus;* from Greek *oikoumenē,* the inhabited world.)

ECUMENICAL COUNCILS. Following are the ecumenical councils of the Roman Catholic Church, with dates and a brief statement of their principal legislation.

1. Nicaea I (325). Condemned Arianism, defined that the Son of God is consubstantial with the Father, formulated the Nicene Creed.

2. Constantinople I (381). Condemned the Macedonians who denied the divinity of the Holy Spirit. Confirmed and extended the Nicene Creed.

3. Ephesus (431). Condemned Nestorianism, which held that there were two distinct persons in the Incarnate Christ, a human and divine. Defended the right of Mary to be called the Mother of God.

4. Chalcedon (451). Condemned Monophysitism or Eutychianism by defining that Christ had two distinct natures, and was therefore true God and true man.

5. Constantinople II (553). Pronounced against certain persons as infected with Nestorianism, notably Theodore of Mopsuestia, Theodoret of Cyrrhus, and Ibas of Edessa.

6. Constantinople III (680–81). Defined against the Monothelites that Christ has two wills, human and divine.

7. Nicaea II (787). Condemned the Iconoclasts or Image-breakers and defined that sacred images may be honored without idolatry.

8. Constantinople IV (869–70). Condemned Photius as Patriarch of Constantinople.

9. Lateran I (1123). First general council in the West, endorsed the Concordat of Worms regarding the investiture of prelates.

10. Lateran II (1139). Took measures against the schism of the antipope Anacletus II and issued disciplinary decrees.

11. Lateran III (1179). Legislated against the Waldenses and Albigensians and decreed papal elections by two-thirds majority of cardinals at conclave.

12. Lateran IV (1215). Made reform decrees, ordered annual confession and Easter Communion, first officially used the term "transubstantiation."

13. Lyons I (1245). Condemned Frederick II for his persecution of the Church.

14. Lyons II (1274). Effected a temporary reunion of the Eastern Churches with Rome and decreed that papal elections should begin ten days after the death of the pope.

15. Vienne (1311–12). Suppressed the Knights Templar, sought aid for the Holy Land, defined the relation of the soul to the human body, and condemned the false mysticism of the Fraticelli, Dulcinists, Beghards, and Beguines.

16. Constance (1414–18). Issued reform decrees in "head and

members," condemned Wyclif and Hus, and put an end to the Western Schism.

17. Florence (1438–45). Affirmed the papal primacy against Conciliarists, who said that a general council was superior to the pope, and sought to effect a reunion of the Eastern Churches separated from Rome.

18. Lateran V (1512–17). Defined the relation of pope to a general council, condemned philosophers who taught the human soul was mortal and only one for all mankind, and called for a crusade against the Turks.

19. Trent (1545–63). Called to meet the crisis of the Protestant Reformation; proclaimed the Bible and tradition as rule of faith; defined doctrine on the Mass, the sacraments, justification, purgatory, indulgences, invocation of saints, veneration of sacred images; issued decrees on marriage and clerical reform.

20. Vatican I (1869–70). Defined the nature of revelation and faith, the relation of faith and reason, and papal infallibility; condemned pantheism, materialism, deism, naturalism, and fideism.

21. Vatican II (1962–65). Convoked by Pope John XXIII "mainly to more effectively preserve and present the sacred deposit of Christian doctrine." Its sixteen documents reaffirmed the principles of Catholic faith and morality, and authorized numerous developments in the Eucharistic liturgy, the ritual of the sacraments, and the Church's administrative structure.

ECUMENISM. The modern movement toward Christian unity whose Protestant origins stem from the Edinburgh World Missionary Conference in 1910, and whose Catholic principles were formulated by the Second Vatican Council in 1964. These principles are mainly three: 1. Christ established his Church on the Apostles and their episcopal successors, whose visible head and principle of unity became Peter and his successor the Bishop of Rome; 2. since the first century there have been divisions in Christianity, but many persons now separated from visible unity with the successors of the Apostles under Peter are nevertheless Christians who possess more or less of the fullness of grace available in the Roman Catholic Church; 3. Catholics are to do everything possible to foster the ecumenical movement, which comprehends all "the initiatives and activities, planned and undertaken to promote Christian unity, according to the Church's various needs and as opportunities offer" (*Decree on Ecumenism,* I, 4).

EDEN. The beautiful garden in which God put Adam and Eve. After they disobeyed him, they were expelled (Genesis 2, 3). It is a word used in Scripture to suggest an ideal place to live (Isaiah 51:3; Ezekiel 31:9).

EFFICACIOUS GRACE. The actual grace to which free consent is given by the will so that the grace produces its divinely intended effect. In the controversy between the Dominicans [led by Báñez (1528–1604)] and the Jesuits [led by Molina (1525–1600)] there was no agreement on what precisely causes an actual grace to become efficacious. In the Báñezian theory, the efficacy of such grace depends on the character of the grace itself; in the Molinist theory, it depends on the fact that it is given under circumstances that God foresees to be congruous with the dispositions of the person receiving the grace. In every Catholic theory, however, it is agreed that efficacious grace does not necessitate the will or destroy human freedom. (Etym. Latin *efficax,* powerful, effective, efficient, *gratia,* favor freely given.) See also AC-TUAL GRACE, GRACE, HABITUAL GRACE, JUSTIFYING GRACE, SACRA-MENTAL GRACE, SANCTIFYING GRACE, SUFFICIENT GRACE.

ELIJAH. One of the greatest religious leaders of the Israelite people. He lived in the ninth century before Christ, and his influence dominated Hebrew thought for centuries although he left no writings. He was an unusual man, unconventional, physically robust, a man who survived many ordeals (I Kings 17–21). In an arduous trip across the desert to Mount Horeb, he reenacted the experiences of Moses when he received the Law. His communications with God amplified the application of the Ten Commandments in an era of more complex social life. To prove the authenticity of his God, Elijah triumphed over the prophets of Baal in a contest, a vindication that established the Hebrew religion firmly and ended the drought that had afflicted Israel (I Kings 18:22–40). In his old age Elijah chose Elisha as his successor (II Kings 2:15). Presumably he went to heaven without dying, and it was an established belief that one day he would reappear on earth to restore Israel's glory (II Kings 2:11). Many people, in fact, mistook Jesus for Elijah (Matthew 16:14). At the Transfiguration it was Moses and Elijah who appeared with Christ (Matthew 17:3). At the Jewish Passover the door is opened in anticipation of his return, and a cup of wine is poured out for him. Elijah is also spelled Elias.

ELIZABETH. A descendant of Aaron, she married Zechariah and, late in life, bore him a son destined to be known as John the Baptist (Luke 1:5–13). During her pregnancy she received a visit from her kinswoman, Mary, who had received the word from the archangel Gabriel that she was to be the mother of Jesus. This meeting of the two mothers-to-be was the occasion of Mary's proclamation of the Magnificat (Luke 1:46–55). Within several months Elizabeth's child was born. Her friends urged her to name him after his father, but in obedience to Gabriel's revelation to Zechariah, he was named John. "And indeed," concluded Luke, "the hand of the Lord was with him" (Luke 1:66). (Etym. Greek form of Hebrew *elishebha,* God is fullness.)

ELOHIM. The Hebrew word most frequently used for God. It appears several thousand times in the Old Testament. It was also used in a plural sense to designate heathen gods (Genesis 35:2; Exodus 18:11). When Jesus was heard to say on the Cross, "Eli, Eli, lama sabachtani," he was using a modified form of Elohim (Matthew 27:46).

ENCHIRIDION SYMBOLORUM. A manual of Catholic doctrine containing essential extracts of all the major definitions and declarations on faith and morals from the first century to the present day. Originally compiled and edited by Heinrich Denzinger (1819–83), one of the pioneers of positive theology in Catholic Germany. The Second Vatican Council relied on the *Enchiridion* for its citations, referred to as "Denzinger."

ENCLOSURE. The cloister of a religious community that reserves certain parts of the residence to the exclusive use of the members of the community. Strict enclosure, called papal, is the standard for other, less restricted forms of cloister. It pertains to religious institutes of women who are strictly contemplative. Its two main provisions, since the Second Vatican Council, are that 1. "the nuns, novices and postulants must live within the confines of the convent prescribed by the enclosure itself, nor may they licitly go beyond them, except in the cases provided for by the law," and 2. "the law of enclosure likewise forbids anyone, of whatever class, condition, sex or age, to enter the cloistered area of the convent, except in the cases provided for by law" (*Venite Seorsum,* 1969, VII, 5, 6).

ENCYCLICAL. A papal document treating of matters related to the general welfare of the Church, sent by the pope to the bishops. Used especially in modern times to express the mind of the pope to the people. Although of themselves not infallible documents, encyclicals may (and generally do) contain pronouncements on faith and morals that are *de facto* infallible because they express the ordinary teaching of the Church. In any case, the faithful are to give the papal encyclicals their interior assent and external respect as statements of the Vicar of Christ. (Etym. Latin *encyclicus;* Greek *enkyklios,* circular, general.)

An encyclical epistle is like an encyclical letter but is addressed to part of the Church—that is, to the bishops and faithful of a particular area. Its contents may be doctrinal, moral, or disciplinary matters of universal significance, but may also commemorate some historical event or treat of conditions in a certain country or locality.

END OF THE WORLD. Revealed truth that the present world of space and time will come to an end. It will be on the day when the dead will rise from the grave and Christ will appear in his majesty to judge the human race. As to the manner of the world's destruction or its time, nothing definite can be said whether from natural science or from the Christian faith. The idea of destruction by fire (II Peter 3:7, 10, 12) can be taken simply as a current mode of expression to state that the present world will be dissolved and a new world will come into existence.

ENDS OF THE MASS. The fourfold purpose for which the Church offers the Eucharistic Sacrifice; namely, adoration, thanksgiving, propitiation, and petition. The Mass is therefore a sacrifice of praise of God's eternal greatness, of gratitude for past and present goodness, of begging mercy for having offended the divine majesty, and of asking for divine favor in the future.

ENVY. Sadness or discontent at the excellence, good fortune, or success of another person. It implies that one considers oneself somehow deprived by what one envies in another or even that an injustice has been done. Essential to envy is this sense of deprivation. Consequently it is not merely sadness that someone else has some desirable talent or possession, nor certainly the ambition to equal or surpass another person, which can be laudable emulation. It is not the same as jealousy, which implies an unwillingness to share one's own possessions.

Envy is a sin against charity and, though serious in itself, allows for degrees of gravity depending on whether it is fully consented to and how important the object envied is. The most serious sin of envy is sadness at the supernatural gifts or graces that another has received from God, i.e., to envy sanctity. (Etym. Latin *invidia*; from *invidere*, to look askance.)

EPHESIANS, EPISTLE TO THE. One of the instructional letters of St. Paul, written from Rome sometime during his first imprisonment (A.D. 61–63). Most likely it was a circular letter whose theme is the union of all the faithful with and in Christ, as members of his one Mystical Body. Its reference to matrimony as a mystery that implies the union of Christ and the Church (5:32) has made this epistle the classic source of the Church's doctrine on the sacrament of marriage.

EPIPHANY. The feast commemorating Christ's manifestation to the Gentiles in the person of the Magi, as well as his baptism and first miracle at Cana. It began in the East in the third century and soon spread to the West, where it is identified with the visit of the Magi. In some countries it is known as Twelfth Night (after Christmas) and is the occasion for special celebrations. For centuries the Epiphany has been a holy day of obligation in many places. (Etym. Greek *epiphaneia*, appearance, manifestation.)

EPISCOPACY. Divine institution of bishops as successors of the Apostles. By virtue of divine right, therefore, bishops possess an ordinary power of government over their dioceses. The episcopal power is ordinary because it belongs to the episcopal office. It is an immediate power because it is exercised in the bishop's own name and not at the order of a superior. Thus bishops are not mere delegates or agents of the pope, nor his mere vicars or representatives. They are autonomous pastors of the flock entrusted to them even though they are subordinated to the pope.

The episcopal power is inherent in the bishops' ordination, though it must be activated by collegial union with the pope and the rest of the Catholic hierarchy. It is a true pastoral power that embraces all the ecclesiastical powers belonging to the exercise of this office, namely teaching, ruling, judging, and, when necessary, punishing refractory members of their diocese. It is, however, a power that is limited locally and materially, since it extends only to a definite segment of the Church and is circumscribed by the papal authority, which is superior to that of any bishop in his diocese. (Etym. Latin *episcopus,* bishop; from Greek *episkopos,* overseer.)

EPISCOPAL CONFERENCE. A form of assembly in which the bishops of a certain country or region exercise their pastoral office jointly in order to enhance the Church's beneficial influence on all men especially by devising forms of the apostolate and apostolic methods suitably adopted to the circumstances of the times (Second Vatican Council, *Christus Dominus,* III, 38). The local ordinaries and coadjutors have a deliberate vote. Each conference draws up its own statutes, which are subject to the approval of Rome. Decisions of an episcopal conference have the force of law when they have been legitimately approved by at least two-thirds of the bishops who have a deliberative vote and confirmed by the Apostolic See, but then only in cases prescribed by common law, or when so declared by a special mandate of the Holy See. This mandate may come from Rome on its own initiative or in response to the conference itself.

EPISCOPALIANS. Anglicans, or members of the Anglican Communion, but called Episcopalians in certain countries such as the United States. Anglicanism came to America in 1607, with the Jamestown, Virginia, settlers, and in 1783 the American Anglicans became the Protestant Episcopal Church. They declared themselves free of all foreign authority, civil or ecclesiastical, but kept their liturgy in conformity with the Church of England. The first convention (1783) also revised the English Book of Common Prayer. Sixty-nine feast days were dropped from the Church calendar, the "Ornaments Rubric" requiring vestments was omitted, and in the catechism the reference to the Eucharist "verily and indeed taken and received by the faithful" was changed to "spiritually taken and received." One result has been that American Episcopalians reflect the whole spectrum of Anglicanism, ranging from Anglo-Catholic churches that are close to Rome in faith and liturgy, through High and Broad, to Low Church groups that are in the mainstream of evangelical Protestantism.

EPISTLE. In the traditional Latin Mass liturgy (Extraordinary Form) most frequently a selection from one of the letters of the Apostles read at Mass after the Collects, at the (priest's) right-hand side of the altar, and therefore called the Epistle side. As a rule there is only one, but on some days there are several. At solemn High Mass, the Epistle is chanted in one tone by the subdeacon. In the revised liturgy of the

Ordinary Form of the Roman Rite, the Epistle has become the First Reading and (on Sundays, Solemnities, and Feasts) the Second Reading. (Etym. Latin *epistola,* letter; from Greek *epistole,* message, letter.)

ERROR. Positive disagreement between the mind and object; a wrong judgment. Essential to an error is that what the mind conceives something to be is contrary to what it really is. Less often the notion of error is applied to a mistake in correctness or validity in reasoning. Error differs from mere ignorance in positively affirming within the mind what is objectively not so outside the mind.

ESCHATOLOGY. The branch of systematic theology that treats of the last things: death, particular and general judgments, heaven, hell, and purgatory. All the essentials of eschatology have been clearly defined by the Church, notably the Fourth Lateran Council (1215) and the constitution *Benedictus Deus* of Pope Benedict XII in 1336. (Etym. Greek *eschatos,* uttermost + *logos,* discourse on.)

ESSENCE. What a thing is. The internal principle whereby a thing is what it is and not something else. Sometimes essence is said to be the same thing as being, but being merely, affirming that a thing is, without specifying its perfections. Essence is not quite the same as nature, which adds to essence the notion of activity, i.e., nature is the essence in action. Or again essence is substance, but not all essences are substantial because accidents also have an essence. (Etym. Latin *essentia,* essence, being.)

ESTHER. The adopted daughter and niece (or cousin) of Mordecai, she was also known as Hadassah (Esther 2:15). She is a traditionally heroic figure to Jews because she outwitted the anti-Semitic Agagite, Haman, a powerful official in King Ahasuerus's court. Following the banishment of Queen Vashti, the king chose Esther to be his wife (Esther 2:17). Using her beauty and intelligence to combat Haman in his attempt to wipe out the Jews, she brought about his execution on the gallows, a fate he had planned for Mordecai (Esther 3–6). The struggle emphasizes patriotic and racial devotion rather than religious aspiration (Esther 7:10). It is a lively, stirring story whose events are celebrated by Jews all over the world in the annual Feast of Purim (Esther 9:27–28). The book of Esther was written by an unknown author, probably not later than the time of Ezra. The text of Esther has come down in two revisions, a shorter Hebrew and a longer Greek.

The Catholic Bible follows the Hebrew and then adds the missing passages (10–16) from the Greek.

ETERNAL DEATH. The lot of the wicked who die estranged from God. It is called death because the person is deprived of the possession of God, who gives life to the soul. And it is eternal because it will never end.

ETERNAL LAW. The plan of divine wisdom, insofar as it directs all the actions and events of the universe. It is, therefore, the unchangeable effective decree of God binding the whole of creation to the fulfillment of its purpose, and to the use of such means for attaining this purpose as are adapted to each nature.

ETERNAL LIFE. The term used by Christ to describe the state of endless happiness enjoyed by the just in heaven (Matthew 25:46; Mark 9:44; Luke 18:30; John 3, 4, 5, 6, 10, 12). It means not only everlasting duration but also fullness of life, which the believer possesses already here and now through participation in the life of God.

ETERNAL PUNISHMENT. The unending penalty suffered in hell by the evil spirits and the human beings who die in mortal sin. The Church bases her teaching about the existence of eternal punishment on the words of Christ in foretelling the final judgment (Matthew 25:34, 41). He compares the sentence of the just with the condemnation of the wicked. Christ as judge will first say, "Come, you whom my Father has blessed, take for your heritage the kingdom prepared for you since the foundation of the world." But to the unjust, "Go away from me, with your curse upon you, to the eternal fire prepared for the devil and his angels." Then he repeats the two judgments with a conclusion, speaking first of the lost and then of the saved, "And they will go into eternal [*aionios*] punishment, and the virtuous to eternal [*aionios*] life" (Matthew 25:46). Since there is no question about the endless duration of heaven, the Church concludes the same about hell. The eternity of hell was defined by the Fourth Lateran Council in 1215.

ETERNITY. In its full sense, duration of being without beginning, succession, or ending. Only God possesses the fullness of eternity, since only he always existed (no beginning), has no succession (no change), and will never end (no cessation). It is defined Catholic doctrine that God possesses the divine Being in a constant undivided now. His eternity is the perfect and simultaneous total possession of interminable life.

Rational creatures share in God's eternity, but only approximate it, by participation. Angels have a beginning, and they have a succession of past, present, and future, but they have no cessation since they are pure spirits that will never die or cease to be. Human beings likewise have a beginning and they have succession, but unlike the angels they will die in body, to be later resurrected, while the souls live on forever. In God's absolute power, however, angels and human souls could be deprived of existence. Their eternity depends on the goodness and will of God.

ETHICS. The science of human conduct as known by natural reason. It is a normative science because it determines the principles of right and wrong in human behavior. It is also a practical science because it does not merely speculate about moral good and evil but also decides what is right or wrong in specific human actions.

Also called moral philosophy, the purpose of ethics is to study this fact of human experience, that people distinguish right from wrong and have an instinctive sense of what they should do. The subject matter of ethics, therefore, is human conduct; its point of view is that of rightness and wrongness.

Although related to other human and social sciences, ethics is different from them by its unique point of view, namely the word "ought." It is also different from moral theology by restricting itself to native reason as opposed to revealed religion.

Ethics is a science, not in the sense of the experimental sciences but as a philosophical science that assumes certain postulates from philosophy and from them derives practical conclusions. It borrows three main premises from natural philosophy: the existence of a personal God, the freedom of the human will, and the immortality of the soul. Implicit in these premises is the idea that a good moral action is done freely by humans, in conformity with the mind and will of God. It is good precisely because it leads a human to the goal or destiny set by God in a future immortality. Ethics comes from the Greek *ethos,* which denotes a fixed custom and is often used to mean a person's character.

EUCHARIST. The true body and blood of Jesus Christ, who is really and substantially present under the appearances of bread and wine, in order to offer himself in the sacrifice of the Mass and to be received as spiritual food in Holy Communion. It is called Eucharist, or "thanksgiving," because at its institution at the Last Supper Christ "gave thanks," and by this fact it is the supreme object and act of Christian gratitude to God.

Although the same name is used, the Eucharist is any one or all three aspects of one mystery, namely the Real Presence, the Sacrifice, and Communion. As Real Presence, the Eucharist is Christ in his abiding existence on earth today; as Sacrifice, it is Christ in his abiding action of High Priest, continuing now to communicate the graces he merited on Calvary; and as Communion, it is Christ coming to enlighten and strengthen the believer by nourishing his or her soul for eternal life. (Etym. Latin *eucharistia*, the virtue of thanksgiving or thankfulness; from Greek *eucharistia*, gratitude; from *eu-*, good + *charizesthai*, to show favor.) See also SACRAMENT OF THE ALTAR.

EUCHARISTIC CONGRESS. An international gathering of the faithful to foster devotion to the Blessed Sacrament of the Altar. The practice originated with a local gathering arranged through the efforts of Monsignor Gaston de Ségur, which met at Lille in France in 1881. In time the congresses developed to their present international character. The congress of 1908, which met in London, was the first occasion on which a papal legate had entered England since the Reformation. Two international Eucharistic congresses were held in the United States, the twenty-eighth at Chicago in 1926 and the forty-first at Philadelphia in 1976.

EUCHARISTIC ELEMENTS. The sensible matter of the Sacrament of the Eucharist, over which the words of consecration are pronounced. They are bread, freshly made of wheaten flour, and wine as the natural uncorrupted juice of the grape. In the Latin Rite the bread is unleavened (without yeast); in the Eastern rites it is leavened.

EUCHARISTIC FAST. The abstinence from food and drink for one hour before receiving Holy Communion. Originally this meant complete abstinence even from water and medicine from midnight. Only those receiving viaticum were dispensed from this law. Pope Pius XII in 1953 reduced the fast to complete abstinence from solid food but permission for liquids (except alcohol) up to one hour before Communion. Pope Paul VI in 1964 further reduced the precept to complete abstinence up to one full hour before actually receiving Communion, but allowing water and medicine to be taken anytime up to reception of the sacrament. In 1973 the Holy See further reduced the fast to fifteen minutes before Communion for the sick and advanced in age, and for those attending them if the hour's fast would be too difficult.

EUCHARISTIC MEAL. Holy Communion as food of the soul. Implied in Christ's words when he told his followers to eat his body and drink his blood, the Eucharist is the principal source of sustenance of the supernatural life. Like food in the natural order, Communion nourishes this divine life, produces a sense of well-being and satiety in the soul, and protects a person from the ravages of spiritual disease or sin.

EUCHARISTIC OBLATION. After the consecration at Mass, the prayer of the Church universal and especially the congregation assembled in which the immaculate Victim is offered to God the Father in the Holy Spirit. The oblation means that the faithful offer up not only Christ but themselves in union with him. He died on his Cross; they are to die to themselves on their cross and thus merit the graces that only sacrifice can merit before God.

EUCHARISTIC PRAYER. The central portion of the Eucharistic liturgy. There are eight parts to this prayer, namely the Preface, Acclamation, Epiclesis, Consecration, Anamnesis, Oblation, Intercessions, and Doxology. Its ritual history goes back to apostolic times.

EUGENICS. The science of hereditary and environmental influences in order to improve the physical and mental qualities of future generations. As a term, it was first used by Francis Galton (1822–1911), cousin of Charles Darwin (1809–82). There are, in general, two types of eugenics. An extreme form advocates the compulsory breeding of the select, contraception among the poor, and sterilization and euthanasia for the unfit. Moderate eugenics promotes the study of how to reduce the number of mentally and physically handicapped without resorting to coercive measures. The Catholic Church strongly supports the idea that people have a right to use suitable, licit means to improve their own physical and mental condition and that of their children. But the Church condemns eugenicists who, in their narrow outlook, exalt eugenics as the supreme good and who, therefore, use illicit means to promote their goal. Eugenics has contributed substantially to the practice of contraception, sterilization, abortion, and euthanasia. (Etym. Greek *eugenēs*, well-born.)

EUGENIC STERILIZATION. Depriving people of their generative powers in order to eliminate offspring having allegedly undesirable traits and to develop an environment more advantageous for human beings having allegedly desirable traits. The Catholic Church forbids the procedure because "public magistrates have no direct power over the bodies of their subjects. Therefore, where no crime has taken place and there is no cause for grave punishment, they can never directly harm or tamper with the integrity of the body, either for reasons of eugenics or for any other reason" (Pius XI *Casti Connubii*, II, 68–70).

EUTHANASIA. Literally "easy death," the act or practice of putting people to death because they or others decide that continued life would be burdensome. Originally the term was used for "mercy killing," which meant administration of an easy, painless death to one who was suffering from an incurable and perhaps agonizing disability or disease. Then, as mass genocide was legalized under Communism and Nazism, the term came to be applied to all forms of inflicting death on persons who are, by legal standards, permitted to take their own lives or others are allowed to do so with the full protection of the civil law.

The Holy See was asked, "Is it permissible upon the mandate of public authority, directly to kill those who, although they have committed no crime deserving of death, are yet, because of psychic or physical defects, unable to be useful to the nation, but rather are considered a burden to its vigor and strength?" The reply was no, and the reason given was that "it is contrary to the natural and the divine positive law" (Venerable Pius XII, *Decree of the Holy Office*, December 1940).

The *Catechism of the Catholic Church* reiterates the Church's traditional condemnation of euthanasia (2277, 2324).

The Catholic Church reprobates euthanasia because it is a usurpation of God's lordship over human life. As creatures of God, to whom human beings owe every element of their existence, humans are entrusted only with the stewardship of their earthly lives. They are bound to accept the life that God gave them, with its limitations and powers; to preserve this life as the first condition of their dependence on the Creator; and to not deliberately curtail their time of probation on earth, during which they are to work out and thereby merit the happiness of their final destiny.

EVANGELICAL OBEDIENCE. The voluntary submission of oneself to obey legitimate ecclesiastical authority beyond the demands of obedience prescribed on all the faithful. It is the free surrender of one's autonomy, according to the Church's directives, in order to better imitate Christ, and to cooperate with him in his work of redemption, who became obedient unto death, even to death on the Cross. This obedience of counsel may be given stability by a vow of obedience made to a superior in an institute of perfection or to one's confessor or spiritual director.

EVANGELIST. In general, a proclaimer of the Gospel. The New Testament uses the term to describe a traveling missionary (Acts 21:8; Ephesians 4:11; and II Timothy 4:5). As such, it denotes a function rather than an office. Since the third century an evangelist has come to mean principally one of the writers of the Gospels: Matthew, Mark, Luke, and John.

EVANGELIUM VITAE. Encyclical of Blessed Pope John Paul II on the intrinsic worth and inviolability of human life (March 25, 1995). The encyclical enumerates the many threats to the dignity of human life in the modern world, including abortion, euthanasia, and infanticide. The pope teaches that the Gospel of Life is at the heart of the message of Jesus Christ, and he calls for the faithful to promote a new culture of life to counteract the culture of death in modern society.

EVANGELIZATION. Zealous proclamation of the Gospel in order to bring others to Christ and his Church. In the words of Pope Paul VI, "Evangelizing means to bring the Good News into all the strata of humanity, and through its influence transforming humanity from within and making it new, 'Now I am making the whole of creation new' (Revelation 21:5). But there is no new humanity if there are not first of all new persons renewed by baptism, and by lives lived according to the Gospel" (*Evangelii Nuntiandi*, 18). Evangelization, therefore, includes three distinctive elements: 1. interior conversion to Christ and his Church; 2. affecting not only the individual person but the whole culture; and 3. as a result, changing this culture and its institutions to make them Christian and Catholic. (Etym. Latin *evangelium;* from Greek *euangelion,* good news, reward for bringing good news; from *euangelos,* bringing good news: *eu-,* good, + *angelos,* messenger.)

EVE. The first woman, wife of Adam and the mother of all the living (Genesis 3:20).

EVENING PRAYER. The fourth hour of the Divine Office, also called Vespers. It consists of a hymn, two Psalms, a New Testament canticle, a short biblical reading, the Magnificat of the Blessed Virgin, responsories, intercessions, and a concluding prayer.

EVIL. The privation of a good that should be present. It is the lack of a good that essentially belongs to a nature; the absence of a good that is natural and due to a being. Evil is therefore the absence of what ought to be there.

EVIL DESIRE. The wish or longing to do something forbidden. An absolute desire for what is sinful is a sin of the same moral species and gravity as the evil action desired, whether the desire is effective or not.

EVIL HABITS. Vices acquired through the repetition of bad moral actions. As a general rule, evil habits do not lessen the imputability of evil actions performed by force of habit if the habit has been recognized as evil and is freely allowed to continue. On the other hand, they do lessen the culpability of evil actions performed by force of habit if one is sincerely repentant and trying to correct the habit.

EVOLUTION. The theory that something was or is in a state of necessary development. Materialistic evolution assumes the eternal existence of uncreated matter and then explains the emergence of all living creatures—of plants, animals, and human beings, both body and soul—through a natural evolutionary process. This is contrary to Christian revelation. Theistic evolution is compatible with Christianity provided it postulates the special Divine Providence as regards the human body and the separate creation of each human soul.

EXAMEN, GENERAL. Prayerful daily periodic examination of one's conscience to determine what faults have been committed, which call for repentance, and what good actions were performed, for which God should be thanked.

EXAMEN, PARTICULAR. Regular prayerful examination of one's conscience by concentrating on some particular moral failing to be overcome or virtue to be exercised. Its focus is on such external manifestations of the fault or virtue as can be remembered for periodic inventory. Particular examens are changed weekly, monthly, or otherwise in order to ensure maximum attention. They are also commonly associated with some brief invocation for divine assistance, as occasions arise for avoiding a sin or acting on a virtue. And after some time another cycle may be started of the same defects that this person has to conquer or good habits he or she needs to develop.

EXAMINATION OF CONSCIENCE. Reflection in God's presence on one's state of soul, e.g., in preparation for the sacrament of penance. See EXAMEN, GENERAL, and EXAMEN, PARTICULAR.

EX CATHEDRA. The term commonly applied to the special and explicit exercise of papal infallibility. When the pope speaks from the chair (*cathedra*) of authority, as visible head of all Christians, his teaching is not dependent on the consent of the Church and is irreformable. (Etym. Latin *ex cathedra,* from the chair.)

EXCOMMUNICATION. An ecclesiastical censure by which one is more or less excluded from communion with the faithful. It is also called *anathema,* especially if it is inflicted with formal solemnities on persons notoriously obstinate to reconciliation. Two basic forms of excommunication are legislated by the Code of Canon Law, namely inflicted penalties (*ferendae sententiae*) and automatic penalties (*latae sententiae*). In the first type, a penalty does not bind until after it has been imposed on the guilty party. In the second type, the excommunication is incurred by the very commission of the offense, if the law or precept expressly determines this (Canon 1314). Most excommunications are of the second type. Among others identified by the Code are the following:

"An apostate from the faith, a heretic or a schismatic incurs automatic excommunication" (Canon 1364).

"A person who throws away the consecrated species or takes them or retains them for a sacrilegious purpose incurs an automatic excommunication reserved to the Apostolic See" (Canon 1367).

"A confessor who directly violates the seal of confession incurs
an automatic excommunication reserved to the Apostolic See"
(Canon 1388).

"A person who procures a successful abortion incurs an automatic
excommunication" (Canon 1398).

There are three principle effects of this penalty, so that "an excommunicated person is forbidden:

to have any ministerial participation in celebrating the Eucharistic
Sacrifice or in any other ceremonies whatsoever of public worship

to celebrate the sacraments and sacramentals and to receive the
sacraments

to discharge any ecclesiastical offices, ministries or functions
whatsoever, or to place acts of governance" (Canon 1331).

(Etym. Latin *ex-*, from + *communicare,* to communicate: *excommunicatio,* exclusion from a community.)

EXISTENTIALISM. In scholastic philosophy the philosophical emphasis on existence and concrete individuals rather than on essences or abstract concepts. Accordingly, it stresses the real over the speculative, the actual over the theoretical, the particular over the general, and the human over the cosmic. It uses history as an instrument of thought and concentrates on the free actions of persons over the broad expanse of ideas or movements that shape human culture and determine human life and destiny.

EXODUS. The second book of the Bible, so named because it relates the departure of the Israelites from Egypt and their wandering through the desert up to Mount Sinai. There are five principal parts to the book: events in Egypt before the exodus (1–12), leaving Egypt and the journey to Mount Sinai (13–18), promulgation of the first precepts of the Mosaic Law (19–31), apostasy of the Jews, reconciliation and renewal of the Covenant (32–34), construction of the Tabernacle (35–40).

EX OPERE OPERANTIS. A term mainly applied to the good dispositions with which a sacrament is received, to distinguish it from the *ex opere operato,* which is the built-in efficacy of a sacrament properly conferred. But it may refer to any subjective factor that at least partially determines the amount of grace obtained by a person who performs some act of piety. Thus in the use of sacramentals or in the gaining of indulgences, the blessings received depend largely on the faith and love of God with which a sacramental is employed or an indulgenced prayer or good work is performed.

EX OPERE OPERATO. A term defined by the Council of Trent to describe how the sacraments confer the grace they signify. Trent condemned the following proposition: "That grace is not conferred 'ex opere operato' by the sacraments of the New Law" (Denzinger 1608). Literally the expression means "from the work performed," stating that grace is always conferred by a sacrament, in virtue of the rite performed and not as a mere sign that grace has already been given, or that the sacrament stimulates the faith of the recipient and thus occasions the obtaining of grace, or that what determines the grace is the virtue of either the minister or recipient of a sacrament. Provided no obstacle (*obex*) is placed in the way, every sacrament properly administered confers the grace intended by the sacrament. In a true sense the sacraments are instrumental causes of grace.

EXORCISM. An adjuration in which the devil is either commanded to depart from a possessed person or forbidden to harm someone. Although commonly referred to as driving the evil spirit from a possessed person, exorcism is essentially the same when used in the case of obsession.

The Gospels are filled with descriptive narratives about exorcisms performed by Christ. St. Mark's Gospel is especially detailed in the number of exorcisms performed by the Master, and the effortless ease with which he delivered those who were under the influence of the evil one. In the account of these exorcisms, the contemporary idiom is unreservedly adopted: the evil spirits cry out in words found in contemporary stories where a devil about to be exorcised acknowledges the power of the exorcist: "I know you. You are . . ." Hence it is noteworthy that Jesus uses none of the contemporary exorcists' rituals and spells, but simply expels them by the power of his command. The deeper significance of these narratives is that Jesus inaugurates the final struggle against all evil and, with emphasis, against the evil spirit, and foreshadows the final victory. Significant, too, are the peace (Mark 4:39, 5:15, 6:51) and awareness of the divine presence (Mark 1:27, 2:12, 5:15) that follow Christ's expulsion of demons. (Etym. Latin *exorcismus;* from Greek *exorkizein,* to drive away by adjuration.) See also RITE OF EXORCISM.

EXPIATION. Atonement for some wrongdoing. It implies an attempt to undo the wrong that one has done, by suffering a penalty, by performing some penance, or by making reparation or redress. (Etym. Latin *ex-*, fully + *piare*, to propitiate: *expiare*, to atone for fully.)

EXPOSITION OF THE BLESSED SACRAMENT. The ceremony in which a priest or deacon removes the Sacred Host from the tabernacle and places it on the altar for adoration. In public exposition the Sacred Host is placed in the lunette of the monstrance and elevated so that all adorers can see it. In private expositions the tabernacle door is opened and the ciborium containing consecrated Hosts is brought forward. Any good cause is reason for private adoration. Public exposition of the Blessed Sacrament requires a period of adoration, in private or public with prescribed hymns and prayers, as well as the blessing with the monstrance. Definite days for public adoration of the Blessed Sacrament are no longer specified for the universal Church; now any days may be chosen for good reasons, and for regular exposition permissions are granted by the local ordinary. The ceremony was introduced in the fourteenth century under the influence of the newly established feast of Corpus Christi. Some religious monasteries and convents with special permission have the Sacred Host perpetually exposed for special honor and devotion with someone in attendance night and day.

EXTERNAL GRACES. Those providential means that God uses as occasions for conferring interior actual graces. External graces are all creatures that are divinely intended to lead us to our eternal destiny. They are any person, place, or thing that can help us attain the end for which we were created.

EXTRAORDINARY MEANS. Such means of preserving human life as cannot be obtained or used without extreme difficulty in terms of pain, expense, or other burdening factors. The burden applies either to the person whose life is at stake or to those on whom his or her welfare depends. In addition, means should be considered extraordinary if, when used, they do not offer a reasonable hope of benefit to the one for whom they are intended.

There is no general obligation to use extraordinary means to keep a person alive, on the premise that God does not exact what is beyond the ordinary power of humans in general. At times, however, one may be bound to employ extraordinary means to preserve life. The two conditions under which such an obligation becomes binding are that a person is necessary to one's family, to the Church, or to society, and the success of the extraordinary means is very probable.

EXTRAORDINARY MINISTER. The person who, in cases of necessity, is permitted or specially delegated to administer one of the sacraments. Baptism, confirmation, and the Eucharist may have extraordinary ministers. Thus baptism is to be ordinarily administered by a priest or deacon, but in emergency any person who has reached the age of reason may validly confer the sacrament. The ordinary minister of confirmation is a bishop, but for special pastoral reasons simple priests may confirm. When they do, their power derives from the papal authorization, which the Holy See actuates in them in virtue of their priestly ordination; it is not a mere extrasacramental delegation. And the ordinary minister of Communion is a priest or deacon, but in cases of real necessity, which have been broadly interpreted since the Second Vatican Council, laypersons and religions may be authorized by a bishop to distribute the Holy Eucharist.

EXTRAVERSION. A personality trait, with moral implications, characterized by outward activity, preoccupation with people and events, and the tendency to avoid thoughtful reflection or prayer.

EXTREME NECESSITY. A very urgent need that a person has for such human goods as food or medical care in order to sustain life or even a minimum of human living. It is extreme poverty or destitution, indicating the want of basic human needs.

EXTREME UNCTION. A term used for centuries for the sacrament of the anointing of the sick. It is unction because a person is anointed with oil; it is extreme because it is conferred on those who are considered *in extremis,* i.e., in extreme physical disability with the likelihood of dying.

EZEKIEL. A prophet of the sixth century B.C. He grew up in Jerusalem and was a contemporary of Jeremiah. He was primarily a preacher profoundly concerned for the spiritual improvement of his people. He disdained the concept of the Messiah as a glorious, militant king; rather he stressed the image of the less dramatic shepherd. Some of his major themes were reproaches addressed to unfaithful Israelites;

"The guilt of the House of Israel and Judah is immense, boundless; the country is full of bloodshed, the city overflows with wickedness" (Ezekiel 9:9); occasional denunciations of foreign nations exerting evil influence on his people, and prophetic anticipation of better days ahead for Israel (Ezekiel 25, 29, 30). "Then they shall be my people and I will be their God" (Ezekiel 11:21). His book concluded on the prophetic note: "The name of the city in future is to be: YHWH-is-there" (Ezekiel 48:35). The Book of Ezekiel is quoted extensively by St. John in the Apocalypse; in fact there are many points of similarity between the writings of the prophet and of the Apostle.

EZRA. A Jewish priest during the reign of the Persian king Artaxerxes (404–358 B.C.). His chief contribution was instituting reforms in the Jewish church and state. In Greek and Latin the name is Esdras. Thanks to the generous policy of the king, Ezra was able to organize a pilgrimage of fifteen hundred families in Babylon to cross the desert to Jerusalem (Ezra 7). He was shocked on arriving to become aware of the great number of Israelites married to foreign women, a practice he described as "treachery" (Ezra 9:2). His denunciation led to the dissolution of many such marriages and considerable unhappiness among the people (Ezra 10). Aiding Ezra in his work was the layman Nehemiah. In fact the biblical report of their ministry carries the joint title "The Book of Ezra and Nehemiah." In the Vulgate, I Esdras is Ezra; II Esdras is Nehemiah. Much of Ezra's accomplishment could be called administrative. He reformed the ecclesiastical ritual, organization of the synagogue improved, and the rise of the rabbinate and eventually the development of the Sanhedrin were tributes to his ability.

F

FACULTIES. Rights granted by the Holy See to bishops and by ordinaries to their priests to enable the latter to exercise their respective powers for the faithful under their jurisdiction. The term is most commonly used in relation to the sacrament of penance, where faculties are needed for the priest to absolve not only licitly but even validly. However, faculties for licit administration are required for all the sacraments, with varying degrees of obligation. On a wider scale, faculties are also required for the exercise of ecclesiastical authority or, in general, for performance of any act of jurisdiction in the Catholic Church. In every case it is assumed that the one giving the faculties has the right to do so and the one receiving them has the power to put them into practice.

FAITH. The acceptance of the word of another, trusting that one knows what the other is saying and is honest in telling the truth. The basic motive of all faith is the authority (or right to be believed) of someone who is speaking. This authority is an adequate knowledge of what he or she is talking about, and integrity in not wanting to deceive. It is called divine faith when the one believed is God and human faith when the persons believed are human beings. (Etym. Latin *fides,* belief; habit of faith; object of faith.)

FAITH, ACT OF. The assent of the mind to what God has revealed. An act of supernatural faith requires divine grace, either actual or sanctifying or both. It is performed under the influence of the will, which requires its own assistance of grace to render a person ready to believe. And if the act of faith is made in the state of grace, it is meritorious before God. Explicit acts of faith are necessary, notably when the virtue of faith is being tested by temptation or one's faith is challenged, or one's belief would be weakened unless strengthened by acts of faith. A simple and widely used act of faith says: "My God, I believe in you and all that your Church teaches, because you have said it, and your word is true. Amen."

FAITH AND REASON. The relationship between human response to God's revelation and use of human native intelligence. This relationship is mainly of three kinds, where the role of reason is to assist divine faith: 1. reason can establish the rational grounds for belief by proving God's existence, his authority or credibility as all-wise and trustworthy, and by proving that God actually made a revelation since he confirmed the fact by working (even now) miracles that testify to God's having spoken to human beings, especially in the person of Jesus Christ; 2. reason can further reflect on what God has revealed and thus come to an even deeper and clearer understanding of the divine mysteries; and 3. reason can both show that the mysteries of faith are in harmony with naturally known truths and can defend their validity against the charge of being contrary to reason.

FAITHFUL, THE. Believing Christians. They are faithful twice over: first by their assent to God's revelation and again by their living up to what they profess.

FAITH HEALER. A person who claims to have extraordinary powers of healing sickness or disability. The healing is effected by the laying on of hands, quoting passages from the Bible, or calling upon God to perform the healing and generally doing so in an atmosphere charged with strong religious feeling.

Most instances of reported faith healing are cases of healing by suggestion. Because of the close relationship between mind and body, hope and courage tend to maintain and restore health, while fear and depression produce an injurious effect on the body. Strong suggestions received from one in whom a person has confidence may be beneficial to health. This is particularly true if the ailment is mainly functional or psychosomatic, or a vivid imagination has made it worse.

Although faith healing by suggestion is not sinful—provided neither superstition, scandal, nor cooperation in fraud is involved, and in serious illness there is recourse to medical help—faith healers who claim to have a divine gift and encourage people to come to them to be cured are traditionally suspect by Catholic standards. Saints are careful not to publicize their sanctity or possible gift of miraculous healing power.

FAITH, VIRTUE OF. The infused theological virtue whereby a person is enabled to "believe that what God has revealed is true—not because its intrinsic truth is seen with the rational light of reason—but because of the authority of God who reveals it, of God who can neither deceive nor be deceived" (First Vatican Council, Denzinger 3008).

FALL. The original sin of Adam and Eve by which they lost the divine friendship and preternatural gifts for themselves and all their human progeny.

FALLEN NATURE. Human nature since the fall of Adam. It is a nature that lacks the right balance it had originally. It is a wounded but not perverted nature. Since the fall, man has a built-in bias away from what is morally good and toward what is wrong. He is weakened in his ability to know the truth and to want the truly good. With the help of grace, however, he can overcome these natural tendencies and become sanctified in the process.

FALL OF ADAM. First sin of the father of the human race. As a result, he lost for himself and his posterity the supernatural gift of sanctifying grace and the preternatural gifts of integrity, bodily immortality, and impassibility. The fall is commonly referred only to Adam because he was appointed the juridical head of the human race, and his guilt was passed on to his progeny. However, Eve also shared in the fall of the human race because she tempted Adam after she yielded to the temptation of the devil. Adam and Eve, although specially gifted by grace, remained free to choose moral evil. They did not yet enjoy the beatific vision of God and consequently had only faith to tell them that what God forbade was truly wrong and what God threatened would really take place. It is uncertain what sin they committed. Most probably it was the disobedience of pride. They yielded to the devil's suggestion that they would become like God.

FALSE CONSCIENCE. The judgment of the mind when it wrongly decides that something is lawful that in fact is unlawful, or vice versa. The error may be due to the false principles used or because the mind was darkened or confused in its reasoning process.

FAMILY. A group of persons who are related by marriage or blood and who typically include a father, mother, and children. A family is a natural society whose right to existence and support is provided by the divine law. According to the Second Vatican Council, "the family is the foundation of society" (*The Church in the Modern World*, II, 52). In addition to the natural family, the Church recognizes also the supernatural family of the diocese and of a religious community, whose members are to cooperate for the upbuilding of the Body of Christ (*Decree on the Bishops' Pastoral Office*, 34; and Dogmatic Constitution on the Church, 43). (Etym. Latin *familia,* a family, the members of a household; from *famulus,* a servant, attendant.)

FAMILY ROSARY. International movement promoting recitation of the Rosary by the members of a family at home. Encouraged by the popes, the practice was singled out for special recommendation by Venerable Pope Paul VI in his apostolic exhortation in 1974 on de- votion to the Blessed Virgin. "There is no doubt," he declared, "that after the celebration of the Liturgy of the Hours, the high point which family prayer can reach, the Rosary, should be considered as one of the best and most efficacious prayers in common that the Christian family is invited to recite" (*Marialis Cultus,* 54).

FASTING. A form of penance that imposes limits on the kind or quan- tity of food or drink. From the first century Christians have observed fasting days of precept, notably during the season of Lent in com- memoration of Christ's Passion and death. In the early Church there was less formal precept and therefore greater variety of custom, but in general fasting was much more severe than in the modern Church. In the East and West the faithful abstained on fasting days from wine as well as from flesh-meat, both being permitted only in cases of weak health. The ancient custom in the Latin Church of celebrating Mass in the evening during Lent was partly due to the fact that in many places the first meal was not taken before sunset.

The modern Church regulations on fasting, until 1966, prescribed taking only one full meal a day, along with some food for breakfast and a collation. Days of fast and abstinence for the universal Church were Ash Wednesday, the Fridays and Saturdays of Lent, Ember days, and the vigils of certain feasts. Days of fast only were the rest of the days of Lent, except Sundays. Special indults affected different na- tions and were provided for by canon law.

With the constitution *Paenitemini* of Venerable Paul VI in 1966, the meaning of the law of fasting remained, but the extent of the ob- ligation was changed. Thus "the law of fasting allows only one full meal a day, but does not prohibit taking some food in the morning and evening, while observing approved local custom as far as quan- tity and quality of food are concerned." To the law of fast are bound those of the faithful who have completed their twenty-first year and up until the beginning of their sixtieth year. Prescribed days of fast and abstinence for the whole Church are Ash Wednesday and Good Friday. Nevertheless, as with abstinence, so with fasting or other forms of penance, "It is up to the bishops, gathered in their episcopal conferences, to establish the norms . . . which they consider the most opportune and efficacious" (*Paenitemini*, III). In the Eastern rites it is the right of the patriarch, together with the synod or supreme authority of every rite, to determine the days of fast and abstinence in accordance with the decree of the Second Vatican Council for Eastern Churches.

FATHER. Theologically, a father is the principal one who produces of his own substance another person like himself. There is, consequently, a Father within the Trinity, who begets God the Son. But the triune God is himself spoken of as Father, with respect to the rational beings whom he made to share in his own possession of knowledge and love. Among human beings a father is the male parent of his own children and, ultimately, the ancestor of all his progeny. In Church usage the term is applied to the early spokesmen and defenders of Christianity, bishops who attend regional and especially ecumenical councils, and priests in general or specific priests in their role as confessors or spiritual counselors of the faithful.

FATHERS OF THE CHURCH. Saintly writers of the early centuries whom the Church recognizes as her special witnesses of the faith. Antiquity, orthodoxy, sanctity, and approval by the Church are their four main prerogatives. They are commonly divided into the Greek and Latin Fathers. It is now generally held that the last of the Western Fathers (Latin) was St. Isidore of Seville (560–636), and the last of the Eastern Fathers (Greek) was St. John Damascene (675–749).

Latin Fathers of the Church

St. Ambrose, Bishop of Milan (340–97)
Arnobius, apologist (d. 327)
St. Augustine, Bishop of Hippo (354–430)
St. Benedict, father of Western monasticism (480–546)
St. Caesarius, Archbishop of Arles (470–542)
St. John Cassian, abbot, ascetical writer (360–435)
St. Celestine I, Pope (d. 432)
St. Cornelius, Pope (d. 253)
St. Cyprian, Bishop of Carthage (d. 258)
St. Damasus I, Pope (d. 384)
St. Dionysius, Pope (d. 268)
St. Ennodius, Bishop of Pavia (473–521)

St. Eucherius, Bishop of Lyons (d. 449)

St. Fulgentius, Bishop of Ruspe (468–533)

St. Gregory of Elvira (died after 392)

St. Gregory (I) the Great, Pope (540–604)

St. Hilary, Bishop of Poitiers (315–68)

St. Innocent I, Pope (d. 417)

St. Irenaeus, Bishop of Lyons (130–200)

St. Isidore, Archbishop of Seville (560–636)

St. Jerome, priest exegete, translator of the Vulgate (343–420)

Lactantius Firmianus, apologist (240–320)

St. Leo the Great Pope (390–461)

Marius Mercator, Latin polemicist (early fifth century)

Marius Victorinus, Roman rhetorician (fourth century)

Minucius Felix, apologist (second or third century)

Novatian, the Schismatic (200–62)

St. Optatus, Bishop of Mileve (late fourth century)

St. Pacian, Bishop of Barcelona (fourth century)

St. Pamphilus, priest (240–309)

St. Paulinus, Bishop of Nola (353–431)

St. Peter Chrysologus, Archbishop of Ravenna (400–50)

St. Phoebadius, Bishop of Agen (d. 395)

St. Prosper of Aquitaine, theologian (390–463)

Rufinus, Latin translator of Greek theology (345–410)

Salvian, priest (400–80)

St. Siricius, Pope (334–99)

Tertullian, apologist founder of Latin theology (160–223)

St. Vincent of Lérins, priest and monk (d. 450)

Greek Fathers of the Church

St. Anastasius Sinaita, apologist monk (d. 700)

St. Andrew of Crete, Archbishop of Gortyna (660–740)

Aphraates, Syriac monk (early fourth century)

St. Archelaus, Bishop of Cascar (d. 282)

St. Athanasius, Archbishop of Alexandria (c. 297–373)

Athenagoras, apologist (second century)

St. Basil the Great, Archbishop of Caesarea (329–79)

St. Caesarius of Nazianzus (330–69)

St. Clement of Alexandria, theologian (150–215)

St. Clement I of Rome, Pope (30–101)

St. Cyril, Bishop of Jerusalem (315–86)

St. Cyril, Patriarch of Alexandria (376–444)

Didymus the Blind, theologian (313–98)

Diodore, Bishop of Tarsus (d. 392)

St. Dionysius the Great, Archbishop of Alexandria (190–264)

Dionysius the Pseudo-Areopagite, mystical theologian (late fifth century)

St. Epiphanius, Bishop of Salamis (315–403)

Eusebius, Bishop of Caesarea (260–340)

St. Eustathius, Bishop of Antioch (fourth century)

St. Firmillian, Bishop of Caesarea (d. 268)

Gennadius I, Patriarch of Constantinople (d. 471)

St. Germanus, Patriarch of Constantinople (634–733)

St. Gregory of Nazianzus, Bishop of Sasima (329–90)

St. Gregory of Nyssa (330–95)

St. Gregory Thaumaturgus, Bishop of Neocaesarea (213–70)

Hermas, author of *The Shepherd* (second century)

St. Hippolytus, martyr (170–236)

St. Ignatius, Bishop of Antioch (35–107)

St. Isidore of Pelusium, abbot (360–c. 450)

St. John Chrysostom, Patriarch of Constantinople (347–407)

St. John Climacus, monk (579–649)

St. John Damascene, defender of sacred images (675–749)

St. Julius I, Pope (d. 352)

St. Justin Martyr, apologist (100–65)

St. Leontius of Byzantium, theologian (sixth century)

St. Macarius the Great, monk (300–90)

St. Maximus, abbot and confessor (580–662)

St. Melito, Bishop of Sardis (d. 190)

St. Methodius, Bishop of Olympus (d. 311)

St. Nilus the Elder, priest and monk (d. 430)

Origen, head of the Catechetical School of Alexandria (184–254)

St. Polycarp, Bishop of Smyrna (69–155)

St. Proclus, Patriarch of Constantinople (d. 446)

St. Serapion, Bishop of Thmuis (died after 362)

St. Sophronius, Patriarch of Jerusalem (560–638)

Tatian the Assyrian, apologist and theologian (120–80)

Theodore, Bishop of Mopsuestia (350–428)

Theodoret, Bishop of Cyrrhus (393–458)

St. Theophilus, Bishop of Antioch (late second century)

FÁTIMA, OUR LADY OF THE ROSARY OF. Shrine of the Blessed Virgin Mary in the mountain region of central Portugal near Cova da Iria. It was the scene of six apparitions of Our Lady, from May 13 to October 13, 1917, to three peasant children, Lucia Santos, Jacinta Marto, and her brother Francisco. During the apparitions Mary told the children to have processions in honor of her Immaculate Conception and to tell the faithful to do penance and pray the Rosary because otherwise the world would be chastised for its sins. During the October apparition seventy thousand people witnessed a spectacular solar phenomenon. In 1930 the bishops of Portugal declared the apparitions to be authentic, and in 1942 Venerable Pope Pius XII, in response to Mary's request, consecrated the world to the Immaculate Heart of Mary. In 1967 Venerable Pope Paul VI personally visited and worshipped at the shrine on the fiftieth anniversary of the apparitions. Blessed Pope John Paul II made a pilgrimage to the shrine in May 1987. Pope Benedict XVI also visited the shrine on May 12 and 13, 2010.

FEAST. Days set apart by the Church for giving special honor to God, the Savior, angels, saints, and sacred mysteries and events. Some are fixed festivals, such as Christmas and the Immaculate Conception; others are movable, occurring earlier or later in different years. Festivals are now divided, excepting those who follow the 1962 liturgical books, into solemnity (*solemnitas*), feast (*festum*), and memorial (*memoria*) in descending order of dignity. Memorials are further classified as prescribed or optional. Below these are ferial, or week, days with no special ritual rank. And in a class by themselves are the Sundays of the year, and the various liturgical seasons, such as Advent and Lent. All of these represent what is called "sacred times," whose religious purpose is to keep the faithful mindful throughout the year of the cardinal mysteries and persons of Christianity.

FETICIDE. The direct killing of an unborn child. It is always murder and therefore gravely sinful. (Etym. Latin *fetus,* the young in the womb + -*cidium,* a killing.)

FIDEISM. A term applied to various theories that claim that faith is the only or ultimate source of all knowledge of God and spiritual things. The name was originally coined by followers of Kant (1724–1804) and Schleiermacher (1768–1834), both of whom denied the capacity of reason to know God or the moral law with certainty. (Etym. Latin *fides,* belief; habit of faith; object of faith.)

FIFTEEN MARKS OF THE CHURCH. The fifteen features of the true Church developed by St. Robert Bellarmine (1542–1621), cardinal,

Archbishop of Capua, and Doctor of the Church. As a contemporary of the original Protestant Reformers, he expanded the traditional four marks to fifteen, as follows: 1. the Church's *name,* Catholic, universal, and worldwide, and not confined to any particular nation or people; 2. *antiquity* in tracing her ancestry directly to Jesus Christ; 3. constant *duration* in lasting substantially unchanged for so many centuries; 4. *extensiveness* in the number of her loyal members; 5. *episcopal succession* of her bishops from the first Apostles at the Last Supper to the present hierarchy; 6. *doctrinal agreement* of her doctrine with the teaching of the ancient Church; 7. *union* of her members among themselves and with their visible head the Roman Pontiff; 8. *holiness* of doctrine in reflecting the sanctity of God; 9. *efficacy* of doctrine in its power to sanctify believers and inspire them to great moral achievement; 10. *holiness of life* of the Church's representative writers and defenders; 11. the glory of *miracles* worked in the Church and under the Church's auspices; 12. the gift of *prophecy* found among the Church's saints and spokesmen; 13. the *opposition* that the Church arouses among those who attack her on the very grounds that Christ was opposed by his enemies; 14. the *unhappy end* of those who fight against her; and 15. the *temporal peace and earthly happiness* of those who live by the Church's teaching and defend her interests.

FILIAL FEAR. Fear of some impending evil based on love and reverence for the one who is feared. Actually filial fear is closer to love that dreads offending the one loved. Thus the filial fear of God is compatible with the highest love of God. A person, knowing his or her moral weakness, fears that he or she might displease or betray the one who is loved. It is selfless fear. (Etym. Latin *filius,* "son," and *filia,* "daughter.") See also SERVILE FEAR.

FILIOQUE. A term meaning "and from the Son," which over the centuries became the center of controversy between the Eastern Churches separated from Rome and the Catholic Church. The Eastern Christians first objected to the insertion of this phrase in the Nicene Creed, which now states that the Holy Spirit "proceeds from the Father *and the Son.*" The last three words had not been in the original creed but were added later, with the approval of Rome. After the ninth century the Eastern leaders challenged not only the addition but the doctrine itself, whether the Holy Spirit proceeded not only from the Father but also from the Son. In recent years the issue has become more historical than doctrinal, since those who believe in Christ's divinity, whether Eastern or Western Christians, all accept the fact that the Third Person proceeds from the Second as well as the First Person of the Trinity. Given this common faith, the verbal expression has become secondary.

FINAL CONSUMMATION. The end of the present world and its renewal as the final conclusion of the work of Christ. As all enemies of the kingdom of God are conquered, he will surrender the overlordship to God the Father (I Corinthians 15:24), but without losing his own dominion founded on the hypostatic union. With the end of the world there begins the perfect sovereignty of the Holy Trinity, which is the object of the whole creation and the final meaning of all human history.

FINAL PERSEVERANCE. Man's steadfastness in good up to the moment of death. It is the work of actual grace. Although man himself cannot merit the gift of final perseverance, he can, by earnest prayer and faithful cooperation with the manifold graces given him during life, secure from God's mercy this most important grace on which eternal happiness depends.

FIRE OF HELL. The physical reality, outside the person, by which those in hell are punished besides their loss of the vision of God. It is called fire in the Scriptures to emphasize the excruciating pain it causes and to identify it as some external agent tormenting the lost. But it is not ordinary fire, since it does not consume what it burns, and although material, it can affect the purely spiritual substance of the soul.

FIRE OF PURGATORY. The external source of suffering in purgatory besides the temporary deprivation of the vision of God. Although many sacred writers, interpreting St. Paul (I Corinthians 3:15), assume a physical fire, the Church's official teaching speaks only of "purifying punishments" and not of purifying fire (Denzinger 1304).

FIRST CAUSE. God as the first cause of all things, because he is the first in the series of all other causes. Also, God as immediately operating in all finite causality, as the underlying cause on which all other causes constantly depend for their activity.

FIRST COMMUNION. The precept of the Church that requires children to receive Holy Communion, along with the sacrament of penance, on reaching the age of reason. First issued by the Fourth Lateran Council (1215), the practice was all but discontinued for centuries, due to the inroads of Jansenism. Pope St. Pius X restored the practice and restated the precept, while he also explained how necessarily related are the two sacraments of penance and the Eucharist. "The age of discretion," he said, "both for confession and for Holy Communion is the time when a child begins to reason." This means that "a full and perfect knowledge of Christian doctrine is not necessary either for first confession or first Communion." Moreover, "the obligation of the precept of confession and Communion which binds the child particularly affects those who have charge of him, namely, parents, confessor, teachers, and the pastor" (*Quam Singulari*, August 8, 1910).

FIRST CONFESSION. The precept of the Church to receive the sacrament of penance on reaching the age of reason. First decreed by the Fourth Lateran Council in 1215, the law was confirmed by the Council of Trent, which condemned anyone who "denies that each and every one of Christ's faithful of both sexes is bound to confess once a year" (Denzinger 1708). The prescription was repeated and clarified by Pope St. Pius X in 1910 and again restated by the Holy See in 1973, ordering an end to experiments that postponed the sacrament of penance until after First Communion: "This precept, accepted into practice throughout the universal Church, brought and continues to bring much fruit for the Christian life and perfection of the spirit."

FIRST FRIDAYS. The customary observance of the first Friday of each month, encouraged by the Church, based on a promise made to St. Margaret Mary Alacoque (1647–90), that special favors, such as the grace of final perseverance, would be given to those who received Holy Communion on nine successive first Fridays.

FIRST PARENTS. Adam and Eve as the original ancestors of the human race (Second Vatican Council, Dogmatic Constitution on the Church, 2, 56).

FIRST SATURDAYS. Devotion to the Immaculate Heart of Mary on the first Saturdays of five successive months, as part of the revelations of the Blessed Virgin at Fátima, Portugal (1917). The faithful are to attend mass on each of the five successive first Saturdays, go to confession, receive Holy Communion, recite five decades of the Rosary, and meditate on the mysteries of the Rosary for at least fifteen minutes. Our Lady promised the grace of final perseverance to those who would do so in reparation for sin.

FISH. Symbol of Christ, seen before the fifth century. The Greek word for fish is *ichthus,* consisting also of the initial letters of Iesous, CHristos, THeou, Uios, Soter—Jesus Christ, Son of God, Savior. The fish is also emblematic of the fishermen Apostles—Andrew, Peter, and the sons of Zebedee—whom Christ would make "fishers of men" (Mark 1:17). The archangel Raphael is often represented with a fish brought back to cure the aged Tobit of his blindness.

FIVE WOUNDS. Devotion to the Passion of Christ by concentrating on the wounds he suffered in his hands and feet and pierced side. A favorite devotion with many great saints, a Feast of the Five Wounds is celebrated in some countries on the fourth Friday of Lent. It also finds expression in the Anima Christi, with the invocation to Christ "Within your wounds hide me."

FORBIDDEN BOOKS. Written material that Catholics are forbidden to read, except for grave reasons, because it is contrary to Christian faith or morals. Lists of forbidden books date from the earliest centuries; for example, Pope Innocent, in 417, forbade the faithful to read the apocryphal Scriptures. The first extensive list, called the *Index Librorum Prohibitorum* (List of Prohibited Books), was issued by the Congregation of the Inquisition under Pope Paul IV in 1557. In 1571 Pope St. Pius V established a special Congregation of the Index, which survived until 1917, when Pope Benedict XV transferred its responsibilities to the Holy Office. When the Code of Canon Law was published in 1918, twenty-one separate laws (1395–1405) dealt with the matter of forbidden books, and severe ecclesiastical penalties were imposed for disobedience. In 1966 the Congregation for the Doctrine of the Faith declared that the Index and its corresponding penalties were no longer binding in law. However, no basic change was made in the Church's attitude toward reading literature contrary to revealed truth. Catholics are still obliged to refrain from reading whatever would be a proximate danger to their faith and Christian virtue.

FORGIVENESS. Pardon or remission of an offense. The Catholic Church believes that sins forgiven are actually removed from the soul (John 20) and not merely covered over by the merits of Christ. Only God can forgive sins, since he alone can restore sanctifying grace to a person who has sinned gravely and thereby lost the state of grace. God forgives sins to the truly repentant either immediately through an act of perfect contrition or mediately through a sacrament. The sacraments primarily directed to the forgiveness of sins are baptism and penance, and secondarily, under certain conditions, also the sacrament of anointing.

FORMAL COOPERATION. The deliberate concurrence in another person's usually sinful action. The cooperation is formal and always sinful if, besides giving external help of whatever kind, one interiorly wants the evil action to be performed. Formal cooperation is at least a sin against charity by doing spiritual harm to one's neighbor; frequently it is also a sin against another virtue, especially justice.

FORNICATION. An act of sexual intercourse between a man and a woman who are not validly married, although they are free to marry. It is by its nature gravely sinful. (Etym. Latin *fornicatio,* fornication; from *fornix,* a vault, arch, brothel.)

FORTITUDE. Firmness of spirit. As a virtue, it is a steadiness of will in doing good in spite of difficulties faced in the performance of one's duty.

There are two levels to the practice of fortitude: one is the suppression of inordinate fear and the other is the curbing of recklessness. The control of fear is the main role of fortitude. Hence the primary effect of fortitude is to keep unreasonable fears under control and not allow them to prevent one from doing what one's mind says should be done. But fortitude or courage also moderates rashness, which tends to lead the headstrong to excess in the face of difficulties and dangers. It is the special virtue of pioneers in any endeavor.

As a human virtue, fortitude is essentially different from what has come to be called animal courage. Animals attack either from pain, as when they are wounded, or from fear of pain, as when they go after humans because they are angered, whom they would leave alone if they were unmolested. They are not virtuously brave, for they face danger from pain or rage or some other sense instinct, not from choice, as do those who act with foresight. True courage is from deliberate choice, not mere emotion. (Etym. Latin *fortitudo,* strength; firmness of soul; courage of soul.)

FORTUNE-TELLING. The art of manifesting to another the fortune (luck), good or bad, that the future has in store for him or her. The real objective in fortune-telling is the disclosure of future events. Quite often, though, to inspire confidence, the fortune-teller will communicate bits of information about a person's past that would be naturally unknown to anyone else. As a presumed help in peering into the world of secret events they employ, for example, tea leaves, a crystal sphere, or a small pool of blood.

The Church considers it gravely wrong to consult a fortune-teller who is known to seriously claim access to the knowledge of future events. It would be a sin of formal cooperation. It is likewise wrong to consult a person who may not actually make such claims but whom the client believes to be a fortune-teller with powers of divination. The gravity of the sin would depend on how seriously one takes the fortune-teller. If neither party takes the thing seriously and someone has a fortune told as a pastime, there is no sin. But even in this case the danger is that if what was predicted actually takes place, one's faith in fortune-telling is (or may be) aroused, and there is danger that what began as amusement may become a temptation to learn about the future through forbidden means.

FORTY HOURS DEVOTION. The solemn exposition of the Blessed Sacrament during forty hours, in honor of the forty hours the body of Christ is believed to have rested in the tomb. The devotion was introduced by St. Anthony Mary Zaccaria in Milan and Vicenza in 1527, and propagated by the Jesuits under St. Ignatius. It was approved by Pope Paul III in 1539. Pope Clement VIII's constitution *Graves et diuturnae* in 1592 and the *Clementine Instructions* of Pope Clement XI in 1705 (later republished by Pope Clement XII in 1731) established the correct form of the devotion. By the end of the eighteenth century, the custom had spread to many countries. St. John Neumann of Philadelphia (1811–60) was the first to hold the devotion in America with any degree of regularity. Where it is more feasible, the forty hours are interrupted during the night and the devotion extends over three days.

FRANCISCANS. The numerous family of men and women religious who trace their spiritual ancestry to St. Francis of Assisi (1181–1226).

The Original Rule written by St. Francis in 1209 is now lost. It was recast in 1221 and brought into final form two years later, when it was approved by Pope Honorius III. Its distinctive feature is the obligation of poverty of dispossession, not only for individual members but for each community. The friars (from *frères,* brothers) were to own no property and were to earn their livelihood by manual labor or begging.

This ideal became the focus of two divergent opinions of poverty in the order. Successive popes gave approval to the more moderate view and, when laxity crept in, favored reform along stricter lines. Eventually three major groups of Franciscans came into being: the Friars Minor, who developed from the Observants allowing no corporate property; the Conventuals, who allowed corporate ownership; and the Capuchins, who strongly emphasized poverty and austerity.

Franciscans have emphasized popular preaching and missionary activity. They have also promoted such popular devotions as the Angelus, the Way of the Cross, and the Crib. They were always strong defenders of the Immaculate Conception, long before the dogma was formally defined by the Church.

The Second Order of Franciscans is contemplative, known as the Poor Clares. There are Third Order Franciscans among men and women engaged in apostolic work and under simple vows. Third Order Secular, popularly called Tertiaries, are laymen and -women in the world who follow the Rule of St. Francis according to their states of life. In 1978 Pope Paul VI approved a new Rule for the Franciscan Third Order and changed the name to Franciscan Secular Order.

FREEDOM OF GOD. The liberty of God relative to creatures. God loves himself of necessity, but he loves and wills outside himself with freedom. This divine liberty is the freedom to act or not to act (liberty of contradiction), for example, to create the world. And it is the freedom to choose various goods or indifferent actions (liberty of specification), for example, to create this or that world.

FREEDOM OF WORSHIP. That part of religious freedom which concerns the worship of God according to the dictates of one's conscience. This refers especially to freedom from constraint by the civil law. As stated by the Second Vatican Council "the private and public acts of religion by which men direct themselves to God according to their consciences transcend by their very nature the earthly and temporal order of things. Therefore the civil authority, the purpose of which is the care of the common good in the temporal order, must recognize and look with favor on the religious life of the citizens. But if it presumes to control or restrict religious activity, it must be said to have exceeded the limits of its power" (*Declaration on Religious Liberty*, I, 3).

FREE WILL. The power of the will to determine itself and to act of itself, without compulsion from within or coercion from without. It is the faculty of an intelligent being to act or not act, to act this way or another way, and is therefore essentially different from the operations of irrational beings that merely respond to a stimulus and are conditioned by sensory objects.

FREQUENT CONFESSION. The practice, going back to the early Church, of receiving the sacrament of penance more often than just once a year or when mortal sins have been committed. Since the beginnings of monasticism, this practice was recommended to religious even in the absence of a priest, and therefore without absolution, as a means of spiritual purification. It was increasingly used by the laity who sought to grow in Christian perfection; then it fell off until modern times, when it became commonplace in the first half of the twentieth century.

Venerable Pope Pius XII defended the practice of frequent confession, presumably of venial sins. "By it," he said, "self-knowledge is increased, Christian humility grows, bad habits are corrected, spiritual neglect and tepidity are resisted, the conscience is purified, the will strengthened, a salutary self-control is attained, and grace is increased in virtue of the sacrament itself" (*Mystici Corporis Christi*, 88). In promulgating the new rite of penance, Venerable Pope Paul VI also stressed the "great value" of "frequent and reverent recourse to this sacrament even when only venial sins are in question." This practice "is a constant effort to bring to perfection the grace of our baptism" (December 2, 1973). Frequent reception of the sacrament of confession is encouraged by the *Catechism of the Catholic Church* (1458).

FRIAR. A brother. Originally a form of address in general use among the Christian faithful, as is clear from the frequent references to "brother" and "brethren" in the New Testament writings. Later the term came to be used more exclusively by members of religious orders, and finally, since the thirteenth century, it referred to those who belonged to one of the mendicant orders, mainly the Franciscans and Dominicans, although extended to others in the monastic tradition. Strictly speaking, however, a friar differs from a monk in that his ministry engages him in work outside the monastery, whereas traditionally the prayer and labors of a monk are identified within the monastery to which he belongs. (Etym. Old French *frère, freire,* brother; Latin *frater,* brother.)

FRIDAY ABSTINENCE. Refraining from meat on Friday in commemoration of Christ's Passion and death. The custom was prevalent among Christians from the first century. It was extended to Saturday in the West at an early date. In 1966, Pope Paul VI issued the apostolic constitution *Paenitemini,* declaring that the "substantial observance" of Fridays as a day of penance, whether by abstinence or in other ways, is a "grave obligation" (Norm II, 2). Since then, the Code of Canon Law explains what the duty to abstain (and fast) now means:

"All Fridays through the year and the time of Lent are penitential days and times throughout the universal Church" (Canon 1250).

"Abstinence from eating meat or another food according to the prescriptions of the conference of bishops is to be observed on Fridays throughout the year unless they are solemnities for the whole Church, with the exception of certain territories that were exempt from the obligation. Since 1966, however, obligatory abstinence for the universal Church applies only to Ash Wednesday and the Fridays of Lent."

"To the law of abstinence are bound all who have completed their fourteenth year of age. The law of abstinence forbids the use of meat, but not of eggs, the products of milk, or condiments made of animal fat."

"The abolition of Friday abstinence is a common misapprehension. Friday abstinence was not abolished; rather the faithful now have a choice either to abstain from meat or to perform some other kind of penance on Fridays."

FRUITS OF THE HOLY SPIRIT. Supernatural works that, according to St. Paul, manifest the presence of the Holy Spirit. The one who performs them recognizes God's presence by the happiness he experiences, and others the divine presence by witnessing these good works (Galatians 5:22–23). They are, in other words, identifiable effects of the Holy Spirit. In the Vulgate text they are charity, joy, peace, patience, benignity, goodness, longanimity, mildness, faith, modesty, continency, and chastity.

FULL OF GRACE. A term applied in the New Testament (Vulgate) to Christ, the Blessed Virgin, the Apostles, and St. Stephen. But traditionally it refers especially to Mary, as occurs in the invocation "Hail Mary, full of grace." This is the Church's official interpretation of the Greek word *Kecharitōmenē* in the angelic salutation, which all Latin translations since the earliest times render as *gratia plena* (Luke 1:28). Applied to Mary, the Mother of God, it is a fullness below that of Christ but above that of all the angels and saints. Assuming that the fullness of grace in Christ was a necessary complement of the hypostatic union, and Mary's was totally gratuitous, some theologians (e.g., Francis Suarez) hold that her sanctifying grace exceeds by far the combined sanctity of all other creatures.

FUNDAMENTAL OPTION. A theory of morals that each person gradually develops in a basic orientation of his or her life, either for or against God. This fundamental direction is said to be for God if one's life is fundamentally devoted to the love and service of others, and against God if one's life is essentially devoted to self-love and self-service.

As such, the idea of a fundamental option is not new. It was reflected in St. Augustine's teaching that the human race is ultimately composed of two cities: the City of God, whose members love God even to the contempt of self, and the City of Man, whose members love themselves even to the contempt of God.

What is new is the use of this idea to explain mortal sin. In 1975 the Holy See issued a formal declaration, *Persona Humana,* in which certain theories involving the fundamental option were condemned. "There are those," the document stated, "who go so far as to affirm that mortal sin, which causes separation from God, only exists in the formal refusal directly opposed to God's call, or in that selfishness which completely and deliberately closes itself to the love of neighbor. They say that it is only then, that there comes into play the 'fundamental option,' that is to say, the decision which totally commits the person and which is necessary if mortal sin is to exist."

The Holy See admitted the description of a person's basic moral disposition as a "fundamental option." What is not admissible is to claim that individual human actions cannot radically change this fundamental option. A person's moral disposition "can be completely changed by particular acts, especially when as often happens, these have been prepared for by previous more superficial acts. Whatever the case, it is wrong to say that particular acts are not enough to constitute a mortal sin" (*Persona Humana,* Congregation for the Doctrine of the Faith, December 29, 1975, number 10).

Blessed Pope John Paul II also opposed the erroneous interpretation of the fundamental option, instructing that one can lose grace by committing a mortal sin, even if he or she perseveres in faith (*Veritatis Splendor,* 68).

Implicit in the proscribed theory is the notion that there can be serious sins, such as murder or adultery, because the actions are gravely wrong. But no mortal sin, with the loss of sanctifying grace, is committed unless a person subjectively rejects God. This would subvert the whole moral order of Christianity, which believes that the essence of mortal sin is the deliberate choice of some creature that is known to be gravely forbidden by God.

FUNERAL RITES. The liturgical functions that the Church performs at the burial of members of the Catholic Church. The Constitution on the Sacred Liturgy of the Second Vatican Council directed that the funeral services be revised to express more clearly the paschal character of Christian death and that the rite for the burial of infants be given a special Mass. Both provisions were implemented in the new rite promulgated by Pope Paul VI. The new emphasis is on Christian hope in eternal life and in the final resurrection from the dead.

G

GABRIEL. One of the seven archangels, used on a number of occasions by God as a messenger (Deuteronomy 8:15–27). He appeared to Daniel and explained a vision to him about future events, telling him, "You are a man specially chosen" (Deuteronomy 9:20–27). In the New Testament he appeared to Zechariah to announce that Elizabeth, his wife, would bear a son and he must name the child John (Luke 1:11–20). Likewise, it was Gabriel who appeared to Mary and told her that she would conceive and bear a Son whom she must name Jesus (Luke 1:26–38).

GALATIANS, EPISTLE TO THE. Letter of St. Paul to the Churches in Galatia, warning them against the Judaizers who wanted the Christians to be circumcised. The faithful were being told that Paul was just another disciple, so he defended his apostleship, directly from Christ. He further explained that salvation is through Christ alone, that Christ's followers are no longer under the yoke of the Old Law, that they must seek only the glory of God and avoid all self-indulgence, and that true glory is found only in the Cross of Christ. St. Paul signed at least the last few lines with his own hand. (Etym. Latin name derived from Gauls who invaded Macedonia, Greece, and Asia Minor in 279 B.C.)

GALILEE. Of the three provinces that made up Palestine (Galilee, Samaria, Judaea) Galilee was the one farthest north. Approximately fifteen hundred square miles in area, it had both fertile plains and rugged mountains (Luke 4:16). Jesus grew up in Galilee, in a small village in the southern part, and most of the Apostles were Galileans (Matthew 4:18; Acts 1:11). He did much of his preaching there, and many of his miracles were performed in Galilee (Matthew 4:23). (Etym. Latin *galilaea;* from Greek *galilaia,* from Hebrew *galil,* circle, district.)

GALILEO CASE. The celebrated case of Galileo Galilei (1564–1642), Italian physicist and astronomer, whose conflict with ecclesiastical authorities has become part of world history. In 1616 he was brought before the Inquisition on the charge of ignoring the implications of the Copernican (heliocentric) theory, which seemed to contradict the biblical story of the stopping of the sun in the book of Joshua. Significantly, the Polish astronomer Copernicus in the previous century had dedicated to Pope Paul III in 1543 his published theory that the sun is the center of a great system and that the earth is a planet revolving about it. In obedience to the ruling of the Inquisition, Galileo promised not to teach Copernicus's theory as anything but a hypothesis, as in fact the proofs for the theory (on modern scientific principles) were not conclusive. In 1632, Galileo was again asked to come to Rome, this time for alleged breach of contract, since he had meantime published a satirical work, *Dialogue,* bitterly attacking his opponents. He was detained for twenty-two days in the buildings of the Holy Office, and he promised not to urge the Copernican system as a proved fact. Before he died in Florence in 1642, he received the special blessing of Pope Urban VIII. No question of papal infallibility was involved. In Galileo's case the Church defined nothing and uttered no doctrine. It made a disciplinary prohibition to protect the faithful from the disturbing effect of a then unproved hypothesis. St. Robert Bellarmine, who was involved in the Galileo affair, wrote that if a real proof were found that the sun was fixed and did not revolve around the earth, "it would be necessary to acknowledge that the passages in Scripture which appear to contradict this fact have been misunderstood." Recent scholarship has shown that the document that led to Galileo's trial in Rome (1633) was a forgery. It had been planted in the Roman Curia by an unscrupulous official. It falsely charged Galileo with having been enjoined seventeen years before from teaching the Copernican system. Galileo's famous trial, therefore, was based on this "document," which he had never before seen. In 2000, Blessed Pope John Paul II apologized for the mistakes made by some Churchmen in attacking Galileo, while also pointing out that the Galileo affair has become a secular "myth" used against the Church.

GAMBLING. The staking of money or other valuables on a future event, chance, or contingency that is unknown or uncertain to the participants. The essential feature of gambling is wagering, or the act of hazarding as such.

The Catholic Church has never condemned gambling outright, in spite of the evident abuses to which it generally gives rise. Yet gambling may become a sin, even a serious sin, when it goes to excess that would destroy personal honesty or expose a person to loss so great as to jeopardize society and, above all, his family dependents.

GAUDETE SUNDAY. Third Sunday of Advent, so named from the opening antiphon of the Introit *Gaudete in Domino semper* (Rejoice in the Lord always). On this Sunday, rose vestments are permitted in the Eucharistic liturgy. (Etym. Latin *gaudete,* rejoice.) See also LAETARE SUNDAY.

GAUDIUM ET SPES. Second Vatican Council's Pastoral Constitution on the Church in the Modern World. The longest document of the council, it has two main divisions: 1. the Church's teaching on human beings, the world they live in, and her relationship to them; 2. various aspects of life today and human society, and in particular the pressing moral issues of our day. Its treatment of the Church's role in the modern world is realistic, recognizing that "atheism must be regarded as one of the most serious problems of our time." It is also practical, noting that with all the media at work today, yet "genuine fraternal dialogue is advanced not so much on this level as at the deeper level of personal fellowship," where individuals share together in spirit. The treatment of marriage and the Christian family is the most extensive in conciliar history. And the strong position on peace and war reflects the Church's mind in the nuclear age (December 7, 1965).

GENERAL CATECHETICAL DIRECTORY. Document of the Sacred Congregation for the Clergy, issued by order of Pope Paul VI, "to provide the basic principles of pastoral theology—these principles having been taken from the magisterium of the Church, and in a special way from the second general council of the Vatican—by which pastoral action in the ministry of the word can be more fittingly directed and governed" (April 11, 1971).

GENERAL CONFESSION. The term has two different meanings, both referring to the reception of the sacrament of penance. Most commonly, it means a private confession where the penitent (exceptionally) resolves to confess as far as he or she can all past sins, and not only those since the last confession. The practice is recommended when a person is entering on a new state of life—the priesthood, religious life, or marriage—and is required in some religious institutes by rule to be done annually. Less often, general confession is associated with the granting of general absolution. When general absolution may be validly given, the provision for general confession is that "the penitents who wish to receive absolution" are invited "to indicate this by some kind of sign." The penitents then say a general formula for confession, for example, "I confess to almighty God." However, one of the necessary dispositions for receiving valid absolution, when only a general confession was made, is that the penitent "resolve to confess in due time each one of the grave sins which he cannot confess at present."

GENESIS. The first book of the Bible, containing an account of the origin of the world, of the human race, and of the Chosen People. These three origins are covered as follows: the creation of the world and the early history of humanity, including the Fall, the promise of a Redeemer, and the Deluge (1–11); the early history of the Jews, including Abraham, Isaac, Jacob, and Joseph (12–50). The prophecy of Jacob (49) contains the celebrated prediction in favor of the tribe of Judah, of which will be born the Messiah.

GENUFLECTION. Bending of the knee as an act of reverence. Customary when passing before the Blessed Sacrament in the tabernacle, entering the pew for divine worship, and during certain ceremonies to the Cross. A double genuflection of both knees simultaneously was commonly made before the Blessed Sacrament exposed in a monstrance. The new directive since the Second Vatican Council specifies: "One knee is bent before the Blessed Sacrament, whether reserved in the tabernacle or exposed for public adoration" (*Eucharistiae Sacramentum*, 1973, number 84).

GETHSEMANE. The garden lying outside Jerusalem on the Mount of Olives where Jesus spent the agonizing hours praying prior to his arrest (Mark 14:32–52; John 18:1–12). (Etym. Aramaic *gat sememe,* oil press; Greek *gethsēmanei.*)

GIFTS OF THE HOLY SPIRIT. The seven forms of supernatural initiative conferred with the reception of sanctifying grace. They are in the nature of supernatural reflexes, or reactive instincts, that spontaneously answer to the divine impulses of grace almost without reflection but always with full consent. The gifts are wisdom (*sapientia*), understanding (*intellectus*), knowledge (*scientia*), fortitude or courage (*fortitudo*), counsel (*consilium*), piety or love (*pietas*), and fear of the Lord (*timor Domini*).

GLORIA PATRI. The lesser doxology, probably an early adaptation of the Jewish blessings addressed to God, as already found in the New Testament (Romans 16:27; Philippians 4:20; Revelation 5:23). Its present form was influenced by the Trinitarian formula of baptism (Matthew 28:19). The English Puritans forbade its use as unscriptural. The Latin text reads: *"Gloria Patri, et Filio, et Spiritui Sancto. Sicut erat in principio, et nunc, et semper: et in saecula saeculorum,"* and in English: "Glory (be) to the Father, and to the Son, and to the Holy Spirit. As it was in the beginning, is now, and ever shall be, world without end. Amen."

GLORIFIED BODY. The human body after its resurrection from the dead and reunion with the soul, which beholds the vision of God. This vision is the source of the body's glorification, described by St. Paul (I Corinthians 15:42–44).

GLORIOUS MYSTERIES. The five mysteries of the Rosary on the glories of Christ and his Mother. They are the Resurrection of Christ from the dead, Christ's Ascension into heaven, the Descent of the Holy Spirit on Pentecost, Mary's bodily Assumption into heaven, and her Coronation in heaven as Queen of the Universe. See also JOYFUL MYSTERIES, LUMINOUS MYSTERIES, SORROWFUL MYSTERIES.

GLORY. The recognition and praise of someone's excellence. Applied to God, the divine (internal) glory is the infinite goodness that the persons of the Trinity constantly behold and mutually praise. His external glory is first of all the share that creatures have in God's goodness. Sometimes called objective glory, it is given to God by all creatures without exception, by their mere existence, insofar as they mirror the divine perfections. Formal glory is rendered to God by his rational creatures, when they acknowledge the divine goodness and praise God for who he is and what he has communicated of himself to the world. (Etym. Latin *gloria,* renown, splendor, glorification.)

GLUTTONY. Inordinate desire for the pleasure connected with food or drink. This desire may become sinful in various ways: by eating or drinking far more than a person needs to maintain bodily strength; by glutting one's taste for certain kinds of food with known detriment to health; by indulging the appetite for exquisite food or drink, especially when it is beyond one's ability to afford a luxurious diet;

by eating or drinking too avidly, i.e., ravenously; by consuming alcoholic beverages to the point of losing full control of one's reasoning powers. Intoxication that ends in complete loss of reason is a mortal sin if brought on without justification, e.g., for medical reasons. (Etym. Latin *glutire,* to devour.)

GNOSTICISM. The theory of salvation by knowledge. Already in the first century of the Christian era there were Gnostics who claimed to know the mysteries of the universe. They were disciples of the various pantheistic sects that existed before Christ. The Gnostics borrowed what suited their purpose from the Gospels, wrote new gospels of their own, and in general proposed a dualistic system of belief. Matter was said to be hostile to spirit, and the universe was held to be a depravation of the Deity. Although extinct as an organized religion, Gnosticism is the invariable element in every major Christian heresy, by its denial of an objective revelation that was completed in the apostolic age and its disclaimer that Christ established in the Church a teaching authority to interpret decisively the meaning of the revealed word of God.

GOD. The one absolutely and infinitely perfect spirit who is the Creator of all. In the definition of the First Vatican Council, fifteen internal attributes of God are affirmed, besides his role as Creator of the universe: "The holy, Catholic, apostolic Roman Church believes and professes that there is one true, living God, the Creator and Lord of heaven and earth. He is almighty, eternal, beyond measure, incomprehensible, and infinite in intellect, will and in every perfection. Since He is one unique spiritual substance, entirely simple and unchangeable, He must be declared really and essentially distinct from the world, perfectly happy in Himself and by his very nature, and inexpressibly exalted over all things that exist or can be conceived other than Himself" (Denzinger 3001).

Reflecting on the nature of God, theology has variously identified what may be called his metaphysical essence, i.e., *what* is God. It is commonly said to be his self-subsistence. God is Being Itself. In God essence and existence coincide. He is the Being who cannot not exist. God alone must be. All other beings exist only because of the will of God.

GODPARENTS. Godparents make a profession of faith for a person being baptized. Solemn baptism requires godparents. The godparent assumes an obligation to instruct the child in the event of the death or neglect of the parents, in order to fulfill the baptismal promises. Being a godparent creates a spiritual relationship that is recognized in ecclesiastical law.

GOD THE FATHER. First Person of the Trinity, who is unbegotten but who eternally begets the Son; from whom and from the Son proceeds the Holy Spirit. To the Father is attributed creation.

GOD THE HOLY SPIRIT. The Third Person of the Trinity, who eternally proceeds from the Father and the Son and is really distinct from them yet coequal with them as God. To him are attributed all the works of the Trinity that pertain to the sanctification of the human race.

GOD THE SON. The Second Person of the Trinity, who is eternally the only-begotten of the Father. He is really distinct from the Father and coeternal with the Father, from both of whom proceeds the Holy Spirit. Through him all things were made. He became incarnate of the Virgin Mary by the power of the Holy Spirit and is known as Jesus Christ.

GOOD. In general, whatever is suitable or befitting someone or something. Practically, however, it is that which all things tend toward or desire. The good is the desirable, and therefore the object of the natural (or supernatural) needs or tendencies of a being.

GOOD FRIDAY. Friday in Holy Week, anniversary of Christ's death on the Cross, and a day of fast and abstinence from the earliest Christian times. The ceremonies of the liturgy consist of a reading of the Gospel according to St. John, special prayers for the Church and the people of all classes of society, the veneration of the Cross, and a Communion service at which all may receive the Eucharist. The Solemn Liturgical Action is to take place between noon and 9 P.M. Good Friday remains the only day in the year on which Mass is not celebrated in the Roman Rite.

GOODNESS OF GOD. The perfect conformity of God's will with his nature (ontological goodness) and the perfect identity of God's will with the supreme norm, which is the divine essence (moral goodness).

God is absolute ontological goodness in himself and in relation to others. In himself, he is infinitely perfect and therefore his will is perfectly and infinitely happy in loving and enjoying himself as the supreme good, the *summum bonum*. He needs no one and nothing outside himself for his beatitude. God is also absolute ontological goodness in relation to others. He communicates his goodness to creatures, as the exemplary, efficient, and final cause of all created things.

God is absolute moral goodness or holiness. He is holy because he is exempt from all profaneness. He is the wholly Other whose will is not dependent on any creature. He is also holy because he is free from sin and, indeed, cannot commit sin. He is finally holy because his goodness is the norm of holiness for his creatures. They are as holy as they are like him.

GOOD NEWS. The Gospel, literally "good things" or "good tidings" or "good announcement," from the New Testament term *evangelion*. This is the whole teaching of Christianity, which those who believe accept with their minds and strive to put into practice. It is "news" because what Christ revealed had previously been hidden from the foundation of the world; and it was "good" because it revealed the infinite goodness of God, who became man, and because, through Christ, all the benefits of divine grace have been conferred on a fallen human race.

GOOD WORKS. Morally good acts that, when performed in the state of grace, merit supernatural reward. The term became highly controverted in Reformation times, when the leaders of Protestantism, notably Martin Luther (1483–1546), claimed that faith alone, and not good works, justifies. Implicit in the Catholic doctrine on good works is the belief that man's nature has not been totally depraved by reason of Adam's fall. Man is able freely to cooperate with divine grace to perform good works. His liberty is not totally enslaved by sin.

GOSPEL. One of the four authentic accounts of the life, death, and Resurrection of Jesus, which the Church teaches have been divinely inspired. They are the Gospels according to Matthew, Mark, Luke, and John. Several stages in the use of the term "Gospel" may be distinguished. In the Old Testament are predictions of the Messianic "Good News of Salvation" (Isaiah 40:9, 41:27, 61:1). The Gospels themselves speak of the "Good News" from the angelic message at Bethlehem (Luke 2:10) to the final commission to the Apostles (Mark 16:15).

Beyond the four narratives of the evangelists the entire New Testament speaks at length, in detail, and with a variety of nuances of the "Gospel of Jesus Christ." Prior to the original, inspired Gospels there was an "Oral Gospel," or tradition, on which the written narratives were based. And after the canonical Gospels were produced, numerous counterfeit Gospels were also written. There is record of twenty-one such apocryphal Gospels. (Etym. Anglo-Saxon *gōdspel*: *god,* good + *spel,* tale.)

GOSPELS, APOCRYPHAL. Spurious narratives of the life of Christ, written between the first and third centuries. Many of these exist, and new manuscripts of some of them have been discovered in the twentieth century. These apocrypha are of different types. Some may embody at least a few trustworthy oral traditions, e.g., the Gospel of Peter, and According to the Hebrews. Others are openly heretical and sought to expound erroneous, especially Gnostic views, e.g., the Gospels of Thomas, Marcion, the Twelve Apostles, and Philip. A third group of writings are pious tales, composed to satisfy popular curiosity, and deal mainly with the childhood of Christ, such as the Childhood Gospel of Thomas, the History of Joseph the Carpenter, and the Departure of Mary. There is record of twenty-one apocryphal Gospels, some available in their full narrative text.

GOSSIP. Idle talk, especially about others. The morality of gossip is determined by the degree to which time is wasted in useless conversation, by the failure in justice or charity committed against others, and by the damage done to people's reputation by those who gossip.

GOVERNMENT. According to Scholastic philosophy, the authoritative direction of a people, requiring them to use certain prescribed means for realizing a predetermined plan for the common good. Essential to the notion of government are authority vested in certain designated persons; management of things pertaining to the common good; an official plan or overview of what needs to be done to promote the welfare of the society; laws that express the will of those in authority relative to the advancement of the public good; sanctions that may be imposed on those who do not observe the laws. (Etym. Latin *gubernare,* to direct, manage, conduct, govern, guide.)

GRACE. In biblical language the condescension or benevolence (Greek *charis*) shown by God toward the human race; it is also the unmerited gift proceeding from this benevolent disposition. Grace, therefore, is a totally gratuitous gift on which man has absolutely no claim. Where on occasion the Scriptures speak of grace as pleasing charm or thanks for favors received, this is a derived and not a primary use of the term.

As the Church has come to explain the meaning of grace, it refers to something more than the gifts of nature, such as creation or the blessings of bodily health. Grace is the supernatural gift that God, of his free benevolence, bestows on rational creatures for their eternal salvation. The gifts of grace are essentially supernatural. They surpass the being, powers, and claims of created nature, namely sanctifying grace, the infused virtues, the gifts of the Holy Spirit, and actual grace. They are the indispensable means necessary to reach the beatific vision. In a secondary sense, grace also includes such blessings as the miraculous gifts of prophecy or healing, or the preternatural gifts of freedom from concupiscence.

The essence of grace, properly so called, is its gratuity, since no creature has a right to the beatific vision, and its finality or purpose is to lead one to eternal life. (Etym. Latin *gratia,* favor; a gift freely given.) See also ACTUAL GRACE, EFFICACIOUS GRACE, HABITUAL GRACE, JUSTIFYING GRACE, SACRAMENTAL GRACE, SANCTIFYING GRACE, SUFFICIENT GRACE.

GRACE AT MEALS. A prayer of invocation before eating and gratitude after eating, acknowledging the divine goodness and recognizing one's total dependence, even for food and drink, on God.

GRACE OF CHRIST. The supernatural life and blessings that God bestowed and continues to bestow on mankind in view of the merits of Christ's Redemption. It goes beyond the grace of God because, in addition to raising man to the divine life, it also heals the wounds inflicted by sin.

GRATITUDE. The virtue by which a person acknowledges, interiorly and exteriorly, gifts received and seeks to make at least some return for the gift conferred. Essentially gratitude consists of an interior disposition, a grateful heart, but when genuine it tries somehow to express itself in words and deeds. Consequently it includes three elements: acknowledgment that a gift has been received, appreciation expressed in thankfulness, and as far as possible some return for what has been freely given with no obligation on the donor's part.

GRAVE SIN. The transgression of a divine law in a grievous matter with full knowledge and consent.

The matter may be serious either in itself (as blasphemy) or because of the circumstances (as striking one's father or mother) or on account of its purpose (as telling a lie in order to destroy a person's character). Sufficient knowledge of the serious nature of a sinful action is present if one is clearly conscious that the act is mortally sinful, say because the Scriptures or the Church identify certain acts as seriously offensive to God. It is enough that one knows that what one intends to do may be a mortal sin, but does it anyhow. Indifference to the laws of God is equivalent to disobeying them.

Full consent is present when one freely wills to commit an action although one clearly knows it is gravely sinful. No sin is committed if one does not will the deed, no matter how clear one's knowledge may be. After all, the essence of sin is in the free will. Thus, too, a person does not sin who, with the best of will, cannot dispel obscene or blasphemous thoughts and desires, even though he or she well knows they are gravely sinful. The resolution to perform an action is not the same as the pleasure or satisfaction experienced in the emotions, nor the same as a compulsive idea "I like the sin." One sign of partial knowledge or not full consent would be the fact that a person does not complete an action when this can easily be done, or is so minded that the person would rather die than commit a grave sin.

GRAVISSIMUM EDUCATIONIS. Declaration of the Second Vatican Council on Christian education. The focus of this declaration is mainly threefold. It tells all Christians that they have a right to a Christian education; it reminds parents that they have the primary duty and right to teach their children; and it warns believers of the danger of state monopoly in education. Catholic schools on every academic level, including universities, are encouraged, their teachers praised, and the right of the Church to conduct educational "institutions under their control" is defended (October 28, 1965).

GREAT SCHISM. The Western Schism, 1378–1417, when there was controversy over the true succession to the papacy. It began with the writings of Marsilius of Padua (c. 1275–c. 1342), who claimed that a pope is subject to a council of bishops, priests, and laymen. Urban VI was elected pope on April 8, 1378, following the seventy-year Avignon residence of the papacy. He was a stern reformer and also harsh. The French cardinals in retaliation declared that Urban had not been validly elected and proceeded to elect Robert of Geneva as the antipope Clement VII (1378–94). Clement withdrew to Avignon and the Great Schism was in full swing. France, Scotland, and Spain gave their allegiance to Clement; England, Italy, Flanders, Hungary, Poland, and most of Germany followed Urban, who died in 1389. There followed a succession of lawful popes at Rome and antipopes at Avignon. The universities of Paris, Oxford, and Prague disputed how the impasse should be resolved. Finally pope and antipope were invited to a council at Pisa (1409); both declined and were declared deposed by the council, which proceeded to elect yet another antipope, Alexander V (1409–10). In desperation Emperor Sigismund of Germany appealed to the antipope John XXIII of Pisa to call a general council at Constance, a German city on the Rhine. John agreed, and the council, later legitimized, was convened in 1414. It lasted four years and finally resolved the schism. The Pisan antipope John XXIII abdicated. Gregory XII, the true Roman Pontiff, having formally convoked the Council of Constance, sent his representatives and then, for the good of the Church, freely resigned his office. The claim of Benedict XIII of Avignon was no longer worthy of serious consideration. The chair of Peter, vacant at last, was filled by the election, November 11, 1417, of Pope Martin V. The Great Schism was ended.

GREED. Avarice or cupidity. It implies a controlling passion for wealth or possessions and suggests not so much a strong as an inordinate desire and is commonly associated with the lust for power.

GREEK. The language of the New Testament and the dominant culture of the Mediterranean world in which Christianity was first established after its origins in Palestine. Its significance in the books of the New Testament lay in the fact that it became the primary linguistic bearer of Christian revelation and ever since has remained normative for the original meaning of the inspired text. The importance of Greek civilization lay in the extraordinary intellectual development, which St. Paul calls the wisdom (*sophia*), of the Greeks and which thus became the cultural incarnation of the Church as the Messianic Kingdom. There was, then, a providential merger of the Jews, who were God's Chosen People of whom the physical Christ was born in the flesh, and of the Greeks, who were the most civilized people of their age, among whom, as the society of believers, the Mystical Christ took root.

GREEK RITES. The form and arrangement of liturgies originally celebrated in Greek in Antioch and Alexandria. Those in use today at Antioch are the pure and modified Greek St. James, Syriac St. James, Maronite, Chaldean, Malabar, Byzantine, and Armenian Rites. At Alexandria the Coptic Liturgies of Sts. Cyril, Basil, and Gregory Nazianzus, and the Ethiopian Liturgy are used.

GREGORIAN CALENDAR. A record of the days, weeks, and months of a current year. The calendar now used is that of Pope Gregory XIII, whose decree established it in 1582. Before then the length of the year was simply the time it took for the earth to travel around the sun. Known as the Julian calendar, it was inaccurate because the earth's journey took a little less than 365.25 days. This error amounted to ten days by Pope Gregory's time. In order to correct this it was calculated that the extra day of leap year would not occur in the century year unless it would be divisible by four hundred, hence 1600 and 2000 would be a leap year; 1700, 1800, 1900 would not be. The pope suppressed ten days in 1582 and made the calendar obligatory on the Catholic faithful. Following the Gregorian calendar, there is an error of one day in thirty-five centuries. Two astronomers, Lilius and Clavius, had made the necessary calculations. At first Protestant countries refused to use it. England did not adopt the Gregorian calendar until 1752. Eastern Churches are gradually adopting it.

GREGORIAN CHANT. The forms of musical worship, as revised and established by Pope Gregory I. It is without definite rhythm and was probably accumulated from Jewish sources. It is accepted as the oldest chant in present-day use. Its revised present form is due largely to the energy and inspiration of the monks at the Benedictine Abbey at Solesmes in northwestern France.

GREGORIAN MASSES. Offering on successive days of thirty Masses said for the same deceased person, to obtain the deliverance of that soul from purgatory, through the benevolent dispensation of God's mercy. The Church has declared that the confidence of the faithful in the special efficacy of the Gregorian Masses is pious and reasonable (Sacred Congregation for Indulgences, August 24, 1888). More than one series of Gregorian Masses may be offered, but not for more than one person at a time. Also the special fruits of these Masses apply only to the deceased. But the Masses need not be said by the same priest or at the same altar. Belief in the efficacy of the Gregorian Masses is based on a private revelation made to Pope St. Gregory I.

GRIEVOUS MATTER. Moral obligations that are binding under pain of mortal sin. The gravity of the matter is determined by the object and circumstance of the action (or omission) and is known in the first place by the teaching authority of the Church, based on divine revelation. Some sins do not admit of slight matter, and these are mortal sins "from their whole nature" (*ex toto genere suo*), as lust and blasphemy. In other sins the matter is not always grave, as in theft or injustice, and these are mortal "from their nature" (*ex genere suo*). In every case, however, for a mortal sin there is also required full advertence of the mind to the fact that the matter is serious, and full consent of the will to do or not do what a person knows is a grave command or prohibition.

GUADALUPE. A shrine of the Blessed Virgin in central Mexico, suburb of Mexico City. One of the principal shrines of Christendom. Scene of the apparition of Our Lady, in December 1531, to a native Aztec peasant, fifty-one-year-old St. Juan Diego. He and his wife had been recent converts to Christianity. Mary appeared on a hillside near the Aztec shrine of Tepeyac and told Juan that she wanted a church built there. When Bishop Zumarraga demanded a sign, Juan was directed by Mary to pick some roses (not in bloom then), which he took to the bishop and found that his cloak had miraculously painted on it a portrait of the Mother of God. Although the material is a coarse fabric made of cactus fiber and totally unsuitable for such painting, the portrait has remained as brilliant as ever and is the principal object of veneration at Guadalupe. The shrine church, originally dedicated in 1709, is annually visited by several million, and numerous miracles are reported to have been worked there. A new basilica was consecrated at the shrine in 1976. The central message of Our Lady of Guadalupe, expressed in the first of her five apparitions, is preserved in an ancient document. Speaking to Juan Diego, Mary says, "You must know, and be very certain in your heart, my son, that I am truly the eternal Virgin, holy Mother of the True God, through whose favor we live, the Creator, Lord of heaven and the Lord of the earth." Blessed Pope John Paul II on January 27, 1979, opened at Guadalupe the Third General Conference of the Latin American Episcopate. He returned later to Guadalupe in 1990, 1999, and 2002. On July 31, 2002, he canonized Juan Diego. St. Pius X in 1910 designated Our

Lady of Guadalupe patroness of Latin America, and Venerable Pope Pius XII in 1945 declared her patroness of the Americas. Her feast is on December 12 and is a holy day of obligation in Mexico.

GUARDIAN ANGEL. A celestial spirit assigned by God to watch over each individual during life. This general doctrine of an angel's care for each person is part of the Church's constant tradition, based on Sacred Scripture and the teaching of the Fathers of the Church. The role of the guardian spirit is both to guide and to guard: to guide as a messenger of God's will to our minds, and to guard as an instrument of God's goodness in protecting us from evil. This protection from evil is mainly from the evil of sin and the malice of the devil. But it is also protection from physical evil insofar as this is useful or necessary to guard the soul from spiritual harm. A feast honoring the guardian angels has been celebrated in October, throughout the universal Church, since the seventeenth century. It now occurs on October 2.

GUILT. A condition of a person who has done moral wrong, who is therefore more or less estranged from the one he offended, and who is liable for punishment before he has been pardoned and has made atonement. (Etym. Anglo-Saxon *gylt*, delinquency, trespass; also a fine for a trespass.)

H

HABAKKUK. The author of the eighth book of the minor prophets, written about 600 B.C. It is a short, philosophic book of three chapters in which he complains of the injustices of life. Evil always triumphs, as evidenced in the ruthlessness of the Chaldeans in trampling on the rights of other peoples (Habakkuk 1:6). One is startled by the insight he shows when he describes them as "A people feared and dreaded; from their might proceeds their right, their greatness" (Habakkuk 1:7). The prophet is comforted, however, by YHWH's assurance that, in time, goodness will triumph. He concludes, "Calmly I await the day of anguish which is dawning on the people now attacking us" (Habakkuk 3:16).

HABIT. A quality that is difficult to change and that disposes a person either well or badly, either in oneself or in relations with others. Natural habits are a partial realization of our potencies. They add to nature by giving it ease of performance, where the acts intensify a habit and the habit facilitates the acts. Habits of acting are acquired by constant repetition and lost by disuse or contrary acts. Good moral habits are virtues; evil ones are vices. (Etym. Latin *habitus*, having, possession; condition, character, from *habere*, to have.)

HABIT, RELIGIOUS. The distinctive garb of a man or woman religious, its use dating back to the beginnings of monasticism. The habit was prescribed for religious by the Second Vatican Council: "The religious habit, an outward mark of consecration to God, should be simple and modest, poor and at the same time becoming. In addition, it must meet the requirements of health and be suited to the circumstances of time and place and to the needs of the ministry involved" (*Perfectae Caritatis,* 17).

HABITUAL GRACE. Constant supernatural quality of the soul that sanctifies a person inherently and makes him or her just and pleasing to God. Also called sanctifying grace or justifying grace. See ACTUAL GRACE, EFFICACIOUS GRACE, GRACE, JUSTIFYING GRACE, SACRAMENTAL GRACE, SANCTIFYING GRACE, SUFFICIENT GRACE.

HAGGAI. Also called Aggeus, the tenth among the minor prophets. About 520 B.C. he appeared among the Jews to rebuke them for apathy in building the second Temple. The book of Haggai contains four utterances: urging the rebuilding of the Temple, foretelling the glory of the new house of the Lord, threatening the Jews with misfortune until the Temple is rebuilt, and promising God's blessings on the people through Zorobabel, the representative of the royal house of David.

HAGIOGRAPHY. The writings or documents about the saints and saintly people. It began with records of the martyrs, including the dates and manner of their deaths. Later it was extended to the lives and data of all the saints. The most scientific form of hagiography is that of the Bollandists in their *Acta Sanctorum*.

HAIL, HOLY QUEEN. See SALVE REGINA.

HAIL MARY. The Ave Maria; the most familiar of all prayers addressed to the Blessed Virgin. It contains the salutation of the archangel Gabriel to Mary, and Elizabeth's greeting to Mary at the Visitation. The petition beginning "Holy Mary, Mother of God" was formulated by the Church and added to the Hail Mary in the Middle Ages. The full text reads:

Hail Mary, full of grace, the Lord is with you.
Blessed are you among women,
And blessed is the fruit of your womb, Jesus.
Holy Mary, Mother of God, pray for us sinners,
now and at the hour of our death. Amen.

HANDBOOK OF INDULGENCES. The official declaration of the Church's teaching on indulgences and collection of the most important prayers and good works to which indulgences are attached.

HEALING MINISTRY. Primarily refers to the ministry of Christ, who during his public life on earth healed the sick; cured the deaf-mutes, paralytics, and blind; and delivered those possessed by the devil. Also refers to the Church's care, since early Christian times, for the sick and those in physical or emotional need. But always in imitation of Christ, the Church's health or healing ministry was understood as not stopping with people's bodily needs. It is concerned with the whole person, body and soul, and seeks to alleviate every human pain or disability, whether physical, psychological, or spiritual. Among the sacraments, penance and anointing are specially directed to healing, both primarily to heal sickness of the soul and anointing also (if it is God's will) to heal the body.

HEART. A symbol of love, showing Christ's enduring love in spite of man's ingratitude. Images representing the heart alone are to be used for private devotion only. Generally the Sacred Heart is pictured as Christ, with his heart more or less exposed, sometimes held in his hands. The love of Christ exhibited in his Passion is often represented as a flaming heart surrounded by a crown of thorns. Mary's heart, pierced by a sword, is usually shown encircled by roses. A number of saints have a heart as their emblem—e.g., St. Augustine, to symbolize his great love for God; St. Teresa of Avila, a pierced heart recalling the wound of the seraph that she received in ecstasy; St. Margaret Mary, because of the role she played in extending the devotion to the Sacred Heart in the modern world.

HEAVEN. The place and condition of perfect supernatural happiness. This happiness consists essentially in the immediate vision and love of God, and secondarily in the knowledge, love, and enjoyment of creatures. Until the final resurrection, except for Christ and his Mother, only the souls of the just are in heaven. After the last day, the just will be in heaven in body and soul. Although the same God will be seen by all and enjoyed by all, not everyone will have the same degree of happiness. The depth of beatitude will depend on the measure of God's grace with which a person dies, and this in turn will be greatly conditioned by the merits that one earns during life on earth. Heaven is eternal because it will never cease. It is continuous because its joys never stop. It is communal because the happiness is shared with the angels and saints and the company of those who were known and loved on earth.

HEBREW CALENDAR. The Jewish era, according to tradition, starts with creation and is dated to add 3760 years before the Christian era. There are twelve months in the Hebrew year, all of them 29 or 30 days, as follows:

1. Tishri (30) September–October
2. Heshvan (29) October–November
3. Kislev (30) November–December
4. Tevet (29) December–January
5. Shevat (30) January–February
6. Adar (29) February–March

7. Nissan (30) March–April
8. Iyar (29) April–May
9. Sivan (30) May–June
10. Tammuz (29) June–July
11. Ab (30) July–August
12. Elul (29) August–September

In every cycle of nineteen years seven are leap years. During a leap year there is added an extra month Adar B (30 days). Thus the lunar year of the Jewish calendar corresponds to the solar year of the Gregorian calendar.

HEBREWS, EPISTLE TO THE. A letter, ascribed to St. Paul, written in Rome about A.D. 63. It was addressed to Christians who were almost exclusively converts from Judaism. It is divided into two main parts. Part One is doctrinal (1:1 to 10:17) and tells of the dignity of Christ as the natural Son of God, the eternal priesthood of Christ, the superiority of the Sacrifice of the New Law over the sacrifices of the Old Law. Part Two is moral (10:19 to 13:17), in which the converts are exhorted to perseverance in the Christian faith and in the difficult virtues required by this faith.

HEGELIANISM. The doctrine and method of the German philosopher Georg Wilhelm Friedrich Hegel (1770–1831). Its main feature is the dialectic process, which postulates the universal existence of opposites, which are absorbed in a higher unity, from which in turn new oppositions generate. Hegelianism rejects identity and contradiction as grounds of thought. All thinking and all development of being follow the scheme of the "triad," thesis, antithesis, and its resulting synthesis—i.e., opposites in conflict producing a higher unity, which then becomes the source of further conflict and another unity, going on ad infinitum. In Hegelianism everything can be explained dialectically. Christianity is represented as the absolute religion of truth and freedom, as the highest so far achieved in human history. But it is neither supernatural nor final, but only a phase in the process of God's self-evaluation as the Absolute Spirit. Marxism is built on Hegelianism.

HELL. The place and state of eternal punishment for the fallen angels and human beings who die deliberately estranged from the love of God. There is a twofold punishment in hell: the pain of loss, which consists in the deprivation of the vision of God, and the pain of sense, which consists in the suffering caused by outside material things. The punishment of hell is eternal, as declared by Christ in his prediction of the last day (Matthew 25:46) and as defined by the Fourth Lateran Council, stating that the wicked will "receive a perpetual punishment with the devil" (Denzinger 801). The existence of hell is consistent with divine justice, since God respects human freedom and those who are lost actually condemn themselves by their resistance to the grace of God.

HERESY. Commonly refers to a doctrinal belief held in opposition to the recognized standards of an established system of thought. Theologically it means an opinion at variance with the authorized teachings of any church, notably the Christian, and especially when this promotes separation from the main body of faithful believers.

In the Roman Catholic Church, heresy has a very specific meaning. Anyone who, after receiving baptism, while remaining nominally a Christian, pertinaciously denies or doubts any of the truths that must be believed with divine and Catholic faith is considered a heretic. Accordingly four elements must be verified to constitute formal heresy: previous valid baptism, which need not have been in the Catholic Church; external profession of still being a Christian, otherwise a person becomes an apostate; outright denial or positive doubt regarding a truth that the Catholic Church has actually proposed as revealed by God; and the disbelief must be morally culpable, where a nominal Christian refuses to accept what he knows is a doctrinal imperative.

Objectively, therefore, to become a heretic in the strict canonical sense and be excommunicated from the faithful, one must deny or question a truth that is taught not merely on the authority of the Church but on the word of God revealed in the Scriptures or sacred tradition. Subjectively a person must recognize his obligation to believe. If he or she acts in good faith, as with most persons brought up in non-Catholic surroundings, the heresy is only material and implies neither guilt nor sin against faith. (Etym. Latin *haeresis,* from the Greek *hairesis,* a taking, choice, sect, heresy.)

HERMENEUTICS. The art and science of interpreting the Sacred Scriptures and of inquiring into their true meaning. It defines the laws that exegetes are to follow in order to determine and explain the sense of the revealed word of God. It presupposes that the interpreter has a knowledge of the biblical languages and of such sciences as contribute to a better understanding of Holy Writ. (Etym. Greek *hermēneus,* interpreter.

HERMIT. A person who dwells alone, devoting himself to prayer and meditation. Dating in Christianity from the early persecutions of the Church, hermits were already known in Old Testament times, as Elijah the Prophet and later St. John the Baptist. More numerous at first in Egypt and Asia Minor, Christian hermits soon spread to the West, where eventually monasteries arose combining the eremitical life with the cenobitical, and isolated hermits were encouraged to form communities. (Etym. Latin *eremita;* from Greek *erēmitēs,* a dweller in the desert).

HEROIC ACT. An act of charity by which a person offers to God, for the benefit of the souls in purgatory, all the works of satisfaction he or she will perform during life, and all the suffrage that will come to him or her after death. It is not a vow but an offering that can be revoked at will. Its heroism consists in the readiness to undergo sufferings here and in purgatory in order to relieve others of their purgatorial pains. The Church has more than once approved such a heroic act of charity.

HEROIC VIRTUE. The performance of extraordinary virtuous actions with readiness and over a period of time. The moral virtues are exercised with ease, while faith, hope, and charity are practiced to an eminent degree. The presence of such virtues is required by the Church as the first step toward canonization. The person who has practiced heroic virtue is declared to be Venerable.

HIERARCHY. The successors of the Apostles under the pope as successor of St. Peter. Three powers are included under the Catholic hierarchy: teaching, pastoral, and sacerdotal. They correspond to the threefold office laid on Christ as man for the redemption of the world: the office of prophet or teacher, the pastoral or royal office of ruler, and the priestly office of sanctifying the faithful. Christ transferred this threefold office, with the corresponding powers, to the Apostles and their successors. A man enters the hierarchy by episcopal ordination when he receives the fullness of the priesthood. But he depends on collegial union with the Bishop of Rome and the rest of the Catholic hierarchy for actually being able to exercise the two other powers of teaching divine truth and of legitimately ruling the believers under his jurisdiction. (Etym. Latin *hierarchia,* holy authority, from

Greek *hierarchia*, power of a *hierarchēs*, a steward or president of sacred rites.)

HOLINESS. In the Old Testament the Hebrew *Kadosch* (holy) meant being separated from the secular or profane, or dedication to God's service, as Israel was said to be holy because it was the people of God. The holiness of God identified his separation from all evil. And among creatures they are holy by their relation to him. Holiness in creatures is either subjective or objective or both. It is subjective essentially by the possession of divine grace and morally by the practice of virtue. Objective holiness in creatures denotes their exclusive consecration to the service of God: priests by their ordination; religious by their vows; sacred places, vessels, and vestments by the blessing they receive and the sacred purpose for which they are reserved.

HOLY COMMUNION. The Eucharist is the sacrament that preserves the soul's union with God and fosters that union by making a person more holy especially in the practice of the supernatural virtue of charity. As a sacrament of the living, to obtain the graces intended, a person must be in the state of God's friendship when receiving, otherwise the reception becomes a sacrilege (I Corinthians 11:27–29).

The union of the communicant with Christ in the Eucharist is effective in the moral order. Though physically present in the communicant, Christ is not physically united with him. Only the consecrated species, since they alone can come in contact with material things, are physically united with the communicant.

Communion aims specifically at producing a likeness to Christ in the communicants. Their acts of mind and will, as a result of Communion, are to become more conformable to the acts of Christ's mind and will. Their body, too, is to become more like Christ's sacred body.

This is the primary purpose of the sacrament, a special union of the soul with Christ. What is special about this union is that the Eucharist is extraordinarily powerful in conferring actual graces that prompt a person to make acts of love for God and one's neighbor. Moreover, these graces inspire one to live for Christ habitually, even under great difficulties, as shown by the readiness to love the unlovable and to promote loving community in spite of great natural diversity.

The secondary purpose of Communion is to assimilate the body of the communicant to the body of Christ in two ways: it curbs or mitigates all disordered passions, especially those against chastity, and it confers a new title to the final resurrection of the body in heavenly glory.

A final effect of Communion is to remove the personal guilt of venial sins, and the temporal punishment due to forgiven sins, whether venial or mortal.

HOLY DAYS OF OBLIGATION. Feast days to be observed by attendance at Mass and rest, as far as possible, from unnecessary servile work. The number and dates of these vary among countries. In the United States there are six holy days: Solemnity of Mary, Mother of God on January 1; Ascension of Our Lord, forty days after Easter (in most dioceses in the United States, the Ascension of Our Lord is transferred to the following Sunday); Assumption of the Blessed Virgin, August 15; All Saints' Day, November 1; Mary's Immaculate Conception, December 8; and Christmas, or the birth of Christ, December 25. On holy days the pastor of every parish is required to offer or have offered a special Mass for his parishioners.

HOLY FATHER. A title of the pope, in common usage as the equivalent of *Beatissimus Pater.* Signifies the pope's position as the spiritual father of all the Christian faithful.

HOLY HOUR. A pious devotional exercise consisting of mental and vocal prayer with exposition of the Blessed Sacrament. It draws its inspiration from Christ's words to the Apostles in Gethsemane: "Can you not watch one hour with me?" It was taught by the Savior to St. Margaret Mary (1647–90) as one of the special practices of the Sacred Heart devotion. In the early nineteenth century a confraternity was founded at Paray-le-Monial, France, to spread the devotion, which has been highly recommended by the popes. If the hour is made publicly it is designated by a priest or the director; if made privately, any hour is suitable but preferably Thursday or Friday evening. The Passion of Christ is the theme during the hour, variously divided into meditation, vocal prayer, and singing. Many religious communities include the devotion as part of the horarium of their day.

HOLY LAND. A name given to the area that witnessed the life, death, and resurrection of Christ. The expression *terra sancta* (holy land) came into general use only in the Middle Ages, although it was found in religious literature since early patristic times.

HOLY MARY. The second part of the prayer "Hail Mary," in which the Blessed Virgin is invoked, "Holy Mary, Mother of God, pray for us sinners, now and at the hour of our death." It began as an invocation added to the Ave Maria in the eleventh century and came into general use by the sixteenth century. Pope St. Pius V gave it official recognition in 1568 by including the Holy Mary in the Roman Breviary.

HOLY NAME. The name of Jesus, from the Aramaic *Yeshu* and the Hebrew *Jehoshua,* which means "YHWH is salvation." It was given to Christ by the angel at the time of the Annunciation (Luke 1:31). It is a common name among Arabic people and is given in baptism to children in Spain and Spanish-speaking countries. A feast in honor of the Holy Name was instituted in the fifteenth century by the bishops of Belgium, England, Scotland, and Germany and extended to the universal Church in 1721. It was celebrated on the Sunday between the first and sixth of January if one occurred. Otherwise it was on January 2. The great apostle of devotion to the Holy Name was St. Bernardine of Siena (1380–1444), who would preach holding a board on which were the first three letters of the Savior's name in its Greek form—IHS—surrounded by rays, and he persuaded people to copy these plaques and erect them over their dwellings and public buildings.

HOLY NAME SOCIETY. Confraternity of men, originating at the ecumenical Council of Lyons in 1274, and promoted by the Dominicans, to whom Pope Gregory X entrusted its direction. The Spanish Friar Didacus (d. 1450) founded a confraternity of the Holy Name and drew up a rule. In time the confraternity merged with the Society of the Holy Name. World membership is several million. The purpose of the organization is twofold: to promote love and reverence for the name of God and Jesus, and to discourage profanity, blasphemy, perjury, and all improper language.

HOLY OILS. Sacramentals blessed by a bishop. There are three kinds: oil of catechumens, holy chrism, and oil of the sick. The first and third are pure olive oil. Chrism has in the oil a mixture of balm or balsam. In 1970, the Congregation for Divine Worship declared that, if necessary, the holy oils may be from any plant and not only from olives. The holy oils are symbols of spiritual nourishment and the light of grace. They are used in the public administration of baptism, confirmation, and anointing of the sick. The blessing of the holy oils normally takes place on Holy Thursday by a bishop at a cathedral church. After distribution locally they are kept in locked boxes in the ambry. Unused oils, a year later, are burned in the sanctuary lamp.

HOLY SATURDAY. The eve of Easter and the day that Christ remained in the tomb. In the early Church no Mass was offered, with services starting about three o'clock in the afternoon and ending with the Mass of the Resurrection on Easter morning. The present Easter Vigil is an approximation of this ancient rite.

HOLY SEE. Synonymous with Apostolic See, designating Rome. The official residence of the pope; the power of the Supreme Pontiff; various Roman offices, especially the tribunals and congregations assisting the pope in the government of the Church.

HOLY SHROUD. Relic of the winding sheet in which Christ was likely buried, and venerated in Turin, Italy. It is a strip of linen cloth, fourteen feet three inches long and three feet seven inches wide, bearing the front and back imprints of a human body. Tradition for its authenticity dates from the seventh century. Originally enshrined in France, it was transferred to Turin in 1578. It is kept in a richly decorated, elaborate case behind the main altar. Recent analysis tends to verify the authenticity of this relic. The marks of the sweat and blood constitute a photographic phenomenon whose nature and preservation have not been explained naturally. An entire science, called sindonology (Latin *sindo,* shroud), has developed to study and draw theological implications from the Holy Shroud.

HOLY SOULS. The souls of those who departed in the grace of God but who are temporarily detained in purgatory for venial faults and for the unremitted punishment due to their forgiven sins. They are the object of the prayers of the faithful, especially the Sacrifice of the Mass offered for them. The feast of All Souls, November 2, and the whole month of November are designated for their remembrance by the Church. The living faithful are daily reminded in the liturgy to pray for the holy souls. See also POOR SOULS.

HOLY SPIRIT. The Third Person of the Holy Trinity, who is distinct from the Father and the Son but one in being, coequal, and coeternal with them, because, like them, he is in the fullest sense God. The Holy Spirit proceeds not only from the Father but also from the Son as from a single principle, through what is called a single spiration. He is the personal infinite term of the eternal act of mutual love of the Father and the Son; hence his name of Spirit, as the issue or term of God's eternal love or act of will. He is also called the Spirit of Truth, the Creator Spirit, the Sanctifier, as the gifts of revelation, of creation (and re-creation), and of sanctification are the outpourings of God's love, and therefore appropriated to the Spirit of Love, though whatever God does outside the Trinity (in the world of creatures) belongs to the common or united action of the three divine persons. He is called Dove, because it was in this form that he descended visibly upon Christ in the Jordan (Mark 1:10).

HOLY THURSDAY. Also called Maundy Thursday, the anniversary of the Last Supper, when Christ instituted the Eucharist, the Sacrifice of the Mass, and the sacrament of the priesthood. On Holy Thursday, since the early Church, the blessing of the holy oils has taken place. The Church's emphasis in the revised liturgy for Holy Thursday is on the institution of the priesthood.

HOLY WATER. Sacramental blessed by a priest, invoking God's blessing on all who use it. Blessed water is a symbol of spiritual cleansing, and its use is advised in moments of physical danger and against temptations from spiritual enemies. It is common practice to dip one's fingers in holy water and reverently make the Sign of the Cross as one enters a Catholic church, and it is recommended for use in the home. Holy water is used in all blessings. There is, besides ordinary holy water, baptismal holy water, used with chrism in the conferring of public baptism, and Easter water specially blessed for use during the paschal time.

HOLY WEEK. The week preceding Easter, from Passion (Palm) Sunday through Holy Saturday inclusive. During this week the Church commemorates the Passion of Christ, and all the ceremonies reflect this attitude of sorrow, yet joined with gratitude for God's mercy in becoming man in order to suffer and die for a sinful mankind.

HOLY YEAR. Essentially, a year during which the pope grants a special indulgence, called the Jubilee, to all the faithful who visit Rome and pray according to specified conditions. First instituted in 1300 by Pope Boniface VIII, whose original intention was that it be celebrated only every hundred years. Since then there have been three changes in the intervals. In 1343, Pope Clement VI decreed that the Holy Year be celebrated every fifty years; Urban VI in 1389 reduced it to thirty-three years in honor of the years of Christ's life; and Paul II in 1470 made it every twenty-five years, which is the period that has been kept ever since. Pope Pius XI made an exception in 1933 to commemorate the nineteenth centennial of Christ's death, Resurrection, and Ascension. And Blessed John Paul II declared 1983 to be the Holy Year of the Redemption. Since 1500 the Jubilee Indulgence could be gained in one's native country, under specified conditions. The opening and closing of the Holy Doors at St. Peter's in Rome marks the opening and closing of each Holy Year.

HOMOOUSIOS. A term first defined by the first general council of the Church to identify Christ's relationship to the Father. It was chosen by the council to clarify the Church's infallible teaching that the Second Person of the Trinity, who became man, is of one and the same substance, or essence, or nature as God the Father. The Arians, who were condemned at Nicaea, held that Christ was "divine" only in the sense that he was from God, and therefore like God, but not that he was literally "God from God, one in being with the Father." (Etym. Greek *homousios,* of one essence, consubstantial.)

HOMOSEXUALITY. In general, some form of sexual relationship among members of the same sex. From a moral standpoint, three levels are to be distinguished: tendency, attraction, and activity. Homosexual tendencies in any person are within the normal range of human nature, whose fallen condition includes every conceivable kind of impulse that with sincere effort and divine grace can be controlled. Sexual attraction for members of the same sex may be partly due to the peculiar makeup of certain individuals or, more often, the result of indiscretion or seduction and presents a graver problem; yet this, too, is not by itself sinful and may in fact be an occasion for great supernatural merit. When the condition is pathological, it requires therapy. Active homosexuality is morally indefensible and has been many times forbidden in revelation and the teaching of the Church. The most extensive declaration on the subject was by the Congregation for the Doctrine of the Faith, *Persona Humana,* approved by Pope Paul VI on November 7, 1975.

HOPE. The confident desire of obtaining a future good that is difficult to attain. It is therefore a desire, which implies seeking and pursuing some future good that is not yet possessed but wanted, unlike fear that shrinks from a future evil. This future good draws out a person's volition. Hope is confident that what is desired will certainly be attained. It is the opposite of despair. Yet it recognizes that the object wanted is not easily obtained and that it requires effort to overcome whatever obstacles stand in the way. (Etym. Latin *spes*, hope.)

HOPE, ACT OF. An act of confident expectation of possessing God in heaven and of obtaining the necessary grace to reach this destiny. Acts of hope are required in times of temptation to discouragement or despair, and are implicit in every supernaturally good work. A simple and highly authorized act of hope says: "My God, I hope in You, for grace and for glory, because of Your promises, Your mercy and Your power. Amen."

HOPE, VIRTUE OF. An infused theological virtue, received at baptism together with sanctifying grace and having the possession of God as its primary object. It belongs to the will and makes a person desire eternal life, which is the heavenly vision of God, and gives one the confidence of receiving the grace necessary to reach heaven. The grounds of hope are the omnipotence of God, his goodness, and his fidelity to what he promised. The virtue of hope is necessary for salvation. Acts of hope are also necessary for salvation and are commanded by God for all who have come to the use of reason.

HOSEA. One of the minor prophets, who carried on his ministry sometime between 783 and 715 B.C. in the kingdom of Israel, which seceded from Judah after the death of Solomon. The book of Hosea consists of fourteen chapters and may be divided into three parts. The first part (1–3) portrays Israel as the faithless bride, whose divine Lover remains true to her in spite of her infidelities and urges her to repent. The second part (4–9:9) is a divine reproach and a cry for vengeance. The third part (9:107–14:10) recalls God's blessings on his people, repeats the exhortation to repentance, and promises salvation. Hosea is frequently quoted in the New Testament, and twice by Christ personally (Matthew 9:13; Hosea 6:6; Luke 23:30; Hosea 10:8).

HOST. A victim of sacrifice, and therefore the consecrated Bread of the Eucharist considered as the sacrifice of the Body of Christ. The word is also used of the round wafers used for consecration. (Etym. Latin *hostia*, sacrificial offering.)

HOUSE BLESSING. One of several liturgical blessings of a home approved by the Church. A standard formula, which the priest recites while sprinkling the house with holy water, begins: "We earnestly beseech You, God the Father Almighty, to bless, and sanctify and endow with every gift this home, its furnishings and those who dwell herein."

HUMANAE VITAE. Encyclical letter of Pope Paul VI, subtitled "The Right Order to Be Followed in the Propagation of Human Offspring." There are four parts to the encyclical: 1. new aspects of a perennial problem; 2. competence of the Church's magisterium to resolve the problem; 3. doctrinal principles to be maintained; and 4. pastoral directives. One of the major issues restated by Paul VI is the Church's right to pass final judgment in moral matters not only where these are formally revealed but also where they "pertain to the natural moral law" (July 25, 1968).

HUMAN NATURE. The nature of humankind considered abstractly and apart from its elevation by grace to a supernatural state with a heavenly destiny. It is the human as such, having a body and soul, capable of rational thought and voluntary decision. Actually human nature has never existed independent either of a supernatural destiny or of free acceptance or rejection of the supernatural invitation of God's grace.

HUMILITY. The moral virtue that keeps a person from reaching beyond himself. It is the virtue that restrains the unruly desire for personal greatness and leads people to an orderly love of themselves based on a true appreciation of their position with respect to God and their neighbors. Religious humility recognizes one's total dependence on God; moral humility recognizes one's creaturely equality with others. Yet humility is not only opposed to pride; it is also opposed to immoderate self-abjection, which would fail to recognize God's gifts and use them according to his will. (Etym. Latin *humilitas,* abasement, humility; from *humus,* ground.)

HYPNOTISM. The phenomenon of artificially induced sleep, which renders the victim abnormally open to suggestion. The subject of hypnosis tends to be dominated by the ideas and suggestions of the hypnotist while under the induced spell and later on. According to Catholic principles, hypnotism is not wrong in itself, so that its use under certain circumstances is permissible. But since it deprives the subject of the full use of reason and free will, a justifying cause is necessary for allowing it to be practiced. Moreover, because hypnotism puts the subject's will in the power of the hypnotist, certain precautions are necessary to safeguard the subject's virtue, and to protect him or her and others against the danger of being guilty of any injurious actions. For grave reasons—e.g., to cure a drunkard or one with a suicide complex—it is licit to exercise hypnotism, given the precaution that it is done in the presence of a trustworthy witness by a competent and upright hypnotist. The consent, at least presumed, of the subject must also be had. Several documents of the Holy See set down the norms to be followed in the use of hypnotism (*The Holy Office*, August 4, 1956; July 26, 1899).

HYPOCRISY. A form of lying in which a person pretends to have virtues or moral qualities that are not possessed. Its motive is pride and its malice depends on the gravity of the pride and on the evil consequences that follow when people take one to be morally good and, perhaps, entrust one with confidences or responsibilities that are not deserved. It is not hypocrisy, however, to be on one's best behavior with those whom one justly wishes to impress favorably. Nor is it hypocrisy when a person, because of human weakness, fails to live up to his or her own principles or profession of faith. (Etym. Latin *hypocrita*, hypocrite; from Greek *hypokritēs*, actor, hypocrite.)

HYPOSTATIC UNION. The union of the human and divine natures in the one divine person of Christ. At the Council of Chalcedon (A.D. 451) the Church declared that the two natures of Christ are joined "in one person and one hypostasis" (Denzinger 302), where "hypostasis" means one substance. It was used to answer the Nestorian error of a merely accidental union of the two natures in Christ. The phrase "hypostatic union" was adopted a century later, at the fifth general council at Constantinople (A.D. 533). It is an adequate expression of Catholic doctrine about Jesus Christ that in him are two perfect natures, divine and human; that the divine person takes to himself, includes in his person a human nature; that the incarnate Son of God is an individual, complete substance; and that the union of the two natures is real (against Arius), no mere indwelling of God in a man (against Nestorius), with a rational soul (against Apollinaris), and the divinity remains unchanged (against Eutyches).

ICON. A flat painting, sacred picture of the Eastern Church. It is generally painted on wood and covered, except the face and hands, with relief of seed pearls and gold or silver. The icon of the saint of the day is usually displayed on an analogion. Icons of Our Lord and Our Lady are reverenced with great devotion, incensed, carried in processions, and normally placed on the iconostasis screen. The icons in the Eastern Church take the place of statues in the West. (Etym. Greek *eikōn*, image.)

ICONOCLASM. A heresy that rejected as superstition the use of religious images and advocated their destruction. It was occasioned by the rise of Islam, which considers all sacred images idolatrous. Moslem pressure on those in political power precipitated the crisis, which came in two phases. The first phase began with Emperor Leo the Isaurian in 726 and closed with the seventh general council and Second Council of Nicaea in 787. The second phase started with Emperor Leo V, the Armenian, and ended when the Feast of Orthodoxy was established in 842 under Empress Theodora. Sts. John Damascene and Theodore were the principal defenders of sacred images. As defined by II Nicaea, these images may be lawfully displayed and venerated. The respect shown them really is given to the person they represent. (Etym. Greek *eikōn*, image + *klaein*, to break.)

IDEA. Originally meant the appearance or visible form of a thing existing apart from the thing itself. Consequently, the likeness within the mind of some reality that exists outside the mind. An idea is clear when it is distinct from other ideas; it is complete when it adequately represents the nature of what is mentally conceived; it is primitive when acquired directly from the object known; and derived when arrived at from other ideas by comparison and contrast (Etym. Greek *idein*, to see.)

IDEOLOGY. The ideas that influence a whole group or society and motivate their conduct. It is immaterial whether these ideas are true or false; they become an ideology when they move a people to action. One of the features of the modern world is its capacity for creating new ideologies, or changing former ones, through the mass communications media.

IDLENESS. Unwillingness to work. The reason may be physical, because a person lacks the strength; or mental, because one does not know what to do; or moral, because of laziness that will not expend the effort needed perhaps even to begin a task or at least perform it as it should be done.

IDOLATRY. Literally "the worship of idols," it is giving divine honors to a creature. In the Decalogue it is part of the first commandment of God, in which YHWH tells the people, "You shall have no gods except me. You shall not make yourself a carved image [Greek *eidōlon*, idol] or any likeness of anything in heaven or on earth or in the waters under the earth; you shall not bow down to them or serve them" (Exodus 20:4–5).

The early Christians were martyred for refusing to worship idols, even externally, but practical idolatry is a perennial threat to the worship of the one true God. Modern secularism is a form of practical idolatry, which claims to give man "freedom to be an end unto himself, the sole artisan and creator of his own history." Such freedom, it is said, "cannot be reconciled with the affirmation of a Lord who is author and purpose of all things," or at least that this freedom "makes such an affirmation altogether superfluous" (Second Vatican Council, Dogmatic Constitution on the Church, 51).

Idolatry is always gravely sinful. Even under threat of death and without interiorly believing in the idol, a Christian may not give divine honors to a creature, thereby violating the duty of professing faith in God.

I.H.S. *Iesus* (*Jesus*) *Hominum Salvator* (usual interpretation), Jesus Savior of Men. Really a faulty Latin transliteration of the first three letters of "Jesus" in Greek (IHS for IHC). See also JESUS.

ILLICIT. That which is unlawful, or contrary to established prescriptions, but not necessarily invalid. Thus, according to ecclesiastical law many elements are prescribed, but not all (or most of them) are strictly necessary for a valid act or, in the sacraments, valid administration. (Etym. Latin *illicitus*, not allowed, forbidden, unlawful; from *licere*, to be permitted.)

ILLUMINATIVE WAY. The intermediary stage between purification and union on the path to Christian perfection. Also called the "Way of the Proficients," the main feature of the Illuminative Way is an enlightenment of the mind in the ways of God and a clear understanding of his will in one's state of life.

ILLUMINISM. A form of Gnosticism, it appears in the history of Christian heresy as a belief in one's own divine enlightenment, with a sense of mission to enlighten others, contrary to the express teachings of the Church's magisterium.

IMAGE. A representation or likeness of something. It corresponds to "exemplar" and implies that one thing (the image) is both a reflection and pattern of something else. In this sense the word has come to mean an attitudinal or judgmental reaction toward a person, an institution, or a people. Thus we now speak of "image makers" or "image builders" to describe the use of publicity and propaganda to create or maintain a favorable impression before the public. (Etym. Latin *imago*, copy, likeness, image, picture, pattern, model.)

IMAGES, VENERATION OF. Honor paid to representations of Christ and the saints. Their purpose is to adorn, instruct, and excite to piety those who behold, wear, or carry images on their persons. According to the Council of Trent, images of Christ, of the Mother of God, and other canonized saints are to be kept in churches and due honor paid to them not because there is any divinity or power inherent in them as images but because the honor shown to them is referred to the prototypes they represent. Through the worship and reverence so shown, the faithful really worship Christ and honor the saints whose likenesses they display. In other words, the veneration is relative, always being referred back to the original, never absolute as though the material object is being venerated in and for itself.

IMITATION OF CHRIST. A devotional book published anonymously in 1418. Sometimes called *The Following of Christ,* it contains counsels of perfection. The authorship is now attributed to Thomas à Kempis, a canon of the Netherlands. It was written in Latin in a familiar style and divided into four books: useful admonitions for a spiritual life; further admonitions relative to spiritual things; interior consolations; and the Blessed Sacrament. It is a popular book also outside of Catholic circles, generally with the fourth book omitted. Its basic theme is that, since Jesus Christ is true God and true man, by imitating Christ as man the Christian becomes more and more like Christ, who is God. Next to the Bible it is the most widely read spiritual book in the world.

IMMACULATE CONCEPTION. Title of the Blessed Virgin as sinless from her first moment of existence. In the words of Pope Pius IX's solemn definition, made in 1854, "The most holy Virgin Mary was, in the first moment of her conception, by a unique gift of grace and privilege of almighty God, in view of the merits of Jesus Christ the Redeemer of mankind, preserved free from all stain of original sin." This means that since the first moment of her human existence the mother of Jesus was preserved from the common defect of estrangement from God, which humanity in general inherits through the sin of Adam. Her freedom from sin was an unmerited gift of God or special *grace* and an exception to the law, or *privilege,* which no other created person has received.

Neither the Greek nor Latin Fathers explicitly taught the Immaculate Conception, but they professed it implicitly in two fundamental ways. Mary, they said, was most perfect in purity of morals and holiness of life. St. Ephrem (c. 306–73) addressed Christ and Mary with the words "You and Your mother are the only ones who are totally beautiful in every way. For in You, O Lord, there is no stain, and in Your mother no stain." Mary was described as the antithesis of Eve. Again in Ephrem: "Mary and Eve [were] two people without guilt. Later one became the cause of our death, the other cause of our life." While implicit in the early writers, the Immaculate Conception had to be clarified before becoming explicit dogma. Main credit for this goes to the Franciscan John Duns Scotus (c. 1264–1308), who introduced the idea of pre-redemption in order to reconcile Mary's freedom from original sin with her conception before the coming of Christ. (Etym. Latin *im-,* not + *maculare,* to stain.)

IMMACULATE HEART. The physical heart of the Blessed Virgin Mary as a sign and symbol of her compassion and sinlessness, and the object of devotion by the faithful. Devotion to the Immaculate Heart of Mary gained international prominence through the Fátima apparitions in 1917 and their subsequent approval by the Holy See. A widely used prayer capsulizing this devotion reads:

Virgin of Fátima, Mother of mercy, Queen of heaven and earth, refuge of sinners, we consecrate ourselves to your Immaculate Heart. To you we consecrate our hearts, our souls, our families, and all we have.

And in order that this consecration may be truly effective and lasting, we renew today the promises of our Baptism and Confirmation; and we undertake to live as good Christians—faithful to God, the Church and the Holy Father. We desire to pray the Rosary, partake in the Holy Eucharist, attach special importance to the first Saturday of the month and work for the conversion of sinners.

Furthermore we promise, O most holy Virgin, that we will zealously spread devotion to you, so that through our consecration to your Immaculate Heart and through your own intercession the coming of the Kingdom of Christ in the world may be hastened. Amen.

IMMERSION. The method of baptism by dipping or plunging the candidate under water while the one baptizing says, "I baptize you in the name of the Father, and of the Son, and of the Holy Spirit." It is one of the three valid forms of baptism and was the method generally used in the early Church. It is still commonly used in the Eastern Church and in certain Protestant Churches, notably in the Baptist tradition. The Catholic Church in the Latin Rite has reintroduced the practice as a permissible option, since the Second Vatican Council.

IMMODEST LOOKS. The conscious looking at a person, picture, or scene that arouses sexual feelings to which a person has no moral right or need to experience. Since sexual feelings are sacred, to which only married persons between themselves have a claim, deliberately to look at something in order to be sexually stimulated is a grave sin (Matthew 5:28).

IMMOLATION. The actual or equivalent destruction of some material object as an act of sacrifice. When the destruction is done actually, the object is radically changed, as when an animal is killed or wine is poured out. When the destruction is not done but is equivalent, it is called mystical or symbolic, as occurs in the sacrifice of the Mass, where the separate consecration of the bread and wine symbolizes the separation of Christ's body and blood on Calvary. Christ does not actually die in the Mass, but he manifests his willingness to die symbolically by the double consecration. (Etym. Latin *immolatio*, sacrifice.)

IMMORTALITY. Freedom from death or the capacity to decay and disintegrate. Absolute immortality is possessed by God alone, who has no body and whose spirit is eternal by essence. He cannot not exist; he always has been and must be. Natural immortality belongs to all spiritual beings, namely the angels and human souls, who are created indeed and therefore begin, but since they are simple by nature and have no parts, they will not die, although absolutely speaking, they could be annihilated by an act of God. Gratuitous immortality is a special grace, given originally by God to the ancestors of the human race and restored by Christ as a promise after the last day. It means freedom from bodily death and from separation of the soul from the human body.

IMMUTABILITY OF GOD. Absolute changelessness. That is mutable which goes from one condition to another. In consequence of its finite nature, every creature is mutable. God is unchangeable because he is infinite. Mutability implies potentiality, composition, and imperfection, and is therefore not reconcilable with God as pure actuality, the absolutely simple and infinitely perfect Being. When God acts outside of himself, as in the creation of the world, he does not produce a new effect in himself but enters on a new realization of the eternal decision of his divine will. The decree of creation is as eternal and immutable as the Divine Essence, with which it is really identical; only its effect, the created world, is temporal and changeable. (Etym. Latin *immutabilis*, unchangeable; changeless.)

IMPASSIBILITY. Quality of the glorified human body in being free from every kind of physical evil, such as sorrow or sickness, injury or death. It may be defined as the impossibility to suffer and to die (Revelation 21:4). The inherent reason for impassibility consists in the perfect compliance of the body and emotions to the soul. (Etym. Latin *in-*, not + *passibilis*, able to suffer; *impassibilis*, incapable of suffering.)

IMPEDIMENT. Any obstacle to progress or activity, and in the moral order whatever hinders a person from achieving the spiritual perfection intended for him or her by God. Such would be inordinate attachments, though not sinful, to some creature that stands in the way of complete surrender to the will of God. In theology and canon law an impediment is any hindrance to the validity or legality of some action or its effects. (Etym. Latin *impedimentum*, an impediment, hindrance; from *impedire*, to entangle the feet.)

IMPENITENCE, FINAL. Dying unreconciled with God, whether through loss of faith, or through despair, or through a blasphemous rejection of God's love.

IMPERFECT CONTRITION. Sorrow for sin animated by a supernatural motive that is less than a perfect love of God. Some of the motives for imperfect contrition are the fear of the pains of hell, of losing heaven, of being punished by God in this life for one's sins, of being judged by God; the sense of disobedience to God or of ingratitude toward him; the realization of lost merit or of sanctifying grace. Also called attrition, imperfect contrition is sufficient for remission of sin in the sacrament of penance. It is also adequate for a valid and fruitful reception of baptism by one who has reached the age of reason. And if a person is unable to go to confession, imperfect contrition remits even grave sin through the sacrament of anointing of the sick.

IMPOSITION OF HANDS. The laying on of hands on a person or thing to convey the communication of some favor, power, duty, or blessing. Patriarchs in the Old Testament used it in blessing children, in consecrating priests, and in sacrifice. In the New Testament it is shown with Christ performing miracles and with the Apostles conferring the sacraments, especially the priesthood. Catholic liturgy employs it now in public baptism, confirmation, and anointing of the sick and holy orders; in other rites and blessings such as exorcisms; and before the consecration of the Mass when the priest extends his hands over the bread and wine.

IMPOTENCE. Incapacity for marital intercourse. Impotence, unlike sterility, hinders the human act of generation, that is, the copula. Impotence that is prior to marriage and is permanent, whether on the part of the man or the woman, whether known to the other party or not, whether absolute or relative, invalidates marriage by the natural law. Absolute impotence prevents marital intercourse with all other persons; relative impotence prevents it only with a certain person or persons.

IMPRIMATUR. The Latin term for "let it be printed," which signifies the approval by a bishop of a religious work for publication. Authors are at liberty to obtain the imprimatur either from the bishop where they reside, or where the book is to be published, or where it is printed. Generally the imprimatur, along with the bishop's name and date of approval, is to be shown in the publication. According to a decree of the Sacred Congregation for the Doctrine of the Faith (1975), "the Pastors of the Church have the duty and the right to be vigilant lest the faith and morals of the faithful be harmed by writings; and consequently even to demand that the publication of writings concerning the faith and morals should be submitted to the Church's approval, and also to condemn books and writings that attack faith or morals." (Etym. Latin *imprimere*, to impress, stamp, imprint.)

IMPRIMI POTEST. It can be printed. Permission that a religious receives from his major superior to publish a manuscript on a religious subject. This implies approval of the writing by the superior and clearance to receive a bishop's imprimatur.

IMPULSE. Any sudden, unreasonable urge to action, often induced by an emotion. Impulses are natural when explainable in terms of antecedent thoughts or feelings. They are supernatural when they incline to something good without any assignable cause, especially when the inclination arises in the context of prayer or resignation to the will of God. They can also be preternatural and demonic, as when they impel a person with a furious intensity to do something particularly offensive, such as blasphemy. (Etym. Latin *impellere*, to impel, incite, urge, instigate, stimulate, persuade, from *im-*, on + *pellere*, to drive.)

IMPURITY. A common term for sins of lust, whether internal or external. Internal sins of lust are interior thoughts or desires that are not carried out in practice; they may take on a variety of forms—e.g., taking pleasure in sexual imaginative representations, complacently enjoying previous sinful venereal experiences, desiring unlawful sexual pleasures. Otherwise the sins are external.

INCARNATION. The union of the divine nature of the Son of God with human nature in the person of Jesus Christ. The Son of God assumed our flesh, body, and soul, and dwelled among us like one of us in order to redeem us. His divine nature was substantially united to our human nature. Formerly the Feast of the Annunciation was called the Feast of the Incarnation. In the Eastern Churches the mystery is commemorated by a special feast on December 26. (Etym. Latin *incarnatio;* from *in-*, in + *caro*, flesh: *incarnare*, to make flesh.)

INCARNATIONAL. Like Christ, who is God become man, the adaptation of the divine to the human, the eternal to the temporal, in the preaching and teaching of the Gospel. Always without compromise of revealed truth, it is the Church's readiness to adjust her message to the culture of the people, even as Christ became incarnate not only in the human nature he assumed as God but in the society and the times in which he lived. (Etym. Latin *incarnare*, to make flesh; Latin *in-* + *caro*, flesh.)

INCENSE. Aromatic gum or resin in the form of powder or grains that give off a fragrant smoke when they are burned. When blessed it is a symbolic sacramental. Its burning signifies zeal or fervor; its fragrance, virtue; its rising smoke, human prayer ascending to God. It is used at Mass, for the Gospel book, the altar, the people, the ministers, and the bread and wine; before consecration; at Benediction of the Blessed Sacrament; during processions; and at absolutions of the dead. When it is to be used, it is carried in a metal, cup-shaped container and burned in a thurible or censer. Five large grains of it are placed in the paschal candle at the Easter Vigil to symbolize the Five Wounds of the Risen Savior. In some countries it is placed in a stationary censer to burn slowly before the Blessed Sacrament, either exposed or reserved on the altar. (Etym. Latin *incensum*, incense; literally, something burned; from *incendere*, to kindle.)

INCEST. Sexual intercourse between those who are related by blood or marriage and whom the Church forbids to marry. It is a sin against both chastity and the virtue of piety or reverence due to those closely related to us. Between parent and child or brother and sister it is also a crime against nature. (Etym. Latin *in-*, not + *castus*, chastity: *incestus*, unchastity, incest.)

INCORRUPTIBILITY. Incapacity of decay or destruction. This may be absolute, as God, who is wholly unchangeable by nature; or natural, as the angels and souls, which, being spirits, cannot disintegrate by decomposition; or substantial, as in physical nature, whose elements can be variously recombined but in their ultimate constituents are not destroyed.

INDEFECTIBILITY. Imperishable duration of the Church and her immutability until the end of time. The First Vatican Council declared that the Church possesses "an unconquered stability" and that, "built on a rock, she will continue to stand until the end of time" (Denzinger 3013, 3056). The Church's indefectibility, therefore, means that she now is and will always remain the institution of salvation, founded by Christ. This affirms that the Church is essentially unchangeable in her teaching, her constitution, and her liturgy. It does not exclude modifications that do not affect her substance, nor does it exclude the decay of individual local churches or even whole dioceses.

INDEX OF FORBIDDEN BOOKS. A list of books that Catholics were forbidden by ecclesiastical authority to read or retain without authorization. The books so condemned were considered heretical, dangerous to morals, or otherwise objectionable. The Index was published by authority of the Holy Office. After the Second Vatican Council its publication was discontinued, but a new set of regulations was published by the Holy See, giving specific norms on the reading of books that are dangerous to the Catholic faith or to Christian morality.

INDISSOLUBILITY. The permanence of marriage that cannot be dissolved either by the withdrawal of consent of the married partners or by civil authorities. Christian marriage is absolutely indissoluble, as defined by the Council of Trent, condemning anyone who says, "The Church errs when she has inculcated and continues to inculcate in accord with evangelical and apostolic teaching, that the bond of marriage cannot be dissolved by reason of adultery on the part of one spouse, and that both parties, even the innocent one who gave no reason for adultery, cannot contract a new marriage while the other spouse is alive; and that both the man who marries another wife after dismissing an adulterous one commits adultery and the wife who marries another husband after dismissing an adulterous one commits adultery" (Denzinger 1807).

INDISSOLUBLE MARRIAGE. Christian marriage, between two baptized persons who enter into a valid contract and consummate their marriage by natural intercourse, cannot be dissolved by any human power, whether civil or ecclesiastical.

INDULGENCE. "The remission before God of the temporal punishment due to sins forgiven as far as their guilt is concerned, which the follower of Christ with the proper dispositions and under certain determined conditions acquires through the intervention of the Church, which, as minister of the redemption, authoritatively dispenses and applies the treasury of the satisfaction won by Christ and the saints" (Venerable Pope Paul VI, apostolic constitution on indulgences).

As originally understood, an indulgence was a mitigation of the severe canonical penances imposed on the faithful for grave sins. The term "indulgence" remained, however, even after these extreme penalties were discontinued. Yet until the Second Vatican Council, the norm for determining the effectiveness of an indulgenced practice was its relationship to the ancient canonical penances, as seen in the numbers, so many years or so many days, attached to every official listing of partial indulgences.

All this was changed by Venerable Pope Paul VI. From now on the measure of how efficacious an indulgenced work is depends on two things: the supernatural charity with which the indulgenced task is done and the perfection of the task itself.

Another innovation is that partial and plenary indulgences can always be applied to the dead by way of suffrage, asking God to remit their sufferings if they are still in purgatory.

INDWELLING. Presence of the Holy Spirit in a person who is in the state of grace. He is present not only by means of the created gifts of grace, which he dispenses, but by his uncreated divine nature. This personal indwelling does not produce a substantial but only an accidental union with the souls of the just. As the indwelling of the Holy Spirit is an operation of God outside himself and as all activity of God outside the Trinity is common to the three persons, the indwelling of the Holy Spirit implies the indwelling of the three divine persons. This indwelling as a manifestation of the love of God, the personal love of the Father and the Son, is appropriated to the Holy Spirit. St. Paul speaks of the Third Person: "Know you not that you are the temples of God and that the Spirit of God dwells in you" (I Corinthians 3:16). But he also says: "You are the temple of the living God" (I Corinthians 6:16), and Christ declares: "If any one loves me, he will keep my word. And my father will love him; and we will come to him and will make our abode with him" (John 14:23).

The immediate effect of the divine indwelling is sanctifying grace, which is the created result of the uncreated grace of God's presence. Its effect on the person is an experience that spiritual writers compare to a foretaste of the beatific vision; the mind is able to understand something of the mystery of God, and the will is enamored of his goodness beyond anything possible by the light of reason or the natural affective powers of humans.

INFALLIBILITY. Freedom from error in teaching the universal Church in matters of faith or morals. As defined by the First Vatican Council, "The Roman Pontiff, when he speaks ex cathedra—that is, when in discharge of the office of pastor and teacher of all Christians, by virtue of his supreme apostolic authority, he defines a doctrine regarding faith or morals to be held by the universal Church, by the divine assistance promised to him in Blessed Peter, is possessed of that infallibility with which the divine Redeemer willed that his Church should be endowed in defining doctrine regarding faith or morals; and therefore such definitions are irreformable of themselves, and not in virtue of consent of the Church" (Denzinger 3074).

The bearer of the infallibility is every lawful pope as successor of Peter, the Prince of the Apostles. But the pope alone is infallible, not others to whom he delegates a part of his teaching authority, for example, the Roman congregations.

The object of his infallibility is his teaching of faith and morals. This means especially revealed doctrine like the Incarnation. But it also includes any nonrevealed teaching that is in any way connected with revelation.

The condition of the infallibility is that the pope speaks ex cathedra. For this is required that 1. he have the intention of declaring something unchangeably true; and 2. he speak as shepherd and teacher of all the faithful with the full weight of his apostolic authority, and not merely as a private theologian or even merely for the people of Rome or some particular segment of the Church of God.

The source of the infallibility is the supernatural assistance of the Holy Spirit, who protects the supreme teacher of the Church from error and therefore from misleading the people of God.

As a result, the ex cathedra pronouncements of the pope are unchangeable "of themselves"—that is, not because others in the Church either first instructed the pope or agree to what he says. (Etym. Latin *in-*, not + *fallibilis*; from *fallere*, to deceive: *infallibilis*, not able to deceive or err.)

INFALLIBILITY, EPISCOPAL. Preservation from error of the bishops of the Catholic Church. They are infallible when all the bishops of the Church are assembled in a general council or, scattered over the earth, they propose a teaching of faith or morals as one to be held by all the faithful. They are assured freedom from error provided they are in union with the Bishop of Rome, and their teaching is subject to his authority. The scope of this infallibility, like that of the pope, includes not only revealed truths but any teaching, even historical facts, principles of philosophy, or norms of the natural law that are in any way connected with divine revelation.

INFANT BAPTISM. The Catholic Church's constant teaching is that children should be baptized soon after birth. The reason being that a child is born with original sin, which, in God's ordinary Providence, cannot be removed before the age of reason except by baptism with water. Through baptism an infant receives sanctifying grace; the infused virtues of faith, hope, and charity; and the gifts of the Holy Spirit.

INFANTS, UNBAPTIZED. See UNBAPTIZED INFANTS.

INFERENCE. A process of reasoning by starting with a proposition as true and arriving at a conclusion as also true because it was already implicit in the original assumption. Inference may be either deductive or inductive, i.e., starting from the general and going to the particular, or vice versa.

INFIDEL. One who does not believe. Formerly applied to all non-Christians, the term is now used only of unbelievers, i.e., professed atheists or agnostics. (Etym. Latin *in-*, not + *fidelis*, true, faithful: *infidelis*, one that cannot be relied upon, faithless.)

INFIDELITY. Either a lack of faith or of faithfulness. As a lack of faith, it may be positive, privative, or negative. Positive infidelity means that a baptized person sufficiently instructed in the Christian faith rejects it by a denial of any of God's revealed truths. Privative infidelity is the culpable neglect either to examine the grounds for divine revelation or to admit one's obligation to embrace the faith once these grounds are seen to be credible. Negative infidelity is simply a lack of faith in the Christian religion by one who has some other faith and, through no fault of his or her own, has not had the Gospel adequately presented. Infidelity as a lack of faithfulness is commonly associated with marriage.

INFINITE. That which has no bounds or limitations. Something can be called infinite in different ways. It can be actually infinite, meaning a positive reality without limit. It can be infinitely perfect when it is unlimited in perfection of being or of operation, when it possesses every pure perfection in every way and in perfect degree. It can be potentially infinite when, as a finite reality, it is capable of actual or conceptual increase without any limit or term; thus the potentially infinite can be multiplied infinitely, but in reality it is finite and limited. On account of the indefiniteness of the limits, it is also called the indefinite. Finally, something can be either relatively or absolutely infinite. The former is infinite in some aspect or particular perfection, such as duration; the latter is infinite in every respect. Only God is actually and absolutely infinite, as only he is infinitely perfect. (Etym. Latin *in-*, not + *finis*, end: *infinitus*, indefinite; boundless.)

IN MEMORIAM. In remembrance of the dead. The full phrase reads, "*In memoriam fidelium defunctorum*," in memory of the faithful departed. It implies faith in the survival of souls of the deceased, and is applied to the Masses, prayers, and good works that are offered to assist the departed if they are still in purgatory, and also refers to the cherished remembrance of the virtues and achievements of the deceased while they lived on earth.

INNOCENCE. Freedom from sin or moral guilt. Applied to Adam and Eve before the Fall, to those who have just been baptized, and to persons who never lost the state of grace because they never committed a grave sin. (Etym. Latin *innocens*: *in-*, not + *nocere*, to harm, hurt.)

INQUISITION. The special court or tribunal appointed by the Catholic Church to discover and suppress heresy and to punish heretics. The Roman Inquisition of the middle twelfth century, with its ecclesiastical courts for trying and punishing heretics, arose during the ravages of the anti-social Albigensian sect, whose doctrines and practices were destructive not only of faith but of Christian morality and public order. While Church authorities would condemn a person found guilty of heresy, it was the civil power that actually inflicted the penalty. The reformation of the heretic was first sought. By exhortations and minor punishments he was urged to give up his heresy. Many did. Only the relapsed heretics who were found guilty were turned over to the civil government for punishment required under civil law. The fact that secular law prescribed death must be understood in the light of those days when heresy was anarchy and treason, and leniency in criminal codes was unknown. Like all institutions that have a human character, abuses crept in.

The Spanish Inquisition, set up by King Ferdinand and Queen Isabella in 1478 and empowered by Pope Sixtus IV, was directed against the lapsed converts from Judaism, crypto-Jews, and other apostates whose secret activities were dangerous to Church and State. The civil government had great influence in the administration of this Inquisition, and the Spanish ecclesiastical tribunal accused of scandalous cruelty must share its condemnations with them. The latter worked during these days in defiance of the Holy See, which often condemned inquisitors because of their cruelties. Even so, these cruelties have been grossly exaggerated, and the fact that the Inquisition did tremendous good in saving the Latin countries from anarchy has been forgotten. Much falsehood surrounds the events of this period, which should be judged by the standards of those times, not by modern ideas of the human person and of religious freedom.

INSANITY. Abnormality of the brain or nervous system producing a morbid mental condition. This condition is accompanied by loss of control of the will, rendering the individual morally irresponsible for what he does. The permanently insane may be baptized, their desire being supposed. If having lapsed into insanity and now incurable, they may be baptized if any, even implicit, desire for baptism was ever expressed by them. The sacrament of anointing of the sick may also be given, and Holy Communion may be received in sane moments or when in danger of death. A temporarily insane person upon recovery may validly receive the sacrament of confirmation and holy orders. The permanently insane may not be sponsors for baptism, nor may they marry, but if they have contracted marriage in a period of lucidity, that marriage may be valid. The Church approves segregation for the insane and sponsors institutions for their care, but sterilization is forbidden as an infringement of their human rights.

INSPIRATION, BIBLICAL. The special influence of the Holy Spirit on the writers of Sacred Scripture in virtue of which God himself becomes the principal author of the books written and the sacred writer is the subordinate author. In using human beings as his instruments in the composition, God does so in harmony with the person's nature and temperament, and with no violence to the free, natural activity of his or her human faculties. According to the Church's teaching, "by supernatural power, God so moved and impelled them to write, He was so present to them, that the things which He ordered and those only they first rightly understood, then willed faithfully to write down, and finally expressed in apt words and with infallible truth" (Pope Leo XIII, *Providentissimus Deus,* Denzinger 3293).

INSTITUTE, DIOCESAN. A religious institute of men or women, erected by a local ordinary, that has not as yet obtained "Pontifical Recognition" from the Holy See.

INSTITUTE, PONTIFICAL. A religious institute of pontifical right (*juris pontificii*), of men or women, that has received the formal approbation, or at least "Pontifical Recognition," from the Holy See.

INSTITUTE, RELIGIOUS. A society approved by legitimate ecclesiastical authority, the members of which strive after evangelical perfection according to the laws proper to their society, by the profession of public vows, either perpetual or temporary, the latter to be renewed after fixed intervals of time. The members also live in community.

INTEGRITY OF CONFESSION. The duty, based on divine law, of confessing in the sacrament of penance all the certainly grave sins committed since one's last valid absolution. All mortal sins are properly confessed when their number and species (distinctive quality), together with the circumstances that change the species of the sins, are exactly indicated.

INTENTION. An act of the will tending effectively to some good, proposed by the mind as desirable and attainable. It differs from simply willing, which is the desire for an end without concern about the means. Intention means desiring not only some good but also the means of obtaining this good. An intention may be actual, virtual, habitual, or interpretative.

INTERCESSION. Entreaty in favor of another person; hence mediation. In biblical language, "there is only one mediator between God and mankind, himself a man, Christ Jesus, who sacrificed himself as a ransom for them all" (I Timothy 2:5–6). The Blessed Virgin, Mediatrix of all graces, the angels, saints in heaven, souls in purgatory, and the faithful on earth intercede for mankind by their merits and prayers.

INTERDICT. A censure forbidding the faithful, while still remaining in communion with the Church, the use of certain sacred privileges, such as Christian burial, some of the sacraments, and attendance at liturgical services. It does not exclude from Church membership, nor does it necessarily imply a personal fault of any individual affected by the interdict. When imposed for a fixed period, it is a vindictive penalty because of some grave act done against the common good of the Church by one or more parishes. Usual religious services are curtailed, but sacraments may be given to the dying, marriages celebrated, and Holy Communion administered if the interdict is general or local (not personal). A general interdict may be inflicted only by the Holy See. Parishes or persons may be interdicted only by the local ordinary.

INTERIOR STRUGGLE. Conflict within a human person between his or her own desires and the will of God. What naturally pleases is not always good. This is the fight of the spirit versus the flesh—human will against human passions, whether bodily or spiritual. This internal struggle varies in intensity for different persons and at different times. Although often difficult, with divine grace it is always possible to overcome self in conflict with the known will of God.

INTER MIRIFICA. Decree on the Means of Social Communication of the Second Vatican Council. After defining the media as those "which of their nature can reach and influence not merely single individuals but the very masses and even the whole of human society," the Council spelled out how these are to be used. Most important, it declared that "the content of what is communicated must be true and—within the limits set by justice and charity—complete" (December 4, 1963).

INTINCTION. The liturgical practice of dipping the consecrated Host into the consecrated wine in giving Holy Communion. Its use was already established by the time of Dionysius of Alexandria (d. 264). In time it became a regular method both in the East and the West. In the East, the intinction was (and is) done by means of the communion spoon (labis). An alternate form of intinction is described in the Ordines Romani (sixth century) and is since discontinued. The consecrated Host would be dipped into unconsecrated wine. Intinction had long disappeared in the West, and has been revived since the Second Vatican Council (1969).

INVALID. Null and void, ineffective. Applied to the sacraments, it means that something essential was missing so that a sacrament was not actually administered or conferred. In ecclesiastical law it means that some document, declaration, or jurisdiction is without effect because some necessary element was not present.

INVESTITURE. The practice in the early Middle Ages of an emperor or other lay prince to invest an abbot or bishop-elect with the ring and staff and to receive homage before consecration. It was condemned by Pope Nicholas II in 1059 and all lay investiture was forbidden in 1075 by Pope Gregory VII (1021–85) and by subsequent popes. The Second Lateran Council (1139) reaffirmed the prohibition but allowed the civil ruler to bestow the temporalities. Variant forms of lay investiture remain to the present day, notably in secular states where the Church's rights are severely restricted, as in countries under Communism.

INVINCIBLE IGNORANCE. Lack of knowledge, either of fact or law, for which a person is not morally responsible. This may be due to the difficulty of the object of the knowledge, or scarcity of evidence, or insufficient time or talent in the person, or any other factor for which he is not culpable. (Etym. Latin *in-,* not + *vincibilis,* easily overcome: *invincibilis.*)

ISAAC. The son of Abraham and Sarah (Genesis 21:2–3). A few years after Isaac's birth, YHWH tested Abraham's obedience by ordering him to sacrifice the growing boy as a burnt offering. Without hesitation Abraham set out with Isaac to the designated spot, built an altar, and prepared to kill his son as an offering to YHWH. But an angel intervened, Isaac was spared, and YHWH praised Abraham for his unquestioning obedience (Genesis 22:1–19). When Isaac was forty years old, his father arranged his marriage to Rebekah, who lived in the land of Abraham's kinfolk (Genesis 24). Eventually they had two sons, Esau and Jacob. In Isaac's old age a bitter enmity developed between the two sons because of Jacob's duplicity (Genesis 25:19–28). Isaac, blind and feeble, wanted to bestow his blessing on Esau, but Jacob, assisted by the conniving Rebekah, received it instead. Many years passed before the brothers were reconciled (Genesis 27:1–40). Isaac died at the age of one hundred eighty and was buried in Hebron (Genesis 35:28–29).

ISAIAH. Author of the longest prophetic book in the Old Testament, he was the son of Amoz, born about 760 B.C. in Jerusalem. His writing paralleled the reigns of three Judaean kings, Jotham, Ahaz, and Hezekiah. His mission was to proclaim the fall of Israel and Judah and the punishment that would befall the nation because of its sinfulness. The beauty of his style and the consistent nobility of his message made him one of the most revered of biblical writers. Constantly he pleaded with his people to place their trust in God and not in military achievements. No other prophet foreshadowed as convincingly the coming of the Messiah, who would be a descendant of David. Biblical students point out numerous incidents in Jesus's life that were foreshadowed in Isaiah's prophetic lines (Isaiah 2:1–5, 7:10–17, 9:1–6, 11:1–5).

ISRAEL. The name given to Jacob by an angel at the Jabbok ford. He was on a journey to hold a reunion with his estranged brother, Esau. During the night a stranger wrestled with him till daybreak and then said to him, "Your name shall no longer be Jacob, but Israel, because you have been strong against God." Was the stranger an angel? Jacob himself thought it was God. He named the place Peniel "because I have seen God face to face and I have survived" (Genesis 32:25–32). Later in Genesis, God appeared to Jacob once again and repeated the statement, "Your name is Jacob, but from now on, you shall be named not Jacob but Israel" (Genesis 35:9–10). This was enough in itself to show the unique niche he occupies in Jewish history: he is the personification of the nation of Israel.

JACOB. The son of Isaac and Rebekah; he became the third of the Hebrew patriarchs and one of the great figures in rabbinical literature. The account of his being renamed "Israel" by God, which thus made him the eponymous ancestor of the nation, is significant comment on his distinctive place in Jewish history (Genesis 35:9–10). In his dealings with Laban, his uncle, over a twenty-year period he acquired the latter's two daughters as wives and considerable wealth (Genesis 32:3–21). All together he had twelve sons, each of whom became the head of one of the tribes of Israel (Genesis 29, 30). One of the most familiar stories in Scripture is the lengthy account of the adventures of Joseph, who was the elder of the two sons of Jacob by Rachel and his father's favorite. Sold into slavery, he eventually became governor of Egypt. During a great famine there was a family reunion, and the overjoyed Jacob regained his son. Jacob and his entire family moved to Goshen in the land of Egypt, and he spent his remaining years there under Joseph's protection. He was buried at his urgent request back in Canaan, where Abraham and Isaac were buried (Genesis 37–50).

JAMES, EPISTLE OF. Traditionally attributed to James the Less, "the brother of the Lord." It was written in Greek, and its style and language were typically Jewish, indicating that it was originally intended for converts from Judaism. Its main stress is on the moral conduct of Christians, notably their perseverance under trial, respect for the poor, and the need to bridle one's tongue. It is especially clear on the duty of living one's faith and not merely professing it (James 2:14–26). Among the good works binding on Christians, the practice of charity and the avoidance of conflict are primary (James 4:1–12). (Etym. Anglicized form of Hebrew, *Jacob,* through Spanish *Jaime.*)

JAMES THE GREATER. The son of Zebedee and older brother of John. Both were Apostles; whenever the Twelve are listed, these names are paired. Jesus called them "the Sons of Thunder" (Matthew 10:3; Mark 3:17). On one occasion he rebuked them for urging violence against some Samaritans who refused to receive him. Both were fishermen and partners with Simon Peter; the trio responded promptly to Jesus's invitation to become fishers of men (Luke 5:10–11, 9:53–56).

That the brothers were especially close to him is indicated by the fact that they were present at the Transfiguration (Matthew 17:1–2) and accompanied him to Gethsemane (Matthew 26:37). James was beheaded by Herod in the early days of the Church (Acts 12:2).

JAMES THE LESS. The son of Alphaeus and Mary (the woman who was present at Calvary). The "Less" means "younger." He was one of the Twelve Apostles (Acts 1:13). He was a brother of Joset and possibly Matthew (Mark 15:40).

JANSENISM. A system of grace developed by Cornelis Jansen, or Cornelius Jansenius (1585–1638), theologian at Louvain and later Bishop of Ypres. As a school of theology, it should be seen in two stages, namely the original position of Jansenius and its later development by his followers.

Jansenius's own teaching is contained in the book *Augustinus,* which he spent years writing and which was published two years after his death. According to Jansenius, man's free will is incapable of any moral goodness. All man's actions proceed either from earthly desires, which stem from concupiscence, or from heavenly desires, which are produced by grace. Each exercises an urgent influence on the human will, which in consequence of its lack of freedom always follows the pressure of the stronger desire. Implicit in Jansenism is the denial of the supernatural order, the possibility of either rejection or acceptance of grace. Accordingly those who receive the grace will be saved; they are the predestined. All others will be lost. Jansenism was condemned as heretical in five major propositions by Pope Innocent X in 1653. It was recondemned by Pope Alexander VII in 1656, when Jansenists claimed that their doctrine was misrepresented.

The later developments of Jansenism were built on the earlier foundations but went beyond them in a number of ways. Stress on God's selective salvation produced a general harshness and moral rigorism, denying God's mercy to all mankind. Disregard of papal teaching led to an arbitrary attitude toward the use of the sacraments, notably reducing the frequency of penance and the Eucharist, and giving rise to Gallicanism, which denied papal primacy and infallibility. In 1794, Pope Pius VI condemned a series of eighty-five propositions of the Italian Jansenists led by Scipione de' Ricci, Bishop of Pistoia and Prato. Among the propositions was the claim that the authority of the Church depends on the consent of its members and that the jurisdiction of a diocesan bishop is independent of the pope.

JEREMIAH. One of the three major prophets. He lived during the seventh and sixth centuries before Christ and witnessed the capture and destruction of Jerusalem. He survived six kings of Judaea: Amon, Josiah, Jehoahaz, Jehoiakim, Jehoiachin, and Zedekiah. It was a time of intrigue and turmoil, with Assyria, Babylon, and Egypt struggling for supremacy. Tiny Judaea was caught in the middle and tried desperately to maintain its independence. Jeremiah was a reforming prophet from childhood, according to his own testimony. When he protested to YHWH, the latter replied, "Do not say 'I am a child.' Go now to those to whom I send you and say whatever I command you" (Jeremiah 1:7). He repeatedly conveyed the anger and resentment of YHWH to his people, deploring their apostasy and the immorality of their lives and the insincerity and superficiality of their leaders. Even his own townspeople of Anathoth were embittered by Jeremiah's denunciations and threatened him with death (Jeremiah 11:21). When he delivered YHWH's condemnation of the pagan practices in Topheth, Pashur, who was in charge of the Temple police, had him beaten and put in the stocks at the Gate of Benjamin (Jeremiah 20:2). After he dictated a scroll to his secretary, Baruch, deploring the offenses of King Jehoiakim, the latter destroyed the scroll, unmoved by Jeremiah's reproaches. The tenacious prophet promptly dictated the entire scroll over again, even adding to his accusation (Jeremiah 36:32). During the reign of King Zedekiah, Jeremiah, acting on YHWH's orders, advised the king to surrender to the Chaldeans, assuring him that he would be well treated. Zedekiah ignored the advice. When the Chaldeans invaded Jerusalem, as Jeremiah had prophesied, the palace was destroyed, the walls leveled, and the king's family killed (Jeremiah 39). Now, in the last year of his life, Jeremiah continued to be the voice of YHWH until he died c. 587 B.C., probably in Egypt.

JERUSALEM. Ancient city in Palestine, the religious and political center of the Jewish people, situated on the crest of a chain of mountains that cross Palestine from north to south. Originally called Salem, it was the capital of King Melchizedek about 2100 B.C. (Genesis 14). First mentioned in the book of Joshua (10, 15), the inhabitants were known as Jebusites. When the Promised Land was parceled out, Jerusalem was assigned to the tribe of Benjamin. Its most famous rulers were King David, who brought the Ark of the Covenant into the city, and his son Solomon, who built the first Temple. A second Temple was built in the sixth century B.C., and the third (and last) was the work of Herod the Great, who ruled as a vassal of Rome from 37 to 4 B.C. The Christian history of Jerusalem begins with the short ministry of the Savior, culminating in his death, Resurrection, and Ascension. The Apostles lived and taught there for some time after Pentecost, and met in Jerusalem for their first council about A.D. 49. The Apostle St. James the Less was the first Bishop of Jerusalem, where he was condemned by the Sanhedrin and martyred in A.D. 62.

JESSE, ROOT OF. A symbol of Christ, "a shoot springs from the root of Jesse" (Isaiah 11:1). St. Ambrose explains the root as the family of the Jews, the stem as Mary, the flower as Christ. The great O antiphon of December 19 is sung "O Root of Jesse who standeth as an ensign of the people before whom kings will keep silence and unto whom the Gentiles will make supplication, come to deliver us and tarry not." Often represented as a flourishing tree, it carries the six-pointed star of Israel at its base and the Cross as its fulfilled blossom at the apex.

JESUITS. The Society of Jesus, founded by St. Ignatius Loyola and approved by Pope Paul III in 1540. As conceived by the founder, it had a twofold aim: to strengthen and where necessary to restore the Catholic faith in the wake of the Protestant Reformation, and to preach the Gospel in non-Christian lands. Typical of the first purpose was the establishment of colleges throughout Europe, and the second purpose was the development of worldwide mission enterprises in Asia, Africa, and the newly developed Americas.

The Society of Jesus grew out of the Spiritual Exercises of St. Ignatius, and its structure and discipline were embodied in the detailed Constitutions, also written by the founder.

Opposition from many quarters, but especially from the Jansenists, led to suppression of the Jesuits by Pope Clement XIV in 1773. They were restored by Pope Pius VII in 1814. After their restoration, they grew in numbers to become the largest single religious institute in the Catholic world through their universities, colleges, secondary schools, scholarly publications, retreat houses, and seminaries.

The Society of Jesus is divided into assistancies, these in turn into provinces, and within the provinces are local communities. The superior general is elected for life; he appoints provincials and also the rectors of the more important local communities.

There are three kinds of finally professed members in the society: the solemnly professed and the spiritual coadjutors who are priests, and the lay brothers who are spiritual coadjutors. The solemnly professed take solemn vows of poverty, chastity, and obedience and four simple vows: special obedience to the pope, not to mitigate the society's poverty, not to accept ecclesiastical dignitaries, and actively seeking to avoid such preferments. The others take simple vows only. But all the finally professed make a total renunciation of private ownership.

JESUS. The name of Our Lord. It is the Latin form of the Greek *Iesous,* whose Hebrew is *Jeshua* or *Joshua,* meaning "YHWH is salvation." It is the name through which God the Father is to be invoked and by which the Apostles worked miracles (Acts 3, 6). In standard usage the name "Jesus" is applied to the Son of Mary, who is also the Son of God; as distinct from "Christ," which refers to his Messianic role as the fulfillment of the ancient prophecies.

JESUS PRAYER. A popular devotion among Eastern Christians. The words of the prayer are "O Lord Jesus Christ, Son of God, have mercy on me, a sinner." It is said by devout Christians at regular intervals during the day and night, and is used by them as the basis of their meditation.

JEWISH DECALOGUE. The Ten Commandments as an essential part of the Jewish religion. Containing only 120 Hebrew words in all, the Decalogue has exercised more profound influence on the moral and social life of humanity than any other group of laws in history. There are two versions of the Decalogue in Scripture: the priestly version (Exodus 20:1–17) and the Deuteronomic (Deuteronomy 5:6–21). They differ mainly in two ways. In Exodus the observance of the Sabbath is based on religious motives, namely the fact that God rested on the seventh day after creation; in Deuteronomy the motive is rather humanitarian. Also in Exodus the prohibition of covetousness classes a man's wife with his other domestic property, whereas in Deuteronomy the wife is treated separately. The first four commandments (in the Catholic version the first three) refer to people's duties toward God; the last six their duties to others. In Temple times, they formed an integral part of the religious service, being recited daily just before the Shema. They are highly honored in modern Judaism. When read in the synagogue, the congregation rises and the commandments are intoned by the reader in a special solemn tone. The Jewish festival of Shavuot (seven weeks after the first day of Passover) commemorates the revelation of the Decalogue on Mount Sinai, and the solemn reading of the Ten Commandments is the highlight of the religious service on that day. See also CHRISTIAN DECALOGUE, DECALOGUE, TEN COMMANDMENTS.

JEWS. Those who adhere to Judaism both as a religion and a people. Originally the name was restricted to the subjects of the kingdom of Judah. But after the Babylonian exile it became the common name for the race descended from Jacob and for the followers of the Mosaic religion.

JOB. The chief character in what many critics consider the most beautifully written book in the Bible. The author is unknown. From internal evidence it is speculated that he was an Israelite who wrote sometime between 600 and 400 B.C. The Book of Job is a profound philosophic discussion of human suffering, with Job and several of his friends taking turns offering possible solutions to the problem of good and evil. Their efforts to find an answer to determine YHWH's reasons for permitting such indignities to afflict a faithful believer were fruitless. Job and his friends realized the fatuousness of the popular belief that goodness and evil are rewarded in this life. Ultimately, there remains the dominant theme: faith in God must endure even when reason and understanding fail (Book of Job).

JOEL. 1. the older son of Samuel, the Israelite judge. He was appointed a judge in turn by his father but failed to win public respect. He accepted bribes and perverted justice. The elders protested to Samuel and urged him to choose a king (I Samuel 8:1–5). Reluctant at first, Samuel was ordered by YHWH to comply with their request. Saul became the new king of Israel (I Samuel 11:15); 2. the son of Pethuel who became a prophet in Judah and wrote one of the books of the Old Testament (book of Joel). He is referred to as the prophet of Pentecost because he emphasized the future coming of the Holy Spirit (Acts 2:17). Peter quoted him in the Acts of the Apostles on Pentecost day in lines that include the familiar promise "Your young men shall see visions; your old men shall dream dreams" (Joel 3:1).

JOHN MARK. The writer of the second Gospel. Several times in the Acts of the Apostles he is referred to as John Mark (Acts 12:12, 25; 15:37). Twice he is referred to simply as John (Acts 13:5, 13). But normally readers of the Bible think of him as Mark. See also MARK.

JOHN THE APOSTLE. A son of Zebedee and a brother of another Apostle, James. Both brothers were fishermen and were among the first to be called to follow Jesus (Mark 1:19). Their mother may have been Salome, the sister of Jesus's mother—which would make the brothers the cousins of Jesus (John 19:25). It seems safe to affirm that John was "the beloved disciple," though nowhere is he specifically named. He was the closest to Jesus at the Last Supper (John 13:23), and it was to John (the only Apostle present on Calvary) that Jesus entrusted his mother (John 19:26–27). On several occasions John was accorded a special place. He was allowed to accompany Jesus to Jairus's home when the latter's daughter was brought back to life. He was present at the Transfiguration (Matthew 17:1–2). Finally, he was one of the three who went with Jesus to Gethsemane (Mark 14:33). It was appropriate that he would be the Apostle to hasten with Peter to the tomb on Easter morning and be the first to proclaim belief in the Risen Christ (John 20:1–10). Several references are made to him in the Acts of the Apostles. He was present in the upper room with the Apostles after the Ascension (Acts 1:13). He accompanied Peter when the lame man was cured in the Temple (Acts 3:1–10). Again he went with Peter to pray for the Samaritans to receive the Holy Spirit (Acts 8:14–17). The most lasting memorial of his work, of course, was his biblical writings. Three short epistles are attributed to him because in style and doctrine they are so closely akin to the fourth Gospel. The book of Revelation, the last book of the New Testament, written during the final quarter of the century, is credited to John. Likewise, the fourth Gospel is Johannine in spirit and tone. It was obviously the work of one close to Jesus, an eyewitness of his ministry, and one who loved him intensely. The style and vocabulary are Semitic. The writer was thoroughly familiar with the customs and geography of Palestine. His close association with Peter and James is significant. John must have been the author. Some have held that he was martyred with his brother in A.D. 44, but if that is true he could not have written either the Gospel or Revelation, which were not written till some years later. In 1907 the Pontifical Biblical Commission denied that the arguments against John's authorship were valid. The weight of evidence indicates that he was the only Apostle not to be martyred. He probably died at the very end of the century. (Etym. Greek *Iôannēs*, from Hebrew *Yochanan*, YHWH is gracious.)

JOHN THE BAPTIST. The son of Zechariah and Elizabeth, John was a few months older than Jesus and destined to become his forerunner (Luke 1:36). Always an austere figure, he was looked upon by the Apostles as a kind of reincarnated Elijah preparing the way for the acceptance of the Lord. Jesus himself said, "I tell you that Elijah has come already and they did not recognize him, but treated him as they pleased; and the Son of Man will suffer similarly at their hands." The disciples understood then that he had been speaking of John the Baptist (Matthew 17:12–13). John lived an ascetic life in the Judaean desert to prepare himself for his ministry in the country about the Jordan. He constantly proclaimed a baptism of penance for the forgiveness of sins (Luke 3:3), and became indeed, in the words of Isaiah, "a voice crying in the wilderness" (Isaiah 40:3). Many were so impressed that they mistook him for the Messiah. He made it clear, though, that "I baptize you with water, but someone is coming, someone who is more powerful than I am; I am not fit to undo the strap of his sandals; he will baptize you with the Holy Spirit and fire" (Luke 3:16). Jesus always spoke of him in the highest terms. "I tell you, of all the children born of women, there is no one greater than John" (Luke 7:28). The common people treated him with reverence, but the Pharisees and the lawyers showed disdain for him and refused to be baptized (Luke 7:30). Surely they had excellent precedent! Jesus himself appeared before John to be baptized. John tried to dissuade him because of his own unworthiness, but Jesus insisted and John baptized him (Matthew 3:13–15). Herod Antipas imprisoned John for boldly denouncing his unlawful marriage to Herodias. Using her daughter to trap Herod into promising her a reward, she demanded and received the head of John the Baptist (Matthew 14:3–12).

JONAH. An Israelite prophet, son of Amittai. Unlike the books of the other minor prophets, the short book of Jonah (only four chapters) is narrative rather than oracular. Though he lived in the eighth century B.C., the book was not written until about the fifth century. To evade YHWH's assignment, Jonah had fled in a ship but a terrible storm led to his being thrown overboard and being swallowed by a huge fish. After three days he was washed ashore and, properly chastened, proceeded to Nineveh to discharge his original task—to warn the people of Nineveh of their impending doom. Their contrition was so genuine that YHWH relented and the catastrophe was averted. But now Jonah was outraged that his effective preaching was negated. He had to learn that YHWH's compassion and love were dominant. The story uses an actual personality to teach a moral lesson: God's mercy is at hand provided man is willing to repent.

JOSEPH. The second youngest of Jacob's twelve sons. Because he was Jacob's favorite, his brothers were jealous of him. When his father gave him "a coat of many colors," they resented the preferential treatment. They even considered killing him, but the prudent Reuben dissuaded them (Genesis 37:3–22). Joseph was sold to the Egyptians as a slave (Genesis 37:28), but with YHWH protecting him he rose rapidly to positions of responsibility (Genesis 39:1–6). During a severe drought that afflicted the entire region he rendered valuable service (Genesis 41:37–49). Unexpectedly he was reunited with his brothers, whom Jacob had sent to Egypt in a desperate search for food. They did not recognize him, but he knew them instantly. After subjecting them to several tests, he disclosed his identity and sent them back to Canaan to get their father. He arranged to have the family settled in Goshen in Egypt, where they would be assured a substantial living as long as they wanted (Genesis 42, 43, 44, 45). Jacob, of course, was delighted to regain his favorite son, and being assured by God that it was a safe move, he entrusted his entire family, seventy strong, to Joseph's protection (Genesis 46). Jacob lived seventeen happy years in Egypt (Genesis 47) but, when he knew that he was dying, asked to be buried in Canaan with Abraham and Isaac (Genesis 49:29–33). His son respected this dying wish. Joseph himself lived to be 110 years old and was buried in Egypt (Genesis 50:26).

JOSEPH, ST. Spouse of the Virgin Mary and foster father of Jesus. His name is an abbreviated form of the Hebrew *Jehoseph,* "may Jahweh give an increase." He was a descendant of David and natural relative of Mary, but the degree of kinship is not known. His father is called Jacob, though he is also said to have been the son of Heli, perhaps by some kind of adoption. Hegesippus in the second century identifies one of his brothers, Cleophas, who is called the "uncle" of Jesus. We do not know where Joseph was born. It may have been at Bethlehem, as the *Apology* of Justin the Martyr suggests, or Nazareth, where Mary lived.

According to the evangelists, he was a workman (Greek *tekton*), which tradition has interpreted to mean carpenter, although he may have engaged in other kinds of labor, too, as circumstances in a Jewish village would require. The *Proto-Evangelium* of James and other apocrypha, wishing to safeguard Mary's virginity and explain the term "brethren of the Lord" (Matthew 13:55), present Joseph as an old man and widower with children by a previous marriage. But the exertions demanded for supporting a family and for making long journeys practically exclude old age. The "brethren" of Jesus are explained as relatives, either on the side of Cleophas or of a sister of Mary.

Joseph's marriage took place before the Incarnation, since he and Mary are called spouses before the Annunciation. When the Gospel says that Mary was a "virgin promised," this refers to Jewish matrimonial rights, which distinguished espousals (regarded as true marriage) from the bride's entering the house of her husband. When Joseph became aware of Mary's pregnancy, he thought of putting her away privately, without exposure, until an angel revealed the mystery to him. He received Mary into his home and acquired the parental right of naming the infant to be born of her.

The census decree of Emperor Augustus sent Joseph with Mary to Bethlehem, where he probably owned a small field, since the law required enrollment in the place where land was held. When the shepherds came to visit the Christ Child, they found him with Joseph and his mother. Forty days after Jesus was born, Joseph accompanied Mary and her Son at the presentation in the Temple, and through angelic direction fled into Egypt to escape the anger of Herod. Twice the evangelist Luke says that Christ lived in Nazareth with Joseph and Mary; first after the presentation and again when Jesus, at the age of twelve, was found in Jerusalem among the doctors after being lost for three days. After this the only references to Joseph in the Gospels are to identify him as the reputed father of Jesus and a workman whose humble origins scandalized the critics of his putative Son. Very probably Joseph died before Christ finished his hidden life, since he is completely absent from the public life, whereas Christ's mother and "brethren" are mentioned more than once. The title "Son of Mary," which the people occasionally used of Christ, also intimates that Mary was a widow by the time her Son began his public ministry.

JOSHUA. Son of Nun, an Ephraimite. A military leader and hero whose name first appeared in the Old Testament when he won a great victory for Moses against the Amalekites (Exodus 17:8–16). His prestige grew, and, obeying YHWH's advice, Moses chose Joshua to be his successor and lead the Israelites out of Egypt and into Canaan (Numbers 27:18–23). Whereas Moses failed to reach it, Joshua succeeded in entering the Promised Land (Deuteronomy 31:2). The history of this great enterprise appears in the book of Joshua, which relates the conquest of Canaan, the partition of the territory among the Twelve Tribes, and his final days (Joshua 1–12, 13–21, 22–24).

Joshua was the dominating figure of the book, but he was not the author. While part of it was written during his lifetime, the writing was spread over a long period and a number of writers contributed. Hence, it is a fabric of many strands. It affords a simple overview of a long, complex historical process, idealized to ensure reverent acceptance by the Jews. Shortly before his death Joshua gathered all the elders, judges, and priests in a great assembly at Shechem. There they agreed unanimously to renounce all other deities and dedicate themselves and their people to the service of YHWH. This was one of the great unifying actions in the history of Israel. His lifework completed, Joshua, the servant of YHWH, died and was buried in Ephraim (Joshua 24:29–31).

JOY. In spiritual literature, the feeling aroused by the expectation or possession of some good. One of the fruits of the Holy Spirit. Joyful emotions affect the body, but they are essentially in the higher faculties of the soul. Differs from pleasure, which may affect the human spirit but originates in some bodily sensation. Thus joy is possessed by angels and human beings, and its source is the rational will.

JOYFUL MYSTERIES. The first chaplet of the Rosary of the Blessed Virgin consisting of 1. the Annunciation to Mary; 2. Mary's Visitation of Elizabeth; 3. the Birth of Jesus in Bethlehem; 4. the Presentation of Christ in the Temple; 5. the Finding of Christ in the Temple. See also GLORIOUS MYSTERIES, LUMINOUS MYSTERIES, SORROWFUL MYSTERIES.

JUBILEE. In the Old Testament the Jewish celebration every fiftieth year to commemorate the deliverance of the Israelites from Egypt. It was commanded by YHWH to Moses, "You will declare this fiftieth year sacred and proclaim the liberation of all the inhabitants of the land. This is to be a jubilee for you; each of you will return to his ancestral home, each to his own clan" (Leviticus 25:10). In the Catholic Church the jubilee year can be traced to Pope Boniface VIII in 1300 and is marked by pilgrimages to Rome, with special services there and throughout the Christian world. Since 1470 the custom has been to hold a regular jubilee every twenty-five years. However, the popes have declared extraordinary jubilees at other times, e.g., in 1933 to commemorate the nineteenth centennial of the Redemption and in 1983 to mark the 1950 years since the Redemption. Jubilees are also celebrated by bishops, priests, religious, and married people to commemorate the fiftieth anniversary of their respective ordination, profession, or marriage. (Etym. Latin *jubilaeus* [*annus*], "[year] of jubilee," alteration [influenced by Latin *jubilare,* to jubilate]; of late Greek *iōbēlaios,* from *iōbēlos,* jubilee; from Hebrew *yōbhēl,* "ram's horn" [used to proclaim the jubilee].) See also HOLY YEAR.

JUDAH. The fourth son of Jacob and Leah; his name was given to one of the Twelve Tribes (Genesis 29:35). From Judah's line Jesse and David came, and ultimately Jesus (Luke 3:23–33). Jacob evidently foresaw potential greatness in Judah, for when he gave his blessing and prophecy to each of his twelve sons, his eulogy of Judah was much more impressive than those of the others (Genesis 49:8). His tribe prospered and acquired additional territory until it was one of the most powerful kingdoms in Palestine. Of the Twelve Tribes only Judah and Benjamin remained loyal to the House of David. The kingdom lasted until Jerusalem fell in 586 B.C.

JUDAISM. The oldest living religion of the Western world, and historically the parent of Christianity and Islam. Present-day Judaism is at once a culture and a religion and should be distinguished accordingly. As a religion, Judaism is the body of a permanent moral tradition, which has its roots in the Old Testament prophets and its hopes in a forthcoming Messiah. As a culture, it is the Jewish people, many of whom are not descendants of Abraham, and among whom is a wide spectrum of faith and worship, yet a mysterious solidarity that is quite unique in the history of mankind.

Modern Judaism may be conveniently divided along religious lines into Orthodox, Reform, and Conservative. Each of these forms builds not only on the Torah or Jewish Bible but also on the Talmud, which is the principal repository of Judaic tradition. Historically, Orthodox Jews are the oldest, reaching back to the synagogues in Palestine and Babylonia in the first century, and theologically they are the most conservative. At the other extreme, and opposed to Orthodoxy, is Reform Judaism, also called Progressive or Liberal, which began in Germany in the eighteenth century as a movement for cultural assimilation. Aroused by this break with historic Judaism, a group of English-speaking rabbis decided to create the Conservative alignment, which seeks to steer a middle course between Orthodoxy and the Reform.

Developments have brought all the segments of Judaism into greater unity, of which the State of Israel is their symbol of a common hope for the future.

JUDAS ISCARIOT. Son of Simon, the only Apostle who did not come from Galilee. His special interest was money, so he was in charge of the common fund of the Apostles (John 13:29). It was an unfortunate assignment, according to John. He referred to Judas as "a thief... who used to help himself to the contributions" (John 12:6). Moreover, Judas remonstrated sharply with Jesus for allowing Mary Magdalene to anoint his feet with a costly ointment, arguing that the money should have gone to the poor (John 12:1–8). His inordinate greed motivated him to betray Jesus. He knew that the high priest, Caiaphas, was anxious to arrest the Master, so he made a deal with the chief priests to identify Jesus at an opportune time for thirty pieces of silver (Matthew 26:14–16). The Apostles were startled at the Last Supper when Jesus said, "I tell you most solemnly, one of you will betray me" (John 13:21). Judas lived up to the terms of his agreement with Caiaphas by leading a number of armed men into Gethsemane and kissing Jesus as a symbol of identification, whereupon they arrested Jesus (Matthew 26:47–56). Scripture reports that when Judas learned that Jesus had been condemned to die, he was filled with remorse (Matthew 27:3–5). There is no way of knowing his motives. He returned the silver, protested that Jesus was innocent, and, when his protest was ignored, went out and hanged himself. The Gospel writers made no attempt to explore Judas's betrayal. They simply said that Satan had entered into him, and they all referred to him as the betrayer (Luke 22:3). His place in the Apostles was taken by Matthias (Acts 1:26). (Etym. Greek *Ioudas;* from Hebrew *Yehudhah,* let him [God] be praised. Greek *iskariōtēs.*)

JUDE, EPISTLE OF. A letter of the Apostle Jude, surnamed Thaddaeus, written to strengthen the faith of Hebrew converts to Christianity. It is therefore a warning against false prophets. Illustrations are drawn from the Old Testament but also from Jewish apocalyptic literature, namely the Assumption of Moses and the book of Enoch. The evidence of previous divine punishments is a prophetic assurance that a similar punishment awaits depraved teachers. Most probably written at Jerusalem before the destruction of the city in A.D. 70, the epistle vindicates the mysterious character of the Christian faith, against those who "abuse anything they do not understand" (Jude 10).

JUDGES, BOOK OF. The seventh book of the Bible, thus called because it relates the events surrounding the temporary leaders of Israel called "judges." This represents the period between the death of Joshua and the days of Samuel. The purpose of the author is especially to illustrate the fact of Divine Providence, that apostasy is always punished and that loyalty to God is always rewarded.

JUDGMENT. In general, an act of the mind affirming or denying something. Philosophically, judgment is the mental act of combining two ideas in affirming their agreement—e.g., God is good—or separating them in denying their agreement—e.g., God is not evil. In ethics, judgment is a right decision about what is just or proper or prudent. It is also the decision of a superior in a natural society (such as the State) or a supernatural society (such as the Church), prescribing what should be done or administering justice.

JUDGMENT, GENERAL. The universal judgment of the human race at the final resurrection of the dead. It is expressed in all the creeds that affirm that Christ now "sits at the right hand of God the Father Almighty, from where He shall come to judge the living and the dead," i.e., the just and the wicked. This will be a social judgment because it will manifest to the world God's justice in condemning sinners and his mercy in those who are saved. It will also be a total judgment by revealing not only people's moral conduct but all the accumulated blessings or injuries that resulted from each person's good or evil deeds.

JUDGMENT, PARTICULAR. The individual judgment of each human being immediately after death. It is a judgment in the sense that God irrevocably determines a person's lot for eternity, depending on his or her cooperation with grace during the stay on earth.

JUDITH. The name means "Jewess." She is the heroine of the book of Judith, which is a historical romance (Judith 7). The details of a great battle are impressive, but the purpose of the book is mainly didactic. When the terrified Israelites were awaiting invasion and annihilation by Nebuchadnezzar's great army under its general, Holofernes, the beautiful, ingenious Judith, inspired by YHWH, visited the Assyrian camp, dazzled the general with her beauty and eloquence, and during the night killed and beheaded him. In the ensuing battle, the demoralized Assyrians were vanquished, and Judith became a national heroine (Judith 10–13). It is an inspiring story to teach the Israelites the importance of depending on YHWH when catastrophe threatens.

JURISDICTION. In ecclesiastical law, the right to exercise official and public authority in some capacity. Thus a bishop has jurisdiction in his diocese, a pastor in his parish, priests in the administration of the sacraments, priests and deacons in preaching, and religious superiors in directing the members of their respective communities. (Etym. Latin *ius*, right + *dicere*, to say: *iurisdictio*, official authority.)

JUSTICE. As a virtue, it is the constant and permanent determination to give everyone his or her rightful due. It is a habitual inclination of the will and therefore always recognizes each one's rights, under any and all circumstances. The rights in question are whatever belongs to a person as an individual who is distinct from the one who practices justice. The essence of justice, then, as compared with charity, consists in the distinction between a person and his or her neighbor; whereas charity is based on the union existing between the one who loves and the person loved so that the practice of charity regards the neighbor as another self.

JUSTIFICATION, THEOLOGY OF. The process of a sinner becoming justified or made right with God. As defined by the Council of Trent, "Justification is the change from the condition in which a person is born as a child of the first Adam into a state of grace and adoption among the children of God through the Second Adam, Jesus Christ our Savior" (Denzinger 1524). On the negative side, justification is a true removal of sin, and not merely having one's sins ignored or no longer held against the sinner by God. On the positive side it is the supernatural sanctification and renewal of a person who thus becomes holy and pleasing to God and an heir of heaven.

The Catholic Church identifies five elements of justification, which collectively define its full meaning. The primary purpose of justification is the honor of God and of Christ; its secondary purpose is the eternal life of mankind. The main efficient cause or agent is the mercy of God; the main instrumental cause is the sacrament of baptism, which is called the "sacrament of faith" to spell out the necessity of faith for salvation. And that which constitutes justification or its essence is the justice of God "not by which He is just Himself, but by which He makes us just," namely sanctifying grace.

Depending on the sins from which a person is to be delivered, there are different kinds of justification. An infant is justified by baptism and the faith of the one who requests or confers the sacrament. Adults are justified for the first time either by personal faith, sorrow for sin and baptism, or by the perfect love of God, which is at least an implicit baptism of desire. Adults who have sinned gravely after being justified can receive justification by sacramental absolution or perfect contrition for their sins. (Etym. Latin *justus,* just + *facere,* to make, do: *justificatio.*)

JUSTIFYING GRACE. The grace by which a person is restored to God's friendship, either for the first time, as in baptism, or after baptism, as in the sacrament of penance. See also ACTUAL GRACE, EFFICACIOUS GRACE, GRACE, HABITUAL GRACE, SACRAMENTAL GRACE, SANCTIFYING GRACE, SUFFICIENT GRACE.

JUST WAR. Armed conflict between nations that is morally tolerated on certain conditions. These conditions, first stated by St. Augustine, have become classic in Catholic moral teaching. In order for a war to be just, it must be on the authority of the sovereign, the cause must be just, the belligerents must have a right intention, and the war must be waged by "proper means." The "just cause" means that a nation's rights are being violated by an actual or at least imminent attack; that other means of preventing aggression—e.g., diplomacy or embargo—have been tried and failed or would be useless; and that there is a proportion between the foreseen evils of conflict and the hoped-for benefits of engaging in war.

K

KAIROS. Literally a "period of time." As used in the Bible, it means time in some religiously significant sense, as "be sure you make the best use of your time" (Colossians 4:5) and "Be on your guard, stay awake, because you never know when the time will come" (Mark 13:33).

KENOSIS. The voluntary renunciation by Christ of his right to divine privilege in his humble acceptance of human status. Paul describes "kenosis" aptly to the Philippians: "His state was divine, yet He did not cling to his equality with God, but emptied Himself to assume the condition of a slave" (Philippians 2:6–7). (Etym. Greek *kenosis,* an emptying.)

KERYGMA. Preaching or proclaiming, as distinct from teaching or instruction (*didache*) in the Gospel of Christ. Before the Gospel was written, it was first preached (Romans 16:25), but beyond preaching it was also to be taught (Matthew 28:19) in order that, as far as possible, it might be understood (Matthew 13:19). (Etym. Greek *kērygma,* proclamation; from *keryks,* herald.)

KINGS, BOOKS OF. In the Douay Bible, translation of the Vulgate, there are four books of Kings, corresponding to Samuel and Kings in the Hebrew Bible. The two Bibles and corresponding versions compare as follows:

ORIGINAL HEBREW	VULGATE AND DOUAY
Samuel	I and II Kings
Kings	III and IV Kings
SEPTUAGINT	RECENT VERSIONS
Kingdoms A and B	I and II Samuel
Kingdoms C and D	I and II Kings

The "Kings" are rulers of a united and divided Hebrew kingdom (c. 1040–561 B.C.). I Kings deals with Samuel, the last of the judges; the origin of the monarchy, and the first king, Saul. II Kings treats the reign of David. III Kings covers the reign of Solomon and the divided kingdom up to Elijah. IV Kings tells the rest of the history of Israel, to the Assyrian captivity, and the history of Judah to the Babylonian captivity.

KISS OF PEACE. Also known as *pax,* it is the mutual greeting of the faithful during Mass as a sign of their union and love of Christ. Certainly in practice by the second century, it became more and more limited in the West. Since the Second Vatican Council it has been restored to being regularly given during the Ordinary Form of the Roman Rite Eucharistic liturgy. The official text of the ritual says, "Then, depending on circumstances [*pro opportunitate*], the deacon or priest adds, 'offer each other the peace,' and all the people, according to local custom, show one another some sign of peace and charity; the priest gives the peace to the deacon or minister."

KNIGHTS OF COLUMBUS. International fraternal benefit organization of Catholic men, founded in 1882 by Rev. Michael J. McGivney, of New Haven, Connecticut. It was established on the principles of charity, unity, and patriotism, and its purpose is to provide a system of fraternal insurance benefits to the members, promote cultural relations, and engage in a variety of religious, educational, and social activities. The Knights represent the modern expression of Catholic Action. Their "purpose has meaning only insofar as they are in perfect accord with the mind of the Church." Worldwide membership is over one million.

KNOCK, OUR LADY OF. Ireland's revered Marian shrine in County Mayo, dating from 1879. On August 21 of that year, during a pouring rain, the figures of Mary, Joseph, and John the Apostle appeared over the gable of the village church, enveloped in a bright light. Beside them was an altar, with a cross surmounting it and a Lamb at its feet. No words came from any of the figures. The parish priest was not informed until the next day, as the onlookers were too stunned to leave the scene. Twice in 1880 the apparition was repeated, but the light was too intense to clearly recognize anyone but Mary. Authenticated miracles brought hundreds to the town. The Archbishop of Tuam started an inquiry. Some fifteen testified that what they saw was no painting or illusion. The Church authorities confirmed the testimony, declaring that the apparitions were "trustworthy and satisfactory." The site is now an object of national pilgrimage. Blessed

Pope John Paul II visited the shrine on September 30, 1979, to mark the centenary of Mary's apparitions and rededicate the Irish people to the Mother of God.

KNOWLEDGE OF GOD. According to the First Vatican Council, "God, one and true, our Creator and Lord [can] be certainly known by the natural light of human reason from the things that are made" (Denzinger 3026). God's first witness of himself, therefore, is in the world of creation as declared by St. Paul: "Ever since God created the world, His everlasting power and deity—however invisible—have been there for the mind to see in the things He has made" (Romans 1:20). Moreover, the human mind "can even demonstrate" his existence and attributes by reasoning from the effects in the universe to their ultimate cause (Pope St. Pius X, *Oath Against Modernism,* Denzinger 3538). However, God has also manifested himself supernaturally in what is commonly called revelation, as found in the Bible and sacred tradition. Such revelation is morally necessary to enable everyone to know God easily, with certitude and without error. Revelation is also absolutely necessary "because God in His infinite goodness has ordained man to a supernatural end," which therefore requires man's knowledge of his destiny and of the means of getting there (Denzinger 3005).

KOINONIA. Community, especially the community of the faithful, of whom St. Luke says they formed a fellowship (koinonia) of believers who worshiped together and held all their possessions in common (Acts 2:42–47). It was also the favorite term of St. Paul to identify the union of the faithful with Christ and among themselves, and it was the Church's term in the earliest creeds for the communion of saints, i.e., the believers on earth, the souls in purgatory, and the elect in glory.

KYRIE ELEISON. The formula of a prayer, "Lord, have mercy," said or sung and repeated in the penitential rite at the beginning of Mass in the Roman Liturgy. Used in conjunction with *Christe Eleison,* "Christ have mercy." One of the few Greek prayers in the Latin Mass, it is most likely the remnant of a liturgical litany. It is also said in the Divine Office and in many litanies, notably the Litany of the Saints. In the Eastern Churches it may appear without *Christe Eleison.*

L

LAETARE SUNDAY. The fourth Sunday of Lent, when the introductory word of the Introit is *laetare,* "Rejoice O Jerusalem." As it is Mid-Lent Sunday, rose vestments are worn, flowers are permitted on the altar, and the organ is played. On this day the Golden Rose is blessed. The day is referred to also as Mediana, Mid-Lent, Mi-Carême, Mothering, Rose, or Refreshment Sunday. See also GAUDETE SUNDAY.

LAIC. *Laicus*—layman.

LAICISM. Exclusive control of Church affairs by the laity. A laicistic program, denying the value of religious ideals for civil, social, and political life, prevents the Church from functioning outside her churches and chapels. Anticlerical proponents of separation of Church and State laicize by government supervision and control functions rightly belonging to the Church, such as education, marriage, hospitals, parishes, convents, churches, and other organizations. It appeared historically as Gallicanism, Febronianism, and Josephinism and in the antireligious laws of France and Mexico. It is part of the political theory of Communism and prevalent in all countries where the government interprets separation of Church and State as subordination of Church to the State. (Etym. Latin *laicus,* pertaining to the people; from Greek *lāos,* people.)

LAICIZATION. The act of reducing an ecclesiastical person or thing to a lay status. The turning over of a church building to a secular purpose; the removal by a civil power of ecclesiastical control in an institution where that control and influence should be operative. In the laicization of clerics, the Holy See, for extraordinary reasons and the greater good of the Church, may laicize a bishop, priest, or deacon. In spite of the term, however, the person does not lose his sacramental powers and remains an ordained person. But he is legitimately dispensed from the ordinary duties attached to his office and, generally also, of his vow of celibacy, giving him the right to marry. In an emergency, a laicized priest can validly administer the sacraments of anointing and penance.

LAITY. The faithful who are not in holy orders and do not belong to a religious state approved by the Church.

LAMB. A symbol of Christ. Rendered in many forms as early as the fourth century. Various aspects show the animal balancing a staff by its right front leg, with a wound in its chest pouring blood into a chalice, representing Christ's Blood in the Passion; the staff bearing a flag signifying Christ's victory in the Resurrection; the lamb resting or standing on a closed book with its seven sealed streamers symbolizing Christ as the judge. The lamb is the emblem of docility; "harshly dealt with, he bore it humbly, he never opened his mouth like the lamb that is led to the slaughter house" (Isaiah 53:7). But the lamb triumphant is portrayed symbolically in the song ascribed to St. Ambrose, "Now at the Lamb's high royal feast," and St. John speaks of the wrath of the Lamb when the sixth seal is broken. As an emblem of St. John the Baptist, it is found in Chartres Cathedral on a banner that reads "Behold the Lamb of God," referring to Christ, "Who takes away the sins of the world." St. Agnes, the child virgin and martyr, is also symbolized by the lamb.

LAMENTATIONS OF JEREMIAH. In the Septuagint and Vulgate, four elegiac poems and one prayer, bewailing the fall of Jerusalem, written by the prophet Jeremiah. The elegies are acrostics, each verse starting with the consecutive letter of the alphabet. Josephus's statement that they were composed after the death of Josiah (608 B.C.) and the claim that Lamentations 4 and 5 date from the Maccabean period are without foundation. They were all composed by Jeremiah after the fall of Jerusalem (586 B.C.).

LANGUAGES, ECCLESIASTICAL. The languages used in the Church's liturgy and in her official teaching. There are two distinct meanings of an ecclesiastical language. In the liturgy there is a further distinction between the Roman Rite and other rites in communion with the Holy See. In the Roman Rite the liturgical language up to the fourth century was mainly Greek. Latin gradually took its place. And this was generally universal until the Second Vatican Council, which opened up the liturgy to the vernacular. On the doctrinal side, the Roman Rite also used Greek in the first three centuries and gradually adopted Latin. The original language of the first seven ecumenical councils, however, was Greek because all the early councils (to A.D. 787) were held in the East. Among the Eastern Christians in communion with Rome the liturgical language was and remains mainly Greek. But other languages have been used from the beginning, e.g., Coptic. The same for doctrine. Some ancient manuscripts of the Bible, including the New Testament, were in Syriac, Armenian, Coptic, and Georgian. Doctrinal statements, except those directly emanating from the Holy See, have also regularly been either in Greek or in the official language of the respective rite.

LAST GOSPEL. The Gospel read in the Extraordinary Form of the Latin Rite at the end of Mass, usually from the first chapter of St. John (verses 1–14), except on days in Lent, vigils, and Sundays when a feast of major rank is celebrated, and the third Mass on Christmas Day.

LAST SACRAMENTS. The sacraments that the faithful receive before death, namely penance, the Eucharist (as Viaticum), and anointing of the sick.

LAST SUPPER. The last meal taken by Christ with his Apostles, the night before his Passion. On this occasion he instituted the Holy Eucharist and the priesthood, and gave the Apostles the long discourse on the Trinity and Christian charity, as recorded by St. John. He then proceeded to Gethsemane and the Agony in the Garden.

LAST WILL. A formal declaration on how a person wants his or her possessions to be disposed of after death. The capacity to make a will is enjoyed by everyone who has the use of reason and the ability to bequeath according to civil or ecclesiastical law. Some of the moral issues affecting wills are 1. the duty to make a will under certain circumstances, e.g., when serious quarrels would follow otherwise among the heirs; 2. the testator who makes a will must leave part of his possessions to his nearest kin, especially the wife and children, who need assistance; 3. on acceptance of the inheritance, heirs are obliged to pay all debts and legacies charged against the estate; 4. the details of the will are to be carried out according to the expressed or even implicit intentions of the testator. Moreover, as long as a person is alive and of sound mind, he may revoke a testament at any time, although conditioned in this matter by the provisions of the civil law.

LATENCY PERIOD. The interval between physical contact with a stimulus and a person's actual reaction. The term mainly applies to the years between five and twelve, when children do not, unless abnormally and unwisely aroused, react to sexual stimulation. The Church advises parents to cultivate this period for teaching children the principles of faith and training them in the moral habits they will need as the foundation of their adult Christian life.

LATERAN TREATY. The agreement signed on February 11, 1929, that finally settled the Roman Question and established Vatican City as a sovereign state under the authority of the pope. At the same time, the Holy See recognized the Italian state with Rome as its political capital. The Italian state recognized "the Catholic, Apostolic and Roman Religion as the sole religion of the State"; it declared "the sovereign independence of the Holy See in the international field" and the Holy See's "sovereign jurisdiction in the Vatican City." At the same time, a concordat was signed, providing for the teaching of the Catholic religion in the public schools, the civil recognition of marriages performed according to canon law, and the freedom of Catholic Action provided it is nonpolitical.

LATIN. Originally the Italic dialect of ancient Rome. It was the ordinary language of the Roman Empire at the time of Christ, and Latin translations of the Bible were made as early as the second century. The liturgy was also celebrated in Latin (along with Coptic, Greek, and Ethiopic) since apostolic times. Latin gradually became the official language of the Western Church, and from the time of Tertullian (c. 160–c. 220) was used extensively in theological writing. A historic change took place at the Second Vatican Council, which declared that "the use of the Latin language . . . is to be preserved in the Latin Rite. But since the use of the vernacular . . . may frequently be of great advantage to the people, a wider use may be made of it" in the liturgy (Constitution on the Sacred Liturgy, I, 36). Since the Council the Church continues to use Latin in her official documents, requires the study of Latin by her future priests, and encourages the use of Latin in those parts of the Mass that are sung or recited by the people, e.g., the Gloria, Credo, Sanctus, Pater Noster, and Agnus Dei. (Etym. Latin *Latinum,* district of Italy in which Rome was situated.)

LATIN CHURCH. The vast portion of the Catholic Church, which uses the Latin liturgies and has its own distinctive canon law. Synonymous with the Latin Rite are the Western Church and Western patriarchate. The expression "Latin Church" is ambiguous, however. It is sometimes used in an uncomplimentary way by the Eastern Orthodox to label all Catholics "Latins" because of their allegiance to the pope. It is also used by some Anglicans to identify what they consider one third of the whole Catholic Church, along with the Anglican and Orthodox. It is finally used, at times, by Catholics belonging to one of the Eastern (or non-Latin) rites to distinguish this from other rites of Roman Catholicism.

LATRIA. The veneration due to God alone for his supreme excellence and to show people's complete submission to him. It is essentially adoration. As absolute latria, it is given only to God, as the Trinity, or one of the Divine Persons, Christ as God and as man, the Sacred Heart of Jesus, and the Holy Eucharist. Representations of God as images connected with the Divinity may receive relative latria, which is given not to the symbol but to the Godhead, whom it signifies. (Etym. Greek *latreiā*, service, worship.)

LAUDS. One of the seven canonical hours, chanted in the Divine Office, taking its name from Psalms 148, 149, and 150. Since the Second Vatican Council it has been replaced in the breviary by "morning prayers." Priests and religious attached to use of the 1962 liturgical books continue to observe Lauds.

LAVABO. The liturgical washing of his hands by a priest at Mass, after the Offertory and before the Preface in the ritual of the Extraordinary Form of the Roman Rite. The sixth verse of Psalm 26 (Vulgate, Psalm 25), recited by the celebrant, begins: "I will wash my hands among the innocent."

LAW. An ordinance of reason for the common good, promulgated by the one who has the care of a community. As an ordinance, law is distinguished from a mere counsel or a suggestion. It is an order or command that imposes obligation or moral necessity to be obeyed. It is the imposition of the superior's will on the will of those who belong to a society, and must be expressed in a mandatory form, no matter how courteously phrased. As an ordinance of reason, though directly imposed by the will of the one in authority, it is first formulated by his intellect as the planning faculty behind the will. Since its purpose is to direct rational beings to do something, it must be reasonable. To be reasonable, a law should be consistent, just, observable, enforceable, and useful. It is consistent when it is neither self-contradictory nor in contradiction with other laws. It is just when it respects higher laws and distributes burdens equitably. It is observable when it does not demand the impossible because it is cruel or too difficult. It is enforceable when not only the law-abiding but everyone can be expected to keep it because it is supported by appropriate sanctions. And it is useful when it serves a valid purpose without needless restriction of human liberty.

A law is for the common good, and in this differs from a command, order, precept, or injunction laid on an individual person. Laws, therefore, always look to the benefit of the community as a whole, not a private or personal good. When they are territorial, they bind all who stay in a certain region, but only when they are there. Laws are relatively permanent. They are always from public authority and last until repealed, and they may bind succeeding generations, whereas personal orders cease with the death or removal from office of the one who gave them.

To promulgate a law is to make it known to those whom it binds. The way it is promulgated depends on the nature of the law, the customs of the people, and on circumstances of time and place. It is properly promulgated if the people can come to know about the law without much difficulty.

A law must be authoritative, which means that it must come from a lawgiver or legislator who has rightful jurisdiction. The lawgiver may be a physical person, which is a single individual, or a moral person, which is a body or a board passing laws by joint action. (Etym. Latin *legere,* to read; *eligere,* to choose; *ligare,* to bind; *lex,* law.)

LAW OF NATURE. The moral law as universally binding on human nature, unchangeable in its essence, and knowable to all mankind. The law of nature is universally binding no matter how many people may violate it. Its universality is not to be confused with the universality of its observance. No matter how many or flagrant the transgressions, they do not change the value or extent of the law.

The law of nature is adaptable but not essentially changeable. There have been modifications adopted at one time or another in the law. On closer study, however, they are seen to be in fact changes in circumstances or in matters to which the law is applied. What cannot change is the substance of the law itself.

Also the law of nature can be perceived, however dimly, by every human being who has the full use of his or her reason. Certain social customs, clearly in opposition to this law, do not change the fact that it can be perceived by all. What such customs prove is that fallen human nature is prone to evil and needs divine assistance as revelation even for a correct and generally available knowledge beyond the primary duties of the moral order. Obscured by passion and exposed to the moral pollution of a secularist culture, human reason is weakened in its perception of what is right and wrong. Nevertheless its light is not completely extinguished, and besides, having access to revelation, the light of grace is also always available. See also NATURAL LAW.

LAX CONSCIENCE. An erroneous conscience when the mind decides on insufficient grounds that a sinful act is permissible or that something gravely wrong is not serious.

LAY APOSTOLATE. Any form of service for the religious welfare of others practiced by the Catholic laity. More commonly refers to apostolic lay activity performed as part of an association or society. The lay apostolate, since the Second Vatican Council, may be one of three types: apostolic work done by the laity but totally supervised by the hierarchy; apostolic work conducted by the laity but officially responsible to the hierarchy; and the apostolic work totally conducted by the laity but approved by the hierarchy.

LAY BROTHER. A member of a clerical religious order or congregation who is not a priest and who is not preparing for the priesthood. The term was originally used to identify those men religious who were not clerics (hence brothers) and who were not bound to the chant or recitation of the Divine Office, hence lay, as distinguished from choir monks, who were also not clerics. But in modern times the term is more commonly applied to all male religious who are not, or will not be, ordained. It is customary, however, to simply call them "brothers" without the prefix "lay." The reason is that brothers are full-fledged members of the religious community to which they belong, although their rights and privileges in the community are determined by their respective rule or constitutions. The term "lay brothers" is not applied to the members of the nonclerical men's religious institutes. They are called brothers.

LAZARUS. 1. the brother of Mary and Martha, who befriended and entertained Jesus in their home in Bethany. While Jesus "was away," Lazarus was taken ill and died. Their faith was so strong that both Mary and Martha greeted Jesus, on his return four days later, with the same words: "If you had been here, my brother would not have died." At the tomb Jesus ordered Lazarus to rise; he came out of the tomb at once in the burial wrappings, to the amazement of the mourning family and friends. The Pharisees were so worried by Jesus's growing popularity that they decided on that day that he must die (John 11); 2. the name Jesus used to represent the poor man in the parable he related concerning the fate of Dives, the rich man who lived luxuriously, and Lazarus, the impoverished beggar, who ate the scraps from Dives's table. When they died, the rich man suffered torment in Hades, while Lazarus rested on Abraham's bosom (Luke 16:19–31). (Etym. Greek *Lazaros* from Hebrew *'El'azar*, God has helped.)

LAZINESS. Disinclination or aversion to effort, whether physical, mental, or moral. It implies idleness, even when a person is supposedly at work.

LEAVENED BREAD. The bread for the Eucharist made of fermented dough, commonly used by the Catholic Christians of the Eastern rite except the Armenians. Natural yeast is used as the leaven. (Etym. Latin *levamen*, alleviation, "that which raises"; from *levare*, to raise.)

LECTERN. A movable reading desk of wood or metal to support the sacred books used in liturgical ceremonies. When stationary, lecterns are sometimes elaborately decorated; those in English churches were conspicuous with eagles with outspread wings and other massive carvings. Two were frequently used, one on the Gospel and the other on the Epistle side of the sanctuary. Since the Second Vatican Council many churches have separate lecterns on either side of the sanctuary: one for the celebrant and the other for the lector of the Mass. A small folding support, sometimes called a lectern, is often placed on the altar to hold the Sacramentary or Gospel book during Mass.

LECTIONARY. The present lectionary for the Ordinary Form of the Roman Rite was introduced March 22, 1970. It contains a three-year cycle of readings for Sundays and solemn feasts, a two-year weekday cycle, and a one-year cycle for the feasts of saints. Moreover, it contains readings for a large variety of other Masses. There are also Responsorial Psalms that follow the first readings for each Mass, along with Gospel or Alleluia verses to follow the second readings.

LECTOR. One of the ministries associated with the Ordinary Form of the Roman Rite. He functions partially as the subdeacon did previously. He is appointed to read the word of God in the liturgical assembly. Accordingly he reads the lesson from Sacred Scripture, except the Gospel, in the Mass and in other sacred celebrations; recites the Psalms between the readings in the absence of the Psalmist; presents the intentions for general intercessions when the deacon or cantor is absent; and may also direct the congregation in the singing. If necessary he also assumes the responsibility of instructing any of the faithful called upon to read the Scriptures in any liturgical celebration. (Etym. Latin *lector,* reader; from *legere,* to read.)

LEGION OF MARY. One of the largest lay organizations in the Catholic Church, founded in Dublin in 1921. Its purpose is entirely spiritual, namely, the sanctification of the members and their practice of charity toward others.

LEGITIMATE MARRIAGE. A true natural marriage between two parties, neither of whom is baptized. Such also is a marriage validly contracted by a baptized person with one who is not baptized. In this case, even the baptized party does not receive the sacrament. The marital bond is said to be a natural one.

LENT. The season of prayer and penance before Easter. Its purpose is to better prepare the faithful for the feast of the Resurrection, and dispose them for a more fruitful reception of the graces that Christ merited by his Passion and death.

In the Latin Rite, Lent begins on Ash Wednesday and continues for forty days, besides Sundays, until Easter Sunday. Ash Wednesday occurs on any day from February 4 to March 11, depending on the date of Easter.

Originally the period of fasting in preparation for Easter did not, as a rule, exceed two or three days. But by the time of the Council of Nicaea (325) forty days were already customary. And ever since, this length of time has been associated with Christ's forty-day fast in the desert before beginning his public life.

According to the prescription of Venerable Pope Paul VI, in revising the Church's laws of fast and abstinence, "The time of Lent preserves its penitential character. The days of penitence to be observed under obligation throughout the Church are all Fridays and Ash Wednesday, that is to say the first days of Great Lent, according to the diversity of rites. Their substantial observance binds gravely" (*Paenitemini,* III, Norm II).

Besides fast and abstinence on specified days, the whole Lenten season is to be penitential, with stress on prayer, reception of the sacraments, almsgiving, and the practice of charity. (Etym. Anglo-Saxon *lengten,* lencten, spring, Lent.)

LEVITATION. Phenomenon in which a human body is raised above ground and sustained in midair without any natural support. At times the body rises to great heights; at other times it glides rapidly just above ground.

Well-documented evidence of levitation is reported in the lives of many saints, e.g., Francis Xavier, Paul of the Cross, Peter of Al-cántara, Philip Neri, and Stephen of Hungary. One of the most celebrated was St. Joseph Cupertino (1603–63), Conventual Franciscan, who was treated with no little severity by his ecclesiastical superiors because of the disturbance caused by his raptures.

According to Benedict XIV, in order to verify genuine levitation it is first of all necessary to make a thorough investigation to eliminate any chance of fraud. Then he states that a well-authenticated levitation cannot be explained on merely natural grounds; that this phenomenon is not, however, beyond the power of angels or demons; and that with the saints it is a kind of anticipation of a prerogative of glorified bodies.

LEVITICUS. Third book of the Bible, named from its contents, which deal entirely with the service of God and the religious ceremonies to be performed by the members of the tribe of Levi, both priests and Levites. Its divisions are the rites of sacrifice (1–7), consecration and installation of priests (8–10), the laws of purity (11–16), the law of holiness (17–22), religious institutions (23–25), blessings and curses (26). The book strongly emphasizes the divine majesty and the duty to honor and obey God as sovereign Lord.

LEX FUNDAMENTALIS. The basic law of the Roman Catholic Church, similar to a constitution for the Church, is a new feature in the history of ecclesiastical legislation. It was called forth by the decisions of the Second Vatican Council.

LIBERALISM. Until the eighteenth century the term generally meant whatever was worthy of a free man, e.g., as applied to the liberal arts or a liberal education. This meaning is still current, but at least since the French Revolution liberalism has become more or less identified with a philosophy that stresses human freedom to the neglect and even denial of the rights of God in religion, the rights of society in civil law, and the rights of the Church in her relations to the State. It was in this sense that liberalism was condemned by Blessed Pope Pius IX in 1864 in the *Syllabus of Errors* (Denzinger 2977–80).

LIBERATION THEOLOGY. A movement in the Roman Catholic Church that makes criticism of oppression essential to the task of theology. The forms of oppression to be criticized are mainly social and economic evils. Originating in Latin America, liberation theology has held as its main concern the exploitation of the poor, but it also seeks to defend the rights of minority and ethnic groups and to support women's liberation. It is, therefore, a theory of deliverance from the injustices caused to people by the power structures of modern society.

It is a new approach to theology, and its leaders urge a reinterpretation of the Christian faith to concentrate on the main task of the Church today, to deliver people everywhere from the inhumanity to which they are being subjected, especially by those in political power. Accordingly all the main doctrines of historic Christianity are to be reassessed and, if need be, revised. Christ becomes an inspired human deliverer of the weak and oppressed; God's kingdom centers on this world, and not on the next; sin is essentially social evil and not an offense against God; the Church's mission is mainly sociopolitical and not eschatological; and objective divine revelation is subordinated to personal experience.

Aware of both the potential and risks of liberation theology, Blessed Pope John Paul II addressed himself mainly to this subject on his visit to Mexico in early 1979. He told the bishops of Latin America, meeting at Puebla for their General Conference: "The Church feels the duty to proclaim the liberation of millions of human beings, the duty to help this liberation become firmly established." At the same time, "she also feels the corresponding duty to proclaim liberation in its integral and profound meaning, as Jesus proclaimed and realized it." Then, drawing on Blessed Pope Paul VI's teaching, he declared that it is "above all, liberation from sin and the evil one, in the joy of knowing God and being known by him."

The pope finally set down the norms "that help to distinguish when the liberation in question is Christian and when on the other hand it is based rather on ideologies that rob it of consistency with an evangelical point of view." Basically these norms refer to the content "of what the evangelizers proclaim" and to "the concrete attitudes that they adopt." On the level of content, "one must see what is their fidelity to the word of God, to the Church's living Tradition and to her Magisterium." On the level of attitudes, "one must consider what sense of communion they have with the bishops, in the first place, and with the other sectors of the People of God; what contribution they make to the real building up of the community; in what form they lovingly show care for the poor, the sick, the dispossessed, the neglected and the oppressed, and in what way they find in them the image of the poor and suffering Jesus, and strive to relieve their need and serve Christ in them" (address to the Third General Conference of the Latin American Episcopate, January 28, 1979).

LIBERTY. Freedom, but with stress on the person who enjoys or exercises the freedom. Liberty, therefore, is more the subjective power of self-determination; freedom is more the objective absence of constraint or coercion, notably with reference to civil society, as freedom of religion, assembly, and education.

LICIT. That which is permitted by law, whether civil or ecclesiastical. Often distinguished from valid, to express what the law prescribes or allows, as distinct from what is necessary to produce the desired effect. (Etym. Latin *licet,* it is lawful, it is allowed or permitted.)

LIFE. Inward activity. The essence of a being to act from within; ranging from the life of God, which is identical with his nature, on through all the forms of life in the created universe. The higher a nature the more intimate what comes from it, for its inwardness of activity corresponds to its rank of being. Life is immanent activity, which begins and terminates within the living being.

LIFE EVERLASTING. The eternal life of heavenly glory, in body and soul, promised by Christ to those who die in God's friendship.

LIMBO. The abode of souls excluded from the full blessedness of the beatific vision but not suffering any other punishment. They enjoy the happiness that would have been human destiny if humans had not been elevated to the supernatural order.

Catholic theology distinguishes two kinds of limbo. The limbo of the Fathers (*limbus patrum*) was the place where the saints of the Old Testament remained until Christ's coming and redemption of the world. The limbo of infants (*limbus infantium*) is the permanent state of those who die in original sin but are innocent of any personal guilt.

Regarding the limbo of infants, it is an article of the Catholic faith that those who die without baptism, and for whom the want of baptism has not been supplied in some other way, cannot enter heaven. This is the teaching of the ecumenical councils of Florence and Trent.

The Church has never defined the existence of limbo, although she has more than once supported the fact by her authority. Those who either deny that heaven is a supernatural destiny to which no creature has a natural claim, or who deny that original sin deprives a person of a right to heaven logically, also deny the very possibility of limbo. On their premises there is no need of such a place. Among others who denied the existence of limbo were the Jansenists, whose theory of selective predestination excluded the need for any mediatorial source of grace, including baptism. They were condemned by Pope Pius VI as teaching something "false, rash and injurious to Catholic education," because they claimed that it was a Pelagian fable to hold that there is a place "which the faithful generally designate by the name of limbo of children," for the souls of those who depart this life with the sole guilt of original sin (Denzinger 2626). Venerable Pope Pius XII declared that "an act of love can suffice for an adult to acquire sanctifying grace and supply for the lack of baptism; to the unborn or newly born infant this way is not open" (*Acta Apostolicae Sedis,* XLIII, 84). At stake is the revealed doctrine that heaven is a sheer gift of divine goodness and that baptism of water or desire is necessary to enter heaven.

The *Catechism of the Catholic Church* states that those children who die without the benefit of baptism the Church can only entrust to the mercy of God (1261). (Etym. Latin *limbo,* ablative form of *limbus,* border; taken from *"in limbo patrum"* [in the border of hell reserved for the fathers (or saints)], a phrase used by the Church Fathers.)

LITANY. A form of prayer consisting of a series of petitions or biddings that are sung or said by a priest, deacon, or leader, and to which the people make fixed responses.

Litanies have a definite structure: first the invocation of the persons of the Trinity, then the petitions corresponding to a distinctive theme, followed by three invocations of the Lamb of God, and closing with a short prayer that summarizes the petitions made.

Since the Second Vatican Council, these litanies have been formally indulgenced—i.e., a partial indulgence for every recitation: the Holy Name, the Sacred Heart, the Precious Blood, the Blessed Virgin, St. Joseph, and the saints. Other litanies, approved for use by the faithful but not thus indulgenced, number over a hundred.

In the Eastern rites, litanies are an outstanding feature of the Eucharistic liturgy, and in the Ambrosian rite are sung every Sunday during Lent in place of the Gloria. (Etym. Latin *litania;* from Greek *litaneiā,* prayer, entreaty, supplication.)

LITANY OF THE BLESSED VIRGIN MARY. In its present form it was approved and indulgenced by Pope Sixtus V in 1587, and again by Pope Clement VIII in 1601. It is a series of invocations of the Blessed Virgin, each with the response "Pray for us." Successive popes have added new invocations—e.g., "Mother of Good Counsel" by Pope Leo XIII, "Queen of Peace" by Pope Benedict XV, "Queen Assumed into Heaven" by Pope Pius XII, and "Mother of the Church" and "Queen of families" by Blessed Pope John Paul II. It is a simplified version of older Litanies of Our Lady that were known already in the twelfth century.

LITANY OF THE HOLY NAME. Invocations expressing various attributes of the Savior, with a petition for mercy repeated after each invocation. Of unknown origin, it has been commonly ascribed to St. Bernardino of Siena and St. John Capistran, zealous preachers of devotion to the Holy Name in their day. In 1588, Pope Sixtus V granted an indulgence for its private recitation. In 1862, Pope Pius IX approved it for any diocese whose bishop requested the litany, and in 1886, Pope Leo XIII extended its use to the universal Church, because of the growing devotion to the Holy Name throughout the world.

LITANY OF ST. JOSEPH. A series of invocations of the foster father of Jesus, approved for the universal Church by Pope St. Pius X on March 18, 1909. After the customary petitions to the Holy Trinity, and one addressed to the Blessed Virgin, the litany is composed of twenty-one invocations expressing the virtues and dignity of St. Joseph.

LITANY OF THE PRECIOUS BLOOD. A series of invocations of the Savior, through his Precious Blood, approved in its present form by Pope John XXIII in 1960. Each of the twenty-four petitions begins with the term "Blood of Christ," to which the response is "Save us." The Blood of Christ either represents Christ himself, as "Blood of Christ, Incarnate Word of God," or refers to the physical Blood of the Savior, as "Blood of Christ, poured out on the Cross," or spans both meanings, as "Blood of Christ, freeing souls from purgatory." The Litany of the Precious Blood is included among the official litanies of the Church in the *Manual of Indulgences*. There is a partial indulgence for each recitation.

LITANY OF THE SACRED HEART. Invocations of Jesus Christ under the title of the Sacred Heart, authorized for recitation in the universal Church by Pope Leo XIII in 1899. After the customary petitions to the Persons of the Holy Trinity, the litany contains thirty-three invocations of the Heart of Jesus. Each invocation reflects an aspect of God's love symbolized by the physical Heart of Christ, the Son of God who became man and died out of love for sinful mankind.

LITANY OF THE SAINTS. Believed to be the most ancient of the litanies used in the Church. Already prescribed by Pope Gregory the Great in 590 for a public procession of thanksgiving at the end of a plague that had devastated Rome. In a somewhat different form, it was mentioned by St. Basil in the fourth century. Called the Litany of the Saints because it is made up of petitions addressed to various saints of different classes and to Mary, the Queen of the Saints. In its present form, after invoking forty-eight individual saints and thirteen groups of saints, the litany begs for deliverance from a dozen evils and makes some thirty intercessions, including "that you would deign to humble the enemies of Holy Church" and "grant peace and unity to all Christian people."

LITTLE OFFICE OF OUR LADY. A shortened form of the Divine Office in honor of the Blessed Virgin. It contains seven hours, but the Psalms do not vary each day. Already known in the tenth century, it originated in the monasteries and was early adopted by the Cistercians and Camaldolese. Retained after the Breviary reform of St. Pius V in 1568, but no longer binding under sin. Recited by many religious communities and used as a private devotion by the faithful.

LITURGICAL BOOKS. Texts approved by the Holy See containing the orderly arrangement of the prayers, hymns, readings, and directives to be followed by the celebrant and ministers in the Church's liturgy.

All the liturgical books have been revised since the Second Vatican Council, including the Sacramentary and Lectionary for Mass, the Liturgy of the Hours, the order for the celebration of each of the sacraments, and for religious profession.

LITURGICAL YEAR. The annual cycle of the mysteries of Christ, the Blessed Virgin, angels, and saints, which the Church commemorates in the Mass, the Divine Office, and other forms of public worship. The liturgical year begins with the first Sunday of Advent and closes with the last Saturday before the First Sunday of Advent.

LITURGY. A public service, duty, or work. In Scripture it refers to the religious duties to be performed by priests and Levites in the Temple, especially those related to the Sacrifice; in Christian use among the Eastern Churches it means the Eucharistic Sacrifice.

In present-day usage liturgy is the official public worship of the Church and is thus distinguished from private devotion. It is the special title of the Eucharist, and the administration of the sacraments with the annexed use of the sacramentals.

From a theological viewpoint, the liturgy is the exercise now on earth of Christ's priestly office, as distinct from his role as teacher and ruler of his people. Christ performs this priestly office as Head of his Mystical Body so that Head and members together offer the sacred liturgy. Its function, therefore, is twofold: to give honor and praise to God, which is worship, and to obtain blessings for the human race, which is sanctification. (Etym. Latin *liturgia;* from Greek *leitos,* of the people + *ergon,* work: *leitourgia,* public duty, public worship.)

LITURGY OF THE EUCHARIST. The most solemn part of the Mass, from the Presentation of the Gifts to the Postcommunion included. The Church has arranged this part of the Mass so that its several parts correspond to the words and actions of Christ at the Last Supper, and specifically in these stages: in the Presentation of the Gifts are brought the bread, wine, and water, even as Christ took these elements into his hands; in the Eucharistic prayer God is thanked for the whole work of redemption and the gifts become the body and blood of Christ; in the breaking of the one bread the unity of the faithful is signified; and in Communion they receive the same Christ who gave himself on Holy Thursday to his Apostles.

LITURGY OF THE HOURS. See DIVINE OFFICE.

LITURGY OF THE WORD. The second part of the Mass, during which the faithful are instructed in the revealed word of God. It consists of readings from Sacred Scripture and the songs occurring between them. The homily, profession of faith, and the prayer of the faithful develop and conclude the Liturgy of the Word.

LIVING WAGE. The compensation given to a worker, based on family responsibilities. Two criteria are recognized in Catholic moral science, according to which a living wage may be either absolute or relative. These criteria are spelled out in the social encyclicals of the modern popes.

An absolute living wage is based on an average wage for family living, in which all workers who perform the same tasks receive the same pay. This is irrespective of whether they are married with children, married without children, or single. A relative living wage is based on the concrete family situation and responsibilities of each worker, in which the pay varies according to one's marital status and the number of dependents to be supported.

LOCUTION. A supernatural communication to the ear or imagination, or directly to the intellect. The locution is supernatural in the manner of communication, that is, beyond the ordinary laws of nature. Spurious locutions may come from the evil spirit and can be recognized by their lack of coherence or clarity, the disquiet they cause in the one who receives them, and the evil effects they produce in those who listen to them. (Etym. Latin *locutio,* a speaking, speech, discourse; from *loqui,* to speak.)

LORD. Title commonly used of God in the Old Testament (*Adonai*) and commonly applied to Christ in the New Testament (*Kyrios*). In the Vulgate it is used in place of YHWH. The consistent way that St. Paul and other New Testament writers use the term of Christ indicates that they regarded him as God.

LORD'S PRAYER. See PATER NOSTER.

LORD'S PRAYER (MASS). The liturgical recitation of the Pater Noster at Mass. Returning to an ancient practice, the Lord's Prayer in the

Ordinary Form of the Roman Rite includes five parts: an invitation by the priest; the Pater Noster, sung or said together with the people; the embolism, which amplifies the last petition of the Lord's Prayer; the doxology; and concluding acclamation by the faithful.

LOURDES. World-famous shrine of the Immaculate Conception, in the department of Hautes-Pyrénées in France. In 1858, the Blessed Virgin appeared eighteen times at Massabielle, at a grotto near Lourdes, to Bernadette Soubirous, a fourteen-year-old peasant girl. At the same time a spring appeared, miraculous healings were reported, and pilgrims began to come to the spot. In 1862 the apparitions received ecclesiastical approbation and a church was built above the grotto. Then beside it, from 1883 to 1901, was built the magnificent Church of the Rosary. Since then millions of people have visited the shrine, and a medical bureau has been established to investigate the character of the cures, of which hundreds have been fully authenticated by medical specialists.

The healings generally take place after the people have bathed in the waters of the spring or during the blessing with the monstrance with the Blessed Sacrament carried in procession. Not all cures are physical, many report marvelous conversions and graces in the spiritual life. In 1891 a local feast of Our Lady of Lourdes (February 11) was established and in 1907 extended to the universal Church by Pope St. Pius X.

LOVE. To will good to someone. Also to please someone, either by sharing with that person what one possesses or by doing what someone wants. Basically there are two kinds of love. The love of concupiscence, or self-interested love, means that another is loved for one's own sake as something useful or pleasant to the one who loves. The love of friendship means selfless love of another for that person's own sake, for his or her good, to please him or her; it is the love of benevolence.

LOVE OF ENEMIES. Christ's commandment of merciful love, shown especially in loving those who are not lovable. The enemies of whom Christ speaks are "those who persecute you" (Matthew 5:44), "those who hate you . . . curse you" (Luke 6:28). This is the highest and truest test of selfless love, to "do good to . . . bless . . . pray for those who treat you badly" (Luke 6:28).

LUCIFER. The name is sometimes applied to a king of Babylon (Isaiah 14:12), but the Fathers of the Church commonly identify Lucifer with Satan, leader of the fallen angels. In the Church's writings it is a synonym for the devil, the Prince of Darkness, who before he fell was an angel of light. In the Scriptures, Christ is also called Phosphoros—Light-Bearer (II Peter 1:19). (Etym. Latin *lucifer*, light-bearer.)

LUKE. He is described in one of Paul's epistles as "my dear friend, Luke, the doctor" (Colossians 4:14). He traveled with Paul on several of his missionary journeys, using the first person plural in giving details. One journey was a sailing from Troas to Samothrace and eventually to Phoenicia. Another was from Phoenicia to Jerusalem. Later they went to Rome together. Scholars estimate that much of his writing was done about the year 70. It seems clear that he was a Greek Gentile directing his message to Gentile Christians. During the two years Paul was imprisoned in Caesarea, Luke had ample time and opportunity to gather material and write his New Testament contributions (Acts 20, 21). He was indebted to Mark for a considerable part of the material that appears in his Gospel. (Etym. Latin *Lucus;* Greek *Loukas*.)

LUMEN GENTIUM. Dogmatic Constitution on the Church, of the Second Vatican Council. Its purpose is declared to be twofold: to explain the Church's nature as "a sign and instrument of communion with God and of unity among all men," and to clarify the Church's universal mission as the sacrament of human salvation. A unique feature of the constitution is the Explanatory Note, added to the conciliar document by order of Venerable Pope Paul VI, clarifying the meaning of episcopal collegiality, that the community of bishops has no authority without dependence on and communion with the Bishop of Rome (November 21, 1964).

LUMINOUS MYSTERIES. The five mysteries of the Rosary dedicated to Christ's public ministry: the Baptism of Jesus, the Wedding Feast of Cana, the Proclamation of the Kingdom, the Transfiguration, and the Institution of the Holy Eucharist. Blessed Pope John Paul II added this set of mysteries to the recitation of the Rosary.

LUST. An inordinate desire for or enjoyment of sexual pleasure. The desires or acts are inordinate when they do not conform to the divinely ordained purpose of sexual pleasure, which is to foster the mutual love of husband and wife and, according to the dispositions of Providence, to procreate and educate their children. (Etym. Anglo-Saxon *lut*, pleasure.)

LUTHERANS. Those Protestants who follow the teaching of Martin Luther (1483–1546), as expressed in distinctive confessions of faith that are contained in the *Book of Concord*, published at Dresden in 1580. In the confessions the Bible is declared to be the only norm of belief, to which even the historic creeds and other traditional statements of faith are to be subordinated. Yet the Bible itself is subordinated to the single basic principle of justification by faith without good works. Since human beings lost their original innocence, which at creation was an essential part of their nature, they are no longer free to do spiritual good but are under the slavery of sin. Redemption means being justified by faith (trust) in Christ, whereby the sinner is considered pleasing to God without any cooperation on a human being's part. Lutherans have remained loyal to this belief, namely confidence that the believer has in fact been saved by the blood of Christ with no merits on a human being's part. To this day it typifies their particular form of Protestantism, which has also been remarkably constant in its allegiance to the person of Luther and to the confessions of personal faith that he inspired.

Besides Germany, where Lutheranism originated, it is the official religion in the Scandinavian countries and has numerous adherents in North America. It is most flourishing where the head of the state is, in effect, also the chief authority in the Church. As such it has contributed substantially to the development of nationalism in the modern world.

LUXURY. The possession and enjoyment of something that gives pleasure to the senses but is not otherwise either useful or necessary. Though not sinful in itself, luxury easily leads to sin or may itself be the result of injustice or failure in charity. As *luxuria*, it is sinful indulgence of sexual pleasure. (Etym. Latin *luxuria*, luxury, voluptuousness.)

LYING. Speaking deliberately against one's mind. The speech is any communication of ideas to another person, and may be done by means of words, spoken or written, and by gestures. By speaking deliberately is meant that the speaker must realize what he is saying; it is not a mere matter of ignorance or misstatement. When a person tells a lie, he or she says something that is contrary to what is on that person's mind; there is real opposition between what one says and what one thinks.

M

MACCABEES. A family that controlled the course of Jewish history from 166 to 63 B.C. and secured some measure of religious freedom and political independence during those troubled years. The Seleucid king, Antiochus Epiphanes, who dominated Palestine, was determined to wipe out Judaism and force Hellenistic culture on the Jews (I Maccabees 1). When he resorted to the crowning indignity of introducing pagan sacrifices to Zeus in the Temple in Jerusalem, the priest Mattathias launched open rebellion, refusing to conduct heathen sacrifices and killing an apostate Jew who agreed to do so. Mattathias and his five sons had to leave Jerusalem, but the struggle had only begun. After the father died, his son, the great Judas Maccabaeus, took over leadership (I Maccabees 2) and re-entered Jerusalem victoriously and purified the Temple (I Maccabees 3–9). He eventually died in battle, but his brother, Jonathan, continued the struggle for eighteen years (I Maccabees 9–12). He was followed by a third brother, Simon, who finally achieved political freedom in 142 B.C. But intrigue and violence never ceased; both Jonathan and Simon were murdered. It was not until the reign of John Hyrcanus, Simon's son, that Judaea became the dominant power in Palestine (I Maccabees 13–16). Several other Maccabees followed (Aristobulus I, Alexander Jannaeus, Alexandra, and Aristobulus II), but increasing internal dissension weakened the government. Finally Roman legions besieged Jerusalem in 63 B.C., took over control, and the Jewish kingship was abolished. The Maccabee dynasty became extinct after a tempestuous century of violence. The history of this heroic struggle is told in detail in the First Book of Maccabees. The Second Book of Maccabees is a more rambling account that parallels the first seven chapters of the First Book of Maccabees but covers only fifteen years.

MADONNA. My lady, the Blessed Virgin Mary, either as a title or representation of the Virgin. Often combined with another title, e.g., Madonna della Strada, Our Lady of the Way. (Etym. Italian *Madonna*, from *mia donna*, my lady; from Latin *mea domina*, my lady.)

MAGDALENE, MARY. A woman from Galilee whose surname was probably derived from her hometown, Magdala. The devotion she showed to Jesus was gratitude for the fact that he had driven seven demons out of her (Mark 16:9). According to tradition, she had been a harlot. Her faithfulness is clearly seen in that she was one of the few on Calvary at the Crucifixion (Matthew 27:56). She watched Jesus being buried and was one of the three women who went to the tomb on Resurrection morning (Mark 15:47, 16:1) and discovered that Jesus had risen (Matthew 28:1–8). The first one to whom he appeared that morning was Mary Magdalene (John 20:14–18).

MAGI. Members of the priestly caste of the Mazdean religion, with special reference to the wise men who brought gifts to Jesus at his birth. The appearance of an unusual star caused them to leave the East in search of a king of whose birth the star was a sign. Herod asked them to return after finding the Infant. But the Magi, warned in a dream, went back to the East by another way. They are described as bringing symbolic gifts of gold, frankincense, and myrrh. Their names, Gaspar, Melchior, and Balthasar, are first mentioned in the sixth century. The Adoration of the Magi early became one of the most popular subjects of representation in art, the first extant painting being in the Capella Greca of the Priscilla Catacomb (Rome), dating from the second century.

MAGIC. The art of making use of the forces of nature by certain occult observances that have a religious appearance, or of courting the secret influences of the invisible world. Magic may be either natural or preternatural.

Natural magic is based on the theory that nature is full of many objects whose hidden protective or curative properties can satisfy practically every need or drive away a host of evils. The problem is to find these objects. With their uncritical mind and animistic prejudice, tribal worshipers easily turn from a valid exploitation of the physical forces of nature to a superstitious cult of the unknown, in the form of charms, philters, auguries, omens, the art of divination, and respect for scores of sacred prohibitions and taboos.

Preternatural magic is a kind of antireligion that has its own orders of worship, incantations, evocations, rites, fetishes, sacrifices, priests, and meeting places. It is black magic when the purpose is malevolent and white magic when the intention is to obtain some benefit for oneself or another. The basis of preternatural magic is some form of animism, which believes that material objects or nonhuman living creatures possess preternatural powers that can be invoked or appeased by hidden or occult means. (Etym. Greek *magikos,* magician, magical, from *magos,* Magus, magician.)

MAGISTERIUM. The Church's teaching authority, vested in the bishops, as successors of the Apostles, under the Roman Pontiff, as successor of St. Peter. Also vested in the pope, as Vicar of Christ and visible head of the Catholic Church. (Etym. Latin *magister,* master.)

MAGISTERIUM, EXTRAORDINARY. The Church's teaching office exercised in a solemn way, as in formal declarations of the pope or of ecumenical councils of bishops approved by the pope. When the extraordinary magisterium takes the form of papal definitions or conciliar decisions binding on the consciences of all the faithful in matters of faith and morals, it is infallible.

MAGISTERIUM, ORDINARY. The teaching office of the hierarchy under the pope, exercised normally, that is, through the regular means of instructing the faithful. These means are all the usual channels of communication, whether written, spoken, or practical. When the ordinary magisterium is also universal—that is, collectively intended for all the faithful—it is, like extraordinary magisterium, also infallible.

MAGNIFICAT. The Canticle of the Blessed Virgin Mary, beginning *"Magnificat anima mea Dominum"* (My soul does magnify the Lord). Mary first recited it on her visit to Elizabeth after the Annunciation and her conception of Christ. It is included in the Roman Breviary, chanted daily at Vespers, and solemnly recited on other occasions.

> My soul proclaims the greatness of the Lord,
> my spirit rejoices in God my Savior
> for he has looked with favor on his lowly servant.
>
> From this day all generations will call me blessed:
> the Almighty has done great things for me,
> and holy is his Name.
>
> He has mercy on those who fear him
> in every generation.
>
> He has shown the strength of his arm,
> he has scattered the proud in their conceit.

He has cast down the mighty from their thrones,
and has lifted up the lowly.

He has filled the hungry with good things,
and the rich he has sent away empty.

He has come to the help of his servant Israel
for he has remembered his promise of mercy,
the promise he made to our fathers,
to Abraham and his children for ever.

MAJOR ORDERS. The diaconate, priesthood, and episcopate. The subdiaconate is also one of the major orders, but it is not a sacrament and may be received in the Institutes of Consecrated Life under the Pontifical Commission *Ecclesia Dei,* and in those that use the liturgical books of the Extraordinary Form of the Roman Rite.

MAJOR SUPERIOR. The abbot primate, the abbot superior of a monastic congregation, the abbot of a monastery, the superior general of an entire religious institute, the provincial superior, the vicars of all the foregoing, and all others who have powers equivalent to those of provincials.

MALACHI. The name appears as the title of the last book of the Old Testament. Since the name means "messenger," it may mean that the author, the last of the minor prophets, is delivering a message from YHWH. No one named Malachi is mentioned or known elsewhere in Scripture. It is a short book of three chapters and offers strong evidence of YHWH's dissatisfaction with the performance of priests and the obedience of the people. It deplores among other evils divorce, marrying Gentiles, and failure to pay tithes. It was probably written in the fifth century before Christ (Malachi 1–3).

MALICE. The evil of a conscious and deliberate transgression of the law of God. It is a contempt of the divine Author of the law and an implicit denial of reverence toward God, who, as Creator, has a right to demand obedience of his creatures. It is the basic evil of sin.

MAN. Latin *homo,* a human being, as distinct from *vir,* a male person. The term *homo* has no perfect English equivalent, but it is part of the Church's official vocabulary and occurs in every major document of the Catholic Church. A living substance, composed of a material body that dies and a spiritual soul that is immortal. Creature made by God to his image and likeness, to praise, reverence, and serve him in this life and thereby attain the eternal possession of God in the life to come. In philosophical terms, "man" is a rational animal, and collectively is the human species or the human race. (Etym. Anglo-Saxon *man,* a person.)

MANICHAEISM. A dualistic heresy initiated in the third century by a Persian named Mani, Manes, or Manichaeus (215–75). He was considered divinely inspired, and he gained a large following. In the Manichaean system there are two ultimate sources of creation, the one good and the other evil. God is the creator of all that is good, and Satan of all that is evil. Man's spirit is from God, his body is from the devil. There is a constant struggle between the forces of good and those of evil. Good triumphs over evil only insofar as spirit rises superior to the body. In practice Manichaeism denies human responsibility for the evil that one does, on the premise that this is not due to one's own free will but to the dominance of Satan's power in one's life.

MANIFESTATION OF CONSCIENCE. Revealing the state of one's moral life to another person for spiritual guidance. It has been a practice in the religious orders since early monastic times. Ecclesiastical law respects those clerical institutes that require a manifestation of conscience. But its general attitude is to forbid superiors to demand such an account of one's interior life. On the other hand, the Church encourages all religious, men and women, to be perfectly open with their superiors and, if they wish, to freely reveal to them even their inmost thoughts and desires. In clerical communities it is assumed that superiors, who are priests, may receive such voluntary manifestations of conscience in the sacrament of penance. In nonclerical communities the Church expects religious to periodically manifest their conscience to a competent priest, in or outside of sacramental confession, as an exercise in humility and a valuable means of growing in sanctity.

MANNA. The name given in Scripture for the miraculous food sent to the Israelites in the desert (Exodus 16:4–36). There are natural exudates from trees and shrubs in Arabia that yield, during two months in the fall, a minute quantity of edible substance. But their limited supply, with characteristic taste, makes them totally unlike what the Bible describes as the manna of the Exodus.

MARIAN ART. The Blessed Virgin in Christian art or architecture. The most ancient image of the Blessed Virgin still extant is a painting in the Roman catacomb of Priscilla on the Via Salaria. Dating from the early second or late first century, the fresco pictures Mary seated with the Child Jesus in her arms and what appears to be a prophet standing next to her, volume in hand and pointing to a star above the Virgin. Three other Marian paintings in the same catacomb date from the second and third centuries. One image on the tomb of a Christian virgin shows Mary, as a type and model of virginity, holding the Child; another gives the scene of the wise men at Bethlehem; and a third is in the less common group of Annunciation paintings. Similar representations, all before the fifth century, are found in the Roman cemeteries of Domitilla, Callistus, Sts. Peter and Marcellus, and St. Agnes. The last mentioned is interesting for the monogram inscriptions of Christ, which are repeated on both sides of the drawing and turned toward the Child.

Paintings and sculpture of Mary in Christian antiquity featured her relations with Jesus, as virgin and mother, generally in one of the Gospel scenes, ranging from the Annunciation to the crucifixion or burial of Christ. The Council of Ephesus (431), which defined the divine maternity against Nestorius, ushered in a new artistic phase that began in the East but was soon introduced into Italy, Spain, and Gaul. Instead of the homely scenes from the Gospel, Mary was now more often depicted as heavenly queen, vestured in gold and seated in royal majesty.

Roman art adopted and propagated the "Byzantine Virgin," but in place of the Oriental posture of Mary at prayer, with hands upraised, Western painters and sculptors favored showing her as the "Seat of Wisdom." This was partly the result of cultural adaptation, but mainly an expression of real development in Marian doctrine. It verged away from the colder Asiatic lines in the direction of greater mildness, tempered by human affection. Historians of the subject have found in each of the great periods, beginning with the early Middle Ages in Europe, an artistic reflection of the dominant Marian relationship to religious thought.

In the Gothic period of architecture it was the "Mother of the Redeemer," featuring the merciful kindness of the Savior and of his mother as companion in the redemptive work of her Son. It corresponds to the "ages of faith" and the time of the Church's pre-occupation with interior reformation of life and ecclesiastical discipline. During the Renaissance "Mother and Child" was the prevalent theme, graced by such names as Fra Angelico, Leonardo da Vinci, Raphael, Lippi, Botticelli, Correggio, Dolci, Perugino, Titian, and Verrocchio in Italy; Van Eyck, Memling, and Rubens in Flanders; and the Younger Holbein and Dürer in Germany. Typical of the Baroque style was Mary's role as "Conqueror of Satan"; and in modern times as "Mediatrix of Grace," strengthened by historical association of the Blessed Virgin with authenticated revelations at La Salette, Lourdes, and Fátima, and to such mystics as Margaret Mary, Catherine Labouré, Don Bosco, and the Curé of Ars.

MARIAN LITERATURE. The Blessed Virgin theme in world literature. She has inspired the literary culture of all nations, not excepting the Oriental and Islamic, but perhaps with more accent in the Latin countries and France, and no less prominently in England and America.

It was said of Chaucer (c. 1340–1400) that he was a good servant of Mary and that in her honor he "wrote full many a line." Taking all his writings together—twenty-nine "lesser works," *Troilus and Cressida,* and the twenty-three Canterbury Tales—we find about five hundred lines that are explicitly Marian poetry, omitting incidental allusions to the Virgin. Almost half are in *The Prioress's Tale* alone. His poem "An A.B.C." (dated about 1366), in which each stanza begins with a letter of the alphabet, is a collection of epithets that have survived to modern times, e.g., "But mercy, Lady, at the great assize / When we shall come before the High Justice," or "Fleeing I flee for succour to thy tent / Me for to hyde from tempest ful of drede."

Among the English poets, Richard Crashaw, Francis Thompson, Coventry Patmore, and Gerard Manley Hopkins; and among essayists, John Henry Newman, G. K. Chesterton, and Hilaire Belloc have left a deep Marian impress. Many of the poems have been put into song, as Crashaw's *Gloriosa Domina* (O Glorious Lady), which begins, "Hail, most high, most humble one / Above the world; below thy Son," and ends, "O boundless hospitality / The Feast of all things feeds on thee." Newman's essay in reply to Edward Pusey is a classic exposition of sober piety, in which he confesses that certain "devotional manifestations in honor of our Lady had been my great *crux.*" They may be fully explained and defended, he said, but sentiment and taste do not run with logic.

Writers in every tradition have described the ennobling influence of faith in Mary's dignity on the life and literature of Western thought. The first of all sentiments that they believe distinguishes an advanced civilization is that of reverence for womanhood. By this norm the honor and respect paid to Mary as the ideal of her sex have done more to elevate the status of women than any other postulate of the Christian religion. And in this sense devotion to the Madonna has ruled the highest arts and purest thoughts of creative genius for over a thousand years.

John Ruskin was persuaded that "the worship of the Madonna has been one of the noblest and most vital graces, and has never been otherwise than productive of true holiness of life and purity of character."

Wordsworth in England and Longfellow in the United States have left memorials of this inspiration. The *Virgin* of Wordsworth is addressed as "Woman, above all women glorified / Our tainted nature's solitary boast." In Longfellow's *Christus,* if Christianity gave us nothing more than "this example of all womanhood," this would be enough to prove it higher than all other religions of humankind.

MARIOLATRY. The worship of Mary with the divine honors (*latria*) due to God alone. Adoration of the Blessed Virgin, which is absolutely forbidden by the Catholic Church. (Etym. Greek *Mariā,* Mary + -*latreiā,* service, worship.)

MARIOLOGY. The branch of theology that studies the life and prerogatives of the Blessed Virgin, and her place in the economy of salvation and sanctification. (Etym. Greek *Mariā,* Mary + *logia,* science, knowledge.)

MARK. A Jerusalem Jew sometimes referred to in the New Testament as John Mark (Acts 12:12). He accompanied Paul and Barnabas, his cousin, to Antioch and traveled with them on their first missionary journey (Acts 12:25). At Perga, however, he left them and went home; no reason is given (Acts 13:13). This caused a split later between Paul and Barnabas when Paul refused to take Mark on their second journey. Barnabas was so incensed that he broke off his partnership with Paul and went on a voyage to Cyprus with Mark (Acts 15:36–39). Some years later, however, Paul and Mark were reunited and joined forces on another missionary trip. Mark was also closely associated with Peter, possibly acting as his interpreter. Peter referred to him affectionately as "my son" (I Peter 5:13), probably considering him a protégé. Mark's greatest contribution was the authorship of the second Gospel. Estimates vary, but it was most probably written in the decade A.D. 60–70. Mark wrote in Greek, evidently for Christians, because he uses terms meaningless to nonbelievers. His Gospel is a blend of history and theology written in simple, forceful language.

MARKS OF THE CHURCH. The four essential notes that characterize the Church of Christ, first fully enumerated in the Nicene-Constantinople Creed: one, holy, Catholic, and apostolic. Since the Eastern Schism and the Protestant Reformation they have become means of identifying the true Church among the rival claimants in Christianity. Some writers add other notes besides the traditional four, e.g., St. Robert Bellarmine with a total of fifteen, including the mark of persecution.

MARONITE LITURGY. Romanized form of the liturgy of St. James, used by the Maronite Church. Similar in some respects to the Roman Rite in using a round Host of unleavened bread and in the priest's vestments at Mass. The Maronite liturgical language is Syriac for the Epistle, Gospel, Creed, and Pater Noster, and Aramaic for the rest of the Mass. Maronites use incense frequently during the liturgy and have a variety of canons for Mass according to different feasts. The words of consecration are always intoned aloud.

MARONITES. The nation and church of most Arabic-speaking Syrians living in Lebanon. The name is also given to one of the Churches in communion with Rome whose members are scattered through Syria, Palestine, Cyprus, Egypt, and the United States. The name is probably derived from St. Maron (d. 443), a Syrian hermit who remained faithful to the Catholic faith during the Monothelite heresy. From the time of the Fifth Lateran Council the Maronite communion with Rome has been uninterrupted. They use the Rite of St. James in ancient Aramaic in their liturgy.

MARRIAGE. As a natural institution, the lasting union of a man and a woman who agree to give and receive rights over each other for the performance of the act of generation and for the fostering of their mutual love.

The state of marriage implies four chief conditions: 1. there must be a union of opposite sexes; it is therefore opposed to all forms of unnatural, homosexual behavior; 2. it is a permanent union until the death of either spouse; 3. it is an exclusive union, so that extramarital acts are a violation of justice; and 4. its permanence and exclusiveness are guaranteed by contract; mere living together, without mutually binding themselves to do so, is concubinage and not marriage.

Christ elevated marriage to a sacrament of the New Law. Christian spouses signify and partake of the mystery of that unity and fruitful love which exists between Christ and his Church, helping each other attain to holiness in their married life and in the rearing and education of their children.

MARTHA. Sister of Mary and Lazarus of Bethany. Jesus and his companions visited their home and enjoyed their hospitality. The close friendship that developed was clearly indicated on the occasion of Jesus's raising Lazarus from the dead. The complete trust the sisters had in Jesus was shown when they both said, "If you had been here, my brother would not have died." Correspondingly, Jesus showed genuine sorrow and wept (John 11:1–44). On another occasion when Jesus visited them, Martha was preparing a meal and remonstrated with Jesus because Mary devoted her whole attention to him and failed to help her. Jesus gently rebuked her and praised Mary (Luke 10:38–42). Were these the same sisters? Martha's complaint does not seem characteristic of the Martha in the Lazarus incident, but there is no evidence to answer the question. (Etym. Aramaic *marta'*, lady.)

MARTYR. A person who chooses to suffer, even to die, rather than renounce his or her faith or Christian principles. After the example of Christ one does not resist one's persecutors when they use violence out of hatred or malice against Christ, or his Church, or some revealed truth of the Catholic religion. (Etym. Greek *martyros*, witness, martyr.)

MARTYROLOGIES. Lists of martyrs of certain cities or countries; catalogues of martyred saints arranged according to the occurrence of their feast days in the liturgical calendar. Originating in the early Middle Ages, they are important as sources of Church history. In some religious communities, the martyrology is read daily in the refectory. The Roman Martyrology, a catalogue of saints honored by the Church, written around the mid-sixteenth century, has been often revised and re-edited. Its total listing gives short accounts of about six thousand saints and blesseds honored by the Catholic Church.

MARXISM. The social philosophy of Karl Marx (1818–83) as developed with his collaborator Friedrich Engels (1820–95) and later embodied in world Communism. There are five essential elements to Marxism, namely dialectical materialism, economic determinism, surplus value, progressive pauperization, and the Revolution.

Marx combined the dialectical method of Hegel with the materialism of Feuerbach. According to Marxism, nothing really exists but matter, which contains within itself the principle of its own development. Man is the spearhead of this necessary evolution.

Economic determinism holds that the underlying motive in all human history is economic. As the economy, so the civilization.

The workman, according to Marx, creates more value than he is paid for, and this surplus value goes to the employer, who exploits the worker to that extent. The employer puts this surplus value back into his business, and this constitutes capital. The lower the wages, the more capital for the capitalist.

As part of his theory of economic determinism, Marx held that the rich necessarily get richer and the poor poorer. Financial crises, inseparable from the capitalist system, accentuate the degrading process.

All the foregoing are preliminary to the Marxist hope of a classless society. Capitalism must inevitably collapse; the masses will revolt, seize the means of production, establish the dictatorship of the proletariat. After a phase of state socialism there will emerge the Communist utopia where no struggles exist because all classes of society will have disappeared.

The classic position of the Catholic Church on Marxism is the encyclical of Pope Pius XI, *Divini Redemptoris,* published in 1937.

MARY, NAME OF. Meaning "lady," "beautiful," or "well beloved." A favorite name given to Jewish women at the time of Christ. It was the name of Moses's sister. Nowadays it is an honored name with Catholics and one of the most popular Christian names of women, in a variety of forms—e.g., Maria, Marie, Miriam—and in combination with other names—e.g., Marianne, Rosemary. The Irish word for Mary, "Muire," is given only to Mary the Mother of God; all other Marys are called Moira. Its special feast in the Western Church was observed on September 12, since 1684, in grateful memory of the Christian victory over the Turks at Vienna in 1683. The feast has been suppressed since the Second Vatican Council, except for those who use the 1962 liturgical books. (Etym. Greek *maria* or *mariam;* from Hebrew *miryam,* exalted one.)

MARY'S DEATH. The passing from mortal life into eternity of the Virgin Mary. Although reliable records are lacking on the time, place, and circumstances of Mary's death, the fact was accepted by the early Church. Sts. Ephrem, Jerome, and Augustine take her death for granted. But Epiphanius (315–403), who had made a careful study of the documents, concluded: "Nobody knows how she departed this world." In the absence of a dogmatic pronouncement, modern theologians generally believe that Mary died. They admit that she was not bound by the law of mortality because of her exemption from sin, but it was fitting that Mary's body, by nature mortal, should conform to that of her Son, who allowed himself to die for the salvation of men.

MARY'S SINLESSNESS. The belief that the Mother of Jesus was never stained with any sin, original or personal, and was also free from all unruly desires or concupiscence. By itself, deliverance from original sin does not mean liberation from the defects that are the result of sin. Mary, like Christ, was not exempt from those limitations that imply no moral imperfection. She lived a normal human life, had to labor, and was subject to pain and fatigue. But concupiscence implies moral blemish because it may lead to sin by exciting the passions to act against the law of God, even when, through lack of consent, a person does not formally do wrong.

Closely tied in with her integrity or absence of concupiscence was Mary's immunity from every personal sin during life. Her sinlessness may be deduced from the Gospel title "full of grace," since moral guilt is irreconcilable with fullness of God's friendship. St. Augustine held that every personal sin must be excluded from the Blessed Virgin "because of the honor of God."

MARY'S VIRGINITY. The belief that the Mother of Jesus was always a virgin. Three stages of virginity are professed in this belief: Mary's conception of her Son without the cooperation of man, giving birth to Christ without violating her integrity, and remaining a virgin after Jesus was born.

The Church's faith in Mary's virginal conception of Jesus found its way into all the ancient professions of belief. In a text dating from the early second century, the Apostles' Creed speaks of "Jesus Christ . . .

who was born by the Holy Spirit of the Virgin Mary." The biblical basis was traceable to the prophecy of Isaiah (7:14), which the first evangelist applies to Mary: "Therefore the Lord Himself shall give a sign. Behold a virgin [halmah] shall conceive and bear a son and his name shall be called Emmanuel [God with us]." From the beginning, Christians understood the passage to refer to the Messiah, since the sign had been fulfilled. Matthew thus interpreted the term in recalling the Isaian prophecy (Matthew 1:23).

All the Fathers affirm Christ's virginal conception by Mary. At the turn of the first century, Ignatius of Antioch spoke of Jesus as "truly born of a virgin." Starting with Justin the Martyr (c. 100–65), ecclesiastical writers uniformly defended the Messianic interpretation of Isaiah, as given by Matthew and confirmed in the Gospel by St. Luke.

Christian tradition went a step further. Not only did Mary conceive without carnal intercourse, but her physical virginity was also not violated in giving birth to Christ. When the monk Jovinian (d. 405) began to teach, "A virgin conceived, but a virgin did not bring forth," he was promptly condemned by a synod at Milan (390), presided over by St. Ambrose. Her integrity during the birth of Jesus is included in the title "perpetual virgin," given to Mary by the fifth general council held at Constantinople (553). Without going into physiological details, ancient writers such as Ambrose, Augustine, and Jerome employ various analogies—the emergence of Christ from the sealed tomb, his going through closed doors, penetration of light through glass, the going out of human thought from the mind.

Mary remained a virgin after Christ was born. Denied in the early Church by Tertullian and Jovinian, the doctrine of virginity *post partum* (after birth) was strenuously defended by the orthodox Fathers and crystallized in the term *aeiparthenos* (ever virgin) coined by the fifth ecumenical council (second of Constantinople). From the fourth century on, such formulas as that of St. Augustine became common: "A virgin conceived, a virgin gave birth, a virgin remained."

MARY, THE BLESSED VIRGIN (IN THE BIBLE). The mother of Jesus, the wife of Joseph, and the greatest of Christian saints. The archangel Gabriel appeared to her in Nazareth, where she lived with Joseph, and announced to her that she would be the mother of the Messiah. "How can this come about," she asked in bewilderment, "since I am a virgin?" When Gabriel assured her that the Most High would overshadow her, she humbly consented (Luke 1:34). She went to visit her kinswoman Elizabeth, who had recently been told by an angel that, despite her age, she would soon bear a child who must be named John (Luke 1:39–40). It was on this occasion that Mary sang the Magnificat (Luke 1:46–55). Joseph was shocked when he became aware that Mary was pregnant. To avoid any public disgrace, he considered putting her away, but an angel comforted him by explaining God's design for Mary. At this difficult time Joseph had to take his wife to Bethlehem in obedience to the census decree of the Roman emperor. Jesus was born during this visit, and all the events familiar to us associated with the Nativity story—the inn, the stable, the manger, the star, the wise men, and the shepherds—are reverently presented (Matthew 1:18–25). After eight days the child was circumcised and given the name Jesus, in accordance with Gabriel's instructions (Luke 2). Then, after forty days, Mary and Joseph appeared at the Temple for the purification ceremonies (Luke 2:21). When the angel warned Joseph that Herod wanted to destroy Jesus, he fled into Egypt with Mary and Jesus and remained there until they learned that Herod was dead. Then they returned to their home in Nazareth (Luke 2:22–28). Only once in the next thirty years do we learn anything more about the Holy Family. When Jesus was twelve and the parents went with him to Jerusalem for the Passover, the boy was missing for three days. His parents finally found him in the Temple with the priests. The first recorded words of Jesus were given in answer to his mother's troubled inquiry: "Did you not know that I must be busy with my father's affairs?" (Luke 2:41–50). His public life began at the age of thirty. At a wedding feast in Cana, he performed his first miracle, converting water into wine at the request of Mary to aid the wedding party (John 2:1–11). Several times she appeared with him during his ministry but always remained in the background. She was present at the Crucifixion and heard her Son tell John to take care of her (John 19:25–27). She waited with the Apostles for the coming of the Holy Spirit on Pentecost. Scripture gives no further biographical information about Mary. She apparently lived in Jerusalem for some time, although there is a tradition that she may have died in Ephesus a few years after Jesus's Ascension. The two basic beliefs concerning Mary, the divine maternity and the virginal conception of Jesus, are unequivocally stated in the Gospels. But other aspects of Mariology are also important. They have a Scriptural basis but are not specifically elaborated in the Gospels.

MASS. The Sacrifice of the Eucharist as the central act of worship of the Catholic Church. The "Mass" is a late form of *missio* (sending), from which the faithful are sent to put into practice what they have learned and use the graces they have received in the Eucharistic liturgy.

As defined by the Church at the Council of Trent, in the Mass, "The same Christ who offered himself once in a bloody manner on the altar of the Cross, is present and offered in an unbloody manner." Consequently, the Mass is a truly propitiatory sacrifice, which means that by this oblation "the Lord is appeased, He grants grace and the gift of repentance, and He pardons wrongdoings and sins, even grave ones. For it is one and the same victim. He who now makes the offering through the ministry of priests and he who then offered himself on the Cross. The only difference is the manner of offering" (Denzinger 1743).

The Mass cannot be understood apart from Calvary, of which it is a re-presentation, memorial, and effective application of the merits gained by Christ.

The re-presentation means that because Christ is really present in his humanity, in heaven and on the altar, he is capable now as he was on Good Friday of freely offering himself to the Father. He can no longer die because he now has a glorified body, but the essence of his oblation remains the same.

The Mass is also a memorial. Christ's death is commemorated not only as a psychological remembrance but as a mystical reality. He voluntarily offers himself, the eternal high priest, as really as he did on Calvary.

The Mass is, moreover, a sacred banquet or paschal meal. The banquet aspect of the Mass is the reception of Holy Communion by the celebrant and the people, when the same Christ who offers himself to the Father as a sacrifice then gives himself to the faithful as their heavenly food. It was this fact that inspired the Holy See, after the Second Vatican Council, to restore the practice of receiving Communion under both kinds for all the faithful: "The entire tradition of the Church teaches that the faithful participate more perfectly in the Eucharistic celebration through sacramental Communion. By Communion, in fact, the faithful share more fully in the Eucharistic Sacrifice. In this way they are not limited to sharing in the sacrifice by faith and prayer, nor to merely spiritual communion with Christ offered on the altar, but receive Christ himself sacramentally, so as to receive more fully the fruits of this most holy sacrifice. In order that the fullness of the sign in the Eucharistic banquet may be seen more clearly by the faithful, the Second Vatican Council prescribed that in certain cases, to be decided by the Holy See, the faithful could receive Holy Communion under both species" (*Sacramentali Communione,* June 29, 1970).

Finally the Mass is the divinely ordained means of applying the merits of Calvary. Christ won for the world all the graces it needs for salvation and sanctification. But these blessings are conferred gradually and continually since Calvary and mainly through the Mass. Their measure of conferral is in proportion to the faith and loving response of the faithful who unite themselves in spirit with the Mass.

It is in this sense that the Mass is an oblation of the whole Mystical Body, head and members. Yet, among the faithful, some have been ordained priests, and their role in the Mass is essentially different from that of the laity. The priest is indispensable, since he alone by his powers can change the elements of bread and wine into the body and blood of Christ. Nevertheless the role of the participants is of great importance, not as though there would be no Mass without a congregation but because the people's "full, active and conscious participation will involve them in both body and soul and will inspire them with faith, hope and charity." The more active this participation, the more glory is given to God and the more grace is bestowed not only on the Church but on all the members of the human race. (Etym. Latin *missa,* from *mittere,* to send; so called from the words of dismissal at the end of the service: *Ite, missa est,* "Go, [the congregation] is dismissed.")

MASS INTENTION. The object for which a priest offers the Eucharistic Sacrifice. This intention is distinct from the priest's decision to offer Mass, which is necessary for valid celebration. It is also distinct from the effects of the Mass, which benefit those who take part in the sacrifice and attend the Mass. These are called the special fruits of the Mass and extensively are without limit, as are also the effects on the entire Church, called the general fruits of the Mass.

Mass intentions refer to the particular purpose for which a specific Mass is offered. This may be to honor God or thank him for blessings received. But technically a Mass intention means that the sacrifice is offered for some person(s) living or dead. Also called the application of a Mass, it pertains to the ministerial fruits of the Mass. These fruits are both extensively and intensively finite in virtue of the positive will of Christ. Other things being equal, the more often the sacrifice is offered, the more benefit is conferred.

The intention for which a priest offers a Mass is determined either by the common law of the Church, or by specific precept, or, most often, by the intention of the donor of a Mass stipend, or by the priest's own devotion. Since it is not absolutely certain that the ministerial fruits of the Mass are limited, a priest may conditionally (if the one giving the stipend suffers no loss thereby) offer the Mass for several intentions. It is assumed that the priest does not intend by these second or third intentions to fulfill an obligation of justice by these conditional applications.

MASS OBLIGATION. A grave obligation of Catholics to assist at Mass on all Sundays and holy days of obligation. As expressed by the Second Vatican Council, referring to Mass on Sunday, "On this day the faithful are bound to come together into one place. They should listen to the word of God and take part in the Eucharist, thus calling to mind the Passion, Resurrection and glory of the Lord Jesus Christ" (Constitution on the Sacred Liturgy, V, 106). The imperative "are bound to come together" indicates the gravity of the obligation, which, according to the Church's tradition, affects all baptized persons who have reached the age of reason. They are obliged under penalty of serious sin to hear Mass on Sundays and holy days, which means that the duty is objectively serious. Subjectively the gravity of the sin will depend on excusing circumstances, notably a person's awareness of the dignity and necessity of the Eucharistic Sacrifice.

MASS RITUAL. The prescribed liturgy for celebrating the Sacrifice of the Eucharist in the Roman Rite. Essentially this ritual consists of two parts: the Liturgy of the Word and the Liturgy of the Eucharist. "In the Mass, both the table of God's word and the table of Christ's body are prepared, so that from them the faithful may be instructed and nourished" (Venerable Paul VI, *General Instruction on the Roman Missal*, 8). There are also some introductory and concluding rites.

Accordingly the Mass ritual is divided into four parts: Introduction, Liturgy of the Word, Liturgy of the Eucharist, Conclusion. While in general the ritual is carefully prescribed, there are also some options left to the discretion of the priest as presiding celebrant.

MASS STIPEND. Offering given to a priest as alms for his maintenance, in return for which he promises to offer a Mass for the donor's intention. The stipend is not given as a price for the Eucharistic Sacrifice. It is rather a voluntary donation whose origins go back to the early

Church, when stipends were made during Mass and later on outside of Mass. Any priest who celebrates and applies Mass to a particular intention may receive a stipend. When a priest accepts a stipend he incurs a grave obligation in justice by virtue of a gratuitous contract, and he is bound to apply the Mass according to the conditions imposed and accepted. The amount of the stipend is determined by the diocesan standard, which must be observed by all priests, diocesan and religious. Nevertheless it is permissible to demand a larger amount if there are special duties attached to the Mass, such as the late hour or the appointment of a definite place.

MASTURBATION. Direct stimulation of the sex organs outside of sexual intercourse. The self-stimulation can be physical, by means of some external object, or psychic, by means of thoughts and the imagination. It is a grave misuse of the procreative faculty and when done with full consent and deliberation is a serious sin. The sinfulness consists in setting in motion the generative powers while preventing them from achieving their natural, divinely intended purpose. (Etym. Latin *manu*, with the hand + *stuprare*, to defile oneself.)

MATERIAL COOPERATION. Assisting in another's wrongdoing without approving it. The help given assists a person to perform the sinful action, although of itself the help is not wrong. To provide necessary information to a thief, because one is forced to, would be material cooperation. Material cooperation with another person's evil action is allowed provided certain conditions are fulfilled. Such collaboration is licit because the cooperator does not internally approve of the sin of another, nor does he or she approve of the sinful use to which the assistance is put by the other. The following principles are standard in resolving this complex moral issue:

Two kinds of material cooperation are to be distinguished: immediate and mediate.

In *immediate material cooperation*, one person actually does something morally wrong with another person. Thus if a surgeon and an assistant are both engaged in actually aborting a fetus, the cooperation of the assistant is immediate. Immediate material cooperation in the sinful act of another is always wrong. It is pointless to say that a person who is not under duress performs a criminal action without intending to do so.

Mediate material cooperation is concurring in the wrong action of another, but not in such a way that one actually performs the act with the other or agrees with the evil intention of the other. While doing something that is in itself good or indifferent, a person rather gives an occasion to another's sin, or contributes something by way of assistance.

The morality of mediate material cooperation is to be judged on the principle of the double effect. In applying this principle, there are four basic norms to be observed. Among these norms are the obligation not to intend the evil effect (as would really be intended in immediate material cooperation) and the need for sufficient reason to permit the evil effect. The presence of a proportionate reason is not sufficient to allow what is called material cooperation. See also DOUBLE EFFECT.

MATERIALISM. The theory that all reality is only matter, or a function of matter, or ultimately derived from matter. There is no real distinction between matter and spirit; even man's soul is essentially material and not uniquely created by God. In ethical philosophy, materialism holds that material goods and interests, the pleasures of the body and emotional experience, are the only or at least the main reason for human existence. In social philosophy, it is the view that economics and this-worldly interests are the main functions of society.

MATINS. The first of the canonical hours. Replaced since the Second Vatican Council by the Office of Readings, followed by Morning Prayer, except for those who use the 1962 liturgical books, in which case it is followed by Lauds. Chanted during the early hours shortly after midnight by enclosed monks and nuns who continue Matins as such, now. (Etym. French *matin,* morning.)

MATRIMONIAL CONTRACT. The voluntary agreement of a man and a woman to enter marriage, and recognized as such by the Church or State. Among the baptized every valid matrimonial contract is also a sacrament.

MATRIMONIAL COURT. A group of clergy attached to a diocesan chancery for reviewing and passing judgment on marriage cases submitted for study and possible decision by the bishop. Besides others, or in duplicate roles, the court consists of a judge, or judges, advocate, secretary, notary, and defender of the bond of union of the married. It meets to consider disputed cases concerning marriage, in which one or both parties are Catholic, or a marriage that must be decided so that a non-Catholic may marry a Catholic. Cases of the "decree of nullity" are the most frequently sought. All decisions to be valid must have the approval of the bishop. An appeal over the matrimonial court's decision may always be made to Rome, or such decision may be sought without recourse to the diocesan court. The ordinary of the diocese has jurisdiction over a true Pauline case. Any Catholic through an advocate has the right to bring any case to any proper Roman congregation for appraisal or decision.

MATRIMONY. Marriage, but a more appropriate term for legal and religious use. It is the proper term for the sacrament of marriage, and refers more to the relationship between husband and wife than to the ceremony or the state of marriage.

MATTER OF A SACRAMENT. That part of a sacrament which is used to perform the sacramental rite. It is that part of a sacrament with which or to which something is done in order to confer grace, e.g., water in baptism, chrism in confirmation, bread and wine in the Eucharist.

MATTHEW. One of the Twelve Apostles and author of the first Gospel. He was a tax collector for the Roman government. Mark and Luke reported that Matthew (also known as Levi) was carrying on his work in the customhouse when Jesus called him to join the band of disciples, and Matthew promptly obeyed (Mark 2:14). Later, when he entertained Jesus and his followers at a reception in his home, it was evident how strongly the Jews resented and despised tax collectors (Luke 5:27–32). Nothing can be learned about his personal life from his writings, because he never spoke about himself in his Gospel. His purpose was to convince Christians of Jewish origin that Jesus was the Messiah and fulfilled the promises of the prophets. It is not surprising, therefore, that Matthew cites the Old Testament more frequently than either Mark or Luke. (Etym. Greek *mathhaios;* from Aramaic *mattai;* a shorter form of Hebrew *mattanyah,* gift of YHWH.)

MATTHIAS. The successor of Judas as an Apostle. Little is known about him. Possibly he was one of the seventy-two disciples Luke referred to (Luke 10:1), because Peter, in arranging the replacement, insisted that it should be someone "who has been with us the whole time that the Lord Jesus was traveling round with us." Matthias and Barsabbas were chosen as worthy candidates. Lots were drawn and Matthias was selected (Acts 1:21–26).

MEAT. The flesh of animals and birds eaten by human beings, as understood in Church law. Its prohibition on days of abstinence and fast has a spiritual value, going back to the Old Testament and practiced since apostolic times. "The law of abstinence forbids the use of meat, but not of eggs, the products of milk or condiments made of animal fat" (Pope Paul VI, *Paenitemini,* Norm III, 1).

MEDALS. Coin-shaped metal disks bearing the image of Christ, Mary, or some saint, shrine, or sacred event. They are blessed by the Church and are used to increase devotion. The use of medals is very ancient; many have been found in the catacombs, some with the Chi-Rho symbol. During the Middle Ages the pilgrims, on leaving a place of pilgrimage, were given medal tokens of the shrine. And today pilgrims to Rome, Lourdes, and elsewhere purchase medals that commemorate their visit. The efficacy of a medal depends on the faith of the person who wears or carries it, and on the Church's indulgenced blessing attached to this sacred object. There are innumerable medals approved by the Church. Among the most commonly used are the scapular and miraculous medals in honor of the Blessed Virgin.

MEDIATOR. A title of Christ as the one who reconciled God and the human race. It is based on the teaching of St. Paul, that "there is only one God, and there is only one mediator between God and mankind, Himself a man, Christ Jesus, who sacrificed Himself as a ransom for them all" (I Timothy 2:5–6). Christ is best qualified to be the mediator, i.e., one who brings estranged parties to agreement. As God, he was the one with whom the human race was to be reconciled; as a human being, he represented the ones who needed reconciliation. Christ continues his work of mediation, no longer to merit the grace of human forgiveness but to communicate the grace already won on the Cross. Moreover, others than Christ may also be called mediators in a totally secondary sense, "in that they co-operate in our reconciliation; disposing and ministering to men's union with God" (St. Thomas Aquinas, *Summa Theologiae,* III, 48, 1). In fact every person, insofar as he or she cooperates with divine grace, is a kind of mediator between himself or herself and God. (Etym. Latin *mediator;* from *mediare,* to stand or divide in the middle.)

MEDIATOR DEI. Encyclical letter of Venerable Pope Pius XII on the Sacred Liturgy (November 30, 1947). A historic document that summarized liturgical development in the Church up to that time and laid the foundations for the liturgical reforms of the Second Vatican Council. It clearly defined the meaning of the liturgy as the Church's official public worship; stressed the primacy of interior worship; insisted on the need for the liturgy to be under the Church's hierarchical authority; traced the development of the liturgy since the Council of Trent but emphasized that to be valid this progress cannot be left to private judgment; declared that the Eucharist is the culmination and center of the Christian religion; urged the importance of the faithful actively participating in divine worship, especially in the Mass; explained how the fruits of Holy Communion are increased by better preparation and a fervent thanksgiving; praised those who are devoted to the Real Presence and promote this devotion among the faithful; placed the Divine Office next to the Eucharist as part of the Church's liturgical life; indicated that the liturgical year should revolve around the mysteries of Christ's life, Passion, and Resurrection; and recommended extraliturgical devotions to increase the piety of priests, religious, and the laity.

MEDIATRIX. A title of the Blessed Virgin as mediator of grace. There are two aspects of this mediation. It is certain in Catholic theology that, since Mary gave birth to the Redeemer, who is the source of all grace, she is in this way the channel of all graces to mankind. But it is only probable, as a legitimate opinion, that since Mary's Assumption into heaven no grace is received by humans without her actual intercessory cooperation.

On the first level of mediation, Mary freely cooperated with God in consenting to the Incarnation, giving birth to her Son and thus sharing with him in spirit the labors of his Passion and death. Yet Christ alone truly offered the sacrifice of atonement on the Cross. Mary gave him moral support in this action. She is therefore not entitled to the name "priest," as several Roman documents legislate. As explained by the Council of Florence in 1441, Christ "conquered the enemy of the human race alone" (Denzinger 1347). In the same way he alone acquired the grace of redemption for the whole human race, including Mary. Her part in the objective redemption, therefore, was indirect and remote, and derived from her voluntary devotion to the service of Christ. Under the Cross she suffered and sacrificed with him, but subordinate to him in such a way that all the efficacy of her oblation depended on that of her Son.

On the second stage of mediation, Mary cooperates by her maternal intercession in applying Christ's redemptive grace to human beings, called the subjective redemption. This does not imply that the faithful must pray for all graces through Mary, nor that her intercession is inherently necessary for the distribution of divine blessing, but that, according to God's special ordinance, the graces merited by Christ are conferred through the actual intercessory mediation of his mother. Recent popes and the Second Vatican Council have spoken in favor of this type of mediation, which finds support in patristic tradition.

MEDIEVAL MUSIC. The period A.D. 600–1400 is here referred to as the medieval period. During these Middle Ages liturgical chant and secular solo public singing saw their greatest development. Polyphony reached fine artistic forms and Gregorian chant had its beginning then, as did Ambrosian chant in the north, the Gallican in France, and Visigothic in Spain. A need for a unified liturgy became most apparent as each geographical section argued its own pre-eminence over Rome until the eleventh century, when the Roman liturgy was universally enforced, with a few limited exceptions. The years between 700 and 800 saw all chants embellished with new words, preludes, and interludes. Sequences had their beginning in the twelfth century and became so elaborate that the Council of Trent felt forced to ban all of them except "Lauda Sion," "Veni Creator Spiritus," "Victimae Paschali Laudes," and "Dies Irae," admitting "Stabat Mater" a little later. A large repertory of secular melodies made their appearance in the same century, but after Rome's fall their impact, musically, was slight. Troubadour melodies appeared in the south of France, spread to the north, then to the German minnesingers. The troubadours occupied prime positions in medieval musical history, with Spain, Italy, and England producing much devotional song composition. The thirteenth century saw the motet developed, using sacred texts, but later the liturgical aspects of the words were lost, dance tunes and troubadour melodies taking their place. Different rhythms were of great interest in the mid-thirteenth century; three-part rhythm dominating in polyphonic music. The ballad form appeared in the fourteenth century, with ornate rhythmic patterns evolving and unusual syncopations being tried. As the period closed a new musical impetus came from England—the new art exploiting thirds and sixths, very important to music.

MEDITATION. Reflective prayer. It is that form of mental prayer in which the mind, in God's presence, thinks about God and divine things. While the affections may also be active, the stress in meditation is on the role of the intellect. Hence this is also called discursive mental prayer. The objects of meditation are mainly three: mysteries of faith; a person's better knowledge of what God wants him or her to do; and the divine will, to know how God wants to be served by the one who is meditating. (Etym. Latin *meditatio,* a thinking over.)

MEEKNESS. The virtue that moderates anger and its disorderly effects. It is a form of temperance that controls every inordinate movement of resentment at another person's character or behavior.

MELCHIZEDEK. A king of Salem and a priest. When Abraham returned from battle after rescuing Lot, Melchizedek greeted him and gave him a blessing in honor of his victory (Genesis 14:18–20). In return Abraham offered him tithes because of his priesthood. In a Psalm devoted to the dual role of priest and king, David exclaimed, "YHWH has sworn an oath which he never will retract, You are a priest of the order of Melchizedek and forever" (Psalm 110:4). There are only two references to this priest-king in the Old Testament. In the New Testament the Epistle to the Hebrews associates Christ's priesthood with Melchizedek's by quoting in three successive chapters the invocation from Psalm 110: "You are a priest of the order of Melchizedek and forever." This is also the biblical basis for the Catholic doctrine that, once a man is ordained a priest, his priesthood, like Christ's "in the line of Melchizedek," is forever (Hebrews 5, 6, 7).

MELKITES. Byzantine Christians descended from those who remained faithful to the Council of Chalcedon (451) when large numbers in the Near East accepted the Monophysite heresy. They gradually became dependent on the Patriarch of Constantinople and joined him in the Greek Schism in the ninth to the eleventh centuries. They were reunited with Rome in the eighteenth century under the patriarch Cyril VI, who, with his successors, represents the original episcopal line of Antioch. Since the twelfth century they have followed the Byzantine Rite, mainly in the Arabic language.

MEMENTO OF THE DEAD. Commemoration of the faithful departed, after the consecration of the Mass. In the Roman Canon, the *Memento* is always made silently, after the brief announcement, "Remember, Lord, those who have died and have gone before us marked with the sign of faith, especially those for whom we now pray." In the other canons, there is a general *Memento* for all the deceased, preceded, in Masses for the Dead, by a special prayer that includes mention by name of those for whom the Mass is being said. (Etym. Latin *memento,* remember [imperative].)

MEMENTO OF THE LIVING. Remembrance at Mass of those for whom the priest and people wish to pray specially. In the Roman Canon, the *Memento* occurs before the consecration, and the persons are mentioned silently by name, followed by a general remembrance of the living. In other canons, there is only a general intercession for the Church but no silent *Memento.*

MEMORARE. Intercessory prayer to the Blessed Virgin, commonly ascribed to St. Bernard of Clairvaux (1090–1153), probably because it was popularized by Claude Bernard, the "Poor Priest" (1588–1641). The real author is unknown. Early texts have been known since the fifteenth century. Frequently indulgenced by the popes, there is now a partial indulgence for its recitation. A standard English version reads:

> Remember, O most gracious Virgin Mary,
> that never was it known that
> anyone who fled to your protection,
> implored your help,
> or sought your intercession,
> was left unaided.
> Inspired with this confidence,
> I fly unto you,
> O Virgin of Virgins, my Mother.
> To you I come,
> before you I stand,
> sinful and sorrowful.
> O Mother of the Word Incarnate,
> despise not my petitions,
> but in your mercy hear and answer me.
> Amen.

(Etym. Latin *memorare,* to call to mind.)

MEMORIZATION. The practice of deliberately committing to memory facts and verbal expressions considered useful or necessary for future recall. Since the earliest times the Church has encouraged memorization, e.g., the directives of the American hierarchy: "The special place of memory in the transmission of the faith of the Church throughout the ages, should be valued and exercised, especially in catechetical programs for the young. Opportunities for memorization should be adapted to the level and ability of the child and presented in a gradual fashion. Among these elements of Catholic faith, tradition and practice which, through an early, gradual, flexible, and never slavish process of memorization, could become lessons learned for a lifetime, contributing to an individual's growth and development in an understanding of the Faith are the following: 1. prayers, such as the Sign of the Cross, the Lord's Prayer, the Hail Mary, the Apostles' Creed, the Acts of Faith, Hope, and Charity, the Act of Contrition; 2. factual information contributing to an appreciation of the place of the Word of God in the Church and the life of the Christian through an awareness and appreciation of: a. the key themes of the history of salvation; b. the major personalities of the Old and New Testaments; c. certain biblical texts expressive of God's love and care; 3. formulas providing factual information regarding worship, the Church year, and major practices in the devotional life of Christians: a. the parts of the Mass; b. the list of the sacraments; c. the liturgical seasons; d. the holy days of obligation; e. the major feasts of Our Lord and Our Lady; f. the various Eucharistic devotions; g. the mysteries of the Rosary of the Blessed Virgin Mary; h. the Stations of the Cross; 4. formulas and practices dealing with the moral life of Christians: a. the Commandments; b. the Beatitudes; c. the gifts of the Holy Spirit; d. the theological and moral virtues; e. the precepts of the Church; f. the examination of conscience" (Amendments to the *National Catechetical Directory*, 1977).

It is assumed that what has been memorized will also be reflected on and, as far as possible, understood. But memorizing is indispensable for any sound pedagogy in the Catholic religion (*General Catechetical Directory*, 73).

MENTAL PRAYER. The form of prayer in which the sentiments expressed are one's own and not those of another person and the expression of these sentiments is mainly, if not entirely, interior and not externalized. Mental prayer is accomplished by internal acts of the mind and affections and is either simple meditation or contemplation. As meditation, it is a loving and discursive (reflective) consideration of religious truths or some mystery of faith. As contemplation, it is a loving and intuitive (immediately perceptive) consideration and admiration of the same truths or mysteries of faith. In mental prayer the three powers of the soul are engaged: the memory, which offers the mind material for meditation or contemplation; the intellect, which ponders or directly perceives the meaning of some religious truth and its implications for practice; and the will, which freely expresses its sentiments of faith, trust, and love, and (as needed) makes good resolutions based on what the memory and intellect have made known to the will.

MENTAL RESERVATION. Speech in which the common and obvious sense of one's words is limited to a particular meaning. The morality of this kind of speech depends on whether the listener can reasonably conclude from the circumstances that a mental reservation is being used.

MERCY. The disposition to be kind and forgiving. Founded on compassion, mercy differs from compassion or the feeling of sympathy in putting this feeling into practice with a readiness to assist. It is therefore the ready willingness to help anyone in need, especially in need of pardon or reconciliation.

MERIT. Divine reward for the practice of virtue. It is Catholic doctrine that by his or her good works a person in the state of grace really acquires a claim to supernatural reward from God. "The reward given for good works is not won by reason of actions which precede grace, but grace, which is unmerited, precedes actions in order that they may be performed meritoriously" (II Council of Orange, Denzinger 388).

Certain conditions must be present to make supernatural merit possible. The meritorious work must be morally good, that is, in accordance with the moral law in its object, intent, and circumstances. It must be done freely, without any external coercion or internal necessity. It must be supernatural, that is, aroused and accompanied by actual grace, and proceeding from a supernatural motive. The person must be a wayfarer, here on earth, since no one can merit after death.

Strictly speaking only a person in the state of grace can merit, as defined by the Church (Denzinger 1576, 1582).

Merit depends on the free ordinance of God to reward with everlasting happiness the good works performed by his grace. On account of the infinite distance between Creator and creature, a human being alone cannot make God his or her debtor, if God does not do so by his own free ordinance. That God has made such an ordinance is clear from his frequent promises, e.g., the Beatitudes and the prediction of the Last Judgment.

The object of supernatural merit is an increase of sanctifying grace, eternal life (if the person dies in divine friendship), and an increase of heavenly glory. (Etym. Latin *merces,* hire, pay, reward.)

MESSIAH. The Hebrew word for "Anointed One." The equivalent word in Greek is Christos. In the Old Testament it was sometimes applied in a general sense to prophets or priests (Exodus 30:30), but more specifically it referred to the coming of one who would usher in a period of righteousness and conquer sin and evil (Daniel 9:26). In the New Testament the evangelists made it clear that they knew Jesus was the long-anticipated Messiah (Acts 2:36; Matthew 16:17; Galatians 3:24–29). Those who refused to accept Jesus interpreted the promised kingdom to be a worldly domain and looked forward to a messiah who would be a military leader to help Israel triumph over her enemies.

METANOIA. Literally "repentance" or "penance." The term is regularly used in the Greek New Testament, especially in the Gospels and the preaching of the Apostles. Repentance is shown by faith, baptism, confession of sins, and producing fruits worthy of penance. It means a change of mind from unbelief to faith, and a change of heart from sin to the practice of virtue. As conversion, it is fundamental to the teaching of Christ, was the first thing demanded by Peter on Pentecost, and is considered essential to the pursuit of Christian perfection. (Etym. Greek *metanoein,* to change one's mind, repent, be converted; from *meta-* + *noein,* to perceive, think; akin to Greek *noos, nous,* mind.)

META-OUSIOSIS. Transubstantiation of the bread and wine at Mass into the body and blood of Christ. The Greek Fathers used this expression to identify what takes place at the Eucharistic consecration. It is a *meta* or change of one *ousia* or being, that of bread and wine, into another *ousia* or being, that of Christ's body and blood.

METAPHYSICS. The science of being, as being; or of the absolutely first principles of being. Also called ontology, first philosophy, the philosophy of being, the philosophy of first causes, wisdom. (Etym. Greek *meta*, after, beyond + *physika,* physics.)

METROPOLITAN. An archbishop who is placed over a certain section of a country, comprising a number of suffragan dioceses. However, not every archbishop is a metropolitan, because there are both titular and resident archbishops.

MICAH. A Judaean prophet, a contemporary of Isaiah, Amos, and Hosea. He was fearless in denouncing the abuses of the times, condemning the rich who defrauded the poor, usurers, swindlers, and venal judges. He warned the people that God would judge and punish them. Among his prophecies was this one: "But you, Bethlehem Ephrathah, the least of the clans of Judah, out of you will be born for me the one who is to rule over Israel" (Micah 5:1).

MICHAEL. An angel sent by God to assure Daniel of God's protection against the Persians (Daniel 10). In the New Testament, Jude refers to the same Michael in contention with Satan (Jude 9), and in Revelation an account is given of Michael and his angels driving Satan out of heaven (Revelation 12:7–9).

MILLENNIUM. A thousand years during which Christ is to rule on earth, before the last day, based on Revelation 20:1–5. Held by some Fathers, such as Justin (A.D. 100–65) and Irenaeus (130–200), the millennium is still professed by a number of Protestant denominations. The Catholic Church interprets the biblical passage as referring to Christ's spiritual reign in the Church and takes "thousand years" to mean simply an indefinitely long time.

MIND OF THE CHURCH. The Church's attitude or policy in matters of faith or morals not explicitly taught in official pronouncements. Where specific doctrine or direction is absent, it is the Church's intention behind her teaching or regulation. To act "according to the mind of the Church" is a mark of Catholic loyalty and frequently urged on the faithful by the modern popes.

MINISTERIAL PRIESTHOOD. The sacrament of holy orders and the permanent state of one who has been ordained a priest, as distinct from the priesthood of all believers, common to all the baptized. Essential to the ministerial priesthood is the conferral of the unique sacerdotal powers of consecrating and offering the true body and blood of Christ in the Mass, and of forgiving sins committed after baptism, through the sacraments of penance and anointing.

MINISTRIES. Formerly called minor orders in the Catholic Church, namely reader and acolyte. They may now be committed to Christian men and are no longer considered as reserved to candidates for the sacraments of orders.

MINISTRY. Authorized service of God in the service of others, according to specified norms revealed by Christ and determined by the Church. In Catholic usage the various forms of ministry include these features: 1. service of God, who is glorified by the loving service given to others; 2. authorization by the Church's hierarchy, whether the pope directly or the local ordinary; this authorization may require ordination, as in the priestly ministry, or consecration, as in religious life; or liturgical blessing, as with lectors and extraordinary ministers of Holy Communion; 3. based on the teaching of Christ, who showed by word and example how to minister to people's spiritual and temporal needs; and 4. under the guidance of the Church in accordance with her directives and decrees.

MINISTRY OF THE WORD. The communication of the message of salvation. It brings the Gospel to the human race. The ministry of the word takes on different forms, according to the different conditions under which it is practiced and the ends that it strives to achieve.

There is the form called evangelization, or missionary preaching. This has as its purpose the arousing of the beginnings of faith, so that men will adhere to the word of God.

Then there is the catechetical form, "which is intended to make men's faith become living, conscious, and active, through the light of instruction" (Second Vatican Council, *Decree on the Bishops' Pastoral Office in the Church*, 14).

There is also the liturgical form, within the setting of a liturgical celebration, especially during the Eucharistic Sacrifice, e.g., through the homily.

Finally there is the theological form, which is the systematic and scientific investigation of the truths of faith. Theologians are ministers of the word insofar as they humbly investigate the resources of Christian revelation and present their findings to the faithful with a view to a more generous service of Christ and his Church.

MINOR ORDERS. The present ministries of acolyte and lector, which for centuries had been called minor orders. They were never considered part of the sacrament of orders and in 1973 were all reduced to Church ministries to which followers can be appointed in a special liturgical ceremony presided over by a bishop or, for religious, a major superior. Those communities that adhere to the use of the Extraordinary Form of the Roman Rite and are attached to the use of the 1962 liturgical books continue to use the minor orders.

MIRACLE. A sensibly perceptible effect, surpassing at least the powers of visible nature, produced by God to witness to some truth or testify to someone's sanctity. (Etym. Latin *miraculum*, miracle, marvel; from *mirari*, to wonder.)

MIRACLE OF GRACE. A sudden and unexpected conversion from ignorance to faith, from doubt to certainty, from sinfulness to holiness. It is not due to ordinary causes but to God's particular special and unmerited grace. It is an effect of divine intervention beyond the ordinary working of Providence.

MIRACLES OF CHRIST. They may be divided into five classes: nature miracles; miracles of healing; deliverance of demoniacs; victories over hostile wills; cases of resurrection.

Nature Miracles

Under this head nine miracles may be enumerated.
Changing of the water into wine at Cana (John 2)
First miraculous draught of fishes (Luke 5)
Calming of the tempest (Matthew 8; Mark 4; Luke 8)
First multiplication of loaves (Matthew 14; Mark 6; Luke 9; John 6)
Jesus's walking on the water (Matthew 14; Mark 6; John 6)
Second multiplication of loaves (Matthew 15; Mark 8)
Stater in the fish's mouth (Matthew 17)
Cursing of the fig tree (Matthew 21; Mark 11)
Second miraculous draught of fishes (John 21)

Miracles of Healing

These were numerous during the public life of Our Lord. There are references to a great many cures that are not related in detail (Matthew 4; Luke 4, 6; Mark 6), and twenty special cases are recorded.
Healing of the nobleman's son (John 4)
Cure of the mother-in-law of Peter (Matthew 8; Mark 1; Luke 4)
Cleansing of the leper (Matthew 8; Mark 1; Luke 5)
Healing of the paralytic (Matthew 9; Mark 2; Luke 5)
Healing of the sick man at Bethesda (John 5)

Restoring of the man with the withered hand (Matthew 12; Mark 3; Luke 6)

Healing of the centurion's servant (Matthew 8; Luke 7)

Healing of one blind and dumb (Matthew 12; Luke 11)

Healing of the woman with an issue of blood (Matthew 9; Mark 5; Luke 8)

Opening of the eyes of two blind men (Matthew 9)

Cure of the dumb man (Matthew 9)

Healing of the deaf and dumb man (Mark 7)

Opening the eyes of one blind at Bethsaida (Mark 8)

Healing the lunatic child (Matthew 17; Mark 9; Luke 9)

Opening the eyes of one born blind (John 9)

Restoring the woman with a spirit of infirmity (Luke 13)

Healing of the man with the dropsy (Luke 14)

Cleansing of the ten lepers (Luke 17)

Opening the eyes of the blind man near Jericho (Matthew 20; Mark 10; Luke 18)

Healing of Malchus's ear (Luke 22)

Deliverance of Demoniacs

General formulas regarding the driving out of devils (Mark 1) indicate that such acts of deliverance were very numerous during Our Lord's public life. Special cases related are as follows:

Demoniac at Capernaum (Mark 1; Luke 4)

Deaf and dumb demoniac (Matthew 12; Luke 11)

Gerasene demoniacs (Matthew 8; Mark 5; Luke 8)

Dumb demoniac (Matthew 9)

Daughter of the Syro-Phoenician woman (Matthew 15; Mark 7)

Lunatic child (Matthew 17; Mark 9; Luke 9)

Woman with the spirit of infirmity (Luke 13)

Victories over Hostile Wills

Under this heading Catholic scholars admit a greater or smaller number of miracles; it is not clear in certain cases whether the incidents in which Our Lord wielded extraordinary power over his enemies were cases of supernatural intervention of Divine Power or the natural effects of the ascendancy of his human will over that of other men. Such are the cases mentioned in John (7:30, 44; 8:20, 59), where the Jews failed to arrest him "because His hour was not yet come" or, in the fourth case, because he hid himself from them. There are two cases that appear to most Catholic commentators to involve a supernatural display of power over wills: 1. the casting out of the vendors (John 2; Matthew 21; Mark 11; Luke 19); 2. the episode of the escape from the hostile crowd at Nazareth (Luke 4).

Cases of Resurrection

Among the signs of his Messiahship which Our Lord gave to the delegates of John the Baptist, we read: "The dead rise again" (Matthew 11; Luke 7). This general statement has made some commentators think that there were cases of resurrection not described in the Gospels. This is possible because the Gospels do not aim at completeness, but the expression quoted would be justified by the three following cases of resurrection, which are related.

Raising of the daughter of Jairus (Matthew 9; Mark 5; Luke 8)
Raising of the son of the widow of Naim (Luke 7)
Raising of Lazarus (John 11)

MIRACULOUS MEDAL. A distinctive oval medal of the Blessed Virgin Mary. Its design was revealed in 1830 to St. Catherine Labouré (canonized in 1947), a Daughter of Charity of St. Vincent de Paul in Paris, in visions she had of Our Lady. On one side the medal bears an image of Mary with arms outstretched with the words "O Mary conceived without sin, pray for us who have recourse to thee," and on the reverse side the letter *M* with a cross and twelve stars above it and the Hearts of Jesus and Mary. The number of miracles attached to the wearing of this medal gave it the popular description of "miraculous." It shares popularity with the Scapular Medal. It is the badge of the Sodality of the Children of Mary. There are numerous special shrines and devotions dedicated to Our Lady of the Miraculous Medal, and weekly devotions to her are on the agenda in thousands of Catholic churches throughout the world.

MISSAL. The book containing the prayers recited by the priest at the altar during Mass. Since the Second Vatican Council, the missal for the Ordinary Form of the Roman Rite includes both the Sacramentary (or ritual part of the Mass) used only by the celebrant, and the Lectionary (containing readings from Scripture) for celebrant and assisting ministers. (Etym. Latin *missalis,* pertaining to Mass.)

MISSION. The term literally denotes "sending" and covers a variety of meanings, all somehow expressing the idea of a going forth from one person to others in order to effect some beneficial change in their favor. At the highest level are the divine missions of the Trinity: the visible mission of the Second Person, sent by the Father in the person of Jesus Christ, and the invisible mission of the Holy Spirit, sent by the Father and the Son. Christ then sent the Apostles to make disciples of all nations. Their mission was to preach the Gospel, baptize, and teach the people "to observe all the commands I gave you" (Matthew 28:19–20). The Apostles, in turn, personally and through their successors have been sending other faithful to continue the work of the Master in evangelizing the human race. Mission, therefore, is the purpose of vocation. All who are called to follow Christ are sent by Christ, in the person of his Church, to extend the Kingdom of God. (Etym. Latin *missio,* a sending.)

MISSIONARIES OF CHARITY. Religious congregations and associations founded by Blessed Teresa of Calcutta. They consist of active and contemplative sisters, active and contemplative brothers, priests, and associations of laity. Their mission is to love and serve Jesus in the poorest of the poor.

MISSIONARY. A person who is sent by Church authority to preach the Gospel or help strengthen the faith already professed, among people in a given place or region. Essential to being a missionary, whether at home or abroad, is the desire to extend the Kingdom of Christ by preaching, teaching, or other means of evangelization and catechesis.

MITER. Liturgical headdress worn by popes, cardinals, abbots, and bishops of the Latin Rite. It is a folding two-piece stiffened cap of silk or linen, often richly ornamented with gold embroidery, united with a piece of soft material allowing the two stiffened pieces to be folded together. It usually has two fringed lappets that hang down the back. It is always removed when the celebrant prays. There are three kinds of miters to be interchanged according to the solemnity of the occasion and the liturgical season: the golden, the precious, and the simple. The last is always of white and worn on Good Friday and at funerals. Usually inferior prelates are restricted to the white miter only. (Etym. Greek *mitrā,* girdle, belt, headband, turban.)

MIXED MARRIAGE. A marriage between a professed member of the Catholic Church and one who is not a Catholic. The mainstream of Roman Catholic tradition on mixed marriages is to discourage them, while recognizing that such marriages are inevitable in pluralistic societies. Two reasons are commonplace as to why the Church discourages mixed unions: the risk to the faith of the Catholic party, and the danger that the children will not be brought up in the Catholic Church. Since the Second Vatican Council the Church has drastically revised her legislation regarding mixed marriages, notably in 1966 and 1970. There is greater leniency on the permission for these marriages, but no change on the basic concern to preserve the faith of the Catholic partner and ensure that all the children are baptized and reared in the Catholic Church.

MIXED-MARRIAGE PROMISES. The commitment required of the Catholic party in a marriage with a non-Catholic. As expressed in the apostolic letter of Pope Paul VI in 1970, this commitment involves two things: "The Catholic party shall declare that he is ready to remove dangers of falling from the faith. He is also gravely bound to make a sincere promise to do all in his power to have all the children baptized and brought up in the Catholic Church" (*Matrimonia Mixta*, Norm 4). In many countries—e.g., the United States—the bishops' conference further specifies that, to obtain a dispensation for a mixed marriage, these promises be made orally or in writing, as the Catholic prefers.

MODERNISM. A theory about the origin and nature of Christianity, first developed into a system by George Tyrrell (1861–1909), Lucien Laberthonnière (1860–1932), and Alfred Loisy (1857–1940). According to Modernism, religion is essentially a matter of experience, personal and collective. There is no objective revelation from God to the human race, on which Christianity is finally based, nor any reasonable grounds for credibility in the Christian faith, based on miracles or the testimony of history. Faith, therefore, is uniquely from within. In fact it is part of human nature, "a kind of motion of the heart," hidden and unconscious. It is, in Modernist terms, a natural instinct belonging to the emotions, a "feeling for the divine" that cannot be expressed in words or doctrinal propositions, an attitude of spirit that all people have naturally but that some are more aware of having. Modernism was condemned by Pope St. Pius X in two formal documents, *Lamentabili* and *Pascendi,* both published in 1907. (Etym. Latin *modernus,* belonging to the present fashion.)

MODESTY. The virtue that moderates all the internal and external movements and appearance of a person according to his or her endowments, possessions, and station in life. Four virtues are commonly included under modesty: humility, studiousness, and two kinds of external modesty, namely in dress and general behavior.

Humility is the ground of modesty in that it curbs the inordinate desire for personal excellence and inclines one to recognize his or her own worth in its true light. Studiousness moderates the desire and pursuit of truth in accordance with faith and right reason. Its contrary vices are curiosity, which is an excessive desire for knowledge, and negligence, which is remissness in acquiring the knowledge that should be had for one's age and position in life. Modesty in dress and bodily adornments inclines a person to avoid not only whatever is offensive to others but whatever is not necessary. Modesty in bodily behavior directs a person to observe proper decorum in bodily movements, according to the dictum of St. Augustine, "In all your movements let nothing be evident that would offend the eyes of another." (Etym. Latin *modestia,* moderation, modesty.)

MONASTERY. The place where religious dwell in seclusion. The term applies mainly to religious men or women who live a cloistered, contemplative life and recite the entire Divine Office in common. (Etym. Greek *monastērion;* from *monazein,* live alone.)

MONASTICISM. The way of life, characterized by asceticism and self-denial, followed by religious who live more or less secluded from the world, according to a fixed rule and under vows, in order to praise God through contemplation and apostolic charity. The principal duty of those living the monastic life is to offer humble service to God within the boundaries of the monastery. Some monastic institutes dedicate themselves wholly to contemplation; others engage in some works of the apostolate or of Christian charity, in accord with the character of monastic life.

MONK. Originally a hermit or anchorite, but already in the early Church applied to men living a community life in a monastery, under vows of poverty, chastity, and obedience, according to a specific rule, such as that of St. Basil or St. Benedict. (Etym. Greek *monachos,* living alone, solitary.)

MONOGAMY. The institution of marriage in which husband and wife may have only one marital partner, who is still living. It is the unity of marriage opposed to polygamy. (Etym. Greek *monos,* only + *gamos,* marriage.)

MONOGENISM. The doctrine that the human race derived from one original human being, identified in Scripture with Adam. This is the Church's constant traditional teaching. In the creed of Pope Pelagius I (r. 556–61) we read: "I confess that all men until the end of time, born of Adam and dying with Adam, his wife, who themselves were not born of other parents . . . will rise and stand firm before the judgment seat of Christ, to receive each one according to his works" (Denzinger 228a). And Venerable Pope Pius XII declared: "No Catholic can hold that after Adam there existed on this earth true men who did not take their origin through natural generation from him as from the first parent of all" (*Humani Generis,* 1950, para. 38). (Etym. Latin *mono,* one + *genus,* race.)

MONOTHEISM. The belief that there is only one God, who is the Creator of the universe. It is first of all theism, because it recognizes the existence of a personal God, with mind and will, who is really distinct from the world he created. It is therefore not monism, which identifies God and the universe. Moreover it affirms that this personal and transcendent God is uniquely one and not plural, hence it is opposed to polytheism and dualism. (Etym. Greek *monos,* single + *theos,* god.)

MONSTRANCE (EMBLEM). A symbol of the Blessed Sacrament since the monstrance is the sacred vessel that contains the consecrated Host when exposed or carried in procession. It is a well-known emblem of St. Clare, who is reported to have repulsed unbelievers who assaulted her convent of nuns by presenting to their gaze Christ in the monstrance. St. Peter Julian Eymard, founder of the Blessed Sacrament Fathers, is symbolized carrying the monstrance and blessing the people with it. St. Thomas Aquinas has the monstrance among his many emblems as the author of the famous hymns "Lauda Sion" and "Pange Lingua," written to honor the Eucharistic Lord. St. John Neumann, who first established the forty hours' devotion in America, and St. Paschal Baylon, patron of Eucharistic Congresses, are both represented in art with the monstrance. (Etym. Latin *monstrans,* from *monstrare,* to show, point out, indicate.) See also OSTENSORIUM.

MORAL. Pertaining to rational beings in the use of free will; therefore pertaining to human conduct or to the science of human behavior. (Etym. Latin *moralis,* relating to conduct; *mos,* a manner, custom.)

MORAL ARGUMENT. The argument for God's existence from the fact of a moral nature in human beings. Given the instinctive human awareness that some actions are good and others wrong, and the sense of peace when one does what is considered good but guilt when one does wrong, it is reasonable to conclude that there must be a God who ultimately inspires these moral sentiments because he is leading the human race to a destiny that must be gained by living a morally good life.

MORAL CERTITUDE. Confident assent concerning human conduct based on people's normal and predictable responses to certain needs, abilities, and motivations.

MORAL DETERMINANTS. Conditions that need to be fulfilled to determine the morality of human conduct. In order to judge the goodness or badness of any particular human act, three elements must be weighed from which every act derives its morality. They are the object of the act, the circumstances surrounding the act, and the purpose that the one performing the act has in mind.

The object of a human act is that which the one acting sets out to do, as distinguished from his or her ultimate purpose in doing it. It is that which the action of its very nature tends to produce. For example, the object of a suicide's act is to take his or her life; the purpose may be to escape evils that person is unwilling to bear.

Moreover, the object is not merely the act considered in its physical makeup. It is the act viewed in its moral nature, i.e., the act considered in its relationship to the moral law. It answers to the question: Does it conform or is it contrary to the standard of right conduct? The circumstances of a human act are accidental modifications that affect its morality. Circumstances are capable of changing an ordinary indifferent act into a sinful one, such as unnecessary servile work on Sunday; an ordinarily venially sinful act into a mortal sin, such as taking even a small amount of urgently needed money from a very poor man; an ordinarily mortally sinful act into a venial sin, such as blaspheming when only half aware of what one is doing; and a sinful action into a doubly sinful, such as unjustly striking a person consecrated to God.

The end or purpose of a human act is the intention that prompts one to perform such an act, as when a person reveals some hidden failing of another in order to injure that person's reputation.

A human action is morally good only if all three elements—namely object, circumstances, and purpose—are substantially good. An action becomes morally bad if even one of these three elements is bad. The reason is that we are always obliged to avoid all evil as far as we can. If an essential part of an action is evil, we cannot avoid that evil part unless we refrain from the whole action. If, then, one does an action in spite of the substantially evil element in it, one is performing a sinful action.

MORAL EVIL. Sin, as distinct from physical evil, which is some form of suffering. It is evil because it is contrary to the will of God; it is moral evil because it is caused by a free created will acting against the law of God, who does not want moral evil as an end or as a means. The Council of Trent condemned the contrary doctrine (Denzinger 816). God simply permits moral evil because of consideration of human freedom, and because he has the wisdom and power to cause good to arise from evil. In the end, moral evil will serve the supreme purpose of the universe, the glorification of God, since it reveals his mercy in forgiving and his justice in punishing.

MORALITY. Relation between a human act and the final destiny of a human being. It is the norm of behavior that flows from each person's ultimate end, which is the possession of God in the beatific vision.

Depending on what is conceived to be this final destiny, morality will be determined accordingly. Since Catholic Christianity believes that this destiny is heaven, a human act is either good or bad according as it leads a person to or away from his or her heavenly goal. The moral norm of human acts, therefore, consists in their aptitude at leading one to that end. Such an aptitude cannot be created by the human will, nor is it entirely at the disposition of some arbitrary divine freedom. It flows necessarily from the nature of God, from the human nature elevated by grace, and from the nature of the acts themselves. Hence the norm of morality contains precepts that transcend every legislative will. The acts related to them are said to have an intrinsic (essential) morality of good or evil. Extrinsic morality, on the other hand, is external to this built-in relationship between action and purpose; they depend exclusively on the free dictate of the legislator.

MORALITY IN MEDIA. Concern of dedicated citizens organized in certain countries like the United States to prevent by legal means the use of the media to morally pervert the press, movie, radio, and television audience.

MORALITY OF MUSIC. The recognized fact that music and song, apart from the words used, have the ability to arouse either noble or base feelings and emotions in the persons who hear a melody. The reason for this emotional influence seems to lie deeper than the familiar association of ideas with certain music or song. It involves something inherent in all musical rhythm to evoke a human response that is either morally elevating or degrading, depending partly on the listener but also on what is heard.

MORAL LAW. The norm of human conduct, whether revealed or known by reason. The term is used to distinguish the law as binding in conscience, from mere statutes or directives intended to ensure good order.

MORAL MIRACLE. Divine intervention that enables a person to perform acts of virtue that are totally beyond the capacity of the unaided human will.

MORAL ORDER. The proper direction of human actions to a person's ultimate end, namely the eternal destiny. On a universal scale, the relationship of all human actions, under Divine Providence, toward the final purpose that God has for the human race. In ecclesiastical and civil law, the legally established body of rights and duties among human beings either in general or in a given society.

MORAL THEOLOGY. The science of human actions insofar as they are directed by natural reason and divine faith to the attainment of a supernatural destiny. The scope of moral theology, therefore, is human conduct precisely as human, that is, whatever people do under the influence of their free will. In this sense, it is the science of human freedom. It differs, however, from ethics or moral philosophy in that human destiny is supernatural twice over: once because heaven is a revealed mystery and once again because heaven cannot be reached without divine grace. On both counts, moral theology deals with the supernatural, since it takes into account a higher end than what reason alone could conceive, and it recognizes the need for God's grace to do what the human will alone could not achieve.

It differs from dogmatic theology, which it presumes, in that moral theology is concerned with the ethical imperatives of Catholic doctrine and how they are to be lived out in practice. Some authors also carefully distinguish moral from ascetical or spiritual theology, on the score that there are two levels of God's manifest will to humankind, one of precept and the other of counsel. Assuming the distinction, moral theology would then cover only the divine precepts, whether directly revealed or as taught by the Church with divine authority. Since the Second Vatican Council, however, the tendency is to include the whole spectrum of divine expectations for the human race under the single discipline of moral theology, not excluding the pursuit of sanctity.

MORNING OFFERING. Prayer of dedication of one's entire day to the Sacred Heart of Jesus, said by members of the Apostleship of Prayer (League of the Sacred Heart) since the first statutes were approved by the Holy See in 1879. A traditional form of the prayer reads:

> O Jesus, through the immaculate heart of Mary I offer You all my prayers, works, joys, and sufferings of this day for all the intentions of Your Sacred Heart, in union with the holy sacrifice of the Mass throughout the world, in reparation for my sins, for the intentions of all our associates, and in particular for the intentions of the Holy Father.

MORTAL SIN. An actual sin that destroys sanctifying grace and causes the supernatural death of the soul. Mortal sin is a turning away from God because of a seriously inordinate adherence to creatures that causes grave injury to a person's rational nature and to the social order, and it deprives the sinner of a right to heaven.

The terms "mortal," "deadly," "grave," and "serious" applied to sin are synonyms, each with a slightly different implication. "Mortal" and "deadly" focus on the effects in the sinner, namely deprivation of the state of friendship with God; "grave" and "serious" refer to the importance of the matter in which a person offends God. But the Church never distinguishes among these terms as though they represented different kinds of sins. There is only one recognized correlative to mortal sin, and that is venial sin, which offends against God but does not cause the loss of one's state of grace. (Etym. Latin *mors,* death.)

MORTIFICATION. The practice of Christian asceticism in order to overcome sin and master one's sinful tendencies, and through penance and austerity to strengthen the will in the practice of virtue and grow in the likeness of Christ. Natural mortification is a normal part of self-discipline; supernatural mortification, based on faith, seeks to grow in holiness through merit gained by cooperating with the grace of God. (Etym. Latin *mortificatio,* a killing, a putting to death.)

MOSAIC LAW. The body of civil, moral, and religious legislation found in the last four books of the Pentateuch and traditionally ascribed to Moses. The foundation of this law is the Decalogue (Exodus 20), and its center is the Book of the Covenant (Exodus 20–23). The civil legislation is mainly in Exodus (18–23) and Deuteronomy (16–26). The moral laws are in Exodus (20–23), supplemented by Leviticus (11–20) and Deuteronomy (5). The religious and ceremonial precepts are in Exodus (25–30) and especially Leviticus (1–27). Compared with similar laws in other nations of that time, the Mosaic code is vastly superior by reason of its strong monotheism, its proclamation of God as the only source and final sanction of all laws, and its summation of the whole law in the love of God and of neighbor.

MOSES. The greatest figure in the Old Testament, the founder of Israel, lawgiver, leader, and proponent of monotheism. Of the tribe of Levi, he was born in Egypt during a persecution when all the Hebrew male children were to be killed. Exposed on the Nile, he was rescued by Pharaoh's daughter and educated at court. God appeared to him in a burning bush and told him to deliver his people with the help of Aaron. The plagues did not make Pharaoh relent, until the death of every firstborn forced him to yield. Moses then led the Israelites through the years-long exodus, but he was excluded from the Promised Land because of his lack of confidence at the "Waters of Contradiction." The prophet died on Mount Nebo after pronouncing the three memorable discourses preserved in Deuteronomy. He was buried in the valley of Moab, but no one knows where.

MOTHER OF GOD. Title of the Blessed Virgin Mary as the physical parent of Jesus, who is God. Although first defined against Nestorius at the Council of Ephesus (431), the concept goes back to subapostolic times. The basis in Scripture is the twofold theme of the Gospels, that Jesus was true God and that Mary was truly the mother of Jesus. St. Ignatius of Antioch (d. 107) wrote to the Ephesians: "Our God Jesus Christ was carried in Mary's womb, according to God's plan of salvation." The title Theotokos (Mother of God) became current after the third century. It was used by Origen (c. 185–c. 254), and St. Gregory Nazianzen, writing about 382, said: "If anyone does not recognize the holy Mary as Mother of God he is separated from the Divinity."

The Nestorian objection that Mary could not be the Mother of God, because she gave birth to the human nature only, was met by Christian apologists who pointed out that not the nature as such but the person was conceived and born. Since Mary conceived him who was the Second Person incarnate, she is truly the Mother of God.

Consequent on her divine maternity, Mary transcends in dignity all created persons and stands next to her divine Son in holiness. Ancient writers stressed the relation between Mary's divine maternity and her fullness of grace, which they found asserted in the angelic greeting "Hail, full of grace" (*kecharitoméne*). Her vocation to become the Mother of God, they reasoned, demanded a special richness of divine friendship.

MOTHER OF THE CHURCH. A title of the Blessed Virgin, formally recognized by the Second Vatican Council (*Lumen Gentium,* 60–65) and solemnly proclaimed by Pope Paul VI at the closing address of the third session of the Council on November 21, 1964. Mary is Mother of the Church by a fivefold title: 1. she gave human life to the Son of God, from whom the whole People of God receive the grace and dignity of election; 2. Christ on the Cross explicitly extended his Mother's maternity, through the disciple John, to all the faithful; 3. the Holy Spirit came upon her, together with the Apostles, when on Pentecost Sunday the Church was born in visible form; 4. since then all generations of Christ's followers, such as John, spiritually took Mary as their Mother; 5. she continues to exercise her maternal care for the Church by her presence and powerful intercession in heaven before the throne of God.

Blessed Pope John Paul II further identified Mary's motherhood of the Church with her Immaculate Heart. "This heart," he said, "the heart of both a virgin and a mother, has always followed the work of her Son and has gone out to all those whom Christ has embraced and continues to embrace with inexhaustible love" (*Redemptor Hominis,* 22).

MOTIVATIONAL HIERARCHY. The theory that all human beings have an implicit hierarchy of motives in all their conscious actions. The hierarchy, it is said, ranges in ascending order as follows: physiological needs, personal security, social relations, prestige, power possession, self-actualization, the need for knowledge, aesthetic needs, and religious needs. Somewhat different sequences are proposed by various writers, but they agree that, unless people are morally perverse, they recognize the priority of the spiritual over the bodily and of the religious over what concerns only space and time.

MOVABLE FEASTS. Those feasts whose dates are variable because of their dependence on the Easter date. Easter may come as early as March 22 and as late as April 25. Lent is shifted back and forth depending on the Easter date, so are Ascension Day, Pentecost, Trinity Sunday, and Corpus Christi. Other feasts are movable because they are placed in relation to certain Sundays.

MURDER. The unjust killing of an innocent person. Directly to intend killing an innocent person is forbidden either to a private citizen or to the State, and this even in order to secure the common good. God has supreme and exclusive ownership over human lives, and so he is the only one who has the right to allow the taking of a human life. He confers on civil authority the right to take the life of a condemned criminal only when this is necessary for achieving the just purposes of the State. In a commentary passage on the Decalogue, divine revelation commands: "See that the man who is innocent and just is not done to death, and do not acquit the guilty" (Exodus 23:7).

MUSICAM SACRAM. Instruction on music in the liturgy of the Sacred Congregation of Rites. An extensive document giving general norms and applying them to every important aspect of liturgical music. Among other provisions there should be choirs, at least one or two properly trained singers especially in churches that cannot have even a small choir. The distinction between solemn, sung, and read Mass is retained; Gregorian chant should be given pride of place; adapting sacred music for regions having a musical tradition of their own requires "a very specialized preparation by experts"; and those instruments which are by common opinion "suitable for secular music only, are to be altogether prohibited from every liturgical celebration and from popular devotions" (March 5, 1967).

MUTILATION. An action that deprives oneself or another of a bodily organ or its use. The mutilation may be either direct or indirect. Direct mutilation is a deliberately intended act that of its very nature can cause mutilation. If the effect is not directly intended, it is called indirect mutilation.

Mutilation belongs to the category of murder. The difference is that mutilation is partial destruction, whereas murder is the total destruction of a person's physical life. Moral law is concerned with mutilation because no one has absolute dominion over the body, and the violation of this principle is an offense against God's sovereignty.

Nevertheless, a person has the right to sacrifice one or more members of the body for the well-being of the whole body. Thus it is permitted to amputate any organ of the body in order to save one's life. However, lesser reasons than danger of death also justify mutilation.

The removal or suppressing the function of any organ of reproduction is in a moral category of its own. It is never permitted when the purpose is directly to prevent conception or pregnancy. (Etym. Latin *mutilare*, to cut off, maim.)

MYSTERY. A divinely revealed truth whose very possibility cannot be rationally conceived before it is revealed and, after revelation, whose inner essence cannot be fully understood by the finite mind. The incomprehensibility of revealed mysteries derives from the fact that they are manifestations of God, who is infinite and therefore beyond the complete grasp of a created intellect. Nevertheless, though incomprehensible, mysteries are intelligible. One of the primary duties of a believer is, through prayer, study, and experience, to grow in faith, i.e., to develop an understanding of what God has revealed. (Etym. Greek *mystērion*, something closed, a secret.)

MYSTERIES OF THE ROSARY. See GLORIOUS MYSTERIES, JOYFUL MYSTERIES, LUMINOUS MYSTERIES, SORROWFUL MYSTERIES.

MYSTERY PLAY. A religious drama during the Middle Ages portraying some mystery of the Christian religion. These plays developed from the dramatic parts of the liturgy and joined to ideas drawn from the Bible and other sources. Biblical dramas featured the Passion of Christ, the Last Supper, the Parable of the Wise and Foolish Virgins, and the End of the World. Saints were featured in these plays, notably martyrs such as St. Catherine of Alexandria and St. George. After the Reformation, mystery dramas practically disappeared, but they have since been restored in many places, notably in the Passion Play at Oberammergau, Bavaria.

MYSTICAL BODY. The Catholic Church established by Christ as an extension and continuation of the Incarnation.

In the words of Venerable Pius XII, "If we would define and describe the true Church of Jesus Christ—which is the one, holy, Catholic, apostolic Roman Church—we shall find nothing more noble, more sublime, or more divine than the expression 'the Mystical Body of Jesus Christ'—an expression that flows spontaneously from the repeated teaching of the sacred Scriptures and the holy Fathers."

The term "body," when referring to the Church, derives its meaning from the analogy used by St. Paul, where he speaks of Christians: "You are the Body of Christ, member for member" (I Corinthians 12:27), and of Christ: "the Head of His Body, the Church" (Colossians 1:18).

Corollary to being a body, the Church must have a multiplicity of discernible members because the possession of parts is an essential feature of anything bodily. And just as a natural body is formed of different organs with different functions arranged in due order, so the Church is bound together by the combination of structurally united parts, and has a variety of members that are reciprocally dependent. Another name for this interdependence is the hierarchy, with its graded levels of orders and jurisdiction, of superiors and subjects, beginning with the Sovereign Pontiff and terminating in the laity.

The body (*soma*) that St. Paul identifies with the Church is a living reality, and like every organism requires suitable means to enter into life, to grow and mature and prosper according to its nature. Similarly in the Catholic Church, the sacraments are available for every spiritual need and circumstance of human life.

Moreover, the Roman Catholic Church regards herself as the Body of Christ. He was the originator of the Church by his preaching and choice of the Apostles to carry on his work, by his death on the Cross when he merited the graces to be channeled through the Mystical Body, and by the descent of the Holy Spirit, whom he sent on Pentecost. He continues to rule the Church from within by supernatural means that are permanent and constantly active within the members.

The Church is called Mystical because she is a mystery, which God revealed to be true but whose inner essence must be accepted on faith and without full comprehension by the mind. Otherwise than in other societies, the end or purpose of the Church is not temporal or earthly but heavenly and eternal; its spiritual bond is the will of God;

incorporation in the Church effects a profound internal change in the members; and the whole reality is called supernatural because it leads to the destiny of seeing God in the beatific vision after death. But the Roman Catholic Church is mainly said to be the *Mystical* Body of Christ because it is sacramental. The Church is the great sacrament of the New Law, instituted by Christ for the communication of invisible grace to the whole world.

MYSTICAL THEOLOGY. The science of the spiritual life, with stress on the operation of divine grace. It deals with the higher forms of mental prayer and with such extraordinary phenomena as are recorded in the lives of the saints. It is the science of the study of mystic states. It is commonly distinguished from ascetical theology, which emphasizes free cooperation with and predisposition for divine grace. See also ASCETICAL THEOLOGY.

MYSTICAL UNION. The union of a soul with God in deep contemplation. It is characterized by a deep awareness of the divine presence and has a variety of grades, not necessarily successive, but distinguished by spiritual writers. They are the two nights of the soul (senses and spirit) before mystical union, the prayer of quiet, the full union, ecstasy, and spiritual marriage or transforming union.

MYSTICI CORPORIS CHRISTI. Encyclical of Venerable Pope Pius XII, published in 1943, on the Church as the Mystical Body of Christ. The Church is a body because she is a visible, living, and growing organism, animated by the Spirit of God. She is a Mystical Body because her essential nature is a mystery, and all her teachings, laws, and rites are sacramental sources of grace. And she is the Mystical Body of Christ because he founded the Church. He remains her invisible Head, and through him all blessings are communicated to her members and through them to the rest of humankind.

MYSTICISM. The supernatural state of soul in which God is known in a way that no human effort or exertion could ever succeed in producing. There is an immediate, personal experience of God that is truly extraordinary, not only in intensity and degree but in kind. It is always the result of a special, totally unmerited grace of God. Christian mysticism differs essentially from the non-Christian mysticism of the Oriental world. It always recognizes that the reality to which it penetrates simply transcends the soul and the cosmos; there is no confusion between I and thou, but always a profound humility before the infinite Majesty of God. And in Christian mysticism all union between the soul and God is a moral union of love, in doing his will even at great sacrifice to self; there is no hint of losing one's being in God or absorption of one's personality into the divine.

NAHUM, BOOK OF. A book of the Old Testament written about 660 B.C. by an author who calls himself Elkosh, or the Elcesite. The prophet was probably a Judaean. Israel had already been destroyed, Judah humbled, and King Mannasseh probably a prisoner in Assyria (II Chronicles 33). To console the Chosen People, Nahum foretells the fall of Nineveh, hence the open line, "Oracle on Nineveh, Book of the Vision of Elkosh."

NAME. In biblical usage, not only the title by which a person is called but the term by which the person is identified. The expressions to profane (Amos 2:7), sanctify (Isaiah 29:23), praise (Isaiah 25:1), and love (Psalm 5:12) the name of YHWH all refer to God himself. In the New Testament this concept is further deepened and refined. The name of Jesus identifies his mission (Matthew 1:21), which is to redeem (Acts 10:43), to save (Acts 4:12), to confer the fullness of supernatural life (Colossians 3:17). Prayer in the name of Jesus, according to his intentions, is always heard (John 15:16); those who invoke his name will be saved (Romans 10:13), and those who believe in his name form the Church (I Corinthians 1:2), so that they can be called Christians (Acts 11:26). They are consequently to pray that the name of God, who became man in the person of Christ, be sanctified (Matthew 6:9), which means honored and glorified.

NAMES, CHRISTIAN. Names given to individuals at their baptism. The custom of giving the name of a saint when a person is baptized goes back to the earliest days of the Church. It is required by ecclesiastical law and means that the saint whose name is chosen becomes a special patron to protect and guide and be the heavenly intercessor for the one who bears his or her name.

NATHANAEL. Another name for Bartholomew. Each time the Apostles are listed in the Gospels, Philip and Bartholomew are grouped together. It was Philip who brought Nathanael to see Jesus for the first time. Despite an initial skepticism, he was instantly impressed by Jesus's superhuman knowledge and became a follower (John 1:45–51). The only other reference to Nathanael was on the occasion of Jesus's appearance after his Resurrection on the shore of the Sea of Tiberias, now known as the Lake of Tiberias, when a group of the Apostles, led by Peter and including Nathanael, went fishing (John 21:1–3). See also BARTHOLOMEW.

NATIONAL CONFERENCES OF BISHOPS. See EPISCOPAL CONFERENCE.

NATURAL FAMILY PLANNING. The controlling of human conception by restricting the marital act to the infertile periods of the wife. This practice is based on the theory that the period of a woman's ovulation can be determined with considerable accuracy. A variety of methods, or their combination, is used to determine the period of ovulation. From the moral standpoint, natural family planning is permissible. As stated by Pope Paul VI: "If there are serious motives to space out births, which derive from physical or psychological conditions of husband or wife, or from external conditions, it is licit to take account of the natural rhythms inherent in the generative functions" (*Humanae Vitae*, II, 16). See also NATURAL FAMILY PLANNING (PRACTICE).

NATURAL FAMILY PLANNING (PRACTICE). A method of determining the fertile and infertile days of a woman. There are three methods currently in use and all rely on the observation and recording of one or more signs of the body: 1. the sympto-thermal method. This is the most comprehensive and surest of the three. It involves the observation and recording of all three signs: a. mucus secreted in the cervical opening: the average menstrual period lasts from three to seven days. Toward the end of this period mucus begins to appear at the opening of the cervix. At first it is tacky and yellowish. After a couple of days it becomes stretchy and turns into a whitish color, like that of an egg white. It reaches this peak quality one to two days prior to ovulation. This indicates the time of greatest fertility; b. body temperature: this is recorded with the use of a basal thermometer, which measures body temperature in tenths of degrees. Twenty-four hours after ovulation, the body temperature will rise approximately .4–.6 degree. About the fourth day after the temperature rise it is safe to assume that the infertile days have begun, provided that the other signs concur; c. cervical opening: before ovulation, the cervix is open, soft, and high. After ovulation, the cervix is closed and firm, and lengthens. The concurrence of all three signs indicates the days on which a woman is ovulating. From this can be charted her fertile and infertile days. Differences in individual cycles must be taken into consideration; 2. the Billings, or ovulation, method relies solely on the recording of the mucus symptom; 3. the third method relies solely on the temperature symptom. The sympto-thermal method is more than 99 percent effective for those who are willing to work with it. The Billings method is also reliable but requires a qualified instructor and somewhat more time and instruction.

NATURAL LAW. As distinct from revealed law, it is "nothing else than the rational creature's participation in the eternal law" (*Summa Theologiae*, 1a, 2ae, quest. 91, art. 2). As coming from God, the natural law is what God has produced in the world of creation; as coming to human beings, it is what they know (or can know) of what God has created.

It is therefore called natural law because everyone is subject to it from birth (*natio*), because it contains only those duties that are derivable from human nature itself, and because, absolutely speaking, its essentials can be grasped by the unaided light of human reason.

St. Paul recognizes the existence of a natural law when he describes the moral responsibility of those ancients who did not have the benefit of Mosaic revelation. "Pagans," he says, "who never heard of the Law but are led by reason to do what the Law commands, may not actually 'possess' the Law, but they can be said to 'be' the Law. They can point to the substance of the Law engraved on their hearts—they can call a witness, that is, their own conscience—they have accusation and defense, that is, their own inner mental dialogue" (Romans 2:14–15). See also LAW OF NATURE.

NATURAL ORDER. The built-in arrangement that belongs to things inherently and that develops them according to the very natures they possess. Contrasted with an artificial or superimposed order. On a universal level, the sum total of all natures, their powers and activities, related to the final end or purpose they have as natural beings. Contrasted with supernatural order.

NATURAL RELIGION. A composite of all those duties to God that human reason can discover by its own power and apart from supernatural revelation. Three principal truths and corresponding duties constitute natural religion: 1. God exists and is a Being of infinite excellence and worth; human beings therefore owe him special reverence; 2. God is the First Cause, as the author and provider of all that anyone is and does; everyone therefore owes him special service;

3. God is the Final Destiny and Highest Good in whom alone the human heart can find happiness; he therefore deserves special love.

NATURAL SINS. A term used to describe those sins against chastity in which the natural purpose of the sexual act is or can be attained, but they are performed outside the legitimate bonds of matrimony. Implicit in such acts is the malice of committing a sin against some other virtue besides chastity. Thus adultery, rape, and abduction are crimes against justice; fornication sins against the justice due to the offspring, the community, and the unmarried partner; incest is opposed to familial piety; and sacrilege offends against the virtue of religion for a person vowed to celibacy.

NATURE. The essence of a being considered as the principle of activity. Also the substance of a thing as distinguished from its properties, considered as the source of its operations. Nature is also definable in contrast to its opposites from a variety of viewpoints. In contrast with God, it is the created universe. In contrast with human activity, it is the world considered prior to or independent of the changes produced by human free will. In contrast to the life and operations of divine grace, it is that to which a human person has claim, as creature, as distinct from a share in God's own life, which is the supernatural. (Etym. Latin *natura,* the inner principle of a thing's operations and activity; from *nasci,* to be born.)

NATURE AND GRACE. The two ultimates of human existence viewed in their mutual relationship. Nature is what human beings are and have when they are born (*nati*). Grace is what they further need by divine favor (*gratia*) to reach their eternal destiny.

NECESSARY REVELATION. Supernatural communication of divine truth as necessary for the human race. There are two kinds of necessity corresponding to the two levels of human need, namely the absolute need of grace to reach the beatific vision and the relative need of help to overcome the limitations of fallen human nature. The human race would have needed revelation even if it had never sinned, once Christianity assumes that it has been elevated to a supernatural destiny. Otherwise how could anyone reach a destiny that is naturally impossible even to conceive? Moreover, humanity sinned. As a result the human mind is darkened, not completely but considerably.

It therefore needs divine guidance, as revelation, to know what is not of itself beyond human discovery but what is difficult to attain clearly, certainly, and by everyone in the present state of the human race.

NECROMANCY. The art of divining the future through alleged communication with the dead. It was mentioned in the Bible and found in every ancient nation. It was forbidden by Mosaic Law in any form, whether as alchemy, magic, or witchcraft. It is also forbidden by the Church. One reason is that the practice lends itself to dependence on the evil spirits who can pretend to foretell the future, but only to deceive and mislead the practitioners. In modern times it is called Spiritism or Spiritualism. (Etym. Greek *nekros,* corpse + *manteia,* divination; Latin *necromania.*)

NEHEMIAH. A rich, well-educated Jew in Persia who learned of the wretched conditions prevailing in Jerusalem and of the defenseless condition of the city without walls and gates. He sought the help of King Artaxerxes and was permitted to return to his homeland (Nehemiah 1–6). He found on careful inspection that the sad reports he had received were true. So he pleaded with the assembled Judaeans, "Come let us rebuild the walls of Jerusalem and suffer this indignity no longer" (Nehemiah 2:17). The Jews in great numbers responded to his plea, and volunteers labored on the repair program day and night. Their enemies ridiculed their efforts but the tremendous campaign persevered. Nehemiah proved to be an excellent organizer. Within a few months Jerusalem was like a new city. Then he concentrated on the civil and religious state of the city, enforcing marriage reform, compliance with the Mosaic Laws (Nehemiah 6), insisting on competent officials, and stressing Sabbath observance. The morale of the people rose to new heights, and neighboring countries marveled at the improvements. Thousands of Jews returned from exile with new hope and pride (Nehemiah 7, 11).

NEO-MODERNISM. The movement attempts to reconcile modern science and philosophy at the expense of the integrity of the Catholic faith. It has its roots in the Modernism condemned by Pope St. Pius X. Like its predecessor, it rejects belief in the supernatural and considers the Church only a human society. Among the main features of Neo-Modernism are the denial of original sin, the claim that Christ was only a human person, and that dogmas of faith are only verbal formulations whose meaning substantially changes with the times. In Neo-Modernism, the philosophies of Hegel and Heidegger replace that of St. Thomas Aquinas, and faith is reduced to a purely subjective experience, apart from an objective divine revelation and independent of the magisterium or teaching authority of the Church.

NEOPHYTE. One who has entered on a new and better state of life. Thus a newly baptized convert from unbelief or a non-Christian religion today or to Christianity from Judaism in the early Church. The name is also given to a novice or postulant in a religious community or to a beginner studying for the priesthood. (Etym. Greek *neos,* new + *phutos,* grown: *neophutos,* lit. newly planted.)

NEO-SCHOLASTICISM. The name given by certain Scholastic philosophers to the revival of medieval Scholasticism since the beginning of the twentieth century. These Catholic thinkers wished to revive among the public and for the people's use the teachings of the great Scholastics of the past, bringing their theories up to date and putting them in touch with modern scientific research. They do not aim to revive unchanged systems of medieval Scholasticism but rather to harmonize modern science with the fundamental doctrines and principles of this school of thought, especially as related to the physical world. The movement was begun in Italy and Germany even before 1879, when Pope Leo XIII's encyclical *Aeterni Patris* gave the movement a major impetus by his approbation. Since then it has become developed, especially in Catholic circles.

NEPOTISM. Preferment in ecclesiastical practice based on blood or family relationship rather than merit. Applied especially to the conferral of Church offices. Historically nepotism plagued the Church for centuries, was practiced by some of the popes and many bishops, and was one of the factors that led to the legislation of celibacy in the Western Church and to the Protestant Reformation. The most important legislation against nepotism was the bull *Romanum decet Pontificem* in 1692, of Pope Innocent XII. (Etym. Latin *nepos,* nephew.)

NESTORIANISM. A fifth-century Christian heresy that held that there were two distinct persons in the Incarnate Christ, one human and the other divine, as against the orthodox teaching that Christ was a divine person who assumed a human nature. Its name was taken from Nestorius (died c. 451), a native of Germanicia in Syria, and later Bishop of Constantinople. Nestorianism was condemned by the ecumenical Council of Ephesus in 431.

Postulating two separate persons in Christ, when Nestorius came to describe their union, he could not have them joined ontologically (in their being) or hypostatically (constituting one person), but only morally or psychologically. They would be united only by a perfect agreement of two wills in Christ, and by a harmonious communication of their respective activities. This harmony of wills (*eudoxia*) and the communion of action to which it gives rise are what forms the composite personality (*henosia*) of Christ.

In the Nestorian system we cannot speak of a true communication of *idioms*, i.e., that while the two natures of Christ are distinct the attributes of one may be predicated on the other in view of their union in the one person of Christ. Accordingly it could not be said that God was born, that he was crucified or died; Mary is not the Mother of God, except in the broad sense of giving birth to a man whose human personality was conjoined to the Word of God.

Nestorian bishops continued to propagate their views, and the confusion this produced among the people contributed to the success of Islam in the seventh century.

"NE TEMERE" DECREE. A declaration of matrimonial law issued by St. Pope Pius X; it went into effect Easter 1908. It was the *Tametsi* decree of the Council of Trent in a modified form. It took its name from the opening words and decreed that 1. marriages involving a Catholic are invalid unless performed by a parish priest in his parish or one delegated by him, or by a bishop or appointed delegate in his own diocese; 2. no pastor can validly perform a marriage outside the limits of his own parish without delegation of the proper pastor of the parish in which he is to perform the wedding, or the bishop in whose diocese he is to perform the wedding. A bishop cannot validly perform a wedding outside his own diocese without delegation from the pastor of the parish in which he is to perform the wedding or the delegation of the bishop of that place; 3. the marriage ought to be celebrated in the parish of the bride; 4. under certain circumstances a marriage may be licit and valid without a priest; 5. all marriages must be registered in the place or places where the contracting parties were baptized. There must be at least two other witnesses for validity besides the pastor or bishop. This decree did not affect persons who had

never been Catholic when they married among themselves. It applied to every marriage of a Catholic, even when marrying someone who was not of his or her faith.

NEW CHRISTIANITY. The name given since the Second Vatican Council by spokesmen for a radically changed Catholic Christianity. Its main features are a man-centered religion, preoccupation with the present world, stress on the Bible to the exclusion of revealed tradition, a classless church in which the hierarchy under the pope does not have binding authority to teach and govern the people, and a church whose purpose is to serve the world and humanity's social needs, with such an emphasis on Christ's humanity as to overshadow to the point of denying his divinity.

NEW COVENANT. Essentially the same as the New Testament but with several distinct connotations. It is a sacred agreement instituted by God in the person of Christ. It is a completion of the Old Covenant that YHWH made with the Jews. It is an eternal covenant whose fulfillment is destined for heaven. It is a promise on God's part to confer the blessings foretold in the Sermon on the Mount and at the Last Supper, provided the followers of Christ are faithful in their generosity toward God.

NEW JERUSALEM. In biblical language the Heavenly City of the angels and saints after the last day. As described by St. John in his prophetic vision: "I saw the holy city, and the New Jerusalem coming down from God out of heaven, as beautiful as a bride all dressed for her husband" (Revelation 21:2).

NEW TESTAMENT. In the sense of new dispensation, it is the fulfillment of the Old Covenant and includes all that Christ did and said during his visible stay on earth. It also means the New Law, operative since the time of Christ and destined to remain until the last day. It most commonly means the canonical books of the Bible, beyond the Jewish Torah, namely the Gospels according to Matthew, Mark, Luke, and John; the Acts of the Apostles, the Pauline Epistles to the Romans, I and II Corinthians, Galatians, Ephesians, Philippians, Colossians, I and II Thessalonians, I and II Timothy, Titus, Philemon, and Hebrews; the Catholic Epistles of James, I and II Peter, I, II, and III John, and Jude; and the book of Revelation of St. John.

NEW WORLD. A term used to describe the restoration of the present world on the last day. Its revealed basis is in the New Testament, where Christ speaks of the "regeneration," i.e., the new formation of the world (Matthew 19:28); St. Paul speaks of the whole of creation being under a curse and awaiting redemption (Romans 8:18–25); St. Peter of a "new heaven and a new earth," concurrent with a destruction of the world, in which justice will dwell (II Peter 3:13); and St. John gives an elaborate description of the New Jerusalem, which is the tabernacle of God among men (Revelation 21:1–8). St. Augustine teaches that the properties of the future world will be just as suited to the immortal existence of the glorified human body as were the properties of the present world to corruptible existence of the mortal body (*De Civitate Dei*, 20, 16).

NICENE CREED. There are two creeds that have the same name. The original Nicene Creed was issued in A.D. 325 by the Council of Nicaea. It was composed by the Fathers of the Council in their conflict with Arianism and contains the term *homoousios* (consubstantial). It is comparatively short, ends with the phrase "and in the Holy Spirit," and has attached to it four anathemas against Arianism. The more common Nicene Creed is more accurately the Nicene-Constantinople Creed. It came after the first ecumenical Council of Constantinople (381), is the creed now used in the liturgy, including the added phrases "and the Son" and "died," and differs from the preceding in that it 1. has more about the person of Christ; 2. says more about the Holy Spirit; 3. adds the articles on the Church, baptism, the Resurrection, and eternal life; and 4. contains no anathemas. The full text reads:

I believe in one God, the Father, the Almighty, maker of heaven and earth, of all things both visible and invisible. I believe in one Lord, Jesus Christ, the only begotten Son of God, born of the Father before all ages. Light from Light, true God from true God, begotten, not made, consubstantial with the Father. Through him all things were made. For us men and for our salvation he came down from heaven and by the Holy Spirit was incarnate of the Virgin Mary, and became man. For our sake he was crucified under Pontius Pilate; he suffered death and was buried, and rose again on the third day in accordance with the Scriptures; he ascended into heaven and is seated at the right hand of the Father. He will come again in glory to judge the living and the dead, and his kingdom will have no end. I believe in the Holy Spirit, the Lord, the giver of life, who proceeds from the Father and the Son, who with the Father and the Son is adored and glorified. He has spoken through the Prophets. I believe in one, holy, Catholic, and apostolic Church. I profess one baptism for the forgiveness of sins. I look for the resurrection of the dead and the life of the world to come. Amen.

NIHILISM. Applied to various theories or systems of thought: that nothing really exists except thought; that nothing really matters, what must be, must be; that the world is an absurdity, so nothing in life is really worth struggling or even living for.

NIHIL OBSTAT. Approved by the diocesan censor to publish a manuscript dealing with faith or morals. The date of the approval and the name of the person approving (*censor deputatus,* delegated censor) are normally printed in the front of the book along with a bishop's imprimatur.

NOAH. Son of Lamech and father of Shem, Ham, and Japheth. YHWH was so embittered by the corruption and faithlessness of the world that he decided he would wipe out the human race in a flood. The one exception he made was Noah and his family. He gave Noah detailed instructions about the construction of an ark strong enough to remain intact (Genesis 6). Then he instructed him to take aboard his family and two specimens of every kind of animal and bird, male and female, so that after the flood the world could be repopulated. Noah obeyed YHWH. Every living being outside the ark was destroyed when the flood submerged the earth (Genesis 7). After several months Noah had proof that the waters receded enough for all to leave the ark, which was now resting on Mount Ararat (Genesis 8). God promised, "Never again will I strike down every living being. . . ." (Genesis 8:21). "There shall be no flood to destroy the earth again" (Genesis 9:11). Noah's sons became the eponymous ancestors of the great races in the repopulation of the world.

NONE. The part of the Divine Office that is said about the ninth hour, that is, three in the afternoon. In the revised Liturgy of the Hours there is an option to say any one of the Middle Hours, Terce, Sext, or None, depending on the time of day when the office is being recited. (Etym. Latin *nona,* ninth.)

NONINFALLIBLE. A term coined by those who distinguish between defined doctrines, which they admit are infallible, and official doctrines not defined by the Church, which they claim are not infallible. Such use of the term is ambiguous and may be erroneous, since many doctrines of the Church in faith and morals—e.g., that contraception is gravely sinful—are infallible from the ordinary universal magisterium. Moreover, even other doctrines, just because they are taught by the Church, are to be accepted in obedience to the hierarchical authority established by Christ.

NORM. Any criterion for determining what is true or false, good or bad. Thus we have norms of truth, to which the mind must conform in order to make correct judgments; and norms of conduct, to which the will must conform in order to perform morally good actions. (Etym. Latin *norma*, rule, pattern.)

NORM OF MORALITY. A standard to which human acts are compared to determine their goodness or badness. A proximate norm is immediately applicable to the acts; the ultimate norm guarantees the validity of the proximate norm.

Human nature is the proximate norm of morality because it is common to everyone, and the rules derived from it will be applicable to all human beings. Moreover, human nature, while essentially unchangeable, is flexible enough to admit of varying applications according to circumstances. It is also constantly present and manifest to all humankind.

The ultimate norm of morality is the divine nature. This assumes that God is the Creator of the universe and the pattern of all things, that he is Being by essence and the Source of all things, so that whatever either exists or can exist is a reflection and participation of Infinite Being. This resemblance between God and creatures—including human beings—should be not only in nature (who God is) but also in action (how God acts). Consequently, the ultimate norm of human morality is the nature and activity of God. A person is as good as his or her character approximates the perfections of God, and his or her conduct is as good as it imitates the activity of God.

NORMS OF ORTHODOXY. Also called "Rules for Thinking with the Church," of St. Ignatius Loyola. They are sixteen norms that form part of the Spiritual Exercises and synthesize, in practical terms, the distinctive qualities of being a Catholic. The first norm is an epitome of the rest. It declares: "We must put aside all judgment of our own and keep the mind ever ready and prompt to obey in all things the true Spouse of Christ our Lord, and Holy Mother, the hierarchical Church."

NOSTRA AETATE. Declaration of the Second Vatican Council on the Relation of the Church to non-Christian religions. It is addressed to Christians and urges them to promote fellowship with persons and groups who do not profess the Christian faith. Singled out are tribal peoples, Hindus, Buddhists, Moslems, and Jews. The principal theme is that Catholics should "enter with prudence and charity into discussion and collaboration with members of other religions."

NOVENA. Nine days of public or private prayer for some special occasion or intention. Its origin goes back to the nine days that the disciples and Mary spent together in prayer between the Ascension and Pentecost Sunday. Over the centuries many novenas have been highly indulgenced by the Church. In modern times the one before Pentecost was prescribed for parochial churches. (Etym. Latin *novem*, nine.)

NOVICE. A person formally admitted to a religious institute to prepare for eventual religious profession. The purpose of the noviceship is also to assist superiors to better know the candidates and therefore be able to pass correct judgment on their suitability for the religious life. The noviceship is of ancient origin, and its duration varied. At present one year at least is required by common law, but many communities require more. A novice receives the religious habit, which in women's communities includes a white veil. He or she may leave or be requested to leave without stated reason during this period of probation. Before first profession the novice must testify to free consent. The minimum age for noviceship is fifteen years. (Etym. Latin *novicius*, new; newly arrived; novice.)

NULLITY. A decree or judgment by a competent ecclesiastical court that a reputed marriage is invalid and hence no marriage was contracted in the first place. The chief ground for nullity is the proved absence of free consent to enter a permanent marital union according to the teaching of the Catholic Church. (Etym. Latin *nullus*, none, not any.) See also ANNULMENT.

NUMBERS. The fourth book of the Bible, so named because the opening chapters deal with the census numbering of the people. It may be divided into four unequal parts: the Hebrews leave Mount Sinai

(1–10); from Sinai to Cades (10, 11–12), Cades (13–20:21); from Cades to the Plains of Moab (20:22–21:35); at the Plains of Moab (22:1–36:13). The last chapter, 36, treats of the Levitical cities and the cities of refuge.

NUMBERS, RELIGIOUS. Numbers, either written or in symbolic form, associated with mysteries of the Christian faith. Drawn from Sacred Scripture, they have become part of the Church's tradition and, in varying degrees, are found everywhere in her liturgy, art, and literature. Among the more common religious numbers are the following:

One stands for the oneness of nature in God; also one divine person in Christ; one true Church founded by Christ; and there is one mortal life, one baptism, one death, and after death one judgment before eternity.

Two represents the two distinct natures in Christ, human and divine; the two covenants of God with the human race, the Old and the New; two ultimate kinds of reality, variously called heaven and earth, soul and body, spirit and matter; there are two basic commandments, to love God and one's neighbor as oneself; and the final separation on the last day into two groups, the saved and the lost.

Three is the number of persons in the Trinity; Christ spent three days in the tomb and rose from the dead on the third day.

Four evangelists wrote the Gospels; the heavenly City of God is perfectly square, with all its dimensions a multiple of four; and there are four cardinal virtues: prudence, justice, temperance, and fortitude.

Five wounds in Christ's two hands and feet and his side are still present in his glorified body.

Six were the days of creation, signifying completion and symbolizing the principal attributes of God, namely his power, majesty, wisdom, love, mercy, and justice.

Seven is the symbolic number of charity, grace, and the Holy Spirit. It is the term that stands for perfection. There are seven sacraments, seven gifts of the Holy Spirit, seven deadly sins, seven joys, and seven sorrows of Our Lady.

Eight is associated with joy and the Resurrection. There are eight beatitudes, and Christ rose from the grave on the eighth day after his triumphal entry into Jerusalem, symbolized in the octagonal shape of many baptismal fonts.

Nine is the angelic number, since the Bible speaks of the nine choirs of angels. It is also the typical number of prayer, because the first Christian novena was the nine full days that the disciples stayed in the Upper Room and prayed after Christ's Ascension until Pentecost Sunday.

Ten stands for the Ten Commandments that Christ confirmed for his followers; it is the basic multiple for fullness, and any number multiplied by ten (or tens) is the highest possible.

Eleven has come to mean incompleteness, as typified among the Apostles after the defection of Judas, who had to be replaced before the Day of Pentecost.

Twelve implies maturity or totality. There were Twelve Apostles, corresponding to the Twelve Tribes of Israel; and the book of Revelation is filled with imagery built around this number. The heavenly Jerusalem will be twelve thousand furlongs on all sides, having twelve jeweled foundations, with twelve gates of twelve pearls. There are twelve fruits of the Holy Spirit.

Thirteen is the symbol of treachery, recalling the presence of the traitor at the Last Supper, beyond Christ and the faithful eleven disciples.

Forty is the biblical number for trial, testing, or waiting. The flood lasted forty days and forty nights; the Israelites wandered forty years in the wilderness; Moses remained forty days on Mount Sinai. After his baptism, Christ was forty days in the desert and there was tempted by the devil. After his Resurrection, he appeared to the disciples for forty days before the Ascension. There are now forty days of Lent, and forty is the symbol of the Church Militant.

Fifty is related to the fulfillment of a divine promise. In later Jewish history the feast of Pentecost was celebrated on the fiftieth day after the Passover to commemorate the giving of the Law through Moses. And the Holy Spirit promised by the Savior descended on the fiftieth day after Easter.

One hundred is the scriptural number for plenitude, whether used alone or as a multiple for other numbers. Christ spoke of a hundredfold harvest and a hundredfold reward.

One thousand often means simply an immense number, too large to be counted. It has come to symbolize eternity, because all higher numbers are either an addition to a thousand or multiplications of the same. God is the Eternal One in whom there is no time element, for "with the Lord, 'a day' can mean a thousand years, and a thousand years is like a day" (II Peter 3:8).

NUN. In general, a member of a religious institute of women living in a community under the vows of poverty, chastity, and obedience. More accurately, nuns are religious women under solemn vows living a cloistered, contemplative life in a monastery.

NUNCIO. An official prelate representing the pope at the capital of a foreign government. He watches over the welfare of the Church in that country and handles the affairs between the Apostolic See and the civil government of the country to which he has been assigned. In Catholic countries the nuncio is the dean of the diplomatic corps. (Etym. Latin *nuntius,* messenger, envoy.)

NUPTIAL MASS. The Mass at which a Catholic is married. With a bishop's permission, a nuptial Mass may be offered in a mixed marriage when the non-Catholic partner is baptized. The ritual provides for the marriage to be performed after the Gospel and homily, with the nuptial blessing after the Lord's Prayer and a special blessing of bride and groom at the end of the Mass.

O

OATH. The invocation of God's name to bear witness to the truth. A person, being conscious of his or her own fallibility, professes by an oath that God is omniscient and the omnipotent avenger of falsehood. For an oath to be licit, the statement sworn to must be true; there must be sufficient reason for swearing, i.e., regarding some matter of importance or because the circumstances demand an oath, as in a court of law; and the statement itself must not be sinful, e.g., not disclosing a secret that should not be revealed.

Oaths are assertive when God is invoked as witness to the truth of a past or present event, e.g., that a crime was not committed. They are promissory when God is invoked to bear witness not only to a future act but also to a person's present intention of doing or omitting something, e.g., the promise to fulfill the duties of one's office.

Oaths may also be distinguished as invocatory and imprecatory. They are invocatory when God is simply called upon as witness to the truth; they are imprecatory when, in addition, he is also invoked as the avenger of falsehood. In the Old Testament oaths of imprecation were very frequent, e.g., in the expression "The Lord do so to me and more also." In current usage they now occur in the familiar form "So help me God." (Etym. Greek *oetos*, a going; fate.)

OATH AGAINST MODERNISM. A solemn declaration against Modernism issued by Pope St. Pius X (September 10, 1910) and required to be taken on oath by all clergy to be advanced to major orders, pastors, confessors, preachers, religious superiors, and by professors of philosophy and theology in seminaries. The first part of the oath is a strong affirmation of the principal Catholic truths opposed to Modernism: the demonstrability of God's existence by human reason, the value of miracles and prophecies as criteria of revelation, the historical institution of the Church founded by Christ, the invariable constancy of the essentials of Catholic tradition, and the reasonableness and supernaturality of the Christian faith. The second part of the oath is an expression of interior assent to the decree *Lamentabili* and the encyclical *Pascendi*. Particular Modernist errors are singled out for censure and rejection. In 1967 the Sacred Congregation for the Doctrine of the Faith issued a new Profession of the Faith to replace the longer Oath against Modernism.

OBADIAH. Unknown author of the shortest prophetic book in the Old Testament, only one chapter of twenty-one verses in length. He condemns the Edomites harshly for their participation in the suppression of Judah by Nebuchadnezzar and offers no hope that YHWH will forgive a treacherous people. "For the slaughter, for the violence done to your brother Jacob, shame will cover you and you will vanish forever" (Obadiah v. 10). In contrast, Obadiah promises that YHWH will restore the glory of the new Israel and its power will reflect the sovereignty of YHWH.

OBEDIENCE. The moral virtue that inclines the will to comply with the will of another who has the right to command. Material obedience is merely to carry out the physical action commanded; formal obedience is to perform an action precisely because it is commanded by a legitimate superior. The extent of obedience is as wide as the authority of the person who commands. Thus obedience to God is without limit, whereas obedience to human beings is limited by higher laws that must not be transgressed, and by the competency or authority of the one who gives the orders. As a virtue, it is pleasing to God because it means the sacrifice of one's will out of love for God. (Etym. Latin *obedientia*, obedience.)

OBERAMMERGAU. Site of the world-famous Passion Play, in Germany, southwest of Munich. The play is staged by the people of the Bavarian village every ten years as the result of a vow made in 1634 because of their deliverance from the Black Death. The oldest existing text was written about 1600 and contains parts of two older dramas. Further revisions include a Passion text by Sebastian Wild and Johann Aelbel. In the eighteenth century the Benedictine Rosner remodeled the text after the Jesuit drama, and later still the script was simplified and put into prose form. Stage and costuming are adapted to modern requirements. The music is by Rochus Dedler. Practically everyone in the village has some part to play in the production of the drama, which was interrupted in 1940 because of World War II.

OBJECTIVE GUILT. Sinful estrangement from God when a person deliberately does something gravely forbidden by God. Those who, with full deliberation and consent, commit adultery, murder, perjury, and similar crimes, estrange themselves from God. He sets down the conditions for human estrangements, not they. It is not up to a human being to decide subjectively whether a deliberate serious sin is also a mortal sin that deprives him or her of God's friendship. God alone has the right to determine what separates a sinner from the Creator; a creature does not have the right to stand in judgment on God and tell him what constitutes a mortal sin.

Consequently "a person sins mortally not only when his action comes from direct contempt for love for God and neighbor, but also when he consciously and freely, for whatever reason, chooses something which is seriously disordered. For in this choice there is already included contempt for the divine commandment; the person turns himself away from God and loses charity" (Paul VI, *Declaration on Sexual Ethics,* December 29, 1975).

Every serious sin, therefore, is a mortal sin when a person freely decides to do whatever he knows God forbids under penalty of exclusion from the kingdom of heaven.

OBLATES. A term that has a long and varied ecclesiastical history, originally designating those children who were sent to monasteries to be brought up by religious. Some of these oblates became religious. After the early Middle Ages oblates were laypersons who were united to a religious order by a simplified rule of life, but who did not become full religious; this practice still continues. In modern times the name has been adopted by a number of fully established religious institutes, of which the best known are the Oblates of Mary Immaculate (O.M.I.), founded in France in 1816 by Bishop Charles de Mazenod, and the Oblates of St. Francis de Sales, originally founded by their namesake and re-established in 1871 by Louis Brisson, a priest of Troyes in France. (Etym. Latin *oblatus,* offered.)

OBLATIONS. The offering of the bread and wine for consecration at Mass, expressed by the offertory procession of the faithful and the offertory prayers of the priest. Also applied to any other gifts presented by the people at Mass, either symbolically on special occasions or actually when the gifts are offered for the use of the clergy, the Church, or the poor. (Etym. Latin *oblatio,* offering.)

OBLIGATION. The moral power of a law commanding obedience. Obligation is moral necessity, imposed on a free will, thus differing from physical necessity, which controls nonfree beings. Moral necessity arises from the final cause, which is from an end or good known by the intellect. This good, perceived by the mind, moves the will either to arouse or to restrain it. Since there is only one way to achieve one's last end, namely by morally good actions, a person is obliged to live what conscience tells him or her is the good life.

OBSCENITY. Whatever is sinfully calculated to arouse sexual pleasure in a person. The nature of the object that arouses the pleasure is immaterial. What is essential is the wrong intent of someone who presents, produces, or depicts something that experience shows will arouse sexual pleasure. The intention is wrong because its purpose is to unnecessarily provoke sexual pleasure outside the privileges of marriage. And the object of the intention is the person, of whatever age, whose sexual desires are inevitably excited by the obscene stimulus. (Etym. Latin *obscaenitas*, offensiveness, filthiness.)

OBSESSION, DIABOLICAL. The exterior control by the devil of a person's actions or of any other activity that affects human beings. The Church's ritual mentions as probable signs of obsession such things as speaking or understanding an unknown tongue or showing strength above one's natural capacity. As in the case of possession, the devil is not allowed to force a person's free will.

OCCASION OF SIN. Any person, place, or thing that of its nature or because of human frailty can lead one to do wrong, thereby committing sin. If the danger is certain and probable, the occasion is proximate; if the danger is slight, the occasion becomes remote. It is voluntary if it can easily be avoided. There is no obligation to avoid a remote occasion unless there is probable danger of its becoming proximate. There is a positive obligation to avoid a voluntary proximate occasion of sin even though the occasion of evildoing is due only to human weakness.

OCCULTISM. The theory and practice of invoking superhuman, but not divine, powers in order to obtain results that are beyond the capacity of mere nature. In this category belong Satanism, fetishism, black and white magic, Spiritism, Theosophy, divination, and witchcraft.

OCTAVES. The seven days following a feast, with the feast day itself included. Prior to the Second Vatican Council octaves were numerous in the Latin Rite. A commemoration was offered at Mass and in the Divine Office each day of the octave, and precedence given over any other feast. The octaves now observed in the universal Church are those of Christmas and Easter. Those using the 1962 liturgical books continue to observe the Octave of Pentecost.

OFFERTORY. That part of the Mass in which the unconsecrated bread and wine are offered to God. The prayers said by a priest in the new ritual are taken almost verbatim from the first-century liturgical document the Didache, discovered at Constantinople in 1873.

> While offering the bread (on a paten), the celebrant says:
> Blessed are you, Lord, God of all creation.
> Through your goodness we have this bread to offer,
> which earth has given and human hands have made.
> It will become for us the bread of life.

> While offering the wine (in the chalice), the celebrant says:
> Blessed are you, Lord, God of all creation.
> Through your goodness we have this wine to offer,
> fruit of the vine and work of human hands.
> It will become our spiritual drink.

OFFICE OF READINGS. The first hour of the Divine Office, still called Matins in those communities attached to the 1962 Latin liturgical books. It consists mainly of three Psalms and two readings, one each from the Bible and a nonbiblical source.

OIL OF CATECHUMENS. One of the three holy oils for the administration of the sacraments. It is used in the ceremonies of baptism, from which its name is derived, the catechumen being the person about to receive the sacrament. It is also used in the consecration of churches, in the blessing of altars, and in the ordination of priests, and has been used in the coronation of Catholic monarchs.

OIL OF THE SICK. The olive oil blessed by the bishop of a diocese for use in the sacrament of anointing of the sick. Commonly abbreviated O.I. (*oleum infirmorum,* oil of the sick) on oil stocks used by priests. Until 1974, when Pope Paul VI published the new *Order of Anointing the Sick,* olive oil was prescribed for the valid administration of the sacrament. This is no longer necessary. Any oil from plants is permissible in case of necessity; and the blessing by a bishop, though ordinarily required, may now be supplied by a duly authorized priest or, in emergency, by any priest.

OLD CATHOLICS. General name for various national churches that at different times separated from the Roman Catholic Church. Three main segments are distinguishable.

The Church of Utrecht in Holland, which separated from Rome in 1724. The immediate occasion for the break was the Jansenism of some of the Dutch Catholics, notably their archbishop, Petrus Codde (1648–1710).

The German, Austrian, and Swiss Old Catholics were organized after certain leaders in these countries rejected the two dogmas of papal infallibility and the universal ordinary magisterium, defined by the First Vatican Council in 1870. Their principal intellectual leader was John Joseph Ignatius Döllinger (1799–1890), Bavarian priest and Church historian.

Slavic Old Catholic Churches, mainly Polish, Croat, and Yugoslav, came into existence in America and elsewhere because of alleged discrimination by Anglo-Saxon bishops but also because of clerical celibacy.

The doctrinal basis of the Old Catholic Churches is the Declaration of Utrecht in 1889. Its main provisions are the rejection of the papal primacy and obligatory auricular confession; married clergy; and in general acceptance of the first seven ecumenical councils as adequate statements of the Christian faith.

In 1925 the Old Catholic communion formally recognized Anglican ordinations, and in 1932 entered into full communion with the Church of England, based on the Bonn Agreement of July 2, 1931.

OLD TESTAMENT. A term denoting the time from the origin of the human race to Christ; also the primitive, patriarchal, and prophetic revelation; and the Old Covenant of YHWH with the Israelites. But most commonly, the Old Testament means the collection of books that the Catholic Church believes are divinely inspired and that are not the New Testament. In biblical order they are Genesis, Exodus, Leviticus, Numbers, Deuteronomy, Joshua, Judges, Ruth, I and II Samuel, I and II Kings, I and II Chronicles, Ezra, Nehemiah, Tobit, Judith, Esther, I and II Maccabees, Job, Psalms, Proverbs, Ecclesiastes, Song of Songs, Wisdom, Ecclesiasticus, Isaiah, Jeremiah, Lamentations, Baruch, Ezekiel, Daniel, Hosea, Joel, Amos, Obadiah, Jonah, Micah, Nahum, Habakkuk, Zephaniah, Haggai, Zechariah, and Malachi.

OMISSION. Willful neglect or positive refusal to perform some good action that one's conscience urges one to do. Such omission is morally culpable, and its gravity depends on the importance of what should have been done, on the person's willfulness, and the circumstances of the situation.

See also ACTUAL SIN, SIN.

OMNIPOTENCE. The almighty power of God. He can do whatever does not deny his nature or that is not self-contradictory. Since God is infinite in being, he must also be infinite in power. (Etym. Latin *omnis*, all + *potentia*, power: *omnipotens*, all-powerful.)

OMNIPRESENCE. God being simultaneously wherever he is, since he is present everywhere. The divine omnipresence is twofold, by nature and by grace.

By nature God is present in all things by essence, knowledge, and power. This is the presence of a cause in the things that share in God's goodness. By his essence, he is substantially in all things, including the created spiritual essences (angels, demons, human souls) as the immediate origin of their existence. By his knowledge, he exercises his wisdom directly in all creation down to the least details. By his power, he operates with divine activity as the First Cause of everything that creatures do.

By grace, God is further present in the souls in whom he dwells as in a temple. Hence the creature is joined, as it were, to God's substance through the activity of mind and heart, by faith cleaving to the First Truth, and by charity to the First Good. He is therefore present by grace as the known is to the knower and the beloved is to the lover. This presence is more than a cause in an effect. It is the possession of God on earth similar to his being possessed by the angels and saints in heaven.

OMNISCIENCE. God's knowledge of all things. Revelation discloses that the wisdom of God is without measure (Psalm 146:5). And the Church teaches that his knowledge is infinite.

The primary object of divine cognition is God himself, whom he knows immediately, that is, without any medium by which he apprehends his nature. He knows himself through himself.

The secondary objects of divine knowledge are everything else, namely, the purely possible, the real, and the conditionally future. He knows all that is merely possible by what is called the knowledge of simple intelligence. This means that, in comprehending his infinite imitability and his omnipotence, God knows therein the whole sphere of the possible.

He knows all real things in the past, present, and future by his knowledge of vision. When God, in his self-consciousness, beholds his infinite operative power, he knows therein all that he, as the main effective cause, actually comprehends, i.e., all reality. The difference between past, present, and future does not exist for the divine knowledge, since for God all is simultaneously present.

By the same knowledge of vision, God also foresees the future free acts of the rational creatures with infallible certainty. As taught by the Church, "All things are naked and open to His eyes, even those things that will happen through the free actions of creatures" (Denzinger 3003). The future free actions foreseen by God follow infallibly not because God substitutes his will for the free wills of his creatures but because he does not interfere with the freedom that he foresees creatures will exercise. (Etym. Latin *omnis,* all + *scire,* to know.)

ONANISM. Theological term for contraception. The name is derived from Onan, son of the patriarch Judah. When Judah asked Onan to marry his (Onan's) brother's widow, in order to raise up progeny to his brother, Onan frustrated conception. "What he did was offensive to YHWH, so He brought about his death also" (Genesis 38:8–10). The more popular terms for onanism are birth control, contraception, planned parenthood, and Neo-Malthusianism.

OPTATAM TOTIUS. Decree of the Second Vatican Council on the training of priests. Aimed at the desired renewal of the whole Church, which "depends in great part upon a priestly ministry animated by the spirit of Christ." The document centers on fostering good priestly vocations, giving more attention to spiritual training, revising ecclesiastical studies, preparing for pastoral work, and continuing studies after ordination. Special attention is given to developing priests whose sense of the Church will find expression in a humble and filial attachment to the Vicar of Christ and, after ordination, in their loyal cooperation with bishops and harmony with their fellow priests (October 28, 1965).

OPTIONAL CELIBACY. A policy advocated in some Catholic circles to change the centuries-old practice of obligatory celibacy for priests in the Latin Rite of the Catholic Church. Although it was strongly promoted before the Second Vatican Council, the Council reaffirmed the Church's tradition on mandatory celibacy, declaring that "the more that perfect continence is considered by many people to be impossible in the world today, so much the more humbly and perseveringly in union with the Church ought priests demand the grace of fidelity, which is never denied to those who ask" (*Decree on the Ministry and Life of Priests,* 11, 16).

OPUS DEI. A personal prelature of Catholic faithful consisting of a prelate, secular priests, and laymen and -women who dedicate themselves to the apostolate and to Christian perfection in the world. Founded in Madrid on October 2, 1928, by St. Josemaría Escrivá, it received its final approval from the Holy See on June 16, 1950. Opus Dei became a personal prelature in 1982. Headquarters are in Rome. There are two branches of Opus Dei, of men and of women, but each so independent of the other that they form two organizations, united only in the person of the president general. The women's branch was founded in 1930. A general council, drawn from persons in different countries, assists the president general in governing the association. Priests belong to Opus Dei, and Opus Dei members have been ordained to the priesthood. Married persons also belong to Opus Dei, dedicating themselves to seeking Christian perfection in their own state of life. Cooperators, who are not official members of the association, help in its numerous apostolic activities.

ORATE FRATRES. The opening words of the prayer addressed to the people at Mass after the Offertory, "Pray, brethren, that my sacrifice and yours may be acceptable to God, the Father almighty." Their response emphasizes both the distinction and the similarity between the priest's sacrifice at the altar and that of the faithful.

ORATORIANS. Members of the Congregation of the Oratory, founded by St. Philip Neri in 1564 and approved by Pope Paul V in 1612. St. Philip's Oratory is a congregation of secular priests, technically a society of common life. For years there was a variety of autonomous oratories, finally formed into a confederation in 1942. Members are priests and brothers living a common life, without public vows. The director is elected every three years. Their purpose is to promote spiritual and cultural development by pastoral work, preaching, and teaching, especially among students and the young.

ORATORY. A place of prayer other than the parish church, set aside by ecclesiastical authority for celebration of the Mass and devotional services. It may be public, semi-public, or private and not intended for the use of the general public.

ORDER, RELIGIOUS. An institute of men or women, at least some of whose members take solemn vows of poverty, chastity, and obedience.

ORDER OF CHARITY. The order to be observed in loving one's neighbor. It is determined by the neighbor's need and relationship. The need of one's neighbor may be spiritual or temporal, and both may be extreme, grave, or ordinary. In extreme spiritual necessity, we must assist the neighbor even at the risk of our life. In extreme temporal necessity, the neighbor should be helped even at great inconvenience, but not necessarily at the risk of one's own life, unless one's position or the good of society demands assistance to the threatened party. In grave spiritual or temporal need, one's neighbor should be helped as far as possible; while position, justice, or piety may even oblige a person to help another. In ordinary spiritual or temporal need, there is no obligation to help the neighbor, certainly not in every case.

Relationship, as grounds for assisting another, is to be calculated in terms of kinship on various levels. Since blood relationship is the basis for all others, relatives, at least in the first degree, should be given first preference. The classic order to be followed is husband or wife, children, parents, brothers and sisters, other relations, benefactors, friends, and acquaintances. In extreme need, one's parents are to be favored because they are the source of one's being.

ORDERS, ANGLICAN. The question of the validity of Anglican ordination to the priesthood was decided negatively by Pope Leo XIII in the document *Apostolicae Curae* (September 13, 1896). They were declared to be "absolutely null and utterly void" on the grounds of defect of form in the rite and defect of intention in the minister. Even if Rome had not made such a declaration, Anglican orders were still considered invalid in practice, since Anglican clergymen were required to be ordained to the priesthood when they entered the Catholic Church. Since Pope Leo XIII's declaration, not a few Anglicans have been ordained by bishops who had themselves been ordained by Orthodox or other prelates whose orders were held to be valid by

Rome. However, the current ordinal in the Episcopal Church in the United States (and elsewhere) provides for two forms of ordination, at the choice of the candidate and the option of a bishop; one form is for the priesthood and the other for the nonsacerdotal ministry.

ORDERS, SACRAMENT OF. The sacrament that, by the imposition of a bishop's hands, confers on a man the grace and spiritual power to sanctify others. There are three forms of this sacrament, also called sacramental orders, namely diaconate, priesthood, and episcopate. They are not, however, three sacraments but only one sacrament that is separately administered with three successively higher sacramental effects. It is certain that every baptized male can be validly ordained, although it would be highly illicit to ordain him before the age of reason. It is likewise certain that every baptized male can be validly ordained a priest without previously being ordained a deacon. However, the more probable teaching is that a baptized male cannot be validly consecrated a bishop unless he has previously been ordained a priest.

ORDINARY. In ecclesiastical law a cleric with ordinary jurisdiction in the external forum over a specified territory; the pope with unlimited jurisdiction; diocesan bishops and their vicars; prelates nullius; capitular vicars and administrators filling the vacancy in a diocese. Also superiors general, abbots primate, provincial abbots of exempt monasteries. Their representatives, too, are called ordinaries. (Etym. Latin *ordinarius,* regular, usual.)

ORDINARY JURISDICTION. The right to exercise authority when this right is attached to an ecclesiastical office. This is the jurisdiction enjoyed by the pope over the entire Church, by a bishop over his diocese, and in the internal forum by the pastor over the members of his parish. Jurisdiction can be either personal or vicarious, depending on whether it is exercised by the officeholder or by someone he delegated.

ORDINARY MEANS. Whatever means are commonly considered ordinary for the preservation of human life. They are ordinary if generally accepted as such or if they are readily available to persons in the time, place, and circumstances in which they find themselves. Such means are food, shelter, and the avoidance of unnecessary bodily danger; also the use of accepted medical and health facilities. Assumed in this matter of preserving life is the sincere desire to remain alive or to keep another person alive according to the dispositions of Divine Providence. There is no question of directly intending to terminate one's own or another's earthly existence.

ORDO. One of several ritual books, published by the Holy See, for the administration of the sacraments or other liturgical offices. Since the Second Vatican Council a number of these have been issued containing the revised rites for all the Masses and all the sacraments. An ordo is also an annual calendar containing abbreviated directions for each day's Mass and Divine Office. Every diocese, or group of dioceses, and every religious order or congregation has its own ordo, or at least a supplement to the general ordo for the Latin (or other) Rite in the Church.

OREMUS. "Let us pray." An invitation to pray, occurring frequently in the Roman Rite and emphasizing the people's participation with the priest in public worship.

ORIENTALIUM ECCLESIARUM. Decree of the Second Vatican Council on the Catholic Eastern Churches, whose purpose was threefold: to encourage Eastern Catholics to remain faithful to their ancient traditions; to reassure them that their distinct privileges would be respected, e.g., the patriarchates and priests administering the sacrament of confirmation; and to urge closer ties with the separated Eastern Churches with a view to fostering Christian unity. An important provision was the permission of intercommunion (along with penance and anointing) between Catholics and those Eastern Christians who have valid orders (November 21, 1964).

ORIGINAL JUSTICE. The state of Adam and Eve before they sinned. It was the simultaneous possession of sanctifying grace, with its right to enter heaven, and the preternatural gifts. Had Adam not sinned, original justice would have been transmitted to all his descendants. Later, through repentance, he personally recovered sanctifying grace but not the other prerogatives of original justice. Since Adam, human beings are said to be deprived of original justice. Jesus Christ, the new head of the human race, by his Passion and death expiated human sin and regained what Adam had lost. Sanctifying grace is restored at justification, but the preternatural gifts are returned only as capacities (such as the ability to overcome concupiscence) or only eventually (such as bodily immortality after the final resurrection).

ORIGINAL SIN. Either the sin committed by Adam as the head of the human race or the sin he passed on to his posterity with which every human being, with the certain exception of Christ and his Mother, is conceived and born. The sin of Adam is called originating original sin (*originale originans*); that of his descendants is originated original sin (*originate originatum*). Adam's sin was personal and grave, and it affected human nature. It was personal because he freely committed it, it was grave because God imposed a serious obligation, and it affected the whole human race by depriving his progeny of the supernatural life and preternatural gifts they would have possessed on entering the world had Adam not sinned. Original sin in his descendants is personal only in the sense that the children of Adam are each personally affected, but not personal as though they had voluntarily chosen to commit the sin; it is grave in the sense that it debars a person from the beatific vision, but not grave in condemning one to hell; and it is natural only in that all human nature, except for divine intervention, has it and can have it removed only by supernatural means. See also ACTUAL SIN, OMISSION, SIN.

ORTHODOXY. Right belief as compared with heterodoxy or heresy. The term is used in the East to identify those churches (not united with Rome) that accepted the ancient councils, notably Ephesus and Chalcedon, and that call themselves "the holy, orthodox, catholic, Eastern Church." In the West the word is sometimes used to describe a justifiable concern for sound doctrine in the Catholic faith. (Etym. Greek *orthos,* right + *doksa,* opinion: *orthodoksa,* having the right opinion.)

"O SALUTARIS HOSTIA." Hymn to the Blessed Sacrament, "O Saving Victim, Opening Wide," sung during Eucharistic Exposition. It forms the last two (fifth and sixth) verses of "Verbum Supernum Prodiens," written by St. Thomas Aquinas, originally for Lauds on the solemnity of Corpus Christi. A standard English translation reads:

O saving Victim, opening wide,
The gate of heaven to man below!
Our foes press on from every side;
Your aid supply, your strength bestow.

To Your great name be endless praise
Immortal Godhead, one in three!
O grant us endless length of days,
In our true native land with thee, Amen.

OSSERVATORE ROMANO, L'. The *Roman Observer,* official newspaper of the Vatican, which began publication in 1861, at first unofficially and then semi-officially under Pope Leo XIII. The editors have been laymen. It is published daily, and more recently also a special edition on Sunday. Besides news of religious interest, it publishes documents, addresses of the pope, reports, and comments on political and social events. Weekly editions in languages other than Italian are also published.

OSTENSORIUM. A monstrance, a metal vessel usually gold- or silver-plated with a transparent section in which the Sacred Host is placed in its lunette when exposed for adoration or carried in procession. It varies in shape and ornamentation, popular models being tower-shaped or round; a metal circlet surrounded with rays or bars resting on a stem rising from a heavy base, many ornamented with jewels. The ostensorium in the Cathedral of Toledo took more than a hundred years to make and is reputed to be of gold brought by Columbus from America. See also MONSTRANCE.

OUR FATHER. The Lord's Prayer, taught by Christ in answer to a request by the disciples to teach them how to pray. As recited in the Catholic Church, it says:

Our Father, Who art in heaven,
hallowed be Thy name.
Thy Kingdom come.
Thy Will be done, on earth as it is in Heaven.
Give us this day our daily bread.
And forgive us our trespasses,
as we forgive those who trespass against us.
And lead us not into temptation, but deliver us from evil. Amen.

It consists of seven petitions, of which the first three are concerned with the interests of God, and the last four are requests for divine assistance to man. The single most commented-on words of the Bible, the Our Father is also the common heritage of all Christians, which synthesizes their common belief in the Fatherhood of God, the primacy of the divine over the human, the need for prayer to obtain grace, the source of morality in doing the will of God, and the struggle with evil as a condition for salvation. The longer ending, with the words "For thine is the kingdom, and the power, and the glory," used by Protestants, is a liturgical addition that found its way into some manuscripts of the New Testament but was not part of the original biblical text, either in Matthew (6:9–13) or Luke (11:2–4).

OUR LADY. The most popular title for the Blessed Virgin in Catholic piety and literature. Its first recorded use in English is in the Anglo-Saxon poet Cynewulf (c. A.D. 750) and is commonly associated with some special prerogative or office of the Blessed Virgin, e.g., Our Lady of Ransom, Our Lady of Divine Providence, Our Lady of the Way. It is equivalent to *Madonna* in Italian and *Domina* in Latin.

OVERPOPULATION. A theory of certain demographers that the natural resources of the earth are becoming too small to meet the needs of the world's growing population. The Church's position is that "overpopulation" is a human construct; that the same Divine Providence that inspired the advances in science to increase human longevity will also ensure the means of sustaining the increased human family.

OWNERSHIP. The exclusive right of disposing of a thing as one's own. It is a right because ownership is more than merely holding a thing in one's possession. The disposition means doing anything possible with what is owned, e.g., keeping, changing, giving away, selling, using, or destroying; yet though of itself ownership is unlimited, the disposition of a thing may be limited from another source, say from the rights of a higher order or from charity to the neighbor. Ownership implies disposing of an object as one's own to distinguish it from mere agency or trusteeship. And the freedom to dispose what is owned is exclusive because others are kept from the use of what is owned, which applies even in corporate ownership. No matter how large the partnership, anyone outside the owners has no claims on the property. Exclusive right to dispose of something is the most distinctive feature of ownership.

OXFORD MOVEMENT. A concerted effort originating around 1833 at Oxford University to restore to the Church of England certain pre-Reformation principles, which through inertia and indifference had been lost. A restoration in faith and worship, with an insistence on its alleged Catholic character without any reference to union with Rome, characterized the movement. It was begun by Dr. Keble at Oxford and was carried on by Blessed John Henry Newman, Edward Pusey, Richard Froude, Frederick Faber, Isaac Williams, Charles Marriott, Bernard Dalgairns, and William Ward. The *Tracts for the Times*, written by the leaders, was a series of doctrinal papers setting forth the aims and teachings of the movement. Many of them were censured and condemned by the Established Church, and Ward's tract cost him his status by the Convocation of the University. Several of the leaders became Catholics, among them Newman and Ward. The movement seemed then to have ended, but its influence continued. The Church of England was transformed, an Anglo-Catholic party was definitely established, and the country at large became familiar with Catholic doctrine and practice.

P

PACIFISM. The doctrine that all war is inherently wrong and, among Christians, that warfare is forbidden by the Gospels. The position of the Catholic Church is that war is, indeed, undesirable and that sinful passions give rise to war, but not all armed conflict is necessarily sinful and Christians may engage in a just war. (Etym. Latin *pacificare*, to make peace.)

PAENITEMINI. Apostolic constitution of Pope Paul VI, issued in 1966, by which the canonical norms of fast and abstinence were changed. While changing the norms, the pope made it clear that divine law requires all the faithful to do penance. Accordingly the purpose of the new regulations was not to weaken the practice of penance but to make it more effective. The Church, therefore, "while preserving—where it can be more readily observed—the custom (observed for many centuries with canonical norms) of practicing penance also through abstinence from meat and fasting, intends to ratify with her prescriptions other forms of penance as well, provided that it seems opportune to episcopal conferences to replace the observance of fast and abstinence with exercises of prayer and works of charity" (*Paenitemini*, III).

PAGAN. A heathen. In general one who practices idolatry. Formerly used to describe anyone who did not profess monotheism, and still used by Christians, Jews, and Moslems to identify a person who does not believe in one God, Creator of heaven and earth. More properly a pagan is a person who has abandoned all religious belief, i.e., an irreligious person. (Etym. Latin *paganus*, countryman, villager, civilian; from *pagus*, district, province, village.)

PAIN OF LOSS. The eternal loss of the beatific vision in hell. Called the *poena damni*, it is the primary punishment of the evil spirits and of the souls who die rejecting God.

PAIN OF SENSE. The suffering in hell caused by some agent called "fire" in Scripture, external to the person and secondary to the main punishment, which is the loss of God.

PALESTINE. Name originally from Philistine of the country on the east shore of the Mediterranean. In the Bible, Palestine is called Canaan before the invasion of Joshua. It was the Holy Land of the ancient Israelites because it was promised them by God and became the Holy Land of the Christians because it was the home of Jesus Christ. Its boundaries have changed many times but, in general, have included the region between the Mediterranean Sea and the Jordan River, bordering southwest on Egypt. In the fourth century B.C., Palestine was conquered by Alexander the Great. In 141 B.C., the Jews revolted under the Maccabees and established a new state, but Rome took it over seventy years later. During the time of Christ, Palestine was ruled by the puppet Herods. The Jewish revolt provoked the Romans to destroy the Temple and either kill or expel the Jews from Palestine. Then followed, in sequence, the Christian occupation of the country until the seventh century, when the Moslems took over. During the Crusades, Palestine was temporarily in Christian hands but reverted to the Moslems by the thirteenth century. Jewish colonization began around 1870, and Zionism entered in the early twentieth century. In 1920 the British, who had acquired the area in World War II as a mandate, designated Palestine as a Jewish homeland, while safeguarding the rights of non-Jews. After many Jewish-Arab clashes, Palestine became the State of Israel in 1948.

PALL. A sacred covering. Most commonly, a pall is the stiff square cardboard covered with linen that is spread over the top of the chalice at Mass. Also a cloth covering, ornamented or plain, placed over the coffin at funeral Masses and over the catafalque at later requiem Masses for the dead; a veil partially covering the bride and groom in marriages of the Mozarabic rite; and a veil placed over the nun at profession ceremonies in some contemplative enclosed orders. (Etym. Latin *pallium*, cloak.)

PALLIUM. A sacred vestment symbolic of the fullness of episcopal authority. It is an inch-wide white wool circular band ornamented with six small crosses with a pendant strip attached in front and another behind, worn about the neck, breast, and shoulders of the pope and archbishops. Made from the wool of two lambs blessed in the Church of St. Agnes in Rome. When granted to a bishop the pallium is purely ornamental. In Eastern rites patriarchs alone are invested with it. It is an outward sign of union with the Holy See. Pope John Paul I was formally invested on September 3, 1978, with the pallium instead of the traditional papal tiara at a Mass he concelebrated with members of the College of Cardinals. His successors, Blessed Pope John Paul II and Pope Benedict XVI were also invested with the pallium.

PALLOTTINES. Members of the Society of the Catholic Apostolate, founded at Rome in 1835 by St. Vincent Pallotti (1795–1850). Their purpose is to preach and teach the faith among Christians and non-Christians, and to cooperate among the faithful in the Catholic apostolate. The Pallottines, according to Pope Pius XI, were the forerunners of modern Catholic Action. There are also Pallottine Sisters, founded by St. Vincent in 1843 as a separate congregation. One of their main interests is to foster reunion of the Oriental separated Christians with Rome.

PALMS, BLESSED. A sacramental of the Church. They are blessed and distributed to the faithful on Palm Sunday, commemorating the multitude bearing palms who triumphantly led Christ in procession on that day in Jerusalem. Already palms were used in the time of St. Bede the Venerable (673–735). The Oriental date palm, when obtainable, is the most popular. But any other twig or woody outgrowth is suitable. The liturgy of Palm Sunday refers simply to branches. In the prayer of blessing, the priest says, "Almighty God, we pray you to bless these branches and make them holy." During the procession with the palms the people walk in joyous public demonstration of their loyalty to Christ.

PALM SUNDAY. The Sunday before Easter and the sixth and last of Lent, and the beginning of Holy Week. On this day the Church commemorates Christ's triumphal entry into Jerusalem, when olive and palm branches were strewn in his path. In the liturgy the memorial of this event is included in every Mass, with the procession or solemn entrance before the principal Mass, and with the simple procession before the other Masses on Palm Sunday.

"PANGE LINGUA." The hymn "Sing, my tongue, the Savior's glory," from Vespers of the Solemnity of Corpus Christi. It is used as a processional hymn on Holy Thursday and Corpus Christi, during Forty Hours' Adoration, and generally in honor of the Blessed Sacrament. The two last verses, the "Tantum Ergo," have long been sung at the Benediction of the Blessed Sacrament. Written by St. Thomas Aquinas, it has numerous translations in all the modern languages.

PANTHEISM. Any of a variety of views that claim that all things are divine, or that God and the universe are really identical, or that there is ultimately no real distinction between God and what believers in creation call the world. (Etym. Greek *pan,* all + *theos,* god.)

PAPACY. A term applied to the office and jurisdiction of the pope as the Vicar of Christ on earth, and also to the papal authority viewed as a religious and social force in history since the beginning of the Christian era. It generally refers to the system of ecclesiastical government in the Catholic Church headed by the pope. (Etym. Latin *papa,* father.)

PAPAL LETTER. A publication or announcement issued directly by the pope or by an official delegated by him. Matters of faith and morals were generally the subjects of these letters, designated as decreta. Others of more dogmatic importance were commonly called *epistolae tractoriae.* They were incorporated in collections of canon law and ranked with canons of synods in importance. Gratian and other canonists insisted that every papal letter of general character was authoritative for the entire Church. There were many forged papal letters during the Middle Ages. From the thirteenth to the twentieth centuries a papal document was given legal form by posting it on the doors of St. Peter's, the Lateran, or the Apostolic Chancery and in the Piazza del Campo di Fiori. Now they acquire force by publication in the *Acta Apostolicae Sedis.* These papal writings are published in a variety of forms, e.g., apostolic letters, constitutions, rescripts, bulls, and briefs. The original letters are deposited in the Roman archives. Private collections of papal letters also exist.

PAPAL STATES. The civil territory subject to the popes as temporal rulers from 754 to 1870. They had their origins in the two donations made in 754 and 756 by Pepin, King of the Franks, to Pope Stephen II, of the Duchy of Rome, the Exarchate of Ravenna, and the Marches of Ancona. This land was enlarged by later additions, e.g., from Charlemagne in 787 and from the Countess Matilda of Tuscany in 1115. Until the French Revolution the Papal States remained substantially what they were in the time of Charlemagne. In the nineteenth century the nationalist movement to unite the principalities of Italy into one country was successful. On September 20, 1870, Rome was taken by Italian troops. However, the legal possession of the Papal States was not recognized by the pope until the Lateran Treaty in 1929.

PAPIST. Opprobrious term used in English-speaking countries to designate a Catholic. Its origin goes back to the Protestant Reformation, when Martin Luther (1483–1546) and John Calvin (1509–64) wrote polemics against the papacy.

PARABLE. A short story based on a familiar life experience used to teach a spiritual lesson. It resembles the fable and the allegory. Jesus used the parable many times in his public ministry. "Why do you teach them in parables?" his disciples asked him. "Because," he replied, "the mysteries of the kingdom of heaven are revealed to you, but they are not revealed to them" (Matthew 13:10–11). It was a means of teaching his doctrine especially to those who accepted him as Messiah. (Etym. Greek *parabolē*, comparison, parable; literally, a throwing beside, juxtaposition.)

NEW TESTAMENT PARABLES

In Matthew

The children who play	Matthew 11:16–19
The sower	Matthew 13:3–8
The tares	Matthew 13:24–30, 36–43
Mustard seed	Matthew 13:31, 32
The leaven	Matthew 13:33
Hidden treasure	Matthew 13:44
Pearl of great price	Matthew 13:44, 45
Dragnet	Matthew 13:47, 48
The lost sheep	Matthew 18:12–14
Unmerciful servant	Matthew 18:23–35
Laborers in the vineyard	Matthew 20:1–6
Prodigal son	Matthew 21:28–32
The wicked husbandman	Matthew 21:33–44
Great supper	Matthew 22:1–14
Marriage feast	Matthew 22:1–14
The ten virgins	Matthew 25:1–13
The talents	Matthew 25:14–30

In Mark

The sower	Mark 4:3–8
Seed growing secretly	Mark 4:26–29
Mustard seed	Mark 4:30–32
The wicked husbandman	Mark 12:1–11

In Luke

The children who play	Luke 7:31, 35
The two debtors	Luke 7:41–43

The sower	Luke 8:5–8
Good Samaritan	Luke 10:25–37
Importunate friend	Luke 11:5–8
Rich fool	Luke 12:16–21
Barren fig tree	Luke 13:6–9
Mustard seed	Luke 13:18, 19
The leaven	Luke 13:20, 21
Great supper	Luke 14:16–24
Marriage feast	Luke 14:16–24
The last place at banquets	Luke 14:7–11
The tower and war	Luke 14:28–32
The lost sheep	Luke 15:4–7
Lost silver piece	Luke 15:8–10
Prodigal son	Luke 15:11–32
The unjust steward	Luke 16:1–8
Dives, the rich man, and Lazarus	Luke 16:19–31
The unjust judge	Luke 18:1–8
Pharisee and publican	Luke 18:9–14
The talents	Luke 19:12–27
The wicked husbandman	Luke 20:9–18

PARACLETE. A title of the Holy Spirit. Christ was and remains the first advocate. When he was to leave earth in visible form, he promised "another Paraclete" so that his followers would not be orphans. That Paraclete came on Pentecost. He is the advocate of the Mystical Body, pleading God's cause for the human family, keeping the Church from error, sanctifying souls through the preaching of God's word and through the sacraments. The Holy Spirit, whose function is to teach, to bear witness, and "to convince the world of sin," is the love of God producing the effects of divine grace on earth, and appropriated to the Third Person of the Trinity. (Etym. Greek *para-*, beside + *kalein*, to call: *parakletōs*, advocate.)

PARADISE. A synonym for heaven. Jesus spoke of it in his promise to the good thief on the Cross (Luke 23:43). In only two other places in Scripture is it used in place of heaven. There is a reference to "the tree of life set in God's paradise" (Revelation 2:7). Paul wrote about a man in Christ "caught up into paradise" (II Corinthians 12:4). (Etym. Greek *paradeisos,* park, the Garden of Eden, paradise; from Persian *pairidaēza,* an enclosure.)

PARADOX. An apparent contradiction that is really true. Christianity is the religion of paradox: that God should be human, that life comes from death, that achievement comes through failure, that folly is wisdom, that happiness is to mourn, that to find one must lose, and that the greatest are the smallest. What is paradoxical about the mysteries of the faith is that reason cannot fully penetrate their meaning, so that what seems contradictory to reason is profoundly true in terms of faith. (Etym. Latin *paradoxum;* from Greek *paradoxon,* contrary to received opinion or to expectation.)

PARALIPOMENON. The Vulgate title for the two books of Chronicles. St. Jerome took over the title from the Greek Septuagint, which reads "things left out," implying that the books are supplementary to the First and Second Book of Kings. The aim of the author of the Paralipomenon was to encourage his fellow countrymen to be faithful to the Law, especially regarding worship in the Temple of Jerusalem.

PARAY-LE-MONIAL. A city in central France where Christ appeared to Margaret Mary Alacoque, a Visitation nun, on December 27, 1763, as she was praying before the Blessed Sacrament. She saw his Sacred Heart surmounted by a cross and a crown of thorns surrounding it. Many other apparitions followed. The Church approved the Communion of Reparation on the First Friday of the Month, the Holy Hour, and a special feast dedicated each year to the Sacred Heart, as a result of Our Lord's requests of Margaret Mary. In 1873 when pilgrimages were revived, English Catholics flocked to Paray-le-Monial, where the convent chapel became the center of attention. The Basilica of the Sacred Heart, once in the priory of the Cluniac monks and now the parish church, shares in the interest of the pilgrims, along with the Eucharistic Museum, which has a remarkable collection of books and objects of art relating to the Blessed Sacrament. Pope Leo XIII called Paray-le-Monial "the town very dear to heaven."

PARDON. Any act of clemency toward a guilty person. It may be release from all or some of the punishment or, more properly, forgiving the offense on the part of the one offended. In civil and ecclesiastical law a pardon is also the document that declares exemption from the penalties for an offense or crime. And until modern times a "pardon" was synonymous with an indulgence. (Etym. Latin *per,* through + *donare,* to give: *perdonare,* to remit.)

PARENTAL OBEDIENCE. The duty of children to obey their parents, as prescribed by the fourth commandment of the Decalogue: "Honor your father and your mother so that you may have a long life in the land that YHWH your God has given you" (Exodus 20:12). The precept obliges children to show love, reverence, and obedience toward their parents. The love that is due should be evident in words, actions, and attitudes. The obedience concerns everything that is part of the parents' care and obliges until the children reach their majority. It does not apply, however, to the children's choice of a state of life or, when they are of age, a choice in a marriage partner.

PARENTS, DUTIES OF. Parents are to provide for the physical and intellectual well-being of their children, but they are especially bound by divine law to educate their children for God and for eternal salvation. According to the Second Vatican Council, "It is the duty of parents to create a family atmosphere inspired by love and devotion to God and their fellow men which will promote an integrated, personal and social education of their children" (*Declaration on Christian Education*, 3).

PARISH. Normally, in a diocese, a definite territorial division that has been assigned its own church, a determined group of the faithful, and its own distinct pastor who is charged with the care of souls. Personal parishes have also been created to meet the needs of people of a certain race or nationality, with no relation to territory. Sometimes subdivisions of vicariates and prefectures apostolic are called quasi parishes. (Etym. Greek *paroikos,* dwelling near.)

PARISH COUNCIL. Modeled on the diocesan council, a group of parishioners organized to cooperate with the pastor in the apostolic work of a parish. After describing the functions of diocesan councils the Second Vatican Council decreed that "Such councils should also be found, if possible, at parochial, inter-parochial and inter-diocesan levels, and also on the national and international plane" (decree *Apostolicam Actuositatem,* 26). As conceived by the Church, parish councils are merely advisory to the pastor and are meant to assist him. Unlike its counterparts among Protestants, a Catholic parish council does not operate under the trustee system. It does not either replace the authority of the pastor or make him juridically dependent on its decisions.

PAROUSIA. The Second Coming of Christ to the earth (I Corinthians 15:23). References to it are frequent in the New Testament, as the writers describe the ultimate triumph of Jesus and the establishment of his kingdom (I Thessalonians 4:15–17; Matthew 24:3–14; II Peter 1:16).

PARTIAL INDULGENCE. An indulgence that removes part of the temporal punishment due to forgiven sin. All particularities in terms of days, months, or years are now removed from partial indulgences. The new norm is based on the dispositions of the person gaining the indulgence and the character of the indulgenced work that person performs.

PARTICLE. A consecrated Host for distribution in Holy Communion, or even a fragment of the Eucharistic species. The Catholic faith teaches as defined doctrine that "in the venerable sacrament of the Eucharist, the whole Christ is contained under each species and under each and every part of either species that is separated from the rest" (Denzinger 1653). (Etym. Latin *particula*, small part; *pars*, a part)

PARTICULAR JUDGMENT. The individual judgment by Christ of each human being a moment after death (Hebrews 9:27).

PASCENDI. Encyclical letter of Pope St. Pius X condemning Modernism. Its full title is *Pascendi Dominici Gregis*, published September 8, 1907.

PASCH. The Jewish feast celebrated annually at God's command to commemorate the deliverance of the Jews from the bondage of Egypt. This deliverance was conditioned on the sacrifice of an unblemished lamb or kid, bones unbroken, whose blood was to be used to sprinkle the doorpost of every Hebrew house on the night before their passage. The deliverance of the Jews from Egypt was a foreshadowing of the Christian Pasch when, through the sacrifice of the Lamb of God and the application of the merits of his blood, the human race would be freed from the bondage of the devil and of sin. Good Friday in the early Church was called the Pasch of the Crucifixion, while Easter day was styled the Pasch of the Resurrection, and the Sundays from Easter to Whitsunday were always referred to as "after the Pasch." Easter is the Christian Passover. See also PASSOVER.

PASCHAL CANDLE. A large candle in which five grains of incense have been encased as a symbol of Christ's wounds. It is blessed on Holy Saturday in a special service and is symbolic of the Risen Savior, Light of the World. It is then used in the blessing of baptismal water and remains during the paschal season in the sanctuary, where it is lit during liturgical services.

PASCHAL LAMB. The lamb eaten at the Passover of the Jews. According to the Mosaic Law, the lambs were first to be sacrificed on the afternoon of the fourteenth of Nisan and then taken to the homes, where the people ate the lamb during the night (Exodus 12). Christ as the Messiah "was sacrificed for us" (I Corinthians 5:7), "and thus became for those who believe in Him the Paschal Lamb who takes away the sins of the world" (John 1:29).

PASCHAL TIME. The fifty-six days from Holy Saturday to Vespers on the Saturday following Pentecost. It corresponds to the time of rejoicing that the risen Jesus spent with his followers on earth and the nine days he told them to wait for the coming of the Holy Spirit. Liturgically it is a period of joy: white vestments are used, the Gloria is said at ferial Masses, the *Te Deum* is daily chanted, *Vidi Aquam* and the *Regina Coeli* replace the Asperges and the Angelus. Every Catholic is to receive the Holy Eucharist during this period.

PASSION. Intense motion of a human appetite. Although commonly associated with bodily desires, such as anger or sex, passions can also arise in the spiritual faculties, as happens in envy and pride. Passions are essentially desires out of control because of fallen human nature. They are concupiscence in action. When passion arises spontaneously before the free will has acted, it is called antecedent and, as such, lessens human freedom and responsibility. When it is intentionally fostered by brooding or preoccupation, it is consequent passion because it comes after the free choice of the will. Consequent passion is morally culpable. (Etym. Latin *passio*, suffering, passion, affection.)

PASSION. The events surrounding the suffering and death of Jesus Christ; part of the religious rite of Holy Week in the Catholic Church.

PASSIONISTS. Members of the Congregation of Discalced Clerics of the Most Holy Cross and Passion of Our Lord Jesus Christ, founded at Monte Argentaro in Tuscany in 1737 by St. Paul of the

Cross (1694–1775). The rule was definitely approved in 1769 by Pope Clement XIV, who conferred many privileges of the old orders on the new congregation. Passionists emphasize contemplation as the basis of their apostolic work, and take a fourth vow to promote devotion to the Passion of Christ. Their traditional apostolates are preaching missions and giving retreats. Passionist nuns, totally distinct from the clerical society, were founded as strict contemplatives.

PASSION PLAYS. The dramatic rendering of Christ's Passion in religious, artistic, and popular forms. They appeared originally as part of the ritual of the Church, first in Latin, then in German, and gradually developed in popular form until they lost their dignified character. By the seventeenth century their presentation was confined to monasteries or isolated villages. Public interest in them received new life in the nineteenth century, in the Austrian Tyrol, in southern Bohemia, and above all at Oberammergau in Bavaria, where now a world-famous literary drama is enacted with appropriate music and setting. It is performed every ten years as an act of thanksgiving for the deliverance of their village from the plague. See also OBERAMMERGAU.

PASSIONS. Human emotions insofar as they are inordinate in purpose, intensity, or duration. They are feelings somehow out of control, and involve a notable change in a person's bodily functions or activity. Less accurately, the passions are sometimes identified with any intense movement of the sensitive appetite, e.g., sex, anger, or hunger, accompanied by some organic change.

PASSOVER. The Jewish Pasch celebrated annually as commanded by God to commemorate the deliverance of the Israelites from the bondage of Egypt. Its main feature is the sacrificial meal, ending with eating the paschal lamb, followed by the seven-day Feast of the Unleavened Bread. At the time of Christ the Passover meal united the Jewish family from sunset to midnight on the fifteenth of Nisan. Its last celebration by the Savior was the occasion for instituting the Eucharist and the priesthood of the New Law. See also PASCH.

PASTOR. An individual priest or a corporate person (religious order or community) to whom a parish has been entrusted by a bishop, with the rights and responsibilities conferred by canon law and the statutes of the diocese. (Etym. Latin *pastor,* shepherd; literally, feeder.)

PASTORAL LETTERS. Official documents sent by a bishop to the clergy only or to all the faithful of a diocese. A group of bishops, of a region or of a whole country, may also issue pastoral letters for the entire territory under their jurisdiction. Pastoral letters may deal with any subject affecting the faith, practice, or worship of the people. They are often published during certain seasons, as in Lent or Advent. Over the centuries they have become expressions of the ordinary teaching authority of the Church. Nowadays important pastorals are also published in the Vatican newspaper, *L'Osservatore Romano.*

PASTORAL THEOLOGY. The practical application of scientific theology to the care of souls in the sacred ministry. Its purpose is to render this ministry more effective by the use of proven methods of dealing with the spiritual needs of individuals or groups of the faithful. A relatively new discipline, it came into being to cope with the increasingly complex and changing circumstances of modern life. It draws on the principles and methodology of both the secular and the sacred sciences, with special concern to help the people live out their Christian commitments in conflict with a hostile or at least indifferent non-Christian society.

PATEN. A saucerlike dish of the same material as the chalice—gold-plated and consecrated by a bishop or his delegate with holy chrism. It must be large enough to cover the chalice. On it rests the bread to be consecrated, and later on the Sacred Host. It was customary to have a subdeacon hold the paten, covered by the humeral veil, from the Offertory to the Pater Noster in solemn Masses. (Etym. Latin *patena,* a broad, shallow dish or pan.)

PATER NOSTER. The prayer composed and taught by Christ to the disciples (Matthew 6:9–13; Luke 11:2–4). Named from the first two words of the prayer in the Latin, Pater Noster (Our Father). The Pater Noster has been part of the Church's liturgy since apostolic times. It was part of the profession of faith for the reception of catechumens into the Church, has more commentary by the Fathers and Doctors of the Church than any other passage in the Bible, and, after baptism, is the best known bond of unity among Christians in every tradition. Its seven petitions are a synthesis of the faith, and its balanced structure is an expression of the true hierarchy of values: first the things of God and then the needs of man. The longer ending among Protestants, "For thine is the kingdom, and the power, and the glory, now and forever," was added in the sixteenth century. It was originally a liturgical ending, which the Catholic Church has recently incorporated into the Eucharistic Prayer of the Ordinary Form of the Roman Rite.

See also OUR FATHER.

PATIENCE. A form of the moral virtue of fortitude. It enables one to endure present evils without sadness or resentment in conformity with the will of God. Patience is mainly concerned with bearing the evils caused by another. The three grades of patience are to bear difficulties without interior complaint, to use hardships to make progress in virtue, and even to desire the cross and afflictions out of love for God and accept them with spiritual joy. (Etym. Latin *patientia,* patience, endurance; from *patiens,* suffering.)

PATRIARCH. The father and ruler of a family, tribe, or race in biblical history. A name commonly applied to Abraham, Isaac, and Jacob. Also a prelate who has the honor of being called the prince of fathers but is without jurisdiction except in virtue of some particular law. He holds precedence over primates, metropolitans, and bishops. In the order of their dignity, the Patriarch of Rome leads those of Constantinople, Alexandria, Antioch, and Jerusalem. In the East there are patriarchs of the Armenian, Maronite, Melkite, and Chaldean rites, with minor patriarchs of Venice, Lisbon, and the West and East Indies. The power and importance of patriarchs, except that of the pope, have diminished since the Eastern Schism. They have the right to ordain all bishops of their patriarchate, consecrate the holy chrism, summon synods, send the omophorion (pallium) to their metropolitans, and hear appeals from lower courts. They are the highest rulers in their churches. The Sovereign Pontiff alone is over them. (Etym. Greek *patriarchēs,* father of a race.)

PATRIARCHATE. The territory ruled ecclesiastically by a patriarch. Rome, Alexandria, and Antioch were the first to enjoy patriarchal rights. The pope as patriarch of the West holds jurisdiction over all the western lands where Latin was once the lingua franca and the liturgical language, where the Roman Rite is now used almost exclusively and Roman canon law still obtains. In the East the patriarchates have become organizations of Catholics observing different rites. The original Eastern patriarchates are now represented by a loose federation of churches differing in liturgies and customs but united in faith, morals, and communion with the Holy See.

PATRIMONY OF ST. PETER. The lands, properties, and revenues from various sources belonging to the Holy See. Before the Peace of Constantine (A.D. 313) the Church's properties were very limited, but after his reign, by his gifts and those of newly converted nobles, the Church found herself possessing large estates. About A.D. 600 the pope might have been called the largest landed proprietor in the world. Large farms, forests, whole villages with their cultivators, though free, constituted a *massa*. Many *massae* formed a patrimony, almost the equivalent in extent of a Roman province. These patrimonies were mainly located in Italy, with a few in the Orient, Gaul, Dalmatia, and Africa. Sicily had the most valuable and Rome the most numerous patrimonies. Naples, Gaeta, Tivoli, Ravenna, and Genoa contributed their share. All together they were called the Patrimony of St. Peter. Hospitals, monasteries, and churches were built and maintained; the freedom of slaves was purchased; and the needy of Italy and elsewhere were relieved by the revenues of Peter's Patrimony. St. Gregory called it the Patrimony of the Poor.

PATRISTIC PHILOSOPHY. The philosophy developed in Christianity during the age of the Fathers, mainly in the first five centuries. It represents the first meeting of Christian revelation with the pagan thought of antiquity. Christian intellectuals were aware that they were at the crossroads of two very different worlds, not necessarily opposed to each other. Patristic philosophy, therefore, represents the fusion of the best heritage of ancient Hellenism and the faith of Christianity, which itself had inherited much from Judaism. Three principal strains of philosophizing are discernible, of which the first two were heretical: that Christianity and paganism are utterly opposed to each other, as in Tertullian; that paganism and Christianity are totally compatible, as among the Gnostics; and that the wisdom of Christ and of pagan thought can cooperate, but always pagan philosophy is subordinate to Christianity and is to be purified by the higher wisdom of revelation. Much of the conflict with heresy in the early patristic age was due to attempts by some Christian thinkers to subordinate their faith to the intellectual theories of the pagan Mediterranean world.

PATRISTIC THEOLOGY. Systematic reasoning on the Christian faith by the Fathers of the Church. There was scarcely any theology among the early Fathers, Clement of Rome and Ignatius of Antioch, who practically repeated the data of Scripture and the apostolic preaching with a minimum of reasoned analysis. In the second and third centuries, however, contact with the pagan world produced a reaction. Two types of apologists arose, traditionalists, such as Tatian, who rejected philosophy, and others such as Justin, who were willing to use Greek speculation in the interests of the faith. Fortunately for the latter, who were in danger of Gnostic absorption, St. Irenaeus urged the need of remaining faithful to the Church's tradition, the living depository of revealed truth.

The more speculative line of St. Justin was developed by Clement of Alexandria and Origen, with consequent influence on the great Cappadocians, Basil, Gregory of Nyssa, and Gregory of Nazianzus. Characteristics of the Alexandrian school were a marked leaning toward Platonism, an allegorical interpretation of Scripture, and a profound mysticism.

By contrast, the more positive Aristotelian school of Antioch produced St. John Chrysostom, Theodore of Mopsuestia, and Theodoret, who affected the movement of theology through the whole patristic age. The high points of subsequent controversies coincided with the first seven ecumenical councils, which profited from both the Alexandrian and Antiochian schools in defining the principal dogmas on the Trinity and the person of Christ. Among the Fathers no one contributed more to theological growth than St. Augustine. He synthesized the four centuries of tradition that preceded him, clarified and in many cases solved the most vexing dogmatic questions, and coordinated the ensemble of sacred knowledge that St. Thomas Aquinas and the Scholastics later organized into a unified system of Christian thought.

PATRON SAINT. A saint or blessed who, since early Christian times, has been chosen as a special intercessor with God for a particular person, place, community, or organization. The custom arose from the biblical fact that a change of personal name indicated a change in the person—e.g., Abram to Abraham, Simon to Peter, Saul to Paul—and from the practice of having churches built over the tombs of martyrs.

PAUL. The most dynamic of Christ's Apostles, even though he was not one of the original twelve. His name was Saul, changed to Paul after his conversion. He was a Jew, born in Tarsus of Cilicia, and his family were Pharisees (Acts 22:3). Saul became a leader among the fanatical Pharisees and developed a reputation for ferocious enmity toward Christians (Acts 8:3). He was traveling on the road to Damascus (on an anti-Christian mission) when he was thrown to the ground and blinded by a dazzling light. Christ appeared to him, and he was instantly converted. "What am I to do, Lord?" he asked (Acts 22:10). He spent a number of years in Arabia (Galatians 1:17). His status when he began to preach Christianity was awkward; the Pharisees considered him a turncoat, and the Christians feared him because of his early reputation. Barnabas was especially helpful to him at this stage; he introduced him to Christian groups and vouched for his sincerity in both Antioch and Jerusalem (Acts 9:27). This association was so effective that the Church in Antioch commissioned Barnabas, as leader, and Paul and Mark, as assistants, to take a missionary voyage through Cyprus, Pamphylia, Iconium, Lystra, and Derbe (Acts 13, 14). This led to a dramatic confrontation. Paul, Barnabas, and Titus proceeded to Jerusalem to urge a more flexible concept of a Christian than that of a circumcised Old Law Jew (Galatians 2). Peter presided. After all viewpoints were presented, Paul's own group won the day: Gentiles did not have to become Jews to become Christians (Acts 15:5–21). Then began Paul's second missionary journey. This time the journey took Paul through Phrygia, Galatia, Philippi, Thessalonica, and Beroea (Acts 18:23). Some of these visits were the first ventures into Europe of Christian apostles. There followed a third journey, through Macedonia and Greece. Only the wariness of his followers saved him from injury or death on several occasions (Acts 19:30). Especially venomous were the Jews in Jerusalem; his Roman citizenship saved his life several times. Some of his finest epistles were written during a two-year period while he was under house arrest awaiting trial. Death came to him finally in Rome during Nero's persecution by decapitation in about 67. He is buried near the present Basilica of St. Paul. (Etym. Latin *Paul[l]us*.)

PAULINE PRIVILEGE. Dissolution of the marriage bond between two persons who were not baptized at the time of their marriage. Its basis in revelation is St. Paul (I Corinthians 7:12–15), and its conditions are the following: both parties are unbaptized at the time of marriage and after the marriage one of the parties receives baptism; one party has embraced the faith through baptism and the other remains unbaptized; the unbaptized person departs either physically by divorce or desertion, or morally by making married life unbearable for the convert; the departure of the unbaptized party is verified by means of interpellations, i.e., being asked if he or she is willing to be baptized or at least willing to live peacefully with the convert to the faith. If the above conditions are fulfilled and are negative, the Church may grant the baptized person the right to marry another Christian.

PAULISTS. Members of the Missionary Society of the Apostle, founded in the United States in 1858 by Isaac Hecker (1819–88). It was established to further the work and interests of the Roman Catholic Church in the United States. Their rule is based on that of the Redemptorists, to which congregation the founder originally belonged.

PAX. Literally "peace." In the revised liturgy the kiss of peace, which the priest celebrant at Mass gives to the ministers at the altar and announces to the congregation with the words, "Let us offer each other the sign of peace." The faithful then extend to one another some appropriate sign of peace, as approved by the national (or regional) conference of bishops. In ancient times the *pax* took place much earlier in the Mass. And for centuries, until the Second Vatican Council, it was given by the celebrant only to those immediately assisting at the altar during a solemn High Mass.

PAX ROMANA. International movement of Catholic students founded in Switzerland in 1921. Its purpose is to instill in its members an awareness of their responsibility to exert a Christian influence on their university environment, to seek Christian solutions to contemporary world problems, and in general to prepare themselves for bringing Christ and his message to all whose lives they will later on affect. These goals are achieved through national and international seminars and through meetings with other student organizations. Another group, Pax Romana—International Catholic Movement for Intellectual and Cultural Affairs, unites Catholic university graduates to help them meet their responsibilities to the Church and to civil society. Pax Romana has a consultative status with the Economic and Social Council of the United Nations and has permanent delegates at the United Nations in New York and Geneva and with UNESCO.

PEACE. The tranquillity of order. Peace is first of all the absence of conflict. But it is also the serenity experienced because there is no conflict. It is the calm that accompanies agreement of human wills, and is the foundation of every well-ordered society.

PECTORAL CROSS. A cross usually of gold and ornamented with precious stones, worn suspended from the neck by a gold chain or silken cord. It may serve as a reliquary enclosing relics of the saints or the True Cross. Although it is the badge of a bishop, other prelates may wear it during public worship. (Etym. Latin *pectoralis,* of the breast.)

PELAGIANISM. Heretical teaching on grace of Pelagius (355–425), the English or Irish lay monk who first propagated his views in Rome in the time of Pope Anastasius (r. 399–401). He was scandalized at St. Augustine's teaching on the need for grace to remain chaste, arguing that this imperiled man's use of his own free will. Pelagius wrote and spoke extensively and was several times condemned by Church councils during his lifetime, notably the Councils of Carthage and Mileve in 416, confirmed the following year by Pope Innocent I. Pelagius deceived the next pope, Zozimus, who at first exonerated the heretic but soon (418) retracted his decision. Pelagianism is a cluster of doctrinal errors, some of which have plagued the Church ever since. Its principal tenets are 1. Adam would have died even if he had not sinned; 2. Adam's fall injured only himself and at worst affected his posterity by giving them a bad example; 3. newborn children are in the same condition as Adam before he fell; 4. mankind will not die because of Adam's sin or rise on the last day because of Christ's redemption; 5. the Law of ancient Israel no less than the Gospel offers equal opportunity to reach heaven. As Pelagianism later developed, it totally denied the supernatural order and the necessity of grace for salvation.

PENAL STERILIZATION. Depriving people of their generative powers as a legally authorized procedure, either to punish certain crimes or to deter a person from committing further crimes. The Church's attitude toward such a procedure is one of great reserve. On the one hand it is granted that in the case of criminals the State has the objective right to inflict this kind of punishment. On the other hand penal sterilization is not considered either a real punishment or a real preventative. It does not effectively deprive a convicted person of anything precious in that person's eyes, while leaving the sex drive intact. Nor does it do anything to a would-be criminal to deter that person from sexual crimes; in fact the sterilized condition may even encourage promiscuity.

PENALTIES. A deprivation of some spiritual or temporal good by a proper authority as a corrective punishment for a criminal or delinquent act. The gravity of a penalty does not depend only on the malice of an act but also on the circumstances and consequences of what was done. Canon law states that the Church founded by Christ has the right and duty to inflict penalties for the correction of delinquent actions but recommends resorting to penal measures only when absolutely necessary, and to use them in moderation. Everyone subject to Church laws may be subject to Church penalties, and the same authority that can exempt a person from such a law may also exempt from the penalty attached to its violation.

PENANCE. The virtue or disposition of heart by which one repents of one's own sins and is converted to God. Also the punishment by which one atones for sins committed, either by oneself or by others. And finally the sacrament of penance, where confessed sins committed after baptism are absolved by a priest in the name of God. (Etym. Latin *paenitentia*, repentance, contrition.) See also SACRAMENT OF CONFESSION, SACRAMENT OF PENANCE, SACRAMENT OF RECONCILIATION.

PENITENT. In the sacrament of penance, the person who confesses sins and seeks absolution. And in general, anyone who sincerely repents of wrongdoing, resolves to amend his or her life, and by appropriate means tries to expiate the guilt and punishment incurred for offending God.

PENTATEUCH. The first five books of the Bible taken collectively— that is, Genesis, Exodus, Leviticus, Numbers, and Deuteronomy, written from about 1400 to 1300 B.C. The name may be traced to Origen (A.D. 254). A decision of the Biblical Commission (June 27, 1906) stated that Moses was the principal and inspired author of the Pentateuch and that the books were finally published under his name. But in 1948 the secretary of the Pontifical Biblical Commission acknowledged that "today there is no longer anyone who questions the existence of sources used in the composition of the Pentateuch or who does not admit the progressive accretion of Mosaic Laws due to the social and religious conditions of later times."

PENTECOST. Feast commemorating the descent of the Holy Spirit on the Apostles. It takes its name from the fact that it comes about fifty days after Easter. The name was originally given to the Jewish Feast of Weeks, which fell on the fiftieth day after Passover, when the first fruits of the corn harvest were offered to the Lord (Deuteronomy 16:9) and, later on, the giving of the Law to Moses was celebrated. In the early Church, Pentecost meant the whole period from Easter to Pentecost Sunday, during which no fasting was allowed, prayer was only made standing, and Alleluia was sung more often. (Etym. Greek *hē pentēkostē*, the fiftieth day.)

PENTECOSTALISM. A revivalist movement in Christianity, originally among Protestant bodies but, since the Second Vatican Council, also among Roman Catholics. The main postulate of Pentecostalism also explains the name. Just as on the first Pentecost in Jerusalem there was an extraordinary descent of the Holy Spirit, so today there is said to be a similar effusion of spiritual gifts. No less than on Pentecost Sunday, so now the descent of the Spirit becomes clearly perceptible especially in three ways: 1. in a personally felt experience of the Spirit's presence in the one who receives him; 2. in external manifestations of a preternatural character, notably speaking in strange tongues, the gift of prophecy, the power of healing, and in fact all the charismata described in the Acts of the Apostles and the letters of St. Paul; 3. in a strong impulse to communicate these blessings to others by becoming a messenger of the Spirit in the modern world. The basic condition required to receive the charismatic outpouring is openness of faith. The only real obstacle, it is claimed, is diffidence or distrust of the Spirit to produce today what he had done in apostolic times.

PEOPLE OF GOD. A biblical term popularized by the Second Vatican Council to describe the members of the Church. The expression brings out the fact that those who belong to the Church form a visible society, that they are distinctive, specially chosen by God, and composed of all baptized believers in Christ throughout the world. Their degree of membership depends on their degree of faith, obedience to the Church's precepts, and sanctity or union with God.

PERFECTAE CARITATIS. Decree of the Second Vatican Council on the Up-to-Date Renewal of Religious Life. This is intended to complement the chapter on religious life in the Council's Dogmatic Constitution on the Church. It is therefore a normative document on how those dedicated to Christian perfection are to renew themselves in spirit and adapt themselves to the changing times. Among the legislative provisions of the decree are community life under superiors, corporate prayer, poverty of sharing, a distinctive religious habit, and continued spiritual and doctrinal education (October 28, 1965).

PERFECT CONTRITION. Sorrow for sin arising from perfect love. In perfect contrition the sinner detests sin more than any other evil, because it offends God, who is supremely good and deserving of all human love. Its motive is founded on God's own personal goodness and not merely his goodness to the sinner or to humanity. This motive, not the intensity of the act and less still the feelings experienced, is what essentially constitutes perfect sorrow. A perfect love of God, which motivates perfect contrition, does not necessarily exclude attachment to venial sin. Venial sin conflicts with a high degree of perfect love of God, but not with the substance of that love. Moreover, in the act of perfect contrition other motives can coexist with the perfect love required. There can be fear or gratitude, or even lesser motives such as self-respect and self-interest, along with the dominant reason for sorrow, which is love for God. Perfect contrition removes the guilt and eternal punishment due to grave sin, even before sacramental absolution. However, a Catholic is obliged to confess his or her grave sins at the earliest opportunity and may not, in normal circumstances, receive Communion before he or she has been absolved by a priest in the sacrament of penance.

PERFECT HAPPINESS. The complete possession of the perfect good. That which fully satisfies all human desires. Imperfect happiness falls short of the perfect in some way by not satisfying all human desires or, if all of them, not all of them fully. Natural happiness, when perfect, is called natural beatitude. It satisfies those cravings that spring from human nature alone. It is the kind of happiness that human beings would have been destined to, had they been left on a purely natural plane. Mere reason cannot pass beyond this point. Christian revelation adds to this the prospect of supernatural happiness. When perfect, in the life to come, it consists of the Beatific Vision, which supposes a free gift of God lifting humanity above its natural capacity and enabling it to share in the very happiness of God.

PERFECTION. That in which nothing is lacking that, according to its nature, it should possess. That is absolutely perfect which in itself has all possible excellence and excludes all deficiencies. Only God is absolutely perfect. That is relatively perfect which has a finite nature and possesses all the advantages corresponding to its nature. The Church teaches that God is infinite in every perfection. Creatures are as perfect as they are like God, and moral perfection consists in becoming like Christ, who is infinite God in human form.

PERJURY. Swearing to a falsehood. Perjury is never permissible even though one swears to the truth of only a slight lie. Even in this case the sin is serious, because great dishonor is shown to God by calling upon him to witness to the truth of what is known to be false. (Etym. Latin *periurium,* false oath, broken oath.)

PERMANENT DIACONATE. The lifelong commitment to serving as deacon in the Catholic Church. Ordination to the permanent diaconate is preceded by a decision as to which form a man wishes to enter, the transitional or the permanent. If permanent, he makes the further choice of a celibate or married diaconate. The public dedication to celibacy is celebrated in a special rite, even by religious, and it is to precede ordination to the diaconate. Celibacy taken in this way is an invalidating impediment to marriage.

PERMISSION. Authorization to act, especially to act in a way other than a particular law allows without the special permission. In philosophy, to permit is to foresee that something will occur and not intending it, yet also not preventing the occurrence although, absolutely speaking, one could have prevented that which is permitted. Thus, foreseeing certain evil effects resulting from a given action, one permits these effects for the sake of some other equal or greater good.

PERMISSIVENESS. The attitude of those in authority that allows great latitude in the exercise of personal choice. Its underlying motives are varied, but as a philosophy of government it subordinates the common good to the primacy of individual freedom.

PERPETUAL ADORATION. Prayer before the Blessed Sacrament, either reserved in the tabernacle or exposed in a monstrance, continued by successive worshipers day and night without intermission. The practice of perpetual adoration of God by Psalm and prayer has been maintained by monks and nuns since early Christian times—e.g., by the *akoimetoi* in the East and the monastery of Agaunum, founded by King Sigismund of Burgundy in A.D. 522. Similar practices were current elsewhere before the ninth century. It was in France that perpetual adoration of the Eucharist began. Mother Mechtilde of the Blessed Sacrament pioneered the custom on request of Père Picotte. The Benedictine convent, founded for this purpose, opened on March 25, 1654. Since then many religious communities have made perpetual Eucharistic adoration either the main or an essential part of their rule of life. Confraternities of the faithful have also been organized to practice the devotion, along with the religious or, in some cases, in their parish churches.

PERPETUAL VOWS. Ordinarily the final vows that a person takes in an institute of Christian perfection, mainly poverty, chastity, and obedience. Other vows may be added, according to the constitutions of the institute. They are also called last vows, although some communities take perpetual vows immediately after the novitiate, and others never take what are technically perpetual vows, but they simply renew their vows regularly, according to their rule of life.

PERSECUTION. The effort by civil authority to suppress or impede the Church's liberty by physical or psychological means. Since the first days after Pentecost the Church has been persecuted by those who felt threatened by her or who sought to enforce religious conformity or who penalized dissent from the accepted or established norms of belief and behavior. Throughout the Gospels, Christ foretold that his followers would be persecuted, and at the Last Supper he predicted, "If they persecuted me, they will persecute you too" (John 15:20). This prediction has been verified in every period of the Church's history, including modern times.

PERSECUTIONS, ROMAN. The ten great persecutions of the Church from apostolic times to the Edict of Milan (A.D. 313) are generally identified by the reign of the ruling emperor: 1. Nero (54–68) accused the Christians of being haters of mankind; 2. Domitian (81–96) took his victims mainly from the Christian nobility; 3. Trajan (98–117) considered Christianity an organized menace to the empire; 4. Marcus Aurelius (161–80) confiscated the property of the faithful and tortured his victims; 5. Septimus Severus (193–211) forbade fresh conversions; 6. Maximinus Thrax (235–38) persecuted the clergy; 7. Decius (249–51) ordered all subjects who would not sacrifice to the state gods to be put to death; 8. Valerian (253–60) forbade all Christian assemblies and concentrated on clergy and nobility; 9. Aurelian (270–75) allowed the anti-Christian legislation to remain but did not seriously enforce it; 10. Diocletian (284–305) reversed Aurelian's policy and unleashed the bloodiest of all Roman persecutions.

PERSEVERANCE. Remaining in the state of grace until the end of life. The Church teaches that it is impossible, without the special help of God, to persevere in the state of grace to the end. Thus the Second Council of Orange, in A.D. 529, teaches, in opposition to the Semi-Pelagians, that the justified also must constantly pray for the help of God so that they may attain to a good end (Denzinger 380). And the Council of Trent in 1547 calls perseverance "a great gift" and says that those in the state of grace cannot persist in God's friendship without special divine aid (Denzinger 1572). Final perseverance cannot be strictly merited, as though a person had a claim on dying in grace because he or she had been faithful all through life. Nevertheless it can, with unfailing success, be achieved by proper prayer, offered regularly and earnestly, in the state of grace. The certainty of the prayer being heard is based on the promise of Jesus (John 16:23). Since, however, the possibility of a fall always remains, one cannot know with infallible certainty whether one will, in fact, persevere unless one receives a special revelation to that effect (*Council of Trent,* Denzinger 1566).

PERSON. "An individual substance of a rational nature" (Boethius). Therefore every individual intellectual substance that is complete in itself, uncommunicated and existing for itself, is a person. Essential to person in theological terms are intelligence and substantiality, wholeness in oneself and especially individuality. From individuality flows such features of personhood as distinctiveness, incommunicability, and uniqueness. Among human persons there are also the elements of responsibility and possession of distinctive rights. (Etym. Latin *persona,* actor's mask; character; supposition of a rational nature.)

PERSONHOOD. The distinctive qualities of each human being as a unique individual.

PETER. The first pope and leader of the Apostles. His original name was Simon, but Jesus gave him the name "Peter," which is Greek, or "Cephas," which is the Aramaic equivalent. "Peter" and "Cephas" mean "the rock" (John 1:42). Such a name was appropriate to the strong character of the man, but the name became a supremely significant metaphor when Christ later made the dramatic assignment, "You are Peter and on this rock I will build my Church" (Matthew

16:18). What made the name distinctive as well was that neither "Peter" nor "Cephas" was ever used as a man's name. It was a career designation. There could be no question about the recognition of Peter's leadership. His name always appeared first in the listing of the Apostles (Mark 3:16). He and his brother were the first chosen. His name appears in the Gospels more often than that of any other Apostle (Luke 5:10). He acted as their spokesman and whenever Jesus questioned them Peter responded on their behalf. He was present at the Transfiguration (Matthew 17:1–8). He was with Jesus when he raised Jairus's daughter (Luke 8:51). He was in Gethsemane during the Lord's agony (Mark 14:33). Jesus paid the Temple tax for himself and Peter (Matthew 17:24–27). When Jesus disappeared from Capernaum, it was Peter who led the disciples in pursuit (Mark 1:36). It was Peter who objected to the washing of the feet (John 13:6–9). The angel in announcing the Resurrection said, "Go and tell the disciples and Peter" (Mark 16:7). Other instances from all four Gospels could be cited that make it clear that Peter's leadership was uncontested. After the Crucifixion it was Peter who directed the meeting to select a successor to Judas (Acts 1:15–26). When Paul and Barnabas attended the first council in Jerusalem, Peter presided and made the speech that silenced discussion (Acts 15:6–12). Through the early chapters of Acts he continues to exercise the leadership role. He was truly obeying the Master's valedictory injunction to "feed my lambs" and "feed my sheep" (John 21:16–17). Peter revealed human shortcomings as well as strengths. He was rebuked by Jesus for misinterpreting the Messianic mission (Mark 8:33). His impetuosity was revealed in the garden when he attacked Malchus (John 18:10). He was bitterly ashamed of the cowardice he revealed in denying Jesus in the courtyard (Luke 22:54–62). But none of these human actions reduce the significance of the assignment he received when Jesus said, "I will give you the keys of the kingdom of heaven" (Matthew 16:19). (Etym. Greek *Petros*, masc. name formed from the fem. noun *petra*, rock.)

PETER, EPISTLES OF. Two letters of St. Peter the Apostle, both addressed to converts from paganism in Asia Minor. Both were sent from Rome. The second intimates his approaching death; the first contains strong admonitions to lead a Christian life, outlining the duties of citizens to civil authority, servants to their masters, wives to husbands, mutual charity, patience, and humility. The Petrine authorship of both letters has been challenged. But in the first letter the author claims to be "Peter, apostle of Jesus Christ" (I Peter 1:1), and the author of the second letter claims to be Peter who witnessed the Transfiguration of the Lord (II Peter 1:1, 16–18), who also wrote another letter (II Peter 3:1), and refers to "our brother Paul, who is so dear to us" (II Peter 3:15).

PETER'S PENCE. The annual contribution from the faithful of various countries to defray the expenses of the Holy See. It seems to have started in England, where each owner of land of certain value gave a penny. It was re-established by Pope Pius IX after having lapsed since the Reformation. In some countries the contributions are gathered by various associations; in others it is an annual collection sent by the bishops to the pope.

PHARISEES. An active, vociferous religious Jewish sect in the centuries before and after Christ appeared on earth. They represented by and large the intellectual sector of their people, because they were avid, contentious students and teachers of Jewish religious law. Their intensity and single-mindedness resulted in a harsh and uncharitable emphasis on the legal aspects of religion at the expense of charity and loving concern. Jesus represented a threat to their intellectual security and leadership. They baited him at every opportunity. They tried to trap him into wrong answers (Matthew 22:15–22). They proposed questions, hoping to prove contradictions (Matthew 22:34–40). They deplored the company he kept. They objected to his Sabbath activities (Mark 2:15–17; Mark 2:23–26). They even plotted against his life (John 11:45–54). Indeed they worked together with the priests and the Sadducees until their plotting culminated in his arrest and Crucifixion (John 18:3). Their hostility, of course, was aggravated by the accusations that Jesus leveled at the Pharisees. He called them hypocrites (Matthew 15:7). He deplored their legalisms as rendering God's word null and void (Mark 7:13). Their self-righteousness he exposed in the parable of the Pharisee and the publican (Luke 18:9–14). The entire chapter 23 of Matthew is a lengthy, detailed indictment of Pharisee mentality. Needless to say, all Pharisees were not fanatics. Gamaliel and Nicodemus were men who kept a sense of balance and were open to the development of Judaism (John 3:1–21; Acts 5:34–39). It is likely that many Pharisees became Christians. (Etym. Hebrew *perusim;* Aramaic *perissayya',* separated, separated ones, separators.)

PHILEMON. A convert of Paul who had the distinction of being the only recorded recipient of a personal letter from the Apostle. Paul had converted a runaway slave named Onesimus and learned that the master he had deserted and robbed was Philemon. He persuaded Onesimus to return to his owner with a warm, beseeching letter urging Philemon to show mercy. He offered to pay whatever the errant slave owed. It was an appeal for compassion that Philemon would not only forgive Onesimus but set him free as a Christian brother (Philemon 1–25). (Etym. Greek *philēmon*, loving.)

PHILIP. 1. the Apostle. Philip must have known Peter and Andrew, because all three came from Bethsaida. When Jesus met him, he invited Philip to join him. Philip must have been instantly impressed. He not only joined the group himself but persuaded Nathanael (better known as Bartholomew) to accompany him (John 1:43, 12:21). Generally, in the listing of the Apostles, Philip and Bartholomew are paired. Apparently Philip took care of the food supply, because it was with him that Jesus discussed the problem of feeding the crowd at the Sea of Galilee (John 6:5–7). Philip must have been painfully literal-minded in learning Jesus's relation to his Father. "Have I been with you all this time," said Jesus to him, "and you still do not know me?" (John 14:9). After the Crucifixion he was among the Apostles waiting for the Holy Spirit (Acts 1:13); 2. the evangelist. One of the seven disciples chosen by the Apostles to supervise the food supply and relief of poor Christians as the Church was growing in numbers. The Apostles feared that preaching and converting would suffer if they consumed their energy in business matters (Acts 6:1–6). Philip himself was an able preacher and performer of miracles, as he proved in Samaria. Two instances of his zeal and eloquence are given in his conversion of Simon, the magician, and the Ethiopian court officer (Acts 8:4–40). His final appearance in Scripture took place when he entertained Paul in his home in Caesarea during his third missionary journey (Acts 21:8). (Etym. Greek *philippos,* lover of horses.)

PHILIPPIANS. One of the four letters of St. Paul written from prison to his converts. It is a letter of gratitude for the kindness the Philippians in Macedonia had shown him. The most significant passage is an exhortation to humility, based on the example of Christ, who, though "His state was divine, yet He did not cling to His equality with God but emptied Himself to assume the condition of a slave, and became as men are" (2:6–7). It is a heart-to-heart communication of Paul to his people, in which the Apostle is disarmingly frank in telling them how much he loves them and wants them to be happy, "happy in the Lord; I repeat what I want is your happiness" (4:4).

PHILOSOPHY. Literally the love of wisdom. It is the science in which natural reason, apart from divine revelation, seeks to understand all things by a knowledge of their first causes. (Etym. Greek *philein*, to love + *sophia*, wisdom: *philosophus*.)

PHILOSOPHY OF RELIGION. The science of human beings as religious persons. It may take on a variety of forms, depending on the subject investigated and the premises of the investigation. Thus it may study the historic religions to determine their common denominator and account for their differences; or it may seek to establish the rational foundations of the historic religions to determine their credibility; or it may assume the validity of a given religion, as Christianity, and analyze its principal tenets and practices on philosophical grounds.

PHYSICAL EVIL. Privation of a natural good desired by a human being. Absence of some satisfaction desired by a human appetite, whether spiritual or bodily. In general, may be equated with pain. It is the loss or deprivation of what a person wants.

PHYSICAL FREEDOM. Absence of external compulsion or violence that would coerce a person to act or not act in a certain way. Lack of physical restraint or pressure compelling a given action. Corresponds to spontaneity of action.

PHYSICAL MIRACLE. An event produced by God that surpasses the powers of physical or bodily nature. Two kinds of physical miracles are known to Catholic theology: 1. those essentially supernatural, such as raising the dead, which only divine power can perform (major miracles); and 2. those relatively supernatural, such as sudden healing, which the angels can perform under Divine Providence (minor miracles).

PIETÀ. A general term applied to representations of the dead Christ in art. The Blessed Virgin is usually included. Among the masters who have represented the Pietà, the best known are Bellini, Botticelli, Caravaggio, Dürer, Fra Angelico, Murillo, Raphael, Rubens, Titian, and Van Dyck. The most famous is the *Pietà* of Michelangelo in St. Peter's Basilica in Rome. (Etym. Latin *pietas*, duty, dutiful, piety, devotion.)

PIETY. Honor and reverence given to someone in any way responsible for our existence or well-being—thus, God as our Creator and constant Provider, parents, near relatives, country, tribe, or people.

PILATE, PONTIUS. The Roman procurator of Judaea from A.D. 26 to 36, appointed by Emperor Tiberius. Several times during his administration there had been turbulent demonstrations by the Jews when their traditions were violated or their rights infringed upon. These demonstrations irritated Tiberius, and Pilate was anxious to placate the Jews so that no further Judaean unrest would be reported to Rome. This was the political situation when Pilate was confronted by the irate delegation of priests and Pharisees demanding Christ's death. All four evangelists testify that Pilate knew full well that the accused was innocent (Luke 23:4; John 18:38). He tried various stratagems in the hope that the charges would be reduced and the fury would abate. He offered to release Christ or Barabbas. He had Jesus flogged (Matthew 27:15–26; Luke 23:14–16). He set up the hand-washing ritual to emphasize his view of the charges in the hope that he could divert Jewish determination. But finally he capitulated and consented to the Crucifixion (Mark 15:15) rather than have the emperor disturbed and his own administration threatened. (Etym. Latin *Pontius Pilatus*.)

PILGRIMAGE. A journey to a sacred place undertaken as an act of religious devotion. Its purpose may be simply to venerate a certain saint or ask some spiritual favor, beg for a physical cure or perform an act of penance, or express thanks or fulfill a promise. From the earliest days pilgrimages were made to the Holy Land, and later on to Rome, where Peter and Paul and so many Christians were martyred. From the eighth century the practice began of imposing a pilgrimage in place of public penance. As a result, during the Middle Ages pilgrimages were organized on a grand scale and became the object of special Church legislation. In modern times, besides Rome and the Holy Land, famous shrines such as Lourdes, Fátima, and Guadalupe draw thousands of pilgrims each year from the Catholic world.

PLAIN CHANT. Sometimes inaccurately called Gregorian chant, but plain chant is a modification of the Gregorian, introduced among the Franks in the ninth century. It is unisonous and free-rhythmed and composed on a scale of four lines. The modes or scales of plain chant are limited to the natural intervals of the human voice and the melodies likewise confined to a person's natural range. Features of this chant are that the "leading note" is commonly avoided; also two choirs may be used while alternately singing the same melody. The beauty of plain chant derives from its pure melody, voice quality, and subtle rhythm.

PLAIN SONG. An ecclesiastical chant, such as Gregorian, having simple, unaccompanied melody.

PLANNED PARENTHOOD. A common term for the practice of contraception or, when this fails, of abortion. Also the organized policy of governments and international cartels to coerce people by means of economic or other sanctions to practice contraception or abortion, or submit to sterilization.

PLATONISM. The system of thought originated by the Greek philosopher Plato (427–347 B.C.), pupil of Socrates. Platonism, in its influence on Christianity, is characterized by its contempt for sense knowledge and empirical studies, by a longing for another and better world, by a frankly spiritual view of life, by its method of discussion or dialogue between persons to acquire more profound insights than could be obtained by cold reasoning, and above all by an unswerving confidence in the human mind to reach absolute truth, and to rely on this inner vision for the direction of one's moral life.

PLEASURE. The satisfaction that accompanies the exercise of a human faculty. Depending on the faculty used, there are different kinds of pleasure, namely sensuous or intellectual. In practice the two forms are never separated, since bodily satisfaction affects the rational part of a human being, and intellectual satisfaction has an influence on the body. Some writers distinguish between pleasure and joy, where pleasure refers to the satisfaction of bodily desires, such as eating and sex, and joy refers to the use of rational powers, such as thinking and loving.

PLENARY COUNCIL. A formal meeting of the archbishops and bishops of a country or region under the leadership of a papal legate, who would decide matters to be considered and ratify the council's decrees. The decrees are binding on all the faithful under the jurisdiction of the bishops assembled. In the Church's history the decisions of some plenary councils were later extended to the universal Church. (Etym. Latin *plenus,* full.)

PLENARY INDULGENCE. An indulgence that can remove all the temporal punishment due to forgiven sin. No one but God knows for certain when a plenary indulgence is actually gained, because only he knows whether a person's dispositions are adequate. One norm for such dispositions is that "all attachment to sin, even venial sin, be absent." If these dispositions are in any way less than complete, the indulgence will be only partial. The same provision applies to the three external conditions necessary to gain a plenary indulgence: sacramental confession, Eucharistic Communion, and prayer for the intentions of the pope. If these conditions are not satisfied, an otherwise plenary indulgence becomes only partial. These conditions may be satisfied several days before or after the performance of the prescribed work, though preferably Communion should be received and the prayers offered for the pope on the same day as the indulgenced work. A plenary indulgence can be gained only once a day.

PLURALISM, DOCTRINAL. The theory that a Catholic may legitimately hold a doctrinal position that is in contradiction to what the Church teaches, either as defined or by her ordinary universal magisterium. This would mean that contradictory doctrines in faith or morals could be professed by different persons, all equally in good standing in the Catholic Church. Doctrinal pluralism was condemned by the First Vatican Council, 1869–70 (Denzinger 3042, 3043).

PLURALISM, THEOLOGICAL. The multiplicity of theological positions present within the Catholic Church. These positions vary according to which premises or postulates are used in reflecting on the sources of revelation, according to the methodology employed, and according to the cultural tradition within which theology does its speculation. On the first basis, the two principal philosophical premises are the Platonic, stressed in Augustinianism; and the Aristotelian, emphasized in Thomism. On the second level, theologies differ in terms of their mainly biblical, or doctrinal, or historical, or pastoral methodology. And on the third basis, the culture of a people helps to shape the theology they develop, as between the more mystical East and the more practical West, or the more reflective Mediterranean and the more scientific Anglo-Saxon. The Church not only permits these diversities but encourages them, always assuming that theologians who are Catholic are also respectful of the rule of faith and obedient to the magisterium of the hierarchy under the Bishop of Rome.

POLARIZATION. The process or state of concentrating on two contrary positions. A phenomenon that has affected many aspects of modern society, due in large measure to the influence of Hegel and Marx, with their stress on the role of conflict as a necessary condition for progress. The term is applied to the conflict, even on essentials of faith and morals, in the Catholic Church since the Second Vatican Council.

POLYGAMY. The status or institution of simultaneous marriage of more than one woman to one man, or of several women to several men. The two forms are polygyny and polyandry. In ordinary use, the term is restricted to polygyny, i.e., where one man is simultaneously married to more than one woman.

Polygamy as polygyny is contrary to divine positive law governing the marriage union (Genesis 2:24; Ephesians 5:31). According to the natural law, even successive polygamy (as in societies that legalize marriage after divorce) hinders the proper care and education of children. And it places an intolerable burden on practicing mutual love between the spouses.

In the Old Testament, God tolerated polygamy for a certain time, as it appears from the examples of men such as Abraham, Jacob, and David. But with the proclamation of the New Law, this concession, almost wrested from God by reason of the moral obtuseness of man, was revoked. Marriage was restored to its original unity. The language of Christ is very explicit (Matthew 19:3–9; Mark 10:1–12; Luke 16:18). Catholic tradition has consistently interpreted Christ's teaching as absolutely forbidding polygamy, and the prohibition was defined by the Council of Trent, pronouncing anathema against anyone who says that "it is lawful for Christians to have several wives at the same time, and that it is not forbidden by any divine law" (Denzinger 1802). (Etym. Greek *polygamos*, having many wives.)

POLYGENISM. The theory that, since evolution is an established fact, all human beings now on earth do not descend from one human pair (Adam and Eve) but from different original human ancestors. This theory is contrary to the official teaching of the Church, e.g., Venerable Pope Pius XII, who declared: "It is unintelligible how such an opinion can be squared with what the sources of revealed truth and the documents of the magisterium of the Church teach on original sin, which proceeds from sin actually committed by an individual, Adam, and which, passed on to all by way of generation, is in everyone as his own" (*Humani Generis*, 1950, para. 38). (Etym. Latin *poly-*, many + *gen*, race + *ism*.)

PONTIFF. High priest, and therefore any bishop, as successor of the Apostles. Now reserved as the title of the pope. In pre-Christian times, the pontifices were the chief priests of Rome and were given this name either because they were "bridge builders" (*pontem facere*) between the gods and men or because they offered sacrifice (*puntis*). (Etym. Latin *pontifex*, high priest; literally, bridgemaker; popular original meaning: waymaker, pathfinder.)

PONTIFICAL. A liturgical book, dating from at least the eighth century and containing the prayers and ceremonies for rites reserved to a bishop. It generally contained 1. prayers and instructions for services without Mass; 2. sacramental ceremonies with blessings and consecrations; and 3. acts of jurisdiction. Such collections were known as *Liber Episcopalis, Liber Pontificalis,* or *Ordinarium Episcopi.* The first Roman Pontifical was published in 1485.

PONTIFICAL MASS. Solemn Mass by a pope, cardinal, bishop, or abbot with prescribed ritual. It is celebrated with full ceremonial when said at the throne of a prelate's own cathedral.

PONTIFICATE. The reign or period of reign of a pope as Roman pontiff. Once legitimately elected, and accepting the election, he immediately receives, by divine right, the full power of supreme jurisdiction over the Christian faithful.

POOR CLARES. A monastic community founded by St. Clare (1194–1253) under the inspiration of St. Francis of Assisi. He first placed her in a Benedictine house, but later, when other women joined Clare, they founded a community along Franciscan lines. Clare became the first abbess (1215), and she occupied the position until her death. Several daughter houses were founded during her life, in Italy, France, and Germany. In keeping with the spirit of St. Francis, the austerity of the Poor Clares was the most severe among women religious up to that time. Some branch houses obtained dispensations from the original rule of absolute poverty not only for individuals but for the community as well. But the community of San Damiano at Assisi, with those of Perugia and Florence, obtained from Pope Gregory IX the "privilege of poverty," which enabled them to keep their primitive rule. In succeeding years modifications and reforms divided the Poor Clares into various religious institutes, mainly the Urbanists and Colettines. Their principal emphasis has been on mortification and Eucharistic adoration, with the chanting of the Divine Office.

POOR SOULS. The souls in purgatory, expiating the temporal punishment due to their sins. They are called "poor" because they cannot merit their own release or mitigation of their sufferings, but depend on the prayers and good works of the faithful on earth. See also HOLY SOULS.

POPE. Title of the visible head of the Catholic Church. He is called pope (Greek *pappas,* a child's word for "father") because his authority is supreme and because it is to be exercised in a paternal way, after the example of Christ.

POPE, ELECTION OF. The choice of the Bishop of Rome, which has gone through various methods over the centuries. In 1975, Pope Paul VI issued an apostolic constitution in which he made certain changes in papal election law. In line with previous legislation, he decreed that only cardinals—a maximum of 120 under the age of eighty—may be electors. There can be no personal attendants for the cardinals during the conclave, and provisions were made for security and means for handling difficult situations that might arise during the election. On February 22, 1996, Blessed John Paul II promulgated the apostolic constitution *Universi Dominici Gregis,* changing the rules governing the election of a new pope. Cardinals gathered in Rome to elect a new pope are to stay in the Domus Sanctae Marthae, but the election will still take place in the Sistine Chapel. Two-thirds of the votes are necessary to elect a new pope, but if after a long succession of ballots no pope is elected, the cardinals can choose to change that rule so that the pope can be elected by an absolute majority of the electors. Pope Benedict XVI in an apostolic letter given as a *motu proprio* (July 11, 2007) amended *Universi Dominici Gregis.* Now two-thirds of the vote is required to elect a new pope, no matter how many ballots it takes. See also CONCLAVE.

PORNOGRAPHY. A description or portrayal of any person or activity that is consciously intended to stimulate immoral sexual feelings. (Etym. Greek *porne,* prostitute + *graphe,* writing.)

POSITIVISM. The view that only the sensibly perceptible is real, that only what is personally experienced is true. Thus nothing but facts can be affirmed with certitude. According to Auguste Comte (1798–1857), who coined the term "positivism," the history of humanity should be described in three stages: the first, when people's minds were dominated by theology and superstition; the second, when reason prevailed; and the third or final stage, when dogmas and philosophies are being replaced by factual knowledge. Hence the supremacy of the physical, psychological, and social sciences in the modern age.

POSSESSION, DEMONIC. The inner control by the devil of the actions of the body of a human being. The victim's liberty of soul always remains intact. Possession can be continual or intermittent, and the victim need not have culpably brought on the devil's control. There is an official exorcism provided by the Church for possessed persons. Public exorcisms must be authorized by ecclesiastical authority.

POSTCONCILIAR. A term used to describe the period since the Second Vatican Council (1962–65). It reflects the developments in Catholic doctrine, liturgy, and ecclesiastical law that were authorized by the council and have been implemented by the Church's hierarchy.

POSTULANT. A person taking the first step in religious life before entering the novitiate and receiving the habit. The purpose of the postulancy is to acquire some knowledge of the religious life and of the particular institute through personal experience. It enables one to become better known to the superiors of the community, and to develop such virtue as will qualify the candidate for acceptance into the novitiate. The length of the postulancy varies, but normally it is not less than six months. (Etym. Latin *postulatum,* a thing demanded; *postulatio,* supplication, intercession.)

POVERTY, EVANGELICAL. A Christian counsel by which a person voluntarily renounces all or part of his right to the ownership of material things.

POVERTY OF DISPOSSESSION. The complete renunciation of ownership and further acquisition of material possessions. The biblical foundation for such poverty is the declaration of Christ to the rich young man: "If you wish to be perfect, go and sell what you own and give the money to the poor, and you will have treasure in heaven; then come, follow me" (Matthew 19:21).

POVERTY OF SHARING. The voluntary sacrifice of one's possessions for the common good of a community. All means of support and activity are provided by the group. Practiced in the Church since apostolic times, it is described by St. Luke as one of the effects of receiving the Holy Spirit: "The faithful all lived together and owned everything in common; they sold their goods and possessions and shared out proceeds among themselves according to what each one needed" (Acts 2:44–45).

PRAGMATISM. A theory that every truth has practical consequences that are the test of its truthfulness. Associated with the American philosopher William James, who defined the true as "only the expedient in our way of thinking." In religious terms, what justifies a creed or ritual is its ability to satisfy psychological needs and generate useful values for society.

PRAISES OF GOD. A hymn of adoration of St. Francis of Assisi. The original paper with these praises is preserved today in a reliquary in the Basilica of St. Francis in Assisi. The praises illustrate the mystical heights to which Francis had attained at the time of his stigmatization. They read:

You are holy, Lord, the only God, and your deeds are wonderful.

You are strong. You are great. You are the Most High. You are almighty. You, holy Father, are King of heaven and earth.

You are Three and One, Lord God, all good. You are Good, all Good, supreme Good, Lord God, living and true.

You are love. You are wisdom. You are humility. You are endurance. You are rest. You are peace. You are joy and gladness. You are justice and moderation. You are all our riches, and You suffice for us.

You are beauty. You are gentleness. You are our protector, You are our guardian and defender. You are courage. You are our haven and our hope.

You are our faith, our great consolation. You are our eternal life, great and wonderful Lord, God Almighty, Merciful Savior.

PRAYER. The voluntary response to the awareness of God's presence. This response may be an acknowledgment of God's greatness and of a person's total dependence on him (adoration), or gratitude for his benefits to oneself and others (thanksgiving), or sorrow for sins committed and begging for mercy (expiation), or asking for graces needed (petition), or affection for God, who is all good (love).

PRAYER, CONSTANT. The Christian practice, advocated by St. Paul, "Pray constantly" (I Thessalonians 5:17), by which a person always remains united with God. Also called the prayer of the heart, it need not be conscious awareness of God's presence. It implies that a person is constantly ready to do the will of God.

PRAYER BOOK. A manual of prayers for private devotion by the faithful or for communal use by members of a religious community or confraternity. There is no Catholic counterpart to the Anglican Book of Common Prayer because Catholic liturgical books of prayer and chant are totally distinct from ordinary prayer books, which may contain a variety of authorized prayers, meditations, or reflective readings.

PRAYER OF QUIET. A peaceful internal repose by which the soul is captivated by the divine presence. It is the result of contemplative love and is a fruit of the gift of wisdom. During the prayer of quiet the mind is specially enlightened by divine grace, and a spiritual delight pervades the whole person. Although the lower faculties and senses are free to exercise their natural activities, God makes himself felt in the subtle part of the soul obscurely as the Great Reality. At first this prayer is of short duration. Under the influence of grace it becomes longer and may eventually become habitual.

PRAYER OF THE FAITHFUL. The General Intercession or Bidding prayer in the Mass of the Ordinary Form of the Roman Rite. In this the people exercise their priestly function by praying for all mankind. The prayer is normally to be included whenever there are people attending the Mass. The normal sequence of intentions recommended is for the needs of the Church, civil authorities, and the salvation of the whole world, those oppressed by any kind of need, and the local community. On special occasions the intentions may be adjusted accordingly. It is the function of the priest to preside over this part of the liturgy by opening and concluding the Prayer of the Faithful, with an assistant reading the intentions and the congregation responding with an appropriate invocation.

PRAYER OF UNION. A most intimate union of the soul with God, accompanied by a certitude of his presence within the soul and a suspension of all interior faculties. With this prayer there is an absence of distractions because the soul is entirely absorbed in God. There is no fatigue, no matter how long the union may last, because no personal effort is involved, but rather an extraordinary experience of joy. The soul is left with an ardent zeal to glorify God, complete detachment from all created things, perfect submission to God's will, and great charity for one's neighbor.

PREACHING. Public discourse on a religious subject by one having authority to do so. Preaching, therefore, can be properly applied only to bishops, priests, and deacons in the exercise of their office of proclaiming the word of God. Speaking of priests, the Second Vatican Council places this office first among the duties of priests, who are "consecrated to preach the Gospel, shepherd the faithful, and celebrate divine worship" (Dogmatic Constitution on the Church, III, 28).

PREAMBLES OF FAITH. The main premises of reason on which the act of divine faith depends as its rational foundation. They are mainly three: 1. the existence of God; 2. his authority, or right to be believed because he knows all things and is perfectly truthful; and 3. the fact that he actually made a revelation, which is proved especially by miracles or fulfilled prophecies performed in testimony of a prophet's (or Christ's) claim to speaking in the name of God. (Etym. Latin *praeambulus,* walking in front: *prae-*, in front + *ambulare*, to walk.)

PRECEPT. A command of God or of legitimate human authority to a definite person or a specific duty. A precept is also distinguished from the whole body of laws as any particular rule or command under the law. Affirmative precepts command a person to act or to do something. Negative precepts forbid some action. (Etym. Latin *praeceptum*, rule, maxim.)

PRECEPTS OF CHARITY. The two great commandments of divine revelation, first stated in the Old Law and confirmed by Christ in the Gospels. They are 1. "You must love the Lord your God with all your heart, with all your soul, with all your mind and with all your strength"; and 2. "You must love your neighbor as yourself" (Deuteronomy 6:4–5; Leviticus 19:18; Mark 12:30–31). The phrase "with all your mind" is Christ's addition to the teaching of the Old Testament, as well as the observation that "there is no greater commandment than these" (Mark 12:31).

PRECEPTS OF THE CHURCH. Certain commandments of a moral and ecclesiastical nature prescribed for observance by all Catholics. Their formulation goes back to the Middle Ages, and their number has varied from four to six or more, depending on the times.

The *Catechism of the Catholic Church* lists these precepts of the Church:

1. Attend Mass on Sundays and holy days of obligation and rest from servile labor.
2. Confess your sins at least once a year.
3. Receive Holy Communion at least during the Easter season.
4. Observe the days of fasting and abstinence established by the Church.
5. Help provide for the needs of the Church, each according to his own ability (2042–2043).

PRECIOUS BLOOD (WORSHIP). The blood of Jesus Christ distinctively mentioned many times in the New Testament. It is the living symbol of the Redemption and of the Savior's death on the Cross. An object of adoration as part of the Sacred Humanity, it is hypostatically united with the Second Person of the Trinity. Moreover, it is an integral part of Christ, who is really present in the Blessed Sacrament. In 1849, Blessed Pope Pius IX extended the Feast of the Precious Blood to the whole Church, assigning to it the first Sunday in July, changed by Pope St. Pius X in 1914 to July 1. Since the Second Vatican Council the feast has been merged with that of Corpus Christi so that the new Feast of the Body and Blood of Christ (*Festum Corporis et Sanguinis Christi*) occurs on the Thursday following Trinity Sunday. In some countries it is transferred to the following Sunday. Those using the 1962 liturgical books continue to celebrate the Feast of the Most Precious Blood on July 1.

PRECURSOR. As the herald of Christ, St. John the Baptist, of whom all four evangelists wrote at length and who was described by his father, Zechariah, in the Benedictus: "You shall be called Prophet of the Most High, for you will go before the Lord to prepare the way for Him" (Luke 1:76). (Etym. Latin *praecursor*, forerunner.)

PREDESTINARIANISM. The theory that denies that God has the will to save all mankind, since he wants only the elect to reach heaven. There is no place in this system for true internal freedom of the human will but only for external freedom from coercion. The eternal decree of God alone predestines to glory or damnation. The elect receive irresistible grace; the others have an impulse of the will to sin and so are not given salvific grace. Predestinarianism is central to the Reformation doctrine of John Calvin. (Etym. Latin *prae-*, before + *destinare*, to destine, ordain.)

PREDESTINATION. In the widest sense it is every eternal decision of God, in a narrower sense it is the supernatural final destination of rational creatures, and in the strictest sense it is God's eternal decision to assume certain rational creatures into heavenly glory. Predestination implies an act of the divine intellect and of the divine will. The first is foreknowledge; the second is predestination.

According to its efficacy in time, predestination is distinguished as incomplete or complete depending on whether it is to grace only or also to glory. Complete predestination is the divine preparation of grace in the present life and of glory in the life to come.

This doctrine is proposed by the ordinary and universal teaching of the Church as a truth of revelation. The reality of predestination is clearly attested by St. Paul: "They are the ones he chose especially long ago and intended to become true images of the Son, so that his Son, might be the eldest of many brothers. He called those he intended for this; those he called he justified and with those he justified he shared his glory" (Romans 8:29–30). All elements of complete predestination are given: the activity of God's mind and will, and the principal stages of its realization in time.

The main difficulty in the doctrine of predestination is whether God's eternal decision has been taken with or without consideration of human freedom. Catholic teaching holds that predestination by God does not deny the human free will. Numerous theories have been offered on how to reconcile the two, but all admit with St. Paul (Romans 11:33) that predestination is an unfathomable mystery. (Etym. Latin *praedestinatio*, a determining beforehand.)

PREDETERMINATION. Also called "physical premotion," to explain how God's sovereignty includes also the free actions of men. According to this theory, first developed by Dominic Bañez (1529–1604) and later adopted by the Dominican Order, God has predetermined from all eternity that certain people shall be saved. For the realization of this he bestows effective grace on these people. In this way he physically affects the free will of the elect and so secures that they decide freely to cooperate with grace. Efficacious grace, by its inner power, therefore, infallibly brings it about that the elect freely consent to do those salutary acts which merit eternal salvation. Thus it is substantially different from sufficient grace, which merely confers the power to do a salutary act. In order that this potency may be translated into act, another new, inherently different grace (efficacious grace) must appear. From all eternity God has decreed the free assent of the human will to the efficacious grace, whereby he brings about salvation for those who fall within his decree.

PRE-EVANGELIZATION. Preparation of a person or people to receive the Gospel. The need for such preparation in the modern world arises from the massive neglect of God and things spiritual. "In the past," the Second Vatican Council explains, "it was the exception to repudiate God and religion to the point of abandoning them, and then only in individual cases; but nowadays it seems a matter of course to reject them as incompatible with scientific progress and a new kind of humanism" (*Gaudium et Spes*, 8). Through the media of social communication, this spirit of unbelief has permeated whole segments of society. Hence the need for predisposing people even to listen to the Gospel, especially in the once Christian affluent cultures of Euro-America.

PREJUDICE. In moral philosophy a preconceived opinion formulated without consideration of known facts and usually based on erroneous knowledge. It leads to wrong judgments and renders a person blind to reason and closed to convincing argument. It often violates justice because prejudiced people tend to ignore others' rights. They are so preoccupied with their own version of persons and societies that they prejudge adversely. Prejudice is the common basis for sinful rash judgment.

PRELATE. A dignitary having jurisdiction in external forum by right of his office. There have been prelates "nullius" who presided over the clergy and people of a certain territory not belonging to an established diocese. Thus abbots, although not bishops, have had the jurisdiction of a prelate. Such prelacies have been drastically reduced since the Second Vatican Council. In exempt religious orders, clerical superiors—such as provincials, guardians, and priors—share in the jurisdictional rank of prelate. The name and rank of prelate may also be given to priests as a mark of papal recognition of their service to the Church. (Etym. Latin *praelatus*, prelate, superior.)

PRESBYTER. In the early Church a member of a group (usually of priests) who advised a bishop. Together they formed the presbytery, which, under a bishop, was the governing body of a community. The presbyter, having no official duties, was often commissioned by the bishop to teach, celebrate Mass, and baptize. Presbyters were usually of advanced age and, like a bishop, chosen by the people. Their rank was above that of deacons but inferior to that of bishops. There was no restriction on their number.

PRESBYTERIANS. Members of various Protestant bodies, following in the tradition of John Calvin (1509–64) and his Scottish disciple John Knox (1513–72). The essential structural feature of historic Presbyterianism was that the Church's government should be in the hands of presbyters. Today, however, many Presbyterians hold that the Church founded by Christ contained episcopal and congregational, as well as presbyterian, elements. A typical Presbyterian church is governed by a hierarchy of authorities, each in the nature of a court: session, presbytery, synod, and general assembly, having clearly defined functions and specific directors.

The substance of Presbyterian belief is contained in the Westminster Confession of Faith, drafted by the Puritan English Parliament in 1643. Its main provisions are the Calvinist predestination belief that the Church founded by Christ was essentially invisible and "consists of the whole number of the elect," a spiritual and not bodily presence of Christ in the Eucharist, and a deference to civil authority that is characteristically Presbyterian. A new confession of the faith, issued by the American Presbyterians in 1967, left the Westminster Confession essentially untouched. Added to the group of now recognized statements of faith, however, was the Theological Declaration of Barmen (1934), published under Karl Barth (1886–1968) during the Nazi regime, to defend the Church's freedom from political oppression.

PRESBYTERORUM ORDINIS. The Second Vatican Council's Decree on the Ministry and Life of Priests. Priests are defined as those men who "hold in the community of the faithful the sacred power of Orders, that of offering sacrifice and forgiving sins, and who exercise the priestly office publicly on behalf of men in the name of Christ." Their ministry flows from their office. It is to share with everyone the truth of the Gospel, which is "often very difficult in present-day conditions." Celibacy for priests is reaffirmed. Their sanctity is declared to be essential and to be fostered by "the double table of holy Scripture and the Eucharist" (December 7, 1965).

PRESENCE OF GOD. The existence of God acting in favor of his creatures. "God is in things, first, because He is their cause, secondly because He is the object of their activity, as the known in the knower and as the desired in the lover, and this . . . which is proper to human souls, is God's special presence by grace to rational creatures who know Him and love Him, actually or habitually" (St. Thomas Aquinas, *Summa Theologiae* I, VIII, 3). Cultivating the awareness of God's presence in the soul, and in the events of Divine Providence, is essential for growth in the spiritual life.

PRESERVATION OF LIFE. The duty that every person has to use at least ordinary means like food, sleep, shelter, and available medication to sustain bodily life. If one's life is specially important for one's family, the Church, or society, that person may be obliged to use proportionally extraordinary means to remain alive.

PRETERNATURAL. That which is beyond the natural but is not strictly supernatural. It is preternatural either because natural forces are used by God to produce effects beyond their native capacity, or because above-human forces, angelic or demonic, are active in the world of space and time. (Etym. Latin *praeter,* beyond + *natura,* nature.)

PRETERNATURAL GIFTS. Favors granted by God above and beyond the powers or capacities of the nature that receives them but not beyond those of all created nature. Such gifts perfect nature but do not carry it beyond the limits of created nature. They include three great privileges to which human beings have no title—infused knowledge, absence of concupiscence, and bodily immortality. Adam and Eve possessed these gifts before the Fall.

PRIDE. An inordinate esteem of oneself. It is inordinate because it is contrary to the truth. It is essentially an act or disposition of the will desiring to be considered better than a person really is. Pride may be expressed in different ways: by taking personal credit for gifts or possessions, as if they had not been received from God; by glorying in achievements, as if they were not primarily the result of divine goodness and grace; by minimizing one's defects or claiming qualities that are not actually possessed; by holding oneself superior to others or disdaining them because they lack what the proud person has; by magnifying the defects of others or dwelling on them. When pride is carried to the extent that a person is unwilling to acknowledge dependence on God and refuses to submit his or her will to God or lawful authority, it is a grave sin. The gravity arises from the fact that a person shows contempt for God or of those who take his place. Otherwise, pride is said to be imperfect and venially wrong.

While not all sins are pride, it can lead to all sorts of sins, notably presumption, ambition, vainglory, boasting, hypocrisy, strife, and disobedience. Pride strives for perverse excellence. It despises others and, depending on its perversity, even looks down upon God. The remedies for pride are a sincere knowledge of oneself, the acceptance of daily humiliations, avoidance of even the least self-complacency, humble acknowledgment of one's faults, and prayerful communion with God.

PRIDE OF LIFE. The natural tendency to egotism, which is partly the result of original sin but mainly the mysterious desire of human beings to do their own will even when this contradicts the will of God. It is an urge to self-worship, or self-deification, and is at the root of all sin.

PRIE-DIEU. A kneeling bench used in many European churches and mainly intended for private devotions. Its present form dates from the seventeenth century. It resembles a wooden desk with a sloping shelf for resting the arms, often with a compartment for books beneath.

PRIEST. An authorized mediator who offers a true sacrifice in acknowledgment of God's supreme dominion over human beings and in expiation for their sins. A priest's mediation is the reverse of that of a prophet, who communicates from God to the people. A priest mediates from the people to God.

Christ, who is God and man, is the first, last, and greatest priest of the New Law. He is the eternal high priest who offered himself once and for all on the Cross, a victim of infinite value, and he continually renews that sacrifice on the altar through the ministry of the Church.

Within the Church are men who are specially ordained as priests to consecrate and offer the body and blood of Christ in the Mass. The Apostles were the first ordained priests, when on Holy Thursday night Christ told them to do in his memory what he had just done at the Last Supper. All priests and bishops trace their ordination to the Apostles. Their second essential priestly power, to forgive sins, was conferred by Christ on Easter Sunday, when he told the Apostles, "For those whose sins you forgive, they are forgiven; for those whose sins you retain, they are retained" (John 20–22, 23).

All the Christian faithful, however, also share in the priesthood by their baptismal character. They are enabled to offer themselves in sacrifice with Christ through the Eucharistic liturgy. They offer the Mass in the sense that they internally unite themselves with the outward offering made by the ordained priest alone.

PRIESTHOOD. Sacrament of the New Law, instituted by Christ at the Last Supper, which confers on a man the power of consecrating and offering the body and blood of Christ, and of remitting and retaining sins. There are two grades or levels of the priesthood: the presbyterate and the episcopate. Normally priesthood refers to the presbyterate and is the second rank of orders, above the diaconate. Only a bishop can ordain priests, who must first have been ordained deacons. In the ordination of priests, the "matter" of the sacrament is the imposition of the bishop's hands upon the individual candidates, which is done in silence before the consecration prayer, of which the following words pertain to the nature of the order and therefore are required for the validity of the act: "We ask you, all powerful Father, give these servants of yours the dignity of the presbyterate. Renew the Spirit of holiness within them. By your divine gift may they attain the second order of the hierarchy and exemplify right conduct in their lives."

PRIESTHOOD OF CHRIST. The role of Christ as ordained to offer sacrifice and prayer for humanity to his heavenly Father. His ordination or anointing to the office of high priest took place at the moment of the Incarnation, i.e., at the moment when the Word of God assumed human flesh in the womb of Mary. During his life on earth Christ exercised his priestly office by all the acts of his will, and then at the Last Supper and on Calvary he united all these mortal acts into one supreme sacrifice to the Father. Along with the sacrifice, Christ also prayed as a priest, notably when he instituted the Eucharist and in the sacerdotal prayer recorded by St. John (17:1–26). Moreover, Christ's priesthood continues everlastingly in heaven, as revealed in the Letter to the Hebrews. Regarding the manner in which he exercises his eternal priesthood, revelation merely says: "He is always making intercession for us" (Hebrews 7:25; Romans 8:34), which is a truly sacerdotal function because, as St. Paul affirms, it bears an intimate relation to the sacrifice of the Cross. In fact, Christ's continuing priesthood is the basis in faith for the existence and efficacy of the sacrifice of the Mass.

PRIESTHOOD OF THE FAITHFUL. The share in the high priesthood of Christ received by everyone at baptism and strengthened by confirmation and the Eucharist. Essential to this priesthood is the right to receive the other sacraments, of participating in the Church's liturgy, and of being united with Christ the eternal priest as he offers himself, with the members of his Mystical Body, to the heavenly Father in the Eucharistic Sacrifice.

PRIESTLY FRATERNITY OF ST. PETER. A community of priests who do not take vows, technically a Clerical Society of Apostolic Life of Pontifical Right, who work together on the mission of the sanctification and formation of priests devoted to the traditional liturgy of the Roman Rite and in pastoral work of the Church.

PRIMACY. First in rank. Applied to the pope as Bishop of Rome, it is a primacy of jurisdiction, which means the possession of full and supreme teaching, legislative, and sacerdotal powers in the Catholic Church. St. Peter was promised the primacy when Christ told him that he was to be the rock on which the Savior would build his Church (Matthew 16:18). Peter received the primacy when the risen Christ told him to "feed my lambs, feed my sheep" (John 21:15–17). It follows from the dogma of the primacy that Paul, like the other Apostles, was subordinate to Peter as the supreme head of the whole Church. Pope Innocent X in 1647 rejected Jansenist teaching that Peter and Paul were joint heads of the Church (Denzinger 1999). According to Christ's ordinance, Peter was to have successors in his primacy over the whole Church and for all time. As defined by the First Vatican Council (1869–70), it is heretical to deny that "in virtue of the decree of Our Lord Jesus Christ Himself, blessed Peter has perpetual successors in his primacy over the universal Church" (Denzinger 3058). Following the precedent of the Second Council of Lyons (1274) and the Council of Florence (1430), the First Vatican Council further defined that the successors of Peter in the primacy are the Bishops of Rome (Denzinger 3058). This doctrine affirms that the Bishop of

Rome at any time is, in fact, the holder of the primacy. On what legal title the association of the Roman pontiff's office with the primacy rests is not defined. The more common position is that it rests not on the historical fact that Peter worked and died as Bishop of Rome but on a positive ordinance of Christ or of the Holy Spirit, who revealed that the bishops of Rome should be the successors of Peter. Accordingly the fact that the bishops of Rome hold primacy over the universal Church is of divine and not merely human origin.

Like other doctrines of faith, the primacy has undergone considerable development over the centuries. Most recently, the role of the bishops to the pope was clarified in the teaching of the Second Vatican Council on collegiality. Notwithstanding this development, the basic elements of the primacy have not changed. They are, in brief, that the pope possesses full and supreme power of jurisdiction over the whole Church and each member in the Church, not only in matters of faith and morals but in Church discipline and in the government of the Church. (Etym. Latin *primus*, first, foremost, primary.)

PRIME MOVER. God as the First Cause, who originally started the world on its course of bodily and spiritual movement and continues to sustain the universe in its process of change.

PRIMITIVE RELIGION. The religion of the early peoples. Strictly speaking, there are no genuine primitives anywhere on earth today. More accurately, the religion of the ancients was archaic, and of this there is extensive evidence in the artifacts, paintings, and symbolic writings they have left. Primitive religion, properly so called, is that of present-day peoples whose relative isolation from the major streams of culture suggests their lineage from the chronological ancestors of the human race. Their religious condition, therefore, is on a par with other phases of conduct and knowledge, ranging from the very undeveloped, or decadent, to a fairly advanced type of civilization.

Two levels of primitive religions should be distinguished. The lower type either has been less directly affected by one of the major religions or shows less speculative development. It corresponds to animism or fetishism; that is, more emphasis is given to attributing souls to every object and to believing in magic or sorcery.

PRINCIPALITIES. The angels who belong to the highest choir in the lowest order of the angelic hosts. With the archangels and angels they form that heavenly multitude who are God's ordinary and immediate servants in what pertains to the visible world. It is probable that whole countries are assigned to the care of certain principalities.

PRINCIPLE OF EVIL. The nonexisting source of all evil postulated by the Manichaeans and others. The immediate basis of this theory was a misconception of God's Providence, as though he could not draw good out of evil or was helpless to prevent evil in the world.

PRIORY. Monastery of men or women governed by a prior or prioress. A conventual priory is autonomous, while one dependent upon an abbey or motherhouse is an obedientiary priory. In England monasteries attached to cathedral churches are termed cathedral priories.

PRISONERS OF CONSCIENCE. A term especially applied to the thousands of persons behind the Bamboo Curtain who have been imprisoned for their religious beliefs. Many are sent, with or without trial, to prison in order to change their thinking or keep them from influencing others.

PRIVATE CONFESSION. The ordinary condition for receiving absolution in the sacrament of penance. It is now distinguished from communal penance, which, under extraordinary circumstances, includes general absolution. It was formerly distinguished from public penance in the early Church when, in some places, the penitents were publicly identified as guilty of certain sins. Private confession of secret sins was practiced in the early Church and, according to the teaching of the popes, was of apostolic origin.

PRIVATE REVELATIONS. Supernatural manifestations by God of hidden truths made to private individuals for their own spiritual welfare or that of others. They differ from the public revelation contained in Scripture and tradition, which is given on behalf of the whole human race and is necessary for human salvation and sanctification. Although recognized by the Church and, at times, approved by her authority, private revelations are not the object of divine faith that binds one in conscience to believe on God's authority. The assent given to them, therefore, is either on human evidence or, when formally approved by the Church, on ecclesiastical authority according to the mind of the Church. Private revelations occur as supernatural visions, words, or divine touches. Often it is impossible to distinguish the three forms in practice, especially since they may be received simultaneously.

PRIVILEGE. A concession, more or less permanent, made against or beyond the law. The popes have granted privileges at least since the eighth century. They are acquired orally or in writing, by direct concession or by communication. Personal privileges are granted to a person; real privileges are attached to things. A personal privilege need not be used and is not lost by lack of use. A real privilege is lost by destruction of the object. Privileges are perpetual unless otherwise stated.

PRIVILEGE, ECCLESIASTICAL. A special concession, not provided in the law, for persons and institutions in the Catholic Church. Privileges can be acquired by direct concession of the competent Church authority, by communication, and even by legitimate custom or prescription. Unless specified to the contrary, privileges are permanent. Typical forms are clerical privileges against violence (*privilegium canonis*), ot ecclesiastical court (*privilegium fori*), of personal immunity, and benefit in case of insolvency. Since these privileges are attached to a person's state of life, they cannot be waived by the individuals who share them. They are lost by degradation, deposition, and reduction to the lay state only.

PROBABILISM. The moral theory that holds that a law against whose existence or application there stands a solidly probable argument does not bind. It is based on the principle that a doubtful law does not bind. It then excludes other theories as either too strict or too lax about the degree of doubt or probability that would exempt one from the obligation of a doubtful law. (Etym. Latin *probabilis,* likely, credible.)

PROCESSION. The origin of one from another. A procession is said to be external when the terminus of the procession goes outside the principle or source from which it proceeds. Thus creatures proceed by external procession from the triune God, their Primary Origin. An internal procession is immanent; the one proceeding remains united with the one from whom he or she proceeds. Thus the processions of the Son and the Holy Spirit are an immanent act of the Holy Trinity. An internal, divine procession signifies the origin of a divine person from another divine person (Son from the Father), or from other divine persons (the Holy Spirit from Father and Son), through the communication of numerically one and the same Divine Essence.

PROCESSIONS. Sacred functions in which clergy and people parade from one place to another. They may be held within a church, between churches, or outside a church or shrine. Processions are public acts of homage to God, to give honor to him or his saints, to ask for divine favor, to thank him for blessings received, and to ask pardon for sins committed. Their practice goes back to Old Testament times to express the faith both of a people as distinct from the worship of a single individual, and of a people who symbolize their cooperative action, as distinct from merely their common profession of faith.

PROCESS THEOLOGY. A view of reality, including what Christianity calls God, that sees everything still in the process of becoming what it will be, but nothing really is. It is called "theology" because it is a form of evolutionary pantheism that postulates a finite god who is becoming perfect but is not (as Christianity believes) infinite and all-perfect from eternity. It is called "process" because it claims that the universe (including God) is moving toward completion, without identifying what this completion is or when or whether it will be reached. On these terms nothing is stable, nothing certain, because nothing really is. There are no determined moral laws, no absolute norms of conduct, no certain principles of thought, and no means of knowing anything. There is no "thing," since what people call "things" are moving functions that keep changing in their very being. Everything, including the thinking mind, is ever becoming what it was not and ceasing to be what it was.

Not all adherents of what is called process theology are consistently evolutionary pantheists. But once they postulate a finite god who is still growing in perfection, logically all the rest follows. The main contributors to present-day process thought were the skeptic David Hume (1711–76); the philosophers Georg Hegel (1770–1831), Herbert Spencer (1820–1903), Henri Bergson (1859–1941), and Alfred North Whitehead (1861–1947); and the Marxist writer Ernst Bloch (1885–1977).

PROCLAMATION. Announcing Christ to the world to make him known and loved by as many people as possible. The proclamation takes on as many forms as there are means of communication, by speaking and writing, and especially by reflecting the virtues of

Christ in one's own life and behavior. The proclamation is also the duty of every Christian. "Jesus Christ," declared Blessed Pope John Paul II, "is the stable principle and fixed center of the mission that God has entrusted to man. We must all share in this mission and concentrate all our forces on it, since it is more necessary than ever for modern mankind" (*Redemptor Hominis*, 11).

PROCREATION. Begetting children. It is a formal term for generation and stresses the role of marital intercourse with the intention of producing offspring. (Etym. Latin *procreare*, to beget.)

PROCREATIVE LOVE. The selfless love of husband with wife for the potential offspring God may wish to give them as the "procreation" of marital intercourse. This love is procreative because it evokes the creative act of God, who requires their cooperation to bring a new human being into the world.

PRODIGY. An unusual event produced by angelic power, whether good or bad, under God's positive or permissive Providence. The term is more commonly associated with the diabolical phenomena, to distinguish true, though minor, miracles performed by the good angels from demonic interventions.

PROFANATION. The desecration of something holy by using or treating a sacred person, place, or thing as though it were not sacred but merely secular or profane. Thus profanity in speech is the use of God's name or the name of one of the saints without due regard for its sacred character.

PROFANE. The secular or merely human as compared with the sacred or divine. "Profane" does not, of itself, imply profanation, since the whole created universe, including human beings, is technically profane in contrast to the Creator, whose essence is to be holy precisely because he is the "totally other" who transcends the world that he made and continually sustains. (Etym. Latin *profanus*, lying outside the temple, ordinary, not holy.)

PROFESSED. Those persons in a religious community who have been admitted to the vows of poverty, chastity, and obedience. In some orders, however, the term is reserved for those religious who have lived in their communities for a definite period of time after the taking of their vows. The term may also apply exclusively to those who have taken final vows. But generally they are said to be "finally professed," as distinct from those who are "temporary professed" or "first professed" or "junior professed."

PROFESSION OF FAITH. The public acceptance of the teachings of the Church. When nonprofession would amount to a denial, the baptized Catholic must profess his faith. Under certain circumstances bishops and priests are required to make an official profession of faith according to canon law.

PRO FORMA. As a matter of formality; as should be done according to ecclesiastical protocol.

PROMISE. A declaration telling God or another person that one will or will not do something. A promise made to God is equivalently a vow, and it binds in conscience according to the gravity of the promise and the intention to obligate oneself under pain of sin. Promises made to people must be kept, and they oblige in justice or charity, with more or less seriousness depending on one's ability to fulfill a promise and the harm caused to another by not keeping one's word.

PROMISED LAND. The land of Canaan, generally thought to be the whole of western Palestine. It was promised to the Israelites by God after their sojourn in the desert (Exodus 12:25).

PROMULGATION. The act of announcing a law publicly, with the effect of obliging its observance from the date expressed. Laws enacted by the Holy See are promulgated by publication in the official *Acta Apostolicae Sedis*. They have binding force three months after the date affixed to the *Acta*. However, in a special case the pope is free to promulgate a law in other ways.

PROPAGANDA. The deliberate and systematic attempt to influence and change the ideas, attitudes, and beliefs of others. On Catholic principles, "a propaganda campaign, with a view to influencing public opinion, is justified only when it serves the truth, when its objectives and methods accord with the dignity of humans, and when it promotes causes that are in the public interest" (*Communio et Progressio*, 1971, 29). (Etym. Latin *propagare*, to generate; to extend, increase.)

PROPAGATION OF THE FAITH. An international association for the assistance, by prayers and alms, of Catholic missionaries throughout the world. Founded in 1822 at Lyons, France, by Pauline Jaricot. It is now under the auspices of the Sacred Congregation for the Evangelization of Peoples (Propagation of the Faith).

PROPER OF THE SAINTS. In the Roman Missal the feast days of the saints commemorated in the universal Church. The feasts are given in sequence, from January through December.

PROPER OF THE SEASON. In the Roman Missal the liturgical feasts of the year, as follows: Advent, Christmas season, Lent, Holy Week, Easter season, the season of the year (also known as Ordinary Time), and solemnities of the Lord throughout the year. In the 1962 liturgical calendar, there is also the Season after the Epiphany and the Season after Pentecost.

PROPERTY. In theology and philosophy an attribute of someone or something that does not constitute its essence but necessarily follows from the essence. Hence a distinctive and characteristic quality of a being. In ethics and morality, property is either that which a person owns or the right of ownership.

PROPHECY. The certain prediction of future events that cannot be known by natural means. However, the biblical meaning of the Hebrew *hozeh* (prophecy) is more general, namely "vision" or "revelation interpreted." Those who were called upon to prophesy did, indeed, on occasion also foretell future events, but these predictions fulfilled were divine confirmations of an authentic vision rather than the vision itself. Prophecies as predictions are consequently part of God's supernatural Providence. God, in whose sight all things future are ever present, is able to communicate to his creatures the knowledge that he has. He alone finally has this power, because certain foreknowledge of the contingent future is possessed only by God. Prophecies are the words of his prescience, just as miracles are the work of his omnipotence. Hence a religion supported by prophecies must be divine. (Etym. Greek *prophētēs,* one who speaks for a god, interpreter, expounder, prophet; literally, one who speaks for another.)

PROPHET. The biblical term *nabi* means "one who spoke, acted, or wrote under the extraordinary influence of God to make known the divine counsels and will." Yet commonly associated with this primary function to proclaim the word of God, a prophet also prophesied by foretelling future events. His role, then, was to both proclaim and to make the proclamation credible.

PROPITIATION. To placate or appease an angry person. It is one of the three fruits of every good work; the others are impetration and merit. It is also one of the four ends of the Sacrifice of the Mass, whose propitiatory power extends to sin, to satisfaction and punishment for the living, and to punishment for the dead. (Etym. Latin *propitiare*, to render favorable.)

PROTESTANTISM. The system of faith, worship, and practice derived from the principles of the Reformation in the sixteenth century. As a name, it comes from the *Protestatio* of the Reformers at the Diet of Speyer (1529) against the decisions of the Catholic majority that no further religious innovations were to be introduced. Although now divided into hundreds of denominations, the original families of Protestantism were only five: the Lutheran, Calvinist, and Zwinglian on the Continent, and the Anglican and Free Church or Congregational in Great Britain. Three premises of Protestantism have remained fairly constant—namely, the Bible as the only rule of faith, excluding tradition and Church authority; justification by faith alone, excluding supernatural merit and good works; and the universal priesthood of believers, excluding a distinct episcopacy or priesthood divinely empowered through ordination to teach, govern, and sanctify the people of God. (Etym. Latin *protestari*, to profess one's belief in or against something, to witness to.)

PROTOCANONICAL. A term applied to those books of the Bible, especially in the Old Testament, whose inspired character had never been questioned, e.g., by any Church Father. But the expression is misleading because it was not the Church Fathers but the Church's magisterium under the pope that was divinely authorized to decide on the canonicity of the Scriptures.

PROTOCOL. Originally the first leaf glued to papyrus rolls; later a sheet with seal affixed, containing a summary of the document's contents by a notary. Now the forms of ceremony to be observed by ecclesiastical and civil officials. In this sense the protocol for bishops and especially for Vatican dignitaries and the pope is highly complex and carefully observed. (Etym. Greek *prōtokollon*, first leaf of a volume, containing an account of the contents.)

PROTOEVANGELIUM. The modern title of the apocryphal Gospel of the Infancy. Also known as the book of James (the Less). Most likely of Docetist origin, it testifies to the early devotion to Mary, dating from the second century. It is the oldest known apocryphal gospel. Protoevangelium (First Gospel) is also applied to the promise of a Redeemer after the Fall. Speaking to the serpent, God said, "I will make you enemies of each other; you and the woman, your offspring and her offspring. It will crush your head and you will strike its heel" (Genesis 3:15). Traditionally the woman and her offspring have been understood to mean Mary and her Son.

PROTO-MARTYR. St. Stephen, whose martyrdom is described by St. Luke (Acts 6:8–7:60). Or anyone who is the first to suffer in any persecution after the example of St. Stephen.

PROVERB. A short statement of a universal truth written in expressive language. There are many proverbial thoughts found in Scripture, expounding spiritual truths and human aspirations. One of the best-known books in the Old Testament is the book of Proverbs, filled with expressions of wisdom and experience.

PROVIDENCE. God's all-wise plan for the universe, and the carrying out of this plan by his loving rule or governance. The eternal world plan and its fulfillment in time are together called Divine Providence. As expressed by the First Vatican Council (1869–70), "God, in His providence watches over and governs all the things that He made, reaching from end to end with might and disposing all things with gentleness" (Denzinger 3003). Divine Providence is universal in that all events, even the most personal decisions of human beings, are part of God's eternal plan. It is infallibly certain because the ultimate purpose that God has for the universe will not fail. And it is immutable because God himself cannot change. (Etym. Latin *providentia*, foresight, foreknowledge.)

PROVINCIAL. A religious superior exercising general supervision over a number of houses that form a division of the order or congregation, called a province. The provincial superior in turn is subject to the superior general according to the constitutions of the institute.

PROXIMATE OCCASIONS. Situations that are likely to lead a' person into sin. They are either circumstances in which any ordinary person is almost sure to sin, or those in which the individual in question as a rule sins. In general, occasions of sin looked upon as proximate for everyone are known to be such from a knowledge of human nature and the way people in general react to situations. Occasions of sin that are proximate only for certain persons are known from experience or from an honest appraisal of one's own moral frailty.

PRUDENCE. Correct knowledge about things to be done or, more broadly, the knowledge of things that ought to be done and of things that ought to be avoided. It is the intellectual virtue whereby a human being recognizes in any matter at hand what is good and what is evil. In this sense, it is the moral virtue that enables a person to devise, choose, and prepare suitable means for the attainment of any purpose or the avoidance of any evil. Prudence resides in the practical intellect and is both acquired by one's own acts and infused at the same time as sanctifying grace. It may be said to be natural as developed by us and supernatural because conferred by God. As an act of virtue, prudence involves three stages of mental operation: to take counsel carefully with oneself and from others, to judge correctly on the basis of the evidence at hand, and to direct the rest of one's activity according to the norms determined after a prudent judgment has been made. (Etym. Latin *prudentia,* foresight in the practical order; from *providentia*, foresight, directive care, providence.)

PSALM. A sacred hymn of praise, usually sung or chanted and taken in whole or in part from the book of Psalms in the Old Testament; originally a harp song. Most of the themes used in Gregorian chant as well as the major part of the Divine Office are composed of such hymns.

PSALMS, BOOK OF. A collection of divinely inspired hymns or poems, also known as the "Psalter of David of 150 Psalms" (Council of Trent, Denzinger 1502). The Hebrew title of the book is *Tehilim,* hymns or songs of praise. Although David is the principal author, he is not the only author of the Psalms. They are divided into five sections, each section closing with a doxology, thus 1–41, 42–72, 73–89, 90–106,

107–150, according to the Vulgate. About one hundred Psalms have titles that indicate the author, historical occasion, musical notation, or type of poetry. These titles, though not inspired, have great historical value. Each Psalm has its own theme and purpose, with eight such themes commonly distinguishable, namely:

1. hymns of praise and gratitude to God (8, 17, 102–6, 145–50)
2. petitions (29, 63, 73, 93)
3. didactic or moral instruction (1, 48, 118)
4. penitential (6, 31, 37, 50, 101, 129, 142)
5. imprecatory (17, 34, 58, 68, 78, 93, 108, 129, 142)
6. historical account of God's providential care of Israel (75, 104, 105, 113, 134, 135)
7. gradual or pilgrim songs (119–33)
8. Messianic (2, 15, 21, 44, 68, 71)

Use of the Psalms for divine worship was adopted by the Church after apostolic times. Today they are the main part of the Liturgy of the Hours.

PSYCHOANALYSIS. A form of practical psychology whose purpose is to diagnose, cure, and prevent mental disorders. Among the many schools of psychoanalysis, including those of Sigmund Freud (1856–1939), Alfred Adler (1870–1937), and Carl Gustav Jung (1875–1961), four principles seem to be agreed upon: 1. the unconscious life of a person is of main importance in determining a person's conscious and overt behavior; 2. early infancy and childhood play a determinant role in shaping one's later life; 3. conversation about one's problems, by bringing the unconscious to the surface, is an essential part of treatment; 4. a reorientation of one's philosophy of life is necessary to avoid the onset or recurrence of mental disorder. (Etym. Greek *psychē*, soul, principle of life, life + *analyein*, to loosen, break up.)

PSYCHOSIS. A mental illness involving emotional disturbances that prevent realistic adjustment to environment. Neurasthenia, hysteria, compulsion phenomena, hypochondria, melancholia, psychopathic inferiority are forms of psychosis. A psychosis is more severe than a neurosis that permits at least some adjustment to reality. Symptoms of psychosis may include hallucinations, severe deviations of mood, absent or inappropriate emotional response, and severe distortion of judgment. Organic psychoses are caused by structural damage of the brain; functional psychoses show no observable organic damage.

Moral imputability is reduced or removed to the extent that

psychopathic ideas and fancies so take possession of a person's mind that he or she cannot at all or only with great difficulty give attention to other considerations. Consequently, depending on the degree of mental illness, freedom of choice is either altogether impeded or at least gravely unpaired. In individual cases it is very difficult to determine to what extent freedom of choice and hence responsibility are nullified. In most instances this must be left to the judgment of God. (Etym. Greek *psychē*, soul + *osis*, process, abnormal condition.)

PUBLICAN. In the ancient Roman Empire, usually a man of equestrian rank. In the Gospels a publican was a Jewish "tax gatherer" employed by these wealthy Roman knights. Universally detested by the Jews, publicans were regarded as traitors to their people and classed as sinners. No publican was admitted as a witness in court. Yet some of these despised men were among the earliest disciples of John the Baptist, and the Apostle and evangelist Matthew had been the publican Levi.

PUBLIC PENANCE. The practice of requiring penitents to give public satisfaction for their sins as a condition for absolution and reconciliation with the Church. In vogue up to the early Middle Ages, public penance could be either solemn or not, depending on the gravity of the offense and the amount of scandal given.

When public penance was also solemn, the reason had to be a grave one. Among the public crimes that might be subject to solemn penance, the most common were adultery, apostasy, fornication, and murder, including abortion. A historic example of public penance was Henry II's walking barefoot in 1174 to the shrine of St. Thomas of Becket to expiate his part in the murder of the archbishop. The more common practice was to limit solemn penance to those crimes that gave such scandal as seemed to call for proportionate expiation.

More generally, public penance was not solemn. The person would secretly confess some grave sin from which he or she was absolved by a priest. His or her satisfaction would be an external penance from which others might conclude the nature of the sin, but there was no formal identification as a public sinner.

PUBLIC REVELATION. The supernatural manifestation of God's wisdom and will for the human race in order to lead humanity to its heavenly destiny. It is entrusted directly to the Church for preservation and interpretation and is contained in Sacred Scripture and sacred tradition.

PUNISHMENT. Any ill suffered in consequence of wrongdoing. It has three functions, which ideally should be retributive as serving the offended person, corrective for the offender, and deterrent for the community at large. Punishment is retributive because it pays back the offender for his or her crime and re-establishes the balance of justice, which has been outraged. It is corrective when directed to improving the offender and rehabilitating him as a member of society. It is deterrent as a means of forestalling similar wrongdoing by others.

Some theorists hold, with Plato, that no one does wrong voluntarily. On these premises, punishment may never be retributive but only corrective or deterrent. Christianity, however, believes that because human beings are free they are responsible for their misdeeds and therefore liable to punishment that gives them their just deserts. It is therefore moral to punish the guilty even if there is no hope of correcting that person or deterring others from crime. (Etym. Latin *poena,* punishment, penalty, pain.)

PUNISHMENT, CAPITAL. Punishment by or involving death, inflicted by legitimate civil authority for crimes regarded as seriously harmful to society. The traditional doctrine of the Church is that capital punishment is not opposed to the divine law, nor is it required by this law as absolutely necessary. The grounds supporting this position are revelation, history, and reason. The Bible regularly attributes to civil authority the right to take the life of a criminal (Genesis 9:6; Exodus 21:22–25; Romans 13:4). Moreover, in all stages of civilization humanity has considered capital punishment in keeping with the moral law. While the *Catechism of the Catholic Church* affirms the traditional Catholic teaching permitting the State to impose capital punishment, it also instructs that capital punishment should be rarely used because other means of protecting society are more in conformity with the dignity of the human person (2267).

PURE ACT. Simple perfection of any kind. Anything that has no imperfection. In the strictest sense, applied to God as *Actus purus,* it is the unqualified perfection of existence, which is neither present in, nor united with, nor limited by any passive potency that could change or improve infinite being.

PURGATIVE WAY. The primary stage in mental prayer, according to the teaching of Sts. Teresa of Avila and John of the Cross. The soul's chief concerns in this stage of perfection are an awareness of its sins, sorrow for the past, and a desire to expiate the offenses against God.

PURGATORY. The place or condition in which the souls of the just are purified after death and before they can enter heaven. They may be purified of the guilt of their venial sins, as in this life, by an act of contrition deriving from charity and performed with the help of grace. This sorrow does not, however, affect the punishment for sins, because in the next world there is no longer any possibility of merit. The souls are certainly purified by atoning for the temporal punishments due to sin by their willing acceptance of suffering imposed by God. The sufferings in purgatory are not the same for all, but proportioned to each person's degree of sinfulness. Moreover, these sufferings can be lessened in duration and intensity through the prayers and good works of the faithful on earth. Nor are the pains incompatible with great peace and joy, since the poor souls deeply love God and are sure they will reach heaven. As members of the Church Suffering, the souls in purgatory can intercede for the persons on earth, who are therefore encouraged to invoke their aid. Purgatory will not continue after the general judgment, but its duration for any particular soul continues until it is free from all guilt and punishment. Immediately on purification the soul is assumed into heaven. (Etym. Latin *purgatio,* cleansing, purifying.)

PURIFICATION. The feast that commemorates the purifying of the Blessed Virgin according to the Mosaic Law, forty days after the birth of Christ. Also called the Feast of the Presentation of Christ in the Temple. The feast was introduced into the Eastern Empire during the reign of Emperor Justinian (527–65) and is mentioned in the Gelasian Sacramentary for the Western Church in the seventh century. Candles are blessed on this day to commemorate Simeon's prophecy about Christ as "a light to enlighten the pagans" (Luke 2:32), and a candlelight procession is held in a church to represent Christ's entry into the Temple of Jerusalem. The popular name is Candlemas Day. See also CANDLEMAS.

PURIFICATOR. A small piece of white linen, marked with a cross in the center, used by the priest in the celebration of Mass. It is folded in three layers and used by the priest to purify his fingers and the chalice and paten after Holy Communion.

PURITY. Freedom from anything that weakens or impairs or changes the nature of a being or its activity. Purity of faith means the absence of error or what is contrary to the revealed truth; purity of intention is the exclusion of self-will in the desire to perform the will of God; purity of conscience is the absence of any sense of guilt in the performance of a moral action; purity of morals commonly refers to the virtue of chastity and therefore freedom from wrongdoing in sexual activity, but on a broader level it means the absence of misbehavior, especially in one's external or publicly recognizable conduct (Etym. Latin *puritas,* clearness, cleanness, uprightness.)

PURITY OF BODY. The state of virginity in the unmarried and of conjugal chastity in those who are married.

PURPOSE OF AMENDMENT. The firm resolution required of a penitent to receive valid absolution in the sacrament of penance. He or she must resolve to avoid, by the grace of God, not only the sins confessed but also the dangerous occasions to sin.

PUTATIVE MARRIAGE. A marriage that is invalid but was contracted in good faith by at least one member. Until there is positive ecclesiastical proof of nullity, such a marriage has all the effects of lawful wedlock. Children of such a marriage are legitimate, and illegitimate children are legitimatized by a putative marriage. (Etym. Latin *putare,* to trim, cleanse; to think over, consider.)

PYX. Any metal box or vessel in which the Blessed Sacrament is kept or carried. The term is more aptly applied to the small round metal case (usually gold-plated) used by a priest to carry a few Hosts on his visitation to the sick. But the larger ciborium is also called a pyx. (Etym. Greek *puxis,* box.)

Q. The symbol of the hypothetical document used by the authors of the first and third Gospels, along with St. Mark, to produce the present Gospels according to Matthew and Luke. The existence of Q is based on the assumption that Mark and not Matthew was the first Gospel and that an unknown document (hence the German *Quelle*, source) must be supposed to account for similarities in Matthew and Luke that are not found in Mark. There are no grounds in historical tradition for the existence of such a source.

QUADRAGESIMO ANNO. The encyclical of Pope Pius XI, dated May 13, 1931, published on the fortieth anniversary of Pope Leo XIII's *Rerum Novarum*. Its theme is a strong condemnation of the control of international finance and credit by a small number of financiers who thus supply "so to speak, the life blood to the entire economic body . . . so that no one can breathe against their will." As a result the State "has become a slave, bound over to the service of human passion and greed."

QUAM SINGULARI. The decree issued August 8, 1910, by the Sacred Congregation of the Sacraments, under the authority of Pope St. Pius X, stating: "The age of discretion, both for Confession and for Holy Communion, is the time when a child begins to reason, that is about the seventh year, more or less. From that time on begins the obligation of fulfilling the precept of both Confession and Communion."

QUID PRO QUO. "Something for something." In moral matters it is either the application of strict justice to a given situation, the giving to someone only what he or she deserves and no more, or the inflicting of a penalty in the exact measure of a crime.

QUIETISM. General name for any view of the spiritual life that minimizes human activity and moral responsibility. But more properly it refers to the theories of Miguel de Molinos (c. 1640–97) and François Fénelon (1651–1715), Archbishop of Cambrai. Its basic position is that, to become perfect, one must be totally passive, annihilate one's will, and so totally abandon oneself to God that one cares for neither heaven nor hell. In prayer, the perfect soul makes no acts of love or petition, nor even of adoration. Such total passivity makes mortification or the sacraments useless. Sin becomes impossible to perfect souls. Quietism was condemned in the person of Molinos by Pope Innocent XI in 1687, and Fénelon by Innocent XII in 1691. (Etym. Latin *quietus,* quiet, at rest, peaceful.)

RACHEL. Daughter of Laban. Isaac was afraid that his son Jacob would marry a Canaanite, so he sent him to live with and work for Laban, his brother-in-law. Jacob fell in love with Rachel and agreed to work for his uncle for seven years in order to marry her. At the end of that time, however, Laban tricked him into marrying Leah, his older daughter (Genesis 29). Jacob had to work for seven more years in order to win Rachel as his second wife. Evidently the ordeal was worth it, for Genesis reports that the additional seven years "seemed to him like a few days, because he loved her so much" (Genesis 29:20). Of all his children Jacob loved Joseph and Benjamin most. They were the two borne by Rachel (Genesis 30:24). She died giving birth to Benjamin (Genesis 35:18), and Jacob erected a tomb in her memory (Genesis 35:20).

RAPE. In ecclesiastical law the crime of forcing a woman, against her will, to have sexual intercourse. Besides the mortal sin against chastity, it is a grave sin against justice to ravish a woman. Rape can be committed by the use of physical or moral force, including fraud and deceit; likewise, in a sin committed with a woman who has not the use of reason, whether mentally deranged or under the influence of drink or drugs. A woman being ravished must offer internal resistance absolutely, in not consenting with the will; and such external resistance as is possible without endangering her life or reputation. (Etym. Latin *rapere,* to seize.)

RASH JUDGMENT. Unquestioning conviction about another person's bad conduct without adequate grounds for the judgment. The sinfulness of rash judgment lies in the hasty imprudence with which the critical appraisal is made and in the loss of reputation that a person suffers in the eyes of the one who judges adversely.

RATIONALISM. A system of thought or attitude of mind which holds that human reason is self-sufficient and does not need the help of divine revelation to know all that is necessary for a person's well-being. Also the view that a priori reasoning can give certitude without experience or verification of facts.

REALISM. Every form of philosophy that recognizes 1. the objective existence of God and the world and their various relationships, independently of human knowledge and desire; 2. that these beings are knowable as they are in themselves; 3. the need for one to conform his or her mind, will, and conduct to this objective reality in order to be happy and attain one's final destiny.

REAL PRESENCE. The manner of Christ's presence in the Holy Eucharist. In its definition on the subject, the Council of Trent in 1551 declared that "in the sacrament of the Holy Eucharist is contained truly, really, and substantially the body and blood, together with the soul and divinity, of our Lord Jesus Christ, and consequently the whole Christ" (Denzinger 1636, 1640). Hence Christ is present truly or actually and not only symbolically. He is present really—that is, objectively—in the Eucharist and not only subjectively in the mind of the believer. And he is present substantially—that is, with all that makes Christ Christ and not only spiritually in imparting blessings on those who receive the sacrament. The one who is present is the whole Christ (*totus Christus*), with all the attributes of his divinity and all the physical parts and properties of his humanity. (Etym. Latin *realis,* of the thing itself; extramental + *prae-esse,* to be at hand, to be immediately efficacious.) See also SACRAMENTAL PRESENCE.

REBAPTISM. The term is inaccurate if taken literally, because baptism imprints an indelible mark on the soul, which means that it cannot, because it need not, be repeated. In the early centuries, Pope St. Stephen insisted with St. Cyprian of Carthage that not even apostasy can eradicate the sacramental character conferred in baptism. See also ABJURATION.

REBEKAH. Daughter of Bethuel and sister of Laban. Abraham did not want his son Isaac to marry a Canaanite, so he sent a trusted servant to the land of his kinfolk to choose a suitable wife. The servant prayed to YHWH for guidance, and Rebekah proved to be the maid who met YHWH's specifications. Rebekah's family rejoiced at the selection, and she willingly returned with the servant and married Isaac (Genesis 24). In time she bore two sons, Esau and Jacob (Genesis 25:24–28). Jacob was her favorite. When the aged, blind Isaac prepared to give his blessing (which involved rights of inheritance) to Esau, Rebekah and Jacob conspired to deceive Isaac into blessing the son she favored (Genesis 27). Then, to frustrate Esau's determination to kill his brother, Rebekah prevailed on Isaac to send Jacob off to her brother's homeland (Genesis 28:1–5). This strategy paved the way for Jacob's marriage to Leah and Rachel, Laban's daughters (Genesis 29). Rebekah and Isaac were buried in Canaan in the same field with Abraham and Sarah (Genesis 49:29–31).

RECOLLECTION. Concentration of the soul on the presence of God. It calls for considerable mental discipline to avoid dissipation of mind but is required of all who aspire after Christian perfection.

RECONCILIATION. The act or state of re-establishing friendship between God and a human being, or between two persons. Reconciliation with God is necessary after a person has lost the divine friendship through grievous sin. It requires repentance on the part of the sinner and forgiveness on the part of God. The willingness to be reconciled with another person is a necessary condition for obtaining God's mercy.

REDEMPTION. The salvation of humanity by Jesus Christ. Literally, to redeem means to free or buy back. Humanity was held captive in that it was enslaved by sin. Since the devil overcame human beings by inducing them to sin, they were said to be in bondage to the devil. Moreover, the human race was held captive as to a debt of punishment, to the payment of which it was bound by divine justice.

On all these counts, the Passion of Christ was sufficient and superabundant satisfaction for human guilt and the consequent debt of punishment. His Passion was a kind of price or ransom that paid the cost of freeing humanity from both obligations. Christ rendered satisfaction not by giving money but by spending what was of the highest value. He gave himself, and therefore his Passion is called humanity's redemption. (Etym. Latin *redemptio*, a buying back, ransoming, redemption.)

REDEMPTORISTS. Members of the Congregation of the Most Holy Redeemer, founded by St. Alphonso Maria de' Liguori at Scala, Italy, in 1732. They form a clerical religious congregation engaged in the preaching and writing apostolate among the faithful, in giving parish missions and spiritual exercises, and in missionary work among non-Christians.

REFORM. Change with a view to improvement. By her nature as a living organism, the Catholic Church has undertaken numerous reforms in her long history. These have been mainly concerned with the moral and spiritual life of the faithful, by the use of the elaborate legislative, administrative, and ritual means at the Church's disposal. The term "reform" occurs in the first paragraph of the first document issued by the Second Vatican Council in its Constitution on the Sacred Liturgy. And the desire "to impart an ever-increasing vigor to the Christian life of the faithful" (Introduction) runs as a theme through all the conciliar teaching and the postconciliar directives of the Holy See.

REFORMATION. A religious, social, and political upheaval (1517–1648) that divided Western Christendom and created world Protestantism. Its causes were manifold: weakening of papal authority through long residence in France and the worldliness of some popes; disloyalty to Rome of many bishops who were really temporal rulers; excessive reservation of ecclesiastical appointments to the Roman Curia; intellectual and moral unfitness of many priests; the wealth of some of the monasteries and dissension in their ranks; superstition and ignorance among the laity; social unrest brought on by the disintegration of the feudal system; support given by political power to dissenters in the Church; unrest and secularism brought on by the new geographical discoveries; and the use of the printing press to propagate the new views. The effects of the Reformation have been far-reaching: Christian unity was shattered, personal liberty in religion affected every sphere of human activity, with the rise of the modern secular state, of capitalism as rugged individualism, and with the loss of the cultural solidarity, founded on a common faith, that had shaped Western civilization for almost a millennium.

REFORMATION DOGMA. The dogmatic teaching of the original Protestant reformers. They were constrained by the logic of separating from Rome to defend their new doctrinal positions. Thus we find Luther writing numerous treatises on faith, grace, and justification, and John Calvin (1509–64) producing in 1536 his *Institutes of the Christian Religion,* as the first systematic compendium of Protestant doctrine. "My design in this work," wrote Calvin in the introduction, "has been to prepare and qualify students of theology for the reading of the divine word." The beginnings of the Reformation were thoroughly dogmatic in character. The earliest Reformation dogma was biblical in the direct sense. It did not take philosophy as a basis or ally. Its first business was to know and expound the Bible. It did not claim

Aristotle and Plato as friends or forerunners. It used reason, but reason derived only from the Bible and put to a biblical use. Actually there was a philosophy behind this dogmatizing, notably the nominalism of William of Ockham (1280–1349), whom Luther called "my teacher" and rated in learning far above Thomas Aquinas.

Two strains in Ockham, sometimes called "the first Protestant," became imbedded in the Reformation: a distrust of reason in dealing with religion, and a theory of voluntarism that made right and wrong depend on the will of God. The first strain appeared prominently in Lutheran or evangelical thought, with the emphasis on revelation and grace as the exclusive media of religious knowledge and salvation. The second affected Calvinism and postulated, in Calvin's words, that "God chooses some for the hope of life, and condemns others to eternal death. . . . For all men are not created on an equal footing, but for some eternal life is preordained, for others eternal damnation." The divine will, therefore, and not as in Catholic doctrine the divine wisdom, is the ultimate norm of man's existence and destiny.

"REGINA COELI." Easter anthem, of unknown authorship, dating from the twelfth century. It has been part of the Liturgy of the Hours, to be said during the Easter season at Compline. It takes the place of the Angelus in Eastertide. The prayer reads:

> O Queen of heaven, rejoice Alleluia.
> For He whom you did merit to bear, Alleluia.
> Has risen as He said, Alleluia.
> Pray for us to God, Alleluia.
> Rejoice and be glad, O Virgin Mary, Alleluia.
> For the Lord has truly risen, Alleluia.
> Let us pray: O God, who by the resurrection of Your Son, our Lord Jesus Christ, have been pleased to fill the world with joy, grant, we beseech You, that through the intercession of the Virgin Mary, His Mother, we may receive the joys of eternal life, through the same Christ our Lord. Amen.

See also ANGELUS.

RELATIVISM. In philosophy, the view that there is no absolute truth or certitude. It is claimed that truth depends entirely on variable factors, such as person, place, time, and circumstances. Moral relativism holds that there are no unchangeable principles of human behavior, either because all truth is relative or because there are no inherently evil actions, since everything depends on other factors, such as customs, conventions, or social approval.

RELIC. An object connected with a saint, e.g., part of the body or clothing or something the person had used or touched. Authentic relics are venerated with the Church's warm approbation. They may not be bought or sold. Those of a martyr are placed in the altar stone at the consecration of an altar. Relics are of three classes: the first is part of the saint's body and is the type placed in the altar stone; the second is part of the clothing or anything used during the saint's life; and the third is any other object, such as a piece of cloth, that has been touched to a first-class relic. (Etym. Latin *reliquiae*, remains.)

RELIGION. The moral virtue by which a person is disposed to render to God the worship and service he deserves. It is sometimes identified with the virtue of justice toward God, whose rights are rooted in his complete dominion over all creation. Religion is also a composite of all the virtues that arise from a human being's relationship to God as the author of his or her being, even as love is a cluster of all the virtues arising from human response to God as the destiny of his or her being. Religion thus corresponds to the practice of piety toward God as Creator of the universe. (Etym. probably Latin *religare*, to tie, fasten, bind; or *relegere*, to gather up, treat with care.)

RELIGION AS FEELING. The view that Christianity is essentially a religion of feeling. It was systematically developed by Friedrich Schleiermacher (1768–1834) in his *Christian Faith*. While rationalists and supernaturalists carried on their struggle, Schleiermacher took the ground from under their contention by removing its main presupposition. The Christian faith, he said, does not consist in any kind of doctrinal propositions. It is a condition of devout feeling and, like all other experience, simply an object to be described. Against the supernaturalists he maintained that Christianity is not something to be received on authority from without but an inward condition of our own self-consciousness. Against the rationalists, he said that religion is not a product of rational thinking but an emotion of the heart, a feeling that occurs independently of the mind. Moreover, this feeling is not merely personal but social in its Protestant form, since it is the common experience of a historical community derived from the Reformation.

RELIGIOUS INDIFFERENCE. The attitude that all religions are equally good and equally capable of leading a person to his or her eternal destiny. In its most extreme form, the theory that there is no one form of religious belief, divine worship, or moral behavior that has been revealed by God.

RELIGIOUS RULE. The plan of life and discipline, approved by the Holy See, under which religious live in order to grow in Christian perfection and perform the works of the apostolate proper to their institute.

REMARRIAGE. In general, the repetition of marriage while a married partner is still living. In the Old Testament remarriage was permitted, but, as Christ explained to the Pharisees, "It was because you were so unteachable that Moses allowed you to divorce your wives, but it was not like this from the beginning" (Matthew 19:8). Christ restored marriage to its former monogamous state and, to provide the necessary grace, raised it to the dignity of a sacrament. A valid sacramental marriage is not dissoluble by any human power, civil or ecclesiastical. Instances of remarriage, therefore, are either cases where the previous marriage was not a sacrament, or the original marriage was not valid, or the partners had not consummated their marriage by natural intercourse.

REMISSION OF SIN. The true and actual forgiveness of sin. When mortal sin is remitted, this includes pardon of the eternal punishment due to it, but temporal penalty may still remain. When venial sin is remitted, the guilt is removed and as much of the temporal punishment as the person's dispositions warrant from the grace of God.

REMOTE OCCASIONS. Situations that can but will not likely lead a person into sin. They may be either circumstances in which sin for any ordinary person is possible but not at all probable, or circumstances in which the person has shown that he or she does not sin as a rule. Remote occasions exist everywhere.

RENEWAL. Renovation in the sense of restoring a practice, custom, or institution to its original meaning or purpose. Used by the Second Vatican Council especially of the spiritual renewal of religious communities, by a return to their Gospel foundations, the charisms of their founders, and the sacred traditions of their history.

RENOUNCING SATAN. Profession of allegiance to Christ and renunciation of the devil as the enemy of Christ, made at baptism by the person being baptized or by the sponsor. It implies the resolution to resist the devil's attempts to seduce the followers of Christ, to live in humility (contrary to Satan's pride), in obedience (contrary to Satan's disobedience), and in holiness (contrary to Satan's total estrangement from God).

RENUNCIATION. To give up something to which a person has a claim. Some renunciations are necessary by divine law; others are permitted and encouraged according to divine counsel. Everyone must renounce sin and those creatures that are proximate occasions to sin. In this category belongs the renunciation of Satan at baptism, either by the person being baptized or by the sponsor. Renunciations of counsel pertain to the exercise of such natural rights as material possessions, marriage, and legitimate autonomy or self-determination, sacrificed for love of God by those who vow themselves to poverty, chastity, and obedience.

REPARATION. The act or fact of making amends. It implies an attempt to restore things to their normal or sound conditions, as they were before something wrong was done. It applies mainly to recompense for the losses sustained or the harm caused by some morally bad action. With respect to God, it means making up with greater love for the failure in love through sin; it means restoring what was unjustly taken and compensating with generosity for the selfishness that caused the injury. (Etym. Latin *reparare,* to prepare anew, restore.)

REPENTANCE. Voluntary sorrow because it offends God, for having done something wrong, together with the resolve to amend one's conduct by taking the necessary means to avoid the occasions of sin. To repent is to be sorry for sin with self-condemnation. (Etym. Latin *repoenitere,* to be very sorry, regret intensely.)

REPROBATION. God's eternal resolve to exclude certain rational creatures from eternal happiness. As taught by the Church, God has eternally predestined certain persons, on account of their sins, to rejection from heaven. Always understood is that God wants all human beings to be saved, but he does not wish to save those who, by their abuse of divine grace, freely separate themselves from his love. (Etym. Latin *reprobare,* to reject, condemn.)

REQUIEM. A Mass celebrated for the dead. The name is derived from the first word of the opening hymn in the Latin Rite (Extraordinary Form) Mass. The invocation says, *"Requiem aeternam dona eis, Domine"* (Eternal rest give unto them, O Lord). (Etym. Latin *requies,* rest after labor, relaxation.)

RERUM NOVARUM. Encyclical of Pope Leo XIII, issued on May 15, 1891, on the condition of labor. It refutes the theories of the socialists and defends the rights of private ownership. It advises employers and workers to organize into both mixed and separate associations for mutual help and self-protection.

RESIGNATION. The acceptance of God's will in all circumstances of life, and especially during heavy trial or suffering. Also called abandonment, it has as its object the submission of one's own preferences or hopes to the dispositions of Providence. In canon law, resignation is the voluntary withdrawal of a person duly elected or appointed to an ecclesiastical office. In order to be valid, the resignation must be accepted by an authorized person or body in the Church.

RESISTING AGGRESSION. The right to use force against an unjust aggressor. This right is present when certain conditions are fulfilled, namely: 1. recourse to civil authority would be impossible. The common good demands that as a rule the State alone uses physical compulsion, for if any private citizen could at will employ force in defending his or her rights, the peace and order of the community would be disturbed; 2. the attack must be actual or immediately imminent; it is wrong to use deadly weapons before the attack, since there is grave danger that such force might be used against an innocent person; nor is it permissible to use such weapons after the attack is over, for then the defense is too late and the act of possible killing would constitute revenge; 3. the attack must be unjust, which really means that it is not provoked; aggression, therefore, is not justified; 4. the force employed must be proportionate to the loss threatened and must not exceed what is necessary; killing is not allowed if wounding would be sufficient for proper defense; wounding is not permitted if disarming the adversary or summoning help would be enough.

RESOLUTION OF AMENDMENT. The firm and sincere decision that a penitent makes to avoid the sins that person is confessing in the sacrament of penance. A true purpose of amendment includes the determination to avoid at least all grievous sins, the near occasions of them, to use the necessary means to amendment, to make due satisfaction for the sins committed, and to be ready to make restitution or repair whatever injury may have been done to others.

RESPONSORIAL PSALM. Antiphonal Psalm that is said or read before the Gospel at Mass. Normally the Psalm is taken from the Lectionary and has some bearing on the particular text from Scripture. After the second reading and before the Gospel the Alleluia is either sung or read, followed by its appropriate verse. If the Alleluia or the verse before the Gospel is not sung, it may be omitted. Except on Easter Sunday and Whitsunday, the sequences (special festive hymns) are optional.

RESTITUTION. Returning to its rightful owner whatever had been unjustly taken from that person. Restitution means the return to an individual of possession or dominion over something rightly owned by that person. Since dominion over certain things cannot be restored, restitution in general means making reparation for a wrong done, whether by returning what had been taken or by some other form of compensation. In this moral sense, restitution belongs to commutative justice (between person and person), whereby one restores to the rightful owner something unjustly taken or repairs damage unjustly caused. Restitution is binding in conscience because a person who does not make restitution, though able to do so, actually continues the theft or injury by depriving others of a good that belongs to them. The common good also requires restitution, since otherwise society would disintegrate if theft could be committed or injury caused with impunity. Moreover, no sin can be pardoned without sincere contrition and a firm purpose of amendment. Both elements are implied in the willingness to make restitution. (Etym. Latin *restitutio*, restoration.)

RESTORATION. The duty to give back or make up for what a person has that does not belong to him or her. It differs from restitution, which implies stealing or unjust acquisition. If something is bought rightfully from an unjust possessor, it must be returned to the rightful owner, but the buyer should be reimbursed for the price paid unless the goods were bought at a suspicious price or under dubious circumstances. Restoration is to be made to the one who suffered the damage. If one is dead, it is due to one's heirs. What must be restored is either what was borrowed or obtained or its equivalent value. And if the object was kept in bad faith, the restoration should include also the fruits accrued from the unjust possession. The obligation to restore is suspended when the one who has borrowed has a physical or moral incapacity that makes repayment impossible. But if one is able to repay gradually, one is held to the obligation, as far as it is possible to make repayment without grave injury to others who depend on him or her for their support. Among the reasons that may cancel the duty altogether are voluntary remission on the part of one who has a right to dispose of one's own goods or a decision of the civil or ecclesiastical authorities.

RESURRECTION, BODILY. The universal return to life of all human beings, to occur soon before the last judgment by God's almighty power. Each individual soul will be reunited with the selfsame body with which it was united on earth. While all the dead will rise, only the just will have their bodies glorified.

RESURRECTION OF CHRIST. The rising from the dead of Christ on the third day after his death and burial. Christ's Resurrection is a basic truth of Christianity, which is expressed in all the Creeds and in all rules of faith of the ancient Church. He rose through his own power. The source of his Resurrection was the hypostatic union. The principal cause was the Word of God, together with the Father and the Holy Spirit; the instrumental cause was the parts of Christ's humanity, soul, and body, which were hypostatically united with the Godhead. When Scripture asserts (Acts 2:24; Galatians 1:1) that Christ was raised by God or by the Father, these statements are to be understood as referring to his humanity. All forms of rationalism in ancient and modern times—deceit hypothesis, apparent death hypothesis, vision hypothesis, symbolism hypothesis—deny Christ's Resurrection. Yet nothing is more central in the faith as attested by Peter's sermon on Pentecost and as defended ever since by the Church's most solemn teaching authority.

The body of the risen Christ was in a state of glory, as is evident from circumstances of the appearances recorded in the Gospels and Acts, and from Christ's supremacy over the limitations of space and time. The risen Christ retained the wounds in his transfigured body as tokens of his triumph over death (John 20:27).

Theologically the Resurrection, unlike the death of Christ, is not the meritorious cause of human redemption. It is the victorious completion of redemption. It belongs to the perfection of redemption and is therefore associated in the Scriptures with Christ's death on the Cross as one complete whole. It is the model and, in the person of the risen Christ, the channel of grace for our spiritual redemption from sin and for our bodily resurrection on the Last Day.

RETREAT. Withdrawal for a period of time from one's usual surroundings and occupation to a place of solitude for meditation, self-examination, and prayer, in order to make certain necessary decisions in one's spiritual life. Although the practice is older than Christianity, the example of Christ's forty days in the desert makes such retreats part of divine revelation, to be imitated, as far as possible, by his followers. As a formal devotion among all classes of the faithful, retreats were introduced with the Counter-Reformation, led by St. Ignatius of Loyola, and followed by St. Francis de Sales and St. Vincent de Paul. Retreats for a specified number of days are required of all priests and religious. "We desire," wrote Pope Pius XI, "that retreat houses, where persons withdraw for a month, or for eight days, or for fewer, to put themselves into training for the perfect Christian life, may come into being and flourish everywhere more numerously" (*Constitution Declaring St. Ignatius Patron of All Spiritual Exercises*, July 25, 1922).

REVEALED LAW. Also called divine positive law, it is the sum total of all the prescriptions that God has communicated to the human race by way of supernatural revelation. It is, therefore, revealed law as distinct from the knowledge of God's will attainable by human reason alone.

Humankind needs a revealed law in addition to the divine natural law because the secondary precepts of the natural law can be obscured by evil passion, bad custom, and the allurement of sinful example. Another and higher reason why God revealed his will supernaturally is that he has elevated human nature to a higher-than-natural destiny. This heavenly destiny cannot be attained without the observance of correspondingly supernatural laws, which are in the character of divine graces with which human beings must cooperate in order to reach the beatific vision.

Three periods may be distinguished in the history of God's revealed will: from the dawn of creation to the time of Moses; the Mosaic period, which spans the whole history of ancient Israel; and in New Testament time from the coming of Christ to the end of the apostolic age.

REVEALING SECRETS. Circumstances under which secrets may be revealed. A reasonable cause for revealing a secret is the urgent necessity of either the public or private good. In such necessity it would be reasonable to presume consent to the revelation of a secret. Since the public good takes precedence over the good of the individual, there are times when the latter's secret should be sacrificed for the good of society. The good of the individual that warrants disclosing a secret may refer either to the one who knows the secret, or someone who benefits from keeping the matter secret, or some third party. Where there exists a real need, it is permissible to reveal a secret for the benefit of any of these three persons. Confessional secrets, however, come under the seal of confession and may never be revealed.

REVELATION. Disclosure by God of himself and his will to the human race. The disclosure comes to human beings by way of communication, which implies the communicator, who is God; the receiver, who is the human being; and a transmitter or intermediary. Depending on the intermediary, there are in general two main forms of revelation, commonly called natural and supernatural.

If the intermediary is the world of space and time, the revelation is said to be natural. In this case, the natural world of creation is the medium through which God communicates himself to humankind. Moreover, humanity's natural use of reason is the means by which it attains the knowledge that God wishes to communicate. It is therefore natural twice over, once in the objective source from which human beings derive knowledge of God and divine things, and once again in the subjective powers that a person uses to appropriate what God is revealing in the universe into which humanity has been placed. In the Old Testament those are said to be "naturally stupid" who have "not known God and who, from the things that are seen, have not been able to discover Him-who-is or, by studying the works, have failed to recognize the Artificer" (Wisdom 13:1). And St. Paul affirmed: "Ever since God created the world his everlasting power and deity—however invisible—have been there for the mind to see in the things he has made" (Romans 1:20).

Supernatural revelation begins where natural revelation ends. It is in the character of a grace from God, who has decided to communicate himself in a manner that far exceeds his manifestation through nature. The Scriptures call this form of communication a divine speech and refer to God as speaking to humankind. There are two levels of this supernatural revelation, as capsulized by the author of Hebrews: "At various times in the past and in various ways, God spoke to our ancestors through the prophets; but in our own time, the last days, he has spoken to us through his Son, the Son that he has appointed to inherit everything and through whom he made everything there is. He is the radiant light of God's glory and the perfect copy of his nature" (Hebrews 1:1–2).

The difference between these two kinds of supernatural communication lies in the fact that, before Christ, God spoke indeed but still indirectly through the prophets who were inspired to tell others what YHWH had told them. In the person of Christ, however, it was no longer God speaking merely through human seers chosen by him; it was God himself speaking as man to his fellow members of the human race. (Etym. Latin *revelatio*, an uncovering; revelation.)

REVENGE. The act or intention of inflicting injury on someone, on one's own authority, to repay an offense committed. It is a manifestation of unjustifiable anger and is one of the most common human failings that takes on a variety of forms, from a momentary silence or frown to defamation of character or physical violence. As a form of sinful anger, it is an unruly desire for vengeance. The desire is immoderate if a person wants the undeserving to be punished, or the guilty to be punished excessively, or the punishment to be meted out in an unlawful manner or in order to vent one's own spite.

REVERENCE. The virtue that inclines a person to show honor and respect for persons who possess some dignity. There are four forms of reverence, corresponding to four forms of dignity: 1. familial reverence toward one's parents or those who take the place of parents; 2. civil reverence toward persons holding civil authority; 3. ecclesiastical reverence toward the pope, bishops, priests, and others in the service of the Church; 4. religious reverence toward any person, place, or object related to God. (Etym. Latin *reverentia*, awe, respect.)

REWARD. Something given in return for performing an action that either could have been left undone or at least might not have been done as well as it was. In theology the merit promised by God is a reward because the human being is physically free either to resist or cooperate with divine grace.

RIGHT. Either opposite to wrong (adjective) or that which is just (noun). In the first sense, right means that which squares with the norm of morality, and so is morally good. In the second sense, right means that which is correlative to duty. As a noun, therefore, right is opposed to might, although both are means to achieve an end. Might is physical power, either as one's own bodily strength or as the physical (and psychological) instruments under a person's command. Physical power accomplishes its purpose by sheer force, which is indifferent to the claims of justice and can be used to help or hinder the observance of the moral law. Might becomes good or evil according to the will that directs it.

Right is moral power and works by appeal to another's will through that person's intellect. It is the moral power to do, hold, or exact something. To *do* here is to be understood both affirmatively and negatively; it means either to perform or omit an action, as a person may have the right to keep silent as well as to speak. To *hold* means to own, keep, or use something, and includes metaphorical meanings, such as to hold an office or job. To *exact* means to demand that someone else perform or omit some action, such as the state requires payment of taxes or a teacher exacts attention from his or her pupils. Right is consequently a subjective moral power that resides in the subject or person possessing it. By a figure of speech, the word "right" may also be applied to the thing over which one has a moral power. Thus we may say that one has been deprived of certain rights, meaning some object that rightfully belongs to him or her. (Etym. Anglo-Saxon *riht,* right; Latin *rectus,* right: straight, upright, conformed to some measure, just, true.)

RIGHTEOUS ANGER. Justifiable indignation. It is permissible and even laudable when accompanied by a reasonable desire to inflict justifiable punishment. Christ himself was filled with righteous anger against the vendors who had desecrated the house of God. Such anger is allowable only if it tends to punish those who deserve punishment, according to the measure of their guilt, and with the sincere intention to redress what harm may have been done or to correct the wrongdoer. Otherwise the anger is sinfully excessive. The necessary provision is always that there is no tinge of hatred and no desire for revenge.

RIGHT TO LIFE MOVEMENT. Organized effort in countries where direct abortion has been legalized. The movement takes on different forms in different places, from the strictly political efforts to change the existing laws of a nation that permit killing the unborn, to the exclusively spiritual promotion of crusades of prayer and penance to obtain divine assistance. The movement is not only Catholic, nor only Christian, although the Catholic Church is outstanding in her defense of the right to life of the unborn child. In the words of Blessed Pope John Paul II, "We can speak of the rights of the child from the moment of conception, and particularly of the right to life" (Address on the Rights of the Child, January 13, 1979).

RIGIDITY. A moral trait characterized by an unwillingness, or inability, to change one's attitudes or way of acting. Great difficulty in adjusting to socially justifiable change. (Etym. Latin *rigidus,* stiff, austere, rigid.)

RITE. In general, the manner and form of a religious function. Hence the words and actions to be carried out in the performance of a given act, e.g., the rite of baptism, the rite of consecration, the Roman Rite. The term in its widest ecclesiastical sense refers to the principal historic rituals in the Catholic Church, whose essentials are the same as derived from Jesus Christ. The four parent rites in Catholicism are the Antiochene, Alexandrine, Roman, and Gallican. Some religious orders have their own rites. In all cases, however, the ritual must be approved by the Holy See. (Etym. Latin *ritus,* religious custom, usage, ceremony.)

RITE OF EXORCISM. A sacramental by which a duly appointed person, generally a priest, is authorized to use the special power he receives to drive out an evil spirit. Until recently this power had been conferred in the minor order of exorcist. Nevertheless the power could not be used except by a priest who had received the special and express permission from ecclesiastical authority. The Church, in her directives to exorcists, warns them not to be too ready to assume that there is diabolical possession, since there are so many cases of hysteria or other kinds of emotional disorder that may seem to be "possession." Moreover, explicit directives are given on how to deal with ostensibly possessed persons, notably to exercise great care not to be either deceived or intimidated by the evil spirit.

Over the centuries the rite of exorcism has been long and detailed, with a variety of ritual forms, numerous signs of the cross, recitation of Psalms and the Athanasian Creed, prayers to St. Michael, use of holy water, and periodic adjurations. Among other formulas, the priest declares, "I adjure you, ancient serpent, by the Judge of the living and the dead, by your Creator, and the Creator of the world, by Him who has power to send you to hell. Depart immediately with fear and with your army of terror. Depart from this servant of God [name], who takes refuge in the bosom of the Church."

Private exorcism, which is the private adjuring of the devil from harming someone, may be performed by any priest and also by a layperson; for example, by the use of sacramentals such as holy water or by invoking the name of Jesus.

ROMAN CANON. The first Eucharistic prayer of the Mass, dating, with very slight changes, from the sixth century. It is based on the Gelasian Sacramentary, ascribed to Pope Gelasius I (r. 492–96).

ROMAN CATACOMBS. A labyrinth of subterranean galleries where the early Christians buried their dead and held religious services. In times of persecution, besides a place to worship, they offered escape and concealment. Begun in apostolic times, they continued in use until A.D. 400. At that time there were twenty-five great catacombs and twenty lesser ones. Like all cemeteries, they were constructed from the first to the third mile outside Rome. The Christians made long recesses in the walls, not small niches for cinerary urns as did the non-Christians, to hold one to three bodies each. When filled they were hermetically sealed, and often the covering slab contained inscriptions or was decorated with various symbols, e.g., the Good Shepherd, dove, anchor, fish, and peacock. These were the first representations of Christian art. The space allotted to a burial was necessarily limited. Larger tombs were only for popes and martyrs. After 313 the catacombs were not really needed, but they remained places of pilgrimage until the seventh century. About this time the demand for relics grew, and quantities of bones were taken from the catacombs to individual churches. The Church finally stopped the universal confiscation of relics. It was reported that twenty-eight cartloads were taken to the Pantheon from the catacombs for burial in the new St. Mary of the Martyrs. The old catacombs became overgrown and soon forgotten except the one under St. Sebastian's Church. In the sixteenth century interest revived, and the search for other catacombs began. Today the Catacombs of Sebastian and Callistus are the most visited, with those of Sts. Domitilla, Agnes, Priscilla, and Pancratius also open to the public. The chief services in the catacombs were the Eucharistic celebration on the anniversaries of the martyrs. The inscriptions on the tomb slabs are among the earliest witnesses to the Christian faith. The 1929 concordat with Italy places the Holy See in charge of the catacombs, with responsibility for their maintenance, supervision, preservation, and expansion.

ROMAN CATHOLICISM. The faith, worship, and practice of all Christians in communion with the Bishop of Rome, whom they acknowledge as the Vicar of Christ and the visible head of the Church founded by Christ. The terms "Roman Church" and "Roman Catholic Church" date from at least the early Middle Ages, but the stress on these terms became prominent after the Protestant Reformation. The reason was to emphasize the distinctive quality of being not only a Christian, because baptized, but of being a Catholic, because in communion with the pope.

ROMAN PRIMACY. The supreme and full power of jurisdiction possessed by divine right by the Bishop of Rome over the whole Church in matters of faith and in matters pertaining to the discipline and government of the Church spread throughout the world. This power is not merely symbolic but real and truly episcopal; it is ordinary in belonging to the office; it is immediate and not dependent on any other human authority; and it affects each and every church, each and every pastor, and every single one of the faithful.

ROMAN RITE. The manner of celebrating Mass, administering the sacraments and sacramentals, reciting the Divine Office, and performing other ecclesiastical functions, as authorized for the city and diocese of Rome. Its origin goes back to the more or less common but variable rite of the first three centuries. From the time of Pope St. Gregory the Great (r. 590–604) the history was uniform, with four major stages of development. In the twelfth century the Roman Rite came to be used wherever Latin was used. During the Middle Ages it branched out into a great number of other rites, differing however only in unimportant details. In the sixteenth century (1570) Pope St. Pius V abolished most of these derived rites, but the Roman Rite by then had been deeply influenced by and received additions from the Gallican and Spanish rites. In the twentieth century, as a result of the Second Vatican Council, major revisions were again made. Yet, as Pope Paul VI declared, these revisions are not to contradict the Roman Rite, since "what is Roman is the foundation of our Catholicity" (Allocution *Facile Conicere*, October 14, 1968).

ROMAN ROTA. Originating as an extension of the Apostolic Chancery, it is essentially a tribunal of appeal for all the ecclesiastical cases in which the Roman Curia is competent and that are not reserved to other jurisdictions. It also receives cases of appeal for Vatican City State and is a tribunal of first instance in cases reserved to the Holy See, or cases that the pope has reserved for himself by means of a special rescript of the Apostolic Signature.

ROMANS, EPISTLE TO THE. Written by St. Paul at Corinth about A.D. 58, when he was about to leave for Jerusalem at the end of his third missionary journey. He was on his way to Rome. It is the only Pauline letter addressed to a church that the apostle had not personally founded, preparing the people for his visit to them. He dwells on the justification of humankind through faith in Jesus Christ, the sinfulness of the world, the meaning and fruits of justification, what faith is, and that its fruits are humility, obedience, unity, and charity. Christ, the second Adam, has more than compensated for the sin of the first Adam.

ROMAN SEE. The primatial see of Christendom, the seat of government of the universal Roman Catholic Church, the papacy, the Apostolic See, the office of the supreme head of the Church. It was founded by St. Peter, the first pope, in A.D. 42 and constitutes the historical foundation of the claim of the Bishops of Rome to Peter's primacy. It was disputed by some on the ground that St. Peter never was in Rome, but it is now fully established that he was in Rome by archaeological discoveries. During the first century the Corinthian Church appealed to the Roman See to heal a schism and St. Ignatius of Antioch (d. A.D. 107) gratefully received instructions from the Roman Church. The bishops of the Roman See alone could summon councils, excommunicate from the Church, judge concerning Christian life and doctrine, and discipline offenders. In times of stress and difficulties as well as for decisions on faith and government, the first Christians regularly appealed to Rome. The Greek schismatics and the Protestants both challenged the authority of the Roman See, but by that time the unbroken succession of Bishops of Rome had established the foundations of Catholic faith and morality. Agreement with the Roman See was a test of orthodoxy according to the Fathers of the Church, e.g., St. Irenaeus (A.D. 180). Even when, during the Western Schism, the popes moved to Avignon, they were still Bishops of Rome, so that by the time of the Second Vatican Council, Pope Paul VI closed the council as the 264th bishop to rule the Roman See. Within the See's territorial limits are located the commissions, offices, and congregations that administer the affairs of the universal Church.

ROME. The diocese of the pope, also called the See of Peter, the Apostolic See, the Holy See, and the Eternal City. According to ancient tradition, St. Peter first came to Rome in A.D. 42; St. Paul arrived about A.D. 60. Both were martyred here under Nero, most probably in 64. The history of the city from that time to the present can be divided into several periods: 1. the age of persecution to the Edict of Milan in 313; 2. freedom recognized by the empire and the building of the first churches to the fall, in 476, of the Roman Empire in the West; 3. the growing power of political rulers, in conflict with the papacy, to the coronation in 800 of Charlemagne as emperor by Pope Leo III; 4. consolidation of the Papal States, irreparably damaged by the Avignon residence of the popes, 1309–77; 5. after the Western Schism to the Reformation; 6. from the Reformation to the loss of the Papal States in 1870, until the Lateran Treaty in 1929; and 7. since the settling of the Roman Question to the present.

ROSARY. A devotional prayer, mental and vocal, honoring the Blessed Mother of God. It is said on a string of beads made up of five sets each of one large and ten smaller beads, called decades. On the large beads the Pater Noster (Our Father) is said; on the small ones, the Ave Maria (Hail Mary). The usual devotion is the twenty decades, on the joyous, sorrowful, luminous, and glorious aspects of Our Lord and Our Lady's lives. It is the most popular of all nonliturgical Catholic devotions and has been highly recommended by many popes. This is the standard Rosary. But there are other Rosaries also approved by the Church, notably of the Holy Trinity, Seven Dolors, Precious Blood, St. Bridget, St. Joseph, and the Rosary of the Lord. (Etym. Latin *rosarium*, rose garden.) See also GLORIOUS MYSTERIES, JOYFUL MYSTERIES, LUMINOUS MYSTERIES, SORROWFUL MYSTERIES.

RUBRICS. Originally red titles of law announcements. They are the directive precepts or liturgical provisions found in the Missal, including the Sacramentary and Lectionary, and in the ritual, to guide bishops, priests, or deacons in the Eucharistic liturgy, the administration of sacraments and sacramentals, and the preaching of the Word of God. Rubrics are printed in red and are either obligatory or merely directive, as the context makes amply clear. (Etym. Latin *rubrica,* red earth; title of law written in red; hence law instruction.)

RULE. A principle or regular mode of action, prescribed by one in authority, for the well-being of those who are members of a society. It is in this sense that the organized methods of living the evangelical counsels are called rules, as the Rule of St. Augustine or St. Benedict. A rule may also be a customary standard that is not necessarily prescribed by authority but voluntarily undertaken in order to regulate one's conduct for more effective moral living or more effective service of others. Finally rule may be distinguished from government, whether civil or ecclesiastical. Rule pertains to the possession or exercise of controlling power, whereas government refers more to actually causing another to obey one's will. (Etym. Latin *regula,* a rule; norm; measure.)

RULE OF FAITH. The norm that enables the faithful to know what to believe. The revealed Word of God in Sacred Scripture and sacred tradition is a remote rule of faith. But the teaching of the Church based on divine revelation is considered the immediate rule of faith.

RULES OF CONSCIENCE. Norms for deciding one's own course of action or advising others in following conscience. Three norms are standard in Catholic moral theology:

1. "We are obliged to use every care to have a true conscience when faced with moral decisions." Conscience is the immediate norm of morality by which a person is to guide his or her whole life and reach eternal destiny. It is imperative that this norm be suitably trained to meet the variety of circumstances that call for moral evaluation. Sound knowledge of the divine and ecclesiastical laws is primary, wise counsel should be readily available, humility of heart and sincere sorrow are necessary to remove the chief obstacles to a true conscience, namely pride and unrepentant sin. Frequent prayer is needed to obtain the light of God's grace.

2. "We must always act on the command of a certain conscience whether it commands or forbids some action, not only when it is true but also when it is in invincible error." The words "commands" and

"forbids" need emphasis, because if conscience permits or merely counsels some line of action there is no strict obligation to follow it. It is obvious why a true conscience must be followed. But even an invincibly erroneous conscience should be obeyed, because failure to do so would mean that a person was acting contrary to the subjective norm of morality and therefore committing sin. Thus a person who is convinced that he or she ought to steal or tell lies in order to save a friend from grave danger is bound to do so. The critical term is "invincible ignorance," which means a lack of knowledge for which the person is not morally responsible. It would be vincible (removable) ignorance if it could have been removed by such reasonable care as a prudent and sincere person would use in similar circumstances.

3. "It is never permissible to act with a doubtful conscience." Thus an action that conscience does not definitely pronounce to be sinless must not be performed. The reason is that one who acts while doubtful, whether his or her action is against the law or not, implicitly wills what is sinful. This person says equivalently, "This action may be offensive to God, but I am going to do it anyway," freely and rashly choosing to act on an attitude of indifference to the will of God.

RUTH, BOOK OF. One of the protocanonical writings of the Old Testament, narrating the story of a Bethlehem family in the time of the judges. Its heroine is Ruth, daughter-in-law of Naomi. Although Ruth is a Moabite, she marries Boaz, a Jew, and becomes the great-grandmother of King David, of whose family Christ was born. The purpose of the book was twofold: to preserve the edifying story of David's ancestry, and to witness to the practice of extraordinary filial piety, rewarded by God.

SABAOTH. A title of majesty applied mainly to God. The Hebrew word means "armies" or "hosts" and is found mainly in the expression "Lord of hosts," which occurs in the Old Testament no less than 282 times, all except 36 of which are in the prophetical books. From an early reference to YHWH as the Lord who defended his people in battle, the term has come to mean God's dominion over the angels, good and bad, and, a fortiori, his power over the destinies of people. In the New Testament, except in a direct quotation from Isaiah, the name becomes "Lord of Sabaoth" (James 5:4).

SABBATH, BIBLICAL. The Jewish day of rest, with elaborate prescriptions for its observance. Failure to observe the Sabbath was one of the principal accusations of the Pharisees against Jesus. It began on Friday night at sundown and ended on Saturday at sundown. No manual labor was done on the Sabbath. This meant complete withdrawal from business and trade interests, and giving oneself to family, friends, and religion. On the preceptive side, the Sabbath was to intensify home life, deepen one's knowledge of religious history and religion, and above all concentrate on prayer and things of the spirit. Already in apostolic times (Acts 20:7) Christians transferred the Sabbath from the seventh to the first day of the week. Moreover, the Catholic understanding of Sunday as a Sabbath (rest) has never been as rigid as that of some Protestant groups, e.g., the Puritans.

SABBATINE PRIVILEGE. The pious belief, approved by the Church, that the Blessed Virgin would be specially propitious to those who have worn the brown scapular of Our Lady of Mount Carmel and observed certain other practices. Specifically, Pope Paul V in 1613 authorized the following decree to be published: "It is permitted to the Carmelite Fathers to preach that the Christian people may believe that the Blessed Virgin will help by her continued assistance and her merits, particularly on Saturdays, the souls of the members of the Scapular Confraternity who have died in the grace of God, if in life they had worn the scapular, observed chastity according to their state of life, and recited the Office of the Blessed Virgin or observed the fasts of the Church, practicing abstinence on Wednesdays and Saturdays." There was an earlier version of the Sabbatine privilege that is now considered certainly erroneous, based on an alleged bull of Pope John XXII, supposedly published in 1322. This apocryphal document has the pope say that Carmelites and others who wear the scapular would be delivered by the Blessed Virgin from purgatory on the Saturday after their death.

SACRAMENT. A sensible sign, instituted by Jesus Christ, by which invisible grace and inward sanctification are communicated to the soul. The essential elements of a sacrament of the New Law are institution by Christ the God-man during his visible stay on earth, and a sensibly perceptible rite that actually confers the supernatural grace it symbolizes. In a broad sense every external sign of internal divine blessing is a sacrament. And in this sense there were already sacraments in the Old Law, such as the practice of circumcision. But, as the Council of Trent defined, these ancient rites differed essentially from the sacraments of the New Law; they did not really contain the grace they signified, nor was the fullness of grace yet available through visible channels merited and established by the Savior. (Etym. Latin *sacramentum,* oath, solemn obligation; from *sacrare,* to set apart as sacred, consecrate.)

SACRAMENTAL. Objects or actions that the Church uses after the manner of sacraments in order to achieve through the merits of the faithful certain effects, mainly of a spiritual nature. They differ from sacraments in not having been instituted by Christ to produce their effect in virtue of the ritual performed. Their efficacy depends not on the rite itself, as in the sacraments, but on the influence of prayerful petition, that of the person who uses them and of the Church in approving their practice. The variety of sacramentals spans the whole range of times and places, words and actions, objects and gestures that, on the Church's authority, draw not only on the personal dispositions of the individual but on the merits and prayers of the whole Mystical Body of Christ.

SACRAMENTAL CHARACTER. The indelible sign imprinted on the soul when the sacraments of baptism, confirmation, and the Holy Orders are received. This sign is indelible because it remains even in a person who may lose the state of grace or even the virtue of faith. It perdures at least until death and most likely into eternity. It is a sign because it signifies that the one baptized, confirmed, and ordained bears a special and unique relationship to Christ. It is a character because it permanently seals the person with a supernatural quality, comparable to the character that identifies each individual as a distinct personality. It is finally a character because it empowers the one who receives with the abilities that no one else possesses. In essence the sacramental character assimilates a person to the priesthood of Christ. From this primary function, secondary functions flow, in increasing order of sublimity, from baptism through confirmation to Holy Orders.

SACRAMENTAL CONFESSION. The auricular confession of one's sins in the sacrament of penance. If they are mortal sins, it is required that they be confessed as to number, type, and such circumstances as affect the gravity of the sins committed.

SACRAMENTAL DISPOSITIONS. Condition of the soul required for the valid and/or fruitful reception of the sacraments. The dispositions differ between minister and recipient. In the minister is required merely the faculty of conferring a given sacrament, and the willingness to carry out the intention of Christ or the Church, even just to satisfy another person's wish or desire. In the recipient who has the use of reason is required merely that no obstacles be placed in the way. Such obstacles are a lack of faith or sanctifying grace or of a right intention.

SACRAMENTAL GRACE. The grace conferred by the valid and fruitful reception of the sacraments. It may be one or more of several kinds:

1. sanctifying grace is communicated in baptism, penance, and in anointing of the sick when needed
2. sanctifying grace is always increased when a sacrament is received in the state of grace
3. actual grace is given by all the sacraments, either actually at the time of reception or also by title as a person needs divine help
4. the sacramental character is indelibly imprinted on the soul in baptism, confirmation, and the priesthood
5. a distinctive sacramental grace is imparted by each of the seven sacraments, corresponding to their respective purpose in the supernatural life of the soul

See also ACTUAL GRACE, EFFICACIOUS GRACE, GRACE, HABITUAL GRACE, JUSTIFYING GRACE, SANCTIFYING GRACE, SUFFICIENT GRACE.

SACRAMENTAL MATTER AND FORM. The rite of each of the seven sacraments, viewed as consisting of the materials used and actions performed, which constitute the matter, and the words pronounced, which constitute the form.

SACRAMENTAL PRESENCE. The manner of presence of Christ in the Holy Eucharist. He is really, truly, and substantially "contained" under the appearances of bread and wine, in such a way that where they are and as long as they are, he is there in the fullness of his divinity and humanity. See also REAL PRESENCE.

SACRAMENTAL SIGN. The external ritual by which a sacrament is performed and through which the distinctive graces of that sacrament are conferred. The Catholic Church believes that the essential element of each sacrament was originally determined by Christ, e.g., the pouring of water and the Trinitarian formula in baptism. Other features of the sacramental ritual have been determined by the Church, acting under the guidance of the Holy Spirit.

SACRAMENTARY. That part of the Roman Missal which contains the prayers and directives for Mass, and a number of sacramental formulas, but does not include the readings of the Mass. In the Western Church, Sacramentaries, as distinct from Lectionaries, were in use down to the thirteenth century. The Leonine, Gelasian, and Gregorian Sacramentaries, the main sources for the early history of the Mass, are the best known. From the ninth century on, the advantage of having everything in one book led to combining the Sacramentary, Lectionary, and Gradual into one book, which came to be known as the Missal. The Sacramentary was restored after the Second Vatican Council.

SACRAMENT OF CONFESSION. A popular name for the sacrament of penance, centering on the accusation of oneself to a priest in order to obtain absolution.

SACRAMENT OF PENANCE. The sacrament that, by means of certain acts of the penitent and by the absolution of a qualified priest, remits sins committed after baptism. As defined by the Catholic Church, it is "truly and properly a sacrament, instituted by Christ our Lord, for reconciling the faithful to God as often as they fall into sin after baptism" (Denzinger 1701). The required acts of the penitent are contrition, confession, and the willingness to make satisfaction. These acts are called the matter of the sacrament. The priest's absolution is the form.

The sacrament of penance was instituted by Christ on Easter Sunday night, when he told the Apostles, "Receive the Holy Spirit. For those whose sins you forgive, they are forgiven; for those whose sins you retain, they are retained" (John 20:22–23). The Catholic Church interprets these words to imply that Christ conferred on the Apostles and their successors not merely the right to declare that a person's sins are forgiven but also the power of forgiving in Christ's name those who are judged worthy of remission and of withholding absolution for those who are not disposed to be absolved.

SACRAMENT OF RECONCILIATION. Another name for the sacrament of penance, focusing on the principal effect of this sacrament, namely the healing of estrangement from God caused by one's sins.

SACRAMENT OF THE ALTAR. The Eucharist viewed as the body and blood of Christ, which are offered on the altar in the Sacrifice of the Mass. Also the Eucharist as reserved on the altar for adoration by the faithful.

SACRAMENTS OF THE DEAD. Those sacraments that can be validly and fruitfully received when a person is not in the state of grace. They are baptism, penance, and, if needed, anointing of the sick. These sacraments confer or restore sanctifying grace and confer actual graces when received by one who is already in God's friendship.

SACRAMENTS OF THE LIVING. The sacraments that require the state of grace to be received fruitfully. They are confirmation, the Eucharist, matrimony, and the priesthood. Of these four, however, confirmation, matrimony, and priesthood are received validly even in the state of grave sin so that a person is really confirmed, married, or ordained but does not obtain the graces associated with the sacraments until the state of grace is recovered. The Eucharist is also truly received by a person not in the state of grace but who commits a grave sin of sacrilege if he or she culpably approaches Holy Communion while estranged from divine friendship. The sacrament of anointing is in a class by itself, since it can be fruitfully received even in the state of grave sin. But it is considered a sacrament of the living because it should be received in the state of grace. Under certain conditions, however, it also restores sanctifying grace.

SACRED. The holy or divine. The sacred is that which pertains to God, as distinguished from what pertains to human beings; that which is eternal, in contrast with the temporal; the heavenly as opposed to the earthly; the mysterious and therefore not the rationally explainable; the infinite and not the finite. In all religions, the sacred is the Absolute, which does not change, whereas the profane is the relative, whose essence is to change. (Etym. Latin *sacrare,* to set apart as sacred, consecrate.)

SACRED CONGREGATIONS. Permanent commissions of cardinals established in Rome for handling the business of the Church. The competence of the various congregations is determined by their administrative responsibilities, although there is not in the Roman Curia a real distinction between legislation and administration. They came into existence as the work of the Apostolic Chancery grew in complexity and the pope needed stable branches of government immediately subject to his jurisdiction. The first such commission with permanent character was the Sacred Congregation of the Inquisition, set up by Pope Paul III in 1542.

SACRED HEART. The physical Heart of Christ as the principal sign and symbol of the threefold love with which he loves his eternal Father and all mankind. It is, therefore, a symbol of the divine love he shares with the Father and the Holy Spirit but that he, the Word made flesh, alone manifests through a weak and perishable body, since "in Him dwells the fullness of the Godhead bodily" (Colossians 2:9). It is, besides, the symbol of that burning love which, infused into his soul, enriches the human will of Christ and enlightens and governs its acts by the most perfect knowledge derived both from the beatific vision and that which is directly infused. And finally it is the symbol also of sensible love, since the body of Christ possesses full powers of feeling and perception, in fact more so than any other human body (Pope Pius XII, *Haurietis Aquas,* II, 55–57).

SACRED HEART DEVOTION. The subjective response of the faithful to the objective fact of Christ's love, divine and human, symbolized in his physical Heart. Historically the Devotion to the Sacred Heart is an outgrowth of devotion to Christ's sacred humanity, which the

Church has more than once defended as adorable because the human nature of Christ forms one Person with the divine nature, and that Person is divine. A series of mystics over centuries contributed to the development of this devotion, notably St. Bernard of Clairvaux (1090–1153), St. Bonaventure (1221–74), St. Mechtilde (1210–80), St. Gertrude (1256–1302), St. Frances of Rome (1384–1440), St. Francis de Sales (1567–1622), and St. John Eudes (1601–80). But it was especially St. Margaret Mary Alacoque (1647–90), whose revelations before the Blessed Sacrament gave the devotion its modern aspect and importance. Through her Jesuit spiritual director, St. Claude de la Colombière (1641–82), the Society of Jesus made promotion of the cultus of the Sacred Heart part of its institute, notably through the Apostleship of Prayer.

SACRIFICE. The highest form of adoration, in which a duly authorized priest in the name of the people offers a victim in acknowledgment of God's supreme dominion and of total human dependence on God. The victim is at least partially removed from human use and to that extent more or less destroyed as an act of submission to the divine majesty. Thus a sacrifice is not only an oblation. Where an oblation offers something to God, a sacrifice immolates or gives up what is offered. In sacrifice the gift offered is something precious completely surrendered by the one making the sacrifice as a token of humble recognition of God's sovereignty. (Etym. Latin *sacrum,* holy, sacred + *facere,* to make, do.)

SACRIFICE, NEW TESTAMENT. While Christ allowed the Mosaic sacrifice in his day, he predicted the end of the Temple and its worship (Mark 13:2; John 4:20–23). At the Last Supper, when instituting the Eucharist, he declared, "This is my body which will be given for you; do this as a memorial of me. . . . This cup is the new covenant in my blood which will be poured out for you" (Luke 22:19–20). Throughout the writings of St. Paul, Christ is identified as the Sacrificial Victim (I Corinthians 5:7; Ephesians 5:2) and further confirmed by the Catholic Epistles (I Peter 1:19; I John 2:2). The eternal nature of the Lord's Sacrifice is assumed (Revelation 13:8), and the whole letter to the Hebrews is about the high priesthood of Christ, who by his perfect obedience has "offered one single sacrifice for sins, and then taken his place forever at the right hand of God" (Hebrews 10:12–13). He is, therefore, the eternal priest who even now intercedes with his heavenly Father for a sinful humanity.

SACRIFICE, OLD TESTAMENT. As described in the books of the Old Law, sacrifice essentially meant honoring God by offering him some of the creatures that are precious to human beings, in acknowledgment of God's sovereignty and human dependence on the Creator. Two kinds of sacrifice are recognized and required of humanity, the bloody and the unbloody. Four kinds of bloody sacrifices are described: 1. the holocaust was the most perfect, also called the whole-burnt offering; the animal or other object was completely consumed by fire, and as the "perpetual sacrifice" it was offered twice daily, morning and evening; 2. the sin offering was to expiate misdeeds committed through ignorance or inadvertence; the kind of victim depended mainly on the dignity of the person offended; 3. the guilt offering was especially prescribed for sins demanding restitution; 4. peace offerings were either in gratitude or in fulfillment of a vow, or simply voluntary; part of the ceremony of this kind of sacrifice was that part of what was offered was returned to the one offering the sacrifice, to be eaten in a sacrificial meal.

Unbloody sacrifices were really oblations and, with the exception of incense, were offerings of articles of solid or liquid food. These food offerings accompanied every holocaust and peace offering, but never a sacrifice for sin or guilt, except at the cleansing of a leper.

SACRILEGE. The deliberate violation of sacred things. Sacred things are persons, places, and objects set aside publicly and by the Church's authority for the worship of God. The violation implies that a sacred thing is desecrated precisely in its sacred character. It is a sin against the virtue of religion.

Personal sacrilege is committed by laying violent hands on clerics or religious of either sex; by unlawfully citing them before secular courts, i.e., without just cause and without express permission of their ecclesiastical superiors; by unlawfully demanding of them the payment of civil taxes or military service; and by the commission of acts of unchastity by or with a person bound by the public vow of chastity.

Sacred places are violated by sacrilege through defilement, e.g., serious and unjust shedding of blood, as in willful homicide or by putting the sacred place (church or shrine) to unseemly use, e.g., secular trading, acts of debauchery; by grave theft from the Church or consecrated edifice; and by violating the immunity of a place as having the right of sanctuary.

Sacred objects are desecrated by sacrilege whenever something sacred is used for an unworthy purpose. This includes the Mass and the sacraments, along with sacramentals; sacred vessels and church furnishings; and ecclesiastical property. Desecration in each of these areas includes the deliberate invalid reception of the sacraments, simulation of Mass, and grave irreverence to the Eucharist; gravely profane use of sacred vessels or vestments; and the unlawful seizure of sacred things or ecclesiastical property.

Sacrilege is many times reprobated in Sacred Scripture, notably in the Second Book of Maccabees and in the writings of St. Paul. Grave sacrilege in the Old Testament was punishable by death and in the Catholic Church is considered a mortal sin. (Etym. Latin *sacrilegium*, the robbing of a temple, the stealing of sacred things.)

SACRISTY. A room attached to a church, usually near the altar, where the clergy vest for ecclesiastical functions. The sacristy affords storage for sacred vessels, vestments, and other articles needed for liturgical use. The sacrarium is usually located there. (Etym. Latin *sacristia*, from *sacrum*, holy, sacred.)

SACROSANCTUM CONCILIUM. The Constitution on the Sacred Liturgy of the Second Vatican Council. It was the first document issued by the Council, whose purpose was expressed in the opening paragraph: "to impart an ever increasing vigor to the life of the faithful; to adapt more closely to the needs of our age those institutions which are subject to change; to foster whatever can promote union among all who believe in Christ; to strengthen whatever can help to call all mankind into the Church's fold" (December 4, 1963).

SADDUCEES. A small group in Jewish society, contemporaneous with Christ, who attracted to their ranks rich, educated, and conservative Jews. In religion, they supported only doctrines that they found in written law. The Pharisees indulged in constant controversy with them over oral and unwritten tradition. The Sadducees were well treated by the Roman government because they supported the established order. Because they had substantial representation in the Sanhedrin, they exercised an influence out of proportion to their numbers in Temple affairs and ceremonies. In one significant activity the Sadducees and the Pharisees were united: ridiculing and denouncing Jesus and his teaching. Frequently they challenged or baited him in his public appearances. John the Baptist called them "a brood of vipers" (Matthew 3:7). Jesus denounced both groups, warning his followers against their false teachings (Matthew 16:12). The Sadducees persisted in their anti-Christian persecution; for instance, they had Peter and John arrested for spreading word of Jesus's Resurrection (Acts 4). Their numbers and influence waned as the first century moved along. Little was heard of them after the destruction of the Temple in the year 70. (Etym. Greek *saddukaioi,* popular meaning "righteous.")

ST. BENEDICT'S MEDAL. A frequently indulgenced medal that bears the image of the Father of Western Monasticism. In his right hand is a cross, next to which is the inscription *Crux Patris Benedicti* (the Cross of the Father Benedict). In his left hand is a copy of the Rule of St. Benedict. At his feet are images of a chalice and raven, symbols of the priesthood and the life of a hermit. Around the edge of the medal are the words *Eius in Obitu Nostro Praesentia Muniamur,* referring to Christ (At our death may we be strengthened by his presence). On the reverse side is a cross on whose vertical bar are the initial letters of the invocation *Crux Sancta Sit Mihi Lux* (The Holy Cross be my light). On the horizontal bar are the initials of *Non Draco Sit Mihi Dux* (Let not the dragon be my guide), referring to Satan. Around the medal are other letters signifying other Latin sayings. At the top is usually the single word *Pax* (Peace), the characteristic motto of St. Benedict, or the monogram *IHS,* the first three letters in Greek of the name Jesus.

ST. BLAISE BLESSING. A special blessing of throats on the feast of St. Blaise (February 3), martyr and Bishop of Sebaste in Armenia (died c. 316). According to legend, he had been a physician who was cast into prison by the pagans in the persecution of Emperor Licinius. He performed a marvelous cure on the throat of a child who was choking on a fishbone he had swallowed. Ever since, St. Blaise has been invoked against throat troubles. He is honored as one of the Fourteen Holy Helpers. On his feast day the faithful receive the blessing of St. Blaise, given by a priest holding two candles against the throat, while saying, "Through the intercession of St. Blaise, bishop and martyr, may God deliver you from illness of the throat and from every other evil. In the name of the Father, and of the Son, and of the Holy Spirit. Amen."

ST. CHRISTOPHER MEDAL. One of the most popular religious medals of our day. St. Christopher is pictured carrying the Child on his shoulder. The story is told that this third-century saint as a big-bodied youth served God and his neighbor well by carrying people over a dangerous river that had taken the lives of many. Among those he carried across was Christ himself, who, on one occasion, appeared to Christopher (Greek, Christ-bearer) in the form of a child. He is the special patron and helper of travelers, especially those who travel by plane and automobile. Hence the custom of having St. Christopher medals (or statuettes) on the dashboard of automobiles. The feast of St. Christopher is on July 25, and his name remains on the Church calendars of particular regions. It no longer appears in the universal calendar because his cultus (like that of many saints) was not originally part of the liturgical tradition of the city of Rome, unlike other early saints, e.g., Sts. Agatha, Agnes, and Cecilia. But the Church has not removed him from veneration by the faithful as a saint.

SAINTE-ANNE-DE-BEAUPRÉ. Canadian shrine dedicated to the mother of Mary, located twenty-seven miles northeast of Quebec on the St. Lawrence River. Hundreds of thousands of ill and crippled people flock to this shrine each year, where it is said that every known disease has been cured at one time or another. Tradition says that the first chapel was built in 1658 by sailors in thanksgiving for their rescue in a storm. However, it was soon swept away, as it was too near the shore. A larger chapel was erected in 1662, but this was demolished through some error of misdirection in 1876. The present Romanesque basilica is the fourth church dedicated to St. Anne of the Meadows.

ST. JOHN LATERAN. One of five great basilicas in Rome and the mother and head of all churches. It was founded by Emperor Constantine (c. 274–337) near the Lateran Palace, which he presented to Pope Sylvester as his episcopal residence and which was used by all the popes until 1309 when the papacy moved to Avignon. The church was dedicated to the Holy Savior and became the prior church of Christendom. Its canons even today take precedence over those from St. Peter's. The primitive church was destroyed by earthquake in 898. The reconstruction was partly burned in 1308 and rebuilt. The present interior is severe but rich in its proportions. Paired columns, with niches between and holding mammoth statues of the Apostles, fill both sides of the nave, while above them are reliefs taken from the Old and New Testaments. Still higher up are medallions of the prophets leading the eye to the gorgeous ceiling with the numerous papal arms and emblems of Christ's Passion. The apse, reconstructed by Pope Leo XIII, contains precious mosaics of the thirteenth century depicting the union of the kingdom of earth and heaven as united in baptism. The high altar covers many relics including the heads of Sts. Peter and Paul, and St. Peter's small altar from the catacombs. Preserved here is the cedar table that according to tradition was used at the Last Supper. As long as the popes were in residence at the Lateran Palace, the basilica saw the coronations and entombments of the popes and was the place where four ecumenical councils were held in 1123, 1139, 1179, and 1215. Connected with the famous basilica is the Lateran Baptistery, for a long time the only one in Rome and since then the model for all others. Constantine was baptized in the year 337 shortly before his death, at the porphyry bath that is still preserved there.

ST. JOSEPH, DEVOTION TO. Manifestation of reverence for the spouse of the Virgin Mary.

In the first centuries of the Church, there was no sign of a liturgical devotion to St. Joseph, which parallels the slow development of Marian piety and is understandable in view of the need first to stabilize the Church's Christology. However, the Eastern Fathers since the fourth century, such as Ephrem, John Damascene, and John Chrysostom, often speak of Joseph and extol his purity of life as in the classic phrase of St. Ephrem (306–73): "No one can worthily praise St. Joseph." The Latin Fathers, notably Jerome and Augustine, stress the justice of Mary's spouse, in the biblical sense of his fidelity to the laws of God. The earliest public cultus of St. Joseph appeared in the East with June 20 the commemorative feast. Later Oriental sources variously assigned December 25, 26, and the Sunday before or after Christmas as feast days honoring St. Joseph at the head of other persons associated with the birth of Christ. By the ninth century the Western martyrologies celebrated his memory on March 19. The Crusades gave great impetus to the devotion, as seen in the basilica that the Crusaders built in honor of St. Joseph at Nazareth.

From the Middle Ages on, the veneration of the foster father of Jesus entered the full stream of Christian piety, through the writings and preaching of Sts. Peter Damian, Bernard of Clairvaux, Thomas Aquinas, and Bernardine of Siena. Before the Council of Trent, the Feast of St. Joseph (March 19) was placed in the Roman Breviary by Pope Sixtus IV in 1479. And after Trent, by a decree of 1621, Pope Gregory XV made it a day of obligatory attendance at Mass and abstention from servile work, which it still remains according to canon law, except in certain countries, such as the United States.

A parallel feast to honor the patronage of St. Joseph was extended by Blessed Pope Pius IX in 1870 to the whole Christian world, and at the same time the saint was declared "Patron of the Universal Church." In 1955, Venerable Pope Pius XII instituted a new feast of St. Joseph the Worker for May 1, and March 19 now commemorates his patronage of the Church.

St. Joseph's pre-eminent sanctity, which places him next to the Blessed Virgin among the saints, was confirmed by many papal documents, especially those of Popes Leo XIII and Pius XII. He is invoked as the patron of a happy death, and by a long-standing custom the month of March and each Wednesday of the week are dedicated to him. In paintings and statues he is usually shown with the Child Jesus and a lily or staff. More recent artists picture him with a carpenter's square or other instrument of his trade in his hand.

ST. LAWRENCE OUTSIDE THE WALLS. The fifth of the major basilicas of Rome. Emperor Constantine erected a church on this site in A.D. 330 over the graves of St. Lawrence and St. Cyriaca. It was remodeled in the sixth century and again in the thirteenth century, and the portico was added. Modern paintings looking like mosaics adorn the façade. The vestibule has many sarcophagi with high relief embellishing them, also frescoes around the walls with stories depicting St. Lawrence, St. Stephen, and Hippolytus. The campanile dates from the twelfth century. In the interior the nave and side aisles are of thirteenth-century construction—grand with their twenty-two antique columns, modern paintings of St. Lawrence and St. Stephen, and the mosaic floor. Here, too, is the crypt containing the bodies of Lawrence, Justin, and Stephen under the high altar, with its magnificent canopy. In the near vicinity the pilgrim sees the tall column with the martyred deacon on its top.

ST. PAUL'S OUTSIDE THE WALLS. One of the five great basilicas of Rome. Founded in 386 by Emperor Valentinian II (375–92), it was finished by his successor, Flavius Honorius, on the site of the church built by Emperor Constantine over the tomb of St. Paul. It was almost totally destroyed by fire in 1823. Rebuilt to the same dimensions as the original with help from many parts of the world, it was consecrated by Pope Pius IX in 1854. The interior is imposing with its broad nave, eighty columns of granite brought from Lake Maggiore, dividing the side aisles and the central area. Above the arches are the mosaic portrait medallions of every pope through Pope Benedict XV. The high altar is surmounted by the famous Arnolfo di Cambio tabernacle, the exterior reliefs on it taken from the Old Testament. Four columns of Oriental alabaster support the canopy over it. Under it in a splendid casket are the mortal remains of St. Paul. The triumphal arch, at the apse end, was saved from the conflagration along with its exquisite fifth-century mosaics of the head of Christ centered in glory and surrounded by the twenty-four elders with St. Peter and St. Paul below them.

SAINTS. A name given in the New Testament to Christians generally (Colossians 1:2) but early restricted to persons who were eminent for holiness. In the strict sense saints are those who distinguish themselves by heroic virtue during life and whom the Church honors as saints either by her ordinary universal teaching authority or by a solemn definition called canonization. The Church's official recognition of sanctity implies that the persons are now in heavenly glory, that they may be publicly invoked everywhere, and that their virtues during life or martyr's death are a witness and example to the Christian faithful. (Etym. Latin *sanctus,* holy, sacred.)

SALESIANS. Members of the Society of St. Francis de Sales (1567–1622), founded near Turin by St. John Bosco (1815–88) in 1859. Their main purpose is to train youth in schools and professional and vocational institutes. They are also active in the missions and have entered the field of social communications. Their rule of life was approved by Pope Pius IX in 1874. St. John Bosco also founded a sister congregation of Daughters of Our Lady Help of Christians in 1872 at Mornese, Italy.

SALUS POPULI ROMANI. Shrine of Our Lady Protectress of Rome, also called Santa Maria Maggiore. The original basilica of the Blessed Virgin was built about A.D. 350 and was called Santa Maria ad Nives because of the legend that the location of the church was determined by the appearance of snow on the Esquiline Hill on a summer day. The first treasure of the present church is a miraculous image of the Madonna with the Infant Jesus attributed to St. Luke and said to have been brought by St. Helena from the Holy Land. Historians rate the painting as being at least fifteen hundred years old. The citizens of Rome flock to the basilica whenever their city is in danger. In 597,

Pope Gregory I carried the painting in solemn procession to St. Peter's when Rome was being decimated by the Black Plague; and when Anzio, only twenty miles away, was being bombed in World War II, the shrine was thronged day and night by the Roman faithful. The original church was built in the fourth century. When Pope Sixtus III rebuilt it in the fifth century, he gave it the further title of Santa Maria ad Praesepe (St. Mary of the Crib) because part of the original manger from Bethlehem was in the basilica's crypt. Venerable Pope Pius XII said his first Mass before Mary's altar in this cathedral, and in 1939 he pontificated at a Mass of thanksgiving at the same altar.

SALUTARY ACT. Human action that is performed under the influence of grace and that positively leads a person to a heavenly destiny. The grace of a salutary act must be at least actual grace, whether a person is in the state of grace or not. If one is in the state of grace, the action is not only salutary but also meritorious. While the Church has not officially pronounced on the subject, it is common teaching that the justified also require actual grace for the performance of salutary acts. (Etym. Latin *salus*, health, well-being.)

SALVATION. In biblical language the deliverance from straitened circumstances or oppression by some evil to a state of freedom and security. As sin is the greatest evil, salvation is mainly liberation from sin and its consequences. This can be deliverance by way of preservation, or by offering the means for being delivered, or by removing the oppressive evil or difficulty, or by rewarding the effort spent in cooperating with grace in order to be delivered. All four aspects of salvation are found in the Scriptures and are taught by the Church. (Etym. Latin *salvare*, to save.)

SALVE REGINA. "Hail, Holy Queen," one of the oldest Marian antiphons in Western Christianity, used for centuries in the Divine Office. The author is not known but was most probably Hermannus Contractus (d. 1054). The final words, "O Clemens, O pia, O dulcis virgo Maria," attributed to St. Bernard, are found in manuscripts before his time and therefore seem to belong to the original prayer. The full text reads:

Hail, holy Queen, Mother of mercy;

hail, our life, our sweetness and our hope.

To you do we cry, poor banished children of Eve.

To you do we send up our sighs,

mourning and weeping in this valley of tears.

Turn, then, most gracious Advocate,

your eyes of mercy toward us.

And after this our exile

show unto us the blessed fruit of your womb, Jesus.

O clement, O loving, O sweet Virgin Mary.

A partial indulgence is gained for every recitation of this prayer.

SAMARITANS. The people of Samaria, who were originally Jews but had intermarried with the pagan Assyrians, who had conquered Israel in 622 B.C. (II Kings 18:9–12). They developed a different form of Judaism, based mainly on their own Pentateuch, which was the only part of the Old Testament the Samaritans accepted. They had their own temple on Mount Gerizim and were bitterly hated by the Jews (John 4:9, 20). They were featured in three narratives of the Gospels: the Good Samaritan (Luke 10:33), the Ten Lepers (Luke 7:16), and the Samaritan Woman (John 4:5–42).

SAMUEL. An Ephraimite, son of Elkanah and Hannah. Deeply religious, he "grew up in stature and in favour both with YHWH and with men" (I Samuel 2:26). "All Israel from Dan to Beersheba came to know that Samuel was accredited as a prophet of YHWH" (I Samuel 3:20). Following a disastrous defeat of the Israelites by the Philistines, Samuel rallied his humiliated people and won for himself recognition as a judge and prophet (I Samuel 7:6). He anointed Saul as YHWH's choice as ruler, and his prestige with the people ensured Saul's elevation to the kingship (I Samuel 11:12–14). But, despite military victories, Saul disappointed YHWH by his disobedience, and Samuel turned against him in favor of young David (I Samuel 15:10–35). Fearful of David's growing popularity, Saul tried in vain repeatedly to have the young man killed, but YHWH protected him (I Samuel 19, 23). Samuel secretly anointed David as future king of Israel (I Samuel 16:12–13), and as soon as the insane Saul died, David succeeded him. Samuel was thus YHWH's instrument in establishing two successive kings who ruled over a sixty-year period. An inspiring, selfless leader, Samuel was held in high regard by his people throughout his life. Two books of the Bible are named after him (I Samuel and II Samuel).

SAMUEL, BOOKS OF. The Hebrew title of what the Vulgate calls the First and Second Books of Kings. They contain the history of Samuel and the two kings, Saul and David, whom he anointed. They are the primary source for the history of Israel in the crucial years of the eleventh and tenth centuries before Christ. Three famous poems are included in these books: Hannah's prayer (I Samuel 2:1–10), David's lament (II Samuel 1:19–27), and David's song of triumph (II Samuel 22).

SANCTIFICATION. Being made holy. The first sanctification takes place at baptism, by which the love of God is infused by the Holy Spirit (Romans 5:5). Newly baptized persons are holy because the Holy Trinity begins to dwell in their souls and they are pleasing to God. The second sanctification is a lifelong process in which a person already in the state of grace grows in the possession of grace and in likeness to God by faithfully corresponding with divine inspirations. The third sanctification takes place when a person enters heaven and becomes totally and irrevocably united with God in the beatific vision. (Etym. Latin *sanctificare*, to make holy.)

SANCTIFYING GRACE. The supernatural state of being infused by God, which permanently inheres in the soul. It is a vital principle of the supernatural life, as the rational soul is the vital principle of a human being's natural life. It is not a substance but a real quality that becomes part of the soul substance. Although commonly associated with the possession of the virtue of charity, sanctifying grace is yet distinct from this virtue. Charity, rather, belongs to the will, whereas sanctifying grace belongs to the whole soul, mind, will, and affections. It is called sanctifying grace because it makes holy those who possess the gift by giving them a participation in the divine life. It is *zoē* (life), which Christ taught that he has in common with the Father and which those who are in the state of grace share. See also ACTUAL GRACE, EFFICACIOUS GRACE, GRACE, HABITUAL GRACE, JUSTIFYING GRACE, SACRAMENTAL GRACE, SUFFICIENT GRACE.

SANCTION. In general, the inviolability of the law, whether divine or human, ecclesiastical or civil. More properly, it is the means adopted to make the law inviolable. These may be natural means and comprehend all the benefits and penalties, personal or social, that naturally follow from keeping or breaking the law. Or they may be supernatural means, which are known to exist only because they have been divinely revealed. Positive sanctions are those set up by legitimate authority in Church or State and, to be valid, must conform to right reason and revelation. Every sanction is only as effective as it is known, whether it acts as a stimulus (in promised rewards) or as a deterrent (in threatened punishments) to motivate people to observe the law. Sanctions are either temporal or eternal, depending on their duration. They are either medicinal or vindicative, depending on their purpose: to act as a remedy for violations of the law or to restore moral order and champion justice against violators of the law. (Etym. Latin *sanctio,* the decreeing of something as sacred, decree, sanction.)

SANCTUARY. The part of a church containing the altar. If there are several altars, the sanctuary is for the high altar. In the Byzantine tradition it is enclosed by the *iconostasis.* It is the center of liturgical ceremony, clearly distinct from the main body of the church. (Etym. Latin *sanctuarium,* holy place, shrine.)

SANCTUARY LAMP. A wax candle, generally in a red glass container, kept burning day and night wherever the Blessed Sacrament is reserved in Catholic churches or chapels. It is an emblem of Christ's abiding love and a reminder to the faithful to respond with loving adoration in return.

SANHEDRIN. The highest Jewish court, which functioned from the third or fourth century B.C. until the fall of Jerusalem in A.D. 70. For several centuries earlier there were courts or councils in existence, but it was impossible to learn when a recognizable Sanhedrin took specific form. Josephus, the Jewish historian, was the first writer to name it specifically as functioning in the reign of Antiochus the Great. It was composed of seventy-one members, chosen from three classes of Jews—the elders of the chief families, the high priests, and the scribes, who were mostly lawyers from the Pharisee sect. The Sadducees were always well represented. The jurisdiction of the Sanhedrin was limited to Judaea, a fact that prevented the court from taking action against Jesus while he was preaching in Galilee. The Sanhedrin met in the Jerusalem Temple area. Any Jew could appear before it to seek clarification of the complexities of the Mosaic Law. The court had the right to mete out punishment to law violators (Matthew 26:47–50; Mark 14:43–46), even to the extent of capital punishment (Mark 14:64; John 11:53). But, as happened in the case of Jesus's Crucifixion, it had to secure the approval of the Roman procurator before such a sentence could be executed (Mark 15:1). Guilt for his unjust condemnation rested partly on the fanatical element in the Sanhedrin (John 18:31) and partly on the cynical Roman official willing to appease a turbulent local group (Mark 15:15). Persecution by the Sanhedrin did not end with Jesus's death. It continued after Pentecost, as in the case of Peter, John, Paul, and Stephen (Acts 4:3; 5:17–18, 33; 7:57–58; 23:1–10). (Etym. Greek *synedrion,* council, a sitting together.)

SANTA CLAUS. An American adaptation of the Dutch form of St. Nicholas (Sint Nikolaas), Bishop of Myra in Lycia, who lived in the time of Diocletian. He was long venerated as the patron saint of children, bringing them gifts on December 6, and his association with Christmas was popularized by the Dutch Protestants in New Amsterdam. They portrayed the saint as a Nordic magician. He is now a secularized personification of the spirit of Christmas.

SARAH. Wife of Abraham. Her original name was Sarai, but when YHWH promised Abraham that his wife would have a son, he instructed him at the same time to change her name to Sarah (Genesis 17:15). Since she was already ninety years old, she scoffed at the promise, but YHWH was as good as his word. The child was born and Abraham obediently named him Isaac (Genesis 21:2–3). An awkward situation developed for Abraham as Isaac grew to boyhood. Years before, Sarah had permitted her servant, Hagar, to become Abraham's second wife (a custom permitted in those days) and a son Ishmael resulted. Now that Sarah had a son of her own, she was meanly resentful of a situation she had initiated herself. "Drive away that slave-girl and her son," she said to Abraham. "That slave-girl's son is not to share the inheritance with my son, Isaac" (Genesis 21:10). Abraham was forced to do so, but YHWH protected Hagar and Ishmael and assured them that Ishmael would head a great nation (Genesis 21:17–21). Sarah lived to be 127 years old and died at Hebron in Canaan (Genesis 23:1–2). When Abraham died years later, his sons Isaac and Ishmael buried him with Sarah (Genesis 25:9–10). (Etym. Hebrew *Sārāh,* "princess.")

SATAN. Chief of the fallen angels. Enemy of God and humanity and everything good. Other names for Satan are the devil, Beelzebul, Belial, and Lucifer. The serpent that tempted Eve was identified with Satan (Genesis 3). In both the Old and New Testaments he is considered the adversary of God, bringing about evil and tempting human beings to defy God's laws (Wisdom 2:24; I Chronicles 21:1; Job 1:6–12). Even Jesus was subjected to temptation by Satan in the wilderness (Matthew 4:1–11). Later the Pharisees accused Jesus of "casting out devils through Beelzebul, the prince of devils" (Matthew 12:24). Paul warned the Corinthians against the temptations of Satan (I Corinthians 7:6). References to Satan are numerous in the Scriptures. The dominant feature of this teaching is that a personal, malign force is active in the world attempting to pervert the designs of God. (Etym. Latin *Satan;* from Greek *Satan;* from Hebrew *sātān,* devil, adversary; from *sātān,* to plot against another.)

SATANISM. The cult of Satan or Satan worship. Known in antiquity, it has long been practiced under a different name among polytheists in their invocation and propitiation of the evil deities. But Satanism properly so called is mainly a revolt against Christianity or the Catholic Church. It rose in the twelfth century and culminated in the Black Mass, a blasphemous parody of the Eucharistic Sacrifice. Modern Satanism has become widespread in circles that venerate the devil, pray for his assistance, perform elaborate rites in his honor (including demonic caricatures of the seven sacraments), establish legally recognized "Churches of Satan," and claim to possess extraordinary power to harm those who oppose them. Philosophically, Satanists hold to a Manichaean view of the universe, that there are ultimately two creative principles in the universe, one good and the other bad. Satanists venerate what Christians call the "principle of evil."

SATISFACTION. The expiation of wrongdoing, especially the penance imposed by a priest before giving sacramental absolution. Essentially the satisfaction consists in the penitent's willingness to accept the penance imposed and its actual fulfillment. The effect of these two elements is to remove more or less the temporal punishment due to the sins confessed. In the early Church, up to the Middle Ages, the penance imposed was generally severe. Later on the severity was mitigated through what have since come to be known as indulgences. (Etym. Latin *satisfacere: satis,* sufficient, enough + *facere,* to do, make.)

SAUL. The son of Kish; he ruled Israel as its first king for twenty years about the year 1000 B.C. He was a tall, handsome, impressive man in appearance (I Samuel 9:2–3), but his complex personality brought him trouble. When the people of Israel begged Samuel, their highly respected prophet and judge, to get them a king in order to protect their security, Samuel consulted YHWH, who recommended Saul (I Samuel 8–10). At first he proved very successful because of his military achievements (I Samuel 11:14–15), but he did not show respect or obedience to YHWH, and Samuel, who had gained the kingship for him, became disenchanted. Instead, Samuel encouraged the advancement of Saul's son-in-law, David, and even secretly anointed him as the future king (I Samuel 13:8–15). Saul became insanely jealous of David and several times tried to have him killed. Ironically, both Saul's daughter, Michal, who was married to David (I Samuel 19:11–12), and Jonathan, his son, sided with the young man against their father and did everything possible to protect David from the maddened king (I Samuel 19:1–7). Finally, in a fierce battle between the Israelites and the Philistines, all three of Saul's sons were killed. Badly wounded, the king killed himself (I Samuel 31:1–6). This cleared the way for David to become King of Israel for the next forty years.

SAVIOR. A title of Jesus Christ, arising from his sacrifice of his life for the salvation of the human race, and thus he won for sinful humanity the graces necessary to reach heaven. It is only because of his satisfaction and the invocation of his name that anyone can be saved (Acts 4:12). (Etym. Latin *salvator*; from *salvare*, to save.)

SCANDAL. Any action or its omission, not necessarily sinful in itself, that is likely to induce another to do something morally wrong. Direct scandal, also called diabolical, has the deliberate intention to induce another to sin. In indirect scandal a person does something that he or she foresees will at least likely lead another to commit sin, but this is rather tolerated than positively desired. (Etym. Latin *scandalum*, stumbling block.)

SCAPULAR. An outer garment consisting of two strips of cloth joined across the shoulders, worn by members of certain religious orders. Originating as the working frock of Benedictines, it was adopted by other religious communities and is now considered a distinctive part of the monastic habit. It symbolizes the yoke of Christ. A scapular is worn under one's secular clothes, in abbreviated form, by tertiaries associated with the religious orders. Tertiary scapulars vary in size and shape; their color corresponds to that of the monastic family. As a further development, the Church has approved some eighteen blessed scapulars as two small pieces of cloth joined by strings and worn around the neck and under the clothes. Best known are the five scapulars of Our Lady of Mount Carmel (brown), the Passion (red), Seven Dolors (black), Immaculate Conception (blue), and the Holy Trinity (white). (Etym. Latin *scapulare, scapularium,* "shoulder cloak," from Latin *scapula,* shoulder.)

SCAPULAR MEDAL. A blessed medal, worn or carried on the person, instead of one or more of the small scapulars. It was authorized as a substitute by St. Pius X in 1910. It bears on one side a representation of the Sacred Heart and on the other an image of the Blessed Virgin. It replaces any (or all) of the small scapulars in which a person has been invested. Investing in each case must be done with the scapular and not the medal. The medal is to be blessed by a priest who has faculties for each scapular investiture.

SCHISM. A willful separation from the unity of the Christian Church. Although St. Paul used the term to condemn the factions at Corinth, these were not properly schismatical, but petty cliques that favored one or another Apostle. A generation later Clement I reprobated the first authentic schism of which there is record. Paul's exhortation to the Corinthians also gives an accurate description of the concept. "Why do we wrench and tear apart the members of Christ," he asks, "and revolt against our own body, and reach such folly as to forget that we are members of one another?" While the early Church was often plagued with heresy and schism, the exact relation between the two divisive elements was not clarified until later in the patristic age. "By false doctrines concerning God," declared St. Augustine, "heretics wound the faith; by sinful dissensions schismatics deviate from fraternal charity, although they believe what we believe." Heresy, therefore, by its nature refers to the mind and is opposed to religious belief, whereas schism is fundamentally volitional and offends against the union of Christian charity. (Etym. Latin *schisma;* from Greek *skhisma,* a split division; from *skhizein,* to tear, rend.)

SCHOLASTICISM. The system of philosophy and theology first developed in the medieval schools of Christian Europe, having a scholastic or technical language and methodology, building on the writings of the Church Fathers, notably St. Augustine (354–430), using many of the philosophical principles and insights of Aristotle and Neoplatonism, and coordinated into a synthesis of human and divine wisdom by St. Thomas Aquinas (1225–74).

Three periods of Scholasticism are commonly distinguished: the medieval period from St. Anselm to Jean Capréolus (1060–1440); the Counter-Reformation or the Spanish-Portuguese Revival (1520–1640), declining after the rise of Protestantism and the spread of Cartesianism; and Neo-Scholasticism, officially recognized by Pope Leo XIII in 1879, beginning in the latter half of the nineteenth century and continuing to the present time. (Etym. Latin *schola,* place of learning, school; from Greek *scholē,* school; discussion; rest, leisure, employment of leisure time.)

SCIENCE OF FAITH. Another name for theology. It is concerned with faith in the objective sense of "that which is believed" and in the subjective sense of "that by which a person believes." Theology accepts Scripture and tradition as the remote rule of faith, and the doctrines of the Church as the proximate rule of faith. But as a science of faith, it seeks by human reason to establish the foundations of faith, to penetrate into the meaning of the mysteries of faith, to show that faith is consistent with reason, and to defend the faith against those who deny the truths of Christianity. See also THEOLOGY.

SCRIBES. A class of well-educated Jews who studied and explained the Law. Occasionally they were referred to as lawyers or rabbis (Matthew 23:7). They were not priests. Some were members of the Sanhedrin (Matthew 26:57). Because they were devoted to defending and preserving the Law, they considered Jesus a threat to their security. They challenged and baited him (Mark 2:16) on numerous occasions and ultimately took part in plotting his death (Luke 22:1–2). (Etym. Latin *scriba,* official writer, clerk, scribe, from *scribere,* to write.)

SCRUPLE. Unreasonable doubt about the morality of an act done or to be done. Its basis is an erroneous conscience combined with a lack of control of the emotion of fear. (Etym. Latin *scrupulus,* small, sharp stone, small weight, scruple, from *scrupus,* rough stone.)

SEAL OF CONFESSION. The grave duty of keeping absolutely secret all sins that are told in sacramental confession and anything else that is told by the penitent and is related to the confession. It is an obligation binding in the natural law, the divine law of Christ, and the positive law of the Church. It binds the confessor and any other person who in any way discovers what was confessed. Under no circumstances may any of this information be revealed unless the penitent freely gives permission.

SEAL OF CONFIRMATION. To establish or determine irrevocably, in the sacrament of confirmation, when a bishop anoints a person with chrism and says, "[Name], be sealed with the Gift of the Holy Spirit." Thus, by confirmation a baptized Christian becomes permanently marked as a witness of Christ and is enabled to preserve, profess, and communicate the faith even (if need be) with the price of his blood.

SECOND ADAM. A title given to Christ, based on St. Paul's teaching that as sin came into the world through the disobedience of the first Adam, so grace has come through the obedience of one man, Christ the Second Adam (Romans 5:12–21).

SECOND COMING OF CHRIST. "I am going now to prepare a place for you and after I have gone and prepared a place for you, I shall return to take you with me" (John 14:3). This promise, which Jesus made to his Apostles the night before he died, will be the culmination of his Incarnation and Redemption. On the occasion of his Ascension, angels repeated the promise. "This same Jesus will come back in the same way as you have seen Him go there" (Acts 1:11). When the Second Coming will be, no one knows. Some of his devoted followers were mistaken in thinking that the return would take place in a short time, possibly in their lifetime. Nevertheless, that promise is the basis of Christian hope. As Paul wrote to Titus: "We must be self-restrained and live good and religious lives here in this present world while we are waiting in hope for the blessing which will come with the Appearing of the glory of our great God and Savior, Christ Jesus" (Titus 2:13).

SECOND VATICAN COUNCIL. The twenty-first ecumenical council of the Catholic Church, first announced by Blessed Pope John XXIII, on January 25, 1959. He opened the council on October 11, 1962, and the first session ended on December 8 of the same year. After Pope John's death, June 3, 1963, Pope Paul VI reconvened the Council for the next three sessions, which ran from September 29 to December 4, 1963; September 14 to November 21, 1964; and September 14 to December 8, 1965. A combined total of 2,865 bishops and prelates took part in the Council proceedings, although 264 could not attend, mainly from Communist countries. Among the sixteen documents issued by the Council, the four constitutions—on divine revelation, the liturgy, and two on the Church—were the basis for the rest.

SECRET SOCIETY. An organization whose members may not disclose the purposes, practices, or activities of their society to civil or ecclesiastical authorities. Because their secrecy often works to the disadvantage of nonmembers, through questionable control, and also to the detriment of the Catholic faith, the Church has for centuries forbidden Catholics to belong to secret societies and has often imposed severe canonical penalties on those who disobey. Under certain restricted conditions Catholics may retain a limited association with such organizations. Forbidden secret societies often sponsor benevolent and charitable enterprises, but they are prohibited mainly because their naturalism is a danger to the true faith. Among the secret societies forbidden by Church law are the Knights of Pythias, Odd Fellows, Sons of Temperance, and the Freemasons.

SECT, RELIGIOUS. An organized body of dissenters from an established or older form of faith, commonly applied to all religious bodies where State churches are established. In countries where many churches are recognized by law, sects are generally identified as religious groups that lack much organization or structure and that are not likely to endure. (Etym. Latin *sequi,* to follow; *secta,* a following.)

SECULAR. That which belongs to this life, in contrast with the sacred, which pertains to the life to come. The secular, therefore, is the earthly and not celestial; the human and not the divine; the created and not the uncreated; the temporal and not the eternal; the visible and not the spiritual; the humanly rational and explainable and not the mysterious and ineffable; the relative and therefore changeable with time, place, and circumstances, and not the absolute, which is immutable because and insofar as it is associated with the unchangeable God. (Etym. Latin *saecularis,* pertaining to the world, *saeculum,* the world.)

SECULAR CLERGY. Clergy who are engaged for the most part in pastoral work and who are not members of a religious institute. They are not bound by a vow of poverty or community life. But their celibacy, in the Latin Church, is under solemn oath, and they promise obedience to a bishop as their immediate superior under the pope.

SECULAR INSTITUTE. A society, whether clerical or lay, whose members profess the evangelical counsels in the world. Their purpose is to enable the members to attain Christian perfection and to exercise a full apostolate. They are distinguished in ecclesiastical law from other common associations of the faithful. They were first approved by Venerable Pope Pius XII on February 2, 1947, in his constitution *Provida Mater,* which still contains the guiding norms for their direction. Secular institutes differ from formal religious institutes or societies of common life because, while their members take vows or promises, these are not technically the public vows of religion, and the members do not live a common life. They are, however, states of Christian perfection, whose apostolate is in the world. The members are to work for the extension of Christ's kingdom in places and circumstances corresponding to people in the secular world.

SECULARISM. Technically the philosophy of naturalism advocated since the nineteenth century, first in England and then elsewhere. It is a closed system that affirms that human existence and destiny are fully explainable in terms of this world without reference to eternity. On its social side, secularism promotes the advancement of humanity's lot in this life, and charges Christianity with indifference to poverty and suffering because of its alleged preoccupation with God and the life to come.

SECULARIZATION. The act of permanent separation of men or women from their obligations to the religious life. They are released from their vows and may return to the world. Except in purely diocesan orders, secularization requires a papal indult. Another form of secularization refers to what occurs when civil power forcibly deprives the Church of the possession and use of her schools, hospitals, and welfare institutions, as happens in Communist countries.

SEE. The seat (*sedes*) of the Church's papal or episcopal authority, vested in the Bishop of Rome for the universal Church and the local ordinary for each diocese. Episcopal sees have definite territorial boundaries, determined by the Holy See.

SEE OF PETER. See APOSTOLIC SEE, HOLY SEE, PAPACY, ROMAN SEE, ROME.

SEGNATURA APOSTOLICA. The highest tribunal of the Holy See; its origins go back to Pope Eugenius IV (r. 1431–47). As reconstituted by Venerable Pope Paul VI in 1967, the Segnatura has two areas of competency, namely: 1. over tribunals already established, pilgrimages to Rome, matrimonial cases of nullity, erection of regional and interregional tribunals, handling cases involving concordats between various nations and the Holy See; 2. settling disputes arising from acts of administrative ecclesiastical power as a court of appeal, deciding on administrative controversies sent to it by the congregations of the Roman Curia, and judging on controversies submitted by the Roman Pontiff.

SELF-CONTROL. The act, power, or habit of having one's desires under the control of the will, enlightened by right reason and faith.

SELF-DECEPTION. The moral failure to recognize one's own limitations and failures or to see the real reasons for one's behavior.

SELF-DEFENSE. The right to use force against an unjust aggressor. The moral premises on which justifiable self-defense is based are the fact that the possession of life includes the right to use the means necessary to protect one's life, provided such means do not violate the rights of others. In the case of unjust aggression, the use of force and even a deathblow may be the only means of saving one's life. The rights of others are not thereby violated, for the assailant's right to live is suspended during the unjust attack. Moreover, the attacker can easily protect his or her life by merely ceasing from the attack.

SELF-LOVE. Inordinate regard for self to the neglect of others and indifference to their needs. In narcissism the attention is centered on the body, especially sexual self-satisfaction.

SEMINARY. A school established for the academic and spiritual training of candidates for the priesthood. The Council of Trent, July 15, 1563, ordered the establishment of a seminary in every diocese. Seminaries that are not houses of study for the regular clergy are of different kinds, depending on the authority that establishes them and has jurisdiction over them. Thus seminaries may be diocesan, regional, interdiocesan, provincial, and pontifical. The decree of the Second Vatican Council, *Optatam Totius,* issued in 1965, treats at length the curriculum and administration of seminarians. In 1979, Blessed Pope John Paul II issued the apostolic constitution *Sapientia Christiana* on ecclesiastical universities and faculties. The document immediately affects all institutions of higher education, including seminaries, which have been canonically erected or approved by the Holy See with the right to confer academic degrees by the authority of the same See. Indirectly it affects all Catholic seminaries. Among other detailed provisions, the constitution requires that "All teachers, before they are given a permanent post . . . must receive a declaration of *nihil obstat* [formal approval] from the Holy See" (Part One, III, 27).

SENSE OF SIN. A salutary fear produced in the believing soul by a clear understanding of the nature and malice of sin. Its keenness depends on a person's holiness and is most sensitive among the saints. Its quality is an awareness of God's sanctity in contrast with one's own weakness, and therefore a sense of constant dependence on divine grace.

SEPARATED BRETHREN. All Christians who are baptized and believe in Christ but are not professed Catholics. More commonly the term is applied to Protestants.

SEPARATION, MARITAL. Temporary or even permanent separation of husband and wife, without the right of remarriage until the death of one of the parties. Permitted by the Church on account of adultery, loss of faith, or other grave reasons. Cohabitation ceases but the marriage bond remains.

SEPTUAGINT. The most important translation of the Hebrew Old Testament into Greek. As the story goes, the Egyptian king Ptolemy II (309–246 B.C.) sought a copy of Jewish Law for his library. Eleazer, the Jewish high priest, sent six scholars from each of the Twelve Tribes to Alexandria to work on the translation. Because of the number of the scholars involved, their joint cooperative production was called the Septuagint, abbreviated LXX. The early Christians used the Septuagint as a basis for their belief in Jesus as the Messiah. As time went on, it steadily became a Christian possession and Jews lost interest in it. (Etym. Latin *septuaginta,* seventy.)

SEPULCHER. The small cavity in an altar stone in which are placed the relics of a saint. According to the Church's provisions since the Second Vatican Council, "The custom of putting relics of saints, whether martyrs or not, into or beneath consecrated altars, is to be commended. But it is important to verify the authenticity of the relics" (*Ordo Missae*, V, 266). (Etym. Latin *sepulcrum*, tomb, from *sepelire*, to bury.)

SERAPHIC BLESSING. The blessing that St. Francis of Assisi wrote down at the request of Brother Leo at Mount Alverna in 1224. It says: "May the Lord bless you and keep you. May He show His face to you and have mercy on you. May He turn His countenance to you and give you peace. May the Lord bless you, Brother Leo." It is based on the words of YHWH to Moses (Numbers 6:22–27) and is now among the solemn blessings in Ordinary Time that a priest may give at the end of the Mass.

SERAPHIM. Angels composing the highest choir of the angelic kingdom. The root meaning of their name is "to consume with fire," indicating their intense love of the Holy Trinity. (Etym. Hebrew *saraf*, plural *serafim*, burning, glowing.)

SERMON ON THE MOUNT. The most comprehensive discourse of Jesus reported in the New Testament. It was delivered to a multitude on one of the hills near Capernaum. It extends over three chapters in Matthew's Gospel (Matthew 5, 6, 7). An abbreviated form appears also in Luke (Luke 6:20–49). The sermon outlined the kind of life that a true follower of Christ should live if he seeks the kingdom of heaven. It opens with the Beatitudes as guides to those who are to be the "salt of the earth." Jesus explained how the New Law fulfills the Old Law but carries it to a new level where love is the ultimate motive for law. He taught the Lord's Prayer as the way the disciple should approach the Father. The Golden Rule should guide people in their relations with others. Marriage is to be monogamous, and the followers of Christ must be willing to carry the cross.

SERVICE. In general, performing one's religious duty as a creature toward God and fulfilling one's moral responsibility of meeting the needs of others. To serve God is the primary obligation of human beings, personally and socially, to be done in acts of worship and prayer, and in acts of virtue as prescribed by the natural and revealed laws of God. This corresponds to the first three commandments of the Decalogue and is summarized in the precept to "love the Lord your God with all your heart, with all your soul, and with all your mind" (Matthew 22:37). To serve others is the secondary obligation of a person, deriving from the preceding duty and depending on it. This corresponds to the last seven commandments of God and is synthesized in the precept "You must love your neighbor as yourself" (Matthew 22:39). On these two commandments of service, Christ says, rest the whole Law and the Prophets also. (Etym. Latin *servus*, a slave, servant, subject to the right of others.)

SERVILE FEAR. Selfish fear based on the dread of pain to oneself that would follow if another were offended. It is the fear of punishment for wrongdoing, without being motivated by honor or a sense of duty, and least of all by love. Theologically, however, servile fear may co-exist with filial fear. There is nothing incompatible in both loving and fearing God. The object of loving him is the divine goodness, of fearing him the divine justice. However, purely servile fear, with no love of God but only self-love that fears the divine punishments, is, at least in theory, inconsistent with the true love of God. See also FILIAL FEAR.

SERVILE WORK. Originally the work done by serfs from which they were freed on Sundays and holy days in order to worship God. Until recently, servile work, forbidden on Sundays, was work that was chiefly physical. At present servile work is heavy manual labor, or such work as in a given society people commonly associate with strenuous effort and do not engage in when they have the freedom to avoid it. Implicit in the Church's prohibition of servile work on Sundays is fidelity to the divine commandment to keep holy the Sabbath. This means avoiding activities that would hinder renewal of soul and body, i.e., needless work or business, unnecessary shopping or housekeeping.

SERVITES. Members of the Order of the Servants of the Blessed Virgin Mary. It was founded at Florence in 1233 by seven councilors of the city, who have since been canonized as the Seven Holy Founders, among whom the first leaders were St. Buonfiglio dei Monaldi and St. Alessio de' Falconieri, who remained a lay brother. The order was approved by the Holy See in 1249 and again in 1304. Its apostolate is among the faithful and non-Christians and includes promoting the devotion to the Blessed Virgin, especially under the title of the Sorrowful Mother. There are several institutes of women religious, pontifical and diocesan, specially devoted to Our Lady of Sorrows. The best known are the contemplative Servite nuns (Second Order) founded by two penitents of St. Philip Benizi (1233–85) about the time of his death; and the nuns of the Third Order, founded by St. Juliana Falconieri in 1306, who care for the sick and the poor and the education of children.

SEVEN COUNCILS. The first seven ecumenical councils of the Church: Nicaea (A.D. 325), Constantinople I (381), Ephesus (431), Chalcedon (451), Constantinople II (553), Constantinople III (680–81), and Nicaea II (787). They are the only councils on which the Eastern and Western Churches agree, and among the Eastern Churches separated from Rome are the only test of orthodoxy.

SEVEN SACRAMENTS. The seven rites instituted by Christ to confer the grace they signify: baptism, confirmation, Eucharist, penance, orders, matrimony, and anointing of the sick. The number and names of the sacraments and their substantial institution by Christ (purpose and essential ritual) were defined on March 3, 1547, by the Council of Trent (Denzinger 1601).

SEVEN WORDS OF CHRIST. The last words of Christ spoken from the Cross, recorded by Mark, Luke, and John. In sequence they are "Father, forgive them for they do not know what they are doing"; "Indeed, I promise you, today you will be with Me in paradise" to the penitent thief; "Woman, this is your son," spoken to Mary; "This is your mother," Christ's bequest to John; "My God, my God, why have you deserted me?" Parched with thirst, Christ called out, "I am thirsty"; and then, "It is accomplished." When every prophecy had been fulfilled, "Father, into your hands I commit my spirit." Several oratorios interpreting them have been written.

SEX EDUCATION. Instruction in the right use of sex, according to the teachings of the Church in the light of sound reason and the norms of Christian revelation. The Church teaches that young people should be given and adequately taught about the facts of human procreation according to their age and mental ability, more so today when they are exposed to so many perversions of sex in the media. It should always be given along with the necessary moral instruction. Parents have the primary right and duty to give this education. If they fail, it should be given by a truly qualified person. Collective or public sex education is discouraged because of the risk of incompetence in the teacher and the practical impossibility of meeting the personal needs of each child in a mass presentation of this intimate subject.

SEXT. The part of the Divine Office that is said at the sixth hour, that is, about midday. Depending on the time of day, the one reciting the office has a choice of saying Terce, Sext, or None.

SHEEP. Symbols of the Twelve Apostles, with Christ in the center as the Good Shepherd. A later symbol early found in the catacombs shows Our Lord either supporting a wounded sheep on his shoulder with the other sheep nearby or the Shepherd rescuing the wandering lost ewe caught in a briary thicket. The Twenty-third Psalm speaks of "the Lord is my shepherd, I shall not want." In song and story it is illustrative of God's Providence and concern. Sheep are symbols of docility, humility, and long suffering, all attributes expected of those who follow the Lamb of God. Sheep are also an emblem of St. Germaine (c. 1579–1601), the poor abandoned child of Pibrac, near Toulouse in France.

SHRINE. In general, a holy place. It may be a box-shaped repository in which relics of a saint are preserved; or the sacred image or statue of Our Lord, the Blessed Virgin, or a saint in church or at home to which special devotion is given. But mainly shrines are prominent sacred localities. They may be the burial place of a saint, or where he or she lived or died, or where a heavenly apparition took place. Shrines are the focuses of pilgrimages by the faithful and often of miraculous phenomena approved by the Church. (Etym. Latin *scrinium,* box, bookcase.)

SICK CALL. The call for a priest to minister to the spiritual needs of a person who is gravely ill. Normally the sacraments administered on a sick call are penance, Holy Communion, and anointing of the sick.

SIGN. Something that leads to something else. It may be an arbitrary or conventional sign that has a connection with what is signified only by agreement among people, as a flag symbolizes a nation. Or it may be a pure sign that leads to the knowledge of something without itself being first known, as our ideas lead to the knowledge of real objects. Instrumental signs give meaning or understanding, as words lead to the knowledge of things and of mental status. Manifestative signs show the existence of something else, as a person's external behavior indicates his or her personality and training.

Each of these types of signs may be either natural or supernatural depending on whether its basis is founded on natural reason or divine revelation.

The whole of the Church's liturgy is built on the function of word, action, and object signs as symbols of the sacred. But among the sacred signs the most important are the sacraments, which not only manifest the special presence of God but actually confer the grace they signify. (Etym. Latin *signum*, mark, sign, characteristic.)

SIGN OF THE CROSS. The most popular profession of the Christian faith in action form. The cruciform sign professes one's belief in human redemption through Christ's death on the Cross. The pronunciation of the names of the Three Divine Persons professes belief in the Holy Trinity. The first of the Church's sacramentals, it has its origins in apostolic times. It is made by saying, "In the name of the Father, and of the Son, and of the Holy Spirit," and its action takes the form of a cross. One touches the forehead, the breast, and the left and right shoulders with the right hand as the words are recited. The prayer ends with "Amen" and is regularly made with holy water as a person enters a church or chapel or, in religious communities, upon entering one's room.

SILENCE. In spiritual terms, the conscious effort to communicate with God or the invisible world of faith in preference to conversation with other people. It is, therefore, not the mere absence of sound or physical stillness, except as either a precondition for recollection of spirit or the perceptible effect of being recollected. (Etym. Latin *silere*, to be still, noiseless.)

SIMON. 1. Simon Peter, the head of the Apostles and the first pope (see also PETER); 2. Simon the Canaanite, called the Zealot. Another one of the Twelve Apostles (Luke 6:15); 3. a leper who was cured by Jesus and who invited him to his home in Bethany for dinner (Mark 14:3); 4. a cousin of Jesus referred to as his "brother" (Mark 6:3); 5. a man from Cyrene who was compelled to help Jesus carry the Cross (Mark 15:21).

SIMONY. A sacrilege that consists in buying and selling what is spiritual in return for what is temporal. In simony the person tries to equate material things, such as money, with spiritual things, such as divine grace, and treats the latter as though he or some other human being had full ownership of what really belongs to God. The term "simony" originated with the biblical account of Simon Magus, who sought to purchase from St. Peter the spiritual power derived from the imposition of hands and the invocation of the Holy Spirit (Acts 8:18). Simony includes both agreements that are illicit by divine law and those that the law of the Church forbids as greater protection and reverence for spiritual goods. Thus to promise prayers only in exchange for a certain sum of money is simony forbidden by divine (natural) law. To confer sacred orders or obtain some position of authority in the Church in return for money or its equivalent is simony forbidden by ecclesiastical law. When simony is against the divine law, it is always a grave sin. Its gravity in other cases depends on the serious nature of what is bought or sold and on the degree of scandal given. (Etym. Latin *simonia*, after Simon Magus.)

SIMPLICITY. As a character trait, the quality of not being affected; therefore, unassuming and unpretentious. A simple person is honest, sincere, and straightforward. Simplicity is single-mindedness. As a supernatural virtue it seeks only to do the will of God without regard to self-sacrifice or self-advantage.

SIN. "A word, deed or desire in opposition to the eternal law" (St. Augustine). Sin is a deliberate transgression of a law of God, which identifies the four essentials of every sin. A law is involved, implying that there are physical laws that operate with necessity and moral laws that can be disregarded by human beings. God is offended, so the divine dimension is never absent from any sin. Sin is a transgression, since Catholicism holds that grace is resistible and the divine will can be disobeyed. And the transgression is deliberate, which means that a sin is committed whenever a person knows that something is contrary to the law of God and then freely does the action anyway. (Etym. Old English *synn, syn,* sin; Old High German *sunta, suntea,* perhaps to Latin *sons,* guilty.) See also ACTUAL SIN, OMISSION, ORIGINAL SIN.

SIN AGAINST FAITH. The deliberate withholding of assent to what God has revealed. As commonly understood, there are five principal sins against faith: profession of a false religion, willful doubt, disbelief of an article of faith, denial of an article of faith, and culpable ignorance of the doctrines of the Catholic Church.

SINLESSNESS. Freedom from moral offenses against God. Absolute sinlessness, including impeccability or the inability to sin, was possessed only by Christ because as a divine person he could not contradict his own divine nature. Mary was also sinless, and could not sin, but only as a unique grace because she was the Mother of God. The rest of humanity is subject to the common weakness of fallen human nature. Except for an extraordinary privilege, accorded to few saints, no one is able to avoid for his whole life at least semideliberate venial sins.

SIN OF OMISSION. See OMISSION.

SINS AGAINST THE HOLY SPIRIT. Major offenses that carry a stubborn resistance to the inspirations of the Holy Spirit and a contempt of his gifts. They are despair of one's salvation, envy of another's spiritual good, opposing known truths of faith, obstinacy in sin, presumption of God's mercy, and final impenitence. Because those who sin in this way, resisting grace, do not wish to repent, we say that their sins cannot be forgiven them.

SINS CRYING TO HEAVEN. The four sins traditionally said to cry to heaven for vengeance: 1. willful murder (Genesis 4:10); 2. sodomy or homosexuality (Genesis 18:20); 3. oppression of the poor (Exodus 2:23); and 4. defrauding laborers of their wages (James 5:4).

SISTERS. A popular term for religious women, whether cloistered nuns or members of congregations under simple vows. The title corresponds to brothers in men's religious institutes and signifies that they are all members of the same spiritual family, share possessions in common, and live together in Christ-like charity.

SISTINE CHAPEL. Main chapel of the Vatican Palace, dedicated to Our Lady of the Assumption and as large as a church. It was designed by de' Dolci under Sixtus IV (r. 1471–84), hence its name. The series of famous frescoes on the left wall of events in the life of Moses and on the right side of the life of Christ were done by Botticelli, Cosimo,

Rosselli, Ghirlandaio, Perugino, and Pinturicchio. The ceiling, which is considered Michelangelo's masterpiece and the most gigantic piece of painting in existence, was begun in 1508 and finished four years later. Between sections of painted simulated vaulting, Michelangelo painted scenes from Creation, the Expulsion from Eden, and the Flood. On the lower part of this created vaulting are the famous series of the seated Prophets and Sibyls. In 1508 Julius II persuaded Michelangelo to paint the ceiling of the Sistine Chapel. It was finished in 1512. Twenty-three years later he began *The Last Judgment,* the most comprehensive painted composition in the world. It was completed in 1541. The marble screens and the choir gallery in the chapel were designed and executed by Mino da Fiesole. The altar, which only the pope may use, is inlaid with mother of pearl. The Sistine Chapel is the private chapel of the pope and the place where the conclaves for papal elections take place.

SLANDER. Detraction. Essentially slander is verbal defamation of a person's character, although it may be either spoken or written. It also implies suffering or positive harm done to the victim of slander. In popular language calumny is a form of slander. (Etym. Latin *scandalum,* stumbling block, offense.)

SLOTH. Sluggishness of soul or boredom because of the exertion necessary for the performance of a good work. The good work may be a corporal task, such as walking; or a mental exercise, such as writing; or a spiritual duty, such as prayer. Implicit in sloth is the unwillingness to exert oneself in the performance of duty because of the sacrifice and the effort required. As a sin, it is not to be confused with mere sadness over the inconvenience involved in fulfilling one's obligations nor with the indeliberate feelings of repugnance when faced with unpleasant work. It becomes sinful when the reluctance is allowed to influence the will and, as a result, what should have been done is either left undone or performed less well than a person is responsible for doing. Sloth may also mean a repugnance to divine inspirations or the friendship of God due to the self-sacrifice and labor needed to cooperate with actual grace or to remain in the state of grace. This kind of laziness is directly opposed to the love of God and is one of the main reasons why some people, perhaps after years of virtuous living, give up in the pursuit of holiness or even become estranged from God. (Etym. Middle-English *slowthe,* slow.)

SOBRIETY. The virtue that regulates a person's desire for and use of intoxicating drink. It is the virtue of temperance exercised in the practice of moderation in the use of alcoholic beverages. (Etym. Latin *sobrietas,* temperance in drinking, moderation.)

SOC. *Socius, socii*—companion, companions.

SOCIAL JUSTICE. The virtue that inclines one to cooperate with others in order to help make the institutions of society better serve the common good. While the obligation of social justice falls upon the individual, that person cannot fulfill the obligation alone, but must work in concert with others, through organized bodies, as a member of a group whose purpose is to identify the needs of society, and, by the use of appropriate means, to meet these needs locally, regionally, nationally, and even globally. Implicit in the virtue of social justice is an awareness that the world has entered into a new phase of social existence, with potential for great good or great harm vested in those who control the media and the structures of modern society. Christians, therefore, are expected to respond to the new obligations created by the extraordinary means of promoting the common good not only of small groups but literally of all humanity.

SOCIETY OF ST. VINCENT DE PAUL. An association of laymen founded by the French scholar Blessed Antoine Frédéric Ozanam (1813–53). Originally called the Conference of Charity, its members are devoted to personal service of the poor through the spiritual and corporal works of mercy. The first conference was formed at Paris in 1833. Under the revised regulations, women are admitted to membership. Emphasis is also placed on opening stores and rehabilitation workshops and employing handicapped persons in the service of their neighbor. A general council is the governing body of the society, now established throughout the world.

SODOM. A town always coupled with Gomorrah in characterizing places of infamy and sinful living. They were probably located on land now completely covered by the southern waters of the Dead Sea. The most likely explanation for this is that about 1900 B.C. an earthquake depressed the plain on which Sodom and Gomorrah were established (Genesis 13:10). Scripture interprets this catastrophe as YHWH's determination to punish an evil population. Abraham tried his best to dissuade YHWH, lest innocent people be punished with guilty, but evidently the only just man who could be found was Lot, Abraham's nephew (Genesis 18:20–32). Frequently in Scripture reference is made to the destruction of the doomed cities as proverbial warnings of YHWH's punishment of evil (Isaiah 3:9; Lamentations 4:6). Indeed, Jesus himself, in instructing his Apostles, told them that towns that refused to listen to their message would suffer the same fate as Sodom and Gomorrah (Matthew 10:15).

SODOMY. In general, unnatural sexual relations. The term is derived from the biblical city of Sodom on the Dead Sea, destroyed with the city of Gomorrah because of the wickedness of the people (Genesis 13:10). More particularly, sodomy is homosexuality between male persons or between a human being and an animal. (Etym. French *sodomie;* from Latin *Sodoma,* Sodom.)

SOLEMN BLESSING. One of a variety of special blessings that may be used at the discretion of the priest, at the end of Mass or after the Liturgy of the Word, the Divine Office, and the administration of the sacraments.

SOLEMNITY. The highest liturgical rank of a feast in the ecclesiastical calendar. Besides the movable feasts such as Easter and Pentecost, fourteen solemnities are celebrated in the universal Church: the Motherhood of God (January 1), Epiphany (January 6), St. Joseph (March 19), the Annunciation (March 25), Trinity Sunday (first after Pentecost), Corpus Christi (Thursday after Trinity Sunday), the Sacred Heart (Friday after the second Sunday after Pentecost), St. John the Baptist (June 24), Sts. Peter and Paul (June 29), the Assumption of the Blessed Virgin (August 15), All Saints (November 1), Christ the King (the last Sunday of the ecclesiastical year), the Immaculate Conception (December 8), and Christmas (December 25). (Etym. Latin *sollemnis,* stated, established, appointed.)

SOLICITUDE. As one of the charisms of administration in the apostolic church, it was the anxious concern of a bishop about the spiritual welfare of his people. St. Paul's solicitude for the churches under his care has been the model for bishops ever since (II Corinthians 11:28). (Etym. Latin *sollicitus,* thoroughly moved, agitated.)

SOLOMON. The third King of Israel, son of David and Bathsheba, ruled his country from 961 to 922 B.C. Because it was a peaceful period in Jewish history, Solomon was able to extend Israel's borders farther than they had ever been before and to increase its prosperity and power to a level never equaled since. His accession to the throne was threatened by his brother, Adonijah, who conspired against him (I Kings 1, 2). But their father, David, preferred Solomon and had him secretly anointed. Eventually Adonijah and his military supporter, Joab, were executed for their conspiratorial efforts. Solomon displayed such remarkable intellectual qualities that his court became a center of culture (I Kings 5:14). He composed an extraordinary number of songs, and it seems certain that a great part of the book of Proverbs had Solomon for its author (I Kings 5:12). He launched an impressive building campaign that included the Temple of YHWH and a magnificent royal palace (I Kings 6:1; 7:1). He built a fleet of ships and extended Israel's trade to many nations. One device Solomon employed to extend his power was marrying many wives who belonged to ruling families in neighboring countries. While this was shrewd strategy, it led to his decline: he antagonized YHWH, who resented this infiltration of pagan religions and threatened punishment (I Kings 11:1–8). During the reign of Solomon's son, Rehoboam, YHWH lived up to his threat. "Israel has been separated from the House of David until the present day" (I Kings 12:19).

SONG OF SONGS. See CANTICLE OF CANTICLES.

SON OF GOD. The Second Person of the Holy Trinity, who became man to suffer and die for the redemption of mankind. Christ is therefore the true, natural Son of God, as testified by the Father in the vision recorded at the baptism of Christ: "You are my Son, the Blessed" (Luke 3:22); and, as described by St. Paul, that "God spoke to our ancestors through the prophets; but in our own time, the last days, He has spoken to us through His Son, the Son that He has appointed to inherit everything and through whom He made everything there is" (Hebrews 1:1–2).

SON OF MAN. The most frequently used title of Christ in the New Testament, occurring eighty-two times, all but once (Acts 7:56) in the Gospels. A messianic title (Daniel 7:2–14), it identifies the heavenly transcendence of the Savior while stressing his humanity, in contrast with the "Son of God," which emphasizes his divinity.

SONS OF GOD. A title used by Scripture for the angels, the Chosen People, the prophets, and, in the New Testament, all who believe in God and do his will.

SORROWFUL MYSTERIES. Second chaplet of the Rosary, consisting of 1. Christ's Agony in the Garden of Gethsemane; 2. his Scourging at the Pillar; 3. the Crowning with Thorns; 4. the Way of the Cross; and 5. the Crucifixion. See also JOYFUL MYSTERIES, LUMINOUS MYSTER-IES, GLORIOUS MYSTERIES.

SOTERIOLOGY. That part of Christology which treats of Christ's work of salvation. It covers the study of man's fall in Adam and the sins of mankind, which needed a Savior; the doctrine of grace by which the guilt and consequences of sin are removed; and especially the two-fold mystery of Christ as Redeemer and Mediator of the human race. (Etym. Greek *sōtērion,* deliverance; from *sōtēr,* savior; from *sōzein,* to save; from *saos,* safe.)

SOUL. The spiritual immortal part in human beings that animates their body. Though a substance in itself, the soul is naturally ordained toward a body; separated, it is an "incomplete" substance. The soul has no parts, it is therefore simple, but it is not without accidents. The faculties are its proper accidents. Every experience adds to its acci-dental form. It is individually created for each person by God and in-fused into the body at the time of human insemination. It is moreover created in respect to the body it will inform so that the substance of bodily features and of mental characteristics insofar as they depend on organic functions is safeguarded. As a simple and spiritual sub-stance, the soul cannot die. Yet it is not the total human nature, since a human person is composed of body animated by the soul. In phi-losophy, animals and plants are also said to have souls, which operate as sensitive and vegetative principles of life. Unlike the human spirit, these souls are perishable. The rational soul contains all the powers of the two other souls and is the origin of the sensitive and vegetative functions in the human being.

SOUL OF THE CHURCH. The Holy Spirit, who animates the Mysti-cal Body of Christ. As Christ is the head of the Church, so the Holy Spirit is her soul. Like the soul in the human body, the Holy Spirit is the source of being and life in the Church. It is the Holy Spirit who welds together the members of the Church among themselves, with

Christ their head, since the same Holy Spirit is entirely in the head and entirely in the members of the Mystical Body. It is he who by his assistance upholds the hierarchy in their exercise of the teaching, pastoral, and priestly office. It is he who by his grace arouses and fosters every solitary activity among the faithful. All the life and growth of Christianity proceed from this divine life principle indwelling in the Church.

SOURCE OF SIN. The principle or root of all sinful human actions. Two sources are commonly found in revelation, deriving from the two sides to every sin: the turning to transient satisfaction and the turning away from everlasting good. As regards the first, the principle of all sin can be called lust—lust in its most general sense, namely, the unbridled desire for one's own pleasure. As regards the second, the principle is pride—pride in its general sense, the lack of submission to God. Lust and pride in this pervasive sense may also be called capital sins, but more properly they are the roots and sprouts of vice, as the desire for happiness is the root of all virtue.

SPECIES. Appearances, especially those of bread and wine, after the Eucharistic consecration. The term "species" is used by the Council of Trent (Denzinger 1652) to identify the accidents—i.e., the size, weight, color, resistance, taste, and odor of bread, which remain exactly the same after transubstantiation. They are not mere appearances as though these physical properties were unreal. But they are appearances because after the consecration they lack any substance that underlies them or in which they inhere.

SPE SALVI. Encyclical by Pope Benedict XVI on the significance of a faith-based hope (November 30, 2007). The encyclical is a meditation on St. Paul's statement "in hope we were saved" (Romans 8:24). Pope Benedict XVI teaches that the message of the Gospel is not just the good news but is a transforming reality; man's only authentic hope comes from a God who loves him; hope relates to eternal life, which comes from Redemption by Jesus Christ; and Christian hope in eternal life is not individualistic but also embraces the hope for the salvation of others. The encyclical also gives some "settings" for learning and practicing hope.

SPIRIT. That which is positively immaterial. It is pure spirit if it has no dependence on matter either for its existence or for any of its activities. God is uncreated pure Spirit; the angels are created pure spirits. The human soul is more properly called spiritual. Although it can exist independent of the body, it nevertheless in this life depends extrinsically on the body for its operations, and in the life to come retains a natural affinity for the body, with which after the resurrection it will be reunited for all eternity. (Etym. Latin *spiritus,* breath, life, soul, mind, spirit, power.)

SPIRITUAL DEATH. The state of the soul in mortal sin, based on the analogy with bodily death. Just as a physical body may be not only ill or suffer injury but cease to retain its principle of life, so the soul can lose sanctifying grace through mortal sin and supernaturally cease to live. It is, therefore, spiritually dead because it is no longer united with God, who gives it supernatural life, even as a body is dead on separation from its animating principle, which is the soul. While still on earth, this union with God is both a possession and a movement. We possess him by grace and in faith, and we are moving toward him in the beatific vision of glory. When persons sin mortally, they are twice dead: once because they lose the gift of divine life they formerly had and again because they are no longer moving toward the consummation of that life in heaven.

Mortal sins are no longer remissible by any power within the soul itself, much as the human body, once dead, cannot be brought back to life except by a special intervention of God. In Patristic literature the restoration is compared with the resuscitation of Lazarus. The exercise of almighty power in either case is the same. "Everyone who sins, dies," says St. Augustine. Only the Lord "by his great grace and great mercy raises souls to life again, that we may not die eternally" (*In Joannis Evangelium,* 49). Only infinite mercy can reconcile the grave sinner.

SPIRITUAL DIRECTION. Assisting persons to understand themselves and, with divine grace, to grow in the practice of Christian virtue.

SPIRITUAL EXERCISES. Any set program of religious duties, notably the prayers, meditations, and spiritual reading required of persons following a distinctive rule of life. Also the period of silence and prayerful reflection practiced annually (or more often) in a retreat. Particularly the Spiritual Exercises by St. Ignatius Loyola, drawn up as a method of arriving at the amendment of one's life and resolving on a determined way of holiness. The Exercises of St. Ignatius were first composed by him in a cave at Manresa, in Spain, after his conversion. They have been recommended by successive popes as a most effective program of spiritual renewal for priests, religious, and the laity. Their underlying principle is their opening statement that "Man was created to praise, reverence and serve our Creator and Lord, and by this means to save his soul." Given this basic purpose of human existence, the believer is told how to reach his or her destiny by overcoming sinful tendencies and imitating Christ in carrying the Cross on earth in order to be glorified with Christ in the life to come.

SPIRITUALISM. Belief that the spirits of the dead in various ways communicate with the living through the agency of a person called a medium. It is also a religious movement that professes to be Christian and has been organized into several denominations, with churches, schools, and an ordained clergy.

The doctrinal position of Spiritualists varies considerably, but one doctrine is common to all of them, namely "that the existence and personal identity of the individual continue after the change called death; and that communication with the so-called dead is a fact scientifically proved by the phenomena of Spiritualism." Moreover, many adherents believe that Christ was a medium, that the Annunciation was a message from the spirit world, and Christ's Resurrection a proof that all human beings live on after death as disembodied spirits.

Religious services and séances are held in churches, in private homes, or in rented halls. They follow the general pattern of Protestant churches, with prayer, singing, music, reading from the *Spiritualist Manual,* a sermon or lecture, and spirit messages from the departed. Communication with the spirit world is not limited to regular church services, not even to public assemblies of professions. "Making contact" with the dead is recommended at other times, even in the privacy of one's room and without the aid of a medium.

Normally, however, spirit communications require a person who acts as a medium between the mortal audience and the world beyond. Mediums are not the ministers in a congregation; they are normally not supported by free-will offerings but through the fees that are charged for classes and séances.

The Catholic Church, through the Holy Office, has declared it is not lawful "to take part in Spiritualistic communications or manifestations of any kind, whether through a so-called medium or without one, whether hypnotism is used or not, even with the best of intentions among the participants, whether for the purpose of interrogating the souls of the departed or spiritual beings, whether by listening to their responses or even in idle curiosity, even with the tacit or express protestation of not having anything to do with the evil spirits" (Denzinger 3642).

Behind the Church's attitude toward Spiritualism is the concern that a Catholic would expose himself to the risk of actually dealing with the evil spirit. The assumption is that if fraud or deception are excluded, and manifestations occur that are beyond natural explanation, the active agent in these cases is neither God nor any one of the good spirits (whether angelic or human) but demonic forces that are sure to mislead the Catholic and endanger the integrity of his faith.

SPIRITUAL LIFE. The life of the Holy Spirit, dwelling in the souls of the faithful and enabling them to praise and love God and serve him in the practice of virtue. It is called the spiritual life because 1. its animating principle is the Spirit of God, the "Soul of the soul" in sanctifying grace; 2. it is the supernatural life of the human spirit; 3. it is mainly lived out in the spiritual faculties of intellect and will, although affecting the whole person, body and soul.

SPIRITUAL MARRIAGE. The calm, abiding, transforming union of the soul with God. Raptures and ecstasies may occur, but they are replaced by a marvelous peace and serenity enjoyed in the presence of a reciprocated love. St. Teresa describes this stage of intimacy with God as one of complete forgetfulness of self, thinking only of God and his glory, leaving her with an insatiable thirst to suffer with Christ in love and in sole conformity with his will. An ardent zeal for the sanctification of other souls follows the repose. Aridities disappear, leaving only a memory of God's tenderness.

SPIRITUAL READING. As the Lectio Divina prescribed in monasticism from the earliest times, it is all reading that is conducive to prayer and closer union with God. The Sacred Scriptures have always held the primacy of honor in such reading, along with writings of the Church's teachers—notably, the popes and bishops, the writings and lives of the saints, and all other forms of composition whose avowed purpose as writing is to enlighten the mind and inspire the will and affections to the worship and service of God.

SPIRITUAL RELATIONSHIP. Religious affinity arising from active participation in the sacraments of baptism and confirmation. The sponsors in both sacraments become spiritually related to those whom they sponsor. Also the one baptizing becomes spiritually related to the person baptized. The relationship arising from sponsorship at baptism becomes an impediment to marriage with the person sponsored.

SPIRITUAL WORKS OF MERCY. The traditional seven forms of Christian charity in favor of the soul or spirit of one's neighbor, in contrast with the corporal works of mercy that minister to people's bodily needs. They are converting the sinner, instructing the ignorant, counseling the doubtful, comforting the sorrowful, bearing wrongs patiently, forgiving injuries, and praying for the living and the dead. Their bases are the teaching of Christ and the practice of the Church since apostolic times.

SPONSOR. The confirmation sponsor undertakes a spiritual responsibility for the confirmand. The confirmand has only one sponsor for the Sacrament of Confirmation. It is desirable, though not necessary, that one of the godparents be the sponsor.

SPOUSE (BRIDE) OF CHRIST. Primarily the Church, founded by Christ, which St. Paul elaborately describes as espoused to Christ. Also a woman who vows her chastity to God in order to be more like Christ and more intimately united with him. Among certain mystics, such as Sts. Teresa of Avila and Catherine of Siena, an extraordinary union in prayer with the Savior.

SPRINKLING. The casting of water from a distance so that it falls upon the head and flows in the administration of baptism. It is the only way in which more than one person can be baptized simultaneously by one minister. It is seldom used now, but in the past was sometimes necessary, as when a large group of people were to be baptized by a single missionary.

"STABAT MATER." A hymn ("At the Cross her station keeping . . .") commonly attributed to Jacopone da Todi (1230–1306), Franciscan poet. It gradually came into liturgical use by the late Middle Ages and since 1727 has been part of the Eucharistic liturgy and the Divine Office for the feast of Our Lady of Sorrows. Its history in music dates largely from modern times. Another hymn, "Stabat Mater Speciosa," apparently modeled on "Stabat Mater Dolorosa," describes Mary's sorrows at Bethlehem, but it has never become part of the liturgy.

STATE OF GRACE. Condition of a person who is free from mortal sin and pleasing to God. It is the state of being in God's friendship and the necessary condition of the soul at death in order to attain heaven. See also SANCTIFYING GRACE.

STATES OF PERFECTION. Those stable forms of living in which some of the faithful bind themselves by vows, or promises equivalent to vows, to practice the evangelical counsels of poverty, chastity, and obedience. They are called states of perfection because those who live in these states agree to follow a particular rule of life, approved by the Church, whose faithful observance will certainly lead to Christian perfection.

STATIONS OF THE CROSS. A devotion performed by meditating on the Passion of Christ successively before fourteen stations of the Cross. The stations are normally wooden crosses that are attached to the interior walls of a church, although they may be erected anywhere—e.g., outside along a pathway. The pictures or representations depicting various scenes from Christ's *Via Crucis* are aids to devotion on the traditional stations:

1. Jesus Is Condemned to Death
2. Jesus Bears His Cross
3. Jesus Falls the First Time
4. Jesus Meets His Mother
5. Jesus Is Helped by Simon
6. Veronica Wipes the Face of Jesus
7. Jesus Falls a Second Time
8. Jesus Consoles the Women of Jerusalem
9. Jesus Falls a Third Time
10. Jesus Is Stripped of His Garments
11. Jesus Is Nailed to the Cross
12. Jesus Dies on the Cross
13. Jesus Is Taken Down from the Cross
14. Jesus Is Laid in the Tomb

A plenary indulgence is gained, once a day, for making the Way of the Cross. But it is only necessary for a person to move from one station to the next and "nothing more is required than a pious meditation on the Passion and Death of the Lord, which need not be a particular consideration of the individual mysteries of the stations."

STERILIZATION. Any action that deprives the body, either temporarily or permanently, of the power either to beget or to bear children. It consists in rendering the faculties of generation unfruitful. Four types of sterilization are distinguished in Catholic morality: therapeutic, contraceptive, eugenic, and penal. (Etym. Latin *sterilis*, unfruitful.)

STEWARDSHIP. In biblical usage the management of whatever a person is entrusted with, not only to preserve but also to profitably administer for his master, ultimately for God. Christ proposed the faithful steward as a model for the responsible Christian (Luke 12:42). The Apostles are chosen stewards of the divine mysteries (I Corinthians 4:1–2), and every Christian is a steward of the mysteries of God (I Peter 4:10). Jesus praised the unjust steward of the parable, not because he was dishonest but because of his foresight, since "the children of this world are more astute in dealing with their own kind than are the children of light" (Luke 16:1–8). This is the ultimate lesson of stewardship: that a human being is not owner but only custodian of God's gifts in this world, to use them and produce with them the fruits of eternal life. (Etym. Old English *stigweard,* "keeper of the hall": *stig,* hall + *weard,* keeper.)

STIGMATA. Phenomenon in which a person bears all or some of the wounds of Christ in his or her own body, i.e., on the feet, hands, side, and brow. The wounds appear spontaneously, from no external source, and periodically there is a flow of fresh blood. The best known stigmatic was St. Francis of Assisi. During an ecstasy on Mount Alvernia on September 17, 1224, he saw a seraph offer him an image of Jesus crucified and imprint upon him the sacred stigmata. Blood used to flow from these wounds until the time of his death two years later. He tried to conceal the phenomenon but not very successfully. Since that time scholarly research has established some 320 cases of stigmatization, among them more than sixty persons who have been canonized.

Authentic stigmatization occurs only among people favored with ecstasy and is preceded and attended by keen physical and moral sufferings that thus make the subject conformable to the suffering Christ. The absence of suffering would cast serious doubt on the validity of the stigmata, whose assumed purpose is to symbolize union with Christ crucified and participation in his own martyrdom.

Through centuries of canonical processes, the Church has established certain criteria for determining genuine stigmata. Thus the wounds are localized in the very spots where Christ received the five wounds, which does not occur if the bloody sweat is produced by hysteria or hypnotism. Generally the wounds bleed afresh and the pains recur on the days or during the seasons associated with the Savior's Passion, such as Fridays or feast days of Our Lord. The wounds do not become festered and the blood flowing from them is pure, whereas the slightest natural lesion in some other part of the body develops an infection. Moreover, the wounds do not yield to the usual medical treatment and may remain for as long as thirty to forty years. The wounds bleed freely and produce a veritable hemorrhage, and this takes place not only at the beginning but again and again. Also the extent of the hemorrhage is phenomenal; the stigmata lie on the surface, removed from the great blood vessels, yet the blood literally streams from them. Finally true stigmata are not found except in persons who practice the most heroic virtues and possess a special love of the Cross. (Etym. Latin *stigma;* from Greek, tattoo mark; from *stizein,* to prick, tattoo.)

STIPEND. Canonically speaking, a means of support for the clergy. Also a part of the revenue of a benefice to which a cleric attached to the benefice is entitled. It is popularly spoken of today as the offering made to a priest on the occasion of having him offer Mass for one's special intention.

STOLE. A liturgical vestment composed of a strip of material, several inches wide, and worn around the neck by priests and bishops; at the left shoulder like a sash by deacons, for the celebration of Mass, administration of the sacraments, and ceremonies of the Blessed Sacrament.

SUBJECTIVISM. Any view of human nature and activity that denies the objective order of reality. It takes on one of three principal forms. In philosophy, it claims that a human being can have no direct knowledge or certitude about the world outside the mind. In theology, it holds that faith is essentially each person's own experience and not the free assent of the mind to God's revelation. In morals, it admits no principles or norms of conduct except those created by each individual's autonomous will, which is then equated with conscience.

SUBSIDIARITY. The principle by which those in authority recognize the rights of the members in a society, and those in higher authority respect the rights of those in lower authority.

SUBTILITY. Quality of the glorified human body, which St. Paul calls "spiritualized." It is not, however, to be conceived as a transformation of the body into spirit or as a refinement into an ethereal substance. The prototype is the risen body of Christ, which emerged from the sealed tomb and penetrated closed doors. The basis for subtility lies in the complete dominion of the body by the transfigured soul.

SUFFERING. The disagreeable experience of the soul that comes with the presence of evil or the privation of some good. Although commonly synonymous with pain, suffering is rather the reaction to pain, and in this sense suffering is a decisive factor in Christian spirituality. Absolutely speaking, suffering is possible because we are creatures, but in the present order of Providence suffering is the result of sin having entered the world. Its purpose, however, is not only to expiate wrongdoing but to enable the believer to offer God a sacrifice of praise of his divine right over creatures, to unite oneself with Christ in his sufferings as an expression of love, and in the process to become more like Christ, who, having joy set before him, chose the Cross, and thus "to make up all that has still to be undergone by Christ for the sake of His body, the Church" (Colossians 1:24). (Etym. Latin *sufferre*, to sustain, to bear up: *sub-*, up from under + *ferre*, to bear.)

SUFFICIENT GRACE. Actual grace considered apart from the supernatural effect for which it was bestowed. It may therefore mean the grace that does not meet with adequate cooperation on the part of the human recipient, and then it is merely sufficient grace. It is enough to enable a person to perform a salutary act, but that person freely declines to cooperate. Or it may simply mean the grace that gives one the power to accomplish a salutary action, as distinct from an efficacious grace, which secures that the salutary act is accomplished. See also ACTUAL GRACE, EFFICACIOUS GRACE, GRACE, HABITUAL GRACE, JUSTIFYING GRACE, SACRAMENTAL GRACE, SANCTIFYING GRACE.

SUICIDE. The direct killing of oneself on one's own authority. It is a grave sin against the natural and revealed law. The suicide offends against the divine precept "You shall not kill." One causes grave injury to the welfare of society and violates the virtue of charity to oneself. God is the supreme and exclusive owner of all things, so exercising ownership over life is lawful only to God. He alone can take human life when he wills. The one who directly takes his or her own life violates the rights of God. (Etym. Latin *sui*, self + *cidium*, a killing.)

SUMMA CONTRA GENTILES. The great apologetical work of St. Thomas Aquinas (1225–74), written from 1258 to 1261. Its purpose is to convince the unbeliever of the inherent reasonableness of the Christian faith. First are set forth those truths that can be discovered by reason alone; then higher truths, beginning with morality; and finally the great mysteries, which though not provable by reason are shown to be consistent with reason and remarkably intelligible.

SUMMA THEOLOGIAE. The principal doctrinal synthesis in Catholic theology, written by St. Thomas Aquinas (1225–74). The method used was the application of Aristotelian philosophy in the systematic and rational explanation of dogma and morals, without any substantial modification of the traditional teaching of the Church. Its central theme is God considered under three aspects: 1. he is studied as *Being*, not only in himself but also outside himself, as the source of all things; 2. he is then seen as the *Good*, that is, as the end of created beings and especially of angels and men; 3. he is finally studied as the *Way* of humanity to God, not humanity in the abstract, but of the fallen human being who needed an incarnate God to be saved.

SUMMORUM PONTIFICUM. *Motu proprio* of Pope Benedict XVI dated July 7, 2007, stating that the Missal of Paul VI and the Missal of Blessed Pope John XXIII are two usages of the one Roman Rite. The Missal of Blessed John XXIII (1962) is called the Extraordinary Form of the Roman Rite. The intent of the *motu proprio* is to permit a greater use of the Missal of Blessed Pope John XXIII published in 1962.

SUNDAY. The first day of the week. Since New Testament times it replaced the Jewish Sabbath (Acts 20:7; I Corinthians 16:2). St. John called it the Lord's Day, which the Western Church later translated *Dominica*. The immediate reason for substituting Sunday for the Sabbath was to commemorate Christ's Resurrection from the dead. Eventually Sunday also became a memorial of the descent of the Holy

Spirit on Pentecost. Moreover, the original purpose of the Sabbath remained as a liturgical day of rest to recall God's lordship of the universe. "On the seventh day, He rested; that is why YHWH has blessed the sabbath day and made it sacred" (Exodus 20:8–11).

SUNDAY OBSERVANCE. The Catholic equivalent of the divine commandment to keep the Sabbath holy. In general, Sunday observance means assisting at Mass and resting from servile work.

SUPERIOR, ECCLESIASTICAL. A member of the Catholic hierarchy who has ordinary or delegated jurisdiction in the Church. The highest ecclesiastical superior is the pope, who has jurisdiction over the whole Church; then the cardinals, archbishops, and bishops, who have jurisdiction over the faithful in the territories under their care; and finally those in sacred orders who have been entrusted with the care of souls, in accordance with the ecclesiastical office that they hold.

SUPERIOR, RELIGIOUS. The person who governs a religious community. His or her powers are defined in the constitutions of the institute and in the common law of the Church. All religious superiors have dominative power over their subjects, i.e., they have the right of authority over the acts of the persons in their community. In a clerical exempt institute, superiors also have ecclesiastical jurisdiction.

SUPERNATURAL ORDER. The sum total of heavenly destiny and all the divinely established means of reaching that destiny, which surpass the mere powers and capacities of human nature.

SUPERNATURAL REVELATION. Divine communication of truth in which either the manner of communication or its content is beyond the capacity of human nature to attain. Thus revelation may be supernatural in its objective source, which is more than the universe naturally tells about its Creator, and again supernatural in the subjective powers by which a person acquires what God desires to reveal. Revelation may also be supernatural in its very essence, as when God discloses such mysteries as the Trinity and the Incarnation. Or it may be, and always is, supernatural in the manner that God chooses to use for communicating himself to human beings. It partakes of a miraculous enlightenment of the seer who then serves as divine legate for sharing with others what God has supernaturally communicated to that person. In every case, however, the acceptance of revelation requires the influx of supernatural grace to enable a person to believe.

SUPERSTITION. The unseemly or irreverent worship of God, or giving to a creature the worship that belongs to God. Rendering unbecoming worship to God may stem either from false devotion or from a tendency toward magic. Giving divine worship to a creature is either idolatry, divination, or vain observance. The term "superstition" more commonly means unbecoming worship to God.

When superstition arises from false devotion, it is really superfluous worship of God, which may take on a variety of forms. Their common denominator is an excessive concern that unless certain external practices, such as multiplication of prayers, are performed God will be displeased.

When superstition stems from a tendency toward magic, it reflects a false mentality that may or may not be the root of false devotion. Behind the false mentality is the notion that certain ritual practices, such as chain prayers or veneration of unapproved objects, carry with them an efficacy that is contrary to sound reason or the teaching of the Church.

SURPLICE. A large-sleeved tunic of half length, made of linen or cotton, without a cincture, and occasionally embroidered at hem and sleeves. It is a liturgical garment worn by all clergy in choir, during processions, and when administering the sacraments. (Etym. Latin *superpellicium* [originally worn by clergymen of northern countries over their fur coats].)

SUSCIPE. A prayer, composed by St. Ignatius Loyola in the Spiritual Exercises, to be said as an act of total self-sacrifice to God. It reads: "Take, O Lord, and receive all my liberty, my memory, my understanding, and all my will, all that I have and possess. You have given all of these to me; to you I restore them. All are yours, dispose of them all according to your will. Give me your love and your grace; having but these I am rich enough and ask for nothing more."

SYLLABUS OF PIUS IX. A series of eighty condemned propositions listing the prevalent errors that aimed at the undermining of society, morality, and religion. Every Catholic is expected to give exterior and interior assent to the condemnation of errors expressed in this syllabus.

SYLLABUS OF PIUS X. A series of propositions condemned by the Congregation of the Holy Office and ratified by the pope as decreed in the encyclical *Lamentabili* (July 3, 1907). It denounced the tenets of Modernism and repudiated their errors. The basis of these false doctrines was the pseudo-scientific theory of evolution on human knowledge and belief. By a subsequent *motu proprio* the pope further confirmed the syllabus by publishing the *Oath Against Modernism* (September 1, 1910).

SYMBOLISM. Investing outward things or actions with an inner meaning. Its effectiveness depends on the depth of personal commitment to the interior truth symbolized and the ability of a symbol to convey its inner meaning. Early Christian symbolism arose partially as a result of persecution. It was necessary to veil beliefs under emblems and figures. Another contributing factor was the instinctive religious desire to envelop the personal and collective life of the people in expressions and reminders of their faith. In time, every detail of Church art and architecture, of the liturgy and private devotion, acquired definable religious meaning. Symbolism is the universal language of every living religion. It is especially rich in Catholic Christianity because of the Church's encouragement, but mainly because the mysteries of the faith are too profound ever to fully understand. Symbols enable the mind to dwell on these mysteries with prayerful reflection and ever greater comprehension.

SYNAGOGUE (BIBLICAL). The Jewish community center where the study and exposition of the Old Testament was conducted. Although its main function was religious, it also served as a meeting place for other kinds of community activities—funerals, meetings, and business affairs. A staff of officials managed the synagogue, directed ceremonies, and supervised educational programs.

SYNCRETISM. The effort to unite different doctrines and practices, especially in religion. Such unions or amalgams are part of cultural history and are typical of what has occurred in every segment of the non-Christian world. Syncretism is also applied to the ecumenical efforts among separated Christian churches and within Catholicism to combine the best elements of different theological schools. But in recent years the term mainly refers to misguided claims that religious unity can be achieved by ignoring the differences between faiths on the assumption that all creeds are essentially one and the same.

(Etym. Greek *synkrētizo,* to unite disunited elements into a harmonious whole; from *synkrētizmos,* federation of Cretan cities.)

SYNOD. An assembly of ecclesiastics, not necessarily all bishops, gathered together under ecclesiastical authority to discuss and decide on matters pertaining to doctrine, discipline, or liturgy under their jurisdiction. The words "synod" and "council" were for centuries synonymous, and the terms are still interchangeable. At the Council of Trent, "synod" referred to a diocesan assembly, which the council decreed should be held once every year. In the Code of Canon Law, diocesan synods were legislated to be held every ten years at least, at which only a bishop was to have legislative authority, everyone else being only a consultor. (Etym. Latin *synodus;* from Greek *sunodos,* meeting: *sun-,* together + *hodos,* road, way, journey.)

SYNOPTIC PROBLEM. The problem of how the Gospels according to Matthew, Mark, and Luke are related, since large areas of these cover the same subject matter, often in similar words and yet sometimes showing remarkable differences. There is no single solution to the Synoptic Problem. In general, Catholic scholarship favors the basic tradition, dating from the second century, that the Gospels bearing the names of Matthew, Mark, and Luke were written by Matthew the Apostle, Mark the disciple of Peter, and Luke the disciple of Paul; that Matthew's original Gospel was in Aramaic, later translated into Greek; and that the similarities among the Synoptics are due to their dealing with the same historical data, and their differences due to each evangelist's perspective, personality, and distinctive purpose in writing a separate Gospel. Among Protestants the Synoptic Problem is commonly resolved by postulating Mark as the first and fundamental Gospel, on which the others built, along with other sources, notably the unknown Q whose existence is inferred purely from the textual evidence.

SYNOPTICS. The first three evangelists, Matthew, Mark, and Luke. They are so named because they follow the same general plan and reflect great similarity in the events related and even in literary expression. They offer the same comprehensive view of the life and teachings of Jesus Christ.

SYRIAN RITE. In the East it is also known as the Chaldean, Assyrian, or Persian Rite and is used by both Catholics and dissident Oriental

Christians. The language is Syriac or Aramaic. Among the Syrian
Nestorians there are only five sacraments, with penance and anointing of the sick practically unknown. In the West, the Syriac Rite is
also used by both Catholics and non-Catholic Orientals, notably the
Syrian Catholics, Maronites, and Jacobites. Among the last mentioned this rite is interspersed with many Arabic prayers.

T

TABERNACLE. A cupboard or boxlike receptacle for the exclusive reservation of the Blessed Sacrament. In early Christian times the sacred species was reserved in the home because of possible persecution. Later dove-shaped tabernacles were suspended by chains before the altar. Nowadays tabernacles may be round or rectangular and made of wood, stone, or metal. They are covered with a veil and lined with precious metal or silk, with a corporal beneath the ciboria or other sacred vessels. According to the directive of the Holy See, since the Second Vatican Council, tabernacles are always solid and inviolable and located in the middle of the main altar or on a side altar, but always in a truly prominent place (*Eucharisticum Mysterium,* May 25, 1967, II, C). (Etym. Latin *tabernaculum,* tent, diminutive of *taberna,* hut, perhaps from Etruscan.)

"TANTUM ERGO." The last two verses of the hymn "Pange Lingua," composed by St. Thomas Aquinas and long prescribed for singing at Benediction of the Blessed Sacrament. A modern English version reads:

> Down in adoration falling,
> Lo, the sacred host we hail.
> Lo, o'er ancient forms departing
> Newer rites of grace prevail;
> Faith for all defects supplying
> Where the feeble senses fail.
>
> To the everlasting Father,
> And the Son who reigns on high.
> With the Holy Spirit proceeding
> Forth from each eternally,
> Be salvation, honor, blessing,
> Might and endless majesty. Amen.

TEILHARDISM. The evolutionary theory of the French Jesuit Teilhard de Chardin (1881–1955). He held that the universe is subject to four stages of development: 1. cosmogenesis, or evolution from the elements to organized matter; 2. biogenesis, or evolution from organized matter to life; 3. noo-genesis, or evolution from living things to rational beings; and 4. Christogenesis, or evolution from individual rational humanity to a society in which Christ was the Lord of the world. Teilhardism was the object of two critical documents from the Holy See, in 1952 and 1967, which stated that his writings abound "in such ambiguities and indeed serious errors as to offend Catholic doctrine."

TELEPATHY. The direct communication of ideas from one mind to another without words, signs, gestures, or any other ordinary means of communicating thought. Extensive data and years of psychical research indicate that such manner of communicating knowledge does occur in exceptional cases or with exceptional people. When verified, the phenomenon is purely natural and the use of telepathic powers by one who possesses them cannot be called divination, nor does their use pose any special moral problems. It should be judged by the general principles applicable to any other human being's behavior.

It is altogether another question whether in a given case of reputed telepathy any preternatural agency has been active. Instances of supposed communication of thought without verbal or other sensory means are reported in the lives of the saints. But the Church does not hold that such phenomena are positive signs of a person's sanctity. (Etym. Greek *tēle*, at a distance + *pathein*, to experience.)

TEMPERANCE. The virtue that moderates the desire for pleasure. In the widest sense, temperance regulates every form of enjoyment that comes from the exercise of a human power or faculty, e.g., purely spiritual joy arising from intellectual activity or even the consolations experienced in prayer and emotional pleasure produced by such things as pleasant music or the sight of a beautiful scene. In the strict sense, however, temperance is the correlative of fortitude. As fortitude controls rashness and fear in the face of the major pains that threaten to unbalance human nature, so temperance controls desire for major pleasures. Since pleasure follows from all natural activity, it is most intense when associated with our most natural activities. On the level of sense feeling, they are the pleasures that serve the individual person through food and drink, and the human race through carnal intercourse. Temperance mainly refers to these appetites. (Etym. Latin *temperare*, to apportion, regulate, qualify.)

TEMPORAL POWER. The rule of the Church in earthly possessions and the authority of the pope over civil territories belonging to the

Church, as in the Papal States. This power is in addition to his dominion in spiritual matters and becomes necessary if freedom from civil power is to be assured. It is presently exercised in relation to Vatican City or State since the Lateran Treaty of 1929. The term may also refer to the exercise of political influence by the bishops formerly through landed estates and currently through financial and other means.

TEMPORAL PUNISHMENT. The penalty that God in his justice inflicts either on earth or in purgatory for sins, even though already forgiven as to guilt.

TEMPORARY VOW. A commitment made to God to practice poverty, chastity, obedience, or some other virtue for a specified length of time. When made in a religious institute, the vows are public, being accepted by the superior in the name of the Church The first vows of religion are generally temporary, to be renewed according to the constitutions and preliminary to perpetual vows. But they do not, therefore, imply only a temporary commitment. They are canonically temporary, so that after they expire the one who made them is free to leave the institute of Christian perfection. But intentionally, even the person who takes only temporary vows should have the desire to persevere in the vowed commitment until death.

TEMPTATION. Solicitation to sin, whether by persuasion or offering some pleasure. It may arise from the world, the flesh, or the devil. Temptation from the world is the attractiveness of bad example and the psychological pressure to conform. Temptations from the flesh are all the urges of concupiscence, whether carnal or spiritual, where man's fallen nature has built-in tendencies to the seven capital sins. Demonic temptations arise from instigations of the evil spirit, whose method is to encourage every form of avarice or selfishness in order to lead one to pride, and through pride to all other sins.

TEMPTING GOD. An act or omission in which a person tries to test God's attributes, notably his love, power, or wisdom. It may be done either explicitly or implicitly.

God is tempted explicitly when something is demanded of him or when something is done or omitted for the actual purpose of ascertaining the extent of God's love, power, or wisdom. An example would be that of an atheist who might give God, say, five minutes to strike him or her dead "if there is a God." To explicitly tempt God is always a grave sin.

God is tempted implicitly when, not doubting his attributes, a person rashly requires a manifestation of divine love, power, or wisdom. Examples of implicitly tempting God are needlessly risking one's life in some dangerous feat or refusing all medical aid simply because it is up to God to cure one of some grave illness or disease. Implicitly tempting God is a serious sin in grave matters, otherwise a venial sin.

TEN COMMANDMENTS. Also called the Decalogue, they are the divinely revealed precepts received by Moses on Mount Sinai. Engraved on two tablets of stone, they occur in two versions in the Bible. The earlier form (Exodus 20:1–17) differs from the later (Deuteronomy 5:6–18) in two ways. It gives a religious motive, instead of a humanitarian one, for observing the Sabbath; and in prohibiting avarice, it classes a man's wife along with the rest of his possessions, instead of separately.

With the exception of forbidding graven images and statues and the precept about the Sabbath, the Ten Commandments are an expression of the natural law. More or less extensive sections of the Decalogue are found in the laws of other ancient people. However, the Ten Commandments excel the moral codes of other religious systems in their explicit monotheism, their doctrine of God's awesome majesty and boundless goodness, and their extension of moral obligation down to the most intimate and hidden desires of the human heart. The following is a standard Catholic expression of the Ten Commandments:

1. I, the Lord, am your God. You shall not have other gods besides me.
2. You shall not take the name of the Lord, your God, in vain.
3. Remember to keep holy the Sabbath day.
4. Honor your father and your mother.
5. You shall not kill.
6. You shall not commit adultery.
7. You shall not steal.
8. You shall not bear false witness against your neighbor.
9. You shall not covet your neighbor's wife.
10. You shall not covet anything that belongs to your neighbor.

See also CHRISTIAN DECALOGUE, DECALOGUE, JEWISH DECALOGUE.

TERCE. The third hour of the Divine Office, which is to be said at about 9 A.M. The beginning hymn is in commemoration of the Holy

Spirit's descent on the Apostles and is followed by three variable Psalms, a short reading, versicle, and response, and the collect of the day. Terce is now technically part of the *hora media* (middle hour), said after Lauds and before Vespers. (Etym. Latin *tertius,* third.)

TERTIARIES. Laypersons living in the world who are striving after Christian perfection as their station in life allows, according to the spirit of a religious order to which they are affiliated and abiding by the rules approved for their association by the Apostolic See. Secular tertiaries generally do not live in community, nor do they wear habits, but they share in the good works of their parent order.

TESTIMONIALS. Letters of recommendation required by ecclesiastical law, witnessing to a person's qualifications for the reception of a sacrament, e.g., ordination to the priesthood. Favorable testimonials are a matter of grave obligation on the one conferring the sacrament.

THADDAEUS. One of the Twelve Apostles, but little is known about him. Matthew and Mark both name him in their listing of the Twelve (Matthew 10:3; Mark 3:18). Luke substitutes the name "Jude son of James" (Acts 1:13). John's Gospel describes him once as "Judas, this was not Judas Iscariot" (John 14:22).

THEFT. The secret taking of an object against the legitimate owner's reasonable will for the purpose of gain. If secrecy is absent, the act is called robbery. If the lawful owner is not reasonably opposed to the act, no theft is committed. And if the purpose of gain is absent, the taking of an object is rather a matter of damage. Consequently it is not theft if the owner consents, expressly or tacitly, or if an object is taken for reasons of extreme necessity, or as occult compensation. Thus, if a wife takes from her husband, either absent or unreasonably opposed as an avaricious man, something necessary for herself, for the support and benefit of her children, for reasons of charity in keeping with the family's financial condition or for helping parents in grave need, it is not theft.

Generally speaking, theft is a serious sin. According to St. Paul, "Thieves, usurers . . . and swindlers will never inherit the kingdom of God" (I Corinthians 6:10). But as an owner may be opposed in different ways to the loss of property belonging to him or her, so too the sin of theft admits of degrees, even to the point of constituting only a slight sin. Moreover, opposition to a loss may be based on the value or quantity of the stolen goods. Finally, theft is more or less grave according to the manner in which it is committed. A person may be more opposed to a large theft committed at one time than to a series of small thefts although amounting to the same value. Yet repeated petty thefts—venial sins if taken separately—may become a mortal sin either because of the intention or because of the conspiracy with which they are perpetrated or because the frequency of small thefts really constitutes a single large act of thievery.

THEISM. Belief in a personal and provident God. It may, however, take on different forms, notably monotheism (one God), polytheism (several gods), or henotheism (one chief god among several). Theism is commonly distinguished from atheism, which denies the existence of a personal, transcendent deity. (Etym. Greek *theos,* god.)

THEOCENTRICITY. God-centeredness. The quality of not only being attentive to God but of making him the principal focus of a course of action or a system of thought. Often distinguished from Christo-centricity.

THEOCRACY. A form of government in which God, acting usually through his priestly or prophetic representatives, is the ruler. Every civil and social act becomes religious. The Jewish nation after its return from exile was a theocracy. Until modern times Moslem nations were essentially theocratic. John Calvin sought to introduce a theocracy at Geneva in 1552. (Etym. Greek *theokratia; theo,* God + -*cracy,* strength, rule.)

THEODICY. Natural theology, or the study of God's existence and attributes as known by the light of natural reason and apart from supernatural revelation. Its main focus is to vindicate God's goodness and Providence in spite of the evident evil in the universe. Gottfried Leibniz (1646–1716) is credited with giving the name to natural theology, which was already known to the ancient Greeks.

THEOLOGICAL CENSURE. A judgment of the Church that characterizes a proposition touching on Catholic faith or morals as contrary to faith or at least doubtful. In the history of the Church's teaching there have been theological censures. A heretical proposition is opposed to a revealed dogma; proximate to heresy is opposed to a truth commonly held to be revealed; erroneous is opposed to conclusions derived from revelation; false is opposed to dogmatic facts; temerarious deviates from the accepted teaching of the Church; badly expressed is subject to misunderstanding; captious is reprehensible because of its intentional ambiguity; and scandalous because it gives rise to error among the faithful.

THEOLOGICAL VIRTUE. A good habit of the mind or will, supernaturally infused into the soul, whose immediate object is God. The theological virtues are faith, hope, and charity.

THEOLOGY. Literally "the science of God," used by the Stoics in the third century B.C. to describe a reasoned analysis of the deity. Earlier uses were more naturalistic. Thus, Plato in the *Republic* and Aristotle in his *Metaphysics* called Homer, Hesiod, and Orpheus theologians because they first determined the genealogies and attributes of the gods.

   With the advent of Christianity, theology came to mean what its etymology suggested and was defined by St. Augustine as "reasoning or discourse about the divinity." Through the patristic age to the period of the Schoolmen, this remained the acceptable generic meaning. Peter Abelard (1079–1142) is credited with first having used the term in its modern connotation. St. Thomas Aquinas (1225–74) defended theology as a science because it investigates the contents of belief by means of reason enlightened by faith (*fides quaerens intellectum*) in order to acquire a deeper understanding or revelation. He also distinguished theology proper from "natural theology" or what Gottfried Leibniz later called "theodicy," which studies God as knowable by reason alone and independent of divine authority. Since the thirteenth century the term has been applied to the whole study of revealed truth and gradually replaced its rival synonyms. (Etym. Latin *theologia;* from Greek: *theo,* God + *-logia,* knowledge.) See also SCIENCE OF FAITH.

THEOPHANY (BIBLICAL). A direct communication or appearance by God to human beings. Instances: God confronting Adam and Eve after their disobedience (Genesis 3:8); God appearing to Moses out of a burning bush (Exodus 3:2–6); Abraham pleading with YHWH to be merciful to the Sodomites (Genesis 18:23). These theophanies were temporary manifestations. They were not like the Incarnation, which, though it began in time, will continue for all eternity. (Etym. Latin *theophania;* from Greek *theophaneia*: *Theo-,* God + *phainein,* to show.)

THEOTOKOS. Mother of God. A term canonized by the Council of Ephesus (A.D. 431) in defense of Mary's divine maternity, against Nestorius, who claimed that she was only the mother of the man Christ (*Christotokos*).

THERAPEUTIC STERILIZATION. The action of depriving persons of their generative powers in order to relieve some pathological condition. Its moral evaluation is based on the norms for mutilation and also the application of "double effect." The reason is that sterilization involves both the loss of bodily integrity (as mutilation) and of the procreative powers.

THESSALONIANS, EPISTLES TO THE. Two letters written by St. Paul to the Christians of the city of Thessalonica. Both were written from Corinth about A.D. 51. In the first, St. Paul sets the people's minds at rest about the fate of the righteous dead. They are alive and at the Second Coming of Christ will rise in their glorified bodies. In the second letter, the Apostle admonishes the new converts to be steadfast in the faith in spite of false teachers who are trying to seduce them.

THIRD ORDERS. Associations of the faithful established by religious orders. Dating from the thirteenth century, they may be either secular or regular. If secular, they are laypersons, commonly called tertiaries. If regular, they are religious, bound by public vows and living in community. Originally, third orders were Franciscan or Dominican, but the Holy See has since approved many others, both secular and regular, e.g., the Augustinians, Carmelites, Servites, and Trinitarians.

THOMAS. One of the Twelve Apostles. In their Gospels, Matthew, Mark, and Luke mention him only once, simply in listing the names of the Twelve. In John's Gospel he is named several times as "Thomas, known as the twin." The disparaging sobriquet he has borne through the centuries, Doubting Thomas, he earned in the familiar story of his refusal to believe that the resurrected Christ had appeared to the other Apostles unless he could examine the marks of the Crucifixion (John 20:24–29). Another incident in John's Gospel reflects great credit on Thomas for strong faith and courage. When Jesus told the Apostles that he would return to Judaea despite the threats against his life, Thomas said to the others, "Let us go, too, and die with him" (John 11:16).

THRONES. Those angels who compose the lowest choir of the highest angelic order. Along with the Seraphim and Cherubim, they form the court of the Heavenly King. Hence they are rarely sent as messengers to humanity.

TIARA. The papal crown, which is a tall headdress of gold cloth ornamented with precious stones, encircled with three coronets and surmounted by a cross. Originating as a plain, helmet-like cap about A.D. 1130, it soon acquired its present form. The first circlet symbolizes the pope's universal episcopate; the second, his primacy of jurisdiction; and the third, his temporal influence. It is placed on the pope's head at coronation, by the second cardinal deacon, with the words "Receive the tiara adorned with three crowns, and know that you are Father of princes and kings, guide of the world, vicar of our Savior Jesus Christ." The tiara is worn only at nonliturgical ceremonies. Paul VI was the last pope to be crowned with the tiara.

TIMOTHY. A companion and helper of Paul. The relationship was notably close and affectionate. Paul speaks of his young protégé as "a dear and faithful son" and as "a true child of mine" (I Corinthians 4:17; I Timothy 1:2). When they separated at Ephesus, Paul recalled the tears that Timothy shed and wrote that he longed to see him again to complete his happiness (II Timothy 1:3–4). They traveled together to many places. Timothy's name appears with Paul's in epistles sent to Corinth, to Philippi, to Thessalonica, to Colossae. They were even in prison together. In writing to Timothy, Paul constantly spurred him on to greater effort, e.g., "I am reminding you now to fan into a flame the gift God gave you" (II Timothy 1:6). Paul's confidence in Timothy was so strong that he set a very high standard of achievement for him. (Etym. Greek *timotheos,* honoring the god.)

TIMOTHY, EPISTLES TO. Two letters of St. Paul to his coworker Timothy, whom he converted on his second missionary journey. In the first, Paul warns him against false doctrines, mainly Gnostic, and erroneous moral practices. In the second, he exhorts Timothy to be faithful to the gifts he has received and to gird himself for hardships in the apostolate and conflict with false teachers.

TITHE, BIBLICAL. The practice regulated by the Pentateuch of giving a tenth part of one's possessions as a tax to a superior. Abraham paid such a tax to Melchizedek (Genesis 14). The Levites, however, did not inherit the prescribed amount of land given to the other tribes, but rather received, as representatives of the Lord, a tenth part of all that the land produced—including flocks and cattle—from all the other tribes of Israel. They in turn were to offer to the priest a tenth part of all they received. Another kind of tithe taken from this yearly produce was to be consumed at the sanctuary (Deuteronomy 14), and the produce of every third year was to be distributed among the Levites and the poor. Tithes were offerings acknowledging the Lord's dominion and expressions of thanksgiving for blessings received from God. The sense of strong obligation to pay tithes is made clear in Leviticus (Leviticus 27:30–33).

TITULAR CHURCH. The particular ancient church in Rome over which a new cardinal receives jurisdiction on receiving the red hat. The name of the church is regularly given in all official listings of the cardinals of the Catholic Church.

TITULAR SEES. Some two thousand ancient Catholic dioceses and archdioceses whose titles are now given to those bishops who do not occupy residential sees, e.g., auxiliary and coadjutor bishops, vicars apostolic, and officials of the Roman Curia. Most of these sees are in Asia Minor, North Africa, the Balkans, and Greece. After the Moslems had destroyed the Church in these lands, the extinct dioceses were called sees "in the lands of the infidels." But in 1882, Pope Leo XIII changed the title to "titular sees."

TITUS. A Greek who was converted to Christianity by Paul and who became one of Paul's trusted and effective assistants. Since Titus was a Gentile, Paul and Barnabas took him with them to Jerusalem to oppose the Jewish contention that, to become a Christian, a prospective convert must be circumcised. Paul "refused to yield to such people for one moment" and reported triumphantly that Titus was not obliged to be circumcised (Galatians 2:3–5). His Epistle to Titus gives the impression that Titus was a strong-minded troubleshooter. Paul left him in Crete with crisp, forthright instructions to reorganize the Church; establish a stable, dependable leadership (Titus 1:9); and insist on an "unchanging message of the tradition." Paul urged him to do so "with full authority" and to be "quite uncompromising" (Titus 2:15, 3:8). On another occasion when Titus represented Paul in Corinth, he evidently won the affection and respect of the people, for Paul commented jubilantly on the success of his assistant's mission (II Corinthians 8:16–17). (Etym. Latin *titus*.)

TITUS, EPISTLE TO. A letter of St. Paul to Titus, a native of Antioch who became one of the Apostle's faithful companions. Paul wrote after Titus became Bishop of Crete, and instructed him about the heresies, mainly Gnosticism, that he had to combat, and about methods of church organization. The letter was written as Paul was on his way east after his first imprisonment in Rome.

TOBIT, BOOK OF. A deuterocanonical book of the Old Testament, not recognized as part of the Bible by Jews and Protestants. It relates the story of Tobit, a pious Jew of the captivity of Nineveh, who, in the practice of charity in his old age, became blind. He sent his son Tobias on a long journey to recover a debt. Tobias's companion, the archangel Raphael, rescued a family relative, Sarah, from the power of the devil, helped recover the debt, and prescribed a remedy to cure Tobit's blindness. The moral lesson of the narrative is to show God's fidelity to those who serve him, especially in the practice of charity, and to teach the special providence of the angels as ministers in the divine service.

TORAH. 1. The first five books of the Old Testament: Genesis, Exodus, Leviticus, Numbers, and Deuteronomy; 2. the entire body of Jewish Law revealed by YHWH and interpreted and taught by priests, prophets, and sages.

TOTAL ABSTINENCE. Complete abstention from alcoholic beverages. The practice was strongly advocated by a number of Protestant leaders, notably John Wesley (1703–91), for whom the drinking of alcohol in any form was a sin. The Catholic Church does not forbid drinking in moderation, but total abstinence may be the only solution for a person with a chronic problem of alcoholism.

TOTALITARIANISM. A theory of society that gives the State total control of the life and conduct of the citizens. Modern totalitarianism is a combination of five movements that were centuries in the making: Machiavellianism, which divorced the public and private morality; Protestantism, which gave princes the right to pass judgment on popes and bishops; Comtism, which favored social development and organization based on exact biological norms; Hegelianism, for which history was the march of the Absolute Idea through the world and incarnated in nineteenth-century Prussia; and Marxism, which merely changed Hegelian idealism to Communist materialism and adapted Hegel's "military class dictatorship" to "dictatorship of the proletariat." All totalitarian regimes in the recent past and the present are greater or lesser expressions of one or more of these contributing philosophies of society.

TOTAL WAR. A modern theory of warfare which claims that all the citizens of a belligerent nation are to be considered combatants. The term has entered the vocabulary of the times since massive destruction of whole segments of the population is inevitable with the use of atomic weapons. With this in mind, the Second Vatican Council declared: "Every act of war directed to the indiscriminate destruction of whole cities or vast areas with their inhabitants is a crime against God and man, which merits firm and unequivocal condemnation" (Pastoral Constitution on the Church in the Modern World, V, 80).

Because of the totally different situation in the world today, while still maintaining that, on principle, war is justifiable, the Church holds that nuclear warfare is next to impossible to justify in practice.

TRADITION. Literally a "handing on," referring to the passing down of God's revealed word. As such it has two closely related but distinct meanings. Tradition first means all of divine revelation, from the dawn of human history to the end of the apostolic age, as passed on from one generation of believers to the next, and as preserved under divine guidance by the Church established by Christ. Sacred Tradition more technically also means, within this transmitted revelation, that part of God's revealed word which is not contained in Sacred Scripture. Referring specifically to how Christian tradition was handed on, the Second Vatican Council says: "It was done by the apostles who handed on, by the spoken word of their preaching, by the example they gave, by the institutions they established, what they themselves had received—whether from the lips of Christ, from His way of life and His works, or whether they had learned it by the prompting of the Holy Spirit" (Dogmatic Constitution on Divine Revelation, II, 7). (Etym. Latin *traditio*, a giving over, delivery, surrender; a handing down: from *tradere*, to give up.)

TRADITIONALISM. The theory that all human knowledge of God and religion comes from tradition. In its extreme form, it denies that reason can arrive at any certain knowledge of divine things. It proceeds from the view that God first made a comprehensive primitive revelation when the human race learned to speak. In this original revelation, God bestowed on people all the basic religious truths that have been handed down by successive generations to the present day. General reason or common sense guarantees the unfalsified transmission of its heritage. The individual receives it by oral teaching. Religious knowledge is entirely and only a knowledge of faith. The chief exponents of traditionalism in its strict form were Viscount de Bonald (1754–1840), Félicité de Lamennais (1782–1854), and Louis Bautain (1796–1867). It was represented in a more modified form by Augustine Bonnetty (d. 1879). Traditionalism is also called fideism insofar as it denies the capacity of reason to attain knowledge of divine matters and correspondingly places an excessive stress on faith.

TRANSCENDENTALS. In Scholastic philosophy, those qualities that are common to all things whatsoever, and to all differences between things. They are not restricted to any category, class, or individual. The classic transcendentals are thing (*res*), being (*ens*), something (*aliquid*), the one (*unum*), the true (*verum*), the good (*bonum*), and, according to some philosophers, the beautiful (*pulchrum*).

TRANSFIGURATION OF OUR LORD. The glorification of the appearance of Jesus before his Resurrection. It took place in the presence of Peter, James, and John. While he was praying on a mountain, suddenly "his face did shine as the sun," while "his garments became glistening, exceeding white." The frightened witnesses saw Moses and Elijah appear before them and converse with Jesus and heard the voice of God. The extraordinary vision vanished as suddenly as it appeared (Luke 9:28–36; Matthew 17:1–8; Mark 9:2–8). The Church's celebration of this event occurs as a feast day on August 6. (Etym. Latin *transfigurare: trans-*, change + *figura*, figure.)

TRANSFINALIZATION. The view of Christ's presence in the Eucharist that the purpose or finality of the bread and wine is changed by the words of consecration. They are said to serve a new function, as sacred elements that arouse the faith of the people in the mystery of Christ's redemptive love. Like transignification, this theory was condemned by Pope Paul VI in the encyclical *Mysterium Fidei* (1965) if transfinalization is taken to deny the substantial change of bread and wine into the body and blood of Christ. (Etym. Latin *trans-*, so as to change + *finis*, end; purpose.)

TRANSIGNIFICATION. The view of Christ's presence in the Eucharist which holds that the meaning or significance of the bread and wine is changed by the words of consecration. The consecrated elements are said to signify all that Christians associate with the Last Supper; they have a higher value than merely food for the body. The theory of transignification was condemned by Pope Paul VI in the encyclical *Mysterium Fidei* (1965), if it is understood as denying transubstantiation. (Etym. Latin *trans-*, so as to change + *significantio*, meaning, sense: *transignificatio*.) See also TRANSFINALIZATION.

TRANSPLANTATION OF ORGANS. The transfer of an organ, or body part, from one body to another. In general, the transplant of organs from living donors is permissible when the expected benefit to the recipient is proportionate to the harm done to the donor. But always the condition is that the loss of such organ does not deprive the donor of life or of functional integrity of the body. Regarding the transplant of single vital organs, such as the heart, two problems are always involved. One is to know precisely when a person is dead. The other is the effectiveness of a transplant if a vital organ is transferred from an actually dead body. The medical temptation is to anticipate death in order to guarantee a successful transplant.

TRANSUBSTANTIATION. The complete change of the substance of bread and wine into the substance of Christ's body and blood by a validly ordained priest during the consecration at Mass so that only the accidents of bread and wine remain. While the faith behind the term was already believed in apostolic times, the term itself was a later development. With the Eastern Fathers before the sixth century, the favored expression was *meta-ousiosis*, "change of being"; the Latin tradition coined the word *transubstantiatio*, "change of substance," which was incorporated into the creed of the Fourth Lateran Council in 1215. The Council of Trent, in defining the "wonderful and singular conversion of the whole substance of the bread into the body, and the whole substance of the wine into the blood" of Christ, added "which conversion the Catholic Church calls transubstantiation" (Denzinger 1652). After transubstantiation, the accidents of bread and wine do not inhere in any subject or substance whatever. Yet they are not make-believe; they are sustained in existence by divine power. (Etym. Latin *trans-,* so as to change + *substantia,* substance: *transubstantiatio,* change of substance.)

TRAPPISTS. Cistercian monks who follow the rule of the abbey at La Trappe, France, as reformed in 1664. They were absorbed into the Cistercians of the Strict Observance in 1892, but the name is now commonly applied to the latter. The reformation of the Trappists, under the Abbé de Rancé in the seventeenth century, was continued by Abbé Lestrange into the early nineteenth century, emphasizing the need for a more penitential life. Separated monasteries were united into an international order in 1892 under an abbot general. Their official name is Cistercians of Strict Observance, or Reformed Cistercians. Monasteries of the order are in many countries.

TRIBUNAL. Ecclesiastical court of justice, established both in Rome and in each diocese. There are three Roman tribunals: the Sacred Apostolic Penitentiary, Supreme Tribunal of the Apostolic Signatura, and the Sacred Roman Rota. Diocesan tribunals are mainly concerned with marriage cases, and their officers, judges, and members are listed in national Catholic directories.

TRIDENTINE MASS. The Eucharistic liturgy celebrated in the Latin Rite according to the Roman Missal promulgated by the apostolic constitution *Quo Primum* of Pope Pius V on July 14, 1570. A revised missal was decreed by the Council of Trent in order to unify what by then had become a variety of "Roman Rites" that had proliferated since the Middle Ages. "For four centuries it furnished the priests of the Latin Rite with norms for the celebration of the Eucharistic Sacrifice, and heralds of the Gospel carried it to almost all the world" (Venerable Pope Paul VI, apostolic constitution promulgating the Roman Missal revised by decree of the Second Vatican Council, April 3, 1969). Pope Benedict XVI's *motu proprio Summorum Pontificum* facilitates greater use of this Mass. (Etym. Latin *Tridentinus,* from *Tridentum,* ancient form of Trent.)

TRIDUUM. A period of three days of prayer, either preceding some special feast or preparing for some major enterprise. Commemorates the biblical three days that Christ lay in the tomb.

TRINITY, THE HOLY. A term used since A.D. 200 to denote the central doctrine of the Christian religion. God, who is one and unique in his infinite substance or nature, is three really distinct persons: the Father, Son, and Holy Spirit. The one and only God is the Father, the Son, and the Holy Spirit. Yet God the Father is not God the Son but generates the Son eternally, as the Son is eternally begotten. The Holy Spirit is neither the Father nor the Son but a distinct person having his divine nature from the Father and the Son by eternal procession. The three divine persons are co-equal, co-eternal, and consubstantial and deserve co-equal glory and adoration.

TRINITY SUNDAY. The first Sunday after Pentecost. Its origins go back to the Arian heresy, when an office with canticle, responses, preface, and hymns was composed by the Fathers and recited on Sundays. Bishop Stephen of Liège (r. 903–20) wrote an office of the Holy Trinity that in some places was recited on the Sunday after Pentecost, and elsewhere on the last Sunday before Advent. St. Thomas à Becket (1118–70) consecrated Archbishop of Canterbury on the Sunday following Pentecost, obtained for England the privilege of a special feast to honor the Trinity on that day. Pope John XXII (r. 1316–34) extended the feast to the universal Church.

TRIUMPHALISM. A term of reproach leveled at the Catholic Church for the claim that she has the fullness of divine revelation and the right to pass judgment on the personal and social obligations of humankind. (Etym. Latin *triumphus,* public rejoicing for a victory.)

TRUE CROSS. The cross on which the Savior died. It was very probably discovered in A.D. 326 by St. Helena, mother of Emperor Constantine. A part of this cross is said to be preserved in the Church of Santa Croce in Rome. The feast of the Exaltation (or Triumph) of the Holy Cross is celebrated on September 14 in the Latin Rite.

TRUTH. Conformity of mind and reality. Three kinds of conformity give rise to three kinds of truth. In *logical* truth, the mind is conformed or in agreement with things outside the mind, either in assenting to what is or in denying what is not. Its opposite is error. In *metaphysical* or *ontological* truth, things conform with the mind. This is primary conformity, when something corresponds to the idea of its maker, and it is secondary conformity when something is intelligible and therefore true to anyone who knows it. In *moral* truth, what is said conforms with what is on one's mind. This is truthfulness, and its opposite is falsehood.

TWELVE FRUITS. The special graces of supernatural satisfaction in the performance of good works, infused by the Holy Spirit at baptism and possessed by everyone in the state of grace. They are charity, joy, peace, patience, benignity, goodness, longanimity, mildness, faith, modesty, continency, and chastity. Their intensity depends on the degree of grace a person has and the generosity with which he or she performs the different virtues.

TWELVE PROMISES. The promises made by Christ to St. Margaret Mary Alacoque, a Visitation nun, in the convent chapel at Paray-le-Monial, France, between 1673 and 1675. They occurred during revelations she received on devotion to the Heart of Jesus, and have been encouraged by the Church as worthy of pious belief. They have been translated into more than two hundred languages. Although the total number is larger, the following are the most important promises made by Christ to those who are devoted to the Sacred Heart:

1. I will give them all the graces necessary in their state of life.
2. I will establish peace in their homes.
3. I will comfort them in all their afflictions.
4. I will be their secure refuge during life and above all in death.
5. I will bestow a large blessing upon all their undertakings.
6. Sinners shall find in my Heart the source and the infinite ocean of mercy.
7. Tepid souls shall grow fervent.
8. Fervent souls shall quickly mount to high perfection.
9. I will bless every place where a picture of my heart shall be set up and honored.
10. I will give to priests the gift of touching the most hardened hearts.
11. Those who shall promote this devotion shall have their names written in my Heart never to be blotted out.
12. I promise you in the excessive mercy of my Heart that my all-powerful love will grant to all those who communicate on the first Friday in nine consecutive months the grace of final penitence; they shall not die under my displeasure, nor without receiving their sacraments; my divine Heart shall be their safe refuge in this last moment.

TYPES, SCRIPTURAL. A biblical person, thing, action, or event that foreshadows new truths, new actions, or new events. In the Old Testament, Melchizedek and Jonah are types of Jesus Christ. A likeness must exist between the type and the archetype, but the latter is always greater. Both are independent of each other. God's call for the return of the Israelites from Pharaoh's bondage typifies the return of Jesus Christ from his flight into Egypt. In the New Testament the destruction of Jerusalem, foretold by Christ, was the antitype of the end of the world. See also ANTITYPE.

U

UNAM SANCTAM. The papal bull of Pope Boniface VIII, issued November 18, 1302, in answer to Philip IV of France, who denied the pope's authority. Only the last sentence is irreversible doctrine, in which Boniface states: "We declare, say, define and pronounce that it is absolutely necessary for the salvation of every human creature to be subject to the Roman Pontiff" (Denzinger 875). The preceding part of the document deals at length with the relation of temporal and spiritual powers in the Church.

UNBAPTIZED INFANTS. Children, whether born or unborn, who die without baptism of water. The difficult question of whether they can attain the beatific vision in heaven has been discussed for centuries and has become especially grave since abortion is now legalized in so many countries. There is no unqualified answer to this question from the Church's magisterium. But there are two principles of Catholic doctrine that must be reconciled.

On the one hand, the Church teaches that even those who die with only original sin on their souls cannot reach the beatific vision. The Second Council of Lyons (1274) and the Council of Florence (1438–45) explicitly define that those who die with "only original sin" (*peccato vel solo originali*) do not reach heaven. There is also the Church's condemnation of the Jansenists, who claimed that it is a myth to hold there is a place "which the faithful generally designate by the name of the limbo of children," for the souls of those who depart this life with only the guilt of original sin (Pius VI, *Errors of the Synod of Pistoia*, Proposition 26, August 28, 1794).

On the other hand, we also know that, according to God's universal salvific will, somehow he gives all persons the opportunity of reaching heaven. This is authoritatively expressed by the Second Vatican Council in its Dogmatic Constitution on the Church: "Those who, through no fault of their own, do not know the Gospel of Christ or His Church, but who nevertheless seek God with a sincere heart, and, moved by grace, try in their actions to do His will as they know it through the dictates of their conscience—those too can achieve eternal salvation" (*Lumen Gentium*, 16). By implication, their children who die before the age of reason can also be saved.

Saying all of this, one should emphasize how deeply the Church is concerned that children be baptized as soon after birth as possible. "As for the time of Baptism," the Roman ritual states, "the first consideration is the welfare of the child, that it may not be deprived of the benefit of the sacrament." Therefore, "if the child is in danger of death, it is to be baptized without delay." See also LIMBO.

UNCREATED GRACE. God himself, insofar as in his love he has predetermined gifts of grace. There are three forms of uncreated grace: the hypostatic union, the divine indwelling, and the beatific vision. In the first of these, God has communicated himself in the Incarnation of Christ's humanity (the grace of union) so intimately that Jesus of Nazareth is a divine person. In the second and third communications, the souls of the justified on earth and of the glorified in heaven are elevated to a share in God's own life. All three are created graces, considered as acts, since they all had a beginning in time. But the gift that is conferred on a creature in these acts is uncreated.

UNCTION. Any anointing with oil with a religious purpose, whether in the actual conferring of a sacrament, as in confirmation and anointing of the sick; as part of the sacrament's ceremony, as in baptism and holy orders; or in using a sacramental, such as the oil of St. Serapion, the martyr. (Etym. Latin *unctio*, from *unguere*, to anoint.)

UNIAT CHURCHES. Eastern Christians who profess the same doctrines as the rest of the Roman Catholic Church. Their rites and discipline, however, vary greatly from those of the Latin Rite. Their liturgies originated in Antioch, Alexandria, and Byzantium, and they usually have a married clergy. Nearly all non-Uniat churches possess corresponding Uniat groups who have reacknowledged their allegiance to the pope. The expression "Uniat," though found in theological literature, is seldom used by Eastern Catholics. They feel that it implies something less than complete allegiance to the Holy See.

UNITATIS REDINTEGRATIO. Decree on Ecumenism of the Second Vatican Council. It deals with the Catholic principles on ecumenism, the practice of ecumenism, and the Churches and ecclesiastical communities separated from the Roman Apostolic See. A careful distinction is made between spiritual ecumenism, mainly through prayer and the practice of virtue, and practical ecumenism, which actively fosters the reunification of Christianity. Also the faithful are told to recognize various levels of nearness to the Catholic Church, in descending order, the Eastern Orthodox, Anglicans, and Protestants (November 21, 1964).

UNITIVE WAY. The third and final stage of Christian perfection, beyond the purgative and illuminative. Its principal features are a more or less constant awareness of God's presence and a habitual disposition of conformity to the will of God. Although commonly regarded as the last stage in the spiritual life, it is recognized that the three traditional levels of progress in holiness are not chronological. They may be present, in greater or lesser degree, at any point in a person's growth in sanctity.

UNIVERSITY OF THE FAITHFUL. An expression of the Second Vatican Council, *universitas fidelium,* declaring that "the whole body [university] of the faithful, whom the holy One has anointed, is incapable of error in belief" (Dogmatic Constitution on the Church, II, 12). This means that the faithful of Christ are joined together by their unerring belief in the mysteries of revelation. They are united by their common allegiance to the faith, which is the truth. Truth unites, error divides.

UNNATURAL SINS. Term used to describe those sexual acts from which conception is impossible. When committed alone, they are called masturbation; when conception is deliberately frustrated, they are some form of onanism; when those engaging in sexual activity are of the same sex, it is sodomy or homosexuality; and if animals are involved, it is bestiality.

UNPARDONABLE SIN. Postbiblical term that means blasphemy against the Holy Spirit. When the Pharisees, baffled by a miracle that Jesus had performed, accused him of using the power of the devil to accomplish it, he warned them, "Let anyone speak against the Holy Spirit and he will not be forgiven either in this world or in the next" (Matthew 12:22–32). Also used as a synonym for the sin of despair.

URSULINES. The oldest teaching order of religious women in the Catholic Church, founded at Brescia, Italy, by St. Angela Merici in 1525. They were approved by Pope Paul III in 1544 as a society of virgins, dedicated to Christian education but living in their own homes. In 1572, Pope Gregory XIII further approved their community life and simple vows at the request of St. Charles Borromeo. In 1612 the Ursulines of Paris were allowed to take solemn vows, and convents along these lines were soon established elsewhere, following a modified Rule of St. Augustine. In 1900 a congress of Ursulines met in Rome and effected a union of many congregations. These take simple vows, but some independent convents take solemn vows. There are twenty-five pontifical institutes of Ursulines, besides those belonging to the Roman Union.

USURY. Taking of excessive interest for the loan of money is the modern understanding of usury. In essence, however, usury is the acceptance of a premium for the mere use of a thing given in loan. Objectively it is the premium paid for a pure loan. The word has come to mean taking advantage of another who is in need. As such, it is forbidden by the natural law, because it is contrary to commutative justice. In the case of the poor, it is also a sin against charity.

Originally, in Jewish and Christian tradition, usury meant taking any interest for a loan. It was forbidden among the Jews (Exodus 22:25; Leviticus 25:35–37) but was permitted in dealing with Gentiles. Christ, explaining the precept of charity, made no distinction between Hebrew and Gentile and stated that loans must be gratuitous (Luke 6:30; Matthew 5:42). The Catholic Church for centuries reflected this concept of usury and still teaches that, where something is loaned and later returned in kind only, no profit may be made by reason of the contract itself. Concrete circumstances, however, relative to the economic position of the lender and borrower may be involved and change the effects of the contract. Four external circumstances have an economic value and therefore constitute titles to a proportionate compensation over and above the restitution of what was loaned. They are actual damage, loss of profit, risk to the object loaned, and danger from delay in returning what was lent. Only such titles, external to the loan, when truly present, justify the right to claim and the duty to pay a just rate of interest on money loaned.

Capitalism, with unlimited opportunities for investment, changed the function of money so that it can fructify. Consequently loaning money did involve loss of profit to the lender and further risk of loss from delay in returning the money loaned. By the end of the eighteenth century the distinction between usury and interest was recognized in civil law. The Church also recognized the distinction so that now only exorbitant interest is called usury and considered morally wrong. In the process, however, the Church's basic teaching on the subject did not change. Injustice surrounding moneylending was and remains condemned. What changed was the economic system. As this changed, the circumstances under which an injustice is committed changed. The Church necessarily permitted what was no longer unjust (Etym. Latin *usura,* use of money lent, interest; from *usus,* use.)

UTOPIA. Any imaginary state whose inhabitants live under perfect circumstances; ideal commonwealths described by Plato, Bacon, and St. Thomas More in his book *Utopia*; in an invidious sense, any visionary reform without consideration of man's human weaknesses and defects.

V

VAIN OBSERVANCE. A form of superstition that tries to achieve a certain effect by the use of unsuitable means. Implicit in vain observance is the belief that there are hidden preternatural forces at work in the world that dispense with the need of using ordinary, natural, or supernatural means for obtaining a desired effect. Vain observance also implies the expectation of an infallible result whenever certain words are said or actions performed. There is only a shade of difference between vain observance and divination. In both cases reliance on the evil spirit is involved. But vain observance, unlike divination, is not concerned with obtaining knowledge of the future or of the occult. Its focus is on obtaining some external results, such as making a successful business deal or recovering one's health.

VALENTINE'S DAY, ST. Traditional lovers' day, going back to the pagan Lupercalia, in mid-February, and the medieval belief that birds began to mate at that time. Eventually this custom and belief became associated with the feast of St. Valentine on February 14, which may refer to any one of three saints by the same name: a priest-physician martyred in Rome in 269; a bishop of Interamna, beheaded at Rome about 273; and a martyr in Africa who was put to death with several companions.

VALIDATION. The making valid of a matrimonial contract that had been null and void because of a diriment impediment. A validation requires that the impediment cease or be removed and that the consent of both parties be renewed. If the impediment is not publicly known, the consent may be renewed in secret. If the impediment is known only to one party, only he or she need renew the consent, provided the other party's consent has persevered. (Etym. Latin *validus*, strong, effective; from *valere*, to be strong.)

VALIDITY. Having not only legal force but actually producing the effect intended. Applied to the sacraments, it refers to the conditions of matter, form, and circumstances required for valid administration. In ecclesiastical law it means that certain prescriptions must be fulfilled for the law or contractual agreement to bind or take effect.

VALUE. That which makes a thing desirable or considered worthwhile. Value stresses the subjective and relative aspect of the good over the objective and absolute character. It means not so much the inherent excellence of an object as how it stands in one's personal estimation; not so much its built-in perfection as its comparative place in that scale of things called the hierarchy of values. The term "value" commends itself to subjectivist and relativist moral philosophies, in preference to the common *good*. Nevertheless, it is also acceptable to Christians provided it includes the notion of an objective moral standard. (Etym. Latin *valere*, to be worth, be strong.)

VASECTOMY. Surgical excision of part of the ducts carrying sperm cells to ejaculation, with the purpose of causing sterilization. If the direct intent of the surgery is to induce sterility, the operation is morally illicit.

VATICAN. A group of buildings in Rome clustered around the palace of the pope. The first to build a residence near the ancient Basilica of St. Peter was Pope Symmachus (r. 498–514). Through subsequent purchase the popes acquired possession of the entire Vatican Hill. The property now is the largest palace in the world. Only a small part is used for living quarters; most of the buildings serve the purpose of the arts and sciences, and the administration of Church affairs.

VATICAN CITY. Official name, Stato della Città del Vaticano. It is the territorial see of the papacy, determined by the Lateran Treaty of 1929. Situated within the geographic boundary of Rome, it covers an area of 108.7 acres and includes the Vatican Palace, St. Peter's Basilica, Vatican Radio Station, and numerous other buildings that serve the pope and the administration of the universal Church. Ultimate authority for Vatican City is vested in the pope but actually administered by the Pontifical Commission for the State of Vatican City. In general, the government is based on canon law or, where this does not apply, on existing laws of the city of Rome. It is politically a neutral state and enjoys all the privileges and duties of a sovereign power. The Papal Secretariat maintains diplomatic relations with other nations. Only the citizens of Vatican City owe allegiance to the pope as temporal ruler.

VATICAN LIBRARY. One of the world's chief depositories of books. The foundation of this famous collection was begun by Pope Martin V

(r. 1417–31), but Pope Nicholas V (r. 1447–55) is considered its real founder. He acquired the imperial library of Constantinople, scattered by the Turks, and donated it to the Vatican. Pope Sixtus IV (r. 1471–84) officially established the modern Vatican Library in 1475, and Pope Sixtus V (r. 1585–90) ordered the construction of new buildings that are still in use. The library is administered by a prefect, writers work on scientifically cataloguing the manuscripts, and assistants catalogue the printed books. The library maintains manuscript repairing, bookbinding, and publishing departments, and as a scientific institution for the use of students it is presently making one of the greatest contributions to human thought.

VATICAN SECRET ARCHIVES. Repository of confidential documents of the Holy See, going back to the early centuries. Deterioration of the original papyri, transfers, and political upheavals caused the almost complete loss of the collections earlier than Pope Innocent III. In the fifteenth century the Archives were kept in Castel Sant'Angelo. In 1810, Napoleon ordered the Archives of the Holy See to be transferred to Paris, and though they were later returned to Rome many documents were lost. The Archives are now housed in a special building off the Piazza of St. Peter's. To the Archives is attached the Vatican School of Palaeography and, since 1968, the School of Archivistry. In 1881, Pope Leo XIII made the Vatican Archives available to consultation by accredited scholars.

VEIL, RELIGIOUS. Covering for the head and shoulders worn by women religious. Historically, different veils have signified different roles. The veil of probation, usually white, was given to novices; the veil of profession was given at the pronunciation of vows; the veil of consecration was given consecrated virgins; the veil of continence was given to widows. In the Church's *Order of Religious Profession,* published in 1970, it is assumed that the veil is part of the distinctive garb of religious women. The veiling of virgins consecrated to divine worship and the service of the Church goes back to early patristic times.

VENERABLE. Title given to Servants of God after the state of their heroic virtue or martyrdom has been proved and a solemn decree to that effect has been signed by the pope. (Etym. Latin *venerabilis;* from *venerari,* to regard with religious awe.)

VENERATION OF SAINTS. Honor paid to the saints who, by their intercession and example and in their possession of God, minister to human sanctification, helping the faithful grow in Christian virtue. Venerating the saints does not detract from the glory given to God, since whatever good they possess is a gift from his bounty. They reflect the divine perfections, and their supernatural qualities result from the graces Christ merited for them by the Cross. In the language of the Church's liturgy, the saints are venerated as sanctuaries of the Trinity, as adopted children of the Father, brethren of Christ, faithful members of his Mystical Body, and temples of the Holy Spirit.

VENEREAL PLEASURE. The bodily and emotional satisfaction that accompanies any form of sexual activity. (Etym. Latin *venereus,* from *venus,* love, lust.)

VENGEANCE. The infliction of punishment on someone who has done moral wrong. In this sense, only God has the right to avenge wrongdoing. He may delegate this right to those in legitimate authority, as St. Paul declares, speaking of civil rulers, that "the authorities are there to serve God; they carry out God's revenge by punishing wrongdoers" (Romans 13:4). (Etym. Latin *vindicare,* to revenge, vindicate.)

VENIAL SIN. An offense against God that does not deprive the sinner of sanctifying grace. It is called venial (from *venia,* pardon) because the soul still has the vital principle that allows a cure from within, similar to the healing of a sick or diseased body whose source of animation (the soul) is still present to restore the ailing bodily function to health.

Deliberate venial sin is a disease that slackens the spiritual powers, lowers one's resistance to evil, and causes one to deviate from the path that leads to heavenly glory. Variously called "daily sins" or "light sins" or "lesser sins," they are committed under a variety of conditions: when a person transgresses with full or partial knowledge and consent to a divine law that does not oblige seriously; when one violates a law that obliges gravely but either one's knowledge or consent is not complete; or when one disobeys what is an objectively grave precept but due to invincible ignorance a person thinks the obligation is not serious.

The essence of venial sin consists in a certain disorder but does not imply complete aversion from humanity's final destiny. It is an illness of the soul rather than its supernatural death. When people commit a venial sin, they do not decisively set themselves on turning away from God but, from overfondness for some created good, fall short of God. They are like persons who loiter without leaving the way.

VERITATIS SPLENDOR. Encyclical by Blessed Pope John Paul II on the moral teaching of the Church (August 6, 1993). The purpose of the encyclical is to recall "certain fundamental truths" of Catholic moral doctrine because of a systematic questioning of the Church's moral teaching and the magisterium's authority in this domain. The pope addresses current trends in moral theology and various related issues including God's sovereignty, the correlation between eternal life and the Decalogue, freedom and law, conscience and truth, fundamental choice and specific kinds of behavior, and the moral act. Blessed John Paul II reaffirms the magisterium's competence and authority in teaching morality and the Church's traditional moral doctrine, especially the "universality and immutability of the moral commandments, particularly those which prohibit always and without exception intrinsically evil acts."

VERNACULAR IN LITURGY. The use of the common spoken language of the people in the Catholic liturgy. It was authorized on principle by the Second Vatican Council, declaring that "since the use of the vernacular, whether in the Mass, the administration of the sacraments, or in other parts of the liturgy, may frequently be of great advantage to the people, a wider use may be made of it" (Constitution on the Sacred Liturgy, I, 36). In practice, within ten years of the Council, the vernacular became the norm in the Roman Rite, and the use of Latin the exception. All translations had to be approved by the Holy See. To obviate difficulties about meaning, Rome declared that "a vernacular translation of a sacramental formula . . . must be understood in accordance with the mind of the Church as expressed in the original Latin text" (*Instauratio Liturgica,* January 25, 1974). (Etym. Latin *vernaculus,* domestic; from *verna,* native slave, probably from Etruscan.)

VERONICA'S VEIL. The cloth with which tradition holds that the saintly Veronica wiped the face of Jesus on his way to Calvary. Christ is said to have left the imprint of his face on the veil. It is honored as a treasured relic at St. Peter's in Rome. The episode is commemorated in the sixth station of the cross. Veronica is sometimes identified with the woman whom Christ healed of an issue of blood (Mark 5:25–32).

VERSES, BIBLICAL. Divisions within the chapters of the books of the Bible. The present numeration for the Old Testament was made by Santes Pagnini in his Latin Bible of 1528. The Paris printer Robert Etienne adopted Pagnini's numeration and himself added the numbers of the verses for the New Testament in his edition of 1555.

VESPERS. Evening service of worship. In the revised Breviary since Second Vatican Council it has been replaced in the Divine Office by "Evening Prayer."

VESSELS, SACRED. The utensils and receptacles used in liturgical celebrations. In the Latin Rite these are the chalice, paten, ciborium, pyx, capsula, lunette, and monstrance—which come into direct contact with the Blessed Sacrament. Other vessels used in the liturgy are cruets, lavabo dish, thurible, boat, and aspergillum.

VESTMENTS. Special garments worn by the clergy, in conformity with Church regulations, at the celebration of the Mass, administration of the sacraments, in procession, when giving blessings, and in general whenever exercising their official priestly duties. The use of vestments goes back to the ritual garb of the priesthood of Aaron. In the Catholic Church, even in catacomb days, priests and bishops were specially, if not always distinctively, garbed when celebrating the liturgy. With the Church's liberation and her emergence into public life, liturgical garments were commonly used to distinguish them from secular dress.

VIATICUM. The reception of Holy Communion when there is probable danger of death. Viaticum should not be deferred too long in sickness lest the dying lose consciousness. It can be given as often as such danger exists and is required of all the faithful who have reached he age of discretion. No laws of fasting persist either for the recipient or for the priest who must consecrate in order to supply the Host in an emergency. (Etym. Latin *viaticum,* traveling provisions; from *viaticus,* of a road or journey, from *via,* way, road.)

VICAR. An ecclesiastic who substitutes for another in the exercise of a clerical office and acts in his name and with his authority according to canon law. (Etym. Latin *vicarius,* a substitute; from *vicarius,* substituting, acting for; from *vicis,* change, turn, office.)

VICARIATE OF ROME. The diocese of Rome administered from the Lateran by a cardinal who is Vicar-General of His Holiness. Its jurisdiction is the city of Rome and the part called Agro Romano. Pope Paul IV in 1558 decreed that the Vicar of Rome should be a member of the Sacred College, and Pope Pius XI in 1929 withdrew the Vatican from the jurisdiction of the vicar.

VICAR OF CHRIST. The pope, visible head of the Church on earth, acting for and in the place of Christ. He possesses supreme ecclesiastical authority in the Catholic Church. This title for the pope dates from at least the eighth century and gradually replaced the former title, "Vicar of St. Peter." Its biblical basis is Christ's commission of Peter to "feed my lambs, feed my sheep" (John 21:15–17).

VICE. A bad moral habit. Technically a vice is the strong tendency to a gravely sinful act acquired through frequent repetition of the same act. Qualities that characterize a vice are spontaneity, ease, and satisfaction in doing what is morally wrong. (Etym. Latin *vitium,* any sort of defect.)

VICTIM. A living being offered in sacrifice to God. The sacrifice implies that the victim is actually or equivalently given up as an act of adoration or of expiation to the Divine Majesty. The destruction of the victim is its immolation; the voluntary surrender of the victim is the offering or oblation. Together they constitute the sacrifice.

VIGIL. The day or eve before a more or less prominent feast or solemnity. It was observed as a preparation for the following day with special offices and prayers and formerly with a fast, honoring the particular mystery of religion or the saint to be venerated on the feast day. The Church today observes solemn vigils for Christmas, Easter, and Pentecost. (Additional vigils are observed in the 1962 liturgical calendar associated with the Extraordinary Form of the Roman Rite.) Although the number of such solemn vigils has been reduced since the Second Vatican Council, the Church still wants the notion of vigils to be kept alive in the minds of the faithful. Thus "it is fitting that Bible services on the vigils of great feasts, on certain ferial days of Lent and Advent, on Sundays and feast days, should also have the same structure as the liturgy of the Word at Mass" (*Inter Oecumenici*, 1964, 38). (Etym. Latin *vigilia,* from *vigil,* alert.)

VINCENTIAN CANON. The famous threefold test of Catholic orthodoxy expressed by St. Vincent of Lérins (400–50) in his two memoranda (*Commonitoria*): "Care must especially be had that that be held which was believed everywhere [*ubique*], always [*semper*], and by all [*ab omnibus*]." By this triple norm of diffusion, endurance, and universality, a Christian can distinguish religious truth from error.

VINCENTIANS. Members of the Congregation of the Mission founded by St. Vincent de Paul in 1625. Also known as Lazarists from the Place de St. Lazare, which was St. Vincent's headquarters in Paris. The original work of the congregation was the preaching of popular missions and conducting retreats. Later on seminaries were established. Vincentians form a society of common life. They are secular priests living in community under religious vows. Their present apostolate is mission work, conducting seminaries, directing the Daughters and Ladies of Charity, and education and spiritual exercises to priests, religious, and the laity.

VINCIBLE IGNORANCE. Lack of knowledge for which a person is morally responsible. It is culpable ignorance because it could be cleared up if the person used sufficient diligence. One is said to be simply (but culpably) ignorant if one fails to make enough effort to learn what should be known; guilt then depends on one's lack of effort to clear up the ignorance. That person is crassly ignorant when the lack of knowledge is not directly willed but rather due to neglect or laziness; as a result the guilt is somewhat lessened, but in grave matters a person would still be gravely responsible. A person has affected ignorance when one deliberately fosters it in order not to be inhibited in what one wants to do; such ignorance is gravely wrong when it concerns serious matters. (Etym. Latin *vincibilis,* easily overcome; *ignorantia,* want of knowledge or information.)

VIOLENCE. Physical or psychological force used to compel one to act against one's choice, or against an inclination to choose in a certain way. Violence may be absolute or relative. Absolute violence demands resistance by all possible means. It destroys free will, and all imputability of the act is then attributed to the violator, if one acts with full freedom of the will. If the victim does not oppose the act with every possible external resistance, or with external resistance internally adheres to the act brought to bear on him or her, violence is called relative. Freedom of the will is not removed but diminished in proportion to the adherence or repugnance present in the mind of the subject.

VIRGIN BIRTH. A popular expression for Christ's conception and birth of a unique mother, Mary. Taught by all the creeds of Christendom, it is an article of faith and a basic norm of Christian orthodoxy.

VIRGINITY. The state of bodily integrity in either sex. This integrity may be physical or moral, and either factual or intentional. Physical virginity is sometimes defined as the absence of any sinfully experienced lustful sensation. But, strictly speaking, a person is physically a virgin unless he or she has had sexual intercourse with a person of the opposite sex. Moral virginity means the absence of any willful consent to venereal pleasure—again, strictly speaking, with a person of the opposite sex. Virginity is factual when, de facto, a person has not in the past sought or indulged in sexual pleasure; it is intentional when a person intends never to experience such pleasure, according to the previous distinctions made. (Etym. Latin *virgo,* maiden, virgin.)

VIRTUE. A good habit that enables a person to act according to right reason enlightened by faith. Also called an operative good habit, it makes its possessor a good person and his or her actions also good. (Etym. Latin *virtus,* virility, strength of character, manliness.)

VIRTUES. Angels who compose the second choir of the second or intermediate order of angels. They are the ones whom God employs for the performance of stupendous works or extraordinary miracles.

VISITANDINES. The Order of the Visitation of the Blessed Virgin Mary, founded in 1610 by St. Francis de Sales and St. Jane Frances de Chantal. It was established for women who wished a contemplative life but under less austere conditions than those of the older orders, stressing humility, gentleness, and sisterly charity. Originally under simple vows, they became a religious order with strict enclosure in 1618, and thus were approved by Pope Paul V. Houses are relatively autonomous. The best known Visitandine was St. Margaret Mary Alacoque, whose revelations helped to promote the modern devotion to the Sacred Heart. There are also several groups of Visitation Sisters, including a native Japanese community based in Yokohama.

VOCAL PRAYER. The form of prayer that is a "conversation" with God, or the angels and saints, and is formed in words or equivalent symbols of expression. More technically, vocal prayer involves the use of some set formulas, since it is assumed that even when a person prays mentally he necessarily employs some form of at least internal speech. So that in practice the distinction between mental and vocal prayer is more a matter of emphasis, whether one's own unrehearsed sentiments predominate (mental prayer) or a person rather employs verbal expressions that are not, at the time, the immediate product of communication with God (vocal prayer). (Etym. Latin *vocalis,* speaking, talking; from *vox,* voice.)

VOCATION. A call from God to a distinctive state of life, in which the person can reach holiness. The Second Vatican Council made it plain that there is a "Universal call [*vocatio*] to holiness in the Church" (*Lumen Gentium,* 39). (Etym. Latin *vocatio,* a calling, summoning; from *vocare,* to call.)

VOLUNTARISM. The doctrine of the primacy of the will. This takes on a variety of forms: 1. that in God his will takes precedence over his intellect, with the result that truth and goodness are what they are because God wants them that way (Duns Scotus); 2. that one's will, including one's freedom, is what makes that person distinctively human (St. Augustine); 3. that the world is the representation of the will, a blind and aimless cosmic power (Schopenhauer); 4. that each person's free will determines for the individual what is morally good or bad (Kant); 5. that what mainly constitutes a human person is his or her lifetime exercise of free will (existentialism). (Etym. Latin *voluntarius,* at one's pleasure, intentional, freely desired.)

VOTIVE CANDLES. Candles burned before some statue or shrine to give honor to Our Lord, Our Lady, or one of the saints. The word "votive" goes back to the ancient custom of lighting candles in fulfillment of some private vow (*votum*).

VOTIVE MASS. A Mass offered in honor of some mystery of the faith, or the Blessed Virgin, or of a saint or all the saints, but not in the liturgical calendar for that day. Votive Masses, with some exceptions, may be offered on any ordinary ferial day in the year, outside of Lent and Advent, and on other days that do not require the Mass of the day to be said. In general, votive Masses may be taken from among those listed as votive in the Roman Missal or from any other Mass of the year. (Etym. Latin *votivus;* from *votum,* vow, vote.)

VOTIVE OFFERING. Any object offered to God or in honor of a saint as an act of appreciation for some favor received, in petition for a favor asked for, and, hence the name, in discharge of a vow (*votum*) or promise made. The votive offering may be a sum of money, or a shrine, or sacred vessel, or jewel, or sculpture or anything that reflects the sentiments of the donor as an act of sacrifice.

VOW. A free, deliberate promise made to God to do something that is good and that is more pleasing to God than its omission would be. The one vowing must realize that a special sin is committed by violating the promise. A vow binds under pain of sin (grave or slight) according to the intention of the one taking the vow. If one vows with regard to grave matter, one is presumed to intend to bind oneself under pain of serious sin. Vows enhance the moral value of human actions on several counts. They unite the soul to God by a new bond of religion, and so the acts included under the vow become also acts of religion. Hence they are more meritorious. By taking a vow, a person surrenders to God the moral freedom of acting otherwise, like the one who not only gives at times the fruit of the tree but gives up the tree itself. And vows forestall human weakness, since they do not leave matters to the indecision or caprice of the moment. Their very purpose is to invoke divine grace to sustain one's resolution until the vow expires or, in the case of perpetual vows, even until death. (Etym. Latin *vovere,* to pledge, promise.)

VOW OF CHASTITY. The vow by which a person freely gives up the right to marriage and adds the obligation of the virtue of religion to the duty of abstaining from all voluntary indulgence of sexual pleasure.

VOW OF OBEDIENCE. The voluntary binding of oneself under oath to obey superiors in a religious institute, or a confessor, or spiritual guide. By this means a person is more permanently and securely united with God's saving will. Speaking of religious, the Second Vatican Council declares: "Moved by the Holy Spirit, they subject themselves in faith to those who hold God's place, their superiors. Through them they are led to serve all their brothers in Christ, just as Christ ministered to his brothers in submission to the Father and laid down his life for the redemption of many. They are thus bound more closely to the Church's service and they endeavor to attain to the measure of the stature of the fullness of Christ" (*Decree on Renewal of Religious Life*, 14). In some institutes of perfection a promise of obedience is taken instead of a formal vow.

VOW OF POVERTY. The vow by which a person freely gives up the ownership, or at least the independent use and administration, of temporal goods.

VULGATE. The Latin translation of the Bible, chiefly the work of St. Jerome, and commissioned by Pope St. Damasus I in 382. In time it became the standard in the Church, but by the sixteenth century several hundred editions were in print, with numerous variants. The Council of Trent declared that the Vulgate "is to be held authentic in public readings, disputations, sermons and exposition" and ordered its careful revision. This decree means that the Vulgate is the official biblical text of the Church. More than once revised, it was the Scripture text used by the First and Second Vatican Councils. (Etym. Latin *vulgata* [editio], "the popular [edition]"; from *vulgatus*, common, popular; from *vulgare*, to make commonly known; from *vulgus*, common people.)

WAKE. A watch or vigil. The term was originally applied to the all-night vigil in Anglo-Saxon times before certain major holidays. By the sixteenth century it was used of the holiday itself, and of the fair held to honor a local saint. In some countries—e.g., Ireland—a wake is the watch over the body of the deceased before burial. And more commonly a wake is the period, one or two days before the funeral, when mourners may visit the body of the deceased and offer their condolences to the bereaved. The Church now provides for a liturgical service, if so desired, during the wake. It is called Vigil for the Deceased.

WAR. Conflict of armed force in which one nation or part of a nation seeks to impose its will on another nation or part of a nation. The basic premise of war is that every right is coercible. Thus a state has the right to use force if necessary to defend just rights or to exact reparation for the violation of rights by another state. Another premise is that since no supernational organization exists with the capacity of enforcing its just decisions, with acceptance by all nations, the right of coercibility can be exercised directly by the aggrieved state itself. (Etym. Old High German *werra*, confusion, strife.)

WASHING OF THE FEET. An action of Christ at the Last Supper (John 13:1–15) when he washed the feet of his disciples to teach them humility as a condition for the practice of charity. This was believed by some early Christians to have been a sacrament of the New Law. As part of the liturgy on Holy Thursday, following the Homily of the Mass, modern popes have performed this ceremony in St. Peter's, washing the feet of a certain number of poor men chosen to participate in the Maundy Thursday liturgy. The ritual is an optional part of the regular Holy Thursday liturgy.

WASHING OF THE HANDS. Liturgical washing of the fingers by a priest before Mass and after Mass, which is not prescribed, and washing the fingers at the Offertory, which is part of the Eucharistic liturgy. It symbolizes the purity of conscience expected of the celebrant at Mass and the respect due to the Eucharistic elements handled during Mass. The hands are also washed by a bishop after using chrism in confirmation and holy orders, and by a priest after using the holy oils at baptism and anointing of the sick.

WASHINGTON, BASILICA OF THE NATIONAL SHRINE OF THE IMMAC-ULATE CONCEPTION. Church dedicated to the Immaculate Conception, who was declared patroness of the United States by the Provincial Council of Baltimore in 1846. The project for the shrine was begun in 1914, after Pope St. Pius X approved the plans, which originated with Bishop Shahan, fourth rector of the Catholic University. Pope Benedict XV sent a mosaic of Murillo's *Immaculate Conception* in 1919, in time for the cornerstone laying by Cardinal Gibbons in 1920. Popes Pius XI and XII sent further favors to the shrine, visited by Cardinal Pacelli in 1936, before his elevation to the papacy. The main church was solemnly dedicated in 1959. More than fifty chapels have been installed since the dedication. The campanile houses a fifty-six-bell carillon. With a seating capacity of six thousand persons, the shrine is one of the largest religious buildings in the world. All the American dioceses and numerous religious communities and organizations have contributed to its erection. Over one million persons visit the shrine each year. Blessed Pope John Paul II addressed several thousand religious women at the shrine (October 7, 1979) to close his seven-day visit to the United States. In 1990, Blessed Pope John Paul II elevated the National Shrine of the Immaculate Conception to the rank of a minor basilica. Pope Benedict XVI visited the shrine on April 16, 2008, to celebrate Solemn Vespers and to meet with the bishops of the United States.

WATER, LITURGICAL USE OF. A symbol of exterior and interior purity, water is used in the administration of baptism to signify the cleansing from sin. At Mass a few drops of water are mingled with the wine to indicate the union of Christ with the faithful and the blood and water that flowed from the side of Christ on Calvary. Sprinkling with holy water is practiced before Mass and during Mass on special occasions (e.g., Easter Vigil), at weddings, funerals, and other functions.

WAX. The viscous or heat-sensitive solid substance used for candles and other lamps in church and for liturgical services. For centuries beeswax was to be used in the service of the sanctuary as far as possible. And even now candles made of 51 (or more) percent beeswax are preferable. But the Church's regulation, since the Second Vatican Council, has been less demanding. According to the directives to episcopal conferences, the materials used are suitable "provided they are generally considered worthy and dignified and properly fulfill a sacred purpose" (*Enchiridion Documentorum Instaurationis Liturgicae*, 1664).

WEALTH. The ownership of a great quantity of material possessions or resources. The Church's teaching on wealth is that 1. riches of themselves do not help to gain eternal life but are rather an obstacle to salvation; 2. the rich should have a salutary fear in the light of what Christ said about those who make evil use of their wealth; 3. the practice of charity is a commandment and all the more pressing as a person has a great deal of this world's goods. The Second Vatican Council added the strong injunction that the more wealthy nations and societies are to share with the less-developed peoples of the world (Pastoral Constitution on the Church in the Modern World, Part Two, III, 69).

WESTERN SCHISM. Widespread division in Catholic unity caused by rival claims to the papacy. In the Western Schism (1378–1417) there were two and later three claimants to the papacy at the same time. The election of Urban VI (1318–89) was challenged post factum by thirteen of his cardinal electors, who in 1378 chose Clement VII as Avignon pope in his stead. After thirty years of fruitless efforts to settle the rift, a council of prelates at Pisa in 1409 sought to depose the Roman and Avignon pontiffs and elected Alexander V. Finally the schism was healed at the Council of Constance (1414–18). Gregory XII, the Roman pope, resigned; the antipopes Benedict XII of Avignon and John XXIII of Pisa were deposed, and Martin V (1368–1431) was chosen to replace them.

WIDOW. A woman who does not remarry after the death of her husband. Widows have been the special object of the Church's care since apostolic times (Acts 6). The early Church formed bodies of such consecrated women. St. Paul's teaching is very detailed about widows who are older, while he recommends that younger widows remarry (I Timothy 5:3–16). The Council of Trent declared that objectively widowhood (as celibacy) is more commendable than remarriage (Denzinger 1810). Each case, however, must be judged on its own merits.

WILL. The power of the human soul, or of a spiritual being, which tends toward a good or away from an evil recognized by the intellect. It is basically a rational appetite with several functions, namely the ability to intend, choose, desire, hope, consent, hate, love, and enjoy.

WILL OF GOD. In spiritual theology the manifest designs of God for a person's whole life or for any part of that life, which the person is to accept though not naturally appealing, or surrender though naturally desirable, or do whether he or she likes it or not. The will of God can be known to some extent by the light of natural reason, more fully and with greater demands on human generosity through revelation, and most clearly from the teachings of the Church that Christ founded precisely to lead the human race to its final destiny. Moreover, frequent prayer for divine guidance, daily reflection on one's moral conduct, and when necessary the counsel of a prudent adviser are part of God's ordinary Providence in showing his will to those who seriously want to serve him as they should.

WILL TO BELIEVE. In Catholic theology the doctrine that in order to assent to God's revealed word a person must receive supernatural grace for the will. The Church calls it "the devout readiness to believe," *pius credulitatis affectus* (Denzinger 375). Also in the psychology of religion the innate tendency of the human will to believe in other people as a precondition for social living. On a higher level the willingness to believe in God beyond all human calculation and with phenomenal results in the achievement of personal sanctity and service of humanity.

WISDOM, BOOK OF. Book of the Septuagint Old Testament placed in the Vulgate and the Church's biblical canon. It is called deuterocanonical because, found in the Greek but not the Hebrew, it was not included in the Jewish canon of the Bible, drawn up by the Pharisees at the close of the first century of the Christian era. In Syriac it is called "The Book of the Great Wisdom of Solomon," but the author was more likely an Alexandrian Jew living toward the beginning of the third century B.C. The book can be divided into two main parts, separated by the famous prayer for wisdom (chapter 19). Part One is an exhortation to rulers to observe justice and wisdom (chapters 1–8). Part Two extols the advantages of wisdom, as seen in the way God dealt with his own people compared with the unwisdom of the idolatrous nations. Wisdom means knowledge that is so perfect it directs the will to obey God's commands. In God wisdom is identified with his Word, a foreshadowing of the revelation of the Trinity.

WITNESS. One who can give evidence based on personal and immediate knowledge of a fact, event, or experience. The Christian concept of witness adds to the popular notion the idea of a religious experience to which a believer testifies by his or her life, words, and actions, and thus gives inspiration and example to others by his or her testimony. Implicit in Christian witness is also the element of courage in giving testimony, either because others are not favorably disposed or because they are openly hostile to the message of faith being proposed.

WOMEN, ORDINATION OF. A speculative question that has become highly controversial since the Second Vatican Council as to whether women could be ordained to the Catholic priesthood and episcopacy. In 1975, Venerable Pope Paul VI declared women's ineligibility for the ministerial priesthood (*Acta Apostolicae Sedis,* 67, 265). And in the following year the Sacred Congregation for the Doctrine of the Faith reaffirmed the fact and gave the reasons why this practice has a normative character. "In the fact of conferring priestly ordination only on men, it is a question of unbroken tradition throughout the history of the Church, universal in the East and in the West, and alert to suppress abuses immediately." Having stated the fact, the Holy See went on to clarify this teaching. Since the priesthood is a sacrament, it is a sign that is not only effective but should be intelligible to the faithful: "When Christ's role in the Eucharist is to be expressed sacramentally, there would not be this 'natural resemblance' which must exist between Christ and His minister if the role of Christ were not taken by a man" (October 15, 1976). Blessed Pope John Paul II in the apostolic letter *Ordinatio Sacerdotalis* of May 22, 1994, solemnly declared that priestly ordination is reserved only to men (males).

WOMEN'S LIBERATION. The movement in modern times to free women from the discrimination to which they have been subject in civil society and in political legislation. As such, it has two discernible roots, one sociological and the other ideological. On the sociological level is the recognized fact that women in all parts of the world are coming more and more into their own, to find their places alongside of men, making their distinctive contribution in the professions, in education, and in the sciences. The other root is not so much factual as ideological, and stands at variance with Christian principles. It argues from a massive discrimination of women by men, and urges women to revolt against men. The best-known proponent of this ideology was Nikolai Lenin (1874-1924), who urged that "the success of a revolution depends upon the degree of participation by women." On these terms, women's liberation is simply part of the larger struggle for the eventual creation of a classless society.

WORDS OF ABSOLUTION. The essential words pronounced by a priest when he absolves a penitent in the sacrament of penance: "I absolve you from your sins, in the name of the Father, and of the Son, and of the Holy Spirit."

WORDS OF INSTITUTION. The words of Christ at the Last Supper, recorded by the Synoptic Gospels (Matthew 26:26-29; Mark 14:22-25; Luke 22:19-21); and St. Paul (I Corinthians 11:23-29). Their essential features are 1. Christ separately consecrated bread and wine; 2. over the bread he said, "This is my body," and over the wine, "This is the chalice of my blood"; 3. the elements of bread and wine were thus changed into the living Christ; 4. he empowered the Apostles and their successors to perform the same consecrating action; 5. he bade his followers to partake of the Eucharist; 6. at the Last Supper, Christ offered his life to the Heavenly Father, but the actual death resulting from the sacrifice was to take place on the following day on Calvary.

WORK. Continued exertion directed to some recognized purpose or end. The exertion may be physical or mental, and the purpose may be determined by the one who works or by someone else, who in turn may have his or her own motive for assigning the task. Christianity does not look upon work as demeaning or evil, as though leisure were more worthy of human dignity. Work ennobles a person's character and assimilates one to the Savior. "We believe by faith that through the homage of work offered to God man is associated with the redemptive work of Jesus Christ, whose labor with his hands at Nazareth greatly ennobled the dignity of work. This is the source of every man's duty to work loyally, as well as his right to work; moreover, it is the duty of society to see to it that, according to the prevailing circumstances, all citizens have the opportunity of finding employment" (Second Vatican Council, Pastoral Constitution on the Church in the Modern World, III, 67).

WORLD. The term has two distinct meanings in revelation and Catholic doctrine. It is generally identified with the visible universe, *kosmos*, in the biblical Greek, and *mundus*, in the Latin Vulgate. As such it is the world of creation, made by God, and therefore totally subject to his divine will. But there is also the world of sin, estranged from God as the creation of man's self-will. It is at variance with the divine will and is what Christ meant when he said, "I am not praying for the world" (John 17:9).

X Y Z

YOKE. A wooden frame used to join two oxen in a team (Deuteronomy 21:3). Metaphorically, it suggested subjection or slavish control and the removal of a yoke, freedom. "When you win your freedom, you shall shake his yoke from your neck" (Genesis 27:40). Christ assured the faithful: "My yoke is easy" (Matthew 11:29).

ZEAL. Love in action. The strong emotion of spirit, based on deep affection, that seeks to obtain what is loved or to remove what stands in the way. In religious terms, zeal is manifested by an impelling desire to advance the Kingdom of Christ, sanctify souls, and advance the glory of God by making him better known and loved, and thus more faithfully served. (Etym. Latin *zelus,* eagerness; from Greek *zēlos*.)

ZEALOT. 1 A Jewish member of a radical, violent group bitterly opposed to Roman domination of Palestine. The group was especially active during the century in which Christ lived on earth. The present-day use of the word "zealot," to mean a fanatical enthusiast, derives from this group's name; 2. Simon was one of the Twelve Apostles. He was referred to in the New Testament as Simon the Zealot (Luke 6:15) to distinguish him from Simon Peter. He had probably been a member of the Jewish group until his conversion to Christianity. (Etym. Latin *zelotes;* from Greek *zēlōtēs;* from *zēlos,* zeal.)

ZECHARIAH. A common name in the Bible; between twenty-five to thirty persons are so called. Variant spellings are Zacharias and Zachariah. Three persons are mainly identified with this name: 1. the father of John the Baptist; he was married to Elizabeth, a kinswoman of the Virgin Mary (Luke 1:5). He was rendered speechless when he doubted the message of the archangel Gabriel that his wife would conceive in her old age (Luke 1:22). At John's circumcision ceremony Zechariah made a prophecy that Israel's Messiah would soon appear and this newborn son of Elizabeth's would "go before the Lord to prepare the way for him" (Luke 1:59-76); 2. a Jewish martyr, son of Jehoiada, in the Old Testament; he was stoned to death for denouncing the faithlessness of the people (II Chronicles 24:20-22). Jesus referred to him when be spoke of the slaughter of the prophets "from the blood of Abel to the blood of Zechariah" (Luke 11:50-51); 3. a book in the Old Testament named after the eleventh minor prophet. This Zechariah was a contemporary of the prophet Haggai. Both wrote in the sixth century B.C.

ZECHARIAH, BOOK OF. Prophetic writing of the Old Testament, containing, for its length, the largest number of predictions about Christ. Three visions concern the foundation of the Messianic kingdom. The fourth makes the promise "to raise my servant Baruch" (3–9b). The fourth through the sixth visions treat of Christ the priest and king. An address stresses the keeping of the commandments and the motive power of the Messianic prophecies (7–8). The rest of the book is mainly two burdens: one over Syria, Phoenicia, and the Philistines; and the other over Israel. In the first is the prophecy of Palm Sunday (9:9–10) and the purchase of Haceldama for the treason money of Judas, who betrayed Christ. In the second (12) is a promise of the restoration of Jerusalem. The author calls himself "son of Berechiah," but he is most probably not the prophet.

ZEITGEIST. Spirit of the times. Used especially to explain why many people are so skeptical of the supernatural and so demanding that Christian faith and morals conform to the modern mentality.

ZEPHANIAH. Author of the ninth book of the minor prophets. The son of Cushi and a descendant of King Hezekiah, he lived in the seventh century B.C. The emphasis in his writing was on the corruption of the people of Judah during the Assyrian rule and the promise of YHWH's punishment. "Seek integrity, seek humility" was Zephaniah's theme. "You may perhaps find shelter on the day of the anger of YHWH" (Zephaniah 2:3).

APPENDIX I

THE CREDO OF THE PEOPLE OF GOD

The Credo of the People of God was proclaimed by Pope Paul VI at the close of the Year of Faith on June 29, 1968. Its purpose was to offer the Christian world, after the Second Vatican Council, a profession of the principal articles of the Catholic faith. It is no mere summary, however, but a carefully assembled synthesis of those revealed truths that today either are most challenged or especially need to be understood by the faithful. It incorporates all the familiar doctrines of the Nicene Creed but goes beyond them in occasionally updating their verbal expression and showing how these mysteries are to be lived by the Christian believer.

POPE PAUL VI
The Credo of the People of God

as published in *The Acts of the Apostolic See,* August 10, 1968

THE SOLEMN PROFESSION OF FAITH
pronounced by Pope Paul VI at St. Peter's Basilica, June 30, 1968, at the end of the "Year of Faith," the nineteenth centenary anniversary of the martyrdom of Sts. Peter and Paul.

VENERABLE BROTHERS AND BELOVED SONS:
1. With this solemn liturgy we end the celebration of the nineteenth centenary of the martyrdom of the holy Apostles Peter and Paul, and thus close the Year of Faith. We dedicated it to the commemoration of the holy Apostles in order that we might give witness to our steadfast will to *guard the deposit* of faith from corruption, that deposit which they transmitted to us, and to demonstrate again our intention of relating this same faith to life at this time when the Church must continue her pilgrimage in this world.

2. We feel it our duty to give public thanks to all who responded to our invitation by bestowing on the Year of Faith a splendid completeness through the deepening of their personal adhesion to the Word of God, through the renewal in various gatherings of the Profession of Faith, and through the testimony of a Christian life. To our brothers in the episcopate especially, and to all the faithful of the Holy Catholic Church, we express our appreciation and we grant our blessing.

3. Likewise we deem that we must fulfill the mandate entrusted by Christ to Peter, whose successor we are, the last in merit; namely, to confirm our brothers in the faith. With the awareness, certainly, of our human weakness, yet with all the strength impressed on our spirit by such a command, we shall accordingly make a Profession of Faith, pronounce a formula which begins

with the word *Credo,* "I believe." Without being strictly speaking a dogmatic definition, it repeats in substance, with some developments called for by the spiritual condition of our time, the Creed of Nicaea, the Creed of the immortal tradition of the Holy Church of God.

4. In making this profession, we are aware of the disquiet which agitates certain groups of men at the present time with regard to the faith. They do not escape the influence of a world being profoundly changed, in which so many truths are being denied outright or made objects of controversy. We see even Catholics allowing themselves to be seized by a kind of passion for change and novelty. The Church, most assuredly, has always the duty to carry on the effort to study more deeply and to present in a manner ever better adapted to successive generations the unfathomable mysteries of God, rich for all in fruits of salvation. But at the same time the greatest care must be taken, while fulfilling the indispensable duty of research, to do no injury to the truths of Christian doctrine. For that would be to give rise, as is unfortunately seen in these days, to disturbance and doubt in many faithful souls.

5. It is supremely important in this respect to recall that, beyond what is observable, analyzed by the work of the sciences, the intellect which God has given us reaches *that which is,* and not merely the subjective expression of the structures and development of consciousness. And, on the other hand, it is important to remember that the task of interpretation—of hermeneutics—is to try to understand and extricate, while respecting the word expressed, the sense conveyed by a text, and not to re-create, in some fashion, this sense in accordance with arbitrary hypotheses.

6. But above all, we place our unshakable confidence in the Holy Spirit, the soul of the Church, and in theological faith upon which rests the life of the Mystical Body. We know that souls await the word of the Vicar of Christ, and we respond to that expectation with the instructions which we regularly give. But today we are given an opportunity to make a more solemn utterance.

7. On this day which is chosen to close the Year of Faith, on this Feast of the Blessed Apostles Peter and Paul, we have wished to offer to the Living God the homage of a Profession of Faith. And as once at Caesarea Philippi the Apostle Peter spoke on behalf of the Twelve to make a true confession, beyond human opinions, of Christ as Son of the Living God, so today his humble successor, pastor of the universal Church, raises his voice to give, on behalf of all the People of God, a firm witness to the divine truth entrusted to the Church to be announced to all nations.

We have wished our Profession of Faith to be to a high degree complete and explicit, in order that it may respond in a fitting way to the need of light felt by so many faithful souls, and by all those in the world to whatever spiritual family they belong, who are in search of the truth.

Therefore, to the glory of God Most Holy and of Our Lord Jesus Christ, trusting in the aid of the Blessed Virgin Mary and of the Holy Apostles Peter and Paul, for the profit and edification of the Church, in the name of all the pastors and all the faithful, we now pronounce this Profession of Faith, in full communion with you all, beloved brothers and sons.

PROFESSION OF FAITH

8. We believe in one only God, Father, Son and Holy Spirit, Creator of things visible such as this world in which our brief life passes, of things invisible such as the pure spirits which are also called angels, and Creator in each man of his spiritual and immortal soul.

9. We believe that this only God is absolutely one in His infinitely holy essence as also in all His perfections, in His omnipotence, His infinite knowledge, His providence, His will and His love. He is *He Who Is,* as He revealed to Moses; and He is *Love,* as the Apostle John teaches us: so that these two names, Being and Love, express ineffably the same divine reality of Him who has wished to make himself known to us, and who "dwelling in light inaccessible," is in himself above every name, above every thing and above every created intellect. God alone can give us right and full knowledge of this reality by revealing himself as Father, Son and Holy Spirit, in whose eternal life we are by grace called to share, here below in the obscurity of faith and after death in eternal light. The mutual bonds which eternally constitute the Three Persons, who are each one and the same Divine Being, are the blessed inmost life of God thrice holy, infinitely beyond all that we can conceive in human measure. We give thanks, however, to the Divine Goodness that very many believers can testify with us before men to the unity of God, even though they know not the mystery of the Most Holy Trinity.

10. We believe then in God who eternally begets the Son, in the Son, the Word of God, who is eternally begotten, in the Holy Spirit, the uncreated Person, who proceeds from the Father and the Son as their eternal Love. Thus in the Three Divine Persons, *coaeternae sibi et coaequales,* the life and beatitude of God perfectly One superabound and are consummated in the supreme excellence and glory proper to uncreated Being, and always "there should be venerated unity in the Trinity and Trinity in the unity."

11. We believe in Our Lord Jesus Christ, who is the Son of God. He is the Eternal Word, born of the Father before time began, and consubstantial with the Father, *homoousios to Patri,* and through Him all things were made. He was incarnate of the Virgin Mary by the power of the Holy Spirit, and was made man: equal therefore to the Father according to His divinity, and inferior to the Father according to His humanity, and himself one, not by some impossible confusion of His natures, but by the unity of His person.

12. He dwelt among us, full of grace and truth. He proclaimed and established the Kingdom of God and made us know in himself the Father. He gave us His new commandment to love one another as He loved us. He taught us the way of the Beatitudes of the Gospel: poverty in spirit, meekness, suffering borne with patience, thirst after justice, mercy, purity of heart, will for peace, persecution suffered for justice sake. He suffered under Pontius Pilate, the Lamb

of God bearing on himself the sins of the world, and He died for us on the Cross, saving us by His redeeming Blood. He was buried, and, of His own power, rose the third day, raising us by His Resurrection to that sharing in the divine life which is the life of grace. He ascended to heaven, and He will come again, this time in glory, to judge the living and the dead: each according to his merits—those who have responded to the love and piety of God going to eternal life, those who have refused them to the end going to the fire that is not extinguished. And His Kingdom will have no end.

13. We believe in the Holy Spirit, Who is Lord, and Giver of life, Who is adored and glorified together with the Father and the Son. He spoke to us by the Prophets, He was sent by Christ after His Resurrection and His Ascension to the Father; He illuminates, vivifies, protects and governs the Church; He purifies the Church's members if they do not shun His grace. His action, which penetrates to the inmost of the soul, enables man to respond to the call of Jesus: *Be perfect as your Heavenly Father is perfect.*

14. We believe that Mary is the Mother, who remained ever a Virgin, of the Incarnate Word, our God and Savior Jesus Christ, and that by reason of this singular election, she was, in consideration of the merits of her Son, redeemed in a more eminent manner, preserved from all stain of original sin and filled with the gift of grace more than all other creatures.

15. Joined by a close and indissoluble bond to the Mysteries of the Incarnation and Redemption, the Blessed Virgin, the Immaculate, was at the end of her earthly life raised body and soul to heavenly glory and likened to her risen Son in anticipation of the future lot of all the just; and We believe that the Blessed Mother of God, the New Eve, Mother of the Church, continues, in heaven her maternal role with regard to Christ's members, co-operating with the birth and growth of divine life in the souls of the redeemed.

16. We believe that in Adam all have sinned, which means that the original offense committed by him caused human nature, common to all men, to fall to a state in which it bears the consequences of that offense, and which is not the state in which it was at first in our first parents, established as they were in holiness and justice, and in which man knew neither evil nor death. It is human nature so fallen, stripped of the grace that clothed it, injured in its own natural powers and subjected to the dominion of death, that is transmitted to all men, and it is in this sense that every man is born in sin. We therefore hold, with the Council of Trent, that original sin is transmitted with human nature, "not by imitation, but by propagation" and that it is thus "in each of us as his own."

17. We believe that Our Lord Jesus Christ, by the Sacrifice of the Cross, redeemed us from original sin and all the personal sins committed by each one of us, so that, in accordance with the word of the Apostle, "where sin abounded, grace did more abound."

18. We believe in one baptism instituted by Our Lord Jesus Christ for the remission of sins. Baptism should be administered even to little children who

have not yet been able to be guilty of any personal sin, in order that, though born deprived of supernatural grace, they may be reborn "of water and the Holy Spirit" to the divine life in Christ Jesus.

19. We believe in one, holy, catholic, and apostolic Church, built by Jesus Christ on that rock which is Peter. She is the Mystical Body of Christ; at the same time a visible society instituted with hierarchical organs, and a spiritual community; the Church on earth, the pilgrim People of God here below, and the Church filled with heavenly blessings; the germ and the first fruits of the Kingdom of God, through which the work and the sufferings of Redemption are continued throughout human history, and which looks for its perfect accomplishment beyond time in glory. In the course of time, the Lord Jesus forms His Church by means of the Sacraments emanating from His plenitude. By these she makes her members participants in the mystery of the Death and Resurrection of Christ, in the grace of the Holy Spirit who gives her life and movement. She is therefore holy, though she has sinners in her bosom, because she herself has no other life but that of grace: it is by living by her life that her members are sanctified; it is by removing themselves from her life that they fall into sins and disorders that prevent the radiation of her sanctity. This is why she suffers and does penance for these offenses, of which she has the power to heal her children through the blood of Christ and the gift of the Holy Spirit.

20. Heiress of the divine promises and daughter of Abraham according to the Spirit, through that Israel whose Scriptures she lovingly guards, and whose patriarchs and prophets she venerates; founded upon the Apostles and handing on from century to century their ever-living word and their powers as pastors in the successor of Peter and the bishops in communion with him; perpetually assisted by the Holy Spirit, she has the charge of guarding, teaching, explaining and spreading the truth which God revealed in a then veiled manner by the Prophets, and fully by the Lord Jesus. We believe *all that is contained in the Word of God written or handed down, and that the Church proposes for belief as divinely revealed, whether by a solemn judgment or by the ordinary and universal magisterium.* We believe in the infallibility enjoyed by the successor of Peter when he teaches ex cathedra as pastor and teacher of all the faithful, and which is assured also to the episcopal body when it exercises with him the supreme magisterium.

21. We believe that the Church founded by Jesus Christ and for which He prayed is indefectibly one in faith, worship and the bond of hierarchical communion. In the bosom of this Church, the rich variety of liturgical rites and the legitimate diversity of theological and spiritual heritages and special disciplines, far from injuring her unity, make it more manifest.

22. Recognizing also the existence, outside the organism of the Church of Christ, of numerous elements of truth and sanctification which belong to her as her own and tend to Catholic unity, and believing in the action of the Holy Spirit who stirs up in the heart of the disciples of Christ love of this unity, we

entertain the hope that Christians who are not yet in the full communion of the one only Church will one day be reunited in one flock with one only Shepherd.

23. We believe that the Church is *necessary for salvation, because Christ who is the sole Mediator and Way of salvation, renders himself present for us in His Body which is the Church.* But the divine design of salvation embraces all men; and those *who without fault on their part do not know the Gospel of Christ and His Church, but seek God sincerely, and under the influence of grace endeavor to do His will as recognized through the promptings of their conscience,* they, in a number known only to God, *can obtain salvation.*

24. We believe that the Mass, celebrated by the priest representing the person of Christ by virtue of the power received through the Sacrament of Orders, and offered by him in the name of Christ and the members of His Mystical Body, is in true reality the Sacrifice of Calvary, rendered sacramentally present on our altars. We believe that as the bread and wine consecrated by the Lord at the Last Supper were changed into His Body and His Blood which were to be offered for us on the Cross, likewise the bread and wine consecrated by the priest are changed into the Body and Blood of Christ enthroned gloriously in heaven, and we believe that the mysterious presence of the Lord, under what continues to appear to our sense as before, is a true, real and substantial presence.

25. Christ cannot be thus present in this sacrament except by the change into His Body of the reality itself of the bread and the change into His Blood of the reality itself of the wine, leaving unchanged only the properties of the bread and wine which our senses perceive. This mysterious change is very appropriately called by the Church *transubstantiation.* Every theological explanation which seeks some understanding of this mystery must, in order to be in accord with Catholic faith, maintain that in the reality itself, independently of our mind, the bread and wine have ceased to exist after the Consecration, so that it is the adorable Body and Blood of the Lord Jesus that from then on are really before us under the sacramental species of bread and wine, as the Lord willed it, in order to give himself to us as food and to associate us with the unity of His Mystical Body.

26. The unique and indivisible existence of the Lord glorious in heaven is not multiplied, but is rendered present by the sacrament in the many places on earth where Mass is celebrated. And this existence remains present, after the sacrifice, in the Blessed Sacrament which is, in the tabernacle, the living heart of each of our churches. And it is our very sweet duty to honor and adore in the Blessed Host which our eyes see, the Incarnate Word Whom they cannot see, and Who, without leaving heaven, is made present before us.

27. We confess that the Kingdom of God begun here below in the Church of Christ *is not of this world whose form is passing,* and that its proper growth cannot be confounded with the progress of civilization, of science or of human technology, but that it consists in an ever more profound knowledge of

the unfathomable riches of Christ, an ever stronger hope in eternal blessings, an ever more ardent response to the Love of God, and an ever more generous bestowal of grace and holiness among men. But it is this same love which induces the Church to concern herself constantly about the true temporal welfare of men. Without ceasing to recall to her children that *they have not here a lasting dwelling,* she also urges them to contribute, each according to his vocation and his means, to the welfare of their earthly city, to promote justice, peace and brotherhood among men, to give their aid freely to their brothers, especially to the poorest and most unfortunate. The deep solicitude of the Church, the spouse of Christ, for the needs of men, for their joys and hopes, their griefs and efforts, is therefore nothing other than her great desire to be present to them, in order to illuminate them with the light of Christ and to gather them all in Him, their only Savior. This solicitude can never mean that the Church conform herself to the things of this world, or that she lessen the ardor of her expectation of her Lord and of the eternal Kingdom.

28. We believe in the life eternal. We believe that the souls of all those who die in the grace of Christ, whether they must still be purified in Purgatory, or whether from the moment they leave their bodies Jesus takes them to Paradise as He did for the Good Thief, are the People of God in the eternity beyond death, which will be finally conquered on the day of the resurrection when these souls will be reunited with their bodies.

29. We believe that the multitude of those gathered around Jesus and Mary in Paradise forms the Church of Heaven, where in eternal beatitude they see God as He is, and where they also, in different degrees, are associated with the holy angels in the divine rule exercised by Christ in glory, interceding for us and helping our weakness by their brotherly care.

30. We believe in the communion of all the faithful of Christ, those who are pilgrims on earth, the dead who are attaining their purification, and the blessed in heaven, all together forming one Church; and we believe that in this communion the merciful love of God and His saints is ever listening to our prayers, as Jesus told us: Ask and you will receive. Thus it is with faith and in hope that we look forward to the resurrection of the dead, and the life of the world to come.

Blessed be God Thrice Holy. Amen.

Pronounced in front of the Basilica of St. Peter, on June 30, 1968, the sixth year of our pontificate.

POPE PAUL VI

APPENDIX II

POPES OF THE CATHOLIC CHURCH

The data give first the name of the pope, for later pontiffs their family names, birthplace or country of origin, date of accession to the papacy, and date of the end of the reign, which is generally the date of death. Double dates include times of election and coronation (installation).

1. ST. PETER (Simon Bar-Jonah): Bethsaida in Galilee; d. 64 or 67
2. ST. LINUS: Tuscany; 67–76
3. ST. ANACLETUS (CLETUS): Rome; 76–88
4. ST. CLEMENT: Rome; 88–97
5. ST. EVARISTUS: Greece; 97–105
6. ST. ALEXANDER I: Rome; 105–15
7. ST. SIXTUS I: Rome; 115–25
8. ST. TELESPHORUS: Greece; 125–36
9. ST. HYGINUS: Greece; 136–40
10. ST. PIUS I: Aquileia; 140–55
11. ST. ANICETUS: Syria; 155–66
12. ST. SOTER: Campania; 166–75
13. ST. ELEUTHERIUS: Nicopolis in Epirus; 175–89
14. ST. VICTOR I: Africa; 189–99
15. ST. ZEPHYRINUS: Rome; 199–217
16. ST. CALLISTUS I: Rome; 217–22
17. ST. URBAN I: Rome; 222–30
18. ST. PONTIAN: Rome; July 21, 230, to Sept. 28, 235
19. ST. ANTERUS: Greece; Nov. 21, 235, to Jan. 3, 236
20. ST. FABIAN: Rome; Jan. 10, 236, to Jan. 20, 250
21. ST. CORNELIUS: Rome; Mar. 251 to June 253
22. ST. LUCIUS I: Rome; June 25, 253, to Mar. 5, 254
23. ST. STEPHEN I: Rome; May 12, 254, to Aug. 2, 257
24. ST. SIXTUS II: Greece; Aug. 30, 257, to Aug. 6, 258
25. ST. DIONYSIUS: July 22, 259, to Dec. 26, 268
26. ST. FELIX I: Rome; Jan. 5, 269, to Dec. 30, 274
27. ST. EUTYCHIAN: Luni; Jan. 4, 275, to Dec. 7, 283
28. ST. CAIUS: Dalmatia; Dec. 17, 283, to Apr. 22, 296
29. ST. MARCELLINUS: Rome; June 30, 296, to Oct. 25, 304
30. ST. MARCELLUS I: Rome; May 27, 308, or June 26, 308, to Jan. 16, 309
31. ST. EUSEBIUS: Greece; Apr. 18, 309 or 310, to Aug. 17, 309 or 310
32. ST. MELCHIADES (MILTIADES): Africa; July 2, 311, to Jan. 11, 314
33. ST. SYLVESTER I: Rome; Jan. 31, 314, to Dec. 31, 335
34. ST. MARK: Rome; Jan. 18, 336, to Oct. 7, 336

35. ST. JULIUS I: Rome; Feb. 6, 337, to Apr. 12, 352

36. LIBERIUS: Rome; May 17, 352, to Sept. 24, 366

37. ST. DAMASUS I: Spain; Oct. 1, 366, to Dec. 11, 384

38. ST. SIRICIUS: Rome; Dec. 15 or 22 or 29, 384, to Nov. 26, 399

39. ST. ANASTASIUS I: Rome; Nov. 27, 399, to Dec. 19, 401

40. ST. INNOCENT I: Albano; Dec. 22, 401, to Mar. 12, 417

41. ST. ZOZIMUS: Greece; Mar. 18, 417, to Dec. 26, 418

42. ST. BONIFACE I: Rome; Dec. 28 or 29, 418, to Sept. 4, 422

43. ST. CELESTINE I: Campania; Sept. 10, 422, to July 27, 432

44. ST. SIXTUS III: Rome; July 31, 432, to Aug. 19, 440

45. ST. LEO I (the Great): Tuscany; Sept. 29, 440, to Nov. 10, 461

46. ST. HILARY: Sardinia; Nov. 19, 461, to Feb. 29, 468

47. ST. SIMPLICUS: Tivoli; Mar. 3, 468, to Mar. 10, 483

48. ST. FELIX III (II): Rome; Mar. 13, 483, to Mar. 1, 492

He should be called Felix II, and his successors numbered accordingly.

49. ST. GELASIUS I: Africa; Mar. 1, 492, to Nov. 21, 496

50. ANASTASIUS II: Rome; Nov. 24, 496, to Nov. 19, 498

51. ST. SYMMACHUS: Sardinia; Nov. 22, 498, to July 19, 514

52. ST. HORMISDAS: Frosinone; July 20, 514, to Aug. 6, 523

53. ST. JOHN I, MARTYR: Tuscany; Aug. 13, 523, to May 18, 526

54. ST. FELIX IV (III): Samnium; July 12, 526, to Sept. 22, 530

55. BONIFACE II: Rome; Sept. 22, 530, to Oct. 17, 532

56. JOHN II: Rome; Jan. 2, 533, to May 8, 535

John II was the first pope to change his name; he was originally called Mercury, the name of a pagan deity.

57. ST. AGAPITUS I: Rome; May 13, 535, to Apr. 22, 536

58. ST. SILVERIUS, MARTYR: Campania; June 1 or 8, 536, to Mar. 537 (d. Dec. 2, 537)

59. VIGILIUS: Rome; Mar. 29, 537, to June 7, 555

60. PELAGIUS I: Rome; Apr. 16, 556, to Mar. 4, 561

61. JOHN III: Rome; July 17, 561, to July 13, 574

62. BENEDICT I: Rome; June 2, 575, to July 30, 579

63. PELAGIUS II: Rome; Nov. 26, 579, to Feb. 7, 590

64. ST. GREGORY I (the Great): Rome; Sept. 3, 590, to Mar. 12, 604

65. SABINIAN: Blera in Tuscany; Sept. 13, 604, to Feb. 22, 606

66. BONIFACE III: Rome; Feb. 19, 607, to Nov. 12, 607

67. ST. BONIFACE IV: Abruzzi; Aug. 25, 608, to May 8, 615

68. ST. DEUSDEDIT (ADEODATUS I): Rome; Oct. 19, 615, to Nov. 8, 618

69. BONIFACE V: Naples; Dec. 23, 619, to Oct. 25, 625

70. HONORIUS I: Campania; Oct. 27, 625, to Oct. 12, 638

71. SEVERINUS: Rome; May 28, 640, to Aug. 2, 640

72. JOHN IV: Dalmatia; Dec. 24, 640, to Oct. 12, 642

73. THEODORE I: Greece; Nov. 24, 642, to May 14, 649

74. ST. MARTIN I, MARTYR: Todi; July 649, to Sept. 16, 655 (in exile from June 17, 653)

His successor, St. Eugene I, was ordained during St. Martin I's exile and, apparently, with the latter's approval.

75. ST. EUGENE I: Rome; Aug. 10, 654, to June 2, 657
76. ST. VITALIAN: Segni; July 30, 657, to Jan. 27, 672
77. ADEODATUS II: Rome; Apr. 11, 672, to June 17, 676
78. DONUS (or DOMNUS): Rome; Nov. 2, 676, to Apr. 11, 678
79. ST. AGATHO: Sicily; June 27, 678, to Jan. 10, 681
80. ST. LEO II: Sicily; Aug. 17, 682, to July 3, 683
81. ST. BENEDICT II: Rome; June 26, 684, to May 8, 685
82. JOHN V: Syria; July 23, 685, to Aug. 2, 686
83. CONON: birthplace unknown; Oct. 21, 686, to Sept. 21, 687
84. ST. SERGIUS I: Syria; Dec. 15, 687, to Sept. 8, 701
85. JOHN VI: Greece; Oct. 30, 701, to Jan. 11, 705
86. JOHN VII: Greece; Mar. 1, 705, to Oct. 18, 707
87. SISINNIUS: Syria; Jan. 15, 708, to Feb. 4, 708
88. CONSTANTINE: Syria; Mar. 25, 708, to Apr. 9, 715
89. ST. GREGORY II: Rome; May 19, 715, to Feb. 11, 731
90. ST. GREGORY III: Syria; Mar. 18, 731, to Nov. 741
91. ST. ZACHARY: Greece; Dec. 10, 741, to Mar. 22, 752
92. STEPHEN II (III): Rome; Mar. 26, 752, to Apr. 26, 757

After the death of St. Zachary, a Roman priest named Stephen was elected but died (four days later) before his consecration as Bishop of Rome, which, according to the canon law of that day, would have marked the beginning of his pontificate. Immediately another man was elected to succeed Zachary as Stephen II. Both Stephens are considered to have been popes.

93. ST. PAUL I: Rome; Apr. (May 29) 757, to June 28, 767
94. STEPHEN III (IV): Sicily; Aug. 1 (7), 768, to Jan. 24, 772
95. ADRIAN I: Rome; Feb. 1 (9), 772, to Dec. 25, 795
96. ST. LEO III: Rome; Dec. 26 (27), 795, to June 12, 816
97. STEPHEN IV (V): Rome; June 22, 816, to Jan. 24, 817
98. ST. PASCHAL I: Rome; Jan. 25, 817, to Feb. 11, 824
99. EUGENE II: Rome; Feb. (May) 824 to Aug. 827
100. VALENTINE: Rome; Aug. 827 to Sept. 827
101. GREGORY IV: Rome; Oct. 827 to Jan. 844
102. SERGIUS II: Rome; Jan. 844 to Jan. 27, 847
103. ST. LEO IV: Rome; Jan. (Apr. 10) 847 to July 17, 855
104. BENEDICT III: Rome; July (Sept. 29) 855 to Apr. 17, 858
105. ST. NICHOLAS I (the Great): Rome; Apr. 24, 858, to Nov. 13, 867
106. ADRIAN II: Rome; Dec. 14, 867, to Dec. 14, 872
107. JOHN VIII: Rome; Dec. 14, 872, to Dec. 16, 882
108. MARINUS I: Gallese; Dec. 16, 882, to May 15, 884

109. ST. ADRIAN III: Rome; May 17, 884, to Sept. 885 (cult confirmed June 2, 1891)

110. STEPHEN V (VI): Rome; Sept. 885 to Sept. 14, 891

111. FORMOSUS: Porto; Oct. 6, 891, to Apr. 4, 896

112. BONIFACE VI: Rome; Apr. 896 to Apr. 896

113. STEPHEN VI (VII): Rome; May 896 to Aug. 897

114. ROMANUS: Gallese; Aug. 897 to Nov. 897

115. THEODORE II: Rome; Dec. 897 to Dec. 897

116. JOHN IX: Tivoli; Jan. 898 to Jan. 900

117. BENEDICT IV: Rome; Jan. (Feb.) 900 to July 903

118. LEO V: Ardea; July 903 to Sept. 903

119. SERGIUS III: Rome; Jan. 29, 904, to Apr. 14, 911

120. ANASTASIUS III: Rome; Apr. 911 to June 913

121. LANDO: Sabina; July 913 to Feb. 914

122. JOHN X: Tossignano (Imola); Mar. 914 to May 928

123. LEO VI: Rome; May 928 to Dec. 928

124. STEPHEN VII (VIII): Rome; Dec. 928 to Feb. 931

125. JOHN XI: Rome; Feb. (Mar.) 931 to Dec. 935

126. LEO VII: Rome; Jan. 3, 936, to July 13, 939

127. STEPHEN VIII (IX): Rome; July 14, 939, to Oct. 942

128. MARINUS II: Rome; Oct. 30, 942, to May 946

129. AGAPITUS II: Rome; May 10, 946, to Dec. 955

130. JOHN XII (Octavius): Tusculum; Dec. 16, 955, to May 14, 964

131. LEO VIII: Rome; Dec. 4 (6), 963, to Mar. 1, 965

132. BENEDICT V: Rome; May 22, 964, to July 4, 966

John XII was deposed Dec. 4, 963, by a Roman council; if the deposition was valid, Leo was the legitimate pope and Benedict was an antipope.

133. JOHN XIII: Rome; Oct. 1, 965, to Sept. 6, 972

134. BENEDICT VI: Rome; Jan. 19, 973, to June 974

135. BENEDICT VII: Rome; Oct. 974 to July 10, 983

136. JOHN XIV (Peter): Pavia; Dec. 983 to Aug. 20, 984

137. JOHN XV: Rome; Aug. 985 to Mar. 996

138. GREGORY V (Bruno of Carinthia): Saxony; May 3, 996, to Feb. 18, 999

139. SYLVESTER II (Gerbert): Auvergne; Apr. 2, 999, to May 12, 1003

140. JOHN XVII (Siccone): Rome; June 1003 to Dec. 1003

141. JOHN XVIII (Phasianus): Rome; Jan. 1004 to July 1009

142. SERGIUS IV (Peter): Rome; July 31, 1009, to May 12, 1012

The custom of changing one's name on election to the papacy traditionally dates from the time of Sergius IV. After his time this became a regular practice, with few exceptions; e.g., Adrian VI and Marcellus II.

143. BENEDICT VIII (Theophylactus): Tusculum; May 18, 1012, to Apr. 9, 1024

144. JOHN XIX (Romanus): Tusculum; Apr. (May) 1024 to 1032

145. BENEDICT IX (Theophylactus): Tusculum; 1032 to 1044

146. SYLVESTER III (John): Rome; Jan. 20, 1045, to Feb. 10, 1045
Sylvester III was an antipope if the forcible removal of Benedict IX in 1044 was not legitimate.

147. BENEDICT IX (second time): Apr. 10, 1045, to May 1, 1045

148. GREGORY VI (John Gratian): Rome; May 5, 1045, to Dec. 20, 1046

149. CLEMENT II (Suitger, Lord of Morsleben and Hornburg): Saxony; Dec. 24 (25), 1046, to Oct. 9, 1047
If the triple removal of Benedict IX in 1044, 1046, and 1047 was invalid, Gregory VI and Clement II were antipopes.

150. BENEDICT IX (third time): Nov. 8, 1047, to July 17, 1048 (died c. 1055)

151. DAMASUS II (Poppo): Bavaria; July 17, 1048, to Aug. 9, 1048

152. ST. LEO IX (Bruno): Alsace; Feb. 12, 1049, to Apr. 19, 1054

153. VICTOR II (Gebhard): Swabia; Apr. 16, 1055, to July 28, 1057

154. STEPHEN IX (X) (Frederick): Lorraine; Aug. 3, 1057, to Mar. 29, 1058

155. NICHOLAS II (Gerard): Burgundy; Jan. 24, 1059, to July 27, 1061

156. ALEXANDER II (Anselmo da Baggio): Milan; Oct. 1, 1061, to Apr. 21, 1073

157. ST. GREGORY VII (Hildebrand): Tuscany; Apr. 22 (June 30), 1073, to May 25, 1085

158. BLESSED VICTOR III (Dauferius, Desiderius): Benevento; May 24, 1086, to Sept. 16, 1087 (cult confirmed July 23, 1887)

159. BLESSED URBAN II (Otto di Lagery): France; Mar. 12, 1088, to July 29, 1099 (cult confirmed July 14, 1881)

160. PASCHAL II (Raniero): Ravenna; Aug. 13 (14), 1099, to Jan. 21, 1118

161. GELASIUS II (Giovanni Caetani): Gaeta; Jan. 24 (Mar. 10), 1118, to Jan. 28, 1119

162. CALLISTUS II (Guido of Burgundy): Burgundy; Feb. 2 (9), 1119, to Dec. 13, 1124

163. HONORIUS II (Lamberto): Fiagnano (Imola); Dec. 15 (21), 1124, to Feb. 13, 1130

164. INNOCENT II (Gregorio Papareschi): Rome; Feb. 14 (23), 1130, to Sept. 24, 1143

165. CELESTINE II (Guido): Città di Castello; Sept. 26 (Oct. 3), 1143, to Mar. 8, 1144

166. LUCIUS II (Gerardo Caccianemici): Bologna; Mar. 12, 1144, to Feb. 15, 1145

167. BLESSED EUGENE III (Bernardo Paganelli di Montemagno): Pisa; Feb. 15 (18), 1145, to July 8, 1153 (cult confirmed Oct. 3, 1872)

168. ANASTASIUS IV (Corrado): Rome; July 12, 1153, to Dec. 3, 1154

169. ADRIAN IV (Nicholas Breakspear): England; Dec. 4 (5), 1154, to Sept. 1, 1159

170. ALEXANDER III (Rolando Bandinelli): Siena; Sept. 7 (20), 1159, to Aug. 30, 1181

171. LUCIUS III (Ubaldo Allucingoli): Lucca; Sept. 1 (6), 1181, to Sept. 25, 1185

172. URBAN III (Uberto Crivelli): Milan; Nov. 25 (Dec. 1), 1185, to Oct. 20, 1187

173. GREGORY VIII (Alberto de Morra): Benevento; Oct. 21 (25), 1187, to Dec. 17, 1187

174. CLEMENT III (Paolo Scolari): Rome; Dec. 19 (20), 1187, to Mar. 1191

175. CELESTINE III (Giacinto Bobone): Rome; Mar. 30 (Apr. 14), 1191, to Jan. 8, 1198

176. INNOCENT III (Lotario dei Conti di Segni): Anagni; Jan. 8 (Feb. 22), 1198, to July 16, 1216

177. HONORIUS III (Cencio Savelli): Rome; July 18 (24), 1216, to Mar. 18, 1227

178. GREGORY IX (Ugolino, Count of Segni): Anagni; Mar. 19 (21), 1227, to Aug. 22, 1241

179. CELESTINE IV (Goffredo Castiglioni): Milan; Oct. 25 (28), 1241, to Nov. 10, 1241

180. INNOCENT IV (Sinibaldo Fieschi): Genoa; June 25 (28), 1243, to Dec. 7, 1254

181. ALEXANDER IV (Rinaldo, Count of Segni): Anagni; Dec. 12 (20), 1254, to May 25, 1261

182. URBAN IV (Jacques Pantaléon): Troyes; Aug. 29 (Sept. 4), 1261, to Oct. 2, 1264

183. CLEMENT IV (Guy Foulques or Guido le Gros): France; Feb. 5 (15), 1265, to Nov. 29, 1268

184. BLESSED GREGORY X (Teobaldo Visconti): Piacenza; Sept. 1, 1271 (Mar. 27, 1272), to Jan. 10, 1276 (cult confirmed Sept. 12, 1713)

185. BLESSED INNOCENT V (Peter of Tarentaise): Savoy; Jan. 21 (Feb. 22), 1276, to June 22, 1276 (cult confirmed Mar. 13, 1898)

186. ADRIAN V (Ottobono Fieschi): Genoa; July 11, 1276, to Aug. 18, 1276

187. JOHN XXI (Petrus Juliani or Petrus Hispanus): Portugal; Sept. 8 (20), 1276, to May 20, 1277

There never was a pope with the title of John XX. This title was dropped to rectify an error in the tenth century when an alleged John XV was mistakenly listed among the popes.

188. NICHOLAS III (Giovanni Gaetano Orsini): Rome; Nov. 25 (Dec. 26), 1277, to Aug. 22, 1280

189. MARTIN IV (Simon de Brie): France; Feb. 22 (Mar. 23), 1281, to Mar. 28, 1285

The names of Marinus I (882–84) and Marinus II (942–46) were mistaken for Martin; because of these two popes and the earlier St. Martin I (649–55) this pope was called Martin IV.

190. HONORIUS IV (Giacomo Savelli): Rome; Apr. 2 (May 20), 1285, to Apr. 3, 1287

191. NICHOLAS IV (Girolamo Masci): Ascoli; Feb. 22, 1288, to Apr. 4, 1292

192. ST. CELESTINE V (Pietro del Murrone): Isernia; July 5 (Aug. 29), 1294, to Dec. 13, 1294

193. BONIFACE VIII (Benedetto Caetani): Anagni; Dec. 24, 1294 (Jan. 23, 1295), to Oct. 11, 1303

194. BLESSED BENEDICT XI (Niccolo Boccasini): Treviso; Oct. 22 (27), 1303, to July 7, 1304 (cult confirmed Apr. 24, 1736)

195. CLEMENT V (Bertrand de Got): France; June 5 (Nov. 14), 1305, to Apr. 20, 1314 (first of the Avignon popes)

196. JOHN XXII (Jacques d'Euse): Cahors; Aug. 7 (Sept. 5), 1316, to Dec. 4, 1334

197. BENEDICT XII (Jacques Fournier): France; Dec. 20, 1334 (Jan. 8, 1335), to Apr. 25, 1342

198. CLEMENT VI (Pierre Roger): France; May 7 (19), 1342, to Dec. 6, 1352

199. INNOCENT VI (Etienne Aubert): France; Dec. 18 (30), 1352, to Sept. 12, 1362

200. BLESSED URBAN V (Guillaume de Grimoard): France; Sept. 28 (Nov. 6), 1362, to Dec. 19, 1370 (cult confirmed Mar. 10, 1870)

201. GREGORY XI (Pierre Roger de Beaufort): France; Dec. 30, 1370 (Jan. 5, 1371), to Mar. 26, 1378 (last of the Avignon popes)

202. URBAN VI (Bartolomeo Prignano): Naples; Apr. 8 (18), 1378, to Oct. 15, 1389

203. BONIFACE IX (Pietro Tomacelli): Naples; Nov. 2 (9), 1389, to Oct. 1, 1404

204. INNOCENT VII (Cosimo de' Migliorati): Sulmona; Oct. 17 (Nov. 11), 1404, to Nov. 6, 1406

205. GREGORY XII (Angelo Correr): Venice; Nov. 30 (Dec. 19), 1406, to July 4, 1415, when he voluntarily resigned from the Western Schism to permit the election of his successor; he died Oct. 18, 1417.

206. MARTIN V (Oddone Colonna): Rome; Nov. 11 (21), 1417, to Feb. 20, 1431

207. EUGENE IV (Gabriele Condulmer): Venice; Mar. 3 (11), 1431, to Feb. 23, 1447

208. NICHOLAS V (Tommaso Parentucelli): Sarzana; Mar. 6 (19), 1447, to Mar. 24, 1455

209. CALLISTUS III (Alfonso Borgia): Jativa (Valencia); Apr. 8 (20), 1455, to Aug. 6, 1458

210. PIUS II (Enea Silvio Piccolomini): Siena; Aug. 19 (Sept. 3), 1458, to Aug. 15, 1464

211. PAUL II (Pietro Barbo): Venice; Aug. 30 (Sept. 16), 1464, to July 26, 1471

212. SIXTUS IV (Francesco della Rovere): Savona; Aug. 9 (25), 1471, to Aug. 12, 1484

213. INNOCENT VIII (Giovanni Battista Cibo): Genoa; Aug. 29 (Sept. 12), 1484, to July 25, 1492

214. ALEXANDER VI (Rodrigo Borgia): Jativa (Valencia); Aug. 11 (26), 1492, to Aug. 18, 1503

215. PIUS III (Francesco Todeschini-Piccolomini): Siena; Sept. 22 (Oct. 18), 1503, to Oct. 18, 1503

216. JULIUS II (Giuliano della Rovere): Savona; Oct. 31 (Nov. 26), 1503, to Feb. 21, 1513

217. LEO X (Giovanni de' Medici): Florence; Mar. 9 (19), 1513, to Dec. 1, 1521

218. ADRIAN VI (Adrian Florensz): Utrecht; Jan. 9 (Aug. 31), 1522, to Sept. 14, 1523

219. CLEMENT VII (Giulio de' Medici): Florence; Nov. 19 (26), 1523, to Sept. 25, 1534

220. PAUL III (Alessandro Farnese): Rome; Oct. 13 (Nov. 3), 1534, to Nov. 10, 1549

221. JULIUS III (Giovanni Maria Ciocchi del Monte): Rome; Feb. 7 (22), 1550, to Mar. 23, 1555

222. MARCELLUS II (Marcello Cervini): Montepulciano; Apr. 9 (10), 1555, to May 1, 1555

223. PAUL IV (Gian Pietro Carafa): Naples; May 23 (26), 1555, to Aug. 18, 1559

224. PIUS IV (Giovan Angelo de' Medici): Milan; Dec. 25, 1559 (Jan. 6, 1560), to Dec. 9, 1565

225. ST. PIUS V (Antonio-Michele Ghislieri): Bosco (Alexandria); Jan. 7 (17), 1566, to May 1, 1572 (beatified April 27, 1672)

226. GREGORY XIII (Ugo Buoncompagni): Bologna; May 13 (25), 1572, to Apr. 10, 1585

227. SIXTUS V (Felice Peretti): Grottammare (Ripatransone); Apr. 24 (May 1), 1585, to Aug. 27, 1590

228. URBAN VII (Giovanni Battista Castagna): Rome; Sept. 15, 1590, to Sept. 27, 1590

229. GREGORY XIV (Niccolo Sfondrati): Cremona; Dec. 5 (8), 1590, to Oct. 16, 1591

230. INNOCENT IX (Giovanni Antonio Facchinetti): Bologna; Oct. 29 (Nov. 3), 1591, to Dec. 30, 1591

231. CLEMENT VIII (Ippolito Aldobrandini): Florence; Jan. 30 (Feb. 9), 1592, to Mar. 3, 1605

232. LEO XI (Alessandro de' Medici): Florence; Apr. 1 (10), 1605, to Apr. 27, 1605

233. PAUL V (Camillo Borghese): Rome; May 16 (29), 1605, to Jan. 28, 1621

234. GREGORY XV (Alessandro Ludovisi): Bologna; Feb. 9 (14), 1621, to July 8, 1623

235. URBAN VIII (Maffeo Barberini): Florence; Aug. 6 (Sept. 29), 1623, to July 29, 1644

236. INNOCENT X (Giovanni Battista Pamfili): Rome; Sept. 15 (Oct. 4), 1644, to Jan. 7, 1655

237. ALEXANDER VII (Fabio Chigi): Siena; Apr. 7 (18), 1655, to May 22, 1667

238. CLEMENT IX (Giulio Rospigliosi): Pistoia; June 20 (26), 1667, to Dec. 9, 1669

239. CLEMENT X (Emilio Altieri): Rome; Apr. 29 (May 11), 1670, to July 22, 1676

240. BLESSED INNOCENT XI (Benedetto Odescalchi): Como; Sept. 21 (Oct. 4), 1676, to Aug. 12, 1689 (beatified Oct. 7, 1956)

241. ALEXANDER VIII (Pietro Ottoboni): Venice; Oct. 6 (16), 1689, to Feb. 1, 1691

242. INNOCENT XII (Antonio Pignatelli): Spinazzola; July 12 (15), 1691, to Sept. 27, 1700

243. CLEMENT XI (Giovanni Francesco Albani): Urbino; Nov. 23, 30 (Dec. 8), 1700, to Mar. 19, 1721

244. INNOCENT XIII (Michelangelo dei Conti): Rome; May 8 (18), 1721, to Mar. 7, 1724

245. BENEDICT XIII (Pietro Francesco-Vincenzo Maria-Orsini): Gravina (Bari); May 29 (June 4), 1724, to Feb. 21, 1730

246. CLEMENT XII (Lorenzo Corsini): Florence; July 12 (16), 1730, to Feb. 6, 1740

247. BENEDICT XIV (Prospero Lambertini): Bologna; Aug. 17 (22), 1740, to May 3, 1758

248. CLEMENT XIII (Carlo Rezzonico): Venice; July 6 (16), 1758, to Feb. 2, 1769

249. CLEMENT XIV (Giovanni Vincenzo Antonio-Lorenzo-Ganganelli): Rimini; May 19, 28 (June 4), 1769, to Sept. 22, 1774

250. PIUS VI (Giovanni Angelo Braschi): Cesena; Feb. 15 (22), 1775, to Aug. 29, 1799

251. PIUS VII (Barnaba-Gregorio-Chiaramonti): Cesena; Mar. 14 (21), 1800, to Aug. 20, 1823

252. LEO XII (Annibale della Genga): Genga (Fabriano); Sept. 28 (Oct. 5), 1823, to Feb. 10, 1829

253. PIUS VIII (Francesco Saverio Castiglioni): Cingoli; Mar. 31 (Apr. 5), 1829, to Nov. 30, 1830

254. GREGORY XVI (Bartolomeo Alberto-Mauro-Cappellari): Belluno; Feb. 2 (6), 1831, to June 1, 1846

255. BLESSED PIUS IX (Giovanni M. Mastai Ferretti): Senigallia; June 16 (21), 1846, to Feb. 7, 1878 (beatified Sept. 3, 2000)

256. LEO XIII (Gioacchino Pecci): Carpineto (Anagni); Feb. 20 (Mar. 3), 1878, to July 20, 1903

257. ST. PIUS X (Giuseppe Sarto): Riese (Treviso); Aug. 4 (9), 1903, to Aug. 20, 1914

258. BENEDICT XV (Giacomo della Chiesa): Genoa; Sept. 3 (6), 1914, to Jan. 22, 1922

259. PIUS XI (Achille Ratti): Desio (Milan); Feb. 6 (12), 1922, to Feb. 10, 1939

260. VENERABLE PIUS XII (Eugenio Pacelli): Rome; Mar. 2 (12), 1939, to Oct. 9, 1958

261. BLESSED JOHN XXIII (Angelo Giuseppe Roncalli): Sotto il Monte (Bergamo); Oct. 28 (Nov. 4), 1958, to June 3, 1963 (beatified Sept. 3, 2000)

262. VENERABLE PAUL VI (Giovanni Battista Montini): Concessio (Brescia); June 21 (30), 1963, to Aug. 6, 1978

263. JOHN PAUL I (Albino Luciani): Forno di Canale (now Canale d'Agordo); Aug. 26 (Sept. 3), 1978, to Sept. 28, 1978

264. BLESSED JOHN PAUL II (Karol Wojtyla): Wadowice, Poland; Oct. 16 (22), 1978, to Apr. 2, 2005 (beatified May 1, 2011)

265. BENEDICT XVI (Joseph Aloysius Ratzinger): Marktl am Inn, Bavaria; Apr. 19 (24), 2005, to February 28, 2013.

266. FRANCIS (Jorge Mario Bergolio): Buenos Aires, Argentina; Mar. 13 (19), 2013, to ———.

ACKNOWLEDGMENTS

The author is deeply grateful to all whose generous assistance has made possible the *Catholic Dictionary* (in earlier editions titled *Modern Catholic Dictionary*). At the editorial offices of Doubleday & Company, the cooperation of Robert Heller, Theresa D'Orsogna, and Cyrus Rogers was indispensable. Readers of the manuscript who shared their professional knowledge and made literally hundreds of incorporated recommendations included Rev. Theodore J. Cunnion, SJ, Rev. James T. O'Connor, Rev. Thomas J. O'Donnell, SJ, Rev. Joseph P. Penna, Rev. William B. Smith, and Rev. William R. Walsh, SJ. Research, editing, and clerical services were provided over a period of several years by numerous people, outstanding of whom were Sr. Mary Gertrude, HPB, Geraldine E. Donovan, and John F. Gonoud; also Rev. Christopher M. Buckner, Sr. Mary Roberta, DM, Sr. Nora Bernardine, RSM, Margaret Aser, Marianne Breiter, Dennis Brown, Colleen Crowell, Dr. Bernard and Jane Donovan, Richard Gill, Robert Horak, Rozanne Joyce, Dr. Jorge and Deborah Juncos, Hannah Kern, Mary Lanzl, Margaret McLoughney, Sandra Munoz, and Priscilla Smith.

Special thanks are due to the editors of the *Annuario Pontificio*, the *Official Catholic Directory*, and *Le Canada Ecclésiastique—Catholic Directory of Canada* for the use of their publications; also to the Byzantine Catholic Seminary Press for the Byzantine calendar and Msgr. Eugene Kevane for the text of the Credo of the People of God.

John O'Connell of Inter Mirifica updated this version of *Pocket Catholic Dictionary*.